Yuri Zieman

How I Lived on an Entirely Different Planet

English translation edited by Cherilyn Davidson Cibelli

BOSTON · 2024

YURI ZIEMAN
How I Lived on an Entirely Different Planet

Translated into English from the Russian-language book
"Как я жил на совсем другой планете," (M·Graphics, 2021)

English translation edited by Cherilyn Davidson Cibelli

ISBN 978-1-960533647

Copyright © 2024 by Yuri Zieman

All rights reserved. No part of this book may be reproduced, stored in a retrieval system, or transmitted by any means, electronic, mechanical, photocopying, recording, or otherwise, without written permission from the copyright holder, except for the brief passages quoted for review.

Published by M·GRAPHICS | BOSTON, MA

   ✉ mgraphics.books@gmail.com
   💻 www.mgraphics-books.com

Printed in the USA

*To my dearest grandchildren
Anna and Andrew Khatutsky
and Natalie, Nadia and Nicola Garibaldi*

CONTENTS

FOREWORD TO THE ENGLISH EDITION, 2024 1
ACKNOWLEDGEMENT TO THE RUSSIAN EDITION, 2021 6
FOREWORD TO THE RUSSIAN EDITION, 2021 7

LIFE FIRST:
A HAPPY SOVIET BOY

    It was a good thing I was born 15
    Out of step with the world 26
    The fatherland is in danger 36
    Back to peaceful life 45
    Named after Gorky 49
    Innulia 56
    The Kagan family 60
    Sunday lunches 80
    Becoming an uncle 81
    Father's illness and death 84
    The Novodevichy epic 87
    My thorny road to college 94
    Epilogue to my first life 100

LIFE SECOND:
I AM A SOVIET YOUNG MAN WITH RECOVERED SIGHT

    Salon at Pushkin street 102
    Someone else's pain 107
    My first and main job 116
    The great reticent person 128
    Down the mother Volga river 135
    How I suddenly found myself married 141
    My first steps of a married man 147
    I am becoming a dad 153

My mother's death 155
My first own apartment 158
My life at the new place. 161
Lumumba park 166
Music for me 169
Everything about her was beautiful 175
Beethoven about Tanya Velikanov 179
Beyond the arctic circle 181
Summer in Koktebel. 188
A wedding behind the barbed wire. 191
My pacifism story. 200
The house that we built. 204
Independent buoy-man 209
The immoral husband. 217
My postgraduate thesis. 219
Kuril expeditions 223
My misadventures with the crab 232
I did find the woman! 235
Was Markish but now—Zieman 245
Preferred "Grass" 249
The return of the Prodigal Son 250
Parting with my Father-in-law 252
Exchange of apartments 256
Denunciation report. 259
Marfuta. 262
The cello bearer 268
Anti-wolf. 273
Tiger of kindness 285
Emotional mentor 291
I am dad, once again. 295
They did not let me into medicine 302
Epilogue to the second life. 307

LIFE THIRD:
MY EFFORTS TO EMIGRATE FROM THE SOVIET UNION

Fears. 309
My despair. 317
Application to emigrate 318

CONTENTS

Suitcases	322
Lyova in Ecstasy	325
Refusal to let us go	330
The old doctor	334
My Little Froggy	340
Tanya Velikanov is arrested	346
Cultural attaché	350
Breach in the Iron Curtain	352
The challenges and joys of a janitor-obstetrician	356
The moments of triumph of a janitor—obstetrician	363
Vodka library	366
My universities	369
Interplanetary trips	373
Hope against hope	380
In search of a better untruth	385
The dictionary of forbidden language	390
Our adopted son	396
A last effort with untruth	400
Our Own Paramedic	403
Vera in the Soviet school	406
My tour to the Gulag country	410
Our Georgian "relatives"	412
Wedding in Upper Svanetia	418
House of the merry beggars	422
Bible stories	428
Starving camels	433
With Little Frogy to the Baltics	435
Aliens from the Land of Dolphinia	440
Becoming father-in-law	449
Becoming grandfather	452
Committee of Fifteen	455
Representative of Israel	458
Music on the water	463
Latin is out of fashion these days	470
With our Little Froggy to Kaluga	479
Symposium of Refuseniks	485
Parting with Galya	488

A hospital epic 493
The new hospital circle 498
The beginning of the "friendship"
      between the two presidents 504
An American with Russian roots. 509
Special gift from the KGB 513
Continuation of the "friendship"
      between the two Presidents 517
Soviet-style hospitality 519
Fourth Summit. 524
Dissidents at the High Reception 527
Opium of the people. 533
To separate or not to separate 538
The dejection of an alien 542
Two worlds — two Shapiros 545
The coveted post card. 548
The dinner that never took place 551
Last days in Russia 555
Last hours in Russia 558
Frankly about Vienna 562
Reuniting with Galechka 567
Epilogue to the third life 571

APPENDIX 1
    When and what 577

APPENDIX 2
    Who is who 580

APPENDIX 3
    Who is mentioned where 615

FOREWORD TO THE ENGLISH EDITION, 2024

First of all, I would like to dedicate the English edition of my memoirs to my dearest grandchildren Anna and Andrew Khatutsky and Natalie, Nadia and Nicola Garibaldi. More than 36 years in the USA taught me that the majority of people in the country, especially young generations, know very little about what is happening beyond the borders. I hope that my book describing very different from the USA country not ruled by the law and WITHOUT freedoms will help these people to understand how lucky they are and never take this for granted. In my opinion, American President Ronald Reagan formulated in 1961 this idea in one of the best possible ways:

> "I would like this generation always remember Freedom is never more than one generation away from extinction. We didn't pass it on to our children in the bloodstream. The only way they can inherit the freedom we have known is if we fight for it, protect it, defend it, and then hand it to them with the well fought lessons of how they in their lifetime must do the same. And if you and I don't do this, then you and I may well spend our sunset years telling our children and our children's children what it once was like in America when men were free."

Now I would like to make a confession. When I decided to write my memoirs in 2018, I arrogantly planned to do it in English. I was motivated with my love for the new homeland and with my passionate willingness to explain the base of this love to the people of the country in their native language. After my several clumsy attempts, I realized clearly, to my great disappointment, that I COULD NOT DO IT! Living such a long time in the United States appeared to be not enough for me to master the language to be able to describe my extremely emotional reflections. This is sad and I want to give my English-speaking readers for this inability sincere apologies.

However, my willing to do the task was so indomitable that I started looking at the ways of still doing this. I could not afford to pay for professional human translation. Therefore, I came to think about starting with a computer translator, most of which seemed to me not good.

In Russian there was saying: *"Better have hundred friends than hundred rubles"*. In my long life, both in Russia and in the USA, I was very lucky with wonderful friends. My dearest American friend, Karen Rahmeier, liked the description of my book and wanted her family to read it. Therefore, she did some research and discovered the German translation software Deepl that looked to her better than other similar products. This software was not free but this did not stop her. She bought it and ran my entire book through this product. I immediately offered her to pay all the money. Karen resolutely said, *"No, it is my gift to you!"* I was overwhelmed with gratitude and my eyes got wet. This was the first miracle that happened to me while creating the English version of the book.

Thus, the "machine" translation of my book into English was born, and Karen gave it to me for revision. I have looked it through and concluded that, though it was much better than I had expected, it was far from what I wanted, it was not "human" translation. Nevertheless, it helped me to believe that I can try to edit the text now and to make it more human. Since that time, I worked hard and it took about few months to edit all 609 pages. At this point, I think, the text became readable and understandable to an English native speaker. But still, though I did my best, I got "lousy human" translation because my English was not proper for native speakers. Since that time, I started thinking what could be the next step of improving the text.

Then the second miracle has happened. I had another dearest friend in California, Cherilyn Davidson Cibelli, who volunteered to improve my English! She had PhD in clinical psychology and was rather busy with her family and with her very demanding job, which she loved. Still she decided to help me and to dedicate a lot of time to do this huge work. Though she never worked as editor

FOREWORD TO THE ENGLISH EDITION, 2024

before, I was absolutely happy to get a native speaker of English to edit my text. Second time I was overwhelmed with gratitude and my eyes got wet again. We started our cooperation: I was sending her chapter by chapter to California using email. She returned to me these chapters after editing. After this I could not help to edit this text finally.

During my long life I did a lot of writing and a lot of translating from the foreign language into Russian. As to writing, my teacher was my beloved Russian poet Bulat Okudhzava. The following lines in his poem "I am writing the historical novel" were instructional to me then and are still today:

> *Everyone writes as he hears.*
> *Everyone hears as he breathes.*
> *As he breathes, so he writes,*
> *Not to please somebody.*
> *That is the nature's way.*
> *Why?*
> *It is not our business.*
> *What is the goal?*
> *This is not for our judgment.*

My comment to these wonderful lines is that in general it is really difficult to decipher and to describe your feeling that you want to describe, even in your native language, to say nothing about a foreign language.

Russian belongs to the group of languages that actively uses patronymic for identification of people both historically and today. English does not have such tradition. That is why in English version of the book I decided to remove patronymic and reduce people names to first and last names.

Also, these two names may change for genders in Russian and usually define the gender of a person. For example, when you read or hear "*Alexandra Ivanova*" and "*Alexander Ivanov*", everybody knows that first is female and the second—male. In English there is no necessary orthographic difference in names for females and males, especially in last names. That is why in English version of the book I decided to take transliteration of the male form of the last name for both genders. I hope nobody would blame me as male chauvinist for this. However, I made exceptions for some famous Russian females whose last name are already well known in the West in female transliteration.

As to translating fiction and poetry, to make choices is much more difficult. And sometimes, I think, it is just not possible at all. Any two different languages are products of very different cultures. That is why, in my opinion, there never can be established exact one-to-one correspondence between pairs of concepts in two different languages. If we agreed on this, than we have to conclude that perfect translation can never be achieved. Then what can we do?

In prose it is possible to RETELL the story trying to keep as much as you can every little nuance of meaning, style and sometime even syntax. On the other hand, in poetry, I think, there are so many extremely fine features that make each poem a miracle. I like poetry very much and in my book there are many poetical quotations. Most of these quotations were originally written in Russian. That is why computer translations of the poems are especially bad. Nevertheless, I love some poetical translations done by the Great Russian poets but I consider them as independent poems in a different language evoked by the original. Every time I tried to mention the name of the translator in this situation.

For the rest of Russian poems in the book I made word for word translation of the original which was not poetry at all. But, it seemed to me, that in this way we can give the best idea of what the original poem was about. When the poems were originally written in English, I tried to find the publication with the original poem and quote from there. It seems to me that is what Copyright requires from us.

In my long life I have done a lot of translation work. Summing up my experience, I came up with the following strict translator's code for myself:

- *I have no right to add, remove or change even a slightest element of original meaning. I still made very few exceptions from this rule when I found it necessary to add a couple of phrases explaining a specific Russian cultural or factual context which, I thought, may be not familiar to English speaking readers.*

- *I have no right to add, remove or change even slightest element of original emotional element.*
- *When quoting any author in target language, I have no right to do any editing at all but I have to quote from original.*

I realize that for many people my rules are too strict nevertheless I always try to never violate these rules. To these people I give my sincere apologies. Among such people I would especially single out my close friend Cherilyn Davidson Cibelly, the great editor of my translation. Dearest Cherilyn, I love you and I appreciate the incredible work you have done. However, I confess that a few of your changes are clearly violating my rules, and I was not able to accept these changes. In these cases, I am sorry, I had to return to my original version equivalent to Russian. Thank you for your understanding! Special thanks to my new planet allowing people to have their own opinion.

Boston MA, USA
February 2024

ACKNOWLEDGEMENT FOR THE RUSSIAN EDITION, 2021

I am happy to use this opportunity to thank my dear daughter Galina Khatutsky and son-in law Victor Khatutsky for their invaluable support beginning with my writing the first lines of the manuscript and ending with the publishing the book in Russian. I think that without their help the book would never see the light of the day.

FOREWORD TO THE RUSSIAN EDITION, 2021

Slowly but surely both my Tanya and I have passed our 80th birthdays. More and more often, I want to look back and recall what I have experienced, and I am sad to realize that much has faded from my memory. No one, I think, has described better how I feel today than Alexander Pushkin in "Boris Godunov:"

> *In my old age, I live anew,*
> *The past passes before me —*
> *Hasn't it recently been flying, full of events,*
> *Wavering like the sea-ocean?*
> *Now it is silent and calm,*
> *Not many faces I can remember,*
> *Not many words are getting through to me,*
> *And the rest have died irretrievably…*

It became clear to me that that Tanya and I needed to follow the desire of our relatives and friends and describe what we still remember. It is not only because 80 years is a lot, but also because a lot has happened in our 80 years. As Thomas Mann rightly noted in The Magic Mountain, *"for not any and every person can have a story happen to them."* Tanya and I just belong to that kind of people to whom stories have happened, and not infrequently. Both of us have a lot to write about.

When I finally decided to become a chronicler, I had a promising plan for how we could do it and it of course included Tanya. First, her memory is clearer than mine is. Secondly, Tanya has a much better sense of style in language than I, be it English or Russian, her prose is sometimes poetry. After she came into my life she has always been a great editor of most everything I have ever written, and I was hoping to write our memoirs side by side.

I envisioned an interesting structure for a book with our memoirs. In the first part of the book, describing events that happened before we found each other, the left-hand page would contain my text and the right-hand page would contain Tanya's about the same time in her life. The rest of the book I planned to write together with her in a regular way. However, to my great regret, nothing of the kind happened to be possible. Everyday worries did not leave enough time and valences for Tanechka to carry out such a big undertaking. I decided to start it myself, hoping and waiting for Tanyusha to join me later. However, this also did not happen. As a result, I am writing alone, and this will of course make the result worse. But please remember, if not Tanya's hand, then Tanya's head and Tanya's heart, albeit indirectly, are undoubtedly present quite a lot everywhere in this book. Don't judge strictly what I've got.

My original intention was to write only about my life and the life of my loved ones, to describe my own experiences and theirs. I thought, when I started, that I might be able to avoid discussing the long-suffering political history of the country in which I was born and lived for the first half-century of my life.

However, I was deeply mistaken. Whether you wish it or not, being a citizen of a country, you become an inevitable participant in its politics. The country's policies and your life intertwine so that they become impossible to separate. Russia was my motherland, but I never treated her as my mother but as my close friend. When a friend behaves unworthily, I cannot continue to love him as before, but I also cannot stop worrying about him.

I could never share M. Lermontov's *"strange love"* for Russia *"contrary to reason"*. I could not love it by *"fame bought with blood,"* and in the Soviet period there was much more blood than in Lermontov's time. Watching *"dancing with stomping and whistling to the chattering of drunken peasants"* never encouraged me to retain my love for Russia, as it did to the poet. When describing my life, I never was able to get away from these sad feelings and thoughts. Infinitely loved by me, A. S. Pushkin, wrote a year before his death in a letter to his wife Natalia *"... the devil cursed me to be born in Russia with a soul and talent!"* Although I never had anything even close to Pushkin's talent but my soul protested vehemently against the immoral and often criminal acts committed by my country like

Pushkin's, my soul protested vehemently against the immoral and often criminal acts committed by my country. When such acts were happening I was each time ashamed to be a Soviet citizen. Some readers may be disappointed and even hurt by my feelings about Soviet Russia, but unfortunately, I did not happen to live in another gentler Russia. Her crimes will remain my crimes. To such readers I offer my sincere apologies and I simply ask for their understanding.

When I sat down with the computer, it suddenly became clear to me that the task I had set for myself was more difficult than I had thought. It feels that I have managed to live not one but SIX different lives, and with the beginning of each of these lives it was as if I had died and been reborn, becoming a completely different person. What makes my storytelling task even more complicated is that I have not much time left to do it: the clock is ticking persistently, and I began this work only in my sixth, I think, last life. I need to follow the rule of Apelles, the court painter and friend of Alexander the Great, "*Nulla dies sine linea.*" In English, it will be "Not a day without a line." The story originally came down to us from the Natural History by Pliny the Elder. It became widely known after the publication of the novel of the same name by the Soviet writer Yuri Olesha. Olesha could not publish his novel in Russia during his lifetime. Similarly, with my political views, I did not risk beginning to describe my life while living in the Soviet Union. The possibility of following the rule of Apelles and later of Olesha came to me only after my rebirth in a free country.

In each of the five rebirths, the new labor turned out to be not easy, but thank God, they all passed without serious complications. At this point, I would like to say that there was no Chinese Great Wall between any two of my subsequent six lives. The boundary between them was not clear in time with one life gradually and smoothly passing into another. The model of my rebirths is certainly interesting, but I like to think that, becoming a completely different person, I nevertheless mostly remained myself. After all, genetics is a stubborn thing.

The saying says, *in for a penny in for a dollar*. First, I will try to list my six lives, to describe who I felt I was in each, how long each lasted, and how well I coped. Here is that list:

1. I am a happy Soviet boy (about my first 20 years).
2. I am a Soviet young man whose sight started to recover (about next 20 years).
3. I am a not too happy and not quite young Soviet person who wished to emigrate from the Soviet Union and was not permittet to (about next 10 years).
4. I am a happy middle-aged US citizen (about 20 years).
5. I am a happy retired US citizen still working to make life easier for the elderly and sick people (about 10 years).
6. I am an elderly and infirm US citizen still trying to be happy. For how many years, will I be able to do that? God only knows.

In each of these lives, there have been many difficulties, but there have also been many significant, valuable, and wonderful things. It seems to me that each life has taught me something and I hope, made me better, wiser, kinder, and more resilient to the waves of time. Lermontov's Mtsyri said:

> *I have not lived much, and I have lived in captivity.*
> *I would exchange if I could*
> *Two lives like that for one,*
> *That will be full of courageous exploits!*

Unlike Mtsyri, I would not want to trade even one of my six lives for a different one. The first three of my lives (I understood this much later) I also lived in captivity, just like Mtsyri, though not militarily, but politically and spiritually. Nonetheless, the first and second lives left me with wonderful memories about the love and care that my parents, relatives, and friends, surrounded me with, protecting me from everything bad and helping me grow and learn. If there is something good in me, it is thanks to their love and teachings. Therefore, those lives are very dear to me to this day. Contrary to the intention of the rulers of my country, I still have managed to live my life according to my norms and not to theirs.

My third life was particularly difficult, when both I together with my closest loved ones found ourselves as refuseniks (those refused the right to leave the country), becoming outcasts in our own country. However, I would not want even this third life not to exist for me. I just wish this period had been shorter. One of our family friends when he returned home after ten years in a Soviet labor camp said, "*The first couple of years were quite instructive and interesting for me, but the other eight were already superfluous.*" I would agree. The first couple of years being a refusenik were quite instructive and interesting for me, but the other nine were unnecessary.

According to my initial plans, I was going to complete the story of my third life just at the moment our plane heading from Moscow to Vienna passed over the Iron Curtain and entered the airspace of the free world. But I changed soon my mind. It seemed wrong to finish the description of the epic on our way to freedom, still in the atmosphere of hostility without describing our triumphant arrival in the United States of America. Therefore, I added an additional two chapters describing our stopover in the Austrian capital of Vienna and, finally, the moment when we set foot on American soil.

In the process of working on the description of my third life, I decided to change the original plan completely. In the beginning I planned to address my memories primarily to my children, grandchildren and their peers, who know either nothing at all or very little about life in Russia. Now it is more than thirty years in the U.S. and I have come to conclude that most citizens of our new country, regardless of their age, have about the same low level of awareness of life in Soviet Russia. And that life in my perception differed so much from life in any civilized country of the Western world that it is appropriate to speak of it as of life ON OTHER PLANET.

My hidden impulse of the way I described it was to make sure that no reader of my book would EVER want to build a similar country again. I realized that my first three lives should be of the greatest interest to anyone living in our country. And as for my next two lives which I lived in the United States, both old and young can tell much more about the country than I can. Therefore, my perception of the last three lives is of much less interest to everyone here. At the same time, I realized that I am not getting any younger and my strength is quietly ebbing. So I have decided, for now, to limit myself to the first three lifetimes I spent in the Soviet Union. This means the end of this part of my biography should be 1988.

I tried to organize entire text, which follows, more or less chronologically. In the last sentence, the words "more or less" are extremely important. I concluded that there cannot and should not be strict chronology in my book. Our memory does not use soulless device like chronometer, but sorts events by heart, in which jumps forward and backward in time are natural, important and have emotional character. I hope that my worsening memory has not deformed much the sequence of facts and I have not lost something essential and important in each of three lives. Though my Tanya did not do actual writing, I, of course, shamelessly used the help of her memory and her wisdom. Without her, the book would never have seen the light of day. For such help from her, I am eternally grateful. Summing up, I would like to ask the readers of this text not to expect STRICT FACTUAL CORRECTNESS. The memory of an old man tends to lose unimportant details. It seems to me that much more important is the EMOTIONAL CORRECTNESS of my history and I tried very diligently to remember and describe my feelings.

Each of the lives I have lived has been filled to the brim and, while not overly easy, each has left me with far more positive than negative memories. The truest blessing has been the wonderful, competent, kind people I have met along the way. I am very happy that among these people there were many who knew more, were more capable and who could do more than I could. Many have played an exceptional role in my life and helped me become the person I am. In the first place, I am talking about close friends and relatives who lived at different times and who had a significant impact on my life. Secondly, I mean historically famous people who influenced the whole of humanity but who have been especially important to me. The lessons learned from these people have often taught me to know clearly the difference between right and wrong.

Essential parts of my memoirs are the three appendices. The first is the main events of my first three lives sorted chronologically. The two others together make the name index of most important people who played an important role during these lives. I am sure that I have left some beloved people out by accident and for this, please forgive me, this old man. This index is a strange mixture of people whom I have personally met, and those whom I have learned about from books, concerts, exhibitions, movies, and theatrical performances. They include people very close and dear to me and those met quite casually, people who lived at the same time with me as well as many centuries earlier, people internationally known and those known to only a select few of us. As a result, the list happens to be quite long, and next to A. S. Pushkin, Johann Sebastian Bach, and President of the United States Ronald Reagan there are the names of our family members and our friends, acquaintances and relatives.

It sounds paradoxical, but some of the people mentioned have taught me a great deal by their negative examples. Therefore, to all in this index, without exception, I express my gratitude, whether they were my contemporaries or not and whether they lived near me or thousands of miles away, whether they shared my views or held views diametrically opposed to mine.

Since November 23, 1973, in my second life, when I met Tanya Markish for the first time, she has occupied the most special place in my life and in my heart. At the beginning of 1974, she honored me by becoming Tanya Zieman. Naturally, before I met her there was no such person in my life. However, after this moment I decided that it makes no sense to refer to her in the name index separately, as there are no references to my name. We have been inseparable and never parted the last 50 years and everything in the book since that time is about both of us, like if both of us became one person. Therefore, I do not make references to Tanya Zieman. as I do not make references to myself. This way I wanted to say that NOTHING significant EVER happened in my life without her.

I would like to say few words about the references in the indexes to my daughters' names. The eldest, Galya Khatutsky, married and changed her last name only two years before she left the Soviet Union in 1987. So, for most of my life in Russia, she carried the surname Zieman. This, I decided, allows me to give myself the pleasure of referring to her as Galya Zieman, I hope, no offense, to our son-in-law Victor. As for my youngest daughter, Vera Garibaldi, she married and changed her surname already in the USA, so she entered our country and got American citizenship as Vera Zieman. Therefore, she is listed in our index as Vera Zieman.

LIFE FIRST
A HAPPY SOVIET BOY

IT WAS A GOOD THING I WAS BORN

I was born on March 2, 1938, in Moscow. My horoscope said I was a fish. An Old Russian horoscope said Pisces have a large nose and forehead. This phrase accurately describes the faces of the men in our family: my face as well as those of my father, my brother, and my nephew. Speaking of my nose, the size of it has never bothered me and has provided me many amusing moments. When I meet small children, I try to joke with them explaining that they are very lucky today: they see the world's longest nose. The funniest thing is that many of them have believed me, though the smartest wondered how I managed to measure the length of the noses of all the people in the world. As for other wisdom about fish, let the reader judge for himself whether this fits me as he turns the last page of these recollections.

Not the best time was it to be born in Russia. The Soviet Union was undergoing not a wave, but a flood of Stalin terror and my parents' friends and acquaintances were disappearing without a trace. I was the last and youngest child for my parents. When I came into the world, my mother was 40 years old. Something was not right for me from the first day of my life. I cried for hours, and nothing could calm me. Back then, it was still possible to get qualified nannies. However, all my mother's attempts to find a good nanny were unsuccessful: none of them wanted to work with such a difficult child. Family folklore tells how once

I am about one-year-old

my parents managed to find an old-fashioned nanny, elegantly dressed, polite, and very experienced, with a white starched apron and a kokoshnik covering her beautiful hair. Just a few days later, this woman came to my mother embarrassed and apologetic: *"Forgive me for God's sake, but I can't stay with you. This is the first time in my practice that I do not know what to do with the child. I am ashamed to take him out for a walk in the yard. He screams and all the people around think I'm a bad nanny."*

My wife Tanya suggests that I cried simply because I was bored like Lermontov's *"bored, and sad, and no one to shake hands..."* or as in Nekrasov: *"bored, and sad, and no one to cheat at card games."* Maybe she's right. I was sickly as a child and my mother quit her job to stay home with me. My illnesses did not go away until I was in high school, and I often felt that I was a burden on my family. In "Bleak House" Dickens described how much trouble Esther Summerson had brought about by her birth, causing her aunt to say to her: *"You had better not to have been born!"* Although I was a cheerful child, Aunt Esther's words remind me of my sad thinking at times, that maybe everyone might have been better off if I had not been born. Thank God, over the years I have battled those worries and self-doubts. I am not sure how old I was when that happened. Although I had met Dickens's Esther at a rather advanced age, the romantic traits in my character had apparently not yet waned, for she joined the ranks of remarkable women in world literature, chiefly of the nineteenth century, whom I admired and worshipped. I was happy and very grateful to Dickens that, despite the difficult circumstances surrounding her parents, Esther was born!

When I think about this today I feel very different. I am happy that I was born, but sometimes the emotions of my childhood still haunt me. I look fondly at my little granddaugh-

I am five-years-old

ters who bring joy to everyone around them. That, I tell myself, is how children should grow up, not like me. But my parents' world was different, and it was not an easy or welcoming one for them either. Of course, I am deeply grateful to my wonderful parents, first of all, and then to my older sister Lena. They had to deal with all the difficulties of my coming to this world. I don't mention my brother Jan in this context. He was 16 when I was born, and he was so involved in a hectic social life with his friends that he, it seemed to me, simply had no valences left for family, much less for such a little cutthroat as I was. And then the war broke out and he went to the front...

Unfortunately, both of my parents are long dead, as well as all the people close to them of their generation. My older brother is also no longer with us, and my sister is ninety five years old, and it is hardly worth relying on her memory. So there is no one to ask about some details of the family history or to specify some facts. I am the only family historian left. That is why I ask your pardon for some factual inaccuracies at once. By way of consolation, not excuse, I want to assure readers that everything I write is emotionally honest and accurate

My father, Lev Zi man, as far as I know, was born in Skopin, in the Ryazan region in 1900, although his family was from Kovno, Lithuania. His birth year of 1900 always seemed "round" to me and always made his age the easiest to figure.

My paternal grandfather, Yakov Ziman, was a pharmacist, and Jews of that profession, unlike millions of other Jews, were allowed to live outside the Pale of Settlement that was originally formed by Catherine the Great in 1855. My father had one sister and two brothers.

He was still a schoolboy when the family moved to Saratov on the Volga River. There he graduated from school and entered the Saratov Institute of Economics. Civil

My father's parents with four children – my father is sitting in the middle

war broke out after the Revolution of 1917 and fascinated by Bolshevik ideas, my father decided that when "the Fatherland was in danger," he had no moral right to stand aside. In 1919, having left classes at the university, he enlisted as a volunteer in the Red Army and went to defend Soviet power. In 1921 he demobilized, returned to the Institute, and successfully graduated early. After that he moved with us to Moscow, where he worked actively in the field of economic geography of the foreign countries and cartography until the beginning of WWII.

When World War II broke out, history repeated itself: Dad left his scientific and pedagogical activities and volunteered for the Soviet Army. From 1942 to 1947 he served in the Navy, providing maps for the Black Sea Fleet operations. After demobilization in the rank of lieutenant-colonel, he returned to his favorite work, being a professor of the largest educational institutions of Moscow, being the editor of major economic and geographical journals, and heading up large scientific collectives. He continued his earlier work in economic geography and cartography and did so until the last days of his life in 1956. By the way, until I grew and developed my own political literacy, I could not understand why my father, studying the economic geography of capitalist countries, had never been to any of them. I repeatedly asked him about it, and never got a coherent answer. Now I know that he just didn't feel comfortable telling me the bitter truth, which was that as a Jew, even one who has been a Soviet officer, he would never have been allowed to leave the Soviet Union, even for a holiday, to go the West. So, there were some things that he could not share with us and yet, he was always a kind and generous man.

Our family of five lived in a cramped communal apartment on Pokrovka Street in Moscow, and my father had been on the waiting list for a private apartment for quite some time. Shortly before the war started, he was offered a nice flat, consisting of three individual rooms and one through room, on the sixth floor of a house in Tikhvinsky Lane in the Oktyabrsky District of Moscow. His subordinate, Anna Evstigneev, a single mother with a young son was also on the waiting list. My father feared that Anna and her son, Vadim would never get out of their communal apartment, so he invited her to move in to the largest of our individual rooms. Vadim was of my age, and it was wonderful to have a playmate close by when you are two years old. So, we ended up in a communal flat again, though incomparably better. I grew up in that apartment as well as my brother's family with children Olya and Lyova. Also, when I got married we lived there with my wife. After my daughter Galya was born she lived there the first year of her life.

In general, I have warm memories of this apartment. Though the country went through hard times, thanks to efforts of my family, those were happy years of childhood and adolescence. I was proud of my dad, who did such a good deed for his subordinate and Vadim. That's why I was very pleased when my nephew Lyova wrote a wonderful, poem "At the Tikhvinsky," which echoes my memories:

> *Here are a couple of windows,*
> *Those are flush with both the sky and the lime tree.*
> *The eternal law of childhood*
> *Sealed in a mysterious scroll…*
> *Out of these windows*
> *The air feels clear and humming,*
> *And the balcony is swaying*
> *Like a cradle over the alley.*

Vadim's mother, Anna, was nice. She reminded me of the main character of S. Mikhalkov's poem "Anna Vanna the Brigadier" and her piglets. Here "Vanna" mimics kids' pronunciation of the Russian patronymic Ivanovna. There were lines that stuck in my memory from my early childhood:

> *Anna Vanna, we all in our squad*
> *Want to see the piglets.*
> *We would not hurt them,*
> *Let's take a look and get out.*

A humble hard worker, Anna had longed to marry a nice man and have a child. She did meet a good man, who fell in love with her and proposed to her. However, Anna did not love him and did not want to marry him but was willing to have a child with him. He agreed, and so Vadim was born. Anna remained a friend with the child's father. I knew this man well and he regularly would come to our apartment to visit both Anna and Vadim.

I would like Anna but at times her actions sadden me to this day, making it impossible to think back on her with warmth. On every occasion that Vadim did something seriously wrong, she would take the belt off his pants, and beat him with it. Every time this abuse outraged me to the core. I even remember my thoughts: "My God! If she really was a pig farmer, she would have beaten the poor piglets!" For some reason it particularly hurt me that the belt was from Vadim's own trousers. I really wanted to tell Anna about Bokelman's sad experience in D. Kharms's poem "Pluh and Plih," the teacher who whipped his pupils when they came to school without doing their homework:

> *It was a very little help, though,*
> *Or it didn't help at all,*
> *Because from the hitting.*
> *You cannot get smart.*

This outrage ended abruptly and permanently when one day Vadim, finally grown and as tall as his mother, resolutely and forcefully seized Anna's belt-wielding hand, and said: *"That's it, it won't happen again!"* And, indeed, he was right, it never happened again. But my respect for this woman never returned.

My father as I remember him

My father was a role model to me in almost everything, and he will always remain for me a model of selflessness, amazing diligence, efficiency, modesty, irreproachable honesty, attention to people and cordiality towards everyone he encountered. This adoration of the father was greatly promoted by the general atmosphere in the family that was set by my mother. We all admired him. My father's authority was unquestionable for all of us. All of us were so proud of this man.

Daddy loved his work and allowed it to possess him. He was on fire at work and, as a result, burned himself out. He died at 56, when I was only 18 years old. I was always jealous of his work, and I always missed him when it took him away. I remember vividly how much I missed my father in the last couple of years when he was seriously ill, and how jealous I was of anyone who could see him more than I did. But the very fact that I grew up around such a man, I think, gave me so many good things. I remember, for example, one of his main lessons was to be never idle, never waste time. *"There are more useful and less useful activities,"* he told me, *"but no matter what you do, there must always be some meaning in it for you or for those around you."* If he passed me and asked, *"What are you doing?"* and I answered, *"Nothing,"* he would get upset with me.

After Daddy was gone, my need for him only increased. I felt that I could have been a better person if I had had the opportunity to talk with him more, to learn from him more, and to have more discussions of important issues with him.

My mother, Hanah Ziman was born in 1898 into a kitchen-master's family. Today, people would probably call the kitchen-master's shop a canteen or a small deli. My mother told me how her father would regularly take a cart and go to market to buy food for his shop. Sometimes he would take his children with him as helpers. Mother loved those trips, and as an adult, she always liked to buy groceries and have extra food in the house. I inherited that

My mother's parents with 11 children,
second from the right standing is my mother

quality from her, too. However, judging from what my mother used to tell me, this business was far from prosperous.

My mother's family lived very modestly. She had ten brothers and sisters, and often one coat for two or even three children. This made a very strong impression on me as a child. I still try to wear out my clothes literally to the holes and buy as few new clothes as possible. I also love to receive gifts or hand-me-downs from my relatives and friends of their used clothing. Not only do I have no prejudice against wearing clothes "from someone else's shoulder", but on the contrary, when I put on, say, a shirt of someone I love, I feel a special pleasure. I like to think about that person and the shirt brings special warmth to me.

I have had a nerdy interest in words since I was a child and I wondered if you can say "from someone else's shoulder," how would you say similar thing about trousers? Finally, I came up with the expression "from someone else's butt." I have been very lucky in this regard: both of my sons-in-law plus a few male friends happen to be about my size, and as a result I have a couple of things from each that I hold dear. This attitude towards clothing, is now unfortunately obsolete and even dying, in the first place, among young people especially in a country as rich as our America. I like the growing sales of vintage clothing and I am charmed by how young mothers will trade children's clothing from family to family.

My mother in the grammar school uniform

Mom's birth year was not as "round" as Dad's was, but it excites me even more. After all, it's still the 19th century!!! I have always had nostalgic feelings about that century. It seems to me that it was warmer and kinder than later centuries. The people in that century seem more beautiful to me than today, and I like their clothes, especially the women's ones. We have made unimaginable technical progress, but as Elie Wiesel remarked in his book about the Feast of the Passover, "... *we have even conquered the cosmos, but we have not conquered our hearts.*" I know I am probably idealizing a bygone time, but if it were possible to transport myself back to the 19th century, taking all my family and friends with me, I would probably do so. If I would classify my father judging on his social and political spirit as one of the noblest persons of the 20th century, then my mother with her emotional richness, I think, was much more suited to the century in which she was born. Dad often could not help but tease my mother's emotionality. I well remember my mother rereading Lev Tolstoy's Anna Karenina many times always with excitement of a young girl. She considered the role of Anna played by her favorite actor, A.Tarasov at the Moscow Art Theatre to be the pinnacle of perfection and mastership, and went to see the play several times. Daddy would repeatedly joke and tease her regularly citing an epigram by N. Nekrasov:

> *Tolstoy, you proved with patience and talent,*
> *That a woman, being a wife and a mother,*
> *Should never have an affair*
> *Neither with a chamberlain, nor with an aide-de-cam*

Each time my father did this, my poor mother become so outraged, she would screech to the ceiling.

It seems to me I learned so much from my mom in the romantic sense. From my childhood until today, I still shed tears over books or movies that touch me. It would seem that my real-life circumstances should have etched in me such sentimentality. However, it has not worked out that way. Here is a little funny story about one experience of about etching.

Around, my seventh or eighth grade in school, my parents had the strange idea of sending me ALONE for two weeks of winter vacation to a union holiday home. I saw their decision as a demonstration of complete trust in me and was therefore very happy. Their experience, I think, had been limited to privileged sanatoriums and holiday camps, and they naively assumed that this was some-

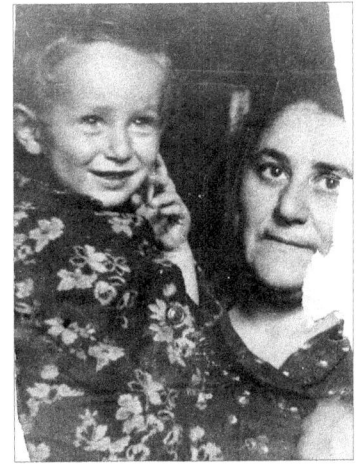

My mother with me

thing similar. Besides, they knew that the holiday home was in the beautiful Kalinin region on a high bank of a river, and they helped me to buy and take with me everything I needed for winter fishing. They could not have known, poor souls, what a honky-tonk they had pushed me to!!

My vacation spot was very different from what they expected. I was in a room and my three roommates were about forty-year-old men, who for two weeks had been drinking from morning till night and running around with local broads. I have to hand it to their tact: seeing such a young and innocent roommate, they, thank God, were ashamed to bring women into our room. It was funny when in the morning we met for the first time. They just appeared in the room with two bottles of vodka, put out four tea glasses, one for each of us!!! and started pouring so we could get acquainted. I don't remember what we snacked on but they took care of this. I was scared to death but silly enough to say "NO". It was a baptism by fire for me: I had never drunk so much vodka before! Nevertheless, I passed the test with flying colors. I do not know how, but I swallowed the whole glass. My roommates immediately disappeared to continue enjoying life. In contrast, I lay in my bed, not knowing what to expect, and closed my eyes. I reasoned this way: if I just died, at least I would not be lying in a dirty corridor and wouldn't do anything embarrassing. In addition, if I got alcohol poisoning and an ambulance came, it would be easier to move me from the bed straight to the stretcher. I could not see other options. But things happened in a completely different way. When I finally opened my eyes, it was already dark outside. I had been asleep all day and into the night. Something terrible was going on inside my head, but I was alive! I was not even vomiting. I remember my thoughts filled with pride: how gallantly I did everything, how grown up I was, and how healthy and manly I was! After all, it could have been much worse.

I had at this place one more very emotional experience. Remember I had with me fishing gear. I came with a plan connected to it. Yes, it was time for me to become a river angler. I had had some fishing experience before near Moscow. If I could manage to catch something at this place, I would keep my catch frozen and bring it home as a gift to my parents in thanks for such a wonderful vacation. I decided to keep my catch frozen by digging a hole deep in the snow at a secluded spot on the shore and burying my catch in it each day. I did manage to pull out 5–10 small fish a day, and my stocking plan was working well. Each day, I added more and more fish to my frozen hole. I anticipated the joy of meeting my parents and their joy at my gift. The day before I left, I arrived at my "freezer" with another catch. What I saw left me in a state of shock. Somebody had trashed my hole and robbed me: not a single fish remained! I searched for a culprit. There was no fresh human track, but there were many of what looked to be dog tracks. I was so angry. In desperation, I threw a few fish from my last fishing trip directly into the snow, yelling: *"eat you bastards!"*! Later that day I brought a man who knew about animal tracks to what was left of my freezer, and he told me beyond any doubt that the thief had been a fox. Well, that was one very contented, wily fox.

As I mentioned before, my mother stopped working soon after I was born. So, I grew up lucky to have my mother at home, giving all the warmth of her generous soul to her family, children and especially to me as the youngest which compensated for much of attention my dad focused on his work. My mom outlived my dad by seven years, so I spent more time with her than with my father. I ended up being a bit of a mother's boy. This is possibly the reason that I learned to appreciate gentle, sensitive people more than supermen.

I was much younger than my siblings were. I was ten years younger than my sister Lena, and sixteen years younger than my brother Jan. I often wished that we were closer. Such a big age difference rather alienated me from them in the first place. As a result, I did not have as close a relationship with them as I would have liked. Jan was always preoccupied with his own life, and rightfully so. Before the war, friends, girls, and the theater quite excitingly filled that life. The move to a new apartment from Pokrovka to Novoslobodskaya, took place without him as he was somewhere having fun with friends and came home only after midnight. I was so young, and he was so busy, that I do not remember much about him before the war and when the war began, he left to join the army. Lena and I were much closer, possibly, because we closer in age and we were evacuated together with my mother during the war.

It would be wrong to end my family description without mentioning the names of several other relatives dear to me. My favorite aunt Raya also played a very important role in my life. Raya was my father's sister, and she dazzled me with her worldly wisdom, strength of character, her dedication to her family and infinite love for all. I also owe a great deal to my mother's brother Semyon, or Senya, a talented musicologist, who instilled in me a love of music. Until the last day of his rather difficult life, he managed to retain his adolescent enthusiasm and love of beauty, which delighted me. The third person I would like to mention is the sweet Balya, my mother's sister Bella. An economist by education, Balya worked with my dad at one time. Each of these people was important to me and I will write more about them in the following pages.

OUT OF STEP WITH THE WORLD

During the WWII people of the Soviet Union were truly out of step with the world fighting the Hitler Nazis. They even were infamiliar with the term Second World War as the whole world called it. The generation of my peers swallowed large doses of propaganda lies about it and did not have right to know truth. We had to believe the Soviet myth that the USSR alone was waging a "holy war" against Hitler's fascism, and since that time till today Russians are calling this war the Great Patriotic War. And what was happening at this time in the rest of the world, we had to be not interested. I was not an exception in this sense and together with others enthusiastically bawled something in the spirit of the "Song about Anxious Youth" by A. Pakhmutov (music) L.Oshanin (lyrics), written after the war in 1958, but exactly reflecting mentality and morality drummed into Soviet people's heads:

> *Our care is simple, and this is our care:*
> *Let our dear country live well, we have no other worries.*

We were not allowed to care that the rest of the world had just undergone a bloody, monstrous Second World War, which became the largest armed conflict in the history of humankind, involving 80% of the population of the globe? We were not allowed to know that more than 60 countries participated in the military conflict or that battles were fought in forty countries. We were unaware that for the first time in human history, the number of civilians killed in the war exceeded the number of soldiers and officers of the armies of the participants. All this was carefully hidden from the Soviet people.

Stalin did not want the people of the world, and especially those of his country, to know the truth about World War II, and the mountains of lies grew. These lies still clog the heads of many Russian citizens and natives of Russia scattered around the world. Moreover, such well-crafted political disinformation has inevitably led to incredible confusion in the statistics published around the world about the war. To this day I personally continue to learn more and more facts about the unsightly role of Stalin the "great leader and teacher" and the Soviet leadership led by him in the struggle against the Nazi atrocities. These facts fill me with bitterness. They are a mockery of the memory of the great number of remarkable people around the world who laid down their lives to free the world from the Nazi monster. They are a bitter mockery of the efforts of my own family, my loved ones, many of whom, including my father and my brother, who served in the Soviet army. About a dozen of people close to me never returned from this terrible war.

A good illustration of what I have said in the previous paragraphs is the history of post-war publications in the Soviet Union on war casualties. All further figures I cite include both the army and the civilian population. For instance, in 1946, Stalin personally stated that Soviet causalities in the War were 7 million, trying to convince people that Russian losses were fewer than Germany's 7.5 million. By 1961, N.Khrushchev estimated that the number was closer to 20 million people. Only in 1990 did the Soviet people learn that the real figure was closer to 26.6 million Russian people lost in the War.

The total losses of all other countries in this war have never appeared in the soviet media in Russia, and they were enormous. The total losses in the world were approximately 80 million people. China lost about 25 million; Poland about 6 million; Japan more than 3 million; Yugoslavia, Philippines about 1 million each; Hungary about 0.9 million; USA, England, France, Italy about 0.5 million each. To say it was a war fought only by the Soviets is a travesty.

And the treachery begins at the beginning. Most historians count the beginning of WWII from September 1, 1939, when Germany crossed the western border of Poland and attacked it. The Russian media referred to this event as the Wehrmacht's invasion of Poland. Just a few days later, Britain and France declared war on Germany. Secretly from the Allies, Hitler and Stalin were acting in a very coordinated, planned way. Almost at the same time, just 17 days after the Germans invaded Poland, the Soviet Union, having crossed the eastern border of Poland, attacked that small country from the other side. Unbeknownst to the world, the Stalin and Hitler had already agreed to divide Poland between them. In the Russian media, this event was referred to as the Red Army's "liberation" march into Poland. The Soviet Union by agreement from Nazi Germany was allowed to take over Western Ukraine and Western Belorussia. So, in November 1939, we were told that Western Belorussia and Western Ukraine "voluntarily" joined the USSR. After that, about 1 million people were forcibly deported from these territories to the eastern regions of the USSR. The Soviet army occupied about 3/5 of the Polish territory. Capture was accompanied by Red Terror and approximately 30 thousand innocent Poles were killed.

After that, the USSR committed with impunity its next steps of undisguised aggression, which, for reasons I do not understand, it was not held accountable. In the same November the Soviet Union, again with "liberating aims," attacked Finland. The Soviet Union was expelled from the League of Nations in December for unleashing this invasion, but that did not stop the Soviet leadership. The outcome of the war was clear because the forces were unequal, and the army of the Soviet Union was many times larger than the Finnish army. However, Soviet losses in this war were much higher than Finnish losses. According to data published in Russia in 2012, 167,976 soviets did not return from the war. According to the latest data from 2005, only 25,904 Finns were killed in the war. The victory was reached by the number, not by the skill. In March 1940, the captured territory, again was "voluntarily" annexed to the USSR.

From June to August 1940, the Soviet Union threatened an ultimatum to Romania, demanding the transfer of Bessarabia and Northern Bukovina to Russia. The transfer of Bessarabia, already in the secret Molotov-Ribbentrop Pact had been previously agreed upon. The Pact did not say a word about Northern Bukovina. The Romanians began to consult with Hitler on what to do. The Führer was surprised by Stalin's insatiable appetite but advised the Romanians to give in. He believed that the suffering of thousands of people inhabiting the territories did not matter and that in any case, very soon everything would be quite different. Romania obeyed the advice and without a single shot withdrew its troops from these territories. This allowed the Soviet army to invade on June 13, 1941, 10 days before the beginning of the Great Patriotic War. Thus, the Soviet Union took away Bessarabia and Northern Bukovina from Romania, which also "voluntarily" joined the Soviet Union. At that, the bastion of socialism did not change its usual tactics and approximately 30 thousand Moldovans were forcibly deported or killed during this rapid invasion.

In June 1940, the Soviet leaders became concerned about the strengthening of the fascist elements in Lithuania, Latvia, and Estonia and, again in fulfillment of the agreement with Nazi Germany, they introduced their troops there. In August 1940, all three countries at once "voluntarily" joined the Soviet Union. In each of the three countries, thousands of citizens were shot or deported to Eastern Siberia for their national patriotism, religious or non-Marxist beliefs. Stalin's "strengthening the borders" of Soviet Russia had increased its territory by more than a million square kilometers. Based on all these facts I do not understand why historians don't name the Soviet Union on a par with Hitler's Germany as one of the main instigators of World War II, and moreover as allies of the Nazis. The Russian rulers, Stalin's heirs kept the Molotov-Ribbentrop Pact secret until 1990. We know so little about other documents that might shed light on the secret affairs between Stalin and Hitler. Moreover, today's Putin government has prolonged the secrecy of many infamous war-related archives The cat knows whose meat he has eaten.

In the previous paragraph, talking about the expansion of the USSR borders, I several times chose the word "voluntarily," a term used and taught when discussing Soviet history. When in eighties I was spending my leave from work in some border areas of the USSR I have heard few very sad true stories afrom the victims survived these "voluntary" assimilations. My hair stood on end from what they were telling me. About 50 years passed since that time, and I sill recall with shudder two of these stories.

In the early seventies I came with friends for a few days to Vilnius, the capital of Lithuania, one of the largest cultural centers in Europe. Tourists from all over Russia loved to visit the city to admire its architecture. Before World War II, the city was one of Europe's largest Jewish centers. Napoleon, passing through Vilnius on his march to Moscow, called it the North Jerusalem. I was lucky to meet there a very interesting Lithuanian architect who showed us around the city. Unfortunately, I don't remember his name.

This man remembered well those days in 1940, when the Soviet Army entered Vilnius. Now documents are available to us, showing that about 2% of the Lithuanian population was then shot or taken to jail. What I heard from this man forms the content of the first story. On the very first day the Soviet army entered Vilnius, one of the large churches of the city was crowded with many families with children seeking sanctuary from the invaders. They locked the doors from the inside. Short talks through the closed doors with those inside did not lead to an agreement. Then the Soviet military command gave the order to blow up the church. The order was carried out, and the church was exploded and all the people inside were killed. At the end of the story my new friend told me, *"Yuri, my son is ten years old now. When he comes of age, I will tell him this story with all the minute details."* I am sure he did.

The second story is about a woman I met during our refusenik summer gatherings between 1986 and 1987, in the Latvian resort town of Melluzhi on the Riga seashore. These gatherings were organized by our good friend, fellow refusenik Alexandr Marjasin who lived in Riga. Two years in line he was inviting many refuseniks from Moscow to come there. From my point of view, these refusenik congresses in Melluzhi were a very remarkable social phenomenon. Many highly educated, energetic and active refuseniks would come together from Moscow and organize endless classes in yoga, Hebrew, tennis, Tai-Chi, English, held academic seminars and concerts of Jewish song. We discussed interesting books, had excursions to local places of interest and music concerts, not to mention time to relax on the wonderful sandy sea beaches.

We lived 15 minutes walk to the sea beach in a small house in a very comfortable room which was rented to us by Sasha Maryasin. The property owner, a former teacher in a Boy Scout school, was an intelligent and kind woman with whom I always enjoyed to talk. Her eyesight was very bad, so of course I asked what was the problem with her eyes. In response, she told me another horrible story. During the first weeks after the invasion, the Soviet administration repeatedly spoke to her rather harshly about her teaching and the mood of her students. At some point, they demanded that she report any anti-Soviet sentiments of her young students. After she refused flatly, the occupiers went from words to torture. They beat her so badly that she lost sight in one eye and 50% of her vision in the other. I was in utter amazement, how this woman endured such torture and yet managed to maintain her unique benevolence! Not a single time did I sense any bitterness in her attitude towards myself as a representative of Russia.

So, let us return to the autumn of 1939 when friendship and love affair between Stalin and Hitler began. It was then that a secret, now infamous conspiracy between two villains called the Molotov -Ribbentrop Pact was prepared and implemented. Ministers of Foreign Affairs of the two powers agreed and signed a treaty of non-aggression and mutual assistance for 25 years (!?). The especially secret part of the protocol contained the map of the agreed division of Europe. Apparently, for all territorial seizures at that time Stalin was inspired by Hitler and had his full agreement and support.

It's incomprehensible to me how Stalin in the maddening division of the world could allow his country to play such games with Hitler, thus making our country at least temporarily his ally. At that very time, a fierce battle against fascist evil was already being fought. Russia's British friend and ally was being subjected to monstrous daily bombing raids (the Blitz, 1940–1941) by the German Luftwaffe that substantially destroyed the major cities of England, killing more than 43 thousand peaceful inhabitants and leaving homeless about one and a half million people. In response to the Blitz, on the initiative of Winston Churchill, about two million children were evacuated away from their families in the major cities of England to strangers in the countryside, leaving many children scarred forever.

In addition to the political treaty, from 1938 onwards the Soviet Union engaged in continuous economic negotiations with Hitler's

Germany. These negotiations resulted in several trade agreements for the exchange of goods up until the time of the Nazi attack on the USSR. The last train with wagons loaded with wheat delivered by the Soviet Union to Germany crossed the border an hour and a half (!?) before Germany invaded Russia on June 22, 1941. Soviet deliveries to the Germans also included raw materials for heavy industry, in particular, various metals, iron ore and petroleum products. Much of this metal soon began returning back to Russia in the form of Nazi planes, tanks, cannons, bombs and shells, destroying the country on an unheard of scale and killing its inhabitants.

Now knowing all these facts, once kept in strictest secrecy for decades, isn't it natural to ask who really unleashed the Second World War? After all, facts are stubborn things! Any open-minded person must agree that two socialisms must be named: German national-socialism and Soviet socialism.

On June 22, 1941, Hitler's hordes crossed the border of the USSR. It looked as if someone had magically switched the brains of at least one side of the conflict. I am not sure if this was the cunning of the rivals, their miscalculation, or just the twist unprincipled villains who always sought not peace, truth, and progress, but power, deception, and domination at all costs. Monstrous as it may seem, up to 1942, when Hitler's army reached the borders of Moscow, Stalin still sent secret messages to his former friend with offers of a peace treaty and territorial compensation. Stalin ruled the territory of the country and his conquests as his personal property. Hitler thank God, rejected these offers. Russia and its allies paid a huge price but won. I will try to tell you how my family and friends passed this terrible time in the next chapter. Here I should thank Heaven that this tragedy ended with Germany surrendered unconditionally.

On 7 May at 02:40 in Reims on the initiative of the Supreme Allied Commander Dwight Eisenhower the Act of Germany's unconditional surrender was signed. German General Alfred Jodl signed it on behalf of Germany. It was accepted on behalf of the victors by American General Beddell Smith and General Francois Sevez of the French Army. Eisenhower suggested that Soviet Major General Ivan Susloparov sign the Act on behalf of the Soviet Union. He immediately sent the text of the Act to Moscow and asked for permission to sign it. Stalin did not wish to acknowledge this date or this Act of Surrender and refused to allow Susloparov to sign the Act. However, Generalissimo's ban did not arrive at the appointed signing time. Susloparov took responsibility and signed the document on behalf of the U.S.S.R. Thank God, the great leader was visited by a good spirit, and no one punished Susloparov for his apparent disobedience. But Stalin demanded that Marshal Zhukov sign a separate surrender act with Field Marshal General Wilhelm Keitel one day later.

As a result, on May 8, the entire world except the USSR exulted, celebrating the victory over Germany, while the citizens of the USSR knew nothing about it. The day was hot in Moscow, and the windows at the British Embassy were wide open. There was laughter and a cannonade of flying champagne corks. After the British anthem the New Orleans jazz sounded. We now know that British diplomats were celebrating victory. We now know that Lady Churchill, 60, easily climbed into a chair in the large embassy hall with her glass and gave a toast: "*Let's drink to victory!*" The embassy staff hugged each other. Then Muscovites were not dignified with the opportunity to learn and rejoice with the Allies, the truth about the war was hidden from them.

By such manipulation, Stalin tried to convince the Soviets that the victory over Germany was won solely by the efforts of the USSR. That is why he was not willing to share the joy of this great event with the Allies and, in general, with the majority of countries of the world. On Stalin's orders, the Soviet people could not know the fact that most of the world, including all Western Europe, the United States, Australia, parts of Asia and Canada, celebrated Victory Day on May 8. In most countries, leaders congratulated each other and their people, on that day. Millions of people around the planet sang, danced, and hugged each other. In London, the royal family and Prime Minister Churchill delivered moving congratulations to their citizens from the balcony of Buckingham Palace. The Soviet press reported none of this. Stalin insisted that Russian citizens celebrate their own victory over Germany the next day, May 9, 1941, separately and independently, as if the allies in the war did not exist at all.

The Soviet Union had the conscience to mislead the ignorant people of the world by claiming, contrary to the real facts, that the

Allies were not really involved in the war with Germany at all and joined Russia to share in its glory when victory had in fact already been achieved. As a result, most Soviet people believed this myth and identified the entry of the Allies into the war with the opening of a second front in Western Europe in 1944. When in fact the allies actively fought Germany and its henchmen on different fronts from the very beginning of World War II in 1939 and did so until the end of the war in 1945. No one in Russia knew or wanted to believe in the enormous contribution of the Allies to the victory over Nazism.

Russia still spreads such propaganda and falsifications. The citizens of the USSR knew very little about the war with Japan or that the surrender of Japan had been signed in Tokyo only on September 2, 1945. They were not told that this was the actual date on which World War II ended. They were not told that it was this day that was declared by President Truman of the United States as Victory Day over Japan. Most countries in the world celebrate this day. The Supreme Soviet of the USSR in September 1945 decided to declare this day a non-working holiday. But after two years, in 1947 this decision was annulled. Since then there is no such holiday in Russia, and few people know about it at all.

I would especially like to mention the extensive program of military and economic aid provided by the United States to the warring Soviet Union and other countries fighting Nazism. This program was carried out under the Lend-Lease Act signed by President Roosevelt. on March 11, 1941. The English word "Lend-Lease" means, "to lend or lease." The scale of this aid is astonishing: America was lending lend-lease aid to 42 countries! The Soviet Union began receiving this aid about a year after the outbreak of war and continued to receive it until the end of the war. The countries that received this aid did not pay a dime for it, neither during nor after the war. Some part of the value was to be returned only for what at the end of the war continued to retain some material value and could still be used.

The Soviet authorities tried to keep the knowledge of the American lend-lease aid from the citizens of the USSR just as it had the knowledge of America's involvement in winning the war. The scale of this aid was always either grossly disparaged or completely failed to mention. And it was by no means negligible, totaling about $17 billion! The country received: 2,150 airplanes; 1,2700 tanks; 13,000 artillery pieces; 35,000 motorcycles; 427,000 trucks; 2,000 steam locomotives; 281 warships; 128 transport ships; 11,000 railway cars; 2.1 million tons of oil; 4.5 million tons of food; 15 million pairs of shoes; 44,600 metal cutting machines; 263,000 tons of aluminum; 387,000 tons of copper; 1.2 million tons of chemicals and explosives; 35,800 broadcasting stations; 5,899 radios; 348 radars, and more. It's interesting that even Stalin himself on November 30, 1943, speaking at a luncheon in honor of Churchill's birthday, said this about the aid: "*The United States is a country of machines. Without these machines received under the Lend-Lease program, we would have lost this war.*" But his statements were not made public until very recently.

The fact of Lady Churchill's visit to the USSR in May 1945 and the purpose of that visit were also hidden from us. And yet Clementine Churchill came to the country not only as the wife of one of the most prominent leaders of England, not only to share the joy of victory with her compatriots in Russia, but as the head of the British Red Cross "Help Russia" program. Since 1941, the British people of all ages, from pensioners to schoolchildren, rich, poor, regardless of belief or attitude to communism, had been donating their pences, and pounds to "Mrs. Churchill's Fund" and in doing so had raised over 8 million pounds. Wikipedia states that to represent this money in the modern equivalent, this amount can be safely multiplied by 100. She also brought to Rostov a complete set of the latest equipment for two hospitals with 1500 beds each.

By the end of the war, my Tanya was 6 years old and I was 7, but we still both remember well the joys of receiving overseas gifts. These gifts were distributed among the families of military service members, and both of our fathers received them regularly until their demobilization. Tanya often recalls how her father received thin Wulen underwear, which kept all family members warm in the frigid Russian winters. Tanya and her sister wore skirts made from the high-quality cloth issued for sewing military uniforms. And I remember the special food rations which we used to take free at a big grocery store on Arbat street. I loved to go to get this ration with my mother and every time I looked forward to the American canned sausage, which seemed like an incredible delicacy. These canned meats and other American foods came to the USSR under the Lend-Lease program.

The history of small post-war payment of the remaining debts is interesting. These debts could be paid in large installments, and all countries paid the required amounts by about 2000, except, of course, the Soviet Union. Stalin was unwilling to pay, saying the Soviet Union had paid it all off in the blood of its citizens. Again, this was based on the great lie, the notorious belief that only the Soviet Union had spilled blood in this brutal war. I am not sure that after the collapse of the USSR, an agreement was reached to partially repay Russia's $2.6 billion debt. Britain's debt to the U.S. at the end of the war was $4.33 billion, and it was repaid in full in 2006. France paid off America in 1946. Negotiations with Russia on this matter have been going on with varying success up to the present day, and as Wikipedia says, Russia has paid part of the debt after all. And it should finally pay off the US in 2030. Now with war brewing, will it ever be repaid?

THE FATHERLAND IS IN DANGER

This was the name of the Declaration of the French Legislative Assembly of 1792, which called on the population to be ready to repel any attack on the French Revolution by its possible enemies. The French Revolution could be reproached for many things, but by issuing this declaration, it was concerned not only with the preservation of its own power, but also with the national security of the country.

Stalin, obsessed with the idea of the communist conquest of the world, did not hesitate to make love to the fascist monster, to begin with, trying to divide with him the world amicably. Hitler saw through his plans and, not wanting to share the world with anyone, attacked the Soviet Union, which was not at all ready for the war, on June 22, 1941.

The war with the USSR began in 1941, when I was only three years old and my sister was 13. My memory did not retain anything remarkable until that time except a general feeling of a happy and carefree childhood. Only much later did it come to me that I owed that feeling mainly to my parents. With the outbreak of war life in the family changed dramatically at once. My father and my brother were called up for military service, and my mother was left alone at this difficult time with two children in her arms.

Father served in the Black Sea Fleet, providing maps for military operations in this sea. He was lucky in military service: in the army he managed to use his knowledge and experience in geography and cartography. Thank God, as he was not on the front line, we regularly received letters from him throughout the war. The thing I was particularly proud of were the letters from my dad to me personally, which I tried to answer. For me, those were the happy moments when my mother would put me on her lap and read me Daddy's letter. From such correspondence, a couple of my letters to Daddy have survived. One of them is before me. I handwrote it on the back of a piece of outline map for high school with ragged edges—no one could get clean paper then. I wrote in large block letters, and I rarely managed to get the letters more or less the same size, because I put them in between the lines that my mother had drawn for me with a pencil especially for this purpose. I was 5 years old, and I give the uncomplicated text of my letter without correcting the spelling and syntax. Oddly enough, punctuation aside, there is only one error in the letter.

My father with me during WWII

> DEAR DADDY
>
> JAN SENT US MONEY. WHY DIDN'T YOU SEND ME THE MANDARINS I ASKED YOU FOR? I HAVE ONE PENNY. CHEERS, I KISS YOU YURI.

The letter was neatly folded into a triangle familiar to everyone during the war, so that the same piece of used paper became not only a letter but also an envelope because no one had those either. On one side of the triangle, right along the pale green lines of continents, rivers, lakes and the address of the cartography factory in

Tbilisi where my father's maps were printed, my mother penned the date, May 1943. Postmarks of Saratov, where we were evacuated, and Tbilisi are also visible on the same side of the triangle. Also visible is the stamp: *"Viewed by the censor. Saratov."* Such "envelops" were never sealed. Only later, the understanding came to me how much such practice made the work of censors easier. Stamps were not required at the time as all letters to the army were sent free. Such a small act of humanity pleased me then and continues to do so today.

This triangle reminded me of a very popular song of that time by Yu. Levitin to lyrics by N. Labkovsky. "Field Post," from which I quote here two verses:

> *Whoever has been with the military at the advanced front line,*
> *Will justify and understand the fighter,*
> *Who, despises death and bullets,*
> *And is ready to dance having received such letter...*
> *While in a distant village, a mother weeps with happiness,*
> *Finding out her son is healthy and alive.*
> *Just such field triangle is bringing to her this news*
> *In spite all the battles and the hardships.*

I find the lyrics of this song very heartfelt, except for one line about despising death and bullets. I find this disdain to be ideological bravado, uncharacteristic of most normal people, not supermen. I doubt that the poet himself, when faced with bullets before death, feels contempt rather than fear.

Back to my brother, Jan. Immediately after graduating high school he entered aviation school in Kharkov, after which he went to the front and served as a navigator-bomber in the Air Force. I must give him credit for writing to mother quite regularly, though not as often as Dad did. But I don't remember him writing to me or to my sister like Dad did.

For some reason everyone was sure that this war would not last long. The official propaganda worked surprisingly effectively: most Soviet people had no doubt that our country was the strongest and our army the most powerful, and of course, we would easily defeat the Nazi scum. Even when the German army approached Moscow and the evacuation began, many thought that it was only for a short time. My parents decided that my mother with the children go to the city of Saratov on the Volga River, where her sisters lived. We planned to live there for a while and then go back to Moscow. No one thought of severe hardships and long deprivations then. Apart from us two children, my mother also agreed to take her nephew, the son of her sister Balia, who was of my age and whose father had been killed in the first days of the war. The aunt of mine could not leave Moscow without loosing her job. At the first time after the outbreak of the war, the transport system had not yet been destroyed. We went to Saratov by steamer via the Moscow-Volga waterway.

Mother's sister Fanya and her husband Misha Michelson were respected people of Saratov: he was the chief of the city's ambulance service and she was the chief gynecologist. They had a wonderful apartment. They had no children, but my mother's other two sisters lived with them. The front line was quite far away from the city and, during some time, our life there was much quieter than it had been in Moscow. My sister, Lena, went to school and always being an excellent student, tried not to miss a single day of classes. We received regular letters from my father and brother.

My grandmother, my mother's mother, who lived with Michelsons and died in Saratov, was no longer alive, but family lore preserves two funny stories of the last period of her life. Grandmother adored her son-in-law Misha. She thought he was the cleverest man in the world. Here is the first story. During the last years she listened daily with interest to the weather forecast and every time when the forecast was not justified she would turn to the wisest member of her family: *"Misha, explain me please, what was the point of lying to them?"* Here is the second story. On election day, Grandma usually had someone from the polling station sent to her house to vote. Grandma would usually ask this person, *"Who do you want me to vote for?"* Let's say she would get the answer, *"For Voroshilov"*. The grandmother would say: *"Nooooo, I won't vote for him!"* A bewildered representative of the polling station asked: *"Why, Granny? He's a very respected person. Who would you like to vote for?"* Granny invariably would reply: *"Only for my son-in-law Misha."* The man went away empty-handed. Not many people in those days dared to show such adherence to their principles. Thank God, Grandma got away with it with impunity.

The German army was advancing swiftly, and the roar of war approached Saratov. The city was bombed, the windows were darkened, and there were escapes to bomb shelters. For some reason, in my memories it was always at night. My mother quickly dressed me sleepy, wrapped me in a blanket on top, took me in her arms, and we all ran to hide in the cellars of the neighboring house. At first, these wake-ups were even somewhat enjoyable. Of course, the first moment, when they woke me up and took me out of a warm bed, was unpleasant. But then the buzz began: I, as a big boy, could stay up so late and be with grown-ups. I remember very well a blue Wool blanket with big oak leaves on it. Apparently it was winter time, because as we ran down the street, huge stars of snowflakes lay on the oak leaves and didn't melt for a long time. I thought it was very beautiful at the time. We kept the blanket and brought it back to Moscow, together with the memory of the amazing warmth that it gave me. It served us well at home for a long time before it became too shabby and fell apart. Gradually the bomb shelter lost its peculiarity and became routine. Mom told me that in the last years of our life in Saratov, when we were escaping to the shelter, she used to dress me and wrap me in a blanket, and sometimes I did not even wake up.

In 1943, the bombing in Saratov became more frequent, and soon it became unsafe to stay in the city. All the evacuees began to move further east. For our family such movement was difficult because we had no acquaintances or relatives in those parts of the country, and we could not count on any help. My father and my brother were in the army, and my mother and the children had to go into total obscurity. In such circumstances, my mother was afraid to take her nephew with us, so we had to contact his mother and somehow arrange for him. So the the three of us set off on our way. Daddy wrote to us that the family of one of his graduate students lived in Uralsk, and he insisted that we go there and contact him. By this time the war had wrecked most of the Soviet systems, especially the transport systems. All the train stations in the country were crowded with people trying to go somewhere. It was almost impossible to get on a train. Exhausted people were waiting for a chance to get a ticket for several days. Some were sleeping one next to another rough on the stone floors of railway stations, some sitting leaning on their bags and suitcases. Some laid out a newspaper on the floor as a tablecloth melancholy were eating their meager food. Most were women with children and the elderly, since most of the able-bodied men were in the army. To this day, when I get into crowded train stations, those gruesome scenes begin to float before my eyes. We were very lucky. My mom's other sister was some kind of military sanitation chief, and her suitor was the head of the sanitation train. So we managed to get on a sanitary train, taking the wounded from the front line to the east of the country, and we started the difficult road of evacuation in the company of some of the first victims of that awful slaughter. I was five years old at the time.

On this very train, I suddenly, for myself and even more so for my mother, I became the breadwinner of the family. Even before the war, my mother often read me nursery rhymes, which I loved very much. I learned many of these verses by heart. One day I recited loudly to my mother, sister and cousin what I had memorized. And at that time, the head of the train was passing through the carriage and heard my performance. He asked my mother to come into his carriage office and he said: "*It turns out we have an artist on the train. We want to employ him. Why doesn't he read poetry to our wounded, and as a paycheck we'll give our artist the food rations that all our employees get.*" Mother could not believe our happiness: today it's hard to imagine what the train manager's offer meant at that time of hunger. And like in a fairy tale, that's what happened. I walked around the wagons and proudly read my favorite poems to the wounded soldiers. Since that time my family began to receive one-person food rations, which we happily divided among three people. My performances were a success. I remember that the wounded with pleasure listened to me. They especially liked the poem by Agniya Barto:

> *Lida is my little sister.*
> *I would not let anyone to hurt her.*
> *You cannot hit them, girls.*
> *We have to love the girls.*
> *I live with her very amicably,*
> *I love her very much.*
> *However when I need it,*
> *I shall beat her up myself.*

As I was writing these lines, I decided to see if I remembered the text accurately today, and I was surprised to notice the changes that had occurred over the years. First of all, the poem somehow got a new title, "What a protector!" which was not there when my mother read it to me. Secondly, the third and the fourth lines disappeared from the poem for some reason. Unfortunately, the poet is dead now and we will never know what she was guided by when she made the changes. I am quoting this verse here as I remembered it in my childhood, and I think the old version is better. The sanitary train brought us without much adventure to the city of Uralsk in the Ural Mountains.

Before I left for the Urals, an event happened that played an important role in my life. My memory has not preserved the details, but during the evacuation, according to my mother's story during one of the German bombing raids, a bomb exploded quite close to us. Thank God none of us was injured but somehow I received neurological trauma. When I got back to Moscow, my mother took me to the district neurologist. It turned out to be a very nice woman. She examined me thoroughly and found some slight disturbance in my symptoms. She said that I could live and study normally, but advised me to register at the neurological dispensary. We will return later to this.

I remember very little of the Ural period. The general feeling is darkness, cold and dirt. Life in Saratov from here was remembered as life in paradise. We tracked down my father's pupil and found out the sad circumstances. He himself had an open form of tuberculosis, and lived in a terribly overcrowded apartment. Living in that apartment was out of the question. Mom went door-to-door trying to find some inexpensive shelter. We were let into a house on the outskirts of town. Our hostess was a harsh and practical woman, one of those who had not been shy about profiting from people's misfortunes during the war. She would never forget to ask my mother money for any little thing. There was a big Russian stove in the house, and we were allowed to boil one kettle of water only once a day. When I later questioned my mother about that time and about that woman, she tried to avoid answering my questions. But I remember one episode myself. There was no central water supply in the house. It was freezing and the water from the well was freezing. One day, when the stove was heating, my mother poured water into a bottle and put it on the floor near the stove to warm it up a little. The landlady noticed this and demanded that Mama pay extra for it.

In general, we remember short frosty days and long dark evenings. Either there were power outages or we were saving it, but often in the evening the only source of light in the room was a small homemade kerosene oil-lamp, or "smokestack" as we called it. I can still see my sister at the counter in front of the smokestack late at night preparing lessons for school. And the school, due to lack of space, worked in four (!?) shifts. Lena was fifteen years old and studied in the fourth shift. Classes would end very late and she would walk home alone in the bitter cold and pitch black. As I write these lines, my heart sinks at the memory of what she went through. But even in such unbearable conditions she did not miss a single year of school! And not only that—all her schooling during the war years took place completely without her mother's participation. Mother had enough troubles with the organization of our life, and, by the way, in that too, Lena was her first assistant. I did not understand it then, but now, when I remember Lena in Uralsk, I can clearly see Dad's leaven in her. How good it would be if today's schoolchildren all over the world knew more about how the best representatives of my sister's generation studied in the Soviet Union during the war years. Looking ahead, we returned to Moscow in 1944, and Lena immediately went to school No. 208 of the Oktyabrsky district, from which she graduated in 1946 with a gold medal. For me personally the story of her schooling remained for the rest of my life an unattainable example of diligence in schoolwork.

During the war, the whole country lived in unsanitary conditions, but a place like Uralsk was breaking all records. Lice were so widespread that it was almost impossible to get rid of them, especially for those who regularly went to public places. My sister, after all, regularly went to school. As a result, my mother had to check thoroughly all Lena's clothes and body every day to remove lice.

By the time we left Saratov for Uralsk, Dad's mapping unit was also moved further east. Now he was serving in Omsk. It was great luck for us, because we found ourselves much closer to each other. In 1944, my father was able to come to Uralsk to visit us. He was horrified when he saw the conditions in which we lived. By that time, the Soviets had begun to push the German army westward, and Dad insisted that we return to Saratov, and then, lo and behold, home to Moscow. So we set off on our way back.

I do not remember our trip back, but when we tried to get into our apartment, squatters occupied it. While we were away, people who lived in barracks in our yard had moved into our apartment. Attempts to persuade them to vacate our flat were unsuccessful. Their arguments were very simple: *"You were hiding somewhere in safety, while we stayed and fought off the Germans. Now this apartment is ours."* The conflict was of a purely class nature, and the house management was clearly on their side. Their representatives said, they did not know how to help us.

In despair, my mother wrote to both my father and my brother. The front line at that time had moved to Eastern Europe. My brother Jan was advancing victoriously with our troops to the German borders. As a navigator-bomber, with the rank of Second Lieutenant in the Air Force, he regularly flew bombing missions against German cities. After he learned about what had happened to our apartment, he arranged a short leave with his commanders and came to see us in Moscow. He arrived from the front line like a conquering hero. With his full regalia and medals, he appeared before the people who occupied our flat. Unlike my mother and me, Jan did not ask them for anything. He simply said that if they did not leave our apartment within a day he would come and throw from the sixth floor window all their belongings into the alley. Only a victorious soldier could afford such clear and ultimate speech. Surprisingly enough, it turned out to be much more productive. Even before Jan's return to his unit, the flat became available and we could, though the war was still rumbling in Eastern Europe, begin gradually to restore our normal Moscow life.

Of course, normality was relative. Electricity and gas, though intermittent, were working, but the water supply was not. We lived on the sixth floor, and there was no elevator in the house. Our men had not yet returned from the war and it was difficult for my mother to fetch water. Our brick house stood in the middle of Tikhvin Lane. I had to go out into the lane for water and walk all the way to the corner of Tikhvinskaya Street where there was a water fountain. I was six years old and I could not carry a regular bucket of water. However, my mother got a two-liter canister especially for me and I went to fetch water with it. My sister Lena used the bucket. When at last the water pipe was switched on, the pump capacity was enough only to lift water to the fourth floor. Nevertheless, it was already much easier: there were nice people living on the fourth floor who allowed us to come to take water from their apartment. Later a more powerful motor was installed, and the water began to rise up to our floor. Still the power of the motor was not enough to provide the water pressure necessary for the normal operation of the gas water heater. It took many years until we had reliable hot water around the clock. What a luxury!

I described the water story as an example of the hardships our country experienced even after the war, and this includes the massive food shortages. Food supply in Moscow was always better than in other regions of the Soviet Union, but there was still rationing of many goods. Most food products, including even bread, were sold on ration cards. Our family was fortunate: we received double rations and ration cards because two members of our family were Soviet Army officers at the front. Once Mom asked me to go to the bakery at the beginning of one week with our bread cards, which were to be used daily and last through the week. I do not know how it happened, but I came home with the bread issued for that day, but without the remaining cards. I cannot say whether somebody stole them from me or whether I dropped them myself. Anyway, I deprived the whole family of bread for the rest of the week. Although it happened more than 65 years ago, to this day I still feel my heart shrinks when I think about it. I was ashamed of myself then.

BACK TO PEACEFUL LIFE

In the spring of 1945, the German army capitulated and on May 9, Moscow celebrated Victory Day. I still remember what an irrepressible jubilation it was. All night long, happy people were walking along the streets and the whole sky was decorated with floodlights. The fireworks were unforgettable. And quite high up in the dark sky, shining like a bright rectangular planet was huge portrait of Stalin. Of course, it was a celebration for our family and me personally because both my father and my brother had survived and their demobilization from the army was very close.

I was seven years old, and I was sure that the terrible evil had been defeated by our country and the happiest period in our lives was beginning. How little I knew then of what was really going on in the world! It took me more than thirty years to learn the truth about what was happening during the war, how it ended, how the victory was achieved and how was it celebrated. The Soviet country refused to acknowledge the role of other countries in the fight against Hitler's fascism.

Anyway, it was great for us that both my dad and my brother soon actually returned to us, alive and well. Dad resumed his academic work. And, although he worked a lot at home, that didn't mean that I could often spend time with him. His workday started around six in the morning, when the whole house was still asleep. He would quietly make himself a glass of tea, grab some bread and a jar of jam, carry it all away to his office and close the door tightly behind him. He would then spend long hours at his desk, and no member of the family could disturb him unless he himself came out of the study to take a break. How often I found an extra excuse to walk past that closed door in the secret hope that that would be the moment, Dad would come out and I would be the first to intercept him! The funny thing is that Dad's morning jam left an indelible mark on my memory and emotions. For many years now, I have been drinking tea without sugar, but always with jam. Generally speaking, jam had for centuries been an important element of life in Russia. A good example would be the hospitable Larin family in Eugene Onegin by A. Pushkin:

> *A simple, Russian family,*
> *With great diligence towards the guests,*
> *With tea and jam, and eternal conversation...*

And, of course, jam was homemade, not store-bought. Even with all the scarcity of berries and fruit in Moscow, every autumn brought to our family a passion for jam making, which I liked very much. My mother would make jam, and I would help her—wash, peel, cut, and we would talk... Inulia, my brother Jan's wife would make jam, and I would help her—wash, peel, cut, and we would talk... To this day, I still love it when my wife Tanya and I would make jam together, and I would help her—wash, peel, cut, and we would talk...

My brother's return to civilian life was more difficult. My father went into the military service, having already had extensive professional experience and established connections, which helped him to return quickly to the job he loved. My brother, on the other hand, had a much harder time. He joined the army voluntarily, literally from his school years, immediately after completing secondary school. After graduating from aviation school, he had become a bomber navigator and flew in the vanguard of our army during the whole war. He was demobilized and came back a victorious hero who had visited most of the countries in Europe and was unprepared to start mastering a new profession. He considered it humiliating to go to school again. But our father intervened very decisively. Although my brother was an adult himself, his father's word was still a law for him. My brother wanted to go to any job, but my father said: *"Forget this nonsense. The war is over, you have to study and acquire a peaceful life profession. It's never too late to study and it's never a shame."* And my brother did what his father wanted. He enrolled in an evening University, worked during the day and in a few years got a degree in higher education in a field related to his service in the army—earth photography from planes.

Things were more complicated for Jan on the personal front as well. Being an emotional man, he fell in love and left his beloved women from a young age. While serving in the army in Austria he also had an affair with a woman, which he never concealed. For me, a boy of seven, brought up on romantic literature, such "amorousness" went against my view of the world. From those days until today, I have remained an old-fashioned man and stuck to my former view. As for the Austrian novel, my brother did not speak German, and I could not understand how it was possible to love a woman with whom one did not speak a common language. My brother's explanation, in the spirit of S.Yesenin:

> *You cannot express love with words,*
> *Love—is just sighing furtively,*
> *With your eyes ablaze, like rubies...*

seemed to me utterly ridiculous. And the ease with which my brother forgot all the objects of his pre-war love, and then his Austrian love, seemed utterly inconceivable to me. After the demobilization, the feeling of being a hero only added to his self-confidence on this "front." It seemed to him that all the women of the world should be at his feet. However, then again, our father intervened. He cooled his ardor and told him that such behavior is not the behavior of a noble man. One should choose a worthy woman and get married.

It seems to me, my brother felt the need to heed father's advice. I do not know exactly how it happened, but soon with our father's approval he married a woman named Inna Kogan. Unfortunately, this marriage did not turn out to be a happy one either for Jan or for Innulia, as we all called her. Although it lasted for almost thirty years, it did not stop my brother's infatuation with other women, as my father and I would have liked it to. Thank God, either Dad did not know about most of these infatuations, or they happened after Dad's death.

I liked Innulia VERY much, and I will try to write about my feelings for her in a separate chapter. I want VERY much to think that both my parents, and my sister had similar to my feelings for Innulia. I loved her kind-heartedness and her humanitarian interests, which we obviously did not have in my family, were important to me. It seems to me that her children inherited these qualities from Innulia. In short, for purely selfish reasons, I am grateful to my brother for giving INNULIA to ME. It sounds paradoxical, but it was a very happy marriage for ME. Moreover, it saddens me that my brother never realized until the end of his days how much he himself got from Innulia.

Innulia's mother, Bluma Kogan was a kind pediatrician who loved and treated all the children around us, including myself. She reminded me the personage of very popular Russian poem for kids by Korney Chukovsky with funny title "Doktor Ahithurts". My parents loved her very much. I was always attracted by her infectious way of laughing. I was also always quite fond of Innulia's brother Genia Kogan with his amazing modesty, education and love of poetry and music. In Genia's eyes I saw the eternal Jewish sadness. My nephew Lyova in his poem "Uncle Genia" found surprisingly precise and touching words to describe this sweetest man. Two stanzas from Lyova's poem I want to quote here:

He wore in his sad eyes
That question in the Beginning,
That still never got any answer.
His days and nights flowed by,
Leaving behind poetic lines
That produced inconspicuous but enduring mark.
Now his granddaughter wears his eyes
In that ill-starred suburb,
In which he recently wandered himself.
And after all, the sun and the wind
Hurried to him with an answer,
It was the quiet day of his funeral.

After the War, there was no problem for my sister Lena to start a peaceful life: she would always take sound decisions and did everything properly. On her return to Moscow, she immediately began to continue her studies at the school next door to our house, from which she graduated a year later with a gold medal. Then she was very lucky: she managed to start studies at the geography department of Moscow University. That was thanks to the fact that geographical community of Moscow new our father. Lena's classmates used to come to see us very often, I liked them a lot, and I was wildly jealous of my sister that she had such friends. I could not wait until I grew up, went to college, and had such friendly company too. Alas, as we shall see next, it never was going to happen. Lena after graduating with honors from Moscow State University went to work at the Research Institute of Geography of the Academy of Sciences. For getting this job, I think, we should also thank my dad's reputation. Again, many people working at the Institute knew well many of Dad's publications and respected his scientific work. I was glad and proud that the happy combination of Lena's abilities and of the Dad's reputation in geography worked so well for her.

NAMED AFTER GORKY

On September 1, 1945, I went to the high school No. 204 in the Oktyabrsky district of Moscow. Since by that time I could already read and even write a little, my parents decided to put me in the second grade at once. Now it seems to me that it was a mistake, but life was not slow to correct it. I was sick all year, missed a significant portion of classes, and my parents and teachers decided that I should go back to the second grade the following year. It was a big trauma for me — after all, I actually stayed in the same class for the second year. In my mind, this only happened to lazybones and slackers. I was ashamed to tell my friends and relatives about it.

But starting from the next school year, everything went well, and I gradually began to forget about such an unhappy start. I remained, for some reason, one of the best students in my class until graduation. The libraries at that time were full of Soviet ideological rubbish that had very little to do with good literature and no one thought to guide my reading. In general, my father, considering me reasonable and conscientious, and often said that school was my own business. As a result, no one in the family was interested in how I read, what I read, or what I learned. However, as far as reading is concerned, I had a great deal of luck with the school librarian who was a lovely, intelligent Jewish woman named Hassi Aronovna. I liked her very much, and every visit to the library turned into a joyous occasion for me. Hassi Aronovna became an unquestionable authority and my reading supervisor. It was thanks to her that I did not leave school being an ignoramus, like many of my classmates.

Dad was the most educated member of our family, and I always wanted to grow up to be as smart as he was. So all my life I have been sad to think how little he was involved in my education during my school years. However, when he did, it always left an indelible mark on me. That was what happened with foreign languages, for example. Dad repeatedly explained to me how knowing languages enriched a person's life. Moreover, he insisted on private lessons in English for me, when I was still in elementary school. It was these lessons that laid the foundation for my interest in translation work and the joy of this work, an interest I have had all my life and still have to this day.

I remember my silly and naive emotions related to school. First, I was so excited that my school was named after A. M. Gorky, in my mind at the time — one of the greatest personalities and writers of the world. After it became a basic school of the Academy of Pedagogical Sciences, my pride had no limits. After the Gorky's name appeared in the school's signboard, I used to bring my friends and boast of it. How naïve I was to have mistaken the bureaucratic propaganda and "show-offs" going on at school until my last grade, as something very important and meaningful.

One incident, however, made me think about the fact that not everything was great about this "best of the best" school. Among my classmates and friends was Vladimir Pluzhnikov, whom I really wanted to be my friend. He seemed to me the cleverest in class and besides he was very good at drawing and was the constant designer of our wall newspapers. One day a very political Soviet story happened to him. At the beginning of the school year, all boys had to write an essay about how everyone spent their summer vacation. Shortly after we handed in this homework, a wild scandal broke out, and it had to do with the content of Volodya's essay. At a class meeting, our teacher read out loud to us the "criminal" phrases from this essay, which caused outrage. I will try to reproduce them close to the original. *"I spent the summer with my parents at the dacha. Most of the time I sat in my room and either read or drew. My mother constantly tried to kick me out of the house to play outside with the kids. I refused and told her that let the goats run and jump, but I like better what I was doing."*

The entire teaching staff at the school went into ferment and resented how parents could bring up such a belligerent individualist. Volodya's parents were summoned to the school, and in their presence and in our presence a proceeding was arranged. The teachers demanded that Volodya and his parents publicly acknowledge the heinousness of such an act, and they succeeded. Volodya, with a heavy heart, told our class meeting that he had committed an immoral act. I was totally embarrassed, but then I did not yet know what "political correctness" meant. Volodya was in my class the only friend I had during my school years, and he was just as "proper" as I was, although more capable and more educated in the humanities. Anyway, I felt very upset and very sorry for Volodya.

I cannot help but end this sad episode by mentioning a humorous fact about goats running and jumping. There were only boys in my school at that time, and in our class alone (41 people) there were three boys with the surname Kozlov and two with the surname Baranov, both family names are transliterations from Russian. But what was really funny, was the meaning of these words: first—"related to a goat" and second—"related to a ram".

In comparison, Tanya, according to her stories, had at this very time very different experience in her school. She was smarter and more well read than me, but she tried to be more free in her behavior. As a result, she had a large group of people with whom she had fun. When she told me about it, I was very jealous of her. She lived near Krasnaya Presnya, which was famous for its hooligans, and there were several such guys in her class. She was the best in her class, but she managed not to stand out among them, not to reject them and thus earned their respect. Together with them, she participated in their pranks, skipped classes, did their homework for them. In the end they all loved her and stood behind her as a wall. When Tanya was graduating from high school, one of them confidentially told her: *"If they don't give you the Gold Medal, we'll blow up the whole school."* Thank God, Tanya got a medal and the school survived. And the jubilant bullies all as one found out somehow before the others about this happy event and, scaring the neighbors in the communal apartment, came to the door of the apartment, flashing their false iron teeth: *"Tanya, buddy, congratulations on the gold!"*

I recall one more funny memory of my school. When I was, I think, in fifth grade, there was a nationwide campaign of labor education. Because our school considered itself an advanced school, we immediately introduced two new subjects, one blacksmithing class and one carpentry class, each once a week. Both subjects were taught by wonderful teachers, whom I liked very much. I do not remember, unfortunately, their surnames. The blacksmithing teacher's first name was "Abram" and his patronymic was "Semyonovich" which in Russian meant "Son of Semyon". The carpentry teacher's first name was "Boris" and his patronymic was "Abramovich" which in Russian meant "Son of 'Abram". Such a funny coincidence with using the biblical Jewish name Abram (Abraham) was quite rare in the anti-Semitic Soviet Union and always carried a negative association. We quickly invented our own full names for then: "Abram Iron" and "Boris Wood" and everybody in our class never called them otherwise. I like to use these names in this book for the purpose of the name index. Perhaps these two men awakened in me an interest in hand made wares that has remained in me to this day. However, to be honest, it saddened me myself that the two very nice people were so "unfortunate" with their names. Apparently, it was thanks to "wooden Abram" that my love of wood, my love of woodwork, developed in me. This love later blossomed into my lifelong hobby, woodcarving, to which I will return. Thank you, Boris Abramovich.

From the early days of school, I was unthinkably politically active. It was probably my father's influence. I was a good student and I never disobeyed school discipline. As a result, I was one of the first in my class to join the Pioneer Organization, and a year after that I was elected Chairman of the Class Squad Pioneer Council. It was my responsibility to prepare and conduct regular meetings of the Unit. For me it was always excruciating, because every time there was nothing to discuss and I had to squeeze a topic out of thin air. My young Leninists (as the pioneers in the Soviet Union were called) were deadly bored at our meetings, and it was quite difficult for me to get them to sit quietly for a while. Nevertheless, it seemed to me that the interests of the "cause" demanded it, and I tried my best. I recall one amusing incident. My pioneers were particularly excited about something, and I could do nothing to silence them. And I must say that almost all of my classmates, including the Pioneers, were actively using obscene language. I was quite a rare exception, and nobody ever heard a curse word from me. However, this time I just became furious, being unable to calm them down. At one point I, unable to cope with myself, loudly slammed my fist on the table and yelled at them, I beg for the readers apology, *"For fuck's sake, can you shut up at least 15 minutes!"* The effect was incredible: a deathly silence came, in which I quickly jabbered the speech I had prepared. I was terribly ashamed, but, on the other hand, it seemed to me that my pioneers were more respectful of me from then on.

In general, I grew up as a quiet and very "homely" child, never fighting, which irritated many of my schoolmates and yard children, including even some of the girls. Getting ahead of time, I must say that, already reaching, I would say, an old age, never in my life I have struck a single person. As a result, I mostly felt like an outsider at school and on the street as a child. Unfortunately, I only had one friend at school—Volodya Pluzhnikov—and none in our yard. I feel pity that my and Volodya's paths went different direction and I do not know anything about him today.

Let us go back to my pacifist ways again. There was one girl in our yard, I would say, rather impudent, whom I particularly disliked for her rudeness and insolence. For some reason she was annoyed that I was so quiet, and she repeatedly tried to provoke me into doing something nasty. Then one fine snowy day in Moscow, when there were many children walking in the yard, she suddenly rushed over to me in full view of everybody, picked up the handfuls of snow and began to rub this snow on my face. Shocked, I barely got out of her hands, bounced a few steps away from her and shouted at her: "*I thought you were smarter than that.*" After that, seeing that no one around me stood up for me, I quickly ran home. The mood was disgusting.

I remember another episode from my relationships with my peers in the yard. When my dad came home and got out of the Navy, he did not need his uniform anymore. I really liked the navy emblem on his cap and asked him to give it to me. Dad did not mind, and I asked my mom to help me take the emblem off the cap and sew it onto my hat. Afer she did it, I quickly got dressed and ran into the courtyard filled with pride. Of course, the children in the yard rounded me up and asked me what I had attached to my hat. "*Oh! You don't know, It is an emblem!*" I replied. In response, I heard friendly laughter. From that day on, no one in the yard ever called me anything other than an emblem. It seems funny to me now, but at the time, it insulted me to tears. First, I found it offensive just because "emblem" was a feminine noun in Russian language. Secondly, I considered it a mockery of our glorious Navy, and finally, I saw in this nickname a reproach that I was different, that I was showing off by using a complicated foreign word. It made me sick. I saw an exceptionally friendly attitude among family members and our friends and naively expected the same attitude from the rest of the world. It was a good lesson for me. From my present life experience, I realize that I was punished justly for my own naivety, insensitivity, and tactlessness.

I have already mentioned my indomitable political activity in my pioneer years. Now, from today's perspective, I relate this to what my family taught me. I was the youngest, and I was brought up completely unaware of the inhumanity and immorality of the "evil empire"—as my beloved president, Ronald Reagan, later summed up the Soviet Union. Wonderful people, in the form of our relatives and friends, surrounded me for the most part, and I naïvely believed that my country's political system ensured that everyone was like that. My parents, unfortunately, not only failed to dissuade me from this delusion but they even actively supported this illusion in me. They did this mostly by their personal example.

My father's authority was unusually high for me. I did not know what was happening before the war, but during the war, when the German army occupied half the country, he joined the Communist Party. Everybody knew well that the Nazis were particularly brutal in their crackdown on Jews and Communists. How much you had to be devoted to your country, how little you should value your own life to perform such a "heroic" act in these hard days: it was not enough to him to be Jewish, he decided to become also a communist. It was clearly a political statement.

Even more to-the subject story happened to my brother. My father never went near or even crossed the front line when he was making military maps for the Navy. My brother, serving in aviation, all the time flew combat missions over the occupied territory. And following my father's example he joined the Communist Party in those days. One day my brother's plane went off the route in close proximity to the front line, and fuel was running out. Both crewmembers — my brother, the bomber navigator, and the pilot managed to land in a small clearing in the woods. About a month, the brother with his comrade-in-arms hid in the woods, risking to be discovered by the occupants. The conversation got on getting rid of the brother's party membership card. However, the brother categorically refused to do it. A physical fight broke out between the comrades-in-arms, and the brother won. Fortunately, they managed to return across the front line to not-occupied territory. My brother returned to his unit, retaining his Party card, thus avoiding, like some of his comrades in arms, political persecution. Some of them were even arrested.

I was proud of those stories, trying to be like my father and my brother. My political zeal was ridiculous. No amount of meaningless pioneer political activity could stop me. The Komsomol (Young Communist League) rules allowed you to join after the age of 14. I just could not wait for that moment. Several of my classmates, being older than me, had already become Komsomol members. Many of them were not a moral example to me at all. This fact depressed me, but did not alarm me. I was asking myself: "*How could it be?"* After all, we are supposed to accept the very, very best. Nevertheless, this did not dampen my enthusiasm. Now there was another campaign for admission to the Komsomol. At that time, I was a few months short of my full age of fourteen. At this time I commit a desperate act: I submit an application for admission, indicating in the documents a false date of birth, adding to myself the missing months. Unbelievable, but true: I was successfully accepted! Funny, but no one bothered to check my documents with those kept in the school and detect the forgery. I myself was convinced I was committing a heroic deed. Of course, that was what we had all been taught: the goal justifies the means.

Proud and happy, I ran home to tell my father what a hero I was. The thunderstorm came out of the blue! To this day my father's terrible rebuke sounds in my ears: *"What a son I have raised! He starts his life in the Komsomol with a lie!! It is a shame on my old head!"* Speaking about the old head — my father was 52 at the time, and four years later he was gone. At that moment I wanted really to burn with shame and stop living. It did take me long to recover from my grandiose political success. This event greatly poisoned the joy of my early years in the Komsomol, and, as I think now, moved me just a little bit towards the epiphany that came much later. However, at that time I still continued to strive to devote all my energies to the improvement of what was already "the best country in the world".

INNULIA

Looking back, I have to say that I am very happy that Jan and Inna got married, though my brother probably felt otherwise. We all fell fondly in love with Inna, or Innulia, as we called her. Innulia became very close to me, the closest person after my parents, even closer than my own brother and sister. She is no longer with us, but I am still overwhelmed with tenderness and gratitude for the fact that she was in my life and gave me so much. So, what did she give me? Although Innulia was only 13 years older than me, I always perceived her, I cannot explain why, as a representative of the older generation, as a kind of a second mother. This is not often the case: I saw in her a motherly love, care, and interest in me personally. To be honest I have never felt being-a-son feelings towards my brother Jan, who was three years older than Innulia. Anyway, even as a child I realized that having a second mother wasn't a bad thing at all. I think it is possible to explain my closeness to Innulia by several circumstances, which I will try to describe.

My sister (on the left) and Innulia with me

First, from the very beginning until I left the apartment we lived together as a family. I moved into my own apartment only about a year after my first daughter Galina was born. So, all this time Innulia shared with us everything that was happening in our everyday life. At the same time her participation was much more than Jan's and Lena's. I think this was because both brother and sister led a rather active life outside the home connected to school, work and friends. However, for Innulia, unfortunately, that kind of life did not work out somehow. Despite being the nicest person and wonderfully kind-hearted with everyone in the family, and with me especially, it was obvious that she was sad and she did not share her life outside the house with us. The situation was, I would say, painful. At communal meals, each of us except Innulia used to talk about coworkers, classmates, and friends. We knew almost nothing of the kind about Innulia.

Somehow, it leaked out that at first she studied at some medical college. However, none of us knew exactly which one, and what's more, we were not sure whether she graduated successfully. After that, it came to our attention that she was working in some laboratory, but no one ever found out what she was doing there. Then at some point, she stopped working at all, and no one ever found out why this happened. It bothered me then and continues to bother me even now when Innulia is no longer with us. It saddens me that none of us, me including, could find a way to help her with her problems or at least make her comfortable to share with us her struggles. Moreover, I never could understand how the closest person to Innulia, my brother, could not support her in her difficult situation. Therefore, it seems to me such a reproach should be addressed to him, in the first place. But as they say, every cloud has a silver lining. As a result, ulia has had more time and mental energy to give her warmth to us. I am happy that I was so fortunate that I personally received a lot of this warmth.

I woud like to mention another circumstance that contributed to my intimacy with Innulia. My brother taught photography out of an airplane at a specialized school. The curriculum of the school required annual summer practice in areas of Russia where weather conditions provided a sufficient number of flying days. For this purpose each summer, Jan went with his students on a business trip for more than a month to the south of the country, usually to Ukraine. Innulia always accompanied him on those trips, and ALWAYS took me with them! I remember these southern vacations with Innulia with great joy. Everything was interesting there: warm weather, frequent bathing, better than in Moscow food, a lot of fruit and berries. The latter made it possible to make preserves: jams and infusions, and I very much liked to assist Innulia in such preparations. We were always proud to bring the results of these harvests back to Moscow to the delight of the rest of the family. On one such trip, Jan took me with him on a plane for a short "walk". They flew in little two-winged PO-2 planes, which everyone called "bookshelf". It was my first and the only flight in my life in an open airplane. I will remember it for the rest of my life, and my happiness was endless.

But even in the cold winters in Moscow, Innulia knew how to bring me joy. She was the only member of our family who would go from time to time to classical music concerts. Much to my regret, there was almost no classical music at all in my childhood. However, sometimes Innulia would take me with her. It was with her that my first visits

Innulia at the time when I already lived in the USA

to the Conservatory and Tchaikovsky Hall took place. A couple of times her brother Genya, a very nice person who knew music very well, was with us, and I was very proud to be in such great company. It was a pity that such cultural trips did not happen more often.

As a child, I was very fond of ice cream. During the war years, all of us had to forget about the existence of this product. I remember well the first time ice cream appeared in Moscow after our return from the evacuation. Our house was in Tikhvinsky Lane and at the corner of our lane and Novoslobodskaya Street a fat woman in a white apron with a trolley started to come and in her trolley she had... ice cream! For 20 pennies, she would take out from the high metal cylinder-shaped box a special spoon of ice cream and put it between two wafer circles of the layer about a thumb. It was a delicacy! So, for my first meetings with the woman in the apron, I went with Innulia.

Later parents would give me 20 pennies and I proudly went to this corner myself to live my life. However, the crowning moment of the ice cream epic was when later Innulia took me to the newly opened Café Ice Cream in Gorky Street (then the only one in Moscow!). We were sitting at a round table TOGETHER and a lovely waiter brought to each of us a metal vase with three different-colored (!) ice-cream balls. I thought I was going to fly to heaven with happiness.

When we left Russia for America in 1988, Innulia was one of the few people I had great difficulty parting with. I cannot resist quoting my congratulations to Innulia in 1995, when she turned 70. I wrote it, imitating my beloved Okudzhava and we emailed it to her. To this day, reading my poem still brings a tear to my eye. Here it is:

> *The windows bring a smell of a fried bred crust,*
> *There is an anniversary behind the curtains.*
> *Of course, we have an invitation but...*
> *Here we are without either dollars, or rubles.*
>
> *A brand-new Boeing is rattling its engines,*
> *Sweet horse, please hurry up, please hurry up.*
> *Ah, Inna-Innulia, I wish we had $1,000*
> *We are ready go either side of your soul!*

She is wearing a rather greasy apron,
It is so unthinkable not to be with her.
Ah, Inna-Innulia, we would be happy
Just bring, please your horses to us.

You would walk here with us in your silk dress,
Things would have been very different in Boston.
Do not stop whipping your horses, Innulia,
Hurry up to get them over here and we will talk...

Alas, Innulia and I did not get to see each other in Boston. The only time I came to Moscow after leaving in 1998 was to say goodbye to Natasha Weisman, the dying sister of my wife Tanya. That was the last time I saw her. Innulia died in 2012 and I, unfortunately, had no opportunity to come to Moscow to say goodbye to her. But she continued to live in me in her children, Olya and Lyova and her grandchildren. And then Olechka also left us. She was only 9 years younger than me... After Olechka's death we talked with her daughter Masha on the phone, but our grand niece has not come to visit us in America since then.

THE KAGAN FAMILY

It so happened that practically I did not know my grandparents at all. My mother's parents and my father's father died before I was born, and as for my father's mother, Berta, I only had a very brief contact with her. The only memory I have is when we returned to Moscow from the evacuation, she came to see us. The war was already ending, and I remember her words: *"I am already old, and my only wish is to live to see the complete defeat of the German invaders."* Alas, she died very shortly before victory. Fate, however, generously rewarded me for this scarcity. Daddy

My father's uncle V. F. Kagan

had a favorite uncle, Veniamin Kagan. His first wife Elena, the sister of my father's mother, died early in 1918, so I could not know her either.

In 1920, Veniamin Kagan married for the second time a wonderful woman named Maria. When they married, they each had two children from their first marriages. The large Kagan family became very close to us, and it played an extremely important role in my parents' life as well as in my own. Although Veniamin formally was only my great-uncle and that by his first wife, I brought from my childhood very warm memories that next to me were great grandparents, whom I loved and was proud of them. I do not mean to say at all that I was unlucky with the families of my parents' siblings. I had very good relationships with them, and with some even very close and important ones. I am writing about those relationships further on. Anyway, the Kagans have occupied a very special place in my life. In my first life, I spent quite a lot of time with them.

The Kagans had a large dacha at the station "42 km" of the Kazan railway. Every summer Maria would invit my parents and me to live with them at the dacha. We loved those summer months, which firstly, allowed me with my parents to spend more time together, and secondly, of course, we were in close touch with our beloved family. Daddy started a cheerful wall newspaper at the cottage, "Sun, Air and Water". Short name for it was the abbreviation for "dacha newspaper" in English, "Dachnews". Dachnews left in me one of the happiest memories of my childhood, and, most likely, this newspaper developed in me both ability and desire to write in general and to be a rhyme writer, which has remained till now. I will come back to "Dachnews" later

A remarkable fact that confirms our closeness to this family: when in the fifties my parents went away for a month to a sanatorium, they left me to live with them in their large apartment on Polyanka Street. For that whole month, while living with them, I went to the local school. Many members of this extremely interesting family had a very great influence on my formation as a person, becoming my mentors for life. Therefore, I feel obliged to tell more about each of them here and to express my deep gratitude to them for being in my life and for everything I have gained from them.

My great-uncle Veniamin, was probably born in 1869 in Kovno province (Kaunas in Lithuania), like the family of my grandfather on father's side. Since 1887, after graduating from the high school with a gold medal, he studied at the Mathematics Department of the University of Novorossiysk. In 1889, when N. G. Chernyshevsky died, V.Kagan together with a large group of students was in the Transfiguration Cathedral at the funeral service for the writer. N. G. Chernyshevsky was the dominant intellectual figure of the 1860s revolutionary democratic movement in Russia. That is why the police persed the assembled, and for participation in the rite, many, including my great-uncle, were expelled from the University and exiled from Odessa. Veniamin was also among the students of this group who organized the sending of a wreath to Chernyshevsky's grave. He was exiled to Ekaterinoslav under police supervision without the right to enter higher education institutions. An application for reinstatement in the university addressed to the Minister of Public Education, promising to observe all the rules of the university, did not help. As a result, V. Kagan studied independently the subjects of university course and in 1892 managed to get permission to try to pass seven examinations for a full course of physics and mathematics faculty of Kyiv University. He passed all of them and received a university diploma.

In 1897 Veniamin went to St. Petersburg, passed the exams and got the degree "Master of abstract mathematics". Outstanding representatives of the St. Petersburg mathematical school petitioned for his appointment as a privat-docent of St. Petersburg University. However, the Minister of Education rejected a personal petition of eminent mathematicians A.Markov and and K.Posse on the grounds of my grandfather's Jewish ancestry. Then in the same year, the Department of Physics and Mathematics of Novorossiysk University brought a similar petition, and Veniamin received this freelance (!) position. This event began the Odessa period of the life of Veniamin. To improve his financial situation, Veniamin actively joined the organization of the famous Odessa Higher Women's Courses, and then he taught there. He became the head of the Mathematics Department. During these years, Veniamin was also the head of the Society for the Assistance to Jewish Teachers, and he cooperated with the Society for the Promotion of Enlightenment among the Jews of Russia. The scientific and pedagogical interests of Veniamin explain his constant attention to the organization of publications in the field of science and education.

An important milestone in this stage of his life was the founding by him in 1904, together with his friend from the university, the mathematician S. O. Shatunovsky, of the publishing house Mathesis, which printed scientific and popular scientific physical and mathematical literature.

"Matesis" is a Greek word, and it means "science" or "knowledge". It is interesting that in the Soviet Union in 1947 an enlightenment organization was created — the Association Znanie (Russian for "Knowledge"), and within the framework of this Association, the Znanie Publishing House. My father took an active part in the work of this Association, gave lectures with it and published his scientific articles in the Znaiye Publishing House. I think it was not without influence of his uncle, who was always a great authority for him. The Society continued to exist after the collapse of the Soviet Union, but slowly and surely fell into decline, the number of its members dwindled. The sad outcome of this process was the liquidation of the Society in 2016.

In 1917, the Provisional Government made a proposal to give privat-docents of Russian universities a full-time paid position of assistant professor. This job would give them the right to qualify for the professorship in any university. The Academic Council of Novorossiysk University submitted its best privat-docents for this position. The University administration blackballed three Jewish candidacies, including Veniamin. A scandal erupted in the department and the Academic Council sent its protest to Rector A. P. Dobroklonsky about this. The rector rejected this protest. I remember the account of Veniamin's wife Maria of the story, Unuversity administration made it clear to Veniamin that he could receive a position only if he converted to Christianity. Considering such a condition morally unacceptable and even humiliating, Veniamin did not accept the offer.

Since 1920, my grandunkle was a professor at the Odessa Institute of Public Education. In 1922, he received personal invitation from O. Schmidt, one of the greatest Soviet scientists and researchers, to move to Moscow in order to head scientific department of the State Publishing House. In the same year, he became a professor at Moscow University, and since 1933 up to the end of his life he was the founder and head of the Department of Differential Geometry of Moskow State University.

At the end of the 20s, the collapse of the New Economic Policy in the USSR began, accompanied by brutal mass repressions against private enterprise. The best representatives of the Russian intelligentsia tried to stand up for the victims of the Bolshevik terror, and I am proud that among them was a very dear man, my great-uncle Veniamin Kagan. In addition, I am bursting with pride that the great poet of our time, O. E. Mandelstam did notice this and mentioned V. Kagan's name at the beginning of the now well-kown text of "The Fourth Prose":

> *Veniamin Kagan approached this case with the wisdom of a Bethlehem sorcerer and a Newton of Odessa-mathematician. He based all his conspiratorial activity on mathematical infinitesimals. Veniamin Kagan saw the law of salvation in the turtle's pace.*
>
> *He would allow shaking himself out of the professor's box; he would take the phone receiver at any time, he would never promise not to give up, he would never refuse to help, but mainly delayed the dangerous development of the disease.*
>
> *Not only professor's, but even mathematician's, presence in the improbable business of saving five lives by mind-blowing, perfectly weightless integral moves, called efforts on behalf, caused universal gratifying.*

I am overwhelmed with pride in my great-uncle, whom O. E. Mandelstam called Newton. After all, all enlightened humanity takes off its hat in front of the scientific discoveries of Newton, this genius of physics. I remember well, as a child, I loved the epigram translated into Russian from English by S. Marshak. Below I give my back word-to-word translation of Marshak's lines:

> *The world was in deep darkness.*
> *Let there be light! And here comes Newton.*
> *However, Satan did not wait long for revenge.*
> *Einstein came! Everything returned back to like it used to be.*

Many years I I liked so much this poem and was remembering this lines by heart. I always wanted to find out who is the author of the poem and to read the English original. Shame on me, I found out the answer to this question only quite recently. It turned out that the first two lines and the second two lines of the epigram were not only written by different poets, but also in very different times. The only thing they have in common is that both authors lived in England. The author of the first part is Alexander Pope, a famous English poet of the 18th century, one of the greatest writers of British classicism who proposed these lines as an epitaph to Isaac Newton's tomb. Pope's original lines are as follows:

> *Nature and nature laws lay hid in the night.*
> *God said, "Let Newton be", and all was light.*

The twentieth-century English poet John Squire wrote the last two lines, as an extension of Pope's epitaph. In the original, it reads as follows:

> *It did not last, the devil howling: "No!*
> *Let Einstein be!" Restored the status quo.*

I have not able to confirm that Pope's lines are today on Isaac Newton's tombstone in Westminster Abbey. Anyway, I love the way S. Marshak expressed everything in Russian.

One can find the historical background of the Mandelstam's Paragraph in, for example, the notes to the book by O. E. Mandelstam "Save My Speech Forever," Poems, Prose. "E" Publishers, 2016. In May 1928, the authorities arrested bank employees of the private Mutual Credit Society and sentenced them to execution. The sentence bothered my granduncle so much that he managed to meet with the member of the Central Committee of the Communist party, N. I. Bukharin and asked him to pardon the convicts. I did not find information about whether my granduncle managed to save lives of innocent people. Shear fact that he tried to do so warms my heart.

In the same 1928 in the USSR, the trials of "saboteurs" on the so-called "Shakhty trial" began, and the head of the publishing department of The Union of the State Publishing Houses A. S. Lizarevich, who was invited to do this job by my grand-uncle, was arrested and sentenced to expulsion. This arrest was followed by the arrest of V. F. Kagan himself after the false denunciation. Then, two mathematicians, his followers managed to get an appointment with V. M. Molotov, the Prime Minister at that time, trying to convince him of the scientist's innocence. In addition, a group of famous mathematicians and physicists wrote a letter to A. Y. Vyshinsky, General Prosecutor at that time, with a request to release V. F. Kagan. The letter was signed by L. I. Mandelstam, A. N. Frumkin, G. B. Gurevich, G. S. Landsberg, Ya. S. Dubnov, A. M. Lopshits, I. N. Bronstein, G. M. Shapiro, M. G. Shestopal, P. K. Rashevsky. Thank to all these efforts, Veniamin Kagan was released.

Concluding the story about the unjust imprisonment of one of the most dignified people in the country, we would like to mention a sad fact. It would seem that knowing the political situation in the country, where illegal arrests took place on a massive scale, citizens, at least educated ones, should be extremely careful in their statements about others, so that the authorities could not consider these statements as political denunciations. The arrest of Veniamin was greatly facilitated by the irresponsible anti-Semitic lines in the diary of the outstanding USSR scientist Academician VladimirVernadsky, who described my grand-uncle this way: *"A sharp semitophil who surrounded himself with Jews and deeply felt their intellectual power. People say that this has been sharply reflected in his professorship."* It is very sad when such a major scientist becomes an informer and sends his fellow scientist to prison without any reason.

V. F. Kagan was the largest specialist in the country on non-Euclidean geometry, surface theory and Lobachevsky geometry. Famous English mathematician Kingdon Clifford William called Lobachevsky "Copernicus of geometry" V. Kagan was the initiator of the first Russian edition of the works of this great Russian scientist and also the editor of his works.

He was also interested in mathematical physics and met with A. Einstein during his stay in Germany. When Maria Kagan showed me a picture taken in Germany with Einstein, you can imagine in what awe it made me. Fascinated by Einstein's theory, my granduncle became one of the pioneers of teaching the general theory of relativity in Russia. He was awarded the title of Honored Scientist (1929) and the Stalin Prize (1943). In addition to innumerable courses for students, during all the post-war years V. F. Kagan was teaching a special seminar on the tensor analysis for professors and graduate students. In 1949, The Moscow University was solemnly celebrated my granduncle's 80-th anniversary.

However, the energy of the scientist was fading. Some time after his jubilee, the principal of the University Academician I. Petrovsky visited V. Kagan at home with a proposal to hold his seminar at his apartment. However, it was not fated to take place. In 1952, V. Kagan has retired from leading the chair of differential geometry in the University due to poor health. My granduncle died on May 8, 1953 and his grave is at the Novodevichy cemetery in Moscow.

An interesting detail about the burial of Veniamin Kagan. From Odessa times, he had a close friend and colleague a professor of Novorossiysk University the algebraist Shatunovsky. This man had a famous apprentice mathematician Fikhtegolts, the author of the reference book for the universities in Differential and Integra Calculus. Everybody in my generation, getting higher education in mathematics, was using this textbook. Shatunovsky died early in 1929 of cancer and was buried at Novodevichy Cemetery. In those years, this cemetery already had graves of celebrities, but then it always remained open to the burial of a wide range of people. Later on times have changed: to be buried at the cemetery they required permission from not less than the Central Committee of the Communist Party of the USSR (!?).

Although V. F. Kagan was one of the most worthy citizens of our country, when he died, there was no chance to get a place for him at this cemetery. Then S. O. Shatunovsky's widow offered my granduncle's widow to bury the body of V. Kagan in their family grave. All of us were happy and grateful to her for that. I will come back to the story of Novodevichy cemetery when I will get to the description of my father's death.

I feel some discomfort for not holding back and devoting a few paragraphs to my granduncle's exceptional scientific and pedagogical talents: of course, it was not what mostly fascinated me about him. Nevertheless, I have to recognize, I am proud of his achievements. I think that his entire professional life demonstrates impeccable morality, and in our mercantile times, I think it is so important to assure as many readers as possible that such people have lived among us. Of course, the first thing I want to do is to tell my wife, my children and my grandchildren about this man and his family. I saw something holy in everything that I knew about him, he seemed to me nobler and higher in every way than others did, and I always wanted to worship him. Probably, I have inherited it from my father, who, as I remember, worshipped his uncle. It always seemed to me that he even had the appearance of a biblical prophet.

He worked very hard, often outdoors on the terrace in the country house. Because of his spinal problems he could not sit for long, for this reason he always worked standing up at his office. I feel a bit embarrassed now, but back then I was glad that he worked standing up, because I could see his face better. I would often creep quietly to the opposite corner of the terrace, lie silently there and for a long time I could not take my eyes off his face. His voice seemed unearthly to me too. There was an unusual softness to it. And those were happy moments for me when Veniamin Fyodorovich paused to rest and sometimes, spotting me on the terrace, could address me with some trifling question. Every time I was terribly embarrassed: it seemed to me then, that I simply had no right to deprive this extraordinary man of his precious minutes for my silly talks. Now I am very sorry that I almost never dared to use such a unique opportunity more often.

However, I did unburden my heart with his wife, Maria. She was freer, of course, and I was extremely lucky that she was nice to me and was willingly telling me about her husband, their children and about their life in Odessa, in Europe, and later in Moscow. I remember well how she used to call him "Geinechka". It always seemed to me that she had invented such form of his name so well because in several languages it sounded to me as affectionate form of the word "genius". He really was a genius in many respects and that is how he remains in my memory. If Veniamin Kagan dwelled somewhere at a height, I think, unattainable for me and for many others, this remarkable woman was here, on earth, next to me and, what was quite incredible, we became friends. She seemed to me a very wise, energetic woman with a wonderful sense of humor, who took on the role of matriarch in the life of a large and extremely interesting family. All her life, Maria had been socially active. Her first husband, Joseph Levintov, worked with Veniamin Kagan at the Mathesis Publishers, and she herself helped him a great deal. I remember her telling me, not without pride, that there were only two people in her family: herself, Maria, and their housekeeper, who did not have a scientific degree. The funny thing was that this was the absolute truth: ALL the others by about thirty years of age became either the doctors of science or, at the worst, the candidates of science (pre-doctoral degree in Russia). Of course, I sat with my mouth open listening to the fascinating stories of my matriarch friend.

Some of these stories about pre-revolutionary Odessa were on the level of Babel's "Odessa Stories" by Isaac Babel. What a pity that none of my adult relatives encouraged me at the time to write down what Maria was telling me. As a result, some seventy years since then have done their work, and I cannot remember today most of what I heard. But here is one story that lingers in my memory. Their niece came to visit the Kagans in Odessa for the summer holidays. The weather was good, and most of the time the girl spent on the beach. One day she came home crying: somehow, her favorite wristwatch had disappeared. Maria asked her niece in details what exactly the missing watch was, and promised to try to help her grief. At that time, the famous Jewish adventuress Sheindlya-Sura Bluivstein, known by the nickname "Son'ka the Golden Hand", was coming to their house to clean it, unbelievably, but it was a fact. Maria told her cleaning lady of her niece's misfortune. After this, everything happened like in a fairy tale. A couple of days later, Son'ka brought back her missing watch stolen by her friends!

Veniamin Kagan's eldest daughter, Nadezhda, was the same age as my father. While working at the Institute of Experimental Medicine, she participated in the research and discovery of the tick-borne encephalitis virus. She developed the first experimental vaccine against this terrible disease. In 1938, Nadya tragically died after being infected with this damned virus while working in the laboratory. Medicine could not save her. To my great regret, I could not know her: Nadya died the year I was born. Since my childhood, I was proud of the fact that I was a nephew of the hero of science, who gave her life to save many and many people. There are many Books and documentaries about her.

Nadya's first husband, Isaac Barenblatt, was a well-known endocrinologist in Moscow, the author of a popular therapeutic handbook. Everyone in the family called him Ize. I remember a joke he made up himself that Ize was the chief specialist in "de-buttocking" the wives of Soviet bosses. I do not know whether he coined the word, but it meant that a large percentage of his female patients were Muscovites, who wanted to get rid of the impressive size of their buttocks. The truth is, Ize surprisingly managed to help them. You may ask, why just the bosses' wives? Because his reputation was so high that it was very difficult to get an appointment with him, and he charged his patients high. Only the bosses' wives could afford it. Ize was a witty person. He loved jokes and used to tell funny stories. I remember, around that time my mother was taking advice from Ize about the regular pain in my knee. After listening to her carefully, Ize gave her some advice that I still remember today. *"Give him less of that damn Mikoyan's food and more cottage cheese, and he will soon forget all about his pain."* Not many people out of Russia know that the main supplier of meat products in Russia since 1798 was the Moscow butchery slaughterhouses. Under Soviet rule, it became the state meat processing plant named after Soviet food industry commissar A. I. Mikoyan. By Mikoyan's food Ize meant meat and sausage products. I liked very much many of Ize's jokes. This one was especially to my liking because the two adjectives "damn" and "Mikoyan" rime in Russian. Ize had to pay dearly for his humor. Some "vigilant" patient of his heard a political joke from Ize and reported to the authorities. They took him to jail and, thank God, he had to stay in prison was not very long.

Mikoyan faithfully served the Bolsheviks for more than 50 years in the highest positions, started under Lenin, and finished under Brezhnev, and for such faithful service they hanged on his chest six (!) Orders of Lenin. Russians were joking about Breznev, that surgeons had to broaden urgently his chest to give enough space for all his awards. Back to Mikoyan, On this occasion there was rhymed joke about him in Moscow: *"From one Ilyich to the other Ilyich without a heart attack or paralysis"* (both Lenin and Brezhnew had patronymic "Ilyich").

My third cousin Grisha Barenblatt, the son of Nadya and Ize, is a well-known expert in theoretical mechanics and applied mathematics not only in Russia, but also in the West, a professor at many universities around the world. However, I want to remember Grisha's quite different achievements. There were rather complicated relations between the members of the Kagan family. Well versed in mathematical logic Grisha liked to joke demonstrating a rigorous proof that he was a third cousin of himself. It is funny to recollect, how I listened to his conclusions dozens of times, with my mouth hanging open in utter amazement.

Another big achievement of Grisha was our garden at the dacha. Each of us knew very little about flowers at that time. Suddenly Grisha took an unusual interest in this field, got in touch with a gardener and the result was brilliant: we grew wonderful phloxes and a fabulous jasmine bush. This way Grisha proved to all of us, not by word but by deed, that he can succeed not only in crack theory. Grisha's jasmine bush became my favorite. Curiously enough, when we became the happy owners of a house and garden in Boston Massachusetts, I wanted passionately to have a similar bush in our garden, but there was no way I could find and buy one here. A good American friend of ours found it somewhere and gave me a small shrub for my birthday. My dream came true: the bush has grown, and every beginning of summer we were enjoying both the view and aroma of a wonderful plant. Every time looking at the bush I remembered Grisha with gratitude. Unfortunately, in 2018 we moved out of our house into an apartment. It was a very sad farewell to the garden and to the beloved jasmine bush.

Nadya's second husband Grigory Sinai like Nadya herself, was a microbiologist and professor at the Moscow Medical School. After Nadya's tragic death, he married Nadya's collaborator Elizabeth Levkovich, who continued after Nadya's death the research on encephalitis virus. The group in which she worked was successful and all members of the group, including Lisa, received the Stalin Prize. All members of the family had mixed feelings: on the one hand, everyone was proud of Lisa, on the other sad that Nadya did not have to live to see this happy day. I think it was fair to award Nadya also this prize posthumously.

The son of Nadya and Grigory Sinai, my third cousin Yasha Sinai, well-known mathematician, expert in probability theory, professor at Moscow University, in recent years professor at Princeton University, member of the US National Academy of Sciences, since 1991 member of the Russian Academy of Sciences. When his mother Nadya died, Yasha was only three years old. He was raised by his grandmother Maria Kagan and his father's new wife Elizabeth Levkovich. On this occasion in our family there was rhyming joke about Yasha's name: "*Yakov Grigorich Sinai-Kagan-Levkovich* " (Grigorich is his patronymic in Russian).

We spent a lot of time with both Grisha and Yasha when we were living together in summer at Kagan's dacha. I remember many funny stories from the dacha years. All Grisha, Yasha and I liked to ride bikes there.

Beginning at some time, Grisha began to ride his bicycle frequently to the other side of the railway. Soon we found out that the object of his interest in these trips was a girl who lived there at the dacha. Her name was Ira Kochin. I remember that on one of his trips to Ira's Grisha had a minor accident and returned home with a bent headlight and a punctured tire. Grisha did not want to tell anybody the exact circumstances of the accident, which led to a merry discussion in the dacha-gazette about how dangerous it is to go to see an "untested" girl. I have in front of me the No.7 of Dachnews for 1950, where the following charade about Grisha's accident was published.

> *The first syllable is a musical note.*
> *The second was the god of sun worshipped on the Nile shores.*
> *The whole word is a long-suffering detail,*
> *Which Grisha's riding ruined.*

This charade is about the Russian word fa-Ra, which means vehicle headlight.

In addition to the charade, the newspaper published a poem signed "Observers" describing the details of the incident in a humorous way. Unfortunately, I have not kept the issue of Dachnews with these poems. But something has remained in my memory, and I recognize my father's style in it. Here is one stanza about Grisha's bicycle, as I remember it:

> *Our cripple is broken,*
> *Now it cannot rush anymore.*
> *A wicked man*
> *Put his hand on it.*

In response Grisha immediately, appealed to Dachnews with an indignant rebuttal (this issue of Dachnews is before my eyes and I am quoting this rebuttal with some cuts):

> *Dear Dachnews!*
> *In the last issue of your paper, some "observers" published verses, which is the most vile slander and fabrication. I feel obliged to make the following revelations: 1) Unnamed observers portray it as though I bent the headlamp. In reality, the headlight bent itself. 2) The observation that the tire has a puncture through it, is a shameless fabrication. Actually, there is a puncture but not a puncture through. 3) It says that the cripple can no longer rush. My bike is not a cripple and it rides just fine. 4) There was no wicked man who broke my headlight. Those are lies! I wonder where these observers come from. May be from Hearst?*

It is interesting to note that at the time multi-millionaire Hearst was the biggest press magnate in the US, owning 15 daily and 36 weekly newspapers and over 300 magazines around the world. The Soviet media always depicted him as a representative of the "yellow press" and a lover of scandalous publications. Our educated Grisha certainly knew the name. I have given here details of our Dachnews publications as an example of how much fun we had at the dacha, no doubt due to my father's ingenuity and sense of humor.

Now let us go back to Ira Kochin and Grisha's trips to see her. I personally as well as most of the family, liked Irochka very much. I do not remember how long the bicycle romance lasted, but Ira became Grisha's wife. Grisha soon after his marriage proudly told us all: "*Both parents of my Ira are academicians, Nikolai and Pelageya Kochin. It happened before only once in history, when the French scientist Frederic Joliot-Curie married Irène Curie, the daughter of Pierre and Marie Curie who were also both academicians.*" I cannot help adding here that Irochka appeared to be exceptionally modest and nice person with both of her parent so famous people.

Incredible development, but starting at some point, Jasha also started taking frequent bike rides to the other side of the railroad, and history repeated itself. The goal of Yasha's trips was Lena Wul, and she was the daughter of a major semiconductor specialist,

B. M. Wul. This time again, I liked Lenochka very much personally and so did other members of the family. This time the "bicycle" romance ended in marriage too. I started thinking that on the other side of the railway there was a special aura helping nice and proper girls to appear. I had to go also there by bicycle, which would guarantee me finding a great wife there.

By that time, I already had a bicycle, so it looked that now it is my turn. And my grand-aunt, Maria Kagan, also had this very idea. Through her friend from her days in Odessa, Lydia Mandelstam, she introduced me to Lidia's granddaughter, Tanya. The Mandelstams also lived on the other side of the railway! They were also an academic family: Lydia was the widow of a great specialist in the theory of oscillations, Academician L. I. Mandelstam.!! And for some time I too had a "bicycle romance" with Tanya Mandelstam!!! However, no matrimonial continuation happened this time and, unfortunately, our ways with Tanya Mandelstam diverged. Today I have absolutely no recollection of how it happened. My visits to Tanya on the other side of the railway left me with very warm memories of her, her parents and her grandmother. More than once, I wanted to find her, but my shyness stopped any such attempt.

Yasha was only three years older than I was. We had a warm, close relationship before we began the epic of emigration. I liked both him and his wife Lenochka, as well as Lena's parents and all of them treated me like a close relative. I appreciated this very much, rejoiced and was very grateful to them for this. In their home, I met some bright, interesting people. Among them, two people made a special impression on me: V. Arnold and M. Levin.

V. I. Arnold was Yasha's university friend. Both were students of A. N. Kolmogorov. Although his full name was Vladimir, I well remember that in Yasha's house everyone, me including, called him Dima. Probably, it was because the Russian VlaDIMir included syllable "dim". Dima became an outstanding mathematician of the century, having solved, when he was only 20 years old, Hilbert's thirteenth problem. In 1900, the German mathematician David Hilbert presented 23 cardinal unsolved mathematical problems at the International Congress of Mathematicians in Paris. In the more than one hundred years since then, 16 of them have been solved. Dima solved one among those 16 problems. He was only one year older than I was. When I met him at Yasha's, he was already a big celebrity in Moscow. At the same time, he struck me then with how modest and friendly he was with everyone. Today it is been thirteen years since Dima, unfortunately, passed away.

I also met the physicist Misha Levin at Yasha's at the height of the campaign to harass big Russian poet Pasternak after his getting Nobel Prize. That evening Misha told us the shameful story of the poet Ilya Selvinsky's involvement in this harassment, a story I did not know. He read us his angry epigram about it. I can not help but briefly relate both the story and the epigram, which I have remembered ever since 1958! While vacationing in Yalta, Ilya Selvinsky heard on the radio about the Nobel Prize awarded to Pasternak and rushed to the telegraph to congratulate the winner with a high award. The next morning the poor man read in the newspaper that all the Soviet people angrily condemned the renegade. Then he rushed to the Yalta "Resort Newspaper" and published there "Letter to the Editor", in which he added his voice to those who branded the traitor. I would like to cite here the text of Misha's epigram, which I consider genial, with two epigraphs (the first from old poems and the second from new ones by I. Selvinsky.):

Epigraph 1: *I love great Russian verse,*
Not yet understood, though,
I love all my teachers
Beginning with Pushkin and ending with Pasternak.

Epigraph 2: *I have missed human happiness*
By never hitting a single nail.

Misha's verse: *All is behind you, both glory and disgrace,*
What has still left is jealousy and stupid anger...
When the crowd crucified your teacher,
Here you came, hammering your first nail.

Dear Lenochka and Yasha. Thank you for a lot of things, including this evening in 1958. Misha, alas, is no longer with us. May he rest in peace! It so happens, that in one evening a person left such a deep trace in my life.

Together with Yasha, I have been on several interesting hikes and trips. For example, he and I had a wonderful trip to Altai.

However, my most memorable recollections are of a trip to the Crimea. I loved the Crimea and had been there many times before with my colleagues from ITM&CT. The trip to the Crimea with Yasha was special. Yasha's scientific adviser Andrey Kolmogorov was with us. This man made a huge impression on me. I have never had a worship of celebrities. Nevertheless, this time I really felt that I was in touch with something very big. He turned out to be a remarkably well educated man. Of course, I knew that he was one of the world's top mathematicians, but I could not have imagined that he knew so much about Russian history, the history of Crimea, and the history of the Crimean Tatars. It turned out that I was not yet born, and he had already been guiding tours around Crimea, telling many interesting things about that land to the youth. His stories were truly fascinating. I liked what he said, I liked the way he spoke, and it was somehow easy and comfortable to be with him.

It was on this trek in the Crimea that I had a funny incident with a telegram. I loved to travel, and I had traveled around the Soviet Union quite a bit. After Galya was born, I made it a custom that wherever I went without her, I would send her a message. It could be a joke letter, postcard or telegram, not very meaningful, with funny rhymes. When I married Tanya and then Vera was born, I extended the custom to them. Most often the postmen liked to send my dispatches which made them smile. But things were different. This time from the Crimea, I tried to send a telegram with the following rhyme:

> *We are walking bravely through the Crimea,*
> *With our bellybuttons exposed for tan.*
> *It is going gloriously well.*
> *I will put the period here: trying to save rubles.*

After reading the telegram, the woman at the window, in all seriousness, shoves the form back into the window and says: "We can't accept this text!" "What is the problem?", I ask her. "Replace the word "bellybuttons", please." "I can't, it'll break my rhyming!" I say. I get a sepulchral silence in response, and I see the irritation on her face growing. I thought that the case takes a scandalous turn, because such a prude could put me in jail for 15 days for hooliganism. I took the form and quickly went out on the street. I sent the same telegram safely to Galecheka from another post office.

At about the same time, maybe a little later, I got interested in the theory of graphs, very popular objects in cybernetics, and came to Latvia to the conference on graph theory. The conference took place in a very beautiful place of the Riga seashore. Unfortunately, at that time somehow my family problems preoccupied me and I could not focus on rather interesting papers. From there I sent a telegram home, the text of which is still in my memory:

> *To the lapping of the waves and the sound of the pines*
> *Graphs would come to my mind.*
> *But as unpleasant as it is,*
> *They would leave back in no time.*

With sending this telegram, I had no problem.

When serious illness of Yasha's son Sasha struck his family, we tried to support both the boy and his parents. What else could it be? We were close people. Unfortunately, politicians do not care about closeness, about kinship, about friendship. When we started our fight to leave Soviet Russia, we put ourselves in the category of *persona non grata*. In this situation, I felt I had no right to jeopardize Yasha's successful career with our closeness. I will write about this in more detail in the future. Slowly but surely we became estranged from each other, and then we lost all contact. This is very sad, but it was the part of my Soviet life.

Veniamin's youngest daughter Lida, five years younger than Nadya, was a specialist in the literature of the Middle Ages and taught at the Library Institute in Moscow. Both my parents and I liked her very much: she was the sweetest and kindest person with a wonderful sense of humor! I was lucky: we communicated with her a lot at the dacha, especially in the issue of Dachnews. Lidochka was an active correspondent of the newspaper, just like my father. I learned a lot from this favorite aunt of mine. I am proud to say that we were friends with her. We loved her until the last day of her life, which tragically ended in 1966 when a car hit her in the street. I think Lida, as well as her sister Nadya was the most worthy daughter of her father and I am grateful that she was in my life.

Until the end of my days, I will remember her. I am jumping now ahead to my last life when I was working as interpreter at the Jewish Rehabilitation Center for Elderly in Boston USA. Among those to whom I translated, I met my aunt Lida's colleague from the Library Institute, Irina Zhivov. She had taught German at Lida's Institute, and she seemed to me a wonderful and most interesting person. Ira remembered our Lida well, and I was proud to hear from her what a wonderful person she was. We became friends with Ira, and I was very glad to have such an unexpected meeting. How nice that the world is so small! I was still working as an interpreter when Irochka died and I was at her memorial service

Now about the two Maria's children, who were adopted by my granduncle. The older one was Ernestina Levintov. We all called her Tasia in the family; she was a Hispanist and professor at the Philology Department of Moscow State University. As far as I remember, Tasia worked all her life on the Big Spanish-Russian Phraseological Dictionary, heading a group of authors of the Moscow State University Spanish department. In 1970, Tasia's team published the Dictionary under her editorship that included over 30,000 vocabulary units. The publication was a major event in the lexicographic world. service.

Tasia's father, Joseph Levintov Sr. (Maria's first husband) was a very educated and interesting man and was well acquainted with no less than the famous Austrian physicist and philosopher Ernst Mach. Mach's philosophical writings formed the basis of the great trend in philosophy that bears his name, Machism. One should not mix up "machism" with "machismo" (exaggerated sense of manliness). E. Mach was Tasya's spiritual mentor and she was named Ernestina. after him. The Bolsheviks, led by Lenin and G. Plekhanov could not stand Mach's philosophy. The word 'Mahist' became a dirty word in Soviet Russia and the Levintov family received nothing but trouble from this friendship with the famous man. However, thanks to my friendship with Tasia, I got a lot. She was one of the most humanitarian educated women I have met in my life. Every time I visited the Kagans I would stay in Tasya's room and always would leave after getting a "cultural injection". I was always very proud that Tasya was my aunt and friend.

When I met Igor Melchuk in the 1960s and became friends with him and his family, I was VERY pleased to know that Tasya was his professor of Spahish language in philology department of the Moscow University. Moreover, she was one of his favorite professors. Here is a reference to Tasia in his recently written memoirs:

> We had a wonderful teacher, an absolutely amazing person, who had a great influence on my scientific life, Ernestina Levintov. As a matter of fact, I fell in love with linguistics because of her.

In addition to her broad philological education, she graduated from a music school, and her knowledge of music was at a professional level. I could learn a lot from Tasia. Meetings with Tasia started in my first life and I continued to enjoy them in my second, and later there will be a talk about those meetings. To my great regret, when we left the Soviet Union, all communication with Tasia and I don't know anything about what happened at the end of her life. I found out from the Internet that she died in 1993.

Maria's youngest child was her son Joseph Levintov Jr. In the family we all called him Zhozya. He was a professor of nuclear physics and chemistry, a man passionate about his science, but not very sociable. As a result, I did not have a special friendship with him. But I loved his wife Ida Levintov, the sweetest and kindest person, a piano teacher at the Moscow Conservatory's College. Remarkably, I don't remember anybody calling her Ida, only Idochka. I think it says a lot about the person. Then again, with our intention to leave Russia all ties with Idochka and Joseph were severed. Zhosya. died in 1970.

One room at the Kagans' dacha belonged to an old friend of theirs, a very nice woman whom all of us loved, Lyubov Loyevetsky. She was a widow: her husband was arrested and shot down in the thirties. She brought up her daughter Ella, whom we called Yolka (furtree in Russian), or, if to say it fondly, Yolchka. My father used to tease her and call her Yel' (old furtree in Russian). Before our eyes, Yolka grew into a pleasant young woman, married Semyon Gurevich, professor of journalism at Moscow State University, and gave birth to a son, Volodya. Another thing that brought us together was that Yolka befriended our Innulia. Every summer we communicated with the Gureviches when we lived in the dacha.

I decided to mention this family because Volodya Gurevich when he was a little boy, gave us a wonderful story. He grew up as a weak and sickly child. Parents and grandmother always tried to feed him properly. An important component of his diet was cottage cheese, which Volodya passionately hated. One day the boy came back from a walk in the yard and firmly declared that from this day on he refused to be Jewish because children in the yard were teasing him. His parents spent a long time explaining to him, that those who tease him are just silly children. There is nothing wrong with being Jewish. Many of the relatives and friends he is so fond of are Jewish, listing famous Jews who make up the glory of the world. Being a reasonable boy, Volodya could not find anything to object to such convincing arguments. At the end of this educational session, he gave in and said: "Well, all right, but if I still have to be a Jew, I would not eat cottage cheese anymore! At least he decided to do away with one evil. Volodya grew up and, following in his father's footsteps, he became a well-known journalist in Moscow and, in his later years, was editor-in-chief of the Moscow News newspaper.

SUNDAY LUNCHES

Even though Dad worked very hard and spent less time with us in absolute terms than I would have liked, in my opinion, the time spent with him was invaluable. I have already told you how he organized the publication of the dacha newspaper, which the editors, correspondents and readers alike remember with delight to this day. Another example of invaluable time with Dad was our Sunday lunches. Dad taught all of us to try not to bring up personal business at lunch time on Sunday so that the whole family could gather around the table. In doing so, he organized two traditions and, of course, played a major role in carrying them out.

The first was that each of us had to come up with and bring a dessert at the end of our Sunday lunch. What dessert in particular, had to be absolute surprise to the rest of the family until the last moment. There were six participants: parents (mom and dad) and children (Jan, Inna, Lena and Yuri). Everyone except me by this time was of legal age and financially independent. Therefore, I was an exception: I did everything together with my dad (that was happiness!) To make this program less financially burdensome for the kids, Dad set up a parent-child line system (Mom-

Jan-Papa-Inna-Mom-Lena-Papa-Yuri), so that each parent's turn came up every third Sunday, and each child's turn came up every seventh Sunday. Strict rule DID NOT ALLOW the repetitions of the same dessert! However, even if the same dessert was accompanied by a new decoration or some sort of new theatricality, it was not only allowed, it was encouraged. This way dad tried to develop creativity in us.

Different candies, for example, were not a repetition.

Nevertheless, we quickly exhausted simple variants, which required some ingenuity. I remember, for example, my turn came up, and I could not come up with anything new. Then dad suggested that we do a circus act. He and I bought type of candy that we already had once, but this time we tied a long (several meters!) chain out of the pieces. When it was time for dessert, Dad and I staged a festive procession: I appeared at the dining room door with one end of the chain in my hands, then the chain itself crawled out, and then Dad already with the other end of it. Although the candy itself was rather cheap, the performance went off by luck!

After a while, we added the second tradition. When dessert was on the table, a second surprise would come: in the same order of precedence, each of us would get and bring a music record. We would play it on the old-fashion turntable and we all would listen to it together sitting at the table. Of course, for musical records we had the same rule of not repetition. However, different arrangements and different performers were OK. Today I feel great regret that nobody, except Innulia, listened to classical music in our family. As a result, it was usually either a song, or an opera aria.

Anyway, of such listening sessions, we knew well many popular singers of the variety of vocal repertoire, such as A. Vedernikov, G. Vishnevskaya, L. Utyosov, K. Shulzhenko, I. Kozlovsky, N. Dorliak, S. Lemeshev, Z. Dolukhanov, L. Gurchenko, M. Magomayev and many others. Thanks to this tradition, music, though not always of the highest quality, became part of our family life.

BECOMING AN UNCLE

In 1947, when I was only nine years old, Innulia became pregnant. It was a joyous event for the whole family, but especially for me for many reasons. First, I liked Innulia so much and I was very happy for her. I was sure that the child would be as wonderful as her mother were. Secondly, with the birth of Olya I instantly grew and ceased to be the smallest in the family. Third, not only did my age increase, but also so did my significance. At only nine years old I had already managed to become an uncle!!! Not everyone manages that, and I was bursting with pride about it. It's amazing why most kids rush to become adults, shortening their carefree and therefore happy childhoods. I was no exception in that regard. Finally, fourthly, everyone expected Olya to come to be my parents' FIRST granddaughter. As for my dad, unfortunately, he did not live to see the next grandchildren...

I could not wait for her birth and it happened on September 2. In 1947, Innulia and Jan got a daughter, Olya. She was a sweet, easy-going and sensible girl.

I do not remember Olya's birth causing me any jealousy towards Innulia. I would even say, on the contrary, we became even closer. I liked Olya a lot, and even though I was not much older than she was, I wanted to help Innulia to raise her. It seemed to me that I not only could, but should do it. It was just time that my being meticulous, peculiar to me from my childhood, created the first and only disagreement between me and Innulia, a disagreement on pedagogical grounds. Such a fool, I thought, you see, that Innulia was not consistent enough and demanding of Olechka. Thank God, Innulia was smarter than I was, and it has not destroyed our friendship, for which I am very grateful to her. I hope that Olya herself did not keep any unpleasant memories about it either. No offense to Olya, but I took her as a part of Innulia. As a result, in addition to my loving Olya for herself she always would get a part of my love for her mother. That is why parting with both of them when I left Russia was difficult for me, and I still regret that they did not follow my and Tanya's example and come after us.

Little Olechka had a surprisingly round head, like

Olechka with two grandmothers

a small round cake, and what delighted me was that her face often showed a smile. I think that all little children should be in a hurry to smile, before the cares and troubles of life come upon them. But our Olechka did not only smile as a baby, but continued to do so later after she received both the cares and troubles of life in full measure.

From the first day we met, I somehow thought that my friendship with Innulia gave me special rights to teach my little Olechka. I myself grew up a boringly "right" child. As a result I tried to teach her to be "right", which was not approved by the rest of the family members, especially by Innulia. When they let me know this, I got very sad and angry: how could they not understand that she is MY NIECE, whom I love so much! Poor girl, she had to put up with that, and when she got a little older, she had to defend herself until I got older and wiser. Thank God, Innulia's anger at me was always short-lived. It was solely my love that, caused my foolish behavior and, thank God, had no effect on our mutual affection. At any rate, that is how I felt then and how I feel today. From that time until her last day, Innulia remained a very close person to me.

My niece Olia and nephew Lev

At the beginning of this chapter I told about my premonitions before the birth of our Olechka. When I wrote these lines, she was already 71, so I had enough time to check whether my premonitions were correct. Of those seventy years, the first fifteen years I watched her very closely, as we lived together in one apartment. In 1962, I got married and soon left Tikhvinsky Lane. For the next 25 years while I was still in Moscow, I tried to see her regularly and these meetings were always pleasant. A special part of our rendezvous were the pies, and Olya was always a great master in baking them. Not long ago we had a visit of my grandnieces, Leova's children. I asked them how good restaurants are in Moscow today. In response, I heard: *"We don't know much about them. Why do we need restaurants when we have Olik!"* I've always been fascinated and moved by the touching way Olya took care of her younger brother Lyova's children. How could I not recall the touching way Innulia took care of me from an early age?

We left Russia in 1988 and came to America. It turns out that up to that moment she and I had been close geographically and emotionally for more than forty years! Almost half a century of such closeness gives me reason to address Olya's Mom: "*Innulia, dear, sleep in peace. You'd be pleased with your daughter.*"

FATHER'S ILLNESS AND DEATH

It makes me sad to ask myself the question, why Daddy even when he was very young, often called himself an old man. He passed on to me this vocabulary somehow against my will. When my Tanya manages to prepare something for our dinner, I express my delight with my dad's words: "*Well, you've pleased the old man!*" At the same time, even though I am behind eighty, I do not feel yet like an old man at all. Ever since I was a child, I've always wanted to be like my father in everything. And when any of my friends or relatives noticed that I looked more like my father than any of us three children, I was overwhelmed with pride. I feel like when I call myself an old man, it comes of course from Dad, but with me it's pure "*façon de parler*". But with Dad — it was a very different case. Years of selfless service to empty communist ideals, which turned out to be propagandistic demagogy, undermined his health and actually aged him. The selfless struggle against windmills comes at a high price. I think that already in his fifties Daddy really felt like an old man. It was as if he felt his years were numbered. Several events, both within our family and political events in the country had finally broken him. I want to mention a few of them, which seem to me to be the most important.

The first event and most distressing event was my brother's severe illness. In the fifties, Jan began to have regular headaches, which crushingly increased and became unbearable. Soon the specialists converged on the terrible diagnosis of tubercular meningitis. The day we learned of the diagnosis, for the first time in my life I saw my father crying. After the war years, it was probably the hardest time for my parents. We experienced the war together with the whole country, which was very supportive. This time it was our own personal grief, the grief of our family. We all felt like we were losing my brother. To add to that, and I have already mentioned this, my father had a special relationship with my brother. I do not know of another person whom my brother respected as much as our father. They were closer in age, both went through the war, both returned to civilian life, and we always lived together. Jan was his first son. Of course, my brother's terrible illness took a heavy toll on my father's health. However, looking ahead, I want to say that thanks to the efforts of doctors and special luck, my brother recovered and for many years after that he lived and worked productively.

The second event is the so-called Doctors-Saboteurs case of 1948. It refers to the criminal case against the *"crème de la crème"* of the Soviet medicine, the 37 country's best Jewish doctors charged with plotting to murder Soviet leaders. All of them were innocent and all were acquitted. Nevertheless, the trial resulted in a state-organized Jewish pogrom on an unprecedented scale. Immediately after Stalin's death, the authorities released, reinstated and fully exonerated ALL those arrested in this case. Thank God, Daddy was still alive when justice prevailed, but, of course, his suffering during the five years left an irreparable mark

The third event was crushing of the Jewish Anti-Fascist Committee in 1948–1952. The 13 victims of this pogrom, the most famous Jewish actors, writers and poets, cultural and public figures, were executed by 1952. Many of their family members were arrested, sent to the concentration camps and exiled. Unfortunately, Daddy did not live to see the full exoneration of all these innocent people, living and dead, in 1988.

The fourth event was Stalin's death in 1953 and the subsequent unmasking of his cult of personality in 1956 with the exposure of the bloody crimes of the Communist regime. I cannot remember exactly my father's reaction when the news came that Stalin was gone. However, I can easily imagine what a shock it was for him. On the one hand, during almost half a century Dad's efforts and attempts to make life better for everyone around him, were associated with the Stalin's name. On the other hand, he was tortured with the painful unanswered questions, why all this took so much blood. About a year after the leader's death, Khrushchev's secret letter to the approaching 20th Party Congress was read at the Party meetings all over the country. This document briefly reported on the bloody crimes of Stalin and his henchmen.

At that time, we only had two Party members in the family: my Dad and my brother. As for the non-party members, they were not supposed to know anything about Stalin's crimes and were supposed to go on living, according to O. Mandelstam *"without feeling the country beneath them."* My mother, my sister and I knew nothing about what was going on behind the closed doors. I still have in my mind the terrible scene of my father returned unhinged from such a meeting and locked himself in his office. Soon my brother Jan came home and joined him. After that, for quite some time the door remained locked and I only remember the tension with which I looked at it, foreboding something terrible. At some time, my brother opened the door and left the office for a minute, then quickly returned and locked the door again. That moment was enough for me to see that my father was crying. After my brother's illness it was the second time I saw my father crying.

The fifth event was my sister Lena's marriage. She married an interesting man, but with a very difficult character. When she left our home with her husband, we all, and of course, Papa felt emptiness, because Lena was always a very active and energetic person, her presence was always significant. However, later we all witnessed how difficult the start of her new family life was for her. It was unbearable for us to see her running home in tears after another conflict with her husband. I do not remember anything like that between my parents or between Jan and Innulia. We had never had such an experience in our family, and we just did not know how to help her. Daddy took my sister's suffering to heart, advised her to return home. This did not happen, but the relationship between everyone in the family and Lena's husband has been seriously damaged. Lena did not return home, and in time she somehow managed to get her life together with her husband. However, it was impossible to recover the health that Dad had lost in that story.

From 1955 onwards, slowly but surely my Father felt worse and worse: the accumulated cardiac fatigue was making itself felt. During 1955–1956, he had several heart attacks. On physicians' advice, all of us tried to disturb him as little as possible to protect him as much as possible from any grievances and worries. Touching the events coming ahead, I had very unfortunate start of my higher education during the last year of father's life. Of course, it was practically impossible to hide from him completely my "achievements" with the admission to the college. It makes me very sad to realize that these bad news of mine undoubtedly shortened his days, too. In September 1956, I started working and studying, and on September 27, my father died. Once again, I remind you: I was only 17 years old! Daddy meant so much to everyone in our family that with his passing away, many things in our lives changed radically.

THE NOVODEVICHY EPIC

Now, I want to tell the story of my father's burial. In the 16th century, Grand Prince Vasily III founded the Novodevichy Convent in Moscow. From that time until the beginning of the 20th century, many famous Russians have found their rest in there in the necropolis of its monastery. The family of Ivan the Terrible, the Tsar Alexei Mikhailovitch, Peter the Great, along with many of the most famous merchants, writers, musicians and scientists had there their graves. After the revolution of 1917, the Bolsheviks closed the monastery, submitted many of the abbots and prioresses to repression, stopped church services, and announced "the protection of the state" of all of the buildings of the monastery, the necropolis and the cemetery. In the 1930s, they decided to "reconstruct" the monastery. The valuable historical monument had been actually destroyed. Most of the family burial sites had been demolished and the few remaining ones had been looted. As for the cemetery, they decided to use it to bury only people with "important social status."

At the time of my father's death, only the Central Committee of the Communist Party of the USSR had right to give permission to bury a person in this cemetery. My brother Jan became obsessed with the idea of getting permission to bury our Father in the Novodevichy cemetery. I would like to say that our father, with his directness and lack of diplomacy (even though he taught at the High Diplomatic School) was never in favor with the authorities. The best illustration of that is the fact that his monograph "Economic

Districts of the USA" waited more than seventeen years to be published because its lack of political correctness. The book was published only after his death, thanks to the considerable efforts of his students and friends. He had no "important social status" and therefore it was impossible even to think about getting the high permission. Nevertheless, my brother did receive permission, from my point of view, in a rather Soviet way.

Since his school he had a friend, Galina Kulikov, a nice and interesting person. She was a journalist by profession, and worked in the editorial office of Novoe Vremya magazine. Everyone in our family liked her, and she had a particularly close relationship with our Father, which, perhaps, I can explain by common professional interests. Galina's personal life did not work out very well: she divorced her husband and was bringing up her son by herself.

Shortly before my father's death, she had an affair with a man who occupied a very high state post, the Chairman of the Presidium of the Supreme Soviet (equivalent of the president) of the Russian Republic of the USSR. His name was Mikhail Tarasov. I had a chance to meet him more than once, and I still have a very pleasant and warm impression of him. These meetings were extremely important for me: I learnt a lesson that even if a man turns out to be one of the leaders of a bandit country, it does not mean that he has to be a bandit and a scoundrel himself.

His feelings for Galina were so serious that he chose to leave his family and marry her. His immediate superior was K. E. Voroshilov, then Chairman of the Presidium of the Supreme Soviet (equivalent of the president) of the USSR. Voroshilov told Mikhail Tarasov that he could have an affair with as many women as he wanted, but an official marriage to Galya would cost him his job. Mikhail acted on his heart rather than on party regulations. He retired and married Galyina. Before he retired, he did a good deed for our family. He got us permission to bury Daddy at Novodevichy Cemetery. My brother was at seventh heaven. You can feel different things about that story, but everyone in our family was deeply grateful to Galina's friend for what he did for us.

Anyway, we became lucky owners of a plot in the cemetery and soon we buried my dad at Novodevichy. Jan, with unbelievable activity went to work to create a monument for the grave. We lived in a country where everything was a problem and there was no suitable stone. I cannot remember, he made a deal somewhere, and the right size and color stone was brought to us. My cousin, Lena Belyaev, an architect by profession, made the design. Jan found a sculptor whom he had ordered a bas-relief bronze portrait of my father. All this has been done. In the Soviet Union at that time, it was almost impossible to achieve all of this either for love or for money, especially in such a short period, which was about a year. Somehow, my brother successfully went through all these steps, and by 1957, the monument was completed. As far as I know today in Moscow, you can get everything for money. However, in that time we have to give credit to my brother, he did the impossible. There was a small plot of land in front of the gravestone. My sister, if I remember correctly, planted forget-me-nots on that land, and that was the final step.

I remember well then how my whole family and I were triumphant that my brother had succeeded, and that Daddy at last received some appreciation. I thought at that time, it was hard to do more for the memory of my deceased father. More than half a century has flown by and I have gone through a reassessment of many values. Today, I think that both the material, moral, and nervous-psychological cost of my brother's efforts for the burial of my father at Novodevichy Cemetery was hardly worth it. I doubt that my father himself would have wanted it. I doubt that with his exceptional modesty he would have wanted to be buried in the company of the high representatives of the Soviet party and state elite, people who were very alien to him in spirit and human qualities. These feelings were gradually growing in me since my Moscow days, and my feeling of uneasiness gradually replaced my pride. Few historical facts that I learned later promoted these changes.

First, the fate of the monastery in Soviet times was very sad. By some miracle in all of the vandalism survived the family crypt of our wonderful friend and mentor Vera Prokhorov, the daughter of the owner of the pre-Revolutionary Trekhgornaya manufacturing factory. There will be a special chapter about this special woman further on.

Second, there was a disgusting process of "corpse shifting" at the cemetery. This term comes from a scathing article by great cellist M. Rostropovich about how the Soviet authorities with incredible vanity sought to transfer the remains of Russia's famous people to their most prestigious Novodevichy cemetery. We are talking here about those people who were buried according to THEIR WILL in other cemeteries in Russia and the world. Rostropovich wrote this article after transferring the remains of F. Shaliapin from Paris in 1984. I do not want to be unfounded and give as an example a short list of those famous Russians "moved": Gogol, Aksakov, Levitan, Yermolova, Shaliapin, Rubinstein, Chekhov, Sechenov, Serov, Taneyev, Khlebnikov, Ogarev, and many others. Such reburials almost always happened against the will of the deceased and their families.

Third, the authorities misappropriated unlawfully the right to rearrange the graves of celebrities in their own way ignoring the will of the deceased and their families. One of the saddest stories for me from this series happened with the grave of N. V. Gogol. From the writer's letters to his friends, we know that he wanted a cross on his grave and did not want any monuments. So, at his burial in Danilovsky cemetery in Moscow in 1852, the stone for the granite base of the cross was specially delivered from the Crimea and received the name "Golgotha" for its shape, resembling the outlines of a Bald Mountain in Jerusalem. The cross was made of dark bronze. On the gravestone, there was a carving of the quote from the book of the prophet Jeremiah (20: 8) "*I will laugh with my bitter word.*" I think, this verse precisely describes the essence of the Great Russian writer's books. However, I did not discover that phrase either in Russian or in English translation of the Bible. It took some research for me to find out that the phrase is the Russian translation from the Church-Slavonic version of the Bible. I wish professional Biblical scholars look at the issue and remove the differences of all translations based on the Hebrew original. In 1909, on the 100th anniversary of the writer, there was the restoration of the tomb. Sculptor Nikolai Andreev designed new cast-iron lattice fence and sarcophagus. This again violated the will of the writer.

In 1930, Bolsheviks closed Danilovsky monastery and opened a colony for juvenile offenders, transferring Gogol's ashes to the Novodevichy. The fence and the sarcophagus traveled with the ashes, the cross was lost and there was no longer need for the "Golgotha" at the base of the cross. They sent it to the cemetery workshop as material for future gravestones.

In 1940, after Mikhail Bulgakov's death, his widow Helen Bulgakov buried her husband at Novodevichy Cemetery and she was thinking how to mark the grave. She recalls, *"I came into the workshop at Novodevichy cemetery and I saw a granite boulder deeply hidden in a hole. When I asked about it, the director of the workshop explained that it was the Golgotha from the tomb of Gogol, removed from his grave, when the new monument was installed."* M.Bulgakov considered N.Gogol as his teacher. Helen bought the stone, arranged its delivery to her husband's grave, which appeared to be very difficult. The old inscription was ground down, and the new one carved. This way, the stone from the grave of the favorite teacher became the headstone of the grave of the student.

By the end of his life, N. V. Gogol was in a state of mental crisis, and whether the admirers of his genius should remember this condition, is a complicated question. On the centenary of the Great writer's life, in 1909 the inauguration of the new monument by sculptor N. A. Andreev took place at the Boulevard Gogol in Moscow. You can see the writer sitting melancholically in his favorite armchair, immersed in deep sad contemplation. The very idea of "grieving" Gogol caused a lot of controversy, the Muscovites sharply divided in their opinions. X

Ilya Repin, for example, was delighted: *"Touching, deep and unusually graceful and simple. What a head turn! How much of suffering in this martyr for the sins of Russia! The resemblance is complete ... Long live N. A. Andreev!"*

However, there were many who just as emotionally would not accept the writer's melancholy. When the Bolsheviks came to power, everything became simple. The depressive Gogol annoyed them all. The rumors say that the great leader and teacher Stalin decreed that the Soviet people needed a more cheerful Gogol. As a result, in 1952, the Soviet authorities replaced the writer who was sadly seating there for 35 years with a cheerfully standing one. An epigram began to circulate in Moscow:

Gogol's humor is sweet to us,
Gogol's tears are a hindrance
Sitting down, he made us sad.
Let him stand now — to make us laugh!

What a good thing that I. Repin was no longer alive at that time.

In 1957 it was decided to set on the grave a bust of N. V. Gogol on a huge cylindrical pedestal made of marble with a golden engraved inscription: *"To the Great Russian artist of word Nikolai Gogol from the Soviet Union government."* Passing the grave, I always would read between the lines *"The writer and we had our own personal relationship, and you had nothing to do with it."* I was ashamed for the country that wrote such a thing. Besides, it is widely known that Gogol was dying in the deepest depression. The marble Gogol on the pedestal was calm and even cheerful. Thank God, in 2009 Gogol's grave returned to almost pristine condition. They moved monument of the cheerful writer by Tomsky to the branch of the Historical Museum, which is located at Novodevichy Cemetery. Instead, they built a new Golgotha with a cross, though, this time it was a shiny and gold cross. Thank God, it did not occur to the Bolsheviks to dig original Gogol's Golgotha from the head of Bulgakov's grave.

The fourth fact of series that caused me to reevaluate my beliefs was that in the seventies the authorities closed the free entrance to the cemetery, and all relatives were given special passes — only one (!?) per family. Who cares about people's convenience? As a result, the cemetery became notorious — the only, I believe, cemetery in the world without free access to its graves. Each time we had to meet with our relatives and friends specifically to give them our pass so that they could come and worship at my father's grave. However, what was even worse, the opportunity to venerate the graves of the most glorious ones in the nation: its great writers, artists, composers and performers, had been taken away from the citizens of the country, as well as from its guests. If you think about it, the authorities acted consistently, believing that everything in the country was their own property and that sharing anything with the common people was unpleasant. They had their OWN closed maternity homes, their OWN closed hospitals, their OWN closed shops and retail chains, their OWN closed factories, their OWN closed cinemas, their OWN closed brothels, and many other closed things. Why could not they have their OWN closed cemetery as well?

Getting ahead of myself, I want to tell a funny story about Novodevichy Cemetery. It happened in the late seventies. We had finally decided to emigrate at that time, filed all the necessary documents, and the authorities denied us the right to leave the country. We will talk about this strange and terrible time ahead. However, every dark cloud has its silver lining. We were outcasts in our own country, so we got a chance to communicate with foreigners working in Moscow. Many of these people were interested in Russian history and culture and wanted to visit Novodevichy Cemetery. Regularly, Tanya and I gladly used our pass to my father's grave to give them that opportunity.

One day we brought to the cemetery our friend Kevin Klose, director of the Moscow office of the American newspaper "Washington Post," to show him the most famous graves. It was a frosty winter day. As I recall, we were standing near the tomb of the painter Levitan and we noticed with a surprise a man not far from us holding a bag of fresh oranges. We could see the contents of the bag, as it was an extremely common Russian "avos'ka": a net bag woven of thin threads. The fact, that in the middle of winter we can see fresh fruit in Moscow, caused our astonishment. Such thing had never happened before. The day was sunny and every orange in the net was shining like a little sun itself. It was impossible not to notice and not to remember something like that! We continued our excursion and a minute later, unbelievably, we saw the man with the oranges next to us again! Those orange orbs became the insignia of the people who appeared around us like a fantasy dream. Here my clever wife found an explanation for the phantasmagoria. It was the "special people" sent to follow and to watch our friend with us walk through the cemetery, and the oranges had been "dumped" for them in locked special dispenser before the assignment was completed! All three of us burst into Homeric laughter.

Later, I think, in 2004 a period of paid admission to the cemetery began. The entrance ticket cost 30 rubles per person, similar to the cost of an expensive theater ticket. When some guests from the Soviet Union told me about it, I could not believe it. However, later I came to understand that by denuding THEIR cemetery of its spiritual aspect, the militant atheists had turned it into a spectacular entertainment — THEIR gallery of THEIR celebrities. Now the authorities have changed, and much has had to be changed. Today, it seems, entry to the cemetery is free again.

Interesting enough, something similar has happened at the Highgate Cemetery in London with the grave of their ideological leader and inspirer of the Bolshevism, Karl Marx. The tombstone was unveiled in 1883. Since that time, the cemetery administration has stopped the free access to the tomb of Marxism's founder and started charging the equivalent of six dollars for visiting it. Curiously, the buried man had fought against private property and profiteering all his life. It seems to me, now he should be rolling over in his coffin, for the people who own the cemetery are profiting from the visitors, those who come to worship the monument of the first Marxist.

When we buried my father in 1956, very few people knew about most of the aforementioned disgusting realities of Soviet life; my parents, protecting me, tried to conceal these things, much of which I myself did not understand at the time because of my youth and innocence. At that time, I rejoiced with my family, believing that my father got what he deserved when he died. More than fifty years have passed since then. Of course, it is easy to be a strong when looking in hindsight. Today I hate to remember all the twists and turns happening with Novodevichy cemetery and I like much less the fact that my parents and brother have their graves there. At first, the Soviet authorities arranged such a difficult life for my father that he left us at the early age of 56. Then we, through connections and tricks, managed to get this handout from them. Reflection about burial of my relatives at Novodevichy cemetery has led me to the conclusion that I absolutely DO NOT WANT any such thing for myself. It seems to me that when a worthy person passes away, there are more important things than a gravestone in a cemetery to keep the memory of their heart alive. I am happy that my wife Tanya fully supports me in this opinion. That is why we left our children and grandchildren a document with instructions to cremate each of us upon our deaths and to scatter the ashes at our favorite spot at Cape Cod from the high and steep ocean shore.

MY THORNY ROAD TO COLLEGE

As I said before, my father had always been the most important authority in the family. From my early age I used to consult him on all my most important matters. I was about to graduate from school, to choose my profession and to start my higher education. However, at this time my father's general health and, his heart in the first place, were failing. With everyone's consent in the family, I stopped discussing with him the problem of choosing my profession and starting a college. Mother by that time was also a rather physically unhealthy person. Both my brother and sister had families of their own. I was 17, my sister was 27, my brother was 33 years old and my father was 55 years old. The role of the main counselor in my life was voluntarily taken over by my older brother Jan at the time.

The Soviet system of higher education then was very different from what it is today in the United States. Institutions such as the American college did not exist in Russia. The structure of all institutions of higher education was similar to the American university, and the only diploma they issued upon graduation corresponded to a master's degree in America. As a result, every entrant to such an institution had to decide on his or her future major subject before enrolling. This made my choice difficult upon graduation from high school. Another major difficulty was the rampant anti-Semitism prevalent in the country. The admission of Jewish youth to the most popular universities was practically impossible.

At that time, I did not really know what I wanted to do with my life. However, I clearly felt that engineering did not appeal to me. I wanted something less applied, and possibly even in the humanities. However, I was even afraid to mention this. It sometimes seemed to me that maybe I would be interested in mathematics. Perhaps this was the influence of V. F. Kagan and his grandsons Grisha and Yasha. All universities in Moscow, especially Moscow University, had at that time a rather high security level. Nobody could even enter the building without special pass confirming that you either worked or studied there. Using my friends and relatives, I managed to obtain such pass and, while still in school, I was attending lectures and seminars on the theoretical foundations of cybernetics (very fashionable then) at the Moscow University. Of course, I realized clearly that in any case, as a Jewish boy, I could not set my sights on the university. During a discussion about my future profession my brother Jan, as if he knew about my doubts, took a very firm stance: no chitchatting no nonsense, only practical engineering. This position I can explain with the fact, that it was much easier, even for a Jew, to enter some technical colleges of higher learning.

Here, with the reader's permission, I would like to give a real example of discrimination in university admissions at that time. To do this I need to skip ahead to the events connected to my wife Tanya, whom I married later, in 1974. We were about the same age and went to college at about the same time. When Tanya finished high school, she was the only gold medalist in her class and in fact, she was a much better educated entrant than I was. About a year before her graduation, Tanya won the FIRST prize in the school Olympiad of the Philological department of Moscow State University. She dreamed of studying languages at this University. Her friends and relatives, unlike my brother, tried to convince her of the possibility of such a plan. Encouraged by their support, she applied. As a medalist, she did not have to take any admissions exams. Having successfully passed the interview, she received from the admissions committee a unique document, the content of which was hard to believe. One could read in black and white that she showed excellent knowledge and training, however they could not accept her due to lack of vacancies!

Now let us go back to the story of my admission. Not daring to ignore my brother's advice, I applied to the Moscow Machine-Tool Institute to major in Precise Instruments. No other specialties interested me at all. As a medalist I also did not have to take any entrance exams, I only had to go for an interview. I was not accepted. On a wave of irritation, I offered them to pass all entrance exams along with non-medal candidates. They sad NO, that also was impossible.

Then my brother insisted that I should apply to the Moscow University of Geodesy, Airplane Photography and Cartography Engineering to major in Instrument-Development. At that place, everybody knew well our father as a cartographer, and my brother himself graduated and taught at that institution. He was sure there would be no problems for me. I obeyed and applied there. I interviewed again, but the Admission Committee told me, that on the specialty chosen by me they had already taken enough students and that they had closed the admission. They agreed to let me major in Geodesy. Having heard from me that this specialty did not interest me at all, they offered: come on Geodesy, finish well the first year, we will transfer you where you want, under the condition of completing in a short time all the classes, which these specialties differ in first year. I agreed and in 1955, I became a first-year student of the University.

I knew whom I was dealing with, and I believed that in order to get what I wanted; I had to finish my first year IRREPROACHABLY. I worked so hard that not only all the credits and exams I passed with honors, but also every single test received an excellent grade. Thus, I completed the first year and, remembering the deal, naively thought that it was in the bag. At once I went to the dean (if I remember correctly, his surname was Bagratuni) to speak about transfer. I walked out of the dean's office literally in shock. He strongly objected to my transfer, as if I had never received any promises. He indignantly yelled at me as if I was a thief trying to steal 10,000 rubles from the state, the cost, according to him, of my tuition for that year. Imagine, he addressed me on familiar terms of course, if we allowed this to happen to you, how many other students would be jumping around like fleas from one specialty to another, without thinking about what it would cost the country.

Mad I slammed the door of his office behind me, already having a plan in my head for what I wanted to do. This time, without consulting my brother, I took all my documents from the Institute and went straight to the admissions office. There, I filed my papers at the Institute to re-enroll in the first year of the specialty CHOSEN BY ME, as if the past year did not exist. Here I got a good lesson in what it means to swim against the tide. First, this time they refused to accept me without entrance examinations! *"All right,"* I decided, *"I'll take the damn exams!"* Secondly, they gave me B's in all the exams and I was NOT ACCEPTED! A funny thing happened during these exercises. The professor who lectured mathematical analysis to us took my math exam. During the school year, he never tired of praising my mathematical abilities. He recognized me, of course, and showed me his amazement... but he also gave me the B as they wanted.

All these petty intrigues took up a lot of time, and it was already too late to try to apply anywhere else. There was a threat of losing a year, not to mention that even after a year the situation is unlikely to change for me. Besides, losing a year in the Soviet Union entailed another problem for young boys. Being called up to the military service at the age of 17 was obligatory but being enrolled to the higher school gave an exemption from being drafted. In other words, my deferment of admission to the institute for a year could inevitably mean three to five years of soldiering. It was at this point that my registration at a neurological dispensary helped me a lot: I obtained draft deferment for medical reasons. Then I decided to break the vicious circle and not to enroll in the university's full-time department at all, but to start working. This coincided with my desire to start bringing money into the house as soon as possible. My father was very sick and had almost stopped working, and my mother, as I have already mentioned, had not worked since I was born. The changed financial situation in the family was very worrisome. Because of this, I planned to continue studying at home in the evenings after finishing my working hours.

Quite soon, I chose where I could study. I was ready for a course by correspondence in the computer department of almost any university. At that time, such a specialty just was emerging. This, at least to some extent, I thought, suited well my longtime interests in cybernetics. I was naïve to expect education in the spirit of lectures and seminars at the Faculty of Mechanics and Mathematics of Moscow State University. However, for admission there I needed a certificate of employment. To start classes at the beginning of the academic year I had to start working urgently. To find quickly a decent job for a Jewish boy was not easy. I decided to start working at any place so I could submit all the papers to the University as soon as possible. Later, I thought I could gradually find something better.

The first thought that came to my mind was to go to the school where I had studied, where I was well known and, as it seemed to me, loved. The headmistress there was still a nice woman who had worked there in my days and she was the one who handed me my silver medal upon graduation. She met me quite nicely and promised to try to find me some kind of job in the school and she kept her promise. After a few days, she offered me a job as a laboratory assistant in the physics department of the school. I was over the moon, especially since both physics teachers I knew well, and I liked them both. In addition, I knew our physics room and the nature of the lab technician's job very well. All through high school,

I was volunteering to help the physics teacher prepare demonstrations for our classes. Fortune was turning its face to me.

However, the details of the beginning of my working life turned out not to be as bright as I had expected. The head of the physics department of the school told me at our first meeting that there was one complication with my taking the job. The thing was that the salary for this position was very low, if I remember correctly, something like 120 rubles a month. Because of this, they could never find a suitable person for the position. As a result, the job was assigned to a semi-literate handicapped guy who had a job somewhere else and who was doing his work for the school through a fake person (!?). He had no idea about physics and as a laboratory assistant in physics he was of little help. Nevertheless, he did not drink much, and his hands were good and did not tremble! He had worked part-time at school for many years, and I remembered him. Well: the school thought it was impossible to take those earnings away from him altogether. I was told that if I agreed, they would be happy to take me on the job, but on the condition that I would give him every month half of my earnings (i.e. 60 rubles). Such a condition did not make me very happy, for it nullified my dream of ever making any appreciable contribution to the family's financial situation. Nevertheless, the job allowed me to get the coveted certificate of employment for admission to college immediately. At the end of August 1956, I started the first in my life job as a laboratory assistant of physical training room of school # 204 in Oktyabrsky district of Moscow.

Thank God, there was no competition for correspondence courses, and everyone could take them, even Jews. I easily collected the required documents and submitted them to the All-Union Correspondence Institute of Energy to major in Electronic Computing. This time my plan worked without a hitch. In a couple of weeks, I happily returned home from Krasnokazarmennaya Street, where the Institute was located at that time, with a briefcase full of training materials for the first year of training. However, it would be wrong to say that giving up what I wanted in terms of higher education came easy to me. First, it was still hard for me to accept that I had to say goodbye forever to the Moscow State University. This was especially painful for me because of my memories about my sister Lena's happy years in the University.

Such thing was not destined to happen for me, I was deprived of carefree and happy days of college. Nevertheless, I knew that far worse things were happening to many people. No ordeals in my first life negated the general conclusion that, though I was Jewish, still I was a happy child in this country.

The epic of my entering the institute reminds me of the story of a wonderful man, professor chemist Lazar Mayants whom I was lucky to meet in the seventies. For many years, he was a member of Scientific Council of one of the leading chemical research centers of the Academy of Sciences. *"I was sitting at the Council meeting and listening to the people defending their scientific thesis. Each times the biography of Russian applicants,"* he recalled, *"would be mortal boredom, everyone has the same thing: high schools, university, sometimes work at a research institute, graduate school. But when a Jewish person defends the thesis, the biography becomes a fascinating detective story: evening school, work as a janitor, training as a turner, work at a factory, correspondence studies at the institute, passing the externship of the candidate's minimum exams—you cannot help but listen!"*

EPILOGUE TO MY FIRST LIFE

As I conclude my description of my first life, I will try to summarize how I feel about it. This period covers my childhood and my adolescence. The all-knowing Wikipedia tells me that a person's childhood is up to the age of 11, and adolescence is from 12 to 18. My division of life ends with the first part before my father's illness and death in 1956, and I was just 18 years old. I was on the threshold of young adulthood. I think that is when the foundations of a person's personality are laid. I was very lucky: my caring and loving family brought me up and formed, which made my childhood and adolescence very happy. Remember, all this happened against the background of the hardest times, through which our country went: the bloody Red Terror, the cruelest war, postwar repression, the last years of the cult of Stalin, the militant state anti-Semitism, the cold war and the Iron Curtain. Nevertheless, wrapped in the care and love of my family, I did not experience all of this. As a result, I can say that my first life was heartwarming and cloudlessly happy, for which I am eternally grateful to ALL members of our family, from young to old. Nevertheless, it is extremely important to me that the reader not get the idea that everything that happened in my first life happened the way I wanted it to. Probably that is never the case for anyone, especially since that life ended when I was only 18 years old. Today, I am 85, and I try to make current evaluation based on my accumulated experience and knowledge.

First, it seems to me that my parents, protecting me from all the nastiness, cruelty and lies of political and economic life in the country, clearly overdid it. They did it undoubtedly for the best of reasons. Now I know that the Soviet authorities did the same nastiness with ALL the citizens of the Soviet Union. It turns out that my parents, even though they hated any evil, helped the evil authorities to inculcate that evil. Moreover, such an attitude of theirs inevitably damaged the closeness between us, practically depriving me of an opportunity to empathize with them. Of course, it delayed my epiphany coming to me apart from them in my next life and made the process very difficult for me. As I said, this situation distanced us from each other.

Secondly, I have had humanitarian interests since childhood. Unfortunately, our family was quite non-humanitarian. The only exception to a certain extent was Innulia, who was the only one in our family to follow the latest literary publications and occasionally listened to musical concerts in the conservatory. As a result, I grew up very poorly educated in literature, theater, music, and the fine arts. I clearly lacked a cultural mentor and it is a pity that my parents did not see this and did not help me with it. As a result, for as long as I can remember, I tried to make up for my lack of general education, which I was not very successful at. The sad outcome is that I still feel this lack in my old age today. However, every dark cloud has its silver lining. This dissatisfaction throughout my life pushed me to people from whom I could borrow knowledge. Such people were very generous and shared with me with great joy. As a result, during my life, something has lingered and eventually accumulated in my head.

LIFE SECOND
I AM A SOVIET YOUNG MAN WITH RECOVERED SIGHT

SALON AT PUSHKIN STREET

Above I have already mentioned my mother's sister Balia, who was my favorite aunt, the closest to our whole family among Moscow aunts. Balia's husband, Yasha. was my father's cousin. He perished at the very beginning of the war in 1941, and Balia remained a single mother for the rest of her life. Her youngest son Lyonya is almost exactly the same age as me—he is two days older than me. We all joked that Lyonya was my one-and-a-half removed cousin, because our mothers were siblings and our fathers were cousins. Not only that, Lyonya and I are also milk brothers. Both were born in the same maternity hospital, and my mother was low on milk, so Balechka breastfed me. Plus because of the kinship of our fathers, both Leonid and I have the same surname –(many of my Russian relatives prefer to spell this name "Ziman").

When we left for evacuation during the war, my mother took Lyonya with us, and we spent the first years with him outside Moscow. Unfortunately, I do not remember Lyonya at all during those years. Only one trifling episode comes to mind. During one of the countless trips from place to place (this time in a truck), everybody heard Lyonya's shrill voice: *"Look, look, the cow is peeing right out of her skin!"* To this, I corrected my older brother, with my meticulousness of the time, *"Not out of the just skin, but out of the animal skin!"* (for these two things there are two DIFFERENT words in Russian). Maybe this exchange of opinions would not have been worth even mentioning but, as I think, it did already express the difference between us. Lyonya was always interested in literature, theater, poetry, reaching for the sublime and never focusing on details, while I, flying much closer to the ground, was thinking about how to help the computer become smarter, and all details were important to me. As a result, after graduating from high school, Lyonya became a student of the Faculty of Philology of the Pedagogical University, and I became a student of the computer department of the Correspondence classes of the Power Engineering University.

In the family, we called Lyonya's mother Balechka. It was surprisingly appropriate to her character, loving and forgiving. My relatives had all grown up atheists, and they called her "Christosic" (in Russian "little Christ") for a reason, though with an element of judgment. I never judged her for anything, and I did not like that label then, and I like it even less now. I loved everything about that aunt of mine! Balechka was a rare treasure collection of Russian poetry, the best examples of which was settled firmly in her memory and just fell from her lips. It is hard to overestimate Balechka's role in my humanities education.

My "double" cousin Lyonia Ziman

Balechka lived in the very centre of Moscow, in a communal flat at the end of Pushkin Street ending at the Theatre Passage, in my day Marx Avenue. At the end of her house was the metro station Sverdlov Square, now Theatre Square. It was simply impossible to live in Moscow "more centrally." The Kremlin was just a stone's throw away from her house. Her warm and hospitable character along with such a central location led to the fact that each of us, being close to the center and having a free half an hour or an hour, just ran into Balechka's with no warning whatsoever. It did not matter if anyone was home at the time. The neighbors knew us all well, and for some reason they always had someone at home. They let us in, and Balechka's rooms were almost always open. As a result, each of us had a wonderful opportunity in the middle of a hectic day to run in there to take a break, for example, to read and run on. To this, we should add that many people, including me, were given the additional privilege of making a cup of tea and having a snack using the refrigerator contents in the absence of the owners. In such apartment, Balechka lived with her son Leonya.

When Balechka read wonderful poetic lines she knew by heart, I always, figuratively speaking, tried to put my palms up, pick these lines up, and immediately shove them into my head to keep them. Every time I was very glad of such a poem-fall, but, apparently, I did something wrong in doing so: when I try to find those poems in my memory today, alas, I do no't find them there. Maybe, at the time, I was not yet ready to hold those lines in my mind. Nevertheles, it seems to me that what I heard has not passed without a trace: the joy I get from good poetry today I certainly owe to Balechka.

Lyonya took an active interest in the theatre quite early when he was still in school. He was a regular reader of "Theatre" magazine, a member of the Central Children's Theatre activists group. He was a well known in our family expert on theater and a major adviser on where and what to watch. This interest continued in him, in any case, until my departure from Russia. Let us remember where the house he lived in was. The house faced the Theatre Square. On this not so large square were the Bolshoi Theatre, the Maly Theatre and the Central Children's Theatre. Maybe there was something theatrical in the air he breathed? I do not remember that Lyonya had vocal abilities, but maybe Lyonya should sing to himself after popular song about Odessa performed by L. Utyosov:

> *There's an air I breathed as a child,*
> *I couldn't get enough of it!*

At any rate, I'm very grateful to our family theatre guy for breathing so actively, and thanks to this breathing he was able to help me so much to learn a lot about theatre.

Balechka's, and afterwards Lyonya's interest in literature and, mainly, in poetry turned their apartment into the literary salon, where many poets and poetry lovers read their own and other authors' poetry. Here I would like to remind readers, there was a special higher meaning in the fact that the salon was on Pushkin Street. These readings aroused my great interest, and I became a habitué at the salon. My visits to the salon at Pushkin Street cause one difficulty. Pieces of literature sounding in the salon, of course, included those, which at that time were not encouraged by the authorities in the country for ideological reasons. No publisher would take risk of printing them. Moreover, storing, reading, and even quoting some of them Soviet authorities considered as anti-Soviet criminal activity. Such poems were distributed "in lists", as they used to say in Pushkin's and in my time. A special word appeared in Russian for such unwelcome literature: "samizdat" (self-publishing). I think, it was thank to Balechka and her salon, that I got acquaintant with the poetry of Osip Mandelstam, Nikolai Gumilev, Zinaida Gippius, Anna Akhmatov and many other excellent poets, who had either become silent or writing underground. Many of them were tortured and destroyed by the Soviet authorities or escaped to the West.

The underground literature in Moscow then included the publications of these poets abroad, which had managed by devious means to be smuggled illegally into Russia. In other words, the salon had a dissident character. This kind of literature would never find its way to our home. This really worried my family a lot. If my parents were just worried about me without saying a word, my brother and sister's worries took on the character of resolute disapproval. They wanted me to stop participating in these "unsafe" gatherings.

I remember very well how painful the situation was for me. It seemed to me, I was personally creating a serious rift in a family, which had previously been in perfect harmony. Even worse, I saw in my brother and sister's position a rebuke that by attending the salon I was endangering the social well-being, successful careers, and even the safety of the rest of the family. It was not easy for me to shake off the guilt and not take the advice of those so close to me. It was then that the realization came to me that I have the right to structure my life as I saw fit after all. Having understood this, I continued to be friends with Balechka and Lyonya, and visits to their salon continued to be important and joyful events for me. Of course, knowing my family's attitude towards the salon, I tried never to tell anything about those visits at home. It was this salon, which opened to me a new chapter in my life; on the one hand, acquaintance with the best examples of Russian literature, and, on the other, involvement in the dissident movement. Such activities were nonexistent at our home, and I thank both fate and Balechka for both of these things happening in my life.

With Lyonya's admission to the Philological Faculty of the Pedagogical University the activity of the salon increased dramatically.

Nobody considered teaching as prestigious in those years in the USSR because of the strict ideological constraints and low salaries. As a result, admission to teacher training colleges was less monstrous, and capable applicants, for whom the doors of elite universities and institutes simply were closed, could go there. Many interesting and talented young people who truly loved literature were Lyonya's classmates and they often took part in the literary readings at Pushkin Street. It was at Balechka's I met Ilya Gabay, Yuliy Kim, Ada Yakushev, Mark Kharitonov, Yuri Vizbor, Vladimir Lukin, Galya Edelman, Galya Gladkov, and many others. The abbreviation for the Moscow State Pedagogical University was MSPU. At that time some people suggested to replace the third letter 'P' to the "S" for 'Singing' to become Moscow State Singing University abbreviated MSSU. That would reflect the fact that the University was one of the centers of the nascent genre of 'amateur' or 'bard' song. I first heard many of the songs that later became well known at Pushkin Street, and they were performed by the authors of those songs.

Many evenings on Pushkin Street became memorable for the rest of my life. Among them was one when Alexander Galich sang his songs there. I did not know his work then as well as I did later. Both the songs and his performance made the STRONGEST impression on me then. Nothing of what he sang was published, and lovers of poetry used to give each other tape recorder cassettes, which were secretly listened in homes. Here I would like to quote two stanzas of poetry "To Galich" by my nephew Lyovochka Ziman from his poem about it:

> *The golden fruit inception of the school years,*
> *Young communist trumpery,*
> *But at night, the forbidden record*
> *That does not let me fall asleep until morning.*
>
> *And like a downpour on a dilapidated roof,*
> *I am still getting a herd of goose bumps*
> *Running through my body the very moment I hear*
> *His voice with the background of the whispering strings.*

I am very surprised and happy at the same time that Lyova and I belong to different generations, but we feel the same way about many things. Speaking of Galich, I would like to recall an episode from his life that I read somewhere. At one of "samizdat" concerts of A.Galich some agitated man started to pester the poet: "*You were in jail, of course. Where was it?*" A slightly irritated Galich answered: "*There was such a big camp, it was called Moscow*".

To conclude this chapter, I would like to say that the Ballechka's salon on Pushkin Street played a very important positive role in shaping me as a person. It became another university for me. I am happy that I managed to cope with my fear, and now I am proud to wear the diploma of this university.

SOMEONE ELSE'S PAIN

About some people, I met at Pushkin Street, we will talk later, but one of them, Ilya Gabai played a special role in my life. I think I met Ilya when he was a classmate of my "one-and-a-half removed" Cousin Lyonya Ziman at the Lenin Pedagogical Institute in Moscow. It was then that we began to meet in the salon on Pushkin Street. From my point of view, he was in many ways a unique man. Only three years older than me, Ilya, became for me in many ways the model of a man I would like to become. I never dared to admit this to him. He was a man of remarkable historical, political, and literary intelligence, and I admired his emotional richness, and his moral purity. I would call him the conscience of a very cruel and difficult time. I think, no one said it better than Ilya himself in 1957 in the final stanza of his poem "Someone Else's Grief":

> ...I would like to feel someone else's pain inside me,
> Like my own heart-oppressing pain.

First I heard this particular cry of his soul just about the time when I became close to him. More than half a century has passed since then, Ilya is long gone, and I still remember, like yesterday, how those lines struck me at that time. I would not want anyone to consider it blasphemy, but they touched me deeper than the commandment "*...love thy neighbor as thyself*". (Luke 10:27). Ilya's words are sort of about the same thing, but I think it's more frontal, more poetic, and more evocative. I think it is more likely that I first heard them at Pushkin street.

Ilya Gabay

The quoted poem by Ilya Gabai has the title "Someone Else's Grief". However, in essence Ilya never considered anybody's grief as someone else's. It seems to me that in this respect he was literally unique. I have never met a second person in my long life who would have been so affected by injustice even connected to a person he didn't know at all. Unfortunately, he lived in a very unkind time. For such a short life like his, there were too many difficulties, and also too much of injustice and grief. He was born in Baku in 1935. He lost his mother when he was five. His father passed away when he was ten. Being an orphan, he first lived with relatives, then for some time found himself in an orphanage. He never had a warm childhood to which we could attribute his unique empathic and warm attitude to people. At 15 Ilya came to Moscow and entered the Moscow Library Training Middle School. The school did not provide a Moscow residence permit and he had nowhere to live in the capital. Ilya's sister was studying at the Moscow Medical School at that time, and he used to come to her dormitory to sleep illegally under her bed in violation of the rules. Miraculously Ilyusha, with his uncompromising political and ethical views, managed to get through these years without a serious conflict with the authorities.

Graduating from Training School he returned to Baku to teach at a high school and in the evenings he studied at Philological department of the Baku University. In 1954 at age 19, he had to go for the full term to the military service,. After his service was over, because of his visual defect, as in the theater of the absurd, he was given a white card, which exempted him from further service in the army (!?). In 1957, Ilya came back to Moscow, enrolled in the Moscow Pedagogical University, and became friends with Lyonya Ziman. Thanks to this happy for me event, our lives crossed.

In 1962, even without waiting for graduation from the Institute, Ilya left to teach literature in a rural school in the Altai region. I have often wondered what made Ilya leave Moscow in such a hurry and go off into the middle of nowhere. Maybe he needed it, as Osip Mandelstam did *"to see no coward, no flimsy mud, and no bloody bones in the wheel."* There he continued his studies in the University come to Moscow on his leave to take his State examinations. In Altai, Ilya had a very productive period as a poet.

After graduating from the university in 1963, he came back to Moscow and taught literature in a secondary school, in a teachers' training school, at preparatory courses of the University of History and Archives. It was during the years when Ilya lived in Moscow that I was lucky enough to see him regularly. However, what following Mandelstam Ilya wanted to escape from, immediately caught up with him. In 1965, KGB summoned him for the first time in connection with his protest against the arrests of writers Andrei Sinyavsky and Yuli Daniel. From that time until the last days of his life, the KGB never stopped going after Ilya. His first arrest was in 1967, associated with participation in a demonstration in defense of A. Ginzburg and Galanskov. What followed was four months of jail in Lefortovo prison. Then he went through a chain of searches and interrogations. In 1969, they arrested him again and sentenced to three years of imprisonment in a general regime camp. This term he served together with criminals. At each "conversation" with his tormentors, Ilya was required to admit the slanderous nature of his activities and to repent. Each time the answer was a firm "never!" Alas, not all of his friends and like-minded people showed such inconceivable strength and fortitude, some could not stand the torture and testified something, which the executioners needed so much! Such thing exactly has happened to P. Yakir and V. Krasin who were in the situation similar to Ilya's. For him it was the hardest blow, and, of course, it added to the feeling of hopelessness. However, the resources of even such a strong man are not limitless. In October 1973, Ilya Gabay, a wonderful man, loyal friend and talented poet committed suicide.

In the description of my first life, I said that the strongest motivation for writing this text was the desire to thank all my mentors, those who I felt helped me to become a better and more interesting person. I have always remembered that as far as mentors are concerned, I have been very, very lucky in my life: I have met on my way many people, whom I happily perceived as my teachers and mentors. I always considered a mentor to be an older, more educated and more experienced person whom you like and revere. However, for Ilya. I had to make an exception. Ilya certainly became one of those mentors for me, although he and I were almost the same age. In this connection, thanks to Ilya, I did some lexicographical research.

My meticulousness pushed me to the dictionaries to see if I could apply the word "mentor" to someone of my age. The next thing happened, as in the poem by Ovsei Driz: *Enyk Benyk Kolobok had made a discovery*. I could not believe my eyes. In the four-volume explanatory dictionary of Russian language edited in 1938 by D. Ushakov that I got from my father, with the word "mentor" was marked *"bookish-archaic, nowadays obsolete."* I was in shock: I had misunderstood the word "mentor" my whole life! I consulted then a four-volume Dictionary of Russian Language, published in 1958 by the Institute of Russian Language of the USSR Academy of Sciences. This scientific publication also said, *"Obsolete, now irrelevant!"* At this point, it began to dawn on me: this is pure Soviet vulgar politicking. Why do the cooking women, whom the revolution have entrusted to rule the state, need mentors? It is high time to throw those "exes" off the steamship of modernity!

It was not without excitement that I rushed to my three-volume New English-Russian Dictionary published in 1993, under the general guidance of Yu. D. Apresian. I was fortunate to know Yuri well in Moscow, a wonderful man, and a talented linguist. In his dictionary, I was pleased to read the short Russian interpretation, without any political nonsense: a "mentor" was *an instructor, teacher, tutor, and educator*. The next natural step after this, I was not lazy to check the interpretation of this word in Russian pre-Revolutionary editions (Broggauz and Efron, 1890–1907, Dahl, 1863–1909), in different editions of Oxford English Dictionary, in several editions of Webster's Dictionary of the English Language, the most popular in USA, etc. As might be expected, I did not find the mentioned politicization anywhere. As a result, I found myself in a good spirits. First, I did understand the word "mentor" correctly. Secondly, I correctly identified Ilya Gabay as one of my mentors (I will return to this statement later). Third, I was correct in my views on the ideological idiocy of "Sofia Vasilievna," which was a euphemism for "Soviet power" in my Moscow days.

As a striking example of how much I learned from Ilya, I want to elaborate on his 1963 poem "Judith." It is a poem that fundamentally changed my understanding of good and evil, and for that reason I present it here in its entirety.

The centuries float by,
One betrayal was giving birth to another one...
Let us leave Azefs along. Much worse,
Much more memorable were a wife's denunciation of her husband,
a sister's slander against her brother,
a stiff stamp
of insane lies, stupid simple-mindedness.
You put yourself at their cradle, Judith!
What an awful thing have you done, Judith!
Earth and sky, swans and geese
Are singing the same importunate tune:
What for did you do it, Judith"?
What for did you do it, Judith?
Was it malice? Was it craftiness? Was it an idea?
Or for the happiness of timid Israelites,
Who rejoice and do not want to forgive you,
Do not accept your cowardice, Judith?
What for did you do it, Judith?
To be remembered in legends?
Or to become the foremother of betrayals,
And to saturate your female arrogance
With the militant blood, Judith?
What for did you do it, Judith?
At the call of fashion, our wives dressed up
In the armor of not-forgiveness, in the appeals of Jeanne d'Arc,
Forgetting, what for they were born:
They came into this world to love, Judith!
What for did you do it, Judith?
Because if you glance back, I think,
You will see how, stepping on the Holofernes' corpses,
The crowd of ugly women is greedy clambering for the myth,
Remember, you were beautiful, Judith?
What for did you do it, Judith?
Out of boredom, did you hanker after a grim feat?

> *Or maybe, implanting in us admiration and envy,*
> *Us, incapable of heroic deeds,*
> *Did you call us to arms, Judith?*
> *No, we cannot. We are ill...*

The Orthodox Church classified the Old Testament Book of Judith as a non-canonical book. This explains the fact that actually all Russian-language editions of the Bible do not include this book. Nor did all editions of the Jewish Bible in Judaism include this book, although it is likely that this book has a Jewish author. The Protestant world also do not include the Book of Judith into the Canon because their Old Testament Canon is the same as the Judaic Canon. The Book of Judith is included in the Catholic Canon, but for reasons I do not understand, for the Soviet government Catholicism was the second most harmful religion after Judaism. Therefore, all Catholic religious publications were under strict prohibition in the Soviet Union. I am going into such detail about the situation of the Book of Judith in Russia to explain how difficult it was to get this book in the country, even on the black market. The described situation has happened, despite the fact that the story of Judith was attracting over the centuries a great deal of European culture, including Russian.

Judith became one of the most popular heroines of the Bible. She has inspired some of the world's greatest artists, such as Titian, Caravaggio, Botticelli, Giorgione, Michelangelo, Veronese, Goya. The world's greatest composers, such as Scarlatti, Vivaldi, Cimarosa, Mozart, Serov and Honegger have written musical compositions about her. The image of Judith spread in world literature, starting before the Renaissance and continuing to the present day. Martin Luther personally recommended the story of the Book of Judith for playwrights. It seems to me that the attention to this plot in Russian poetry is especially striking. You'll find poems about Judith by Mei, Gumilev, Balmont, Akhmatova, Mandelstam, Tsvetaeva.

As a result, when I became friends with Ilyusha I hadn't read the Biblical Book of Judith although I knew its contents well in various versions. First time I heard Ilya's "Judith" on Pushkin Street in 1963 and the story appeared to me in a completely different light. His ethical stance struck me out of the blue like a bomb. All the great figures of art, music and literature praised Judith as a folk hero, and only Ilya explained to me that she was *"the mother of treachery."* It was then that I wanted to see the original story and, of course, I tracked down the text of the Catholic Book of Judith. It became clear to me, as clear as daylight, that Ilya was absolutely right! More than 60 years passed, but to this day I ask together with the author: *"What for did you do it, Judith???"*

The first time I heard in Ilyusha's "Judith the question *"But what about the Azefs?"* I had no idea what they meant. It was at Ilya's prompting I later read about the Russian revolutionary provocateur and informer, and terrorist, head of the Socialist Revolutionary Organization and at the same time a secret police officer Evno Fishelevich Azef. Gabay, put this name in his poem as a common name in plural not by chance. What a shit (in Russian "govno", rhyming with Evno!) this man was, indeed, Evno! His hands were up to his elbows in blood. On the one hand, he directed the assassination attempt on the Grand Duke Sergei Alexandrovich and, on the other hand, he tracked down and turned in more than one revolutionary to the police. Many thanks to people like Ilyusha, who help us to see the extent of our illiteracy. I did not know until very recently that in the Explanatory Dictionary of the Russian Language by Ushakov there is a term "AZEFOVSHCHINA" (equivalent in English may be "azefing") meaning "major political provocation". I did not know that A. N. Tolstoy had a play called "Azef: two sides of the coin", that Azef's name was mentioned by V. V. Mayakovsky in "Cloud in Pants" (*"the night is black like Azef"*), and that there are several films, in Russia and in the West about this "hero."

Speaking here about how much I got from Ilyusha, I cannot help but tell you about how, thanks to him, I have read and come to love Thomas Mann's novel "Dr. Faustus." I had heard from the most educated people that it was, after the Goethe's "Faust", one of the most important books in world literature. Both Goethe's text and that of Thomas Mann were at the time, I describe, beyond my comprehension. To my shame, my many attempts in my school years to wade through this very difficult text for me ended in total failure. I complained about my lack with Ilyusha at Pushkin Street.

Fortunately, Ilya took our conversation very seriously. We talked with him a lot about the German legend of the 16th century, about "Dr. Faustus", about how it incited the best minds of the 20th century to think deeply about morality, about how educated and good people can sell their souls to the devil without noticing it. He confirmed that Goethes text is, actually, harder to understand and further removed in time. He advised me to try Thomas Mann again. In doing so, he recommended me to try not to lose the main ethical issue behind the details.

I followed this advice, and the result exceeded all my expectations. Not only did I come through the entire text of the novel from beginning to end, but I went back to some places several times, not because I didn't understand something, but because I just wanted to repeat my experience and make sure I hadn't missed anything. Maybe it happened not only because of Ilya's amazing persuasiveness in our conversation, but also because by the time of reading I had become, thanks to Ilya, a little wiser and better prepared to perceive the main moral problem. Of course, I hastened to report to my mentor on my unthinkable success. Then I also had a plan: to repeat this experiment with Goethe and, if it succeeded again, to run out again and report everything to Ilyablokhin. I must repent; alas, none of this happened. My mentor is no longer with us, and I have not yet fully read Goethe's Faust. Forgive me, dear Ilyusha. I continue to hope to become better and more worthy of our friendship. When it will be a success, I promise certainly tell you about it.

Now I would like to tell, how I said goodbye to Ilya forever. I lived on Novatorov Street in the South-West at the time. And the Gabays, lived on the 11th floor of a tall house on Novolesnaya Street, not far from Novoslobodskaya Street, but one block closer to the center. In the afternoon of October 20, 1973, the phone rang, and I, thank God, was at home and picked up. My aunt Bella (Balechka) was on the other side, but she was not speaking in her usual voice: I didn't even recognize her at first. "*Yurochka,*" said the voice, "*terrible things have happened to Ilyusha. Can you run to him right away?*" I hung up without saying goodbye and rushed to Novolesnaya Street. There was a group of people standing by their house, of which I knew only one: Yuliy Kim. A minute later I learned the terrible news: Ilyusha, had thrown himself out of the window of his apartment. There was a one-story store attached to the house, and the window looked out over the store's flat roof. The police had not yet arrived and Ilyusha,'s body was lying on the roof of the shop. No one had dared touch him.

The rest was like a bad dream and I do not remember the details very well. I was with Yulik the whole time. Somehow, we got in touch with the people in the building who lived directly above the shop and got permission to go into their apartment and then climb out onto the roof of the shop through the open window. Yulik was the first to climb out, and I followed him. The sight was not for people with weak nerves. Fortunately, I could not see Ilyusha,'s face, it was turned towards the roof. When he fell, his shoes had bounced off somewhere, and I could see his smashed feet. After that I somehow turned off and do not remember anything. I do not know how I got back to myself, but before that, I walked Ilyusha's Galya home.

Memory has preserved only that mentally I repeated long and frantically, like a record on a broken gramophone, following Ilyusha's periphrasis from his "Judith": *Why have you done this, you beast?!* Almost fifty years have passed since then, and I still cannot get my inner gramophone fixed. To this day I still keep hearing in my head, *Why did you do that, you brute?!* And just recently, I read a poem by my nephew Lev in memory of his close friend Sasha Rosenstrom, a talented man who died untimely of a heart attack. The poem took my thoughts back to the terrible day when I saw Ilyusha Gabai for the last time. It is short, and I'm quoting it in full:

> *Who says he is dead?*
> *He just moved.*
> *Escaped from the captivity*
> *Of the daily lie.*
> *Not in peace with himself,*
> *He was just a hindrance to himself.*
> *He lived by my side.*
> *However, who said that it was life?*

To end the chapter about Ilyusha on a more cheerful note, I want to tell you that it happened that Ilyusha's wife, Galya, came to Boston before we did and brought her children, Alyosha and Mashen'ka, here. For a moment, I was pleased to know that Galechka had joined her life with a good and kind man whom we liked. Galechka also published in the US a large, wonderful book about Ilyusha and she gave us a copy as a gift. Both she and the children are healthy and we hope that they will never have to pass through Calvary like Ilya, did. I personally have always liked Galya Gabay,. I worshipped her courage and strength, her ability to endure unimaginably difficult circumstances of Ilya,'s life and support him in everything. I was worried when her relationship with Ilya, became difficult, and he moved to live with Balechka at Pushkin Street. I did not want to blame anyone, realizing that they both lead extremely difficult lives, and I just prayed that everything would work out. Even though I cannot communicate with Galya as often as I would like, from time to time, we do communicate, and it warms my soul and brings me a lot of joy. It is a little bit like a compensation for the fact that those monsters took Ilya away from us so early. When I wrote this chapter Galina's book about Ilya was lying on my desk and Ilyusha was looking at me from the cover strictly watching that my writing be truth and only truth. I tried very hard

When I finished the chapter about Ilyusha, I felt it necessary to show the text to Galya Gabay to see if I had made any mistakes. I got her full approval in the form of a quote from A.Tvardovsky's poem "One Far Away after another": *"There's nothing to diminish or add, it was exactly like that on the Earth."* I considered it the best compliment.

MY FIRST AND MAIN JOB

As was most often the case with getting a good job in my former homeland, the easiest way to solve this problem would be "through acquaintance." My brother had a friend who worked at the Institute of Precise Mechanics and Computer Technology (IPM&CT) of the USSR Academy of Sciences, which was the leading research institute in Moscow for computers. With the help of this person a miracle has happened: I got a job as a technician in the laboratory of computer elements. His name was Victor Zeidenberg. We will talk about him below. I was employed with IPM&CT for twenty years (1958–1977), having worked my way up from a junior technician to a senior researcher.

It was a great luck to work at this institution for so long because it played a leading role in the creation and development of the computer industry in Russia. I think, I could not acquire anywhere else in my country better professional experience in computer specialty. In other words, I found myself at the computer forefront. Here I would like to list the first steps of computing machinery in the world:

> the first in the world program-controlled calculating automat on telephone relays (Germany,1941);
> the first calculating device on vacuum tubes (U.S.A., 1942);
> the first calculating machine on electronic lamps (U.S.A., 1943);
> the first electronic computer in the world Eniac (U.S.A., 1946);
> the second electronic computer in the world MARK-1 (England, 1948);
> the first electronic computer in Russia, Small Electronic Calculating Machine SECM (Russia, 1950).

Everyone familiar with the history of electronics knows that Russia lagged behind the developed countries of the West by about ten years. One has to wonder how, under the conditions of the Iron Curtain and general economic lag, the first Soviet computer scientists managed to literally step on the toes of their Western counterparts!

This was happening despite the even greater backwardness of electronic technology in the country. I joined the Institute in 1958. It was the time of the painful start of the Soviet semiconductor computer industry. First Soviet large semiconductor computer BESM-6 was born at the place I worked in 1965. I still admire my colleagues who were able to build such powerful WORKING computer on domestic semiconductors of such a low quality. I remember very well that testing ALL the production of such semiconductors in the country showed that only 5% (!?) met technical requirements. The military industry would receive all this 5%. Our head research institute of the Academy of Sciences and the Ministry of Radio Industry selected from the remainder.

Our Institute was founded in 1948 by the Decree of the USSR Council of Ministers signed personally by I. V. Stalin. Its first director was the Academician Bruevich Nikolay, first director of my IPM&CT, specialist in theory of precision mechanisms.

My first direct manager was a wonderful woman, Lena Lander. Together with Viktor Zeidenberg they became my close friends and remained so until the last day of my work at the Institute.

Lena was the most talented woman-engineer I have ever known. From her I learned a great many technical things, big and small. It seems to me that it is to her that I owe much of my love of manual work, which throughout my life has brought me much both joy and benefit. The feature of Lena Lander's style of engineering was the ability to find fast a solution that WORKED, even if it did not have an outward gloss. Speaking about my own handicrafts, their main critic was always my wife Tanya. I often hear from her that my work is often not perfect because it lacks a "clean" finish. I think it was Lena Lander who "gave" me this virus.

I cannot help telling here funny story about Lena's son Sasha. The boy was reading a lot and and he was compiling the catalogue of all the books he have read. Once we talked and I asked him what did he read last month. He got his catalogue, looked in it and answered: *"I have read books for 127 rubles 93 kopecks."* I did not understand him and asked: *"What does this mean?"* *"I am summing up the prices of all the books I have read and I gave you the total"*, responded the boy. Never before I heard about such measure for loving to read!

Since one of the main processes determining my second life was "recovery of sight", it is appropriate here to tell a sad story related to Lena Lander. This story helped me a lot to understand what kind of country I was living in. Victor, Lena's husband was a worthy man whom I liked a lot. When Soviet Union was involved into Second World War, though he was very young, he went to the front. Soon he was wounded and became disabled: it was difficult for him to walk because after the wound he started dragging his leg. Victor was successfully engaged in research in radiolocation. Physically he was quite strong, and his willpower was amazing. For example, once I happened to be together with him in a hike BY FOOT along the Crimean Mountain chain. If I had not seen it with my own eyes, I would have never believed that a disabled person like Victor could on pure willpower do such a thing. In the sixties, to the joy of the Landers themselves and their relatives, they bought a car, a small Zaporozhets. Lena obtained her driving license, and the car not only gave joy to the family, but also made the life of the whole family and especially of Victor much easier.

One day the Landers were driving their Zaporozhets along a quiet and rather deserted Moscow street, Lena, as usual, was at the wheel. They saw a group of people ahead of them making signs asking them to stop. Lena stopped the car near the people and opened her window fully. Judging by their accent, the people were of Caucasian and looked very drunk. They asked or rather demanded in a rude tone for a ride somewhere. Lena tried to explain to them politely that she was an inexperienced driver, that they urgently needed to take a disabled person somewhere, and that their car was too small to give a lift to such a large group of people. The negotiator responded by swinging his fist across Lena's face. Lena was wearing glasses, which broke and seriously injured her eye. Today I no longer remember the details, but somehow Landers managed to get away from the hooligans and rushed her to the emergency room of the nearest hospital. Doctors diagnosed a serious retinal detachment and Lena ended up on the operating table. After the surgery, the Lander family became two disabled people.

However, the story did not end there. A few days later a doorbell rang in Lena's apartment. There was a woman on the doorstep who turned out to be the mother of the bandit who mutilated Lena. How this woman found Landers, we do not know. The woman gave Lena the details of what had happened. The raiders turned out to be mostly Dagestanis, "scientific workers" associated with the Department of the History of the Communist Party in Moscow University. The horde was returning from a banquet after successfully defending the dissertation "History of the Communist Party of Dagestan." The woman begged her not to sue her son and was ready to pay Lena any money for this. Lena promised to fulfill her request and said she would not charge her a penny. The only condition Lena set was that she would never see the woman, her son or her son's friends again.

I remember well how I was upset with this story. First, I felt sorry for them both: Lena and Victor. This couple was absolutely an example of high morality, kindness and modesty for me. I think they never offended a single person in their life, but they helped many people. Besides, at that time, I still had many naïve illusions about what scientific workers and university professors, communists should be. What happened shattered such type of illusions in me.

I often went to Lena Lander's house Smolenskaya Square, right above the famous Gastronome. Usually nice people have nice friends. Some of such pople became my friends which I consider as a present from Landers. There was her neighbor Liolya, a rare kind and benevolent person. I do not remember her last name, so let us call her Liolya Nice. Liolya had a son, Tim, an interesting boy, small and thin, and very clever.

Liolya told us the story of her giving birth to Tim, both funny and sad. In the maternity ward, she met a woman who caught her attention with her sad appearance and nervousness. They quickly became friends. Both of them were admitted to the maternity hospital early due to some pregnancy complications and were in the same room. When they got to talking, the woman told Liolya what was bothering her. She had a difficult relationship with her husband, a strange man, to put it mildly. He really wanted a son, so she finally got pregnant, hoping that with the birth of a son everything would go better. But when she left for the maternity hospital, her husband told her in all seriousness that if she gave birth to a girl, let her take the baby anywhere, but not return home. Time came for both women to go into labor. Imagine, Liolya is giving birth to Tim and her roommate is giving birth to a big girl! The poor woman returned to her room in tears, and her grief was inconsolable. Seeing this Liolya decides to take the unthinkable step, very few people are capable to do this—she offers her roommate to switch children, without telling anyone about it! Grief-stricken, the woman did not respond immediately. There was one more woman in their room, who the next day told Liolya about her conversation with the unhappy woman. "*Can you imagine,*" the woman said about Liolya, "*what a sly Jewish woman: she wanted to exchange her little baby boy who weighs 2900 grams for my baby girl, 4,300 grams!*" As we say: "*No need for comments!*"

The second person who worked with me from day one in Lena Lander's group was Viktor Zeidenberg, the one who interceded for me when I applied for the job. He was older than I was and had been single for quite a long time. He had very few friends, and the only person who was really close to him was his sister. He had worked with Lena Lander for quite a long time and was her devoted friend. He was a very mild and kind man, who tried to do everything in his life punctiliously and correctly down to the smallest detail. Such people, I think, are not usually very happy. We immediately reached out to each other because, I think, there were several things we had in common.

First, neither he nor I were born into this world as engineers. In computers, Victor was primarily interested in informatics. He knew computer vocabulary well in both Russian and English. He liked to browse through all the most serious American computer magazines, and he would always find there interesting facts for our design engineers. In computer science, I was primarily interested in logic: how to combine optimally the logical elements that already work, so that together they optimally perform a more complex logical function. This was a new field for me, and I wanted to be acquainted with solutions to this problem from publications in the American literature. Both he and I eventually changed the nature of our work at the Institute, and moved to other departments to be able to do more of what interested us.

The second thing we had in common, was that by that time I was doing a lot of translation for a living and I became interested in dictionaries. Victor was very interested in computer terminology. It was developing so fast, mostly in the United States, that new terms did not have time to appear in Russian. Our lively conversations on this subject turned into a big joint project. Victor formed a team, which began to work on compiling an English-Russian Dictionary of computer language. The director of the Institute, the academician Sergey Lebedev agreed to be the editor of the dictionary, and the work began. Victor and I became the main authors. Looking ahead, the first Soviet English-Russian dictionary of computers was published through our efforts in 1964. It contained 12,000 terms. I remember with great pleasure our collaboration in the preparation of this dictionary, and I am very grateful to Victor for everything I have learned from him, particularly his meticulousness in all the details. Victor was extremely demanding, I would even say painstakingly demanding, of both himself and his colleagues, even in smallest things. One way or another, it was working in this project that I developed an interest in dictionaries and lexicography in general, which has continued through my life.

One can't help but think in this context of the closing line in the movie "Casablanca", one of the most memorable phrases in the history of cinema. The main characters, Rick (Humphrey Bogart) and Louis (Claude Rains)) walk off into the fog and the former says to the latter: *"Louie, I think this is the beginning of a beautiful friendship."* This work on our dictionary really turned out to be the beginning of a beautiful friendship for me with both Victor and the dictionaries. Dictionaries became my best friends. You can imagine how excited I was when I found S. Marshak's poem "Dictionary" describing poet's admiration of the richness of Russian language vocabulary. The poem demonstrates a variety of idioms including the word "century." For English speakers I will literally translate the Russian expression and add in parentheses the meaning of it. I can't refrain from quoting the poem here in full.

> *I look more and more diligently every day into the dictionary.*
> *I can see sparks of feeling twinkle in its columns.*
> *The art will descend into the sellers of words more than once,*
> *Each time it will have a mysterious lantern.*
> *There are stamps of events on all words.*
> *They were given to man for a reason.*
> *I read, "Century.*
> *Centuries since* (beginning since old time ago).
> *To live your century* (to pass a lifetime, to exist).
> *God did not give his son a century* (about a person young).
> *To drag down one's century* (make one's life difficult).
> *To woke over somebody's century* (to live to a great age).
> *You can hear all in the words: reproach, anger, and conscience.*
> *No, it is not a dictionary in my hands,*
> *It is an ancient scattered tale.*

The third thing we had in common was that he and I both loved being outdoors traveling. Lena Lander was always our wonderful companion in this and together we made many interesting trips. Two of them were the most memorable: hiking on the Crimean Mountains and rafting down the Volga River. The second turned out to be a milestone in my life, and I will talk about it separately.

Fourthly, Victor, Lena, and I were buying piano concert subscriptions to the Moscow Conservatory every year and several times a year we enjoyed together wonderful music performed by the best Soviet pianists. In music all three of us were at about the same level and all three wanted to go up with this level. These concerts helped us to be closer to each other.

Before finishing about Victor, I think it is necessary to mention an important event in our friendship. In the early sixties, he had a serious heart attack and the doctors strongly advised him to stop all work and to remain in bed for at least a couple of weeks. This recommendation was not easy to carry out. Victor lived alone in a room in a communal apartment, and the only person who could take care of him at this time was his sister. However, she lived quite far away from him and worked. My mother was still alive at that time (she died in 1963) and she offered to bring Victor to our place. My mother was ready to take care of him, and that had happened. Victor became friends with my mom and all subsequent years he was deeply grateful to us for our help. The intense communication with my mother and me during the "hospitalization" at our home served as an important therapeutic factor in the healing process and all involved enjoyed it. Victor recovered and returned safely to work.

I was working in Lena Lander's group for about ten years, and in terms of human qualities I could not have wished for better colleagues than Lena and Victor. However, as I have already mentioned, for both Victor and me, the work was not in the nature that I would have liked it to be. Neither he nor I enjoyed debugging electronic circuits with a soldering iron in hand. I was looking for opportunities to work with computer logic circuits and Victor was looking for opportunities to work with information documents. Ironically, in the late sixties, both he and I had such an opportunity inside IPM&CT. Fortunately the style and practice of the Institute was always to go out of its way to help each employee to do the work he or she wanted to do. As a result, I moved to the department of logic circuits and software, and Victor received the position of head of the information department. These transitions did not weaken our friendship in any way. We still would often meet both inside and outside the Institute.

My new boss turned out to be a very nice man, Lyova Korolev. He is no longer alive, and I, alas, cannot thank him enough for the many good things he did for me personally. Lyova played an important role in the defense of my PhD in 1970. After he graduated from the Moscow State University in 1952, he immediately started working at IPM&CT, where he worked his way up from an ordinary worker to head of the department (1956), to Candidate of Science (1960), Doctor of Science (1967), and Laureate of the State Prize of the USSR (1969). After I left the Institute he became a Corresponding Member of the USSR Academy of Sciences (1981), he was awarded the Prize of the USSR Council of Ministers (1982), became Corresponding Member of the Russian Academy of Sciences (1991), he was awarded the Lomonosov Prize of the Russian Academy of Sciences (1995). He became a Honorary Professor at Moscow State University (1996). Since I have listed here many regalia and awards of Lyova, I cannot refrain from telling, how the epic of the election of Lyova as a corresponding member of the Academy of Sciences of the USSR began.

I had to leave the Institute in 1977, when my odyssey with emigration began. I remember well one episode that happened in my last year at the Institute. So it was either 1976 or 1977. I ran into Lyova's office on some trivial matter and found him clearly in a highly nervous state. Our relationship allowed me to ask him directly, *"Lyova, is something wrong with you!?"* My question sounded more like a statement than a question. He did not immediately respond, but after a pause, it poured out of him as from a horn of plenty. Then he told me a rather sordid story.

It was the time, when they first decided to nominate him as a corresponding member of the Academy of Sciences. The Presidium of the Academy of Sciences began to prepare documents for him. On this case, they summoned him for an interview with some "pawn" of the Presidium. This "pawn" after stupid meaningless questions like *"How are you?"*, *"How is your tummy?"* got down to business. The first meaningful question was, *"How well does he know his family history?"* Lyova's answer was, *"Not much."* The second question was, *"Does you recall any Jewish people among your ancestors?"* According to his story to me, he was at this point speechless with indignation. This visit took place the day before we met. What I saw of him the next day at work told me that his indignation was still there and that he had not yet completely recovered his gift of speech. *"Yuri,"* he told me, *"I still can't believe what I heard!"* When he came to his senses, according to his story, he told the "pawn," *"I am sorry, but I've never done any ethnic research on my ancestry."* *"It is a shame!"* the "pawn" reacted. In conclusion, of the description of this episode, I remind you that Lyova became Corresponding Member of the Soviet Academy of Sciences only in 1981. This means that it took about five years to clarify the purity of his Aryan descent.

All my years working in Lyova's department, I never questioned his logical-mathematical abilities. It was always easy for me to talk to him about any work issue. But on this day, I came home completely happy. First, I was proud of the complete confidence my boss had shown in me. Secondly, I rejoiced at the fact that Lyova had a "brain group" and a "heart group" (compare blood group) just like me. And, of course, I was surprised at how acute his reaction was. How had he managed to live to this age and not know that this was happening regularly and everywhere?

Until my last day at the Institute, he and I remained good friends. I was lucky that with my immediate supervisor I also had a friendly relationship, and he was always ready to help me and support me. But there were times when he was not able to help me. I would like to recall here one sad and ridiculous example.

Since I was young, my favorite movie actor was Sophia Loren. I liked her in every movie where I saw her. Interestingly, to this day I feel attracted to this woman. In the room where I worked in Lyova's department, there were four of us sitting, and three of my colleagues were all quite nice people to me. Beginning at some time, of course, with their consent, I began to hang pictures of this prominent woman on the wall when I managed to cut out such pictures in some magazine. Gradually, one of the bare walls of our room became an interesting, from my point of view, photo exhibition. All my colleagues liked this exhibition too. Moreover, some of them sometimes would bring me additional photos for Sophia Loren's gallery. It seemed to be a good thing for everybody. As for me personally, Sophia Loren looking at me from the wall only increased my productivity.

We had in our Institute the secret documents department with the conspiratorial name "First Department". One day a lady from this Department came to our room on business. Looking at my exhibition, she squeamishly asked: *"What is this?"* I politely answered her: *"These are pictures of Sophia Loren, an actress my friends and I are very fond of."* She snorted angrily and left the room. Half an hour later, Lyova came into our room. He felt guilty and told me that the Head of the First Department had summoned him and demanded that all the pictures be removed from the wall immediately. Lyova told me that of course it was stupid, but we had to comply with his demand. That was the inglorious end of my cultural outburst within the walls of the Institute. To this day, I don't understand how photographs of such an enchanting woman could violate even the strictest rules of a confidential research.

Color television did not start to spread in Moscow until the seventies. Lyova was then one of the few happy owners of this technology. I well remember him coming to work one day and talking excitedly about how his family was enjoying the novelty of technology. At that time, an international figure skating competition was taking place, and the broadcast of the competition was shown on color television. The conversation turned to how wonderful it was to see the skaters' colorful costumes. Unintentionally I mentioned that my daughter Galina loved figure skating. Lyova immediately invited us to come over to his place to watch the competition. They lived near us and all three of us, Galka, Tanya and I, went there. Galka's excitement was boundless. Lyova himself and his wife, also Galya, turned out to be very hospitable hosts. We still remember that visit with joy and gratitude.

Besides the good friends I made in IPM&CT, there were simply co-workers, some of whom left a vivid trace in my memory. A wonderful example is Sasha Semyonov, who worked at the photocopier machine. Today it is hard to believe it, but at that time, the work of any copier was strictly registered, and Sasha had to document in a special journal each page copied. This strict rule thought to prevent the seditious copying of confidential or ideologically unsound documents. As a result, the lord guardian of our security in the laboratory was Sasha Semenov. Suffering from chronic alcoholism, this semi-literate man was, from my point of view, a very interesting and bright in his own way personality.

In the first place, Sasha had an amazing sense of humor. He asserted that in order to live life to the fullest, *"Everyone should ALWAYS be on low speed and a little bit tipsy."* Sasha demonstrated this philosophical principle very successfully by his own life. During all twenty years of my work at the Institute I never once saw him unpleasantly drunk, but I ALWAYS noticed that every day he had already touched a bottle. And strangely enough, I would say that this state suited him. Sasha elaborated in detail his theory, the essence of which was that vodka contains all the nutrients necessary and sufficient for human life. *"Look, Yuri,"* he used to say to me, *"at the formula of alcohol C_2H_5OH, it contains carbon, hydrogen, and oxygen,* *and a man really needs nothing else!"* Apparently, Sasha noticed my sympathy, and chose me, not as much as a friend, but as a confidant. Before all other people in the laboratory he would come to me to borrow three rubles, that is how low was at that time the price of a bottle of vodka, and I must give him credit, he always would pay back his debt.

There were four of us working in the room. From time to time our door would get ajar, and Sasha silently beckoned me in with his finger. I already knew: he was here for the three rubles. If I tell him this day that I didn't have three rubles for him, he would always nod his head in the direction of my colleagues asking me the same question: *"And what about the scientists?"* On such occasions I would ask my enlightened colleagues for financial help, and sometimes I got it. If during these few minutes any of my three roommates would pay attention to the requestor, Sasha in a whisper, not to disturb the others, said: *"And you, you multiply, multiply, multiply..."*. It always amused me a lot that in his head the arithmetic operation of multiplication was the symbol of the complexity of our mathematical research.

Sasha also regularly wrote "literary" opuses that clearly expressed highly individual and very personal relationship of him with Russian spelling and syntax. For all my meticulously strictness about respecting language, these works did not really annoy me, and I even liked something about them, probably the humor and lack of rudeness. They were all exclusively about drinking. Again, he chose me as his first reader and critic. What was funny, he listened respectfully to my comments and sometimes even made appropriate changes to his text. I still grieve that I did not ask him for one of his masterpieces to keep it for history.

Another one of my Institute coworkers, Vitya Pankov, was like me, a programmer, and we worked in the same room at the adjacent desks. Vitya had also a wonderful sense of humor, and I had loved jokes since I was a kid and I loved his "aphorisms." Today I even forget what Vitya looked like, but some of his sayings are with me, and I never stop telling them to my friends.

Being quite conscientious and working quite hard, from time to time Vitya did not disdain relaxing. He was very fond of the Russian steam room and set up a club with his friends that met in the steam room. The members of the club elected Vitya unanimously as the president of the club. They had picked a place in Moscow where there was good steam, good as the doctor would prescribe, and every Thursday they would meet there, never forgetting to bring plenty of beer with them. On Wednesday afternoon, right from work, he would call his "steam friends" and I could hear him discussing tomorrow's event with each of them: *"I remind you that tomorrow is the professional development day. Are you going to come to our thermodynamics seminar?"* The seminar, as agreed, would take place, and the improving qualification would go very successful.

When Vitya and I would meet in the morning at work on a sunny, warm day, he always asked me if I could hear the weather whispering: *"Get fired!"* Vitya, a very nice, though naïve, Russian man, did not realize that the weather was whispering me a bad advice. After all, for a Jew it would be very difficult get any decent job afterwards.

It seems to me, that the unusually nice nature of the director of our Institute resulted in the fact that the majority of my colleagues were unusually good people. Only some of them I have mentioned in this book, and I apologize if I have forgotten anyone. Getting ahead in my writing, I have to say that all my Institute friendships and acquaintances, to my great regret, disappeared overnight and forever from my life, when I left the Institute to embark on an epic of emigration. Human relations in my ugly country had no right to exist if they did not meet the requirements of political correctness. In this connection, it is important for me to tell that I am grateful to fate for the meetings with all those who made my life and work at the Institute richer, more pleasant, and interesting. There were very many of such people, who left me with the warmest memories about these decades. I wish wholeheartedly all the best to those of them who are still alive today.

THE GREAT RETICENT PERSON

Having said many good things about the place where I worked for 20 years, I feel obligated to talk about the Director of our Institute, Sergey Lebedev, from whom, I believe, most of this good was coming. In my first years at the Institute, my knowledge of the Director was limited to superficial observations at meetings and, of course, to the stories of my colleagues, who new him much better an even visited Lebedev's house. As a result, I must confess that, knowing very little about him, I made a wrong impression of S. Lebedev. He seemed to me a very decent and kind person, an exceptionally talented, hardworking, and conscientious engineer, but a kind of Soviet technician, devoid of humanitarian interests. In other words, I imagined him as my brother Jan wanted me to be and as he himself was. In that sense, I considered his marriage to his wife Alice, nicest person and musician, as a misalliance in the same sense in which I saw Jan's own marriage to Innulia. But much later, especially when writing these memories, I managed to read a lot about the Lebedev family, and I realized, in the words of B. Okudzhava:

> *Ah, my childhood dreams — what a mistake,*
> *In what clouds I was foolishly flying!*

One is smart in hindsight, I have dramatically changed now my opinion of this man.

Sergey Lebedev was born and lived his childhood in Nizhny Novgorod. His parents, teachers, were members of the Russian democratic party Narodnaya Volya, engaged in enlightenment. His father's brother closely knew Gorky. His mother was a hereditary noblewoman, who had one brother and eleven sisters (almost like my mother!). The house was full of books; there were shelves even in the cold porch. Sergey's sister, Tatyana Mavrina was an internationally renowned artist, a famous illustrator of fairy tales by A. S. Pushkin. Young Sergey as a child read a lot and was quiet, focused, and shy. People, who new him then, used to call him *"great reticent boy"*.

In the early 20s, the Lebedevs moved to Moscow and Sergey entered the Moscow Higher Technical School (MHTS) named after Bauman. Shortly before graduating in 1927, Sergey Lebedev had a life-changing meeting with cellist Alice Steinberg on one of the beaches near Moscow. She was swimming along the shore, and he has dived and came up, unexpectedly, right in front of her. That day their fate was sealed. Two years later, they became husband and wife and happily lived together for 47 years. Years later, Sergey admits that he *"experienced with Alice the whole gamut of feelings, except boredom."* I really like this description of their family life.

When I started working at IPM&CT, they already had four wonderful children. In Russian language, there are two different words for pronoun "you": one polite, formal and it is in plural, and another informal in singular. Before they were married, Sergey addressed Alice using informal one in singular but after the wedding, polite one in plural. When his wife asked him *"why so?"* he replied *"There are so much of you!"* This was exactly true: there was so much in this special woman! Her brilliance and activity attracted to the house many wonderful people, including famous writers and poets. Among the guests, one could see Ilf and Petrov, and Olesha and Kataev, and Fadeyev, and Svetlov. Alice herself worked as a secretary for Korney Chukovsky.

Director of my Institute Lebedev S.A.

All members of the Lebedev family had a keen sense of justice. The road roller of first Tsar's and later Bolsheviks' repressions could not pass this type of people. Sergey's father found himself imprisoned for two years for supporting the views of Narodnaya Volya and was under surveillance for a long time. The husband of Sergey's sister and the husband of Alice's sister perished in Stalin's camps. Alice's father spent several years in the camps. However, as far as I was able to find out, only the older generation of Lebedev family suffered in that meat-grinder. Thank God, Sergey himself and his wife were not touched.

Lebedev A.G., the wife of Lebedev S.A.

There was always music in Lebedev's family, his father played a bit, Sergey himself played the piano from his childhood, and he liked to listen to Beethoven and Grieg. He had many friends who were musicians. I even had the impression that young Sergey, pushed with his strong intuition, foresaw that he would marry a musician, and he did. The children's favorite pastime was home theatre. The children were studying foreign languages, French and German. What a shame that I did not know at all this about the Lebedev family. If I, a fool, had done so, with the simplicity and friendliness of both Alice and Sergey, I, of course, would try to make friends with such wonderful people. I wish, my family was more like Lebedev's, I was especially lacking music in ours.

Alice belonged to the line of women in my life whom I liked, but whom I was too shy to approach. But I do remember my admiration of her as a beautiful decoration of our Institute banquets. Recently I was, going through the poems written by me, I came across one I wrote on her birthday in the mid-70s:

> *Technocrats and nerds,*
> *We wasted piles of paper with writing,*
> *Without thinking about a shortage of paper in the Institute,*
> *Like everywhere else.*
> *Still we were not able to find worthy enough words,*
> *Let them be playful, but decent,*
> *To glorify the earthly namesake of Alice in Wonderland.*
> *From one banquet to another*
> *We were tortured with this problem.*
> *To solve which was a trickier,*
> *Than to, design BESM-6.*
> *We cannot help ourselves,*
> *Our feelings are getting out of hand.*
> *However, there can be a song without proper words,*
> *Here it is today*

In these lines, I think I made it clear how I felt about Alice. I am an emotional person and it seemed to me that she really appeared to us from the land of miracles. I was very happy for our Sergey Lebedev.

Lebedev came to our Institute from Ukraine, and his MECM was born in Kiev. It was extremely important for my formation as a computer specialist that I was lucky to work my first and most important years in the organization headed by such a remarkably talented and amazingly intelligent, modest, and kind person. He reminded me something of my father by his human qualities. During the twenty years of his leadership of the Institute, Sergey would always set the tone in everything by his own example. As a result, the atmosphere at the Institute was unique. Over those years I NEVER encountered anti-Semitism (his wife Alice was Jewish). Almost every employee, regardless of his or her position, felt comfortable approaching the director on any issue, asking him for any help. It is still incomprehensible to me how this man, who had received every possible award and distinction in the country, managed not to be infected by such a widespread virus of haughtiness, arrogance, conceit, and indifference to those around him. The incredible simplicity of Sergey resulted in the fact that most employees in IPM&CT considered him not only as their boss, but also as a FELLOW COWORKER. His wife Alice, nice, clever, affable, and well-educated woman, was a participant and a true pleasure at all Institute celebrations and feasts.

In 1972 our whole institute widely celebrated his 70th anniversary of the director. It should be said that at the Institute I was known as a reliable rhymester: I was oftenly composing cheerful poems about different events. This time I wrote humorous congratulatory verse from our laboratory to the jubilee. Until now I am a little bit embarrassed by my impertinent hail-fellow-well met verses in these poems. I made them public only at the insistence of my co-worker friends, who not only approved the poems, but also convinced me to do so. But finally I agreed to present my verse to jubilee only after I was told about their approval by Alice. Here is the text of this congratulation, preserved in my archives:

> *It is already the third decade,*
> *That from the crown of your head to your toes*
> *You are OUR academician, Sergey.*
> *We feel not bad to work with you,*
> *That is why we have decided, old fox,*
> *YOU DID DESERVE AN ANNIVERSARY!*
>
> *You have been cooking computers*
> *Since time in Ukraine,*
> *You have been giving the world many of your ideas.*

They were, uh, not bad,
You knew, did not you, old fox,
YOU DID DESERVE AN ANNIVERSARY!

You organized for fun a bold team of graduates
From the physics technology university,
They all really were big forehead people.
You were not a bad teacher.
You knew, did not you, old fox,
YOU DID DESERVE AN ANNIVERSARY!

All things were running alone as smooth as grease,
Your enemies were annoyed with envy:
Your house already was full of kids.
You did not a bad job,
You knew, did not you, old fox,
YOU DID DESERVE AN ANNIVERSARY!

We are common people,
We are not going to blather,
We are not going to drip the unction.
Your pushing was not bad, keep it going,
However, remember you, old fox,
IT WAS NOT FOR NOTHING,
THAT YOU DESERVED YOUR ANNIVERSARY!

I am happy to say that Lebedev's response to my poem was exceptionally positive.

I often remember with great gratitude, the help and support S. Lebedev gave me personally. However, what he did for Russia, was immense. In October 1955, a letter signed by the largest scientists of the country addressed the Presidium of the Central Committee of the Communist Party of the Soviet Union on the unacceptable situation in the biological science in the USSR. It was imposed by a pseudo-scientist T. Lysenko, protégé of the country's leadership and the communists. This letter, known as the "Letter of Three Hundred," played a historic role in ending the obscurantism in biological science of the country. It stopped the stagnation of the development of genetic science, and literally cruel punishment of all opponents of this scoundrel. There were three hundred signatures under the letter and one of them belonged to Sergey Lebedev. As they say, comments are unnecessary here.

To maintain justice and even decency in the Soviet Union of those years was already an act of courage. Alice Lebedev, a worthy companion of Sergey Lebedev, repeatedly showed such courage. One good example was her organization in the '70s, together with Andrei Sakharov the so-called academic aid fund. I am talking here about a secret fund to help four "humiliated and insulted" (the title of the novel by Dostoevsky) writers: A.Galich, V.Dudintsev, V.Voynovich and A.Solzhenitsyn. For this, three famous academicians: P. Kapitsa, A.Sakharov, and S. Lebedev,— would contribute their money, and the cashier was Alice Lebedev. She personally sent monthly to each of the four an envelope containing 100 rubles. I salute and praise these three scholars and this amazing woman!

Sergey Lebedev's constant helper for twenty years, Valentina Elksnin was worthy of her boss. Pleasant and intelligent, I personally remember that when I passed the director's office and was in no hurry, I always wanted to open the door and, if she was not busy, to have a word with her. She was always ready to share her vast professional and life experience, to advise me when I had to make a difficult decision. Once, when I was hesitating whether it was appropriate for me to address her boss with my personal request, I asked for her opinion and saw in her understanding and a desire to help. I could trust her 100%, and I could tell her anything about my friends and myself. When my friend Konstantin Babitsky ended up in exile for participating in a protest of the Soviet invasion of Czechoslovakia, I decided that I had to go and visit him there. Most of my relatives and friends had exhorted me not to do so, lest I lose my job. I went to Valentina, told her everything, and asked for her advice. She not only supported my decision, but also helped me arrange my vacation days quickly. I remember well how happy I was when I left the waiting room. Almost fifty years have passed since then, and I often remember this wonderful woman with gratitude.

I remind the reader, Sergey Lebedev was the General Designer of the first universal computer in Russia; since 1950, he was Head of the Laboratory of IPM&CT and from 1953 and practically until his death, he was its director. He has organized and led few extremely important projects in applying computers for military defense. The Government appreciated the work of the Institute and personally the work of Sergey Lebedev according to their merits. He got the highest awards of the country: the Stalin Prize (1950), the title of Member of the USSR Academy of Sciences (1953), the title of Hero of Socialist Labor (1956), the Lenin Prize (1966), the State Prize of USSR (1969), numerous orders and medals. In 1973, his health sharply worsened, and he had to retire, but continued to work at home. In 1974, he passed away. He died three years before I left the Institute. I knew well personally two first members of staff of our Institute, students of S. Lebedev, who succeeded him as director, I worked with them side by side for 20 years. Both were highly respected people and specialists, but, in my opinion, they were succeeding, but not replacing. It was impossible to replace Sergey Lebedev!

DOWN THE MOTHER VOLGA RIVER

During my vacations and holidays, I loved to travel around Russia, mostly with a backpack behind my shoulders. However, until I left the country for good, I had never crossed the borders of the Soviet Union. Traveling abroad had always been the privilege of Party activists and certainly not of Jews. I remember the summer of 1960 traveling in a tourist bus on the road along the amazingly picturesque Tissa River in the Karpat Mountains. In this area, Tissa was a border river between Romania and the Soviet Ukraine. The day was warm, and the bus windows were open. I was holding a paper bag with plums in my hands, eating them and throwing the stones out the window, trying to make them reach the river and fall into the water. The thought came to me that my bones were falling in a foreign and inaccessible world, as if flying to another planet. Thank God, I turned out to be not 100% right about that. It was at that moment that I, without realizing it, took a small mental step in the direction of emigration.

In the summer of 1961, together with my friends and colleagues, I went on one of my most interesting hikes. This trip turned out to be a historical milestone in my life: I left home as a BACHELOR, and returned home as MARRIED MAN. In 1958, a translation of the book by the Norwegian explorer Thor Heyerdahl "Kon-Tiki" about crossing the Pacific Ocean (about 5000 miles) on a self-made raft has appeared on the Russian shelves. This book created a furor all over the world, including Russia. It was that time, when my friends and I decided to build lightweight rafts and float on them down the Volga river, one of the biggest rivers in Europe. The title of this chapter is the quote from very popular in Russia volk song. We planned to start from the source of the great river (Lake Seliger) and finishing as far as we would have guts. Some participants of the expedition gradually dropped out as they went along the route, depending on free time resources available. The most persistent ones reached Tver (then Kalinin).

There was a special group of linguists working in my department on automatic language translation software. A very interesting man named Kostya Babitsky joined this group, and I quickly became friends with him. Destiny connected me closely with him and his family from that time up to my departure from Russia. I will mention Kostya more than once in this book.

First, Kostya was a man of amazing civic courage. His mother was Russian and his father was Jewish. To make his future life easier, when he was born, he was registered as a Russian. When the time came to him to obtain a passport, there, too, appeared the notation "Russian" in the appropriate column. At the height of the cosmopolitan campaign and at the height of anti-Semitism in 1948, Kostya showed up at the police station and demanded a new passport that contained the ill-starred clause "Jewish." In respond, he received such a passport! For his noble aspirations, he paid dearly during the following years. However, the real trouble came 1968, when he got to jale. I will tell about this in detail later.

Secondly, Kostya had golden hands, and in this respect, I had much to learn from him. That said, in all our company only the two of us had any idea how to approach practically the construction of light rafts. When we discussed the details of our journey, I felt that it would be much safer for me to have such a handy man in our group. But the idea of rafting down the Volga was born in our conversations with Kostya, as we were wandering with him through the mountains and forests, much earlier.

Thirdly, Kostya's romantic mood absolutely won me over. He was a dreamer by nature and loved Russia and Russian culture with the ardor of a young man. By that time Kostya became, as well as myself, distrustful of the possibility of a happy future for his country. He and I had very serious conversations on this topic. When I talked to him about leaving the country, he would say to me, "*Are not you sorry, Yuri, to give up this country to THEM?*" In response, he would invite me to participate in his plan. He had found a place in the Krasnoyarsk Region of Siberia, far removed from any manifestations of Soviet power. The Podkamennaya Tunguska River flows there. He suggested we build a house on the river and work as buoy-keepers, to drive around buoys on a boat and to light and extinguish lamps on them. "*Can you imagine, my friend, we will build a windmill that will give us electricity. Then we will be able to take nothing at all from the Soviets!*" I remember how I tried to criticize his, in my opinion, completely unrealistic plan: "*Do you really think*," I would say to him, "*such a flight from your home, from your favorite job, from the people close to you, does not mean to cede this country to THEM? Do not you think that you are a stranger for them and that THEY will be only happy to get such easy chance to rid of you and continue their dirty business? Or, on the contrary, they will finish you with a million of accusations? THEY will blame you of violating the stupid registration of your residence, or of parasitism (he who does not work — doesn't eat!), or of plundering state property (from what materials did you build the house?)*" Unfortunately, the sad circumstances of his life ended his romanticism. Last years of his life, sadly, Kostya's thinking looked much more realistic.

Our expedition crew consisted of Kostya, me and my old friends and colleagues Lena Lander, Victor Zeidenberg and Maria Sychiov, a veteran of my Institute, who was also our frequent summer kayak companion. Kostya took his little daughter Natasha with him. She was about seven years old at the time. This sweet girl endured all the difficulties of the trip and was never a burden. One day Kostya came over and started a conversation with me asking if we would mind inviting his acquaintance Renata Ravich who was interested in our floating. Being a linguist himself, Kostya had many friends among Moscow linguists and Renata was one of them. We met her, and no one had any reservations about her joining our company. She seemed to like all of us, so Renata got involved in the preparations for the expedition. I had no idea at the time how much this woman would change my whole life.

Because Renata happened to play a special role in my life, I am going to pay more attention to her than any other participant of the trip. By the time we met, I was 23 and she was 25. I had grown up a very shy young man. I had, you could say, ZERO experience with girls or women. I graduated from a men's school and then studied by correspondence. During my high school years, girls and boys in Russia were studying in different schools. I only saw girls invited to our school parties from the girls' school. I never once dared to meet any of them, much less ask any of them to dance. At school dances I always was, they used to say back then, propping up the walls. It is not that girls did not interest me. I even chose one who was coming to these parties that I liked more than others. Every time she would come over, I secretly kept my eyes on her, imagining that I was dancing with her. One day I saw her by chance near my house: she was coming back with her friends from the girl's school opposite our house. This was how I found out where she was studying, but her name remained unknown to me, and she remained a beautiful stranger. I never dared to make a move to meet and talk to her. After I finished school, my father died. I started working, and in the evenings after work I studied by corresponding. Somehow, I did not have time even to think about girls. As a result, by the time I met Renata, I had never touched a girl, never hugged or kissed one.

Renata, as I found out later, was the exact opposite of me in this respect. She never had any problems with getting acquainted and flirting with other people, especially men. By the time, I met her, she was in many respects already an experienced woman, had few boyfriends and was familiar with intimate relationship. Of course, such social "freedom" of hers bothered me a bit. However, after I learned the very sad story of her family, I put all such worries on the back burner. My strong desire to brighten the life of her family and of Renata herself came to the fore. I was young, inexperienced, and overconfident. I thought I could do anything. Of course, before the trip and in the beginning of the trip, I had no idea that Renata would become my wife. My thoughts were simply to be supportive of a friend whose family had endured so much grief. Below I describe the short story of her family.

Renata's father, David Ravich, was an experimental chemist, who specialized in gunpowders. Originally, from Romania, he lived and worked in Germany, was an active Bolshevik, and a member of the Communist parties of both countries. Her mother, Leah Ravich, a pianist, trained at the Sorbonne in Paris. In the 1930's they returned to Russia. He worked as the director of one of the gunpowder factories. In 1936, an explosion happened at his factory. The director was charged falsely of an act of sabotage, tried, and sent to a prison camp. He served 17 years and came to freedom only in 1953. The family lost everything: their house, their savings, their jobs, and their piano. To feed their two children, Renata and her elder brother Yakov, her mother worked sweeping the streets. When the war started. Renata's brother was one of the first volunteers mobilized to the front line and was killed a few months later.

Her father returned from imprisonment with complete legal exoneration. However, it was impossible to restore ruined life. Strange as it may seem, her father managed to preserve his health in jail much better than her mother did. Life had made her frightened and anxious; and she had lost much of her sight. Her task in life was now to devote the rest of her feeble powers entirely to the welfare of her daughter. For herself, she needed nothing more. She walked around in old shabby dresses, not wanting to spend a penny on herself, saving everything for her daughter. Being half-blind, she was cooking for everyone, and would not let Renata near the kitchen. *"My life was ruined,"* she would say, *"so I want to spend the rest of it to help my daughter live hers in a different way."* I understood and respected her self-sacrifice. However, as a result, Renata grew up taking this selfless service from her mother for granted. I never saw Renata display appreciation or attempt to repay her mother with special gratitude, care, affection or love. Now let us return to our trip.

The voyage along the Volga began right at the source of the river at Lake Seliger. Having studied the maps, we decided to unload from the Moscow-Leningrad train at a small half-station near Valday because it was the closest to the shore of the lake. Though we tried not to be overloaded, we had accumulated quite a lot of luggage, and we did not want to carry it far. I remind readers that we carried most of the groceries from Moscow, as we could not count on buying them in the half-starved coastal villages on the Volga. That said, the train stood at our half-station for just a few minutes. So, we had to lighten our load but we coped with this task with honor. The sailing itself turned out to be very enjoyable and interesting.

Kostya and I together had designed the rafts. The main consideration was to have a low weight so that the rafts would not be difficult to manipulate during the trip. We had only two men in our team, which gave us a goal to haul as little as possible from Moscow and back to Moscow, as well as to haul as little as possible in the evenings to organize overnight stays on the bank of the river.

Four huge tire inner tubes (from heavy trucks of Minsk Automobile Plant, short for MAP) were the basis of each raft. To get these inner tubes for a bottle of vodka was not a problem in any major automotive facility in Moscow. First two inner tubes touched each other in the shape of an "8". Then we added two more inner tubes to the "8", one from each side, into a rhombic 4-leaf clover shape. Each pare of tubes touching each other held together by strips of tarp closed with buttons. We sewed the tarps beforehand at home. The rigidity of the construction we provided by planking with wooden poles cut from the woods. Kostya and I built the floor planking out of poles fastened with nails. At the trip's end, we disassembled the decking, and burned the poles. We constructed three such rafts. Each one had a decent carrying capacity (for three adults plus about 600 lbs. of cargo). In addition to this, we had triangle shape three-inner tube raft used as our floating food warehouse, which made it possible not to overload the passenger rafts with food. This stockpile traveled on a tether, attached with a rope to one of the passenger rafts, like a dog on leash. We rafted during the daylight hours, landing only in nice places to stretch our legs and to use the "facilities" on solid ground. When it was evening, we again chose a nice place, docked, unloaded, and camped for the night.

Immediately a problem arose as to how to arrange for refreshments afloat. After all, we had to find a way to transfer easily food between rafts without docking on shore. I think we found an ingenious solution for which we could receive a patent. Each raft needed two oars which we constructed by attaching aluminum plates with screws to the long wooden handles of floor brushes. Our oars were lightweight enough to float if someone accidentally dropped them in the water. We also used them as bowls and plates for meals. As a result, there was no need to go ashore to wash the dishes: we could soap the plates and use then as oars and they were clean. In addition, the length of the sticks made it very convenient to pass food, and anything else from one raft to another *"Our raft presents to your raft!"* Our oars created an added element of fun. More than once, as we paddled past the village, the kids would run along the shore shouting, "Look, look: paddling with frying-pans!"

Kostya's daughter, Natasha, loved the water and swam often. For the most part the weather was fine and the water in the Volga River was warm. Natasha's swimming was a special amusement for her and for all of us. Kostya had a children's inflatable life belt for Natasha that did not fit over her shoulders. When Natasha slid her thin body through it from underneath, she looked like a big fishing float, and her arms and legs were free. Here came the idea of tying this "float" to Kostya's raft on good days, which allowed the girl to float for a while as if independently, by herself, picking lilies as she went and talking to the fish, having her own special fun.

Volga rafting trip was a true success. Due to various family and work circumstances my coworkers had to finish the voyage somewhere above Kalinin, I do not remember exactly where. They left for Moscow and four of us: Kostya and Natasha, Renata and me, reached Kalinin. There, Kostya and I got rid of the decking for the rafts, dismantled and packed the rest of the rafts and sent them with mail at a slow speed to Moscow. After that, Babitskys returned home to Moscow. By that time, Renata and I got already so close to each other that we decided to use our remaining week of vacation for a hiking trip on the Karelian Isthmus.

Kostya has gone from this world already a long time ago. The connection with the rest of my coworkers was permanently broken with my departure to America in 1988. They were older than I was so I think that today they are not alive any more. The only person who could remember today some detail of this magic trip could have been Natasha Babitsky but I lost contact with Kostya's children after both of their parents died...

HOW I SUDDENLY FOUND MYSELF MARRIED

Now is the moment to describe in more detail the week during which everything was so swiftly resolved both for me and for my companion with whom I went to Karelia. First, I would like to make one thing clear. Many of my relatives and friends thought, and still think, that Renata had me wrapped around her finger. Yes, that what it was, however with a big BUT. To be fair, I wanted to say, that I at the time wanted very much this to happen. The situation reminded me of the Military Procedural and Penal Code of 1715, issued by the Russian Tsar Peter I. There, the timeliness of the victim's statements was crucial in determining whether she was a victim of rape. It said that if the victim *"kept silent for a day or more it will mean that she was willing to do so as well."* My silence as a victim has lasted for more than 60 years now! Yes, it is true, the initiative of our rapprochement was on her side, but she was the FIRST woman in my life who took such an initiative. It got me so excited that I could not and DID NOT WANT to say NO. In the end, I think, it is me who should decide who was wrapped around the finger. I take full responsibility for everything that happened. To sum up this thought, I want to reiterate that this was not a case of getting married without my consent at all.

Being philologically meticulous, of course, from the moment I met Renata, I started thinking about the etymology of her first name. I immediately assumed that it was from the Latin *"renatus,"* meaning *"reborn,"* and after checking with the dictionary of names, I was convinced that I was right. However, after we were married, I asked her parents why they had named, her that. The answer was: the name is the abbreviation of Russian "REvoliutsiya, Nauka i Trud". English translation of these words is: *"Revolution, Science and Labor"*!? How sad, that even educated members of our fathers' generation were to such an extent infected with the virus of vulgar Marxism.

Renata had luxurious red hair, and I had been partial to redheads from a young age. It was O. Renoir's fault. I have loved his red-haired beauties since I was a kid. True, I had some differences of opinion with the great artist. I always felt most of his models had too much body. However, there is no one for every taste or color. I still liked his big-bodied redheads. So, believe me, when Renata, who had no extra body at all, stood on the raft and the sun shone on the mop of her red hair, this sight brought a special uniqueness to the already wonderful beauty of the Upper Volga shores. Perhaps then, a parody on my beloved Okudzhava's lines was born in me.:

> *She was floating on tire inserts with him,*
> *She waved with her red braid.*
> *And then the passion grasped Zieman*
> *With its callous hand!*

To be precise, at first it was not yet a dead grip. It all happened later, when Renata and I, not wanting to part, went for another week to the Karelia. It was only there that I felt the calloused hand. Since I have talked about my weakness for redheads, I should mention here the funny verses that I had memorized and sung since my school days:

> *I am sure, no doubt,*
> *I will definitely get married!*
> *Absolutely, absolutely, I will do it.*
> *I'll take wife matching my taste.*
> *I want her to be a 250-pounder.*
> *And able to hum like a steam engine:*
> *"Oooooh!"*
> *Absolutely, absolutely,*
> *She has to have red hair.*
> *Because blondes and brunettes*
> *Good while they are young.*
> *They're getting old, they're growing ugly,*
> *They're no good at all.*
> *And the redhead is,*
> *Always, always young!*
> *Wherever you touch her,*
> *You feel fire!!!*

These verses are the best example of how far my moral "degradation" had gone by the time I met Renata. Nevertheless, as for the red hair, I am very happy that my daughter inherited it from her mother, and to this day, I cannot stop admiring Galya's wonderful red hair.

Renata and I found ourselves together in one of the most beautiful places in Russia, and the weather was as if to order. To my senses, the combination of my inexperience and her maturity carried us like a rushing mountain stream. It seemed that both nature and weather were executing a preconceived plan. During first night, we camped on a high shore of lake. This night the inevitable happened... For some time, I completely disconnected, did not understand where I was, with whom I was and what happened to me. What I saw and heard when I came to my senses, I was literally dejected. Renata was shaking with sobs. Then, between sobs, I heard the words that just horrified me. *"Of course,"* she said, *"Now you will do as most men do, and leave me!"* I was tormenting myself, trying to recall what I had done or said that made her think of me in such a way. Of course, remembering nothing of the kind, I rushed to comfort her and assure her that I would never, under any circumstances... Then I remember well how I was shoked with pity for her: *"Poor girl, how can she live with such horrible ideas about the world and people around her? How good is it, that now I can be there for her all the time and do everything I can to get her out of this emotional maelstrom."* For the next ten years, I tirelessly made endless fruitless attempts to accomplish the impossible. Back then, I still naively thought I could... That is long gone now. I know how terribly wrong I was!

The events described in the previous paragraph took place at dawn. The morning was coming, and the tragic tone of the scene suddenly changed in the most unexpected way to a comic one. At one of the pauses in my sermon, I suddenly heard a low male voice somewhere very close to our tent. This was more than unexpected: I supposed that there was not a soul around us for miles. However, the worst were the words that this voice was uttering. Never in my life, neither before, nor after this incident, had I heard such a heavily sophisticated Russian obscene language. Wow: under the noise of the wind, I turned to my lady of the heart with a serious comforting speech about love and fidelity, and suddenly in a completely deserted place such an accompaniment comes to me!? I felt terribly guilty for such an embarrassment and was ready to fall through the earth in shame right across the floor of the tent. In a hurry, I was dressed and jumped out of the tent to look at the troublemaker. Right below our tent, by the water on a snag, an angler was sitting with a fishing rod, and he continued to swear. What had upset him so much? Instead of fish, he hooked a huge crayfish. He took it off the hook not without difficulties, and threw it aside, and it fell down into the grass. I went up to him, said hello and politely asked, "*Why, don't you want it for yourself?*" I apologize for exact reproducing the language of his response. "*You can have this fucking thing!*", he said to me sternly. I took advantage of his gruff but generous offer in anticipation of an unusual breakfast, took the crayfish and went up to the tent.

Renata had already cleaned herself up by then and came out of the tent. I had already started making a fire by that time. Speaking of fires, dealing with them is one of my favorite things in life. It is not in vain that Igor Melchuk made a joke about me that I am the best kostrator (do not think, castrator) of the world. It is a phonetic joke: fires like I did this morning in transliteration from Russian would be "kostry." An infinite number of hikes, which I have participated in, resulted indeed in acquiring considerable experience making and maintaining a fire in the woods at any time of year and in any weather conditions. I have learned to do it in dryness, rain, cold, heat, calm, and wind. When the fire was already lit, I cannot take my eyes off the fire. I think there is some special magic in fires that really affects me. I can understand fire worshippers. So, on that overly emotional morning, I made a fire, looked at the fire, and that magic helped me come to my senses.

However, our crayfish misadventures did not end there. I decided to cook crayfish for breakfast to improve my companion's mood. Apparently, I was still out of sorts, and my best intentions led to a moment of my unheard-of embarrassment. I fetched water from the lake and put the crayfish in the cauldron for safekeeping while the fire was kindling. When the time came, oh horror, I hung the kettle with the live crayfish, as it were, over the fire and, satisfied with myself, began trying to entertain Renata with intelligent conversation. The water began to warm, and then the crayfish said all what he thought of me. He jumped high into the air, raising fountains of spray. As I took the cauldron off the fire in agony, I feared it would end up in the fire. I was disgusted with myself and burned with shame. I wish that day had never happened in my life! After that, I did not even remember if it tasted good.

To be honest, my memory has retained little of this momentous week in Karelia. The reason was simple: of course, I was very nervous, my head was filled with thoughts about how I would return to Moscow, how I would inform my mother and relatives about my decision to get married, how I would ask Renata's parents for her hand, how and where we would live, etc., etc. There was no time for contemplation of the Karelian beauties. I was in a hurry to get home.

The first time in Moscow was very difficult for me. Almost all my relatives and friends were in shock at my news. Now that I remember what was going on, I have to admit that I was in a state of shock myself too. Whenever I informed my relatives about big changes in my life, everybody tried to stop me, advised me to be cautious and not to make haste in my deeds. Frankly speaking, such unanimity did not make me happy: I really do not remember any exceptions. No matter how much I tried to explain to everyone that after what had happened, I had no other choice, I heard back that my naivety was foolish. However, I knew for sure that there was no other way for me! Of course, I told myself, with all my determination, that time would tell, and I would prove everyone wrong.

I do not know why my memory has preserved so few details about what exactly happened during the first weeks in Moscow. I do not remember anything at all about the celebration of my union with Renata, whether there was such a celebration at all, and if there was, how it was held, where it was, who was involved. We had to solve urgently a housing problem in Moscow, which was very difficult at that time. Renata's parents got a room in a three-room flat in a communal apartment right after her father's exoneration. I never considered it possible for me to live there. At that time, my family had managed to redeem a room from our neighbor on Tikhvinsky Lane and since that time, we became owners of a detached four-room flat! My sister Lena was married and lived in her husband's apartment. So, in our apartment lived besides me my mother, my brother Jan with Innulia and their two children, Olechka and then little Lyova.

Our Lyovochka was everyone's favorite from birth, although, when he grew up, he would get rather often into trouble in full form. In the last sentence, for the Russian original of the expression *"to get often into trouble in full form"* there is one verb "kurolecit". When I used it, I started doubting whether I had chosen this verb correctly. After checking with a dictionary, I discovered an interesting etymology of the word. The verb comes from the Greek "Kyrie Eleison" and means, "*Lord, have mercies, please.*" Lyova used to give us rather often the reason to come to the Lord with a favor of asking about this. So I was convinced that it expresses exactly what I wanted.

Although neither my mother, nor my brother's family was thrilled with my choice of wife, they generously agreed to give us one of our four rooms, in which we settled. It seemed to me that each of them did his best to make us feel good and to make Renata feel comfortable in our home. For the rest of my life I will be grateful to them all for such a desire to help me, for such understanding, for such participation. It was to this room that I brought my eldest daughter Galya from the maternity hospital in 1962.

MY FIRST STEPS OF A MARRIED MAN

Although my new life began too quickly and, frankly, not quite the way I would have liked it to, I strongly do not want to leave the impression that everything in this beginning was not to my liking. With Renata, many new things came into my life at once, some good and some bad. I immediately plunged into the good with joy. Since then, I have been trying to remove the bad things from my memory and heart not always successfully. And there were a lot of these things, and they caused me a lot of pain. Forgetting the deep pain was not an easy task at all, but I continue to work on it even today. So I would like still to start with the good. Let me try going this way.

Renata, after graduating from the English Department of the Moscow University of Foreign Languages, got a job at the Institute of Linguistics of the USSR Academy of Sciences. Her immediate supervisor there was Igor Melchuk, one of the country's leading linguists. It is a small world, the boss of both Igor and Renata turned out to be an old friend of my father's, Alexander Reformatsky. When my father was actively involved in cartography, he engaged Reformatsky as a consultant in toponymy, a branch of linguistics that studies toponyms, place names.

The acquaintance and friendship with Igor was one of the wonderful gifts I received through Renata. Igor is an extraordinary person. Devilishly capable, with an extraordinary humanitarian education, a language researcher, a man of unimaginable public temperament and activity, he was like a magnet, attracting to himself the most interesting and brightest people in Moscow. When was initiating walking or hiking with his friends on Sundays, crowds of both "physicists" and "lyricists" in dozens gathered, reminding me strongly of the exodus of the Jews from Egypt. He walked among the crowd like Moses, but unlike the latter, he was not pestering others with theological moral teachings, but entertaining everyone by discussing interesting scientific problems and phenomena or historical and literary facts, and by telling funny stories and anecdotes, which he could remember in great numbers. What was common to our meetings in the woods and those in the desert over three thousand years ago was not only the phonetic similarity between Exodus (in Russian "Iskhod") and the hike (in Russian "pokhod"), not only the fact that many of the participants were Jewish, but also our desire to escape from lies and injustice. I think that this can explain the popularity of hiking as a form of recreation among the Soviet intelligentsia.

Igor left Russia in 1977, the year we filed our emigration papers. There were dozens of his most interesting colleagues and friends revolving around Igor. Acquaintance with Igor as a gift came to me with a huge bonus, I got to know and become friends with many remarkable people in his entourage. Foremost among them, of course, were linguists: Apresyan, Kasatkin, Smorgunova, Kibrik, Glovinskaya, Zholkowsky, Iordanskaja, Rosenzweig, Leontiev, Kadzasov, Babitsky etc. But there were also mathematicians: Natalia Svetlov and Gladky, physicists: Blokhintsev, Braginsky, and Plakida, and physicians: Marshak and Freidin. For some reason I want to remember Anna Marshak the wife of Victor Rosenzweig. A lovely woman, Anna was the head of the department at the Research Institute of Antibiotics. She happened to be a constant consultant on many health issues for most of the participants in our Sunday Exoduses. It was Anna's anniversary that I dedicated my poem, which included the following lines:

> *Whose antibiotics*
> *We all have in our tummies.*
> *If not these antibiotics,*
> *Our tummies ache.*
> *They are from Anna MARSHAK!!!*

I would very much like that if I have not mentioned someone from Igor's entourage in these lines. It does not mean that these people have played less important role in my life. All of them generously shared with me both their knowledge and their spiritual riches, for which I will be grateful to them for the rest of my life.

There was another wonderful thing, which, I think, can be considered even more of a gift from Renata to me personally. It was she who initiated our joint and regular visits to classical music halls in Moscow. To my great regret, there was practically no classical music in my childhood. The only person in our family who was interested in this music was my brother's wife Innulia. Among many good things Innulia did for me were several visits to Moscow Conservatory. That was all. As result I, unfortunately, didn't get even an elementary musical education. Nobody has explained to me in my childhood that, regardless of natural ear for music, some knowledge of music is as necessary for a person as is some knowledge in mathematics, in fine arts and some knowledge in all branches of humanities.

Later when I started working at IPM&CT, I joined my friends and colleagues in acquiring season tickets for solo pianist concerts at Moscow Conservatory. The annual subscription, if I remember correctly, included only six concerts. These were crumbs, of course, and could not remedy my blatant musical illiteracy. Now, when more than sixty years have passed since then, I bitterly think what a fool I was that I did not realize then how much brighter my life would have been if I had been persistent enough and made an effort to learn more about music.

Of course, it is a shame that I did not take advantage of my exceptional opportunities to get closer to music. After all, my own uncle Senya, my mother's brother, was a well-known musicologist who knew much about music and was personally acquainted with many major figures in the world of music. Through him, I could have witnessed the most interesting musical events at the Union of Composers. But I did not do any of that! By the way, I remember a remarkable conversation with Senya. He asked me if I had been to a concert of some amazing musician. Of course, I had not been and I commented my negative answer with the stupid assertion: I am on such a low level in music, that to let me listen to such a great musician is to cast pearls before a swine. Senya was a very emotional person. He started telling me, with all his heat, how I do not understand even the basics of music. After all, the less a man knows about music, he said, the higher-level performance he needs. I learned that lesson from him forever.

To be honest, it is not entirely accurate to say that I never tried to learn about music. Just at the time I am now describing, I made a desperate attempt to take piano lessons. Senya's wife Liolya, music pedagogue, wife of my mother's brother was a piano teacher in the Music Middle School at the Conservatory. I got up the nerve and asked to be her student. I liked her wildly as a woman. Every time I went to her lesson, I felt it was a blessing. Unfortunately, at the same time, it was also an agony, because I had a feeling that my fingers were made of wood, they did not want to do what Liolya asked them to. My lessons turned into torture, and I was ashamed that I was torturing such a beautiful woman. After a while, I gave up in shame and firmly decided that never again... My musical impulse ended so sadly.

The collapse of my musical dream did not prevent Renata's pregnancy from developing normally and her own enjoyment of good music. So, she and I continued to listen to music. And then a terrible thing happened to me: I started falling asleep right in the concert hall. Every time I was dying of embarrassment, but I was falling peacefully asleep. Every time I wanted to just vanish through the earth, but I fell asleep peacefully. It happened especially easily at symphony concerts. Yes, I was working very hard at the time, but that was just an explanation, not an excuse. I remember well how I came to my aunt Ernestina (Tasia) Levintov, Maria's daughter, to complain bitterly and to ask for advice. Tasia was an exceptionally educated woman, including music. Her advice gave me considerable encouragement. Stop worrying, she said. It is natural that a good but tired person feels sleepy from good music. Don't get upset, it will pass. And Tasia appeared to be absolutely right. IT DID PASS!!!

Falling asleep to music does not detract from my gratitude to Renata for her tolerance of my narcolepsy and for her help in getting me through such a difficult time for me, and for those around me. More than half a century has passed since those days. Not only did I practically stop falling asleep while listening to classical music, but also I learned to enjoy it. Music has become an integral and important part of my life. Moreover, it was my love of music, that subsequently brought many interesting and talented musicians into my life. I am happy to call them my acquaintances and some even friends. Among them are cellists Natalia Gutman and Arkady Beletsky, the conductor Lev Markiz, violinists Oleg Kagan, Alexander Brussilovsky and Sofia Wilker, violist Mikhail Zaretsky, pianists Eliso Virsaladze, Vladimir Feltsman, Sally Pinkas and Evan Hirsch, clarinetist Julian Milkis, flutist Fenwick Smith, French horn player Mikhail Weinstein and many others.

In listing the good things that came into my life with Renata, I really should not end but rather begin with the most important thing, our daughter, born in 1962. This girl has had a difficult fate: her mother left her when she was eight years old. Today she is indomitable as she started her sixties. I have been incredibly lucky to have her: We have never been even temporarily apart since she was born. On my part on a grand scale, it has been years of unclouded joy and pride in such a wonderful daughter. Until my last hour of life, I will remember that in times of the toughest trials and tribulations, I knew I had my little helper I could always rely on. Thank you, Renata, for such an invaluable gift.

Having described in such detail all the good things that came into my life with Renata I want to put a full stop at this point, without touching the unhealed bitterness and pain she brought into my life. Later I will return to this sad side too, so that the reader has a chance to imagine an objective picture.

Speaking of the beginning of my family life, I would like to start with sharing my memories of meeting my newly acquired mother-in-law and father-in-law. I remember well that the acquaintance and rapprochement with parents left quite a pleasant impression. They both treated me very warmly; I would even dare to say as their own son. I had never forgotten that, among other hardships, the war had taken their son from them, and from the first days of my marriage, I had hoped that I could make up for that terrible loss in some way for them.

Her father's name was David Ravich. He was an unusually friendly man, even though he had a zealous revolutionary past. Since his gymnasium years, he had been friends with the greatest Soviet military leader, Iona Yakir, who was executed in 1937. Almost everybody in the Yakir family was prosecuted, but the Ravichs continued their friendship with unscathed splinters who survived until their exoneration. I met Iona Yakir's widow, Sara at the house of Renata's parents. David Ravich was one of the authors of the collection of memoirs "Commander Yakir" about the great commander of post-revolutionary Russia.

I have to give my ex-father-in law a credit: seventeen years in confinement did not leave in my ex-father-in law any bitterness to people at all. He even preserved some gentleness and faith in the achievement of the bright ideas of communism. Of course, I did not do without political discussions on this theme with him. However, these discussions were quite friendly and I immediately appreciated his tolerance and respect towards my interlocutor's opinion. *"Of course, Yuri,"* he used to say to me, *"Stalin, the scoundrel, discredited wonderful ideas. But what a contra are you!"* It was Bolsheviks, who introduced the noun "contra" to the Russian language. The term acquired a sinister meaning, for it was used left and right to hand down death sentences to "counter-revolutionaries". However, in the mouth of my father-in-law it did not sound any militant and fearful, even, I would say, it sounded affectionate. As if there were good contras and bad "contras", and you may be friends and peacefully argue with them, but you have to destroy immediately the bad ones. Thank God, he counted me among the good ones.

Renata's mother Leah Ravich, never managed to recover mentally from the unimaginable misfortunes that had plagued her life. It sounds paradoxical, but it seems to me that she, who was outside had a much more difficult fate than her incarcerated husband did. For example, it was very difficult for me to accept that among the irrecoverable losses of Leah was that music, stopped sounding in her house for more than twenty-five years. After her husband's arrest, the pianist's fingers never touched the keys of the instrument for all these years. I literally became obsessed with the idea of buying them a piano so that she could return to her favorite pastime. The irony of fate was that literally a few hundred yards from the house, where the Ravichs lived, was a store where you could theoretically buy a piano. However, to become a happy owner of an instrument in Moscow at that time one should have stood in a line for years. Without saying anything to anyone, I joined that queue, and then got a secret agreement with my father-in-law, when the queue came up, to divide the expenses in half.

We said and we did it: time was running out, and my turn came up. The event happened a few years after the birth of our daughter. My mother-in-law rejoiced: she would have the opportunity to teach our daughter music. I rejoiced with her. She insisted that a piano stand in our home, which has happened. However, it resulted in my becoming suddenly a witness to a heart-breaking scene. It was the first time that Leah Ravich came to get acquainted with the instrument. She resolutely sat down at the piano and began to play something familiar fluently and vigorously. It seemed to be Mozart. I was in seventh heaven. It went on like that for about a minute. Then suddenly, as if somebody had shot her down, the playing broke off on some note, and her head literally fell on the keys. I was scared if it was a heart attack, and the next moment I heard her moaning, interrupted by sobs: *"How could I have forgotten that!?"* We all tried to calm her down and persuade her to give it another try. After a while, she came to her senses and started playing again, and the same thing repeated itself. After that day, Leah never came up to the piano to play again.

Looking ahead, when Galka grew up, Leah tried unsuccessfully to teach her music, it did not work either. Now, remembering those events, I felt twice as sad. First, I felt endless pity for my mother-in-law. Secondly, I still feel guilty that I failed to provide my daughter with a musical education. All my life I have blamed my parents for not doing that, but I was no better than they were! Talking about my mother-in-law, my plan of getting her back into music had completely failed. Her progressive blindness made it impossible for her to play from the sheet music, and there was no other option.

I AM BECOMING A DAD

In the meantime, my first child's due birth date was approaching, and I was busy preparing for the big event. I was trying to make the room cozy and provide everything I needed for the baby. It is hard to imagine, but every step in that direction turned out to be a problem. Not only did we have little money, but also in Moscow, even with money, it was almost impossible to buy anything. Say, the curtains I wanted, was difficult to find, and I remember how it took me several trips to the shop "Fabrics" on Lenin Avenue, before I managed to buy material with a cheerful pattern for a child, which I hemmed on my mother's sewing machine and attached rings for them to hang. Wooden cribs were in sale in "Children's World" store on Lubyanka Street but very seldom, so you had to become a lucky buyer to get one. I ended up picking up a discarded crib on the street and bringing it home, washed it with soap and water, repaired it, sanded and re-lacquered it, so it shone like new. A friend gave us his used stroller as a gift. I washed it, cleaned it thoroughly, oiled the moving parts and it started rolling like a new one.

Slowly but surely we solved all such problems and were ready to meet the brand new girl. On April 16, 1962 a new person, my Galyusha was born. The day came, and we took her to the lovingly made room for her on Tikhvinsky lane. To my shame, I have no recollection of the maternity hospital where she was born, of my visits to that place or of any details of Renata's pregnancy and delivery. The saddest part is that I have absolutely no recollection of Renata's empathy or even my own about it. I want to caution readers of this text against concluding that there were none at all. They certainly were, but I remember how, after all the unpleasant things in my relationship with Renata, I tried very hard to blot out all the sad details from my memory. But the dominant part of my memories of her will forever remain my gratitude for such a wonderful daughter. I have to say that the birth of this little girl was one of the most important events in my life. More than half a century later, this little girl has grown into a wonderful woman, and she continues to bring great joy to my life.

In connection with her birth, I often recalled a lovely autobiographical book by A. Brushtein "The Road Goes Away", describing the world of Soneczka Yanovskaya's childhood. I have read book few years before Galya's birth. It describes the events in Vilna, not far from Kovno, where my dad's family lived at the very end of the 19th century and the beginning of the 20th century. These events happened during the decade when my parents were born. The girl's father was a Jewish doctor, and my father's side grandfather was a Jewish pharmacist. Sonechka was small from birth, and in the family, all called her affectionately "Little button". My little gal was born very little and I (not without memories of the book by A.Brushtein called her "Little drop." May be thanks to the listed similarities, I fell in love with this book, and the book, in turn, added to the joy of my girl's birth and tenderness of my feelings. Though not everything in my married life was happening, as I would have liked it to, the joy of having my little girl overrode everything and made me happy.

I In Moscow, especially in Jewish families, it was customary to regularly weigh the newborn and thereby make sure that the child was getting enough nutrition and was growing well. I remember how I was running around Moscow trying to find among people, I knew, the owners of scales for babies, whose children had already grown. *He who seeks, he will always finds.* One day I triumphantly returned home with a scale for newborns, washed it, debugged and installed next to the crib. I immediately constructed a chart on graph paper on which I marked the weights I read after each weighing. I hung the graph above Galya's crib and the growth curve began to climb upward, slowly but surely, to the delight of all relatives.

MY MOTHER'S DEATH

When I lost my father, I was only eighteen years old. Everything in my life changed drastically, its carefree period ended once and forever. Mom was not in a very good shape before, but the death of her closest loved one really took its toll on her. Heart arrhythmias plagued her more and more, and I was the one who helped her and took care of her. With my days at work and study in the evening, it was not easy. Nevertheless, I bless heaven that it happened this way: if it were not for these circumstances, there never would have been such closeness between me and Mom. At that time, both my brother and sister already had families of their own, so they lacked the emotional and physical energy to help my mother as I could. I tried my best to help her cope with the unbearable emptiness of loss at that time. When I think about the period between my dad's death (1956) and my mom's death (1963), I am literally flooded with incredibly warm memories. The year after Dad's death, on my birthday, Mom gave me a newly published volume of Russian poet Tyutchev, in the Poet's Library series. She liked these verses very much. There was a bookmark on page 254 with a quatrain in it:

> *The punishing God took everything from me,*
> *Everything: health, willpower, air, sleep.*
> *He left you alone with me,*
> *So that still I can pray to Him.*

In the bookmark, my mother made a full bibliographical reference to this poem, and in the margin of said page, against the third line, my mother's hand made a pencil mark suggesting replacing of the feminine form of "you alone" in the original by the masculine form. In reliving these lines of her favorite poet, my mother was thinking of ME! It is hard to overestimate how much those Tyutchev's lines meant to me then and still do today. In general, the memory of my exceptional relationship with my mother, especially in the last years of her life, does not cease to warm me to this day. Until the end of my days, I will be deeply grateful to fate that I was destined to experience the happiness of that relationship. Often, I take out Mother's book of Tyutchev Fyodor, open it on page 254, and tears come to my eyes. It is as if I am talking to my mother once again.

Over the years, I have grown even fonder of Tyutchev, and it warms up my heart that the poetry of this wonderful poet happened to help my dearest Mother to describe the closeness between her and me. Quite recently, I found out an interesting detail from the poet's biography. In 1848, Marx and Engels published their "Manifesto of the Communist Party" in England. The language of the publication was German. In the same year, the Russian revolutionaries translated it into Russian and wished to publish the translation in Russia. It was then that the Tsar appointed Tyutchev, as one of the most educated people in the country, a senior censor. The question of distribution of the "Manifesto" came to the poet's attention. He imposed a ban on its distribution, and his resolution is well known: *"... those who need it will read it in German."* I personally was delighted with such a decision and my worship of the poet grew more. Nevertheless, communists, unfortunately, found their way not only to publish the Manifesto in Russian but later to implement many of its ideas in the country.

One of my main worries at this time was financial. The period of material prosperity given to a professor's family was gone. It tormented me that in the rush to get a certificate for higher education, I grabbed the first job that came my way. The school administration was very pleased with me, but I have already mentioned the stupid circumstances that caused me to bring home very little money. Therefore, I had to change my job urgently. I believed, in addition, that I needed to do it as soon as possible to begin to gain knowledge and experience in my current specialty of computers. For these two reasons I was looking for a job and it was hard to get one in Moscow because of my Jewish nationality.

Everything written about my relationship with my mother was true until 1961–1962, which is when I married Renata. It is incredibly sad, but the relationship between my mother and my wife failed to work out from the first day. I brought Renata to Tikhvinsky Lane. I did not understand the animosity between the two women and I still do not understand it today. It seems to me that my mother had never hurt a single person in her life. I have very painful and bitter memories from the last year of my mom's life. In 1962 my daughter, Galya was born. We are going to talk later about this.

Many Moscow residents, especially those with small children, tried to leave the city for their dachas in the summer. We also rented a dacha near Moscow, at Odintsovo station of Belorussian railroad. The tremendous job of coordinating and moving to the dacha, in addition to my already numerous duties, fell on me. The arranging of everyday life in Soviet dachas at that time demanded a lot of work. Everything turned into a problem: buying and bringing food from Moscow, organizing the baby's laundry and bathing, heating the room, etc. After a full day of work, I simply did not know what to do first.

These circumstances never bothered my wife, who had strong objections to my mother's coming and living with us. Luckily, my wonderful aunt Raya, my father's sister, took care of my mother and offered to let Mother come to her dacha for the summer. Unfortunately, her dacha was quite far from ours, at the "41st km" station of the Yaroslavl railway (25.5 miles). Though my mother lived with someone close to her and to all of us, it was FAR AWAY from me. For the rest of my life, I will appreciate this good deed of Rayachka's. After my father's death, my mother's health slowly but surely deteriorated. For her to get to our dacha without any assistance was out of the question.

With my work, my home duties and a newborn baby, I had no opportunity to see my mother regularly, let alone to go and fetch her to see my granddaughter. This situation was unbearably sad and difficult for me. At Rayachka's dacha, my mother did well but her health continued to deteriorate. She was fading, and in 1963, she passed away. She died in the early autumn, when we were living in our dacha. She was not able to say goodbye to my girl and me. She died in my aunt's arms and I WAS NOT THERE with her. Sixty years has passed since my mother's death, and I still cannot shake the guilt and the bitterness. No amount of hardship in my life can excuse what happened. Forgive me, Mommy, my darling! Of course, I should have found a way and been there with you, the dearest person in my life. However, I failed to do so.

Our friend Bobby Brown, Vera and I visiting my parents grave

After cremation, my aunt buried Mom temporally on a picturesque edge of the woods, half a mile from Raya's dacha. Later, we moved the urn with her ashes to Dad's grave at Novodevichy Cemetery in Moscow.

I still have a priceless picture of my mother in high school. I think Mom is no more than 15 years old on the photograph. This allows me to date the portrait to about 1913. It travels with me through my life. Today it hangs over my bed, and as I lie on my back, our gazes meet. At such moments, I feel as if we are talking, and I try to express everything that I did not say at the proper time...

MY FIRST OWN APARTMENT

Of course, the departure of my mother unsettled me completely. However, time did its job. I had a wonderful little girl in my arms, and the task of surrounding her with warmth, care, and love gave me a lot of strength and joy. My Galyusha was only one year old at the time. She was very pretty, and it was she more than anyone else, who helped me to keep hope alive. Later she has provided me more than once with similar occasions to thank her, but, when I lost my Mom was probably, the most important one. In any case, it was clear that I had an obligation to move forward with life.

Although I was very happy to live with Innulia, the sad history of my mother living with us pushed me to think hard about how to start living separately and thus avoid the risk of my wife's conflicts with my dear relatives. However, did not have money even close to what I needed at that time to buy an apartment, and there was no prospect of earning such money in the near future. Nevertheless, these thoughts tortured me. Then was a miracle that happened. After my mother's death, there was a little money left over and we three siblings decided to divide it among ourselves. My share was just enough to pay the entry fee to the cooperative for the smallest apartment in the so-called Khrushchoba: one of the cheapest buildings in Moscow at the time of Khrushchev. In Russian, there is a pun: "slum" is "trushchoba", so "Khrushchoba" means "Khrushchev's slum." That is what people would call the cheap and ugly houses built during the Khrushchev's rule.

Although I absolutely overwhelmed with remorse: after such an inadmissible parting with my mother, I still did not hesitate to spend HER MONEY FOR MY OWN IMPROVEMENT and settle Renata in the new apartment, who was so cruel to my Mom. Still I did not want to wait a single day and signed up for a "burning" apartment on the ground floor of the Academy of Sciences cooperative at the very end of Lenin Avenue (Novatorov Street). After about a month, the builders finished their job and in my pocket were the keys to my own apartment! The only thing that comforted me was my confidence that I was doing it for my little girl, and no doubt, my mother would approve it.

The hustle and bustle of moving and improving our new home began immediately. Psychologically, it was not easy for me. First, as I have mentioned, I was depressed by the thought that my mother could no longer see and approve of the way I had used her money really depressed me. I thought a lot about it and came to the firm conclusion that my mother would agree with me and that I had done the right thing. That firmness helped me make such a difficult move. The second difficulty with my move was the separation from my family. Mentally, I was well aware that there comes a time when a young family is better off living separately. However, my heart did not want to go along with that. Ever since I left my apartment on Tikhvinsky Lane, I have never forgotten the warm atmosphere that surrounded me there for the first quarter century of my life. The longer I live, the more I realize what a happiness it is to have a warm parental home! My sister Lena gave that warmth to me while she was living with us, also my brother Jan, however different we were, and, of course, Innulia with her children Olya and Lyova. The warmth received over the years has helped me a lot, especially in the last years of my life there. Thank you, my dear ones, for a warm start in my life.

Now let us go back to the description of the apartment itself. Our new apartment was a panel building that had five floors without an elevator, and exactly the same looking houses, not different from each other at all, like identical twins. The huge block consisted completely of such creations. Architecturally, the sight was depressing. Muscovites joked then that the proliferation of "khrushchobas" led to a social problem: elementary school children, returning home after classes, could not recognize their house and their apartment, because they were all indistinguishable, like chickens from the same incubator. Someone suggested as a joke an ingenious solution to the problem: display a large picture of kid's mothers in the window. I wondered at the time why no one mentioned that such a solution would also lead to a wonderful side effect: decorating faceless houses with portraits of young and interesting women.

Our type of apartment was called a "wing apartment." Through a small corridor, bypassing the passage to a very small kitchen, bathroom and toilet doors (our bathroom was separate) we came to two doors to the left and right into two isolated rooms with windows on opposite sides of the house. At the time, this apartment seemed like a palace to us. We moved all the unpretentious stuff that stood in our room at Tikhvinsky into our palace, and a dozen trips to Moscow shops added everything we needed. After that, from our point of view, the apartment took on quite a homey appearance. It looked like home to us.

There is indeed a silver lining around every dark cloud.

I was young and healthy then, so the lack of an elevator did not bother me at all, especially since I agreed to the first floor. Later I discovered even the advantages of the first floor. Several times when I left the house, I forgot to take the key and slammed the door. Waking my soundly sleeping daughter with the bell would fail. All those times, I climbed in through the window, when it was not locked, and opened the door from the inside. After I have married Tanya, we moved together to the new apartment that was again on the ground floor. Therefore, I could continue to use my experience with break-ins, requiring climbing skills. Once, I remember, she was staying alone in the apartment, went to sleep and left the key in the keyhole so we could not open the door from the outside with our key. This time, again, I had to crawl in through the window.

MY LIFE AT THE NEW PLACE

According to Moscow standards, the apartment was quite convenient for both Renata and me in terms of transportation to and from work. The Institute of Linguistics, where Renata worked, was near the Kropotkinskaya metro station. To get there it was either a 20–30 min walk or a 10 min bus ride to the closest subway station. After that, it was a 20-minute subway ride. As for me, my institute was located on Lenin Avenue. It took me about 10 minutes to walk to the avenue, and then I had to take a bus for about 20 minutes. At peak hours, however, my buses were unthinkably jammed. As a rule, I would hang on the open doorstep, as it was impossible to close the doors. For the first few minutes, I did so, ventilating my rear end, until the passengers inside made room for me. I was young and strong then, and that did not bother me too much.

The situation changed by 1965, when Galka was three years old and we had to solve the problem of kindergarten. The choice was between the new district kindergarten right in front of our house (a huge advantage!) and the old academic kindergarten in the same block where my Institute was located. I did a wide poll of opinions around me, and the voting certainly spoke in favor of the academic kindergarten. This way, my hesitation was resolved, and the matter and we made our decision. Of course, the neighborhood of the kindergarten with my Institute was very convenient for me, but the problem of transportation was greatly complicated. I feel scared even today when I recall how it was happening. The bus would pull up, the doors would barely open, but it was literally impossible to get in. I would lift my girl over the heads of those standing on the steps as high as I could and ask a stranger to hold her until I managed to squeeze into the bus. The wonderful thing was that there were always nice people willing to take my Galya and the nice driver only ever moved off after he made sure in the mirror that I was hanging on tightly. The bus would move, and for the first few minutes, I was riding in the breeze, just like before. For almost 30 years of our life in America, I gradually began to forget such "amusement" of our everyday lives in Moscow. I think I should not.

Talking about Galka's kindergarten, I want to tell you about the first day. I was very worried about the transition so she would not have a big trauma. I decided that if the reaction to the separation was strongly negative, I would not leave her there in tears. In that case, I thought I would have to think about some way to smooth the transition. We went with her early in the morning in the way already described, I introduced her to the caregivers and spent about 15 minutes there with them and her. So far everything had been, thank God, peaceful. After that I left the day care center, surrounded by a wooden fence, and closed the gate behind me. The weather was good, and all the children were playing outside.

But I just could not go to my office in peace. I managed to find an observation point with a crack between the boards of the fence through which I could see my girl. Peeking there, I spent there about the next 20 excruciating minutes. At some point my Galochka seemed very sad to me, and I was ready to run back and rescue her. But then she was distracted by another child, and I realized that my worries were probably in vain.

I ran to work, but of course, I could not focus at my working problems at all. Much earlier than the standard time, I rushed to pick her up. It is funny to recall now, but I was so nervous that for couple of minutes I could not open the gate. My joy had no limits: the girl was perfectly fine. And soon a trip to the kindergarten became the daily routine for both of us. By the way, the acrobatic tricks with boarding the bus were somewhat facilitated by the fact that Galya was always small in both weight and size, which justified the fact that I called her "Little Drop."

Igor Melchuk of course, was not slow to make fun of my sentimentality, jokingly calling such a sweet girl in his own style a "Little snot." Such a parody of my "Little Drop" made me a little angry but did not reduce my sympathy and even affection for him. Interesting fact: if someone else allowed himself such jokes, I would have wanted to distance myself from that person. Some attractive force always was and still is in Igor for me, which transcends such sentiments. Without scatological-sexual humor, it always has been, and continues to be difficult to imagine this man. He would always say that he does this solely for the enjoyment of those around him. Ironically, the Melchukes got an apartment in the Galyanovo district of Moscow. In order to give Igor a pleasure, as well as to the delight of many admirers of his sense of humor, I would rename the area of his residence into Galyunovo ("latrine" in Russian is "galyun"). I think he would like such my initiative.

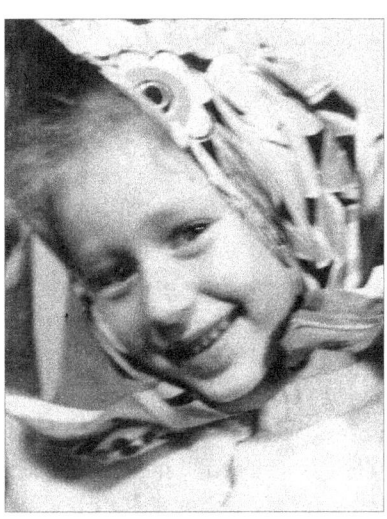

My kindergarten girl

Curiously enough, Igor's wife Lidochka is in this sense the exact opposite of Igor. Her thoughts, speech and deeds presented a striking example of purity. Even Igor himself often tenderly called her "Tiny Lidochka." Igor would use adjective "tiny" for many women, but he did not use the diminutive form of the name for many. Pay attention, not Lida, but Lidochka. Following him, I think, in our circle, almost everyone called her "Lidochka," and it was to my great pleasure. If I am not mistaken, it was also Igor who came up with an ingenious synonym for the adverb "indecently" (in Russian "neprilichno") — "neprilidochno", that should be translated as something like "not-for-use-in-the-presence-of-Lidochka".

At this point, at the end of my years, I would like to make an important confession, and this is the first time I have done so. From the first moment of our acquaintance (1961!) up to present day, I am a silent, but passionate admirer from the distance of Lidochka Iordanskaya. Just like in the poem by Pushkin: "I loved you, my love may be..."

loved you silently, hopelessly,
Exhausted now with shyness, now with jealousy.

Since I mentioned Galyanovo, a limerick comes to mind that I wrote about Igor around that time. Its text requires some preliminary explanation. The limerick was about one of the most interesting works in the world of linguistics, started by Igor, and contributed to by another talented linguist in his environment, Alik Zholkovsky. This was the creation of the Explanatory Combinatorial Dictionary of the Modern Russian Language. Igor managed to infect wonderful people in his circle with his enthusiasm, and they joined the project. Some of them I knew well, and liked such as Yuri Apresyan, Lida Iordanskaya, Kostya Babitsky, Lyova Yelnitsky and many others. Before both of the initiators of the dictionary emigrated from the Soviet Union (Igor in 1977, and Alik in 1979), endless unsuccessful attempts were made to reach an agreement about the publication of the dictionary in Russia. As a result, in the known traditions, the publication of the the Dictionary happened not in Russia, but in Vienna in 1984. As Hermann Plisetsky very accurately said about this in his poem "In Memory of Pasternak ":

We gave our glory for free, as a present,
Our barns are, probably, not big enough for it ...".

Igor and Alik had very different interests. Igor had a unique talent for focusing on scientific problems, but never shied away from the practical applications of his results, such as a machine translation (MT). Alik, on the other hand, leaned towards much broader humanitarian interests. It was his scientific interest, which gave rise to his work on poetics. Igor with his characteristic passionate nature, which rather seldom goes along with justice, was very skeptical about Alik's works: "Why are you doing such nonsense? You're a linguist!" That is what my humorous limerick was about:

There lived once Melchuk from Galyanovo,
Who tried to redo the entire MT from scratch.
But about the poetics
He never new a thing,
He was even worse than comrade Zhdanov.

Zhdanov was communist leader and chief ideologist and propagandist who authored many vulgar political articles and speeches in the domain of culture.

Two circumstances: the move to Novatorov Street, and the beginning of my friendship with Kostya Babitsky, somehow contributed to my rapprochement with a circle of remarkable people, many of whom were associated with the human rights movement in the Soviet Union. I am mentioning just a few names here as examples. In our house lived the children of Pavel Shapiro and his wife, who belonged to a previous generation of Russian intellectuals. They were so attractive to me because of their education and modesty. Bolsheviks hated this type of people. As a result, they lived years exiled to Vorkuta. We met them at the house of Renata's parents'. Through the Shapiros we became acquainted with the elder Bogorazes, pleasant people, parents of Larissa Bogoraz, who had passed through Stalin's gulag. Sister of Kostya's wife Asya Velikanov also lived in our house with her husband Sergei Muge. Sergei had been caught in the Stalinist meat grinder for the mere fact that at a student meeting of the biological faculty of Moscow State University he had said kind words about his biology professors who had been arrested for their anti-Lysenko's genetic views. I was fortunate to recognize among these people the real "crème de la crème" of the Soviet society, and I consider my acquaintance and friendship with them as an incredibly good fortune.

It was thanks to these people, that my eyes slowly but surely began to open wider and wider to what was going on in a country. It was they, who helped me to see lies in the song by Lebedev-Kumach and Dunayevsky, which included the following stanza:

> *From Moscow to the outskirts of our land,*
> *From the southern mountains to the northern seas*
> *A man passes as a master*
> *Of his unbounded mother country*

Russian wits have turned these lines into both a sad and funny parody-joke without a violation of the structure of rhythm and riming:

> From Moscow to the outskirts of our land,
> From the southern mountains to the northern seas
> The man passes as a master,
> Of course, except he is Jewish!

As a result, everybody could sing these lines using Dunayevsky's tune. Anyway, the process of my epiphany in the mid-sixties was well underway.

However, the center of this circle of people was undoubtedly an extraordinary woman, then K.Babitsky's wife, Tanya Velikanov. Tanya played a huge role in my life, and I will be grateful until the end of my days to the fate for my friendship with this woman and for so many good things, she gave me. I will mention Tanya's name more than once in my memoirs, and I will devote an separate chapter to her.

LUMUMBA PARK

One of the advantages of our new place of residence was the pleasant forest park in the next block. I loved going there for walks with Galechka, especially sledding or skiing in the winter. We called it Lumumba Park because on the border of the park was Volgin Street, where has been opened the University of People's Friendship for foreigners named after Patrice Lumumba. For some reason there were many students from African countries, we often met during our walks. After a while, there was a general meeting of our housing cooperative, at which, to my great dismay, all members got an advice not to go to Lumumba Park after dark, because there were cases of robbery and even rape.

Patrice Lumumba was a black African pro-Soviet Congo left-wing nationalist politician who was highly praised by the Soviet authorities. There were more than 30 streets named after him in the cities of the Soviet Union. Particularly happy, I believe, were the people of Buryatia that in their village of Kyren a street was named after Patrice Lumumba. I find the liberator's biography remarkable. Born into a family of farmers, he had worked as a beer seller when he finished high school. Then the Belgian colonial authorities sent him to a class for postal workers and paid completely all expenses. The post workers at that time were considered as privileged "enlightened citizens" in the country. Upon the completion of the course, he served as a postal official. At some point, he went with a group on a free tour of Belgium. He had chance to get the job with the Belgian Ministry of Colonies, but his successful career was interrupted by his arrest on a charge of embezzlement of remittances to the tune of about two and a half thousand dollars. I suspect that this was no ordinary theft, but a class-action attempt to redistribute wealth "properly". Sick socialist ideas turned upside down everything: robbery became an act of justice.

The story reminds me of Mayakovsky's lines from the poem "All right!". They describe a gentle, of course, worker from the Putilov (at soviet time Kirov) factory, speaking illiterate Russian and grabbing by force a wrist watch from an embarrassed "bourgeois" son of a bitch, naturally:

> *Some confused son of a bitch,*
> *Pressed to the soil by Putilov factory worker,*
> *Nicerer than a papa:*
> *"You, fellow, put out the stolen watch—*
> *Now all watches are ours!"*

After six months in prison, Lumumba came to love new radical ideas and dedicated himself entirely to politics. Already in October 1958, he became the leader of the leftist party National Movement of the Congo. This party won 40 of the 137 seats in Parliament in the country's first elections in May 1960. Lumumba became prime minister. The leadership of the Soviet Union, I think, rejoiced: the faithful disciple of Lenin had proved by personal example the claim of the soviet leader that any cook may be taught to run the state.

By this time, there appeared Lumumba's political opponent, Moise Chombe, a pro-Western white leader of Congo's richest province, which had a significant white population. A month later, the independence of Congo was declared in a solemn ceremony attended by the King of Belgium. The president spoke of national modernization, a multiracial society and cooperation with the former metropolis. Contrary to agreement and protocol, Lumumba took the podium with an angry and rude speech, ending with the words: *"We are no longer your monkeys!"*

In protest, Chombe declared the independence of its province of Catana. Another province followed suit. What historians today call the Congolese crisis was ignited. A civil war had actually broken out. Lumumba asked for help from the UN, which surprisingly rejected it and sided with Chombe. Then he turned to the Soviet Union for help. Khrushchev sent him advisers and 10 military transport planes, one of which was given as a gift to Lumumba personally. Chombe, for his part, asked for help from the former metropolis and received Belgian professional soldiers.

At Chombe's insistence, the president issued the warrant for Lumumba's arrest. Lumumba attempted to escape but was captured and handed over to the separatists. Without any investigation and trial they summarily executed by shooting him and his comrades-in-arms. Even today, the exact circumstances of the murders are still unknown. However, what happened next was something that is hard to believe even in the wildest corners of the any civilized world. They buried the corpses just at the scene of the shooting. To conceal the criminal affair, the executers exhumed the corpses a few days later and then buried the remains.

As to Lumumba's body, it was dismembered, dissolved in acid and then the remains burned. There were rumors, attributing the murder to villagers. Recent years disclosed that the USA England and Belgium, all knew about the plans to kill Lumumba, although I would like to think that no one had any idea of the details. I remember well that in the 60's there was a poem going around Moscow:

> *Would Lumumba*
> *Have some brain in his head,*
> *Nobody would need*
> *To have anything to do with Chombe.*

That may be true. Many today believe that it was Lumumba's intransigence, his leftist views and his pro-Soviet sympathies, that caused his elimination.

Today we know that the Congolese crisis has claimed 100,000 lives. It is a well-known fact that all liberators with the noblest intentions first of all free themselves from any remorse of having walked to freedom on the corpses of those who disagreed with them. It remains to add, that after the collapse of the Soviet Union, all the streets named after Patrice Lumumba in the country disappeared from maps and got new names. The same fate befell the Peoples' Friendship University named after Patrice Lumumba. Now it is Peoples' Friendship University of Russia (PFUR). I personally for the rest of my life will call our beloved park Lumumba Park. This story teaches us not to hurry with perpetuating the names of politicians.

MUSIC FOR ME

Now I would like to change the subject and, returning to the chronological path, to talk about music. From my young years until today, complexes related to my musical illiteracy torment me. The title of this chapter echoes the title of one of my favorite books, "Poetry for Me" by Peter Weill. The conclusion of the preface to his book explains clearly, why about him. Because without the poems he chose for the book, his *"life would be different, duller, not as rich it was, dimmer, it would be worse."* I have to confess that I personally realized how much worse my life would be without music, only after W. Shakespeare's personage Lorenzo explained it to me quite radically. I quote it from the translation by Shchepkina-Kupernik in the first scene of the fifth act of his "Merchant of Venice":

> *The man that hath no music in himself,*
> *Nor is not moved with concord of sweet sounds,*
> *Is fit for treasons, stratagems, and spoils;*
> *The motions of his spirit are dull as night,*
> *And his affections dark as Erebus.*
> *Let no such man be trusted...*

Before going further, I would like to say that Erebus in Greek mythology is an embodiment of eternal darkness.

Today I have similar feelings about music in general and especially about the music of my favorite composer Johann Sebastian Bach. It started in 1965–1966, when I got a fever of interest and love to the works of Bach. I decided that if I did not get proper musical education in my childhood, I should make up for lost time now myself. I was 27 years old and with all the energy of a young man, I rushed to fill the gap in my education: listen to the music of Bach, read about the great composer.

What was my dismay when I discovered that there were surprisingly few records of Bach music in the music stores. I became a regular visitor to the central record store "Melody" on Kalinin Avenue. Quite soon, I became convinced that there were very few domestic Bach records for sale. I managed to buy just a few discs, most of which were a compilation of instrumental fragments of works by various composers, including Bach. Vocal Bach was, naturally, almost not present in records: Soviet citizens did not need this religious nonsense. The bookstore of the socialist countries on Gorky street, where in the GDR department German plastics were sometimes "thrown out" (suddenly appeared in sale), turned out to be a lifesaver. No one even heard of CDs in Moscow at the time. Thus began my Bach records library, in a year I was the happy owner of about one and the half a dozen records.

The trips to the Melody store brought me not only musical joy, but also an additional bonus: meeting a wonderful person, Sandro Kadzasov, who became a close friend of mine. Once, being in the store, I started to ask the sales clerk some questions related to the records of Bach's works. As, unfortunately, it often happens, the seller was unable to answer my questions. But next to me stood a nice-looking man of my age who, on hearing my questions, answered them very sensibly. I immediately thought that he was a professional musician. We began talking, and he turned out to be a linguist and a great music lover, who knew much more about music, at least at the time, than I did. We left the shop, being already friends, on New Arbat Avenue. We both bought the same record with music of Bach's contemporary, G. F. Telemann, which piece exactly, I don't remember now. Until our departure from Russia, we were close friends with Sandro and his lovely and interesting wife, Tamara Kazavchinsky. After our departure from Russia, they also immigrated with their children to Germany. However, we never saw them again, and today both of them passed away.

During those same years, I made regular raids on sellers of used books, buying up just anything about Bach and his music. Much of it was vulgarly political, militantly atheistic Soviet "musicology". To prove my point, once I purchased at this time in a Soviet sheet music store publication of excerpts from Johann Sebastian Bach's vocal works under the original title "Lieder". This unique Soviet publication contained the original text of pieces in German, as well as a "translation" of this text into Russian. I was literally shocked when I started reading these texts. For example, in the original, it was about the sufferings of the crucified Christ, but in Russian, we read about little birds, cheerfully singing in the sun-drenched forest. I don't know what other country has come down to such cultural crimes and what kind of idiots the Soviet publishers took their readers for, putting in their publication together both the original text and its "translation".

But in 1965 in Moscow a great event in music life has happened: publishing house "Music" has printed the Russian translation of the remarkable book "Johann Sebastian Bach" by outstanding man and humanist, musicologist and organist, philosopher (Nobel Prize 1952) and theologian, self-sacrificing doctor Albert Schweitzer. It was the last year of the life of our great contemporary, and I do not know whether he knew about this publication in Russia. In any case, Soviet musicians and music lovers received, I think, a wonderful present from the departing great Man with a capital letter. I, of course, bought this book at the time, seeing it as an incredibly timely gift to me personally.

I did not only read it thoroughly, I worked through it. I want to confess right away that some parts of the book were not one hundred percent up my alley because of my musical illiteracy. I am talking here, for example, about the specific details of some of the musical expressions suggested by Bach, and tips on how a performer can try to convey exactly these musical ideas of the composer to the listeners. Nevertheless, overall, Schweitzer really helped me with his book to hear, feel and understand better that the Bach's music is written FOR ME really. This music opened my eyes, literally, to the way in which Bach was having a direct and intimate conversation with God, to the point that I sometimes felt uncomfortable for seemingly overhearing their conversation.

One of the lessons Schweitzer taught me was the importance of texts in Bach's vocal music. Schweitzer begins the chapter "Word and Sound in Bach" in his book: "*It is difficult to imagine a livelier, closer connection between music and text, than in the works of Bach,*". When I was "*...wading through the fog from the prologue to the epilogue*" in the words of Okudzhava, I tried, for those of my recordings for which I could get the text, to carefully read the corresponding paragraph in Schweitzer's book, to carefully parse the text, then listen to the recording. After this I would try to go back to the text, then back to the recording, and so on several times. I once did these steps with Aria 39 of The Passion According to Matthew. From then until today, I personally agree with many people that this is not only Bach's own supreme vocal achievement, but also the greatest achievement of the world's vocal art in general. I want to cite here for this short aria the original German text and my English translation:

Erbarme dich, mein Gott,	*Have mercy, my God,*
um meiner Zähren willen!	*Do it the sake of my tears!*
Schaue hier, Herz und Auge	*Look here; look at my heart and my eyes*
weint vor dir bitterlich.	*They are sobbing bitterly before you.*
Erbarme dich, mein Gott!	*Have mercy, my God.*

The translation here is slightly different from the literal Russian translation commonly used today, and I allowed myself to make these changes only because in this form these lines are more "for me".

On the record I had, one of Russia's best mezzo-sopranos, Zara Dolukhanov, performed this aria. Since then I loved the singer tenderly, and her voice would forever remind me about this aria by Bach. Moreover, this recording prompted me to read the full text of Bach's great work. My plan was simple: find the sheet music of the Passion and read the text under the notation. To my amazement, the task was not an easy one. The Internet did not exist then, so I went to the best of Moscow's libraries, the Lenin Library. The electronic catalog did not exist then, I do not know if it exists today. The card catalog then occupied a large room. In that catalog, I began to look for "Passion". Contrary to my expectations I managed to find only one (!?) card of a German edition of the end of XIX century with full sheet music and text.

That same day, using the card I found, I placed an order for this publication. The answer, which came to me the next day, was of little comfort. The edition, I was interested in, lived in a special music room, access to which was restricted to professional musicians. I had to talk to several library administrators, and they all said that in order to gain access to this specialized room, I had to bring a certificate stating that I needed it in my line of work (!?). For the life of me, I cannot remember how I got over that problem. However, I prevailed and got the coveted clearance.

Armed with a school notebook and pen, I could not wait and went to my first meeting the next day with the long-awaited text, to begin rewriting it word for word. The sight was impressive: a small and thin librarian brought me a huge folio. She set it on the floor in front of her to rest before setting it on the table at which I was about to work. On that table, the sheet music, uncovered, took up almost its entire surface. I was overwhelmed with both joy and pride, as if a magic power transported me to Bach's time. Then the working evenings of rewriting began. I remember well that, for greater pleasure, I armed myself with a German-Russian dictionary, which could help me to understand on the fly at least a little bit, of what I was copying. About two weeks passed, and I was the happy owner of the complete text to the composer's great work. By the way, this text did not fit into one school notebook, and I wrote half of the second.

Now let us say a few words about the text itself, the author of which was a contemporary of Bach, the poet and librettist Christine Friedrich Henrici with the literary pseudonym of Picander. I was interested to learn that Henrici was a lawyer by main profession, and that poetry was his hobby as well as a means of making extra money. He published his spiritual poems in Leipzig magazines, to which Bach drew attention. They met and became friends. Picander. was not a great poet, but his education, depth of faith and conscientiousness appealed to Bach, and they began to collaborate. Thereafter, Bach wrote quite a few of his own works to Picander's words. I liked Picander's text for Bach's Passion as well. Besides, looking around today, I cannot see any lawyers that, like this man in 18th century, wrote and published poetry and were friends and collaborators with the great musicians of their time. As a result, this jurist went down in history not by his practice of law, but precisely by his hobby.

Once I had the text, I rolled up my sleeves and got to work on translating this text into Russian. The further I progressed with the translation, the more I liked the text I was working with. To be honest, I still do not know how I had the time and patience to do it. However, the work progressed steadily, slowly but surely. From time to time, I reopened the pages of the Schweitzer's book dedicated to the Passion, and I became convinced with great satisfaction how knowledge of the text now revealed more and more to me in those pages.

In the spring of 1966 I finished my translation. It reminds me of Alexander Galich's lines from the poem "We are no worse than Horace":

> *"Erica" takes four copies,*
> *That is it!*
> *That is enough.*
> *Let us say there are only four copies so far.*
> *That is enough!*

Erika is a German typewriter and I had my own one left to me by my dad, and it did take four copies. Using it I typed my translation and made four copies: one for me, and three for my friends. We should pay attention to the lines from Galich that tell us: samizdat circulation is only four copies for now, but four is better than nothing is. My friends were delighted to receive the Bach text. In addition, the reward was not long in coming, just a present for my birthday! On 1st and 2nd March 1966 in the Large Hall of the Conservatory and in the Tchaikovsky Hall a historical event for Moscow took place: the Symphony Orchestra of the Latvian Radio and Television with the State Academic Choir of the Latvian USSR performed Bach's oratorio "Matthew Passion". Such incredible coincidences do happen!!! Of course, I was at the concert with my text in my hands and felt fully that this was the MUSIC FOR ME.

During all the years I lived in Moscow, this great work by Johann Sebastian Bach was performed literally only a handful of times. It goes without saying that the original text, let alone the Russian translation, has never been included in the program. The previous time the same Latvian group played "Passion" in the Great Hall of Conservatory on November 15, 1964. I managed to be in the hall again, but at that time, I did not have the text yet. Since the 50's I saved the programs of all interesting events, which I attended. By the time of the remarkable concert in 1964, I had already accumulated four 3 rings folders with such programs. As with many other things in the Soviet Union, there was also regularly a shortage of concert programs, there were often not enough for everyone. To my great chagrin I was not able to buy (they always sold for money!) the programs for such an important concert for me. Fortunately, I saw my friends Marina and Yuri Apresyan in the audience. They knew about my collection, and Marina promised to give me her program at the end of the concert. I was over the moon! We saw each other before going home, and I received a precious item in my collection. However, I had no idea, before I looked at it, how precious it was to me. On the title page right above the portrait of Bach, Marina wrote: *"To the sleepy concertgoer from the sympathetic M. Glovinskaya. 15.11.64."*. Glovinskaya was the maiden surname of Yui Apresyan's wife. I've already mentioned before my problem with falling asleep to music. Marinochka, darling, your gift is like a love letter to me. Thank you is not the right word! Now that I mentioned Apresyans, I can not help saying that I really miss them in my life in the USA.

From many people who know music well, I was happy to receive support for my choice of favorite composer. But I was especially delighted when I learned that my revered musician and composer Sophia Gubaidullin said in an interview that she would never consider ANY COMPOSER equal to Bach.

EVERYTHING ABOUT HER WAS BEAUTIFUL

When I was still in school and memorized Dr. Astrov's words from "Uncle Vanya" by A. Chekhov *"Everything in a man should be beautiful: his face, his clothes, his soul, his thoughts..."* These words seemed to me too abstract and therefore not interesting and banal. However, as time passed, life taught me that I was very wrong; fortunately, it showed me real people in whom I could see all these qualities with my own eyes, and not just for an instant, but I could observe them for many years, enjoying what I saw. Yes, actually, there were very few of them, but they were! It seems to me that we can name Tanya Velikanov among such people. I really liked everything about Tanya: how she looked, how she treated people, including those with whom she disagreed, how she spoke, how she acted, how she raised her children, and how she treated her teaching job. I had to get to know many people in the dissident movement in Moscow, and I do not think there was a second person like her.

Unfortunately, I did not have a chance to get to know personally A. Sakharov. I do not know Andrei D. Sakharov intimately, but my impressions of my meetings with him allow me to think that maybe he was this kind of person. I think it is natural to feel the joy of communicating with a person who thinks the same way you do on many issues. However, oh how difficult it is to maintain benevolence and respect for someone who disagrees with you, and about whom you are sure they are wrong. Back to Tanya, the uniqueness of her was that she never had this difficulty. According to the testimony of many people among my close ones, I personally never managed to achieve such emotional wisdom though I tried very hard.

I met Tanya Velikanov in 1961 through her husband Kostya Babitsky. I left Moscow and Russia in 1988. It turns out that I was fortunate to be able to see her regularly for 27 years. And we did see each other a lot. She used to come to our house. I often visited her apartment on Profsoyuznaya Street. Many years we celebrated the New Year together at her dacha in New Jerusalem. We would gather at our mutual friends' houses and, first of all, at the house of her closest friend Lena Smorgunova.

However, the most remarkable meetings and the most memorable communication with her for me took place when we wandered together with backpacks through the mountains and forests. Lenochka worked at the Russian Language Research Institute, and she knew and loved the history of Russian culture, primarily literature and Russian church architecture. It was Lenochka who infected both Tanya and me with her interest and knowledge, and what was especially valuable, her knowledge poured out at us in a violent flow even without our questions. She was the initiator of many of our itineraries, usually passing near the pearls of Russian building genius. In the company of these two very special women, I went quite thoroughly around Moscow suburbs and some part of the north. The latter particularly attracted me with its wooden architecture and woodcarvings, and I was the initiator of some of these trips. One of the most remarkable such trips with Tanya was building a log cabin in the forests of the Arkhangelsk region, about which there will be a separate chapter further on.

As for my woodcarving, the roots of this hobby go back to my childhood. When I was a boy, it was very common for kids to carve plywood with a jigsaw. In Moscow, they used to sell hand-jigsaws and sets of patterns for carving. I really enjoyed this activity. However, woodcarving became my hobby seriously after I was more than forty years old. That means I have about forty years of woodcarving experience. Over the next forty years, I carved about few HUNDRED pieces that were distributed to family and friends all over the world. Photos of many of them I still have in the memory of my computer.

My dearest friend Tanya Velikanov

The North of Russia is in many ways very interesting area. Lena, being a linguist, participated in many dialectological expeditions, studying various dialects of the Russian language, traveled much more than Tanya and me. She knew this part of Russia very well. Besides, being a very generous person, she was glad to go with us to the places she had been many times before, to share the joy of a new meeting this time with us. From her expeditions, Lenochka used to bring back wonderful stories, many of which were pieces of literature to me. It is a pity that my memory has not kept most of them. I cannot refrain here from telling one of my favorite stories that I remember well. In some godforsaken Northern village, Lena went into a hut to interview the host, an old woman, and record her answers on a tape recorder. When she came, grandmother was baking pancakes and feeding her family, who were enthusiastically nibbling on the pancakes. Lena, wanting to hear how Grandma pronounces the third person plural form of the verb "bake," asked: *"Grandma, here you are baking pancakes, and, if they do, how do you say this about them?"* and she nodded towards those sitting at the table, *"What are they doing?" "And they guzzle!"* replied Granny, with dignity.

If from Lena I learned many elements of the history of Russian culture, from Tanya I learned some, I think, things that are even more important. They concerned the emotional reactions that arise in the relationship between people, between man and knowledge, between man and nature. I have already mentioned

Tanya's extraordinary ability to respect her opponent's opinions in the case of divergent views. To this day, I try to follow Tanya's example in this respect with varying success. I have learned another lesson more successfully. In our travels, she would often tell me: *"If the route of your trek is aimed at meeting something interesting in terms of history, culture or nature, you should not arrive to this place by car, bus or even horse, as it is often done by tourists in a foreign country. One should not be lazy to come to the place on foot, so that the place emerges from the misty distance through the trees like legendary Kitezh Castle".*

The Russian legend tells us about the 13th – 16th centuries war with Thatar-Mongol army which wanted to take the glorious city of Kitezh. However, on the prayer of the inhabitants, springs gushed from the ground and flooded the city. The cross of the cathedral was the last to disappear under the water from sight of the frightened Tatars. Only when you come to the place Tanya's way you can experience the true joy of the encounter. Together with Tanya, I have repeatedly shared such joy. I did learn this lesson from her. In many circumstances of my life, I miss my wonderful friend Tanya Velikanov very much. I will return later many times to this special woman.

Tanya was well known human rights fighter in Moscow, and my friendship with Tanya Velikanov did not go unnoticed by the KGB. I think it was 1976. I was in my office when I got a call from our department, which worked with secret documents, and they asked me to come in. There were two visitors waiting for me, who introduced themselves as KGB officers. The conversation started out silly, and for a while, I did not understand what they wanted from me. They sang dithyrambs to me about how smart and talented I was. They asked me if I was going to write a doctoral dissertation. In Soviet Russia, they had two scientific degrees: Candidate of Science and Doctor of Science. The first was about the level of PhD and the second was higher. When they heard that not yet, they advised me to start and offered their assistance. I politely thanked them and said that I could do it myself, and that I think that their department has very different tasks.

However, at some point, all this nonsense stopped, and one of the men asked, if it was true, that Tanya Velikanov was a good friend of mine, and that we often communicate. That is when it all became clear to me. I new well, that these people new about

Tanya's human rights activity and were watching her closely. I replied that it was true. After that, they said that they wanted to ask me for a small favor that would cost me nothing, but would help them a lot. They would like things to continue as they were, and they would meet with me from time to time for a short chat. I told them emphatically that what they expected me to do, I categorically could not do. The tone of our conversation immediately changed: the previous friendliness was gone. They rather harshly told me that ALL Soviet people help them, and if I did not want to help them, they had to bring this fact to the notice of our Institute's administration. I responded that I thought they knew better than I did how they should do their jobs. We said our dry goodbyes. Before parting, they said: *"We hope you understand that nobody must know about our conversation"*. I said *"Of course"*. *"And you also would not say a word to your wife,"* they added in the affirmative way. To which I replied, "I am sorry, but there was and is absolutely nothing in my life that my wife doesn't know about me. And we should not even talk about it." These pygmies had to swallow my response, and the determination of my voice made it clear to them that there was no further discussion of the subject. I never saw these people again.

BEETHOVEN ABOUT TANYA VELIKANOV

Tanya's husband Kostya was talented in many ways, including poetry and music. He composed poems and songs, which we all liked very much. Among them there was one song that played a special role in my life. From the day when Kostya sang it for the first time in my presence, and to this day, every time I hear it or mentally recall it, I am overwhelmed with emotions. Kostya dedicated this song to his wife Tanya, a very close and important person for me. I think he found very touching words and found an equally touching melody to them. I will be mentioning this outstanding woman more than once. Here are the lyrics of this song:

> *Finally, it was just the two of us.*
> *The song of concern got silent for an hour.*
> *Everything in our little house is in order,*
> *There is a light burning in the fireplace.*
> *We manage rarely to get any leisure time.*

Our life flies by in struggle, jingling.
Let us not scare away, my tried-and-true friend,
The low sounds of music of this day.
Let us get some wine out of the cupboard,
Let us sit down at the table and converse.
It is all right that the wind beats with its chest the window,
It is all right that it drives the gray mist across the sky.
It is all right that steady rains come down,
It is all right that my heart aches for dampness.
Listen to the song being born in your chest-
That is how the pain converts into sadness.

Knowing Kostya well, I want to comment on one line to avoid misreading it: "*Our life flies by in struggle, jingling*". Kostya was never a fighter in any sense, he never would fight with anyone, he would run from the ringing of the struggle to the "*quiet music of the day*". In all the people around him, he tried to see something good, including even the interrogator who questioned him after his arrest. He was an exceptionally quiet and peaceful man. At the same time, he had a keen sense of honesty and justice. When he saw lies and injustice around him, which, alas, was so often the case in the country, he, following L. N. Tolstoy, would say "*I cannot keep silent!*"

Kostya borrowed a Beethoven motif as the music for these touching words addressed to Tanya. From the first day, I heard Kostya play this song on his guitar, I was very impressed by how the music he had chosen matched the heartfelt words. All the years I talked to Kostya, I was going to get exact reference to the particular Beethoven's melody which he borrowed. Ashamed to say, I never did. Kostya has long been gone, and there is no one to ask. However, I still cherish these stirring memories and it tormented me all these years that I never bothered to talk to Kostya about it when he was next to me. For sure, as the saying goes, *never put off until tomorrow what you can do today.*

I've been telling many of my friends and family about the melody of this song, hoping that someone who loves and listens to Beethoven's music would help me find the actual opus that Kostya was using. The task was even more complicate by the fact that with my lack of musical ear I NEEDED TO BE ABLE MYSELF TO

HEAR AND RECOGNIZE, if it is possible at all, Beethoven's melody in Kostya s song. And here I was lucky: our acquaintance Vitaly Khomanko whom I gave a link to an Internet page, where Kostya performs *"Finally, it was just the two of us"* seems to have succeeded. Vitaly is very fond of Beethoven's music and listens to it often. Just recently, I received a text message from him including a piece of video of the pianist Valentina Lisitsa performing the third movement, Allegretto, from Beethoven's "The Tempest" Sonata in D minor 17. (Opus 31 No. 2), written by the composer at a difficult time when he was struggling with his deafness.

When I have listened to this piece, I cried with excitement. In my soul, the Beethoven melody in this performance DID CLICK with Kostya's song. I admit that Kostya could mean another work of the great composer. But I have already told in the beginning of my memoirs, that though I am rather meticulous, for me the emotional truth is more important than the documentary one. Vitaly's finding became even more important to me after I read on Wikipedia about this sonata, that it represents a struggle with fate, a confrontation. And that was the main content of Kostya Babitsky's and Tanya Velikanov's life. Thank you, dear Vitaly, you can't even imagine how much you have done for me.

BEYOND THE ARCTIC CIRCLE

In the middle 60-th for several years in a row I had a chance to take part in very interesting winter skiing trips in the Khibin mountains on the Kolsky Peninsula. Why did I like these hikes so much?

Firstly, they took place in one of the first weeks of April. In Moscow the snow usually disappears at this time, and warm spring days have already arrived. On the Kolsky Peninsula it is also getting noticeably warmer and sunnier, although the snow cover is still over three feet there.

Secondly, the fact that the most part of the peninsula, and consequently, practically all Khibin mountains are BEHIND THE POLAR CIRCLE, would always excite me! I think there is no polar region closer to Moscow. I must confess that the challenge to cope with practical difficulties of the polar hike would please my vanity. And there were many of such difficulties: how to make fire when snow cover is about 3 to 6 feet, how to keep the fire going in frosty evenings for a long time, sufficient for cooking and warming of participants, how not to freeze in a tent at night.

Thirdly, I was always pleased with the participants of our expeditions: in our company there were the most pleasant, interesting and educated people of Russia and not only Russia. Among them were representatives of the best of linguists, such as Y. Apresyan, A. Zholkovsky, I. Mel'chuk, K. Babitsky, A. Wierzbicka, a Polish linguist who settled in Australia, mathematician N. Svetlova, geodesist E. Boyarsky. In the evenings at a fire Kostya delighted us, me certainly, with his songs. Exactly there I heard for the first time in his performance a song with LINES, very typical for Kostya-philosopher, defining the most important concepts in life:

> *Happiness is the descent from the heights taken*
> *Memory is a means of possessing friends*
> *Time is what you pass through.*

As for happiness, when we were descending after a difficult crossing the mountain chain in the Khibin, I felt exactly as Kostya wrote. As to a memory, I read much later Brodsky's obituary on the death of Nadezhda Mandelstam, and there were words in it that surprisingly resonated with Kostya's: *To remember is to restore intimacy.*

It really hit me there, in Khibin, when Alik Zholkovsky, as it was typical of him, with completely inappropriate tactlessness, from my point of view, allowed himself to parody Kostya's naive emotionality in the above song: "*Skiing is a means to apply the repair base*". I must say that, in fact, of all the company Alik more than anyone else, would had talent to break something in the ski bindings. Each time he held everyone up, and Kostya or I had to fix the defect. He for sure was the first user of our repair base. In his place, I would rather appreciate help than making fun of it.

Fourth, I knew that our routes passed through the sites of former Stalin's camps. The possibility to see with my own eyes the places, where Soviet political prisoners had served their sentences, intrigued me. The actuality of the theme affected Russian language during the decades of Bolsheviks terror. A special meaning for the word "zone" was born for secret and closed areas for prisoners. I could not know then, that I would later visit an ACTIVE Soviet concentration camp zone in Mordovia. When our Khibin ski track was crossing the area of the former camp, only scraps of the rusty barbed wire reminded me of the history. All the buildings were demolished during the liquidation of the camp. When writing this paragraph, I was thinking of the lines by Yuliy Kim describing the prisoner's zone:

> There is *so much of air around.*
> *There are pine trees, oak trees — all for you.*
> *In addition to the recreation zone*
> *There is just a zone.*

During the soviet epoch, the word "zone" without any adjective clearly meant guarded area where prisoners lived and worked. The only difference between the Kim's zone and Khibin zone was that the climatic conditions in Khibin resulted in not so much pine and oak forests, rather spruce forests.

Now, I would like to say a few words about the peculiarities of the Khibin hikes. As the snow layer exceeded three feet almost everywhere, there was no strength to dig down to the ground when setting up each tent, and it was cold to put the tent directly on the snow. In addition, the warmth of our bodies allowed the snow to melt even through the sleeping bag, and we were at risk of waking up in the morning in a puddle. Therefore, every night we had to prepare a fir tree branches "mattress", much thicker than when we hike in the central region, under the bottom of the tent. This ensured a dry and warm overnight stay.

The fire was especially troublesome: each time we had to dig a hole in snow until the ground about three to six feet deep to start the fire there. The hole had to be rather big to have enough room for the fire itself and all people around the fire. As a result, the fire was as if in the middle of a snowy room without a ceiling. Luckily, the walls of the "room" would gradually melt by the heat of the fire, and they reliably protected those who were inside from the wind or falling snow. Moreover, they have allowed a better retention of heat from the fire inside the "room" and created a kind of comfort. The fire itself was also special. Eskimo people call it "nodja". The name comes from the languages of the Ugro-Finnic group and means just fire. Our nodja consisted of a couple of thick

At Khibin Mountains from the left to the right:
Melchuk I., me, Apresyan Yu., Martemyanov Yu,
on the rock Plakida N.

dry timbers about five feet long. It is necessary that the logs should touch each other tightly. To do this we had to choose level trunks and carefully grind the limbs with the hatchet to form two even cylinders. For better adhesion, you can hammer pegs into the ground from the outside. After that, it is necessary to contrive with the help of thin dry twigs to light the line of contact of the logs along the whole length. When all described steps are done correctly, the nodya, without any effort on your part, will thank you with many hours of slow burning, giving enough both heat and pleasure.

During several years of Khibin expeditions, only a couple of times we did not have to make any significant efforts to arrange our lodging. During our first expedition, we found a small house in one place, built by geologists during their time, and it was well preserved. This cabin was the size of a small room with a door and a very small window. The room had a dry plank floor, noticeably elevated above the frozen ground, which, one might say, was a luxury in those conditions.

The laying of the routes in the Khibin expeditions was in the hands of Eric Boyarsky, a geodesist by profession, who had spent half his life in expeditions and had traveled half a world around. Eric was an irreplaceable person in mountaineering expeditions, especially in complicated conditions. Wherever I went with Eric, he always carried a portable Italian espresso machine, which he ran over the embers of the fire. It is impossible to describe the feelings one gets over when, after a hard day of battling snow and frost in the middle of the taiga forests, Eric brings you a few sips of great espresso of the quality, you cannot always find in a gourmet restaurant. Erics itinerary was different every year, but always, when it was not difficult, he tried to include one night at the geologists' lodge. We called such night a "night of relaxation." At the end of this paragraph, with saddness I have to say that Eric is no longer with us: after a painful battle with cancer, he passed away.

One of the nights of relaxation was quite remarkable. The day had been rather hard, everyone was tired and, having eaten and sat by the fire, everybody gladly retired to his or her sleeping bags on the flat, dry floor. The weather did not seem to be an omen for anything bad: it was snowing lightly. Everybody slept well. When in the morning one of us had to go outside, we found out that the door not only could not open, but it was impossible to move it even for a one eights of an inch. The small window, heavily covered with snow, did not give a good view of what was going on outside. However, it was clear that there had been a heavy snowfall during the night and about two feet of snow had fallen. The door was opening to the outside, and there was absolutely no way to get out of the lodge without cleaning the snow outside. We found ourselves in a trap.

Nevertheless, I remind, the most part of the trapped people were masters of scientific researches aimed at solution of "almost unsolvable" problems. Therefore, these masters arranged a scientific council in a small hut in the Khibin Polar region. They discussed how to get out from the cabin strewn with the fresh snow to the outside world and outlined the plan. I personally have undertaken to expose a frame from a window aperture accurately in such way that we could keep it later and then insert back to its place. After that, we have planned to push the thinnest member of our expedition through the formed square hole. This person would then be able to dig out the blocked door from outside and open it just enough so that everyone could get out with all our junk. After that, the intention was to put the frame back in place. Encouraged by such daring decision, the scientific council did not hesitate to discuss candidates for such an unusual taiga action.

There were two unusually slender, unusually beautiful, unusually pleasant, and unusually intelligent women among us: Lida Iordanskaya and Anya Wierzbicka, both quite small. None of us had any doubt that if anyone in our company could slip through the resulting square hole, it would be one of them. Alas, this assertion turned out to be untrue as both of them got their hips stuck while trying to do so. Then it was my historic hour: I volunteered to try next, and to everyone's surprise, including myself, in a minute I was up to my ears in the snowdrift below the hut's window. Difficult to believe, I beat in a fair contest two of the finest and most graceful women I had ever met in my life. The story reminded me of an old joke in which representatives of different countries argued over whose wife was thinner, and one of them, I think the Frenchman, said: *"When my wife takes a bath, I always worry that she won't slip down the drain hole in the bath."*

Another very interesting experience in the Khibin hikes was an overnight stay in an Eskimo snow dwelling: igloo. In Soviet Russia we, children, were taught not to be interested and not to care about how other countries and people of the world live, anyway, we live better than anyone else does. Being a proper silly Soviet boy, I followed this advice. I got all my knowledge about life of Eskimos from a idiotic song, popular at that time, about this small, less than hundred thousand, people, who hardly survived in the cold Arctic. From my point of view, this song is rather silly and racist, and makes fun of the broken Russian language that many Russian Eskimos as if spoke. By the way, I learnt later, that the language of Eskimos is in the Guinness Book of Records as one of the most difficult languages to learn. There were the following lines in the song:

> *In the far north*
> *The Eskimos were running,*
> *The Eskimos were running,*
> *They wanted to catch a walrus.*
> *An Eskimo did catch a walrus*
> *And stabbed her,*
> *He stabbed her,*
> *And his knife went ve-e-ery deep in.*

May be, yes, the Eskimos were not strong in Russian language. However, the only thing that was possible to learn from the song about the life of these people was that many of them, like our hero, had sadistic tendencies. Otherwise, why would he with such passion put his knife deep into the poor body of the caught walrus?

However, bad the song was, it did not excuse my complete ignorance of Eskimo life at the time. Therefore, I was very grateful to Eric Boyarsky, the irreplaceable participant of our Khibin expeditions, who told us much about the life of Eskimos and both initiated and headed in one of our trips to Khibin a construction of a snow igloo. As a result, to everyone's delight, we built the igloo and spent one night in it. Here it is appropriate to say that at that time it was not yet possible to Google "Eskimo igloo" and find out the history of Eskimos using igloo and all the details of its construction. I do not know how, but Eric dug up all the information somewhere, and the success was tremendous.

In Moscow before starting our hike, we built homemade machete knives to cut building blocks out of the snow and took them with us. Eric showed us how to use such a knife to cut out of hard snow blocks about 20 inches long, 12 inches high and 12 inches deep. Next, at the spot where we decided to build the igloo, we drew a circle about 10 feet diameter. The igloo is a dome-shaped structure like a yurt. The walls of the base of the yurt Eskimos would lay along this circle out of cut out blocks. They would smoothly go up and converge at a point at the top of the dome. The depth of the blocks would determine the thickness of the walls and it was about 12 inches. The wall at one point had an arch-shaped opening for entry and exit. The main requirement for putting of blocks was tight adjacency of the blocks touching each other. We managed to achieve this easily by correcting inclination angles of adjacent blocks with the help of machete.

We did build the igloo and we did sleep in it overnight. The results exceeded all my expectations. I cannot remember a single cold night in a tent that was as warm and comfortable as this one in the igloo. Our warm breath melted the walls of the blocks inside the igloo and sealed them tightly. Even though outside there were a heavy wind and a snowstorm, in the igloo we felt windless and calm. For complete comfort, of course, we had to close somehow the entrance. For this purpose, the Eskimos made a short (1–2 feet) "corridor" out of snow blocks. We have simply stuffed the entrance with our backpacks. About a half a century has passed since that unique experience, and I still remember it with great pleasure. Thanks to dear Eric Boyarsky!

SUMMER IN KOKTEBEL

In Moscow, every family with children tried to get them out of the city for the summer. The cheapest option was dachas near Moscow. We always belonged to people with a limited budget, which meant that we tried to rent a dacha not far away and for the cheapest price. Cheaper is understandable, but not far because food supply was atrocious in Moscow region and we had to carry all the food to the dacha from the city. Automobiles were very, very rare at that time. As a result, the dachas we managed to rent were cramped and uncomfortable. Therefore, when in 1967 (my Galka was 5 years old) my friends with kids of her age started discussing with me renting a house in the Crimea in Koktebel and organizing a commune there, I was very interested in this plan.

The commune included three participants, me including. My first companion was Natasha Svetlov with her son Dima from her first marriage with Andrey Tyurin. I knew her well from two sides: from hiking together in the company of Igor Melchuk, and as a graduate student of my brother Yasha Sinai in the Department of Probability Theory at Moscow State University. I liked Natasha. She always was a pleasant companion in in our hiking trips, she called in me all respect as a single mother, but my special admiration was her knowledge of Russian literature and especially poetry. Her Dima was not an easy but interesting boy, exactly the same age as my Galya. My second companion was Varya Blokhintsev with her two boys, the eldest of which was also Galya's age. I also knew Varya and her husband, Lyonya, from hiking with Igor. Both were very knowledgeable and modest people, Leonya was a physicist, and Varya, if I remember correctly, was a biologist, and I was always glad of their company. I never crossed paths with Lyonya in Koktebel. The third participant was your humble servant with his daughter Galya.

We agreed that any time with children in Crimea should be at least two parents. This plan worked perfectly, I still with pleasure recollect the time, which I have spent then in Koktebel both with children, and with their parents. My girl as a result has lived all summer in one of the best places in the country of rest and with wonderful people. Of course, I missed Galyusha very much when I was not on my shift in Moscow and she was in the Crimea. In one of such periods, a letter flew from me to her with the following lines:

> *It's so hot in here, and so stuffy,*
> *And it's so boring without my Little Drop,*
> *That I want to rush to the woods,*
> *And in the woods, I want to climb a big spruce,*
> *So that the top of this spruce*
> *One could see in Koktebel.*
> *Then I would be sitting on a spruce,*
> *And be able to look at my dear Little Drop.*

My life turned out so that, to my great regret, my connections with many of my good friends from Russia, including Natasha Svetlov and the Blokhintsevs, died off after we left Russia. It is most likely my fault: I did not make enough effort to find my friends and try to restore our friendship, although the ocean that separated us did not make it easier. Starting new life in the new country was rather difficult, which also did not help to do this.

Just the next year, Natasha met the writer A. I. Solhzenitsyn and soon after this became his wife. The following years they were with three kids and she dived deep into her new life. Political views of this courageous talent caused hatred of the soviet authorities. I was worrying about Natasha but felt that there was no place for me in this life at all. It was very difficult for me to come to terms, especially after closeness in Koktebel. It seemed to me, I lost her forever. When we lived in Moscow, I regularly inquired about her life from Arina Zholkovsky, who was her close friend. I would like to tell one story about Natasha's children. A family is riding somewhere in an elevator, and a woman, lightly cooing, addresses, I think, the youngest: *"What a good boy, how old are you?"* He answers her glumly and not very politely, *"But, I am Solzhenitsyn!"*, meaning: "do not talk to me, I am persona non grata!". After all, if you think about it, this is a very sad story about how the country maimed not only its conscious citizens for their political views, but also destroyed the happy childhood of their very innocent children. However, in Russia not many people cared then and care now about that.

Losing friends is always difficult, but the feeling of losing Natasha I was especially tormented when I thought that if I got permission to come to the U.S., we might be quite close: the Solzhenitsyns had lived in Vermont since 1976. I could probably get their phone number and call them, but, silly me, I was afraid that I would hear the voice of Natasha, different from the one I knew and loved so much. But one day some time before we left Russia (1988) the unbelievable thing has happened: the telephone rang in my Moscow apartment and I got to the phone. I heard Natasha's voice, and it was the voice of the same Natasha, I knew and loved. She told me she had seen me in a dream and she wanted to hear my voice. I do not know how she got my number. Anyway, I was happy and I can feel still the warmth of our conversation to this day.

In the United States, we really lived not far away: the Solzhenitsyns lived in Vermont, and we lived in Massachusetts. Nevertheless, I was embarrassed to impose myself on her, and as a result, to my great regret, we never saw each other until their departure from America. In the US I received the sad news that Natasha's Dima died tragically in 1994 in an accident.

Similar miracle never happened with Varya Blokhintsev: we lost each other and have not seen and talked since that summer in Koktebel. I found out from the Internet that Lyonya Blokhintsev became a professor, head of the department of the Research Institute of Nuclear Physics at the Faculty of Physics of Moscow State University. He is four years older than me, so he must be 90 years old now, if he is still alive. I do not know anything about their boys.

Concluding the chapter on our good days in Koktebel I am full of gratitude to both, Natasha, and Varya, for the fact that they treated my girl as their own daughter and gave us with her a very happy summer. I had wonderful vacation together with Galya. The rest of the of the summer time I was working in peace being sure that very nice people are taking care of my girl. She really was in good hands and she felt very comfortable. By the way, it was this summer, thank you, dear Natasha and Varya, I managed to complete and publish in the journal "Foreign Radioelectronics" "Dictionary of English terms on the use of digital computer systems" a very brief English-American terminology on the use of computers.

A WEDDING BEHIND THE BARBED WIRE

In the previous chapter I spoke with great warmth about Natasha Svetlova, now it is natural to tell about her close friend Arina Zholkovsky-Ginzburg. I got acquainted with Arina in the beginning of the 60-s, when she was the wife of Alik Zholkovsky. But that time somehow did not leave anything remarkable in my memory. For me my friendship with Arina begins from the time of her rapprochement with Alik Ginzburg in the mid-sixties.

Several generations of Alik Ginzburg's family had been victims of the red terror. In 1918 his grandfather was arrested and died in custody of a fabricated case. In the 20s, his grandmother had to spend a couple of years in Lubyanka (prison in Moscow). Alik himself was only 2 months old when his father was taken to custody and they killed him. Before I left Russia, three times he was arrested and served his term time after time in prisons and camps. I learned from Arina that he called himself a third-generation convict. Did not this noble man get too much? Alik only a year older than me, but the circumstances of the life of this most worthy citizen of Russia were such, that during fifty years of my life in Russia, we, unfortunately, have never met. The point is that we had many common friends, but most part of 14 years, starting, I think, from his acquaintance with Arina in 1965 up to his expulsion from Russia in 1979, Alik had spent in places of detention.

At some point in my rather intense communication with Arina there was so much about Alik that I began to think that we knew each other and had met more than once. So I found out that Alik's first arrest took place in 1960 before my acquaintance with Arina. Alik was only 23 and had prepared several self-published collections of poetry "Syntax". The collections included "criminal" poems by Brodsky, Okudzhava, Akhmadulina, Sapgir and other best poets in Russia. A large number of poems were confiscated during the search of his home, he was arrested, and soon he received 2 years in a labor camp as a punishment.

If I remember correctly, Arina and Alik met after his return from the camp, I think, in 1965, and at the end of 1966, they officially applied to register their marriage. From that time until the last day of Alik's life (he died in 2002 from heart failure with a severe form of camp tuberculosis) Arina was his support, faithful friend and helper in all his misfortunes with the Soviet authorities. Let me get back to their marriage: the registration of the marriage was planned for January 1967 and a week before Alik was arrested again. This time the occasion was to compile the White Book, a collection of facts about the arrest of writers Sinyavsky and Daniel in 1965. Ironically, he ended up later in the same Mordovia labor camp as Yuli Daniel. For both Yuli and Alik, it seems to me, this was a great stroke of luck.

In 2019, Novaya Gazeta in Moscow published an interview with Arina, in which she describes how Alik proposed to her.

> *He was trying to convince me to marry him for a year and a half. Finally, when I realized that the authorities were going to arrest him again, we filed the papers. But the conversation about our marriage happened before that. There is a trolleybus park near Miussky Square. Back then, it was famous for the fact that trolleybuses stayed there overnight to rest, but they did not close the doors. And you could sit there like in a café. That was what we did, and he was talking me into the marriage. He said, you know, it really would be great... You would be... And I was then such a university teacher, a young girl in high heels, you know, and he already was an experienced convict, not exactly a bohemian, well, partly, yes, of course. Exhibitions, meeting artists, and so on. He told me then: here you are going to create stability, and I am going to bring my share of anxiety to the family. I said, "That's a very tempting prospect!"*

From that time on Arina fought relentlessly with the authorities about her and Alik's marriage registration, about bringing him to the camp means of sustenance, and about very seldom allowed visits. It was during this time that I tried my best to help her. Arina lived in the southwest, as I did, which made our communication easier. I will briefly mention some of the projects that I worked on with Arina. It's been about fifty years since then, and I'm wildly pleased that I was able to participate in those projects back then.

In prison and in a camp in 1965–1966, Yuli Daniel wrote, from my point of view, a cycle of wonderful poems. Kostya Babitsky, talented, again from my point of view, set some of them to music. We liked these songs very much and often listened to them accompanied by guitar. I cannot help but bring here one of, it seems to me, the strongest verses of this cycle. The title of this poem was "Romance about the Motherland"!

> *My country, please, utter at least a word to me.*
> *I have no mean deeds or thoughts in my soul about you.*
> *I cannot believe that the slander will sever us,*
> *Sever so shamelessly and forever.*
>
> *Rocks are giving my dreams bleeding wounds,*
> *When I walked to you through the heat and the cold,*
> *I was walking with you. I was walking, and the cities*
> *Were floating to my eyes, like tears.*
>
> *I conceal neither evil thought,*
> *Nor any regrets about my fate.*
> *My country, utter a word,*
> *Because you know, I never lied to you.*
>
> *Because you know, I never throw my crushes on the scales*
> *And never broke my passion into fraction—*
> *I loved you so much, my Russia,*
> *Like, maybe, I never loved a woman.*
>
> *My country, touch me with the palm of your hand,*
> *So that I will never complain about my share,*
> *That I will never fall pressede by the weight of the cross.*
> *Here is my soul, blameless in front of you*

One stanza, however, in this poem is personally perplexing me. It is incomprehensible to me how someone can even compare feelings for the closest person in the world who gives you her life, and possibly the lives of your children, with feelings for a soulless country, and any country is soulless. This seems to me all the more unthinkable when we are talking about a country that has ruined millions of lives like this someone, and sometimes even better than this someone. No, I cannot agree with the author of the poem and I differ greatly from him in understanding of what a motherland is, what love is and what intimacy is.

When Alik happened to be in the same camp as Julius, many of us had a dream to record these songs as performed by Kostya on tape and somehow give the tape to Julius so that he could listen to his poems in the form of songs. This plan also arose because everyone knew that Alik was very handy and well versed in all sorts of electronics. Everybody in the camp turned to him about using an old tape recorder, which somehow happened to be there and which Alik fixed up. The legend tells that Alik fixed the tape recorder simply by chasing away the cockroaches living in it and by cleaning it well. The work on this and similar projects has always been in the apartment of Arina, and I spent there a lot of time with her. The plan was very simple. First, we recorded the whole Daniel -Babitsky songs cycle on a cassette recorder. Then, having noted the beginning and the end of Kostya's performance and unwinding reels, we carefully cut a suitable piece of tape and spun it tightly. The result is a very small cylinder, which was waiting unnoticed until handed over to Alik during a date with Arina. I cannot remember today exactly how it happened: most likely, it happened with the warmth of Arina's body during the private rendezvous. But it turned out!

Once a year Arina was entitled to a personal visit (1 day) and to a general visit (3 hours in the presence of a warden), but the authorities always tried to find a thousand reasons not to have such a visit. However, it was difficult to stop Arina: like a wolf-mother, she wrested from the Gulag administration what she was entitled to. In my opinion, Arina demonstrated unparalleled loyalty and support for the person she loved who found himself in the Soviet prisons. Just her courage and tenacity alone, with which she fought the authorities for about two years to register her marriage to Alik, caused then and continues to cause me infinite respect today. So many people around her advised her to give up and abandon the unrealistic plan to join Alik legally. Even Arina's parents and her lawyer were among those people. Arina did not even want to hear such advice. At that time, Arina was working at the Moscow State University, teaching foreigners Russian. University administration demanded of her to renounce Alik. She, of course, refused, and they kicked her out of the department. Three Academic Councils: first of the Department, then of the Faculty, then of the entire University for some reason had to discuss her relations with Alik. As a result, they showed humanity: she was not expelled from the university at all, but transferred to the "basement", to the storage room of the library. In the light of all these facts, her actions always seemed to me even more heroic than those of the Decembrists' wives.

As I remember, Arina did get a private date in 1968, and many friends helped her in preparation for that date. The songs of Daniel -Babitsky went to the camp, I think, just then. Of course, it was a very pleasant surprise for Julius Daniel, and Alik did only the necessary technical work on the other side of the barbed wire. With the same chance went to the camp also a pleasant surprise for Alik himself. The matter is that many friends empathized with Alik's epopee and tried their best to do something pleasant for him. I remember that someone got a bottle of matured cognac of rare quality and there was a problem how to bring the contents of such a valuable bottle to Alik. I do not remember who suggested such an ingenious and very unusual solution. We bought at a drugstore, I am sorry, condoms, and thoroughly washed them of all coating and powder. Then we used a double condom, for safety, as a soft gift bottle, filled with precious cognac and carefully closed this bottle. Although I was very curious, I was too shy then to ask Arina in what intimate places she had hidden this soft bottle. Anyway, Alik was able to appreciate the quality of such an extraordinary drink.

The story of Arina and Alik would be incomplete if I did not briefly recount the odyssey of their marriage registration. It seems to me that even such sub humans as the Gulag gang bosses were impressed by the courage and steadfastness of this couple in their seemingly hopeless struggle for their happiness. Arina pounded every doorstep of this nightmarish organization. When Alik was still in prison, they advised to wait until he was in the camp. When they took him to the camp, they told that she should have done it while he was in prison. These taunts continued until 1969, when they both reached the breaking point and decided to take the last desperate step: it was on May 16 that Alik has announced in the camp his hunger strike.

Astonishingly, several of his fellow camp mates, all political prisoners, have joined the hunger strike to support Alik. I would like to name these heroes: Valery Ronkin, Yuri Galanskov, Leonid Borodin and Vyacheslav Platonov. Those prisoners who could not go on hunger strike for health reasons (Juli Daniel) pelted the administration with letters, expressing their indignation. The hunger strike became a group protest. Here the authorities became alarmed. During those anxious days, Alik's campmate Juli Daniel was able to keep a sense of humor, which once again amazed me so pleasantly. He wrote a wonderful witty rhyme about the hunger strike and Arina:

> *Arina is certainly more expensive than Paris,*
> *The riddle of the comparison is easy and simple.*
> *The worth of Paris is the mass, and the worth of our Arina*
> *Is the Lenten fast.*

The verse refers to an expression *"Paris is worth the mass"* that became catchwords. The history attributes it to Henry of Navarre in connection with his decision in 1593 to adopt Catholicism to become King of France as Henry IV. Thus, the French Bourbon dynasty started. To me the easiness of politicians as Hery IV to change their religion is rather sad: he wanted the French crown and he became catholic. The poetical joke uses the play of words. The etymology of the word "mass" in Russian language is connected with the word "dinner" because the Liturgy was usually served before the dinnertime, and *"the Lenten fast" refers* to the hunger strike in the camp.

To punish Arina, as a human rights activist, Soviet authorities disconnected her home phone for rather long time. After about three weeks of hunger strike in the camp, this phone suddenly rang. The person on the other side of the line invited Arina to see General Kuznetsov at the Main Gulag Headquarters. Here is how Arina herself described the meeting. *"Smiling broadly, he holds out his hand to me and says: 'Well, congratulations, you have got your way.' He said this just in a way, as if he was giving his daughter in marriage."*

On the 21 of August, they appointed the registration, and Arina went to the camp with Alik's mother. This time she was allowed an exceptional "wedding" date of three days plus to take with her about 11 pounds of goodies for Alik! Arina vividly described how they prepared for this "wedding". According to her, inside such a huge scary country indifferent to its citizens, there existed "their own" little kind country. Inside the big and cruel Moscow, there existed "their own" little touchingly responsive Moscow. Therefore, all the wonderful people of this good country and good Moscow with their own rules of friendship and honor prepared Arina on such an important for her trip. Someone brought a jar of caviar, someone baked pies, someone fried cutlets. In addition, Arina received a list of Alik's friends among his campmates with the information what each of them liked: Roquefort cheese, special kinds of coffee, etc. Our friends helped her to get and prepare it all. The same circle of people got for the bride a white wedding dress to make everything as it should be. I remember well how happy I was to be among the inhabitants of the mentioned above good Moscow.

The deadline approached, and with huge rucksacks, Arina and her escorts set off on a difficult journey: first by regular train, then by narrow gauge railroad, and finally 20 km by bus. But the bus broke down and Arina reached the camp by a truck loaded with coal. The small house chosen for the marriage registration was on the territory of the camp zone just behind the entrance gate. It was also the same house, where family visits with prisoners took place. When Arina arrived at the camp, she found herself in this house, which with a funny name "house of assignation". It did not even occur to the camp organizers that in few European languages, including Russian, these two words stood for a brothel. I am able to mention here some of the details of what went on inside the house, thanks to the fact that Arina wrote them down in detail in her time. The description of hers reads today like a farce. The next few paragraphs are an abridged excerpt of her description.

> *In the specially allotted room, the camp personnel frisked our huge backpacks. Then I was told that I had to go to the red room named after Leni n. They brought Ginzburg there. When they entered the room with Alik, I almost fell down laughing. The camp rule for a private visit required that the convict had to change his clothes completely. The explanation was that you never know what one could hide in the seams... For this occasion there was one uniform for ALL people, a medium-sized one. Alik was short and very thin and therefore in this form he looked, well, very comically. In addition, as it was a prison uniform, so there were no belts, buttons, and laces on it, of course. Thus, my man in the prison uniform entered the room, and I met him in a white English dress. He was supporting his*

trousers with one hand, so they would not fall down, and with the other holding the shirt on his chest. The groom's first question to the bride was, "Don't you have a safety pin?" I, of course, had no safety pin, so the poor man, had to stand like this for the whole ceremony.

However, he did bring, and it was very touching, a bouquet of flowers. Usually convicts used to grow flowers in the summer in attempts to occupy themselves with something meaningful. The camp inspectors encouraged this activity, because before September 1, they would cut the flowers off, and their kids would go to school with these flowers. At this time there was only August 21 on the calendar and the convicts cut the flowers themselves. In general, the bouquet which Alik held was simply remarkable: it was made of small bouquets from different groups of convicts: a bouquet from Lithuanians, a bouquet from the Latvians, a bouquet from Ukrainians etc. So the groom showed up, and he managed somehow to support with his hands the ghastly clothes, but also to hold a luxurious bouquet.

The registrar was the head of the special unit in the camp, a scary, huge woman with several gold teeth. When she opened her jaws, it was creepy. They tried to reproduce the ritual of a Soviet marriage ceremony in the registry office, which looked, of course, insanely ridiculous. Finally, this woman with gold teeth stood up, she was very moved by the whole story, and said: "May the feeling that brought you here stays with you for life". (!?)

The wardens had no time yet to finish registering when the voices began to echo from behind the fence, such friendly male voices. The camp was not very big, but there must have been about seventy people in it, so the chorus was loud enough. They were declaiming loudly: "Bitter! Bitter!" (In several Slavic countries, Russia including, there is a wedding tradition according to which at some moment of the celebration all gests pretend, that vine and food became very bitter. To remove this bitterness the newly wedded have to kiss each other.) *Alik became very animated and said, "Bitter—they shouting, it's time to kiss!" The gloomy woman with gold teeth said: "You have waited a long time, you shall have to wait some more" and she went on with the "ceremony."*

One way or another, three-year struggle with the authorities ended in victory: Arina and Alik officially became husband and wife. After the 1969 registration, I had only one more episode of contact with Arina shortly before Alik's release in 1972. Special order of the court did not allow Ginzburgs to return to Moscow, they could settle no closer than 101 km from the capital. Friends helped them to get a house in the town of Tarusa and, by the time, Alik returned, to try to arrange this house. There was no toilet in the house and I was on the construction team to build it. I saw that as an honor. I am not joking about the honor, as I remember well that the brigade consisted almost entirely of the refined intellectuals, many of them had PhDs and were scholars. I participated only once in my life in such a high-ranking "Saturday work". The name was for the soviet tradition founded by V.Lenin: day of unpaid labor, usually on a Saturday. Originally, it was voluntary, and it had the idea of uniting the revolutionary minded masses and promoting the ideas of socialism through labor. At my time, it became obligatory and everyone refusing to participate would have problems.

Unfortunately, I never met Alik and never saw Arina after this "Saturday work". Our paths were somehow parted. But I know that their ordeal in the Soviet Union did not end there. In 1977, Alik again was arrested for his active participation in the dissident activity and was sentenced to 8 years of a forced labor camp. But in two years, in 1979, the Soviet authorities suddenly decided to expel him from the country and deprive him of citizenship. They did it by exchanging five political prisoners, Alik among them, for two Soviet spies arrested in the United States. Such expulsion once again demonstrated the bigotry of the authorities: neither the prisoners knew where they were going before arriving in America, nor their relatives got informed about the deportation. They learned the news when the deportees had already been in America for several days. Even that was not enough for such not-humans. Arina having learnt about the decision of the authorities has rushed to liquidate the dwelling and to make out documents on departure for herself, mother of Alik and children. At this time, she received the last blow in this dreadful country: the authorities would not give permission for her adopted son Sergei to leave the country. Arina postponed her departure for several months because of this, and she could not get anything done. She left the boy in Moscow, and he soon died under circumstances unknown to me. In 1980, Arina reunited with Alik in America. The authorities did their black business: they took the son away from his mother forever.

MY PACIFISM STORY

Most full-time universities in the USSR included a compulsory military education program and studying at such an institution exempted students from the military draft. Graduates of such universities received the title of junior reserve officer, so the successful completion of such an institute spared students from compulsory military service in peacetime. I was studying by correspondence and had no such privilege. My military rank on my military ID card was " regular soldiery, untrained " I could afford such a luxury, because as a child I was very sickly and had been registered in a neurological clinic. This gave me an exemption from obligatory draft into the army. With my pacifist views, I appreciated this.

In most of the civilized western countries with compulsory military service, the law allows anyone who cannot serve in the army for ethical or religious reasons to substitute the military service with civilian service. There is even a name for such people: "conscientious objectors." Nothing like that existed in Soviet Russia. Although there was no article in the Soviet criminal code punishing pacifist views, Soviet authorities considered such views as anti-patriotic and therefore anti-Soviet. Soviet lawyers were very inventive in finding ways to imprison people. Pacifists were imprisoned under "parasitism," "evasion of conscription into the armed forces," "malignant hooliganism," "anti-Soviet agitation and propaganda", "slandering the state and social system" etc.

After I graduated from the institute, in the early 1960s, I was summoned by the military enlistment office. IPM&CT was an academic institute, and at that time, I worked as a junior researcher. At my meeting, the military commissar made a speech. *"Yuri! We respect your education and your specialty (computers). If, God forbid, a war breaks out, no, not now, of course, but if war breaks out, we would like our army to make full use of your knowledge and your abilities."* These words made me extremely wary. "No doubt," I replied, *"if war breaks out, of course I will do all I can to help the army. You need not worry about it at all, and there is nothing to be done for that."* "You are not quite right in that respect," continued the military officer, *"we would like you* to become a reserve officer, and then we can use you more efficiently." This alarmed me and I went into a long explanation of how very busy I was, and how work plus a small child left me little time to improve my military qualifications. The military commissar continued: "*Please, Yuri, do not worry, nothing will be required of you. We will prepare all the necessary documents, after which we will ask you to come again to obtain a new military card.*" Having said goodbye to such a surprisingly polite military inspector, I went home in total confusion, sure, that something was wrong. I could not believe it, but all my worries were in vain. A couple of weeks later I was called up again, congratulated, shook hands, and was ceremonially presented with my military ID card as a junior lieutenant in the reserves! They took me aback by this unexpected promotion in my military career, and I still suspected some sort of intrigue. A line from a thieves' song came to mind:

> *The authorities, than the prosecutor were shaking my hand,*
> *After this, they put me under heavy supervision!*

However, this time nobody put me under supervision. I was beginning to get used to my new military rank, though I was a little sorry to give up my status as an untrained private. Further events confirmed that my regrets were not in vain.

A 1967 law introduced the conscription of reserve officers younger than 30 years of age. In 1967, I was 29 years old and so came under that law. I was at risk of the draft into the army for 2–3 years. It was terrifying and I did not know who could help me. Few friends told me that if I was a graduate student, the recruitment office could give me a deferment, and by graduation I would be older than 30. I new, even the universities give an exemption from the draft, then the graduate schools should do the same, of course. Fortunately, the director of the Institute, Segey Lebedev, was an amazing person, and I felt comfortable to come to him with any of my personal problems.

The next day I was already in his office and described him everything. I said to him that I would rather go to prison for evasion of military duties than to the army. Even my extreme intentions Sergei Lebedev accepted with understanding and sympathy. The result surpassed all my expectations. When he learned of my situation, he helped me become a postgraduate student at his Institute of Precise Mechanics and Computer Technology (IPM&CT) of the Academy of Sciences of the USSR. It was unbelievable. In such a terribly anti-Semitic country, a Jew had been accepted into a daytime graduate school in a matter of days, bypassing all the bureaucratic rules and the Party Bureau!?

As soon as I received a certificate of enrollment in graduate school, I flew like on wings to the military commissar, anticipating his surprise and distress. However, another blow waited for me. The military commissar met me with unperturbed calm: *"Your graduate school will not run anywhere,"* he told me in a fatherly way. *"Come back in a few years from the army and start your studies then."* Completely distraught by this turn of events, I crawled back to my Institute. Luckily, it was very close to the military registration and enrollment office. I managed to see Lebedev again that same day. *"For God's sake,"* I begged him, *"please hide me anywhere from these monsters"*

And my savior did it. A week later, I left home on a business trip to a military unit about 25 miles from Moscow where one of our laboratories was doing important work. A computer center was located within that gave me access to a powerful computer where I could work on my dissertation. 1967 was ending. The draft applied to officers under 30, so I just had to wait this out until March 1968. Family members learned from me that I was on a long secret business trip. I asked them not to respond in any way to any mail that came in my name and to save it for my return.!

I need to say that this escape from military service was only possible because of the complete understanding and love of my mother-in-law, who selflessly took over ALL the care of my little girl. For as long as I live, I will never forget her devotion. This was not easy for me, and the hardest part was the separation from my Little Drop. I was determined that I should see her at least once a week. On the other hand, I was paranoid that if someone from the neighborhood saw me entering the apartment, this person might report me (Soviet habituation!) to the Military Commissar. Therefore, I always arrived after dark and, with my collar up and my hat pulled low over my head, I would sneak like a thief into my own apartment. If I saw anybody in front of the door, I would usually wait round the corner until the way opened. Galyusha was asleep at that time, of course. I would go quietly to her crib, stroke her, and kiss her, and then, having received a full account of her life, would disappear the same way I appeared.

I have to say right away that this escape from military service was only possible thanks to the complete understanding and love of my mother-in-law, Leah Ravich, who selflessly took over ALL the care of my little girl during a long year. For as long as I live, I will never forget her devotion. This was not easy for me, and the hardest part was the separation from my Little Drop. I was determined that I should see her at least once a week. On the other hand, I was paranoid that if someone from the neighborhood saw me entering the apartment, they might report me (Soviet habituation!) to the Military Commissar. Therefore, I would always arrive after dark and, with my collar up and my hat pulled low over my head, I would sneak like a thief into my own apartment. If I saw anybody in front of the door, I would usually wait round the corner until the way opened. At the time of my visits Galyusha was asleep, of course. I would go quietly to her crib, stroke her, and kiss her, and then, having received a full account of her life, would disappear the same way I came.

To relieve the tension, I will describe one comical episode from my life in the military unit. The computer center where I worked was in a multistory building, on the third floor. The whole building consisted of several sections, floors or parts of a floor, each with a different level of secrecy. A pass for each person working in the building marked the sections to which that person might go. At the borders between the sections, there were soldiers who checked the passes. It was my Jewish luck that the section on the third floor where my computer was located did not include the men's room. The closest precinct with a toilet allowed by my pass was on the sixth floor. The office next door to mine had a men's room with the door just 10 feet from the guard post. What happened was this. Each time, shifting from foot to foot, I would approach the post and beg the soldier: "*Listen, guy, take pity, and allow me to pee here. I cannot make it to the sixth floor.*" Often, the soldier did take pity on me, waved his hand and said, "*Well, go fast!*"

Today I wonder how I was so lucky, but my plan did work. The enlistment office lost me, and after several attempts with summons commanding me to appear, they gave up. At the beginning of March, I returned home, with the lines by Mayakovsky in his poem "Cloud in Pants" in my head:

Expressing my joy so loudly that the whole world could hear me,
I marsh — as happy as a clam,
I am thirty years old!

In all honesty, my happiness was limited, for I knew well that the Soviet authorities could do anything and, if they wanted to, would find a way to lay their long hands on me. I was right, they did. Ten years later, in 1977, we tried to leave Russia and the authorities gladly remembered my staying in a military unit and used it as an excuse to refuse to let us out of the country for 11 years!!!

THE HOUSE THAT WE BUILT

The title of this chapter is inspired by the "This Is the House That Jack Built": a popular English nursery rhyme and cumulative volk tale. An ancient wisdom says, *"A man should first build a house and plant a vineyard, and then marry. (Talmud, Sotah, 44b)* As a very young man, I read this advice and it stuck in my head. Unfortunately, I married early for the first time (23 years old), and it was already too late for me to literally fulfill both the first and second requirements. Who knows, maybe that's why my first marriage was such a failure. I figured, however, better to fulfill those requirements later than never. Since then, the desire to build a house has never left me.

With my love to wooden buildings, I have already mentioned that I wandered a lot in the north of Russia, mainly in the Arkhangelsk region. There I was utterly fascinated by the log structures of the 12th to 18th centuries, built without the use of a single nail! The north of Russia is very rich in wood and people continued to build log houses for themselves. In every trip whenever I passed constructors building a new log house in a village, I would stop and carefully watch how they do it, and sometimes I asked the workers dozens of silly questions. As a result, it seemed to me that I mostly knew what to do and how to do it. Gradually, the dream of building just such a log cabin was growing inside me more and more. As for the vineyard, I did not yet have a clear idea of how and when

I would be able to do it. I was saving that for later. Looking ahead, I cannot wait to tell you that when we bought a house in Boston in the 90s, I built a pergola and planted vines on either side of it!

It was clear that I would not be able to accomplish the task of building a log house on my own: I could not carry even a small log by myself. I had to find a partner and an enthusiast among my friends. I was very lucky: I managed to involve Kostya Babitsky, the handiest person in my entourage, into my idea. I could not have made a better choice: Kostya had golden hands, and he was even more of an idealist than I was. I myself was handy, and Kostya's golden hands were of a much higher gold standard than mine were. The summer of 1968 was passing, Galka was 6 years old, and I, of course, planned to take her on this expedition. Her mother was not usually eager to spend the summer with us, much less take part in such construction adventures. To my great joy, Kostya's wife Tanya Velikanov wanted to come with us, and she was going to take all three of her children with her. So my Galka had a wonderful company. Besides, her close friend Lena Smorgunov also wanted to go with us. I have already said that I always enjoyed wandering through the forests and mountains with these two women.

After I mentioned Lena Smorgunov let me say a few words about Lena's mother. Her name was Praskovya. A simple Russian woman, she was an amazing example of kindness, modesty and dedication. On top of that, she was a wonderful cook. When any of Lena's friends dropped by for any reason, she would always try to treat that person to something delicious. On most of my and Lena's trips it turned out that Praskovya baked something for the participants. Getting ahead of myself, I would like to tell you a funny episode. When we went to build a house up north, she also baked and sent us something wonderfully delicious. At the first opportunity to send her a telegram, I composed the following text:

> *Holding back moans of raptures*
> *We bow low to you.*
> *When we will have again*
> *A chance to eat similar delights?!*

When we returned to Moscow, we learned that Praskovya, having received the telegram, got quite agitated. "*I thought you were very ill (moans!) and hungry (chance to eat),*" she said. This is an example of how jokes do not always hit the mark.

Kostya and I prepared the tools for our project needed to build a house. All the tools, naturally, were hand-held, for there were no, of course, electrical outlets in the forest. This, to my delight, brought us closer to the Russian artisans of kind old days.

Since I always tried to take my Galya with me on hikes, I had a blue dream of getting her a storm jacket, a hiking jacket with a hood. A little backpack she already had. Nobody could even dream to buy at that time such thing for a child in Moscow. I decided in preparation for our trip to the north to try to sew such a storm jacket for my girl. Someone I knew brought from Europe, though for an adult, just the jacket I wanted: it had a large pocket on its belly, opening upward, reminding a kangaroo's poach. I carefully measured my little girl, and then this jacket and, proportionally reducing all sizes, prepared a pattern. Then I got, which was not easy, a piece of tarpaulin, of the protective color similar to the material my own storm jacket was made of. I had an old Singer sewing machine from my mother, with which I had a tender friendship. I set to work. I was passionate about the project and the work was progressing well. By the time our construction plans took concrete shape, the storm proof jacket was ready. I was quite pleased with the result. I still have a lovely photo of those days, taken from the back and which has become my favorite. I am walking hand in hand with my Little Drop down a small village street somewhere in the area where we were building a house. Both in tarpaulin gear, both having rucksacks, and the road goes far away. This photograph is today in my living room and I often approach it, look at it an, like in A. Brushtein's novel, warm-warm memories come back to me.

Favorite photo on the hike at the north of Russia with my Little Drop

The plan was like this. The first, we hoped, shorter phase of the trip was to end with the selection of a location. With the abundance of lakes in the area, we hoped to find a high enough shore of a picturesque lake for our house. All the rest of our vocation time we wanted to devote to the constructing work. Everyone agreed that Kostya and I would spend most of our time at the construction site, while the women and children would gather mushrooms, pick berries, fish, cook and walk around. As a law-abiding person, I was somewhat concerned about the legal side: getting permission from the authorities to build the house and to use the forest trees for this purpose.

It was hard to believe, but everything turned out exactly as we wanted. In a remote place, about 7 miles to the nearest village, we found the lake of a rare beauty with a high rather dry shore. The place was especially attractive to us because close to it we discovered a typical result of the Soviet mismanagement: dozens of big spruce trees sawn down by someone and already dried up. They were piled on the ground very close to the lake shore. There were more than would be needed for our log cabin, and certainly more than we would need for firewood. We set up our tents and first thing we did was to explore the nearest village. We found out that it was about two hours on foot walk! Everything was adding up perfectly.

The village had a small grocery store and a post office, but no telegraph office. The main luck was that a local forester lived in this village. We tracked him down and talked to him. Of course, the wild idea of Muscovites surprised him a lot, but he was nice and friendly. What a pity, nothing has survived in my memory to describe him as a person. I only remember that there were many small children running around him, all snotty for some reason. Of course, he laughed at our question about permission, *"Go ahead guys, no one cares!"* We learned from him, too, a couple of years ago a geological expedition was clearing a place for a helicopter to land and they cut down the spruces. *"They are of no use to anybody,"* said the forester, *"they will rot away all the same. At least hunters and anglers will be*

I am at the construction site

able to spend a night in your log cabin". How can I not say, going back again to Peter Weil's idea of his book "Poems for me", I felt that we found a place exactly for me!

We brought with us most of the food products, such as cereals, canned meat, tea and coffee, without counting on the village shops, where at that time there was not much to find except bread and vodka. However, once we happened to be in the village, we loaded our rucksacks with some things that still were to our liking, and, satisfied with our negotiations with the ranger, we went back to walk our 7 miles to our lake.

The next day already, we began to work. First, the dimensions of our house were determined. The maximum length of the logs that Kostya and I could carry turned out to be 20 feet. Since we wanted the house to be rectangular, we put the dimensions of the house at 20 by 19 feet. The long side of the house faced the lake, and there was a about 7 feet bench planned on the outside of that wall, and an oblong window above it. There were many huge boulders in the water near the shore. With great difficulty, we dragged and rolled up four of these boulders. We laid one of these boulders as a base under each of the corners of the house. From the façade, we buried a silver Russian ruble under one of the two, someone advised me to do this for good luck. We, like all local builders, decided to use dry moss as insulation between the timbers.

After this, the serene happy days went on. Kostya and I worked like clockwork from sunrise until sunset, hurrying to put the house under the roof before we got home. It was physically demanding but joyful work. We were making breaks only for eating and talking with our children and lovely women. We saw that they felt good too, and it added to our strength. I do not think there are builders either in Russia or in America who work that hard. Our log cabin was slowly but surely rising. However, it soon became clear that we would not be able to complete the construction in one season; there remained a lot of work to do on the floor, roof, door and window. It was not without pleasure that we began to discuss the possibility of continuing the construction the following summer.

I must say that Tanya was very good with children. She knew a lot about the forest and its gifts, and the children enjoyed listening to her stories about herbs, mushrooms and berries. She somehow cleverly managed to organize them into any useful work. My

Galya very much liked to collect and clean mushrooms together with Tanya. Tanya laughed: my girl got these tasks as a reward for good behavior. About fifty years has passed, and my Galiusha remained "mushroom-phile" up to now: very much loves everything about mushrooms: to pick up wild mushrooms, to cook mushroom dishes, and to treat guests with them. I am only feeling pity that she does not enjoy drinking a shot glass of liquor with mushrooms.

Tanya Velikanov had a special talent to cope with children's illnesses and even injuries. Once, her son Fedya, incompetently waving a sharp axe, cut his head. The wound was quite deep, and although I am not panicked, but I was terrified of what we will do. Where and how far away the nearest hospital was, we had no idea. Amazing how calmly and skillfully Tanechka dealt with this surgical problem, but, moreover, managed to convey to us somehow her calmness and confidence that everything necessary she did. It appeared to be true: Fedya's wound, indeed, healed quite soon.

Time flew by, and it seemed that in the second half of August the end of our leave from work was approaching. No one wanted to return home, we felt that nothing good awaited us in Moscow. Tanya was the first to run out of her vacation. She decided in advance to send a telegram to her boss with the request to prolong the vacation for a week without pay. A 7 miles "walk" to the post office was required. A surprise awaited her there. There was also about seven miles between the post office and the telegraph office, and to receive and to send telegrams they were using a horse. The poor horse got sick and could not deliver Tanya's telegram for sending. Nice postal worker promised Tanya to solve her problem within a week.

It was the twentieth day of August 1968. All we managed to do was raise our log cabin walls to the level of the roof. We could not stay any longer. It was very sad to part with our cabin, but we had to go. We folded up our camp on the lake and headed back to Moscow. We even stashed some things away until next summer, confident that we would definitely come back to continue building our cabin.

INDEPENDENT BUOY-MAN

I do no remember exactly, I think, we arrived in Moscow on August 23. There we learned terrible news that on the night of August

20th-21st Warsaw Pact tanks led by the Soviets (Albania, Romania and East Germany did not participate) had entered Prague, the capital of Czechoslovakia, to suppress the social and political reforms in the country that everybody knows as the "Prague Spring". Soviet media cited a call for help from unnamed representatives as the cause of the "fraternal intervention". Leader of the Country, the initiator of the reforms A.Dubček and some of his supporters found themselves in the Soviet custody. We were all dispirited. It was a shock for all of us, but especially for Kostya, who had a close cooperation and friendship with Czech linguists. Kostya had been to Prague and loved the city very much.

On August 25, at exactly 12 noon, eight people came to Red Square to the historic monument of the Execution Ground and unfurled posters: *"We are losing our best friends"*, *"Long live free and independent Czechoslovakia!"*), *"Shame on the invaders!"*, *"Hands off Czechoslovakia!"*, *"For your and our freedom!"*, *"Freedom for Dubcek!"* Here are the names of eight heroes who condemned the Soviet aggression: Konstantin Babitsky, Tanya Baev, Larisa Bogoraz, Natalia Gorbanevskaya with the Czechoslovak flag in her hands, Vadim Delaune, Vladimir Dremlyuga, Pavel Litvinov and Viktor Feinberg.

There was an interesting historic detail. Before the demonstration, these eight people met together to discuss the plan. Seeing that, there were too few of them, some were suggesting to cancel the demonstration. Then Larisa Bogoraz said: *"OK, I will go alone."* *"Being a gentleman, I cannot let a lonely lady go to such a thing,"* said Kostya and took Larisa by the arm. The others followed these two.

Later I learned about the history of the slogan "For your and our freedom!", which was in the hands of Kostya. This slogan first appeared at a patriotic demonstration, held in Warsaw on January 25th 1831. The demonstration was in support of the Russian Decembrists revolt in Saint Petersburg in December 1825. Since then, it has become a popular political motto of Poland. It is believed that the author of the slogan was Joachim Lelewel, a Polish historian of the 18th – 19th centuries. The completely original motto sounded like *"In the name of God, for our and your freedom!"*

Within few minutes secret police rushed to the demonstrators and all of them were arrested. The protesters managed to convince the investigators that 21-year-old Tanya Baev did not participate in the rally, but simply happened to be nearby. As a result, they released her. Later, Tanya Baev described these terrible minutes as follows:

> ... 6–7 men in civilian clothes are running from the mausoleum, they all seemed tall to me, 26–30 years old. They flew in with shouts: "They sold themselves for dollars!" Then they pulled the slogans out of the hands of the protesters, after a minute of confusion, also little flag. One of them, shouting "Kill the Jews!", began to kick Feinberg in the face with his feet. Kostya tries to cover him with his body. Blood! I jump up in horror. Another man was beating Pavlik with a bag.

All demonstrators, including Kostya, were arrested. In October 1968, the Moscow City Court found him guilty of "slandering the Soviet system" and "group actions grossly violating public order", and sentenced him to 3 years of exile, which he served in the Komi ASSR. Before sending him into exile, they held him in Krasnopresnenskaya prison. The authorities faced some difficulties with Feinberg's sentence. Attackers knocked out all his front teeth in Red Square, and showing the man in the court for this reason was undesirable. The authorities found the way out of the situation in sending Feinberg to a SPECIAL psychiatric hospital. The court has made this decision without the presence of the accused and without the right to appeal to a higher court.

I would like to draw readers attention to the peculiar popularity of the adjective "special" in the Soviet Union (SPECIAL forces, SPECIAL department, SPECIAL hospital, etc.). The country's rulers used it mainly for their structures, which had right to violate existing laws. For example, special psychiatric hospitals were engaged in "curing allergic reaction" to the Soviet regime. As a result, "doctors" in the hospital declared Feinberg insane and forcibly sent him to the Leningrad mental hospital, where he was

That is how Kostya looked on August 25, 1968

for 4 years. It seems to me that such "medical" institutions were worse for an intelligent "patient" than prisons and correctional camps.

I have often wondered why it happened, that I absolutely do not remember my trip to visit Kostya, in exile in the Komi ASSR. Probably because Kostin's arrest and exile from Moscow left me in a state of deep shock. By that time, I had already read a lot about the horrors of the Gulag or heard many stories of acquaintances and friends. However, these were explosions at a distance, and here the bomb exploded in the immediate vicinity of me personally. In addition, it has happened right after the serene days of building a house in the Arkhangelsk region.

When Kostya returned to Moscow from exile he was a completely different person. I invariably started seeing a breakdown in him, both physical and mental. It showed me that the demonstration, arrest and exile can break even such a strong person as Kostya was. This impression was greatly facilitated by a very sad event for me: Kostya's break with Tanya Velikanov. After his return from exile, they no longer lived together. Fortunately, they kept respectful and even friendly relations, and I continued to meet with both, but with Kostya less often. Neither in my heart nor in my head did it fit how it was possible to leave such a woman as Tanya. But, on the other hand, I'm not sure how I myself would have coped with what fell on Kostya.

In one of my meetings with Kostya, I, of course, started a conversation about our cabin in the north. By the way, at the same time I caught myself thinking that I myself had never even once remembered about it during these tense years. Nevertheless, Kostya's answer upset me very much. *"Yuri,"* he said, *"I do not play toys anymore!"* He has changed a lot in this too. These weeks have never been a toy for me. To this day, these are some of the most important and happy times in my life. This month, I think, was also extremely important for my Galya. Although the construction took too much time and energy from me, leaving not enough for personal contact with her, what she received from life on the lake in human terms is difficult to overestimate.

After his release from exile, the country, which Kostya loved so ardently, renounced him, expelled him from the society. He found himself transferred into the outcast people group. In Moscow, he could not get ANY job, nothing to say about his favorite specialty: linguistics. Our good friend Miroslava Kikot worked at that time in the museum of A. N. Ostrovsky in the village of Shchelykovo, Kostroma region. Thanks to her, it was possible to settle Kostya in this village and to give him the unskilled work. In the beginning it was the job of a carpenter and later of a stoker. Is it not sad when this happens to a person who received a double higher education? Kostya had diplomas of the Institute of Communications and of the Faculty of Philology of the University. Before arrest, he has worked for years at the forefront of Russian linguistics. However, Kostya himself rejoiced in Shchelykovo's Berendey forests. His attitude to resettlement in the wilderness of the Kostroma region remind me of Lermontov's lines:

> *Farewell, unclean Russia,*
> *Land of slaves, land of masters.*
> *Farewell, blue uniforms*
> *Together with the people, who obey them.*
> *Maybe over the ridge of the Caucasus*
> *I will hide from your pashas,*
> *I will hide from their all-seeing eyes,*
> *Hide from their all-hearing ears.*

Kostya took refuge in the small village of Kudryaevo not far from Ostrovsky's estate. People in those years were fleeing from starving villages, and it was not difficult either to find an abandoned house or to buy a house for a pittance. Friends helped him find such a house. He put it in order, built furniture by himself, took a big dog, mongrel by name Marik. The dog had always followed Kostya, who became very fond of his four-legged friend. Kostya brought his linguistic file cabinet to his house in the hope that he could return to his favorite activities in the quietness of the village. He also tried then to translate Romanian poetry.

Everyone wanted to think that somehow things were getting better in the life of this rebellious man. Unfortunately, that was not the case! Some time later Marik fell terminally ill with rectal cancer. Under the description of friends from Kudryaevo, Kostya was trying to do something with him up to the last, categorically refusing to put him to sleep, considering it treachery to give his friend in strange hands. When the dog's suffering became unbearable, Kostya took out his gun and shot Marik dead himself. I do not know anyone who would dare to take such a step: a step very much in the spirit of Kostya.

Apparently, loneliness was hard for him. He put his eye on a museum worker named Valya. It was not long before Valya gave birth to his baby girl, and he got even more to worry about. I personally was very upset by this his step, as many of our mutual friends. In the first place, because we all knew Tanya Velikanov too well and involuntarily compared the two women. For me, there was no second person, like Tanya, and will never be. I do not want to say anything negative about Valya and, most likely, her joining Kostya improved his life. However, as a result Kostya distanced from us: Valya did not belong to our circle of people. As Yunna Morits had once told my Tanya about one of their mutual acquaintance, *"What do you want from him, he has a different brain group?"*

A little later there was trouble again. I do not remember, in 1979 or 1980 a fire broke out in Kostya's house. Thank God, no one was hurt. Kostya himself was at home, and he never understood how it happened. Everything burnt to the ground, including his books and the file cabinet he had been working on for years. Some friends familiar with the situation in Kudryaevo said it was arson. It was easy for me personally, familiar with the ways of the Soviet authorities, to believe this. However, I do remember well the words of Kostya in our conversation after the fire: *"It was a reminder to me from above that one should accumulate things not on the earth but in the sky!"* Again, typical Kostya. Such was the sad end to his last attempts to do what he loved.

After some time he and Valya found another house in the village of Tverdovo. However, in the last decade, it seems to me, he has changed a lot, in particular, he abandoned his desire to live in silence. They would only spend the summer months in Tverdovo, and would come to Moscow for the winter. For me, the 1980s were a time of desperate struggle for permission to leave Russia. Kostya never supported my decision to leave the country. As a result we became estranged and saw each other only a few times in Moscow and in 1988 I left Russia for good and the connection disappeared completely. All I know is that his health was deteriorating rapidly and he developed nightmarish sclerosis. He would go out to the shop and forget where he was going.

Kostya's daughter Natasha posted her memories of her father on the Internet. There she recalled her favorite very sad Kostya's verse, which I forgot about when I wrote these lines. Thank you, dear Natasha, for reminding me. I went back to that place and added these lines from Kostya, which I think say a lot about him and about life in general. Unfortunately, I cannot exactly date when he wrote it. I am sure that this poem he wrote most likely, in Shchelykovo, when his life was already ruined.

> It is time to return home. It is time to get out to freedom,
> It is about a time to return my share of a human
> Back to the earth, back to the earth.
> Our planet is black, red, and scary,
> We conduct unequal fight, unequal fight.
> But all that was loved and sung,
> All, connected here with the spirit and with the light,
> I shall take with me, I shall take with me!

I want to express my dissenting opinion here. My Kostya, I think, made a mistake in the last three lines of that so special verse. He thought that when he will leave us, he would be able to take with him ALL that was *"loved and sung,"* that was in him *"connected with the spirit and with the light"*. However, it seems to me impossible, it does not work that way in life. Kostya was, in my opinion, a very significant person. Significant people spread something lightfull and spiritual around them, and that falls on those around them and sometimes penetrates into these people. I have been fortunate enough to meet several significant people in my life. After EVERY meeting with such a person, when I parted with him, I took away something of his spirit and his light. So was it with Kostya. Luckily, because we communicated with him quite a lot, I got quite a lot. With Kostya's departure, of course, a lot went away, but a lot continues to live inside me and with me today.

In the context of this verse, I would like to remind you that Kostya was not the first who refused the "harmony" of our cruel world and wished to return the ticket to the Creator. Back in 1879,

Fyodor Dostoyevsky in his novel "The Brothers Karamazov", said with the Ivan's mouth, "*It is not that I, Aliosha, do not believe in God, I only would like to return him respectfully the ticket.*" After this, in 1939, Marina Tsvetaeva in her poem "O tears in my eyes..." came to a similar thought:

> *Oh, black mountain,*
> *That obscured the whole world!*
> *It is time, it is time, yes, it is time*
> *To return to the Creator my ticket back.*

I cannot refrain myself from comparing Kostya with Dostoevsky and Tsvetaeva. He saw clearly, no less than his great predecessors did, how *"black, red, and scary"* the planet is, how sometimes it is not possible on this unhappy planet to preserve all connected *"with the spirit and with the light"*. Yet, unlike them, he was a dreamer, he, in his departure, could not resign himself to the fact that what was dearest to him remained on our sinful earth.

The last GOOD news about Kostya that I heard back already in America, was the news from the Czech Republic in 1990 that Chech authorities awarded to Konstantin Babitsky honorary citizenship of the city of Prague. How wonderful that Kostya lived to see this day! What a pity I could not have hugged him on that day! On September 14, 1993, he passed away. He was only 64 years old. His memorial service was in the Moscow Temple of Elijah the Prophet of the Ordinary. It is interesting that it was in this church that Natasha Svetlov was married with Alexander Solzhenitsyn. Kostya's burial was at the Golovinsky cemetery in Moscow. Before revolution the cemetery was next to the Golovinsky monastery, which was destroyed during the Soviet era. I would like to think that Kostya did not know that he would find his resting place at the site of one of the many atrocities committed by the Soviet authorities.

In conclusion of this chapter about Kostya Babitsky, I would like again to thank fate for the fact that it brought me into close contact with such an extraordinary person, who has influenced me greatly and from whom I have learned so much.

THE IMMORAL HUSBAND

There are very few people among my friends, for whom I have such mixed feelings as Liosha Gladky. Professor of mathematics of the Novosibirsk University, he started coming to Moscow as a friend and colleague of Igor Melchuk in 1969. At that time, he and Igor were working on a book called "Elements of Mathematical Linguistics". He attracted me by the breadth of his education, including the humanities, and his interest in languages. I was pleased and interested in mixing up with him. Apparently, my wife was much more attracted to him than I was. It did not take long that Renata started explaining to everyone around her, including me, how sad that Liosha lives with his wife who had nothing in common with him. I was not sure how she came to this conclusion without ever meeting her. Living with an unloved woman, she insisted, was immoral. It seems to me that Liosha was a nice and kind man, and he simply could not withstand such an attack and succumbed to her sermons. His family lived in Novosibirsk scholars' settlement and he taught at Novosibirsk University. In some time, it seems to me now not without the help of Renata, Liosha left his family in Novosibirsk and moved to Kalinin (now Tver) where he got a professorship at Kalinin University. This way he came closer to Moscow, which made it easier to him working with Igor, so the move contributed a lot to the success of such cooperation.

Who really was happy with the move, was Renata. Without saying a word to me, she arranged with my good friend and colleague, Lena Lander, for Igor and Liosha to stay at her dacha in Mamontovka and work in quietness on their book. The Landers used their dacha only in summer, and all the rest of the time, nobody lived there. She voluntarily offered herself for a role of a housekeeper; she fed and served them so that both of them could focus on their scientific work. It was sort of her job and Igor, as her boss, I assume, approved this. To be honest, her eagerness embarrassed me a little, but I could not even in a bad dream think about where all this was going. After all, Liosha had three children, and she had such a beautiful daughter.

Anyway, Renata contributed to the progress of the work on the book until its successful publication at the end of 1969. Some of my friends tried to draw my attention to the fact that the situation was becoming unhealthy, but I naively dismissed all their suspicions for a long time. It took me a while to believe what my eyes had now seen. What kind of "morality" could demand to deprive Liosha's underage children of their father and our 7-year-old girl of her mother? Also, how can a woman, a mother, be the bearer of such "morality"? It turned out that she could!

Things moved quickly, and in 1970, I think, Renata announced that she could not live without Liosha and intended to join him. From then on, they spent more and more time together, and she weekly started to spend a few days with him in Kalinin. For me the most difficult period of my life began. What had happened, according to my naïve notions, could not and should not ever happen. It took me several years to get rid of this bitterness. Maybe it is strange, but the departure of my girl's mother only strengthened my love for Galyusha and, I think, even brought us closer.

In this connection, I want to tell about one episode from that time. My little girl was eight years old and of course, she knew what was going on. One Sunday we went on a camping trip together with her in the Moscow region, where there were also Igor and Lidochka with their daughter Sveta, Galka's age. As for Igor, he was a known women's man and, sometimes, without brakes. Even before our story with Liosha, he had an affair with a woman from Novosibirsk, I think a student of the same Liosha. As a result, this woman gave birth to his son. For me all these years, it was incomprehensible how he could take his eyes off Lydochka and look in the direction of another woman. Nevertheless, people are different, and he did it and then never hid this connection and his paternity.

Let us return to our hike. At some point, my Galya and Sveta Melchuk disappeared together from sight. I even began to worry that our girls might have gotten lost. After a while, they returned, and I forgot about this story. It was after Renata finally left us, someone, I do not remember who, reminded me of their disappearance. It turned out that the girls wanted privacy and, being just the two of them, swore to each other that Sveta would never leave her mother and Galka — her father. Weren't our girls great? I still do not know how this information leaked out and reached me, but it really helped me to live all these years and warms me up to this day. Svetochka, I am speechless in loving and thanking you!

The story of Lesha Gladky's invasion into the Renata's life would not be complete if I did not tell you about both nice and sad reaction of my mother-in-law Leah Ravich began to correct decisively the moral climate in Liosha's family life, and even after that, Leah treated me like her own son, and our Galiusha was just a light in the window for her. I have already mentioned that her dedication knew no limits. There was not a thing she would not do for both me and Galya. I had been this woman's son-in-law for about ten years and all those years I was overwhelmed with respect and gratitude. When the story I described happened, it broke my heart to see the poor woman's bitter tears and her desperate but futile attempts to stop her daughter's madness.

MY POSTGRADUATE THESIS

I would like to remind here the readers how I was full of gratitude to the director for saving me from the army by arranging my postgraduate studies. I felt that now it is my duty to prepare everything as soon as possible and as well as possible for my thesis defense so that the director of my Institute Sergei Lebedev would never regret his efforts to help me. In fact, my dissertation was purely applied in nature and summarized and formulated the results of my work in IPM&CT before I fled Moscow. I proposed to use the hydraulic model of wave propagation on discrete grids developed by the American mathematician for optimal designing of connections in computer units. Most of the results I received experimentally and they turned out to be good. I tried to complete the all pre-defense huddle noticeably ahead of the graduate school deadline. All the feedback on the dissertation was positive. I submitted my dissertation for defense. I was glad that my supervisor, I remind you, was the head of our department, Lyova Korolev, with whom I was on friendly terms. I could always count on his goodwill and support.

On defense day, I managed to make a strong impression on my mother-in-law. The thing is that in Moscow there has always been a problem with recycling empty bottles and jars. Sometimes there was no tare, sometimes the collector was sick, or else you would bring a huge bag of bottles (almost no one had a car!) and find an announcement like the one in Winnie the Pooh: *"No and un-*

known!" There were not many collection points and you had to go to who knows where. My defense time, as I recall, was scheduled for about 3 p.m. I got up in the morning, had breakfast, gathered the bottles and went to the collection point to drop them off. I was inconceivably lucky, the operation was a success and I returned home with empty bags. My excited mother-in-law told everyone she knew: *"Can you imagine, on the day of his thesis defense, he went to the collection point to return the dishes!"*

Even before my defense, I surprised and disappointed many friends and relatives with my appearance. In Russia, I absolutely could not stand ties. Such strong emotions of mine against this apparel were caused by the fact that all the party bosses in the country looked as if they had been hatched from the same incubator: gray suits, white shirts, and necessarily dim ties. I disdained these people and I hated looking like them. As a result, oh horror, I went to the ceremony WITHOUT a tie! Interestingly, after coming to America, many things changed in me. I began to meet people, quite sympathetic to me, who came to work wearing ties. First of all this applied to doctors in the hospitals where I worked in America for many years. As a result, I started going to work in a tie myself. I felt I was thereby expressing my attitude towards these nice people and their noble profession. But in Russia I strongly disapproved of the tie.

Regarding my relationship with ties, I recall a funny detail. Eighteen years after my dissertation, in 1988, when we already had our permission to leave the country, several friends were giving us a party celebrating our departure from Russia. One of such dinners took place at the apartment of our dear American friends journalists Anne Blackman and Michael Putzel. Both of them knew about my "love" for ties. At one point, Michael got up from the table, went to his office, and returned to the dining room with a tie in hand. As I remember now, this tie was red. "Yura," he said to me, *"it may happen that when you come to the United States, you will be invited to a meeting with our President. I ask you as a friend, please, when you go to the meeting, wear this tie."* At that time, I was sure it was a joke. I could not think of any meeting with the President at that moment, but I was terribly glad of the joke. However, our dear Michael was a visionary. Indeed, the Reagans did invite us upon our arrival in the country, and, of course, I remembered the episode and went to the White House wearing a tie given me by Michael. After this for more than twenty years in the USA I worked in hospitals, and at work I always wore a tie, often the one I got from my friend. New life came with new surroundings and new habits.

Talking about my relationship with ties, I want to mention that much later, when I was already writing these memoirs, I read in Irina Uvarov's book "Daniel and All, all, all" that the friend of Yuli Daniel, my very favorite poet, Bulat Okudzhava, hated ties and NEVER wore them. The book mentioned above tells how, after many years when the Soviet authorities did not allow Okudzhava to go abroad, he got finally permission to go to Spain. But on the questionnaire photo everybody was required to be in a tie. The poet refused and DID NOT GO! I do not know what triggered such strong emotions in Bulat Okudzhava. It's probably ridiculous, but my resemblance to this, in my opinion, remarkable man and poet pleased me wildly.

Some of the members of the scientific council I knew well as our staff and a few others as regular participants in our seminars. Therefore, I felt quite comfortable and did not worry too much. The defense went quite smoothly. I had no difficulty answering the questions posed. The vote was unanimous. I was quite satisfied. All my papers went for approval to the Highest Attestation Commission. I was well aware that this was not an easy step, especially for a Jewish applicant, but the smooth start almost eliminated my worries.

Russian tradition required a gala dinner at a restaurant with colleagues and friends to celebrate after the thesis defense. I booked a banquet at the restaurant in the Ukraine Hotel on Kutuzovsky Prospect, and there were more than a hundred people invited. We had such a good time that to my shame I did not remember how I got home. Worse, there was a piece of material torn out of the pants of my almost-new suit!? That had never happened to me before. After such tumultuous events, the working routine of worrisome waiting for the decision of the Higher Attestation Commission went on.

I did not receive a decision for longer than usual and I already started to expect bad news, and sure, they came. I have received an invitation from the Commission to come to talk to them. When I arrived, I was brought into the room so that I could be acquainted with the review of the "black" opponent". The adjective "black" meant that I should not know his name. There was a page of typed text on the table, with a white strip of paper attached at the bottom with two staples to cover the signature. The clerk prompted me to read the review and left the room. Taking advantage of the fact that I was alone in the room and risking a scandal, I peered under the strip of paper and managed to read there the name of my opponent: Yablonsky Sergey. Everybody connected with mathematics already knew that this person was a faithful follower of the academicians Vinogradov and Pontryagin in their anti-Semitic pogroms in Soviet science.

Today we can read in the article "Anti-Semitism in Soviet Mathematics" in Russian Wikipedia, for example: *"Grigory Freiman, a doctor of physical and mathematical sciences addressing in 1977 with a letter to the President of the Academy of Sciences Alexandrov A. called Vinogradov, Karatsuba, Ershov, Shirshov, Yablonsky and Ulyanov as the main inspirers of anti-Semitism."* Our friend Mikhail Tsalenko, a doctor of physical and mathematical sciences, also wrote about it: *"Today, the inspirers of anti-Semitism in Soviet mathematics, I. M. Vinogradov and L. S. Pontryagin, are no longer alive. There are new academicians in the Department of Mathematics of the USSR Academy of Sciences who were not involved in the events of the 1970s. However, both academician V. S. Vladimirov, and new academicians A. A. Gonchar and V. P. Platonov, and a number of old academicians A. N. Tikhonov, A. A. Dorodnitsyn, S. V. Yablonsky, etc. etc. are directly responsible for the lawlessness that occurred in those years."* Yet the chests of anti-Semites, named here, did not have enough space for their orders, medals, Stalin, Lenin, and State Prize awards.

However, it seems to me, that besides the type of personality of my "black" opponent, his review itself deserves an attention. There was only page in this review that I managed to read at the Higher Attestation Commission. This page correctly stated the content of my thesis chapter by chapter, repeating almost verbatim the relevant paragraphs from my thesis abstract. After that followed only ONE phrase, which I reproduce here from my memory: *"The thesis does not contain any new results, and therefore the author cannot be awarded the degree of candidate of physical and mathematical sciences"*. Having recovered from the shock, I thanked the employee of the Commission for acquaintance with the review and went straight to my scientific supervisor Lyova Korolev to consult, what I can do now.

After listening to me carefully, Lyova asked for a day to discuss it with someone else. The next day he made a concrete proposal. He discussed and arranged my next steps with a highly respected professor in our field, with the unusual surname Mikhail Shura-Bura. This man was the head of the department at the Institute of Applied Mathematics and the member of the Highest Attestation Commission's section on Computational Mathematics. Lyova wanted me to meet him and tell him the content of my thesis. Professor Shura-Bura said, if during our meeting I could convince him that the thesis contained new material, he would try to help me. I was still sure that it was impossible to resurrect my thesis, but I was interested to know professor's personal opinion.

A couple of days later this meeting took place. I came back very happy, because Mikhail Shura-Bura understood at once everything I told him and he seemed to be interested in trying to help me. What happened after this was just like a fairy tale! A couple of weeks later I was invited again to meet a member of the Commission, congratulated, shook hands with this person and was handed a diploma of Candidate of Sciences in Physics and Mathematics. I sill treasure in my archives the Diploma, I have received this memorable day. More than fifty years passed since the day and I am still positively shocked.

KURIL EXPEDITIONS

After Renata has made public her plans with Gladky I had the hardest time. She lived between Moscow and Kalinin, and when she would come to Moscow, she felt free to visit our apartment as often as she wanted, sometimes even bringing Liosha there. She had no idea that it was difficult and unpleasant for me to see her or Liosha at our home, let alone them together. Each her coming she would always explain with her motherly feelings, with her desire to be with Galya. It seemed to me that she was doing everything, as it was convenient to her, not caring at all how I felt about it. She never even tried to move her Moscow life into her mother's apartment, including communication with her daughter, which would have been easy enough to do and poor girl's grandmother would be very happy. As a result, more and more often I wanted to run away from home anywhere. The only thing that stopped me was that there was no place, where I could run WITH Galya when Renata was in Moscow. At the same time, actually, I understood that I had no right to hide the child from her mother. A vicious circle was forming: she did not want to meet with the girl outside my home, and each such meeting just tortured me. I was ashamed of my desire to run away from home and not see my beloved child, but I could not help it. I have to say that I kept thinking about it only because of the dedication, kindness, and love for our girl of her grandmother, Renata's mother. I firmly knew that even if I managed to leave, my Galya would be in loving hands.

Some sympathetic friend advised me to go away for a couple of summer months on an expedition and even recommended talking to an acquaintance from the Institute of Hydrogeology of the Academy of Sciences USSR on the subject. After a long struggle with myself, I went to this Institute and met there a very pleasant woman. Her name was Nelya Otman. Just at that time, Nelya was forming a small group of five people for an expedition to the Kuril Islands to study the hot springs there. They needed a worker to carry bottles of water samples on the day's passage. The prospect of carrying a heavy backpack with bottles did not concern me: I was young and healthy then. Besides, I got excited about the opportunity to see places so far away, of unimaginable beauty to my knowledge. The whole area of the islands was a border zone at the time and a special pass was required to visit, which was almost impossible to obtain for a private person. In other words, it was a unique chance for me in that sense.

A couple of words about "closed" borders of Russia. Already after the Kuril expedition, I had seen enough of monstrous picture of such borders. For example, dozens of kilometers of beautiful beaches in Estonia resembled a concentration camp: the splash of the sea came to us from behind barbed wire, and it was impossible to approach the water. The population did not have right to come close to water, to swim or to go boating. The sea looked kind of died out. The Soviet authorities were paranoid: their concern was that somebody could dive in Estonia, but to surface in Finland. The border zone was a narrow strip of sand, less than 100 yards wide. According to the Moscow newspaper Kommersant, the width of the border strip in some parts of Russia was up to 20 miles, and the total area along the borders, which was under the control of the KGB, exceeded the area of the whole France!

I was also attracted to the Kurils because I was looking forward to seeing the remnants of the Japanese culture that, I hoped, was still there. If you add to all this that my personal impressions of Nelya were quite positive, and I thought she liked me too, the overall picture was that I should try to go away with her. When I told her about my intentions, of course, I never mentioned my family affair. She said that it was necessary to start requesting for permissions, and if successful, the further paper work would not be difficult. However, I thought to myself that my dissident connections might come out with the request, and then the whole plan would fall apart: I would not get a security clearance. Therefore, I had to be patient and wait."

About a couple of weeks later, I got a call from Nelya and she informed me that we have my security clearance and the paperwork was well underway. We agreed with her on an unskilled worker's salary that barely covered transportation costs, lodging in hotels along the way, and meals, leaving very little as net income. That suited me fine: My plan solved my personal problems at home for at least two months. After this, either, as they say, the donkey dies or Mohammed dies. Besides, it promised many interesting things and allowed me to leave my full IPM&CT salary for my child's mother and grandmother to live on.

Soon, Nelya invited me to come, prepare, and pack the expedition luggage. It turned out to be a memorable meeting where I met first time the other three members of the expedition. There were two young people: a girl technician who worked with Nelya and a boy, a geology student at Moscow State University. There was nothing special about them. I very rarely remember these two people, they were and passed me by, without leaving much of a trace. However, the third man did turn out to be very special. His name was Juli Blank. He was a design engineer from Moscow, and a very kind and modest man. I have at once visited his house and was acquainted with his wife Galya, and we became close friends. We brought our friendship from the Kurils to Moscow and from Moscow to Boston. Unfortunately, neither Galya nor Yuli are with us today. This remarkable couple, as well as their son Yuri with his family, brightened up our life in Boston. This friendship is time-tested, it is 45 years old today (!), Juli is one of the most wonderful gifts of fate to me personally.

Getting ahead of myself, I would like to say that not only did I go to the Kurils in 1972, but also I brought the strongest impressions from there, it would be no exaggeration to say that this trip was the most important in my life in terms of my formation as a person. The next year, when Nelya went to the Kurils second time and invited me to take part again, I gladly said *"YES"*. When I think back on those two expeditions, they merged into one for me. Unfortunately, I catch myself that I can no longer reconstruct what was in the first, and what was in the second. That's why, with few exceptions, the rest of my story about the Kuril Islands is structured as if everything happened during one trip between 1972 and 1973.

Before turning to both of my two unique trips to the Kuril Islands, I would like to say here a few words about Nelya Otman here. Till the end of my years I will have a feeling of deep gratitude to her for those happy weeks she gave me. I tried not to show it, but I really was depressed about what had happened between Galina's mother and me. I was worried sick about how I was going to be both father and mother to my beautiful girl. Thanks to Nelya, the Kurils turned out to be an intensive care ward for me after a major surgery. I cannot remember now how much Nelya was aware of my personal affairs. In any case, thank you, thank you, dear Nelya for your therapy! Thank you for your kindness and understanding! I felt very comfortable in your expeditions. When I remember these years, I become a bit sad that the cataclysms of my life, and then the departure from Russia led to our estrangement. Nelya still lives in Moscow and from time to time, I am happy to talk with her by phone.

Now back to the beginning of the first trip. Time flew by, it were first summer days of 1972. The plane with me on the board started in Moscow, crossed almost all of Russia and landed in Vladivostok. All the way on the plane, I was looking out the window, and I was amazed at what an immense country I was living in and how little of this immensity is mastered. Of course, I knew that at the end of the war Soviet army seized the islands we were going to explore. Japan had made endless unsuccessful attempts to buy the islands back. But after seeing with my own eyes from a bird's eye view the vast expanse of almost unused land, while the Japanese lived incredibly crowded in a very limited area, I became ashamed to imagine a country living by the ethical rule "Though I am not using it myself I will never give it to other people."

I had little memory of the town, we were in it briefly, and were very busy preparing our cargo for shipment by sea to Sakhalin island. In Sakhalin, there was an office of the representatives of the Nelya's Institute, from which we received much useful information, maps, etc. The few days I spent on Sakhalin made quite a sad impression upon me, first of all I have in mind the ethnic "cleansing". By the end of WWII Russia had taken over the island. There were about 400,000 Japanese, Koreans and other natives of the Japanese islands living on the island at that time. All of them were forcibly deported, and the Soviets destroyed all traces of their residence on the island. We were on Sakhalin for several days, but I did not manage to see A SINGLE Japanese or Korean buildings.

Koreans played a special role in the history of Sakhalin and the Kuril Islands. The Japanese brought them there as a cheap labor force to work in the sulfur mines. They quickly adapted and demonstrated how hard work and diligence can change the face of a country. They soon made a name for themselves as the best gardeners and horticulturists, growing vegetables and fruits, including even watermelons, in rather harsh climatic conditions. The Korean market on Sakhalin became a remarkable sight for all islands. Nevertheless, the Soviet authorities managed to put a quick end to it by expelling the entire Korean population from the area. A curious detail: most of the deportees wanted to go to their relatives in South Korea. They absolutely could not get the permission to do so and Soviet administration forced all of them to move to North Korea.

There were no Koreans, vegetables and fruits disappeared from the islands. The recruitment from central Russia brought new Russian, Ukrainian and Belarusian residents to the islands. They settled in the blooming Korean farms—go forward and keep it up. In a couple of years, the gardens and orchards died out. During all the weeks I worked on the islands, I did not see a single fresh vegetable or fruit in the shops. Only once a ship brought green unripe tomatoes from the mainland. The island administration organized selling them right on the shore. The local residents stood in line for hours just to get a taste of that forgotten vegetable. Getting ahead of myself, one day later we were sailing from island to island on a small boat, and I got into a conversation with a local man, a stranger to me. He turned out to be the first secretary of the South-Kurilsk District Party Committee (on Kunashir). I, of course, began to ask him about the problem of supplying the population with vegetables. I remembered his answer well. *"What can I do? If I was allowed to bring at least 10 (!?) Koreans here, I would provide the district with vegetables."* Alas, that has never happened!

After some time at Sakhalin Island, we sailed to the southernmost Kuril island of Kunashir. This island was the main object of our research in our expedition, and we spent more time on it than anywhere else did. It is the second largest island in the ridge. Kunashir strait, which separates it from the already Japanese island of Hokkaido, in its narrowest part has only 15 miles. When the north wind blew, it brought children's inflatable toys, bright and colorful, from Japanese beaches. Collecting these toys turned into a kind of pleasant hunting.

As is often the case, nasty people are capable of ruining the nicest things. On one of my first days on Kunashir, I went for a walk along the water's edge. Most of the people you can meet in the Kuril Islands are military, serving in the border guards. A soldier that I spotted from afar was walking toward me as he was carrying a Japanese kids inflatable swimming circle and the colors of the circle glinted in the sun. I immediately thought that perhaps the soldier himself, or his family, had a child who would enjoy such a wonderful thing. However, the idyll was instantly shattered when the soldier and I leveled off. Behind me, an officer and a soldier were catching up, apparently on patrol along the shore. The officer swiftly approached the soldier with the toy and barked, *"Give me that!"* The soldier, obediently, without uttering a sound, handed him his find. Then the patrol swiftly continued its way, and the soldier staggered on sadly. I was angry and wanted to catch up with the officer and to strike him at his head. However, I was afraid to start the conflict and I realized that such my reaction could cause an security scandal at the strictly guarded border of my great motherland.

Later on in our expedition, I had enough opportunities to see this kind of attitude of officers and soldiers. As they say, God is high, and the tsar is far away. No one can find here a justice! Thousands of miles away from their superiors, to whom one could complain, the officers were in absolute arrogance and treated the soldiers as their serfs. For example, they forced them to clean their houses or work in vegetable gardens, and the soldiers did it for them without complaint, indeed as under serfdom. More than once, seeing all this, I thought how lucky I was to avoid serving in SUCH an army.

On Kuril Islands, sitting right to left: Juli Blank, Nelia Otman and me

From the point of view of natural environment, Kunashir is amazingly beautiful and diverse. According to descriptions, its fauna is much richer than that of the other islands of the ridge. I personally managed to see on the routes the brown bear, sable, mink, dozens of waterfowl birds, seals and walruses, and of course, in countless quantities of far-eastern salmon.

The situation with salmon was typically Soviet. This fish swims in the coastal ocean waters, but for spawning millions of specimens, like being possessed, always go up the freshwater rivers and streams. The river literally boils, filled with fish. Such a spectacle I have never seen before or after the expedition. After spawning all those millions of fish die, and if nobody immediately fished them out, they float to the surface of the water and then waves throw them onto the banks of the shore. Nobody needs them. Nevertheless, the stupid law does not allow population to catch this fish. There is an unimaginable smell of rot along the river. It was sad to see how something considered for centuries as high-class delicacy in Russia and in the rest of the world, and very expensive too, here became mountains of rot.

Of course, we fished the fish anyway while it was alive, cooked and ate them in all kinds: after all, there was never any fish inspectorate on the islands. Our way of hauling out would be the envy of any angler at any place of the world. All what we needed was a big hook and a thin rope (nobody needed a fishing line). As a weight, you could use any stone or some piece of iron. Then you are throwing this "tackle" away in the river and yanking hard. Typically, the hook sinks into the side of the first-class fish, and it is yours! As a bonus, you also get about a pound of the freshest red caviar. Remember, the fish was rushing to spawn!

It was even sadder to see the state's clumsy attempts to solve the problem of processing and using this fish. During salmon spawning periods, there were not enough local people to do the job. Significant injection of labor was required. I recall with horror the relocation from island to island on a ship carrying such "workforce" recruited in Russia and Ukraine. They were so-called "girls" of 16–20 years old, brought in for fish-processing work. I have never had the chance to see such dregs of society. The ship's administration warned all passengers in all seriousness never to stay alone with the recruits. This was especially true of the men, upon whom these savage females, reeking of vodka, smoke, and sweat, pounced for sexual gratification. Their speech was hardly more than foul language. I still do not understand how they managed to find these "girls", who had completely lost attributes of human beings.

One of the strongest impressions connected with the island's nature was the eruption of the Kunashir volcano Tyatya, which occurred in 1973. Some specialists in volcanism rank Tyatya among the most beautiful volcanoes in the world. They describe it as the third after Vesuvius and Mount Fuji. In terms of type, it belongs to the volcanoes of Vesuvius group with a double crater. However, Tyatia is one and a half times higher than Vesuvius, about 6000 feet, and the outer ancient crater is better preserved. In clear weather, the volcano is visible from everywhere on the island. On my second Kuril visit, I was lucky to be very close to the foot of erupting giant, a little over 6 miles. To come closer it was already dangerous, stone kernels flying out of the crater landed within sight. From time to time above the crater flashed yellow-red glow of red-hot lava. A circle with a radius of over 30 miles around the volcano was painted black with ash from the crater. The sight was unforgettable, majestic and scary. However, all the rivers and streams within this circle looked even more terrible. They turned into streams of black water.

I hope that most of the wildlife in the river survived and managed to swim away from such end of the world.

No story about the Kurils can be complete without mentioning hot and warm springs, rivers and lakes. Moreover, thermal springs were the main subject of our expedition's research. On the coldest days, we could take nice warm baths, very well prepared for us by nature. Using these springs the Japanese have built their famous water therapy centers. Specialists proved that water in such springs, rich in sulfur, has a very beneficial effect on human health. Our routes passed many times by such places. None of them functions today: the Russian occupants ruined them all. It is impossible for a reasonable person to understand whose way all these were in?! We do not even speak about attractiveness for tourism of such wonders of the Kuril Islands, as boiling rivers and lakes. However, the Soviet idea of border zone does not combine with tourism. By the way, there are several rich deposits of good quality sulfur on the islands, extraction of which used to be a notable part of Japanese industry. All the remains of the sulfur mines were destroyed and one can see there only ruins. A similar fate has befallen the asphalt roads on the islands. Since the time when Soviet army captured Kuril Islands and turned them into a border zone, troops have used the roads for tanks. As a result, already at the time when I was there only the all-terrain vehicles could use all roads besides the tanks.

I cannot help but tell you about another one of the Soviet Union's unparalleled diabolical desecration of another country's history and culture, and in fact, its own as well. There was an old Japanese cemetery in Southkurilsk, the main town of Kunashir island. Unfortunately, walking there, I could not make out the Japanese text, but the architecture of the tombstones and the years inspired reverence. One horrible day I went there and could not believe my eyes: a bulldozer was turning all the gravestones out of the ground, and then they were loaded on dump trucks and taken away somewhere. With all my knowledge of the bolshevism evil, I did not expect such vandalism from the Soviet authorities. However, this was also not enough for them. At the end of the atrocity in the "cleaned" territory, these criminals set up a city garbage dump. Later I learned the backgrounds of this horror: the Soviet Union had signed an international agreement obliging every country to issue entry visas to the people trying to visit the graves of relatives on the territory. The authorities decided to remove all traces of such burials from the face of the earth.

I want to finish my story about the Kuril Islands with one of the most important emotional experiences in my life, which happened exactly there. It happened also on Kunashir Island. We settled down on a coast of the narrow part of Kunashir strait. It was a fine quiet evening, and I went for a walk along the shore. The light haze did not provide a good visibility. However, I was able to see the blue outlines of Japanese Hokkaido in the distance. I did not want to leave this place. In the rocks, I saw an inviting stone chair calling out to me, "*Sit down, it's nice here!*" I sat down and, looking into the distance, pondered about my return to my Moscow life. It was getting evening, and I did not notice how darkness fell. At some moment, I raised my head, and a wonderful picture appeared before my eyes. The lights of Japan seemed to be flickering, just ahead of me! I had a feeling that I might just swim to reach them. This very moment some thoughts dawned on me. What a crazy world I live in, I thought to myself. I was sitting here now so close to a place that I would NEVER be able to visit. Suddenly, I felt very strongly and clearly that I do not want to live in THIS mad world any more! Tsvetaev's lines came to my mind: "*To your mad world my response is one: rejection.*" Unlike Marina Tsvetaev, I was sure that in addition to my crazy world there was another world. I would not call it completely healthy, but much less crazy.

I do not want the reader to misunderstand my feelings I just described. I am not saying that this evening, I was suddenly ripe to part ways with Russia. It did not happen until four years later. The day I described it was simply the first time I had a clear revelation that I wanted to live in a different world. The Kuril Islands moved many of my thoughts in the right direction and contributed a lot to my understanding things.

MY MISADVENTURES WITH THE CRAB

Long before the end of my second trip to the Kurils, I started racking my brains as to what I should bring to Moscow for my Little Drop, something memorable from such an amazing place. When I was there, I saw anglers once, who were sorting out just pulled out nets. In their catch among fish, there was a huge, bigger than the biggest dinner plate, Pacific crab. Then it dawned on me that there could be no better gift for my girl. I told these people that in Moscow, I have remained eleven-year-daughter, and asked them to give this crab her. These nice people gladly gave me a crab. I rejoiced and thought that nobody in Moscow ever saw such beautiful thing. This crab was burgundy-chocolate color. I naively thought that the most difficult part of the problem I have solved and, of course, I will be able to keep and bring it to Moscow. How wrong I was!

First, there was big problem of how to preserve the magic coloring of the crab. Whomever I tried to consult, the general opinion was that it is just generally impossible. If to do nothing, the crab will fade and turn gray. Most recommended to simply boil it, as we do in America with lobsters. Then, at least, it will get a bright red color that can last indefinitely. After painful hesitation, I took the second route.

The next serious problem turned out to be how to dry the flesh of the animal so that at least before arriving in Moscow those around me would not kill me for the stench that would spread due to decay. Here I must pay tribute to my colleagues on the expedition: not only they did not kill me, not only they did not throw me together with my crab into the Pacific Ocean, just the opposite, they showed rare tolerance and understanding. For such kindness, I want to thank them very much! After all, I naively believed that immediately on my arrival to the capital of our motherland I could easily find specialists, who could teach me how to preserve crabs professionally. After all, in museums there are also stuffed animals that do not stink! After numerous referendums among my acquaintances, I have found nothing better than to take every opportunity and to expose my gift on an open sunny place for airing and drying. You can imagine how easy it was to do this with the incessant moving using transport or by feet. In order not to break the fragile piece of art created by nature, I attached it to a plywood mat with thin wires, on which it made all the way to Moscow. I was happy and proud that I had managed to do this without any major injuries both to crab and to myself.

After arriving in Moscow the first place I went with my crab was the Zoological Museum of Moscow State University. Before I talked to the Museum people, I decided to be acquainted with their collection. What was my joy when in one of the halls, I saw a Pacific crab like my. However, what made me happy: mine was bigger! I had an additional satisfaction of seeing that their crab had lost its natural color and was gray. Yep, I thought, I like my red one better. There was no way I expected such a precise hit from the first shot. Encouraged: at last, I will learn all I need to know, I went to the people working in the museum to find out what to do with stuffed crab. Here I was deeply disappointed. It turned out that the museum bought this exhibit about 20 years ago, and at that time, they had a person who knew how to do it. Today, unfortunately, they do not have such a specialist. They advised me to contact the Department of Zoology at the University.

With this experience, I decided to make a phone call first before going anywhere. When I called the Department of Zoology, I heard from a person there that they have experts on snakes, frogs and, I think, even octopuses, but, alas, on crabs they have no one. I cannot vouch that here my memory exactly retained the specific animals for which they did have specialists. Another piece of advice I got there, to go to the Institute of Ocean Studies, the Benthos laboratory. Shame on my old head for my illiteracy, but at the time I did not know that "benthos" is the word for animals that live near the bottom of the ocean. I was sure it was just the name of another smart Jew, the head of the laboratory. I call there and, without a second hesitation ask for Professor Benthos on the phone. On the other end of the line, I hear a woman's Homeric laughter. When the pleasant woman came to her senses from laughing, she cheerfully explained to me the meaning of the word "benthos" and asked what exactly I wanted to discuss with Professor Benthos. I laid out the gist of my problem. In reply, I heard: *"Unfortunately, we will not be able to help you. We have experts on starfish, oysters, stingrays, but no one on crabs today"*. That was the end of my patience. I realized that even in our capital I could not find a person who knows how to do it. So I had to do what I thought was right. I have done so with this crab before, and should continue doing so.

I cleaned and varnished the plywood base for my crab and made it so that hanging it on the wall in Galya's room will not make the wall look ugly. In addition, I reinforced more all the parts of the crab on the backing. After that, the crab took its rightful place on the wall in Galya's room and lived there for many years. As a result, I still do not know, unfortunately, how to make a stuffed crab.

I DID FIND THE WOMAN!

It was autumn 1973. The Kuril trips, of course, did not eliminate my problems, but they gave me an opportunity to think calmly about how I should build my future life. My Little Drop was 11 years old, and I did not stop worrying about my obligations to her. I knew firmly that if I succeeded in getting married again, it would have to be a woman capable of replacing the girl's mother to the maximum and help me to put her on her feet. I was aware of how unthinkably difficult this task was, and this additionally depressed me. I doubted I could I find such a woman.

However, not only did such a woman exist, but also she lived just a few blocks away, and her name was Tanya Markish. This famous name she kept after her first marriage to my namesake Yuri, the nephew of the poet Peretz Markish. Tanya was teaching English literature and English stylistics at the Institute of Foreign Languages. We, of course, knew nothing about each other, but by happy circumstances, we had many mutual friends. These friends, God bless them, conspired to organize our meeting. I would like to say at once that before this story, I had not believed in matchmaking, now I do! It was November 23, the birthday of Nina Leontiev, lovely woman from the linguistic company, we both hung out with people from this company. I knew Nina and her family well. A secret group of friends had sent that day, both to me and to Tanya, Svetlana Yelnitsky with the strict instructions not to retreat, not to accept any objections and to bring both of us to the gathering celebrating the birthday. With both Tanya and me, Svetlana carried out her task, playing her part brilliantly.

I personally remember well refusing flatly, citing a bad mood, but the messenger's persistence did the trick, and I gave in. As for Tanya, she recollected later that on that day she was not feeling well at all, lying in bed, and strictly did not want to go anywhere. However, Svetlana literally took her out of bed, forced her to get dressed, and there was a taxi waiting outside the door. Therefore, Svetlana did not leave to the poor Tanya any choice at all. In addition, for her the decision was even more difficult than for me:

she did not know most of people in the company, while I knew almost everyone. Anyway, on November 23 we DID MEET. Since that time, we celebrate this day every year. To me it is one of the happiest days of my life. I would like to think that Tanya feels the same way. Our friends, of course, introduced us and took care that we sit at the table next to each other and have a chance to talk.

I cannot help to mention one funny detail. It came as a complete surprise to me that already that evening I had an "unplanned" competitor. At the party there was Nina's brother Leontiev Anatoly, whom I had known for a long time and whom I had always liked. Tanya got his fancy. However, our friends were on guard to make sure that everything went "according to plan".

When it was time to leave, my friends sent the two of us to the nearest taxi rank. Tolya Leontiev volunteered to take over from me the role of an escort, but my friends very decisively and effectively rebuffed his attempts. As a result, I took a taxi to accompany Tanya to her house. Interestingly, my lexicographic interests played a crucial role on this pivotal day. I told Tanya about my interest in dictionaries. As we parted outside her house, she gave me her phone number and said, *"I have a couple of dictionaries that might get your attention, so give me a call sometime and stop by."*

My impressions of my new acquaintance were the best, however when we parted, I foolishly returned home, then completely unaware of what had happened. My little girl was sleeping peacefully. The next day I was plunged back into my daily routine: Galya, work, and home were leaving me very little time for anything else. Nevertheless, several times I picked up a little piece of paper with Tanya's phone number and every time I put it off, without calling her, ashamed of being annoying. I realize now how silly of me that was, especially as it turned out later, Tanya had been expecting my call.

While I continued to struggle with my shyness, our conspirators did not letup and, wasting no time, continued to do their work. On the December 1, I received a call from my good friends Tamara and Sandro and they invited me to come over for tea in the evening. I loved these two people very much and was heartily grateful to them for their active and unconditional support at such a difficult time for me. Fortunately, they lived close to me, so after putting my Galya to bed, I ran over to them. Sandro opened the door and the first thing I noticed was a brown fur coat hanging on a coat rack in the hall, exactly similar to one, that Tanya wore when she and I were coming back from Nina Leontiev's birthday party. I thought I was hallucinating. However, as soon as Sandro opened the door to the room I saw that no, I was not dreaming: at the table was really sitting live Tanya Markish!

If our acquaintance and our first meeting left me just with a pleasant memory, our second meeting had an effect on me like an emotional explosion. I sat down at the table, and another guest, linguist Kostya Erastov was asking Tanya about her teaching the children English. Later I found out that children and lessons with them were always an important part of Tanya's life. From the childhood she dreamed that she had 12 (!?) children of her own. However, God never gives horns to a cow that butts. Tanya had no children of her own. Answering Kostya's questions, Tanya told us a story that absolutely fascinated me.

Every Sunday she gathered children of her relatives and friends about my Galya's age and had a wonderful time with them. It would be wrong to call these meetings simply English lessons. Rather, I would call what she did, introducing children to culture in general, to English culture in particular, to history in general, to English history in particular, to languages in general, to the English language in particular. Some of these "lessons" turned out to be meetings with interesting people, trips to interesting places, visits to interesting exhibitions, concerts and plays. As an example, once Tanya said to her students that the next class would be dedicated to the culture of cooking sandwiches in England and related English vocabulary. Planning to teach kids not only the theory, but also the practices of cooking, she has already prepared all the necessary ingredients to make and fry everything. The class will end with a general tasting.

From all this I was in a state of positive shock, unable to think about anything else except how to get my Galya accepted into Tanya's class. I improved the moment when Tamara was alone in the kitchen, and quietly asked her opinion if it was all right to ask Tanya to take my girl into her children's group. I was somewhat surprised by the confident tone of her reply, "*Of course it is all right, and I'm convinced she would never say no to you.*" Encouraged by Tamara, I decided to ask Tanya about it and could not wait until she will be ready to go home. I planned to go with her and have an appropriate conversation.

Everything worked out exactly as I wanted it to! It had been an uncommonly beautiful evening. Tanya lived only a couple of trolley stops away from my friends, so we decided to walk. The rare large snowflakes were falling, swirling. Somehow, they managed to get into the brown curls of her coat and stayed there for quite a long time, sparkling like little lanterns. Tanechka looked like a fairy out of a tale. I spoke about my Galya, how I want to give her as much as possible, at least in some way to compensate the loss of her mother's family. I told her that the story about her working with children touched me and that I would be eternally grateful to her if she would take my girl to her group and give her some of her knowledge and of her warmth. It was very difficult for me to begin this conversation, but she responded with such understanding and sympathy that the conversation ended simply and naturally. *"Sure, bring her to me. We're getting together next Sunday at such and such an hour, I would love to meet her"*, Tanya said. I was in seventh heaven and could not wait for Sunday.

On Sunday, a little before the appointed time, my Galechka and I showed up at Tanya's door. I was so worried that when I pressed her doorbell, my hand trembled. Tanya opened the door, very kindly, I would even say, affectionately, took Galya inside, and asked me to come and get her in a couple of hours. I went outside, and my head was swarming with thoughts about how I should better organize my and Galya's, lives now. I was discussing with myself how I could defend myself from the Renata's and Gladky's visits, how I build my relationships with Renata's mother, with many of my friends. Of course, I could not help thinking about Tanya and her role in Galya's and my present life. I decided not to go home and started walking in circles around Tanya's house. I needed some time to bring minimal order to my thoughts.

As for Renata, I was racking my brains as to how can I minimize her visits to our house, and I could think of nothing better than to wait for it to work itself out. As to my ex-mother-in-law, I always had respect, sympathy, and deep gratitude for her selfless and unfailing help with Galya after I found myself alone with my daughter. I decided that, as before, I should, help the poor old sick and half-blind woman, for example, by continuing to buy her groceries.

I was just lucky with our mutual friends, after we broke up with Renata, most remained close with me, which was a huge support for me. The best example of that support was their initiative to introduce me to Tanya. Going my circles, I thought a lot about our getting to know her. A little over a week had passed since our first meeting, and with each passing day, I was more and more glad that it had happened. I could not help, of course, to worry how the first lesson went and whether Galya liked Tanya. All these thoughts were swirling around chaotically in my head, and I did not notice how the two hours flew by and it was time to go and pick up the child.

Again, I was at Tanya's door, and pressed the same bell button. The teacher opens the door with a smile. *"Come in, please, and please take off your jacket Galyusha, Daddy is here."* However, my Galyusha does not hear, she is engrossed in something. That is already a good sign, I thought at this moment, hung up my coat, and we went into the room.

Everything around was very different from the place where we lived: it is difficult for me to explain in detail, but somehow everything looked much more elegant and beautiful. I was even a bit sad because I had put a lot of effort into decorating our place, especially Galya's room, but now my apartment seemed to me like a soldier's barracks compared to Tanya's flat. There were lots of interesting pictures, small objects and "gizmos" to be seen everywhere in her apartment. My child was sitting on the sofa and was happily looking at one of these "things". It struck me that the girl already felt at home here. She was impatient to play the role of guide and urgently told me about some local pictures, things and "gizmos". Slightly stunned by my new impressions, I heard from the neighboring kitchen Tanya's voice: *"Galyusha, let us give Daddy some tea."* My Galya exclaimed with unusual enthusiasm *"Yeees!"* and we moved into the kitchen.

The tea party, it is not difficult to guess, was an extension of the pleasantness and elegancy of the house. My memory, unfortunately, has not preserved what exactly Tanya offered with tea, but I remember well that it looked beautiful. Again, enthusiasm and pleasure, with which my daughter acted as Tanya's assistant, surprised me a lot. It looked as if she had done this with her more than once before. After tea, I hurried home, not wanting to abuse the hospitality of the host. However, there was a problem: our pupil did not want to leave the house of the teacher. I had to act as a drag, explaining that the teachers are people too, and they should rest too. My strongest and most efficient argument was that the week would fly by quickly and we would come here again.

In fact, even after everything I had already learned about Tanya, I had never expected SUCH success! It is amazing how a real teacher knows the ways to turn a lesson into a celebration! We both went home happy, thinking about how we were going to visit Tanya again in a week. I was also glad that since the trouble had come to my family, the beginning of my lessons with Tanya was the best thing I had done for my child.

Unfortunately, problem with Tanya's health suddenly interrupted our joy. Tanya's chronic pneumonia, which had been bothering her since childhood, got worse. She had to go to the hospital, where she stayed until the end of December. During those weeks, Galya and I went out twice to visit her there.

Time was moving irresistibly towards the New Year, 1974. According to an established tradition, I spent New Year's Eve in New Jerusalem at Tanya Velikanov's dacha with her relatives and friends. Of course, I wanted to invite my new friend there, but I decided not to do that, firstly, because of her illness it was rather risky and, secondly, I was very shy to force events in our relations. As a result, I, foolishly, left without even seeing her before. I still blame myself for such my insensitivity. In New Jerusalem, I felt warm and happy, as always, although, for the first time in years, my thoughts returned regularly to the woman I had left behind in Moscow.

When I returned home, I started calling her many times, but no one picked up the phone. After a couple of days, I called the hospital and found out that the ward she was in has closed, and Markish Tanya asked to discharge her from the hospital on December 31. Later I found out that after her discharge she left Moscow for the country with her friends. God luckily protected her: on January 1, there was a terrible fire in her ward. The hospital personnel had to evacuate urgently poor lung patients through the windows in the freezing cold...

On January 9 I called again to find out that Tanya is back. With her permission, I ran over to see her. That week a new small CD of my very favorite poet Okudzhava had arrived in the shops and I went to see her with this little present. In the chronicle of the history of our family, my visit went down as "a visit with Okudzhava". That day was significant because on that day I felt clearly that I WANTED to see Tanya every day.

Meanwhile, the meetings of Tanya's little students were going on. I want to mention one of them here, which, I think, was special. When Tanya left Moscow for the countryside at the beginning of January, she met a pleasant woman who was a single mother raising a little boy. In no time Tanya, of course, befriended the child, and he confided in her his innermost dream: he terribly wanted a little crocodile and that thing must be green. When Tanya returned to Moscow looked for a place where she could buy such a crocodile. Her mind immediately made a plan for the next "lesson" with children. With all her brood, she went to choose a crocodile, and then they all went together with the gift to the boy. All participants of the mission, including my girl, were endlessly happy.

In Moscow, there was an ensemble of early music "Madrigal" founded and directed by Andrey Volkonsky. I liked very much both the musicians of the ensemble and the pieces they performed. One of my friends called me a lover of "dusty" music, meaning the music covered with dust of time. I tried not to miss any of their concerts. It was 1974, January 25, Tanya's Name Day, in the Big Hall of Conservatory was announced concert of "Madrigal". I had arranged for tickets in advance and was thrilled, I would invite her on her day to the concert. I call her and ask her what plans she has for the day. She answers that she was going to be home because she usually has crowds of friends coming to greet her. I get ready to get upset, *"So you cannot go to the concert with me?"* Her answer immediately threw me up to the seventh heaven, *"No, why not? I would love to!"* Then we both recalled the conversation of ours with laughter, because she never even ask me what the concert was about. She immediately told me an English joke on the subject. The telephone rings, and the girl hears the question on the receiver, *"Mary, will you be my wife?" "Of course,"* replies Mary, *"and who is speaking?"*

Tanya's Name Day came, and everything happened like in a fairy tale. The concert was wonderful. I cannot remember lately when I have been in such high spirits. Tanya could not have shared my joy more. It was a real celebration. I still felt a little guilty before her friends, having stolen the name-day girl from them so unexpectedly. One of Tanya's friends and admirers called the next day and asked why she was gone on her day. Tanya replied that she was at a Madrigal concert. A moment's pause followed, and then her friend said; *"I see! Comrade Madrigal showed up."* After that, some of her old friends did not call me anything other than Comrade Madrigal.

I remember a funny story of those days, when I often was coming to Tanya's house on Lobachevsky Street. Everyone who visited Tanya, as well as she herself, were amusing himself or herself by the announcement in her entranceway that read: *"Citizen Markin, who lost her passport, please come to the garbage chute."* We all giggled until one day a police officer ringed the bell at her apartment door. *"Does Tanya Markish live here?"* he asked. *"Yes, it's me,"* replied Tanya. *"Don't you need your passport?"* the man asked and handed her passport. It turned out to be funnier than we all thought. The garbage collectors, having found the passport in the garbage and transformed the surname "Markish" into the more familiar Russian "Markin", put up a stupid announcement. In the heat of another clean up, Tanya accidentally threw her passport together with other unnecessary papers to the garbage chute. I would not wish anyone to lose and then restore passport in such a bureaucratic country as Russia was then. This was a scary tale with a happy and cheerful ending.

Then came very big day February 1, the day when the last barriers between the two of us disappeared. I was at Tanya's place. We had made the final decision to be together, and that night we really did. We had been celebrating this day ever since as our wedding day. After that day we both racked our brains trying to figure out how to best present our decision to my Galya, how to make her feel like she was a part of this important decision too, which was very true. We soon became convinced that our worries were in vain.

At the beginning of February, I dropped in on Tanya and found her mother, Maria there. We were acquainted. Our conversation was quite small talk, and I did not make any definite impression about her. However, when we parted, mother, unlike me, expressed to Tanya her opinion about me very strongly: he does not look right, he is dressed God knows how, and works as a technician (where did she get that from?). He DOES NOT FIT in any parameters. Interestingly enough, Tanya's father after seeing me later was in the subsequent discussion much more positive: *"Do not worry, Mashenka, it is no problem to dress him up, and as to technician, it's nothing wrong, as long as he is a good person!"* Such discussion of my person reminded me of the lines in "Merry conversation" by A.Galich:

> *She blew them all off, but she did not blow one.*
> *She called him affectionately Aliosha.*
> *He was a counting-machine technician,*
> *He was rather bald Jewish man, nevertheless a good one.*

The reason I cited these lines is that there is an obvious allusion. Tanya had had quite a few men with whom she had romantic relationship. Most of them were in humanities: artists, poets, literary scholars, translators, architects, actors. I have only had two women in my life: first Renataand then Tanya. I did have my PhD in computers but still I was a modest representative of the technology domain, much less dressed up and finery than Tanya's humanities suitors. In a way, her mother was right, and in fact, I still do not understand myself how it happened that Tanya chose me over all of them. In addition, I think, I was never a good Jew, but, maybe, I was not a bad one. However, I never really had a bald spot, and I still do not. I liked Tanya's dad right away, and, of course, his words about me, after we met, were a great comfort to me. As for her mother, she, from the beginning to the end of her life, was never the hero of my affair. However, I can say with satisfaction that in the course of time, I managed to change her opinion about me for the better and she has loved me, as far as she was able to love somebody. As for my Galechka, unfortunately my mother-in-law never came to love her.

Here I would like to mention Tanya's sister Natasha Weissman, who actively welcomed both Galya and me as new family members from the very first days. She was a person of boundless kindness and readiness to help people in general, and, in the first place, those close to her. I was very happy to see that Natasha unconditionally accepted us and fell in love with us. As a cardiologist by profession, Natasha always was taking care of our sick relatives and friends. Until her last days, and she died early, she tried to take care of my little girl and do something nice for her. She was one of the few people who regularly invited my little Galya for walks, theatrical performances and concerts. Natasha passed on her good feelings for us to her husband Zhenya and daughter Masha. Their home was always a welcome home for us. Tanya and I wished that Natasha's family had joined us when we left for America, but alas, they did not want to. Natasha struggled long and painfully with her illnesses and died in Moscow in 1998.

On February 9 in the Great Hall of the Conservatory was announced concert of the German soprano Adele Stolte, the renowned performer of Bach's cantatas. I really wanted to hear her. I told about it to Tanya and she told about the event to her father Boris Gershman, a great classical music lover. He moved me to tears. He got tickets for the concert and invited me. It was a big event for me. There were four of us at the concert: Tanya-, Tanya's parents, and me. On that day for the first time, I performed as a member of their family. Of course, I was nervous, but everything was very pleasant, both her father and mother were very friendly with me. We sat in the "general's" seats in one of the first rows of the parquet. I myself had never bought such expensive tickets at the conservatory. The singer was wonderful and the music was divine, so the concert turned into a holiday.

Unexpectedly, during intermission a meeting happened: we bumped into Renata in the foyer. I paid no attention to this meeting, said a discreet greeting and passed on. However, the consequences turned out to be, to put it mildly, not very pleasant. That day I came home late and did not see Renata. The next day, when I saw her, she gave me an unimaginable scandal. To my horror, it happened in the presence of her mother and Galya. To this day, I still do not understand what caused her hysterical screaming. After my repeated unsuccessful attempts to stop the tantrum and find out what it was that made her so angry, I felt I could not stay in this bedlam any longer. After calling Tanya and getting her invitation to come immediately, I rushed out of the house. At the door, I said, "*I am leaving. I have, thank God, where to go now. I would not set my foot here until Renata leaves the apartment.*"

I did not walk, I ran, panting, all the way to the door of Tanya's apartment, and could not come to my senses for a long time, even after I fell into her arms. At this moment I thought what a blessing, it was to have Tanya now! Half an hour later the phone rang. It was my girl on the other end of the line, and she was begging me to come back home. Barely holding back tears, I told her something not very coherent about how much I loved her, that I would never leave her under any circumstances and that I would of course come home as soon as her mother calmed down and gone. It would be better for all of us. Both Tanya and I were sure that it was my girl's grandma, who asked Galya to call me.

It was Monday, when I escaped from home. Renata stayed in Moscow all week until Saturday. Apparently, she needed it for work, so she was all these days at our apartment. I lived with Tanya until Saturday. Of course, I felt wonderful and warm, but I wore myself out with worry that for the sake of my own warmth I had let her separate me from Galya. However, as saying goes, every dark cloud has a silver lining: this stupid situation once again shook me by how sensitive my girl. was and how she understood everything without words. I wish many adults around me to be able to understand and feel as my 12-year-old Galyusha. Every day when Renata was not with her at home, she would call and talk to Tanya for a long time. I do not know what their conversation was about, but I do not think it matters that much. I was happy that she wanted to talk to Tanya. On this occasion, I remember in Tanya's group of children there was a girl, Galya's age, Natasha. Her father was a well-known Moscow psychiatrist, Anatoly.Smulevich, a very educated man. He repeatedly would tell Tanya that he did not care what Tanya and his daughter were talking about when they were together. All that mattered to him was that they were breathing the same air.

WAS MARKISH BUT NOW — ZIEMAN

On February 18, my sister Lena turned 46 years old. All three of us went to her birthday party. I was worried about introducing Tanya to my relatives. But all went quite well, and everyone liked my Tanya. Lena had always been a wonderful cook, so we had a very tasty evening. Satisfied and happy, the three of us drove home in the evening. Tanya offered to put our little girl to bed. The offer to my great pleasure went off with a bang: over the past two months

Galya had become used to her and felt quite comfortable with her. Nevertheless, I was a little worried, and several times passed by Galya's room to peep through the door to see what was happening inside. Everything was going fine. Tanya was holding Galya's little hand in her hand and they were having a heart-to-heart talk

Later they called me in for "Goodnight." Then my daughter said to me, *"Daddy, I don't want Tanya to leave us. Let her stay with us."* Tanya says, *"Galyusha, I have to teach my students tomorrow morning, and I have all the materials and clothes at home."* However, my child was not confused: *"It's very simple. We'll ask Daddy to go to your house and get everything you need."* Tanya and I just looked at each other in mute amazement. That evening, everything happened just the way the child wanted it to. That was how Tanya stayed with us overnight for the first time.

On the February 20, we made our historic submission of marriage registration documents to one of Moscow's registry offices (the Civil Registry Office). All the three of us showed up, of course. My child unfortunately had to listen to an idiotic lecture given to us by a Soviet clerk. She clearly explained that we were not serious people (for both of us it was our second marriage!) and therefore she was going to put us on probation for six months. Then we bickered long and tediously with her which ended in our great victory. The clerk scheduled our registration for April 9. It was such a frosty day in Moscow that it took my Galyusha quite a while to take off her mittens when she entered the room. However, she was so worried about our bickering with the official that she took her hand covered with the mitten into her mouth and by the end of our discussion, she had chewed the mitten almost to the end.

That is how we looked when we got together

After this hard-won victory, all three of us felt that something good and important was happening. We wanted this day to be a celebration. There was a hotel very close to the registry office on Vernadsky Avenue, and we dropped by its restaurant. It was daytime and there were very few people there. We ordered something light and pleasant with champagne, made toasts, and even allowed the child to taste the wine. The mood was great for all three of us. It never occurred to anyone how much our "extravagant life" would cost us.

The formal registration was still a month and a half away, but all three of us felt that we did a good job, and we could start building a new life. Therefore, we began to do it very actively. However, this was Russia! It was impossible to buy a modest wedding ring. Upon learning of our problem, the parents of Lily, Tanya's student from the children's group, Masha and Misha Tsalenko, gave us as present wedding rings, exactly like we wanted, which somehow they happened to have. Of course, we, like small children, could not refrain from wearing them on the same day. We did not care at all what the Soviet officials thought about it after their resolute refusal to register us as soon as possible as we asked them. This had ridiculous consequences. A few days later, Tanechka and I found ourselves not far from her parents' house and decided to drop in on them for a while. In the semi-darkness of the entryway, we took the rings off our fingers and hid them in Tanya's purse so as not to upset the old-fashioned feelings of the older generation.

One day, the three of us went to the hardware store to buy all sorts of little things, and a funny conversation happened there. We lived in a strange country and in a strange time, where buying any object was often a big problem. Some time before, I was lucky enough to be able to buy a German blender, which we liked to use while cooking. So, in the store, Galya ran up to Tanya and, very excited, said: *"Tanya, they sell blenders here, but our blender was taken away by my mother!"* Tanya answered her: *"Don't worry, Galyusha, I have a blender."* Then Galyusha turned to me and with her loud voice exclaims to the whole shop, *"Daddy, daddy, how lucky we got married—Tanechka has blender!"* The people around us laughed, and I was happy to think that it was not in vain that Tanya and I tried so hard to involve the child in all our decisions. It had turned out just the way we wanted. All three of us indeed had gotten married.

And Renata took more than the blender. After I started my life with Tanya, I believed that everything that happened to me was for the best, I did notice, that Renata took many things, including those, which I liked, but I saw this as a change for the better too. I saw it as evidence of the irreversibility of the process and a confirmation of the principle that one had to pay for all good things. Sometimes, though, I felt offended by the cavalier way in which she handled it. The best example was the two volumes of Van Gogh's letters that I had found and bought at a second hand bookshop. She was well aware of my special interest in the artist and in this particular edition, and yet she took it away from home without saying a word to me. If she had discussed with me that she wanted to have these two volumes, I would have been pleased to give them to her as a keepsake of the good that was between us. However, that never happened.

I remember few funny conversations with my Galechka at this time. One example: Tanya had asked her when she thought it would be best to hold a children's group session. The girl replied, *"We seem to have twinned, after all. Why do we have to study now?"*

Time flew by and our registration in April approached. We did not have a traditional wedding party, but relatives from both sides and close friends gathered together. My whole family was very happy, and everyone welcomed my new chosen one. It was very touching: some of Tanya's friends took our union as their own personal celebration. I, unfortunately, remember very little about it. There was a lot of delicious food and booze. Tanya assures me that I drank heavily. Anyway, my formally new and this time very happy family life began. Tanya Markish from that day on no longer existed. Instead, there was Tanya Zieman. When I am editing these lines in English translation, we are only few months to celebrating our GOLDEN WEDDING, fifty years of our cloudlessly happy lives together.

As a present for my happy wedding day, Moscow Publishing House "Russian Language" issued a revised and considerably enlarged second edition of our "English-Russian Dictionary on Computers." The first edition contained only 279 pages and the second edition had 535 pages. The co-authors of this edition were my colleagues from IPM&CT and friends Victor Zeidenberg and Alexei Zimarev. I thank them for the pleasure I have always had in collaborating with them, and for the fact that it was they who helped my lexicographic interests to emerge in our joint work on the compilation of dictionaries.

PREFERRED "GRASS"

In the previous chapter, I described the very good news of the arrival of Tanya into my family. A short time before that another piece of news came to our family, but unfortunately, it was not good at all. My brother Jan left his wife Innulia whom we all loved very much and with whom he had lived for almost thirty years. When he left home, he also separated from his two wonderful children Olya and Lyova and joined up with a woman who was much younger than he was, whom none of us liked. Tanya called her Grass in the sense that she was nothing special. She lacked everything that distinguished a pleasant and interesting person, like a pleasant and interesting flower. She easily built her happines on the grief of the whole family. I liked Innulia very much, and I was bitter and offended for her. The woman's name was Vera Baratov.

First, I personally would like that the name Vera by its literal meaning in Russian, which was "faith", should be given only to a nice person. Secondly, it was a very dear name to Tanya and me and belonged to an extremely close woman of rare merit. It was Vera Prokhorov, Tanya's beloved teacher and colleague, who became a mentor for both of us. In this book, there will be a special chapter about her. In her honor and memory, our daughter. was named Vera. In addition, as a child, I was completely crazy about Goncharov's Vera from his novel "The Precipice." Now suddenly this nonentity with the name Vera became my brother's wife! It seemed a mistake of the fate to me!

Secondly, It was even worse with her surname. The Russian dictionaries suggest synonyms for the verb "baratsia'" "such as "to sin" or "to have sex with," not counting the obscene words. For this reason, I cannot help to beg my readers for apology for suggestion to replace transliteration of her Russian surname into English with the translation of its meaning: "Fucking".

Of course, I remembered how at the end of the war, after my father's return from the army, he insisted that my brother marry Innulia. And Daddy's opinion always meant a lot to my brother, and he would do what my father wanted. I have mixed feeling about this Father's insistence. On the one hand, it made me sad to think that if my father was alive, he would have met my brother's decision with as much bitterness as I did. In this case maybe what happened would not have happened. I am sure Dad would never have approved of him breaking up the family for Grass. On the other hand, nobody may give orders to one's heart.

I have my own explanation as to why this misfortune happened. It seems to me that Innulia was better educated, primarily in the humanities, than Jan, had a firmer moral fiber, and, I would say, was more sensitive and kinder. Therefore, I think she was a more interesting, more pleasant person than he was. For many people it would be very hard to accept that, and I think, for my brother it was just completely unbearable. Therefore, he traded it for blind worship of the "Gras": *"Janochka, Janochka"*... Each person makes his own choices.

I do not know, if there was anyone around us who approved of my brother's move. From my recollection, everyone felt some unease. However, it was particularly hard on the family, and even harder on the children, especially, for Lyova. A kind and sweet boy, he was angry beyond his years. *"My father is a scoundrel,"* he said, *"and I do not want to know him anymore!"* Poor Innulia, who felt trampled on, was sickened by this and lacked the strength to help Lyova out of this crisis. What was even sadder is that in the 12-year-old Lyova's strong attitude against his father, she felt like she had some kind of support.

I would like to notice that in our family children's life-changing moments were happening not once at the age of 12. Galka, have lost her mother and got her "stepmother" Tanya in return, when she was 12. Lyovochka have lost his father when he was 12. Our Vera. left her birth country when she was 12!? These coincidences seem to me interesting.

THE RETURN OF THE PRODIGAL SON

The title of this chapter quotes the name of the famous oil painting by Rembrandt, part of the collection of the Hermitage Museum in St. Petersburg, Russia. It is among the Dutch master's final works, likely completed within two years of his death in 1669.

With the departure of my brother from home, Tanya immediately joined a family in upheaval. I must say that all my relatives were happy about my new marriage, but my brother was most impressed with Tanya. He loved everything about her. I think she made him feel better about me, too. It is funny to say, but he thought she was the smartest, so he even consulted her on his official business. Tanya empathized with all of us in everything, connected with Jan's divorce from Innulia. In addition, she tried to support Innulia as much as she could. However, for her the children always came first. She said that Jan was a foolish egotist, but it was urgent to help Lyova, a child that she immediately fell in love with. She rushed eagerly to carry out a peacemaking mission between the son and the father.

Tanya had long conversations with Lyova and I actively assisted her in this. The essence of her message was that no matter how much we might judge his father's actions, he was still a loving father and to deny and reject this love was wrong. On the other side, she told Jan that he hurt his son very badly, and if he did not want to lose him forever, he needed to be sympathetic and understanding towards the child's grief. To rebuild the relationship, Jan needed to strive for reconciliation without anger or posturing or judgment. This Kissinger-style shuttle work between father and son bore fruit: they met and started talking! We were both very happy about this success, although Innulia's painful reaction to our peacemaking activities was overshadowing our joy. Perhaps she would have felt better if no one in the family had continued their relationship with Jan as a punishment for what he had done.

Tanya's close friend Miroslava Kikot, worked then at A. Ostrovsky's Shchelykovo museum-reserve in the Kostroma region. Jan had a car at the time, and Tanya had an ingenious plan to seal the reconciliation. She suggested all of us, including both father and son, to drive in his car to the reserve. Jan agreed, and she arranged our coming with Miroslava. For the company of Lyova, we also took with us two of his peers: my Galya and Tanya's niece Masha. The trip was a rare success. We picked out wild mushrooms and berries in the forests well known from Russian folklore as the Berendei Kingdom. We lit a fire and roasted a chicken. Everyone was happy, and most importantly, Leovochka and his father. This development reminded me the parable of the prodigal son in chapter 15 of the Gospel by St. Luke in Bible.

It was impossible to imagine a better solution at that time. Of course, it was only a step forward, and this trip was not a complete solution to the problem. Lyova stopped cursing his father and agreed to see him, but the pain and bitterness remained in him. Jan returned and lived with his Grass, which no one in the family, including Tanya and me wanted to know. Alas, neither my brother nor his chosen one cared at all. The saddest thing was that the children, Olya and Lyova, never accepted her into the family and tried to keep their contacts with her to a minimum. The Grass herself did not lift a finger to establish any kind of relationship with the children. On the contrary, I would say that she behaved in a way that made rapprochement out of the question. It seemed to me that her primary interest was financial—she tried to grab from her husband as much as possible. She had a disgusting squabble with the children and Olya's daughter Masha over their use of Jan's dacha. All the members of our family hated these disgusting disputes.

I am still in pain when I remember how depressed Innulia remained. The hardest part was that our efforts to reconcile Lyova with his father caused poor Innulia additional pain. I could not find the way to help her to change her attitude. Remember, she continued to be a very dear person to me. Moreover, my love for her did not decrease, but increased. Besides, she had no idea that many of our efforts at that time related to the naïve hope of getting Jan back to Innulia. However, pretty soon it became clear to me that it was IMPOSSIBLE.

PARTING WITH MY FATHER-IN-LAW

Boris Gershman, Tanya's father, was a very specialperson in many ways. It is sad and sorry, that our lives entwined for so short a time. I met Tanya in October 1973 and her father in February 1974, and in May 1974, he died. From the day of our first acquaintance, everything in this man aroused only respect and sympathy. I will try here to tell briefly, how he started his life and how he got education. Naturally, I got these stories from Tanya.

Boris was born into a Jewish family in Lithuania. Curiously enough, my father's father also came from Lithuania. Boris was the eldest of five children, followed by three sisters and a brother. Although his father, Tanya's grandfather, owned some small business, perhaps due to his poor health it was quite difficult for him to support a large family. He was often ill. When the eldest boy,

Boris, was only ten years old, his father suffered a massive stroke that left him completely incapacitated. Boris' mother found herself alone without any means of livelihood with a completely disabled husband and five small children. They had difficult time for a couple of years, and then moved to Samara, where their relatives lived. These relatives sheltered them and tried to help.

In Samara, the 13-year-old Boris, being the head of the family, could not afford to go to school and went to work in a print shop. School was out of the question for his younger brother who found work in a confectionery factory. However, the world is not without good people. In the printing house worked a wonderful man, who spotted the bright and inquisitive boy. He tried to help Boris to study, to pass an external exam for school and to receive a certificate of maturity. This kind man suggested that he himself would do as much of Boris' work as possible so that Boris could use this time to study. A child like Boris did not need someone to repeat such an offer. He worked during the day and studied at night, stealing hours from sleep. After a while, he successfully passed his school exams and got his diploma.

My father-in-law Gershman B.G.

Boris' next dream was to study chemistry at the Moscow State University. However, nothing was easy for people in this country. The authorities reminded Boris of his father's failed business. The children of the "bourgeois" found themselves, according to the Constitution, in the category of "deprived" which meant that the authorities could refuse these people of many rights, including the right to get the higher education. It was not so easy, however, to stop this boy. He followed Lenin's instruction *"To study, study and study again!"* Boris hid his "bourgeois" origins, "lost" his parents' occupation papers that were used to denounce him. He applied to the university as a proletarian, successfully passed the entrance exams, matriculated, and began to study. However, it did not take long for the music to play. There appeared a do-gooder, obsessed with the idea of class purity in soviet higher education, which found the forgery and wrote a report to the school. The vigilant administration immediately threw Boris out of the university.

Then Boris, without saying a word to anyone, lest there be also a snitch, went to the Bauman Moscow State Technical University and re-applied for a chemical specialty. Again, they accepted him and once again, he became a Moscow student. I admire persistence of a provincial boy and his indomitable thirst for acquiring knowledge. In addition, it amazes me how high a bar he set for himself. After all, both times he chose the BEST universities in the country. For those who are not familiar, Bauman College is the Moscow equivalent of the American Massachusetts Institute of Technology. Now fate was more favorable to him: he happily studied, worked at night and used the money to support his family. He rented a room, into which he later brought his two sisters, so that they too could be educated in Moscow.

I have described only the beginning of the life of this special person. The years and decades that followed did not indulge him. Political accusations, exile, war, the delights of an overcrowded communal apartment, army service, anti-Semitism: all these did not help him maintain his health. When I met him, he was 66 years old and already a seriously ill man. What absolutely captivated me, was having lived such a life, he managed not to harden himself but maintained an amazing kindness and benevolence. One of his most obnoxious communal flat mates shared: *"All Jews are bastards, only our Boris is good!"* For me personally, it is significant that even such a racist woman could not speak ill of this man.

As a retired military officer, Boris Gershman could receive medical care in military hospitals. The last time I saw him was in beginning of May 1984 in Lefortovo military hospital, where Tanya and I visited him. Slowly but surely his strength was leaving him. He died on May 8, on the eve of the Soviet Victory Day. Such a coincidence turned out by a sad irony of fate and the last difficulty in Boris's life. The whole country got ready to rejoice Victory Day. Most of the services were not working these days. Organizing funerals had always been a difficult business in Russia, but when the holidays came, it was next to impossible to get anything out of anyone at all. It seems to me that V. Mayakovsky was completely wrong when he wrote:

It is not hard to die in this life.
To make life is a much more difficult task.

In my experience, with bureaucrats and often anti-Semites working in the funeral parlors, dying with dignity in Soviet Russia was no easier than living. One way or another, we managed with incredible effort to get everything done in a proper and timely fashion. Tanya's mother wanted the funeral to happen in the German Cemetery in Moscow. This was an old city cemetery and of course, there were no free burial places there. As always in Russia, friends came to the rescue. Gershman's friends had a family grave at the cemetery and they offered to bury Boris in their grave. It is significant that history repeats itself. When my beloved great-uncle, a world-famous professor of mathematics, died, the family was unable to get a burial place in a decent cemetery within the city. Friends came to the rescue and offered to bury him in their old family grave at Novodevichy Cemetery. When my father died as an eminent professor of economics and geography, we could not get a burial place accessible in terms of transportation for my sick and fading mother. Friends again came to the rescue and, we were able to bury him in the Novodevichy cemetery through an acquaintance with a high-ranking governmental person.

Many people gathered for Boris's funeral, and a mountain of flowers grew on the fresh grave. But the funeral ended ominously. All the people began to disperse. At the gate of the cemetery, my mother-in-law found that she had hung her purse on the fence of the grave and had forgotten to take it when leaving. I volunteered to run back and fetch it. When I ran up to the grave, I couldn't believe it. The purse was hanging where it was left, but on the grave, there was NOT A SINGLE FLOWER!!! Shocked, I went back to the gate and whispered about it to Tanya. We decided not to tell anyone. I felt that my farewell with this remarkable man ended with a heinous abuse of the person who just passed away, and in general, of everything sacred. In Russia, people believe that one should never even speak ill of dead people. However, what happened is a hundred times worse. What could be more disgusting than stealing from the dead? This felt like the Nazis pulling gold teeth out of a corpse's jaw. I wandered towards the exit from the cemetery and thought how lucky it was that Boris could no longer be a witness to this outrage!

I would like the reader to remember, such thing had happened in one of the oldest and most famous cemeteries in Moscow, the German Cemetery. Here was buried a famous saint, a Moscow doctor who came to Russia from Germany in the 19th century to do good deeds. Dr. F. Haass lived and worked in Russia for almost fifty years, and all these years he did good, he treated and eased the suffering of many people. The doctor was a Catholic, and in 2011, the Catholic Church canonized him. On his tombstone, located close to my father-in-law's grave, you can see engraving of the doctor's motto: *"Hasten to do good deeds!"* As a response to the call of the saint person, some scoundrels hastened to do evil! Poor Dr. Haass should turn over in his coffin.

EXCHANGE OF APARTMENTS

Immediately after we got married, the first thing on both Tanya's and my minds was to get the apartments exchanged in the best way for everybody. We wanted to move out as soon as possible and to separate from Renata and her mother. We wanted a home for our new family. We also tried not to lose the apartment that Renata and I lived in. To that end, we included in the exchange Renata's mother Leah Ravich and her one-room apartment. As a result, we were looking for a three-room flat for Galyusha, Tanya and me. Renata wanted to join her mother in our old flat, and one more participant in the exchange got the accommodation for two one-room flats: Tanya's and Leah Ravich's. I have to give credit to Renata: she immediately agreed to have Galya registered in our apartment and to live with us. The girl also wanted it, so everyone's interests happily coincided. I would not like to discuss what motivated whom. I naively thought that such exchange would not be a problem. We just needed to find an option that suited everyone. How wrong I was!

From the very beginning, even before we started looking for suitable apartments, the head of the exchange bureau did not want to accept our documents and put all kinds of obstacles in our way. He turned out to be a very unpleasant person and, to all appearances, an anti-Semite. *"Why is the girl not going with her mother, that happens more often, but with her father?"* he asked me. *"For a very* simple reason," I answered, "it's what the girl herself wants, it's what both parents want, it's what the family wants." "That's not enough for us," he said, "you will have to get approval of such an exchange from the custody inspector of the District Department of Public Education (?!), only after this I can accept the documents from you." I could not believe my ears. "Who," I asked him, "should decide who my daughter lives with, the education inspector or the family?" "Of course, the inspector," he answered me. Seeing the pointlessness of continuing our discussion, I made an appointment to see the damned inspector.

After about a week, I showed up at the office of a formally polite but boring woman who questioned me at great length and in detail about, when and with whom my Galya lived, and at which address. She then told me that I had to provide her with certificates from all the House managements where we lived, confirming everything that she had heard from me. Based on these certificates they would decide my "question". Cursing with a grin, I left the building and went to get the requested certificates from, thank God, only two administrations of the houses where my girl had lived. When I received the desired certificates, I got an audience with the District Education Office inspector again and put these certificates on her table. Some more days passed and ...HOORAY!!!, VICTORY!!! We got permission for a father to live with his own beloved daughter. The preliminary phase was over, and we could begin the actual exchange process.

It did not take us long to find a apartments to exchange after a very active search. We found what we wanted and, happy as we were, we thought we had it in the bag. However, no such luck, the regional executive committee would not allow us to make the exchanges. The formal, completely ridiculous reason for this refusal was that both Tanya and I were to receive, in the exchange, about hundred square feet more than we had given up. I was terribly upset and could not understand their decision. Firstly, why would anyone care about the participants of the exchange winning and loosing, as long as everyone was satisfied and happy with the exchange? Secondly, the perception of the quality of the apartment seemed to me a purely individual matter: for one, the most important thing was view from the window, for another: noise from the street, for the third: hearing between the floors, and for the fourth: floor area. After failing to get this option and remembering all our misfortunes with the exchange bureau and its head, Tanya and I realized that the real reason for all our difficulties was of quite a different nature. This Soviet bureaucrat simply did not like the shape of our Jewish noses.

Soon, we received prove that our assumption was true. The apartment, into which Tanya and I could move, belonged to a handsome man, a retired Soviet Air Force pilot, who wanted to move into a smaller 2-room apartment. A man with the funny double surname Borkin-Yolkin vacated this small apartment. In Russian "bor" is "forest" and "yolka" is "fur tree". The pilot was very upset that the deal did not go through. In an outburst of candor and sympathy for us, he shared with us that the head of the exchange office informed him that the exchange was not possible. In their conversation he said, "*Do not get upset, please, I am even glad that you should not get mixed up with those three Jewish crooks, it will not be good for you.*" At first, I did not understand how this man could count three Jewish participants of the exchange. After a while, I understood, and my laughter began to choke me. The clerk in his anti-Semitic gusto counted Borkin-Yolkin, as two Jews. Thus, Borkin-Yolkin received the honorary distinction of the Double Jew of the Soviet Union, which he did not even know about.

This was really a bad joke. However, only at this moment the hopelessness of our efforts became clear to Tanya and me. I recalled here Lenin's immortal directive "*We have to go another way*". Soviet propaganda had this phrase in every history textbook. According to Soviet legend, after the execution of his brother, terrorist Alexander in 1887 for organizing an unsuccessful assassination attempt on Tsar Alexander III, Lenin said these words to his grief-stricken mother.

Through the parents of Tanya's students, we found an old colleague, moreover friend of our hero, the head of another exchange office. We managed to arrange for this woman to call her old friend and say "*Listen, why do you pester them? Leave them alone and let them do what they want!*" After this, a miracle happened: it was as if somebody smeared this very official with honey. He became nice and helpful, and the result was not long in coming, very soon, we found an exchange option similar to the one that had just fallen apart. By the way, we again slightly increased the size of our apartment, but this time it did not bother anyone. We got an approval for our exchange and soon had the keys for our new apartment and moved in.

Our new apartment was in the Moscow Southwest on Maria Ulyanov Street. We lived there until we left for America in 1988. There was not yet privatization at that time and when we left Russia, we gave it as a gift to the country. This was a token of our celebration of the parting with Soviet regime and of the gratitude for the honor of residing in this area named for famous Soviet leaders. Our street named after Lenin's sister Maria Ulyanov was off Lenin Avenue. The next street, named after Lenin's wife Krupskaya, ran parallel to ours, closer to the city center. One more street, named after Lenin's brother Dmvitry Ulyanov, was off Lenin Avenue even closer to the city center.

I recall a conversation I had once with a Moscow taxi driver. One evening I was returning home, and I asked this man if he knew how to get to Maria Ulyanov Street. He replied *"I remember once being requested to drive to a street named after one of Lenin's female companion but which one, I can't remember."*

DENUNCIATION REPORT

From the very first days of life on Maria Ulyanov Street, many fun and joyful things happened. Tanya played the guitar a little at that time, and at such moments my child would be in seventh heaven, and I, looking at them, even higher. Her rendition of the popular Yiddish song "Di mizinke ois gegeben" was a particular success. A father at his youngest daughter's wedding sings this song, and in Russian, the name of the song would be "I give you my youngest." My Galya asked Tanya to repeat this song repeatedly and again. My child, of course, let both her mother and grandmother hear her delight. Both of those women felt pain about my new life: the girl had left them for me, and, I think, they were especially grieved that she was most happy when she was WITH ME!

Unable to contain her irritation at such a development, Grandma decided to take an unthinkable and insane step. I was this very woman whom I came to love and whom I was helpng for years. Nevertheless, she made mad and baseless claims that could have ruined our lives. At the German faculty of the university, where Tanya worked, Renata's mother knew one professor.

She contacted this woman and asked her to go to the rector and tell her that Tanya, their professor in the English Department, corrupted her 12-year-old granddaughter (!?). The denunciation contained two very serious charges. Firstly, she told that Tanya taught the child to drink alcohol. As an example, she described our going with the girl to the restaurant on the day of registration. Secondly, she told how Tanya taught the girl harmful Zionist ideas, referring to Tanya's performance of the wedding song in Yiddish. In fact, to this day I cannot get over how this could have happened. After all, the woman's husband spent 17 years in torture chambers because of false denunciation, and that report ruined his life and the life of the whole family. Now his wife comes with false denunciation that could ruin the life of her beloved granddaughter and her father (!?)

Just the next day Maria Borodulin, the rector of the Institute, urgently summoned Tanya, informed her of the complaint and shouted at her in her foul language: *"How you can allow yourself to do such things?"* Tanya was not embarrassed and answered her, from my point of view, in the best possible way: *"I refuse now,"* she said, *"to discuss with you here anything whatsoever. I am ready to give any explanation, but in the presence of the reporter."* Borodulin agreed and immediately summoned this friend of Renata's mother.

The reporter DID NOT COME at the appointed time. This miracle could happen only in a country of bedlam and lawlessness. On the one hand, the university professor ignored a summons by the rector, and no one ever called her to account neither for disobedience, nor for slander. On the other hand, there were no "practical consequences" on the basis of the denunciation received, even though the whole institution as a whole was terribly Soviet and anti-Semitic.

True, Tanya had a special relationship with the rector of her institute. The fortunate circumstance was that this woman happened to know Tanya quite well and as well as her attitude towards children. She might believe anything about Tanya, but she knew for sure that never in her life would Tanya do anything bad to a child. This was the only thing that saved Tanya from immediate dismissal after the denunciation. In the next chapter, I will discuss M. K. Borodulin, the rector of the University and her friendship with Tanya.

The whole story of the denunciation made a depressing impression on me. It felt like I had touched something vile and dirty. I do not know what role Renata played in this story. I did not want to know about this then and I still do not want to know about it. The more so, I flatly did not want to discuss this issue with my ex-mother-in-law and my ex-wife. However, I told Liosha Gladky that I wanted to meet him urgently. On his next visit to Moscow this meeting happened in the street, I did not want to come to their house or invite them to mine. We arranged to meet at the corner of Lenin Avenue and Maria Ulyanov Street.

When I told Gladky what had happened, he was genuinely stunned and kept repeating: "Yuri, *you have got it all wrong. It cannot be.*" I would very much like to think that he meant it sincerely. To this, I recommended that he ask his current mother-in-law for details. I directly described to him the arrangement with Renata's mother. As they had left an old, ill and half-blind woman in Moscow, I considered it my duty to look after her and help her in every possible way. I regularly visited her, brought her groceries, and tried to run errands around the house. However, from now on, I told him, things would be different. After what had happened, I would not set foot in her house: the person I had known and respected had ceased to exist for me. She was dead to me. She had instantly destroyed all the good things built between us for years. I told him I just wanted to inform him and to let him do as he pleased. As we were saying goodbye, I asked him to tell Renata about our conversation. I have never seen Liosha since. On such a sad note, my relationship with Leah Ravich ended. When she died, I did not attend her funeral. Perhaps I should have been more tolerant and kind, but I was not strong enough to do so. I am no saint.

It has been almost 50 years since it all happened, but time has not erased our sad memories. You can imagine how strong that feeling was back then. Both of us, Tanya and I, were just in shock. It was that day that Tanya received a call from her department they asked: *"Tanya, what happened to you, are you ill?"* It turned out that on this day in the schedule she was to give a lesson. Her group came, and she was not there! She completely forgot about the class. During all the years that she worked in the University, nothing similar had ever happened to her before or after.

After Renata left my family, I was not at all interested in what was going on with her and Liosha Gladky. However, through mutual friends I heard that they had a son named Jasha. That was the name of Renata's brother, who was killed during the war. When I still used to visit Galya's grandmother, I would sometimes see the boy. I myself witnessed how Jasha's mother would bring and leave him with his grandmother. When that poor child would be late for a walk, the half-blind grandmother, losing her head with worry, would run around the block looking for the boy. She could not see the walking children and tried to get him to come to her desperate cries, "*Yasha! Yasha!* " After a while, I heard a rumor that Renata had parted with Liosha Gladky and had begun to live with his graduate student. This time she destroyed the normal family life of the FIFTH child! Nothing good had happened to this boy: he had grown up, "dabbled" in drugs, changed several professions, married early, and had a child. I was glad to hear from my Galya lately that after all the ordeals, Yasha turned into a good, kind person.

After I was describing my last meeting with Gladky in the spring of 2018, Galya told me from her mother's words the sad story of Liosha's last days. When he could no longer do his beloved science and no one needed him, he came to Moscow and Yasha sheltered him in his apartment. Later circumstances changed, and when Yasha could no longer keep his senile father at home, he moved him to his mother's apartment with her consent. Renata at that time was old, sick and helpless herself, alone in that apartment. When I think about the life of Yasha and his parents, I cannot help thinking about the extremely sad story-song about the miserable life of the girl growing up into a woman by A. Galich "Jolly talk." Its refrain at the end of many verses, repeats the words "*Akh, what a jolly talk!*" The adjective "jolly" in this context only amplifies the tragedy. This refrain, seems to me, sums up the sad description of these two people's lives.

MARFUTA

After very sad previous chapter, this paragraph is an introduction to a few of following chapters that would be, I hope, more cheerful. Before I met Tanya, each of us had a extensive circle of friends and acquaintances, and each of us knew quite a few interesting *people*. Here I remember Yuri Apresyan's joke about it. He used to say, *"When you walk down the street and meet a person, if that person is not a relative of Yuri Ziman, he is probably a good acquaintance of his"*. When we started living together with Tanya, we each gave each other our own circle of friends. In general, it seems to me that we cannot give a close person anything better than a friend with whom this person has not been acquainted before. As a result, such presents enrich everyone's life. The next few chapters summarize the people Tanya gave me. I have intentionally arranged them alphabetically by last name to eliminate the assumption that the order indicates a preference, an interest, a role this person has played in my life, or my liking for him or her. It is simply alphabetical order.

The rector of the Moscow University of Foregn Languages, Borodulin M.K

First is Maria Borodulin who was the rector of the University of Foreign Languages, where Tanya had studied and then taught until the day we decided to leave Russia. Maria was a curious phenomenon. She was born in a remote village of the Ruza district, where there were only 12 households, all belonging to the Borodulins. She loved her native village and regularly went there with friends, bringing a car full of vodka and logs of scarce sausages. When she arrived in the village, she would get out of the car, throw herself down, and kiss her native land. This ritual was neither posing nor playing, she would do it choked with sincere emotion.

As a girl, Maria came to Moscow to enroll in the Agricultural Academy. They did not accept her, so, may be a great manager of the collective farm or agronomist was lost for the country. In sad contemplation, she walked down Metrostroevskaya Street, and her gaze fell on the open doors of the University of Foreign Languages. *"Why do not I try this?"* She applied there and was accepted. After years of study, followed by work at the front during the WWII as a German interpreter, she began pedagogical work in the

German department of the University. A triumphant career march led her to the principal's chair of one of the largest universities in the country.

Fate arranged it in an intersting way. When my Tanya married Yuri Markish they moved into a small cooperative apartment in southwest Moscow. Soon after moving in, Tanya was shocked to learn that her NEXT-DOOR NEIGHBOR was the principal of her University, Maria Borodulin! Both were depressed, the rector even more than Tanya. One can imagine that unlike Tanya, this woman had a wide choice of apartments and she moved to the one where the chance of meeting her employees was minimal. Subsequently, Tanya heard her neighbor's curious account of those days. *"For several days in a row I howled. Then the first test came up: boozing in my apartment with lots of vodka and foul language. The first week goes by, all quiet, she did not report me, I conclude in mute amazement! Then the second time, the same thing! Then a third time and it is the same again! That's when I fell in love with you!"* It is not funny, I think Tanya heard an honest and heartfelt confession. After that, her principal, being a single woman, poured out upon Tanya her unspent maternal feelings.

After a while, her attachment to Tanya became so strong that even with the traditional anti-Semitism of a Soviet high-ranking official, she forced herself to pretend that she also liked Tanya's husband Yuri Markish. Nevertheless, she was delighted when Tanya and Yuri Markish divorced, but when Yuri left for Israel, she became hysterical. *"You are a fool; you do not understand that he is going to write a feuilleton about you and me there!"* I personally found it curious that Maria understood that our life in this country could be the subject for a published article criticizing the evils of the state.

Now both single, they seemed to get closer. Tanya even invented a special name for her neighbor: Marfuta. This name was commonly used for an ironic description of a village granny who could be at times kind and sympathetic. I also started calling her Marfuta and remembered a Russian folk ditty every time:

> *Where are you, girls?*
> *Here we are, here we are.*
> *But where is my Marfuta*
> *She is not here!*

Running ahead, our Marfuta is really not here today. Her body found rest at the Novodevichy cemetery in Moscow.

When Tanya told her that she was marrying me, Marfuta wanted to see me. "*A Jew again?*" she asked, and as if embarrassed, she turned her head away from Tanya. "Yes," replied Tanyusha, "*what can I do when only Jewish men love me?*" "*It's you who love them!*" retorted Marfuta. My reception was "in a warm, friendly atmosphere." She treated us to a nice cognac. We drank to our alliance with Tanya. The lines of A. Galich went round in my head:

> *She drank Champaign and I drank pepper vodka*
> *Toasting the new Soviet family, an exemplary family.*

I was surprised to find that in Marfuta's apartment I did not feel any discomfort. I had the feeling that I was on a tour in an ethnographic museum, becoming acquainted with the social types of man in the "Homo soveticus" hall. It is not without pride that I can say that I passed the test and received high approval from Marfuta, despite the shape of my nose.

One day, Tanya Markish had to take the English entrance exams for those applying to the Institute. Just before it started, a member of the department came into the classroom. This woman came up to Tanya with a list of all the applicants present in the class. Tanya looked at the list, and her eyes darkened: against all the Jewish surnames there were pencil marks indicating "no." Tanya ran after her into the corridor and saw with horror that this woman entered all the classes where the exams were starting. Unaware of herself, Tanya rushed to the chairperson of the admissions committee to complain. This woman told her: "*God be with you, Tanya, you didn't understand, go back to class and take the exam as you see fit.*"

Tanya felt as if in a fog, could not continue taking the exam, and paid no attention to the marks in the list she had received. Before she left for home, she stopped for a bite to eat in the University cafeteria and shared her indignation with a member of staff from their department. This woman was Jewish, so the sharing, she thought, should have been safe.

The journey home took her about half an hour. By the time she reached her floor, Marfuta was waiting for her on the landing in an absolute rage. Pushing her into her apartment, she pounced on her like a tigress. *"Someday I'll have to rip your tongue out! How many times do I have to tell you that every other person who works for us is reporter?"* Two things still amaze me. First, the inconceivable speed with which the denunciation system worked: after all, no more than half an hour had passed since the conversation in the cafeteria! Secondly, how could something real and human awake from time to time, in, the Soviet party bureaucrat, who had climbed so high!

Since Marfuta lived with Tanya literally next door, she was a living witness of Tanya's Sunday English school for children. Marfuta could not understand WHY Tanya spent so much effort and time on other people's children, without getting a penny nor a crumb of honor or fame. Nevertheless, Marfuta appreciated Tanya's depth of knowledge, cultural intelligence, brilliant pedagogical skills and her extraordinary love of children. *"You are silly, you are foolish, you could live so..."* How she could have lived, Tanya never heard from her boss. However, in the critical situation of Tanya's denunciation report, Marfuta did NOT BELIEVE that Tanya could corrupt children. Mafuta did understand what kind of person her young friend was and this saved Tanya this time.

About a similar question "WHY" we can read in the poem about Janush Korczak by A.Galich called "Kaddish", Judaism uses the word for the memorial prayer. In 1942, as the Polish police interrogated the most dignified Pole, grenadier and invalid of the First World War Piotr Zalewski, who worked as a janitor in the house of Jewish orphans in the Warsaw Ghetto, they addressed to him the same eternal question "WHY":

> *You, stumpy, you want to live,*
> *Why, the hell,*
> *You are in the ghetto babysitting like a kike,*
> *With the kike kids?!*

These not-humans never got an explanation from the hero as to WHY, just as Marfuta did not get one from Tanya. Failing to satisfy their curiosity, the conquerors of Poland shot the most dignified man on the spot. Thank God, times have changed. Nobody ever tried to kill neither Tanya nor her pupils like Korczak's orphans and their great educator. I suppose that Marfuta had never read A.Galich and this saved her from doubt and remorse, which would have made her life much more difficult. Since that time Tanya, now for more than 50 years, continues to baby-sit the Jews' children like a Jew.

Regretfully, I have not had the chance to hear about many of Marfuta's brilliant performances myself. However, the stories were so remarkable that I cannot refrain from telling some of them here as they sounded in Tanya's presentation to me. One such story has to do with her trip to West Germany. Of course, she was worried to look dignified, representing the happiest country in the world. Of course, her main adviser turned out to be Tanya. "*Ms. Borodulina, may I advise you to dress in a different way,*" said the consultant in a friendly manner. "*You should never wear red shoes with a green skirt.*" The funny thing was that Marfuta really appreciated such a qualified consultant and listened very much to her advice. Anyway, the preparations were over, and Marfuta was ready to go.

The name "Dun'ka" was for some reason used in Russia for an uneducated woman. When an uneducated person would go abroad, Russians would joke, "*Dun'ka was allowed to go to Europe*". This time it was not Dun'ka but Marfuta who went with the business trip to Europe. From the corrupt West she returned alive, unharmed, and enthralled. "*Well, I will tell you, Tanya, they live there so..., they live there so...*" Her excitement did not let her to breathe normally. "*It is high time they were closed!*" How she really thought about "closing" West Germany, the most economically developed country in Europe, I would be very curious to know.

Everyone among Tanya's colleagues remembers that Marfuta had a clinical paranoia that poisoned all her joy of working at the University. She constantly lived in fear of sabotage, most of all political sabotage, which she, as principal, could not prevent. Tanya's University was to publish its research related to general philology and the science and practice of translation. Our very close friend Vera Prokhorov, who worked in Tanya's department, prepared one such publication. This wonderful woman, Tanya's mentor and teacher, was one of the best human gifts I received from Tanya, and there will be a separate chapter about her later on.

Our dear Verochka's pamphlet was devoted to the role of political factors in the semantics of a text. The soviet propaganda demanded that most of the people in the West had to be bad, whereas most of the soviet people had to be nice. For instance, a person employed for an intelligence job by a government of one's own country or of a friendly country is always an INTELLIGENCE OFFICER whereas one employed by the government of a hostile country, is always a SPY. In both cases, we are talking about the people performing exactly the same job. This was the topic of Vera's article. Somehow, the communist party authorities have seen a draft of this publication and a scandal broke out. The party bosses found the article ideologically wrong and ordered its publication cancelled. At that time, Tanya rang Marfuta's doorbell and found her hysterical. *"What luck that the article was intercepted,"* she told Tanya, *"it is all your friends! It is high time we grabbed some of them by the ass"*. Tanya at this time was sick and irritable and could not contain her indignation. *"All right, Maria, then start with those closest to you, namely, go and grab me!"* After this being said, Tanya stormed home. Ten minutes later, the bell at her door rang. Tanya opened it, and on the threshold stood Marfuta with a plate in her hands. *"Here's some warm soup, eat it, you're not going to make it yourself. You'll feel better."* It appeared that normal human warmth periodically broke out in this party official probably against her will.

I have mixed feelings about this woman. Today, I regret belatedly, not talking more to Marfuta and not asking her more questions. However, that train is gone. The country she loved and served so faithfully no longer exists, Russia has become very different, but the mentality of many people is still the same as Marfuta's. Soviet heroes continue to be in honor. Nevertheless, I am still grateful to this unhappy woman for the good she did for Tanya. Today, our Marfuta is no longer with us. She passed away and her body found rest in 2005 in the Novodevichy Cemetery.

THE CELLO BEARER

I was fortunate to hear Natalia Gutman play the cello many times, and every time I was reminded of Okudzhava's verse "Musician," and following the poet, I always marveled at *"how these hands could produce these sounds."* I agree with those people who call Natasha the cello queen. Knowing Natasha was truly a royal gift from Tanya. Unfortunately, it is not always the case that brilliant, genius professionals are nice. Natasha is an absolute exception in this regard. Almost fifty years of our friendship have been years of pure joy.

Throughout, I have been her admirer, both as a music lover and as a man. There was one question, which I never dared to ask Natasha: in our friendship, did she ever felt joy similar to one Tanya and I did, or it was one-way street. It seems to me, Natasha has truly valued our friendship in return.

We were always happy to get a confirmation of this from a person very close to Natasha, Vera Prokhorov who introduced Tanya to Natasha. Unfortunately, Verochka is no longer with us. When we saw her the last time, it felt as if we were saying good-bye to her forever. Then she uttered words that I will never forget. Verochka never had a husband or children and she told us: *"You are my children!"* She also said this to Natasha. It turns out that through Verochka, Natasha is our sister!

After Natasha's concerts, Tanya and I would often visit her in the dressing room to share our enthusiasm and pride. Natasha ALWAYS responded to our wows by saying: *"No, you just did not hear it, it was awful!"* It was during these conversations that Natasha helped me understand that dissatisfaction with yourself is the road for you to perfection, and one who is fully satisfied with him or herself is a finished person with no growth left. Being unsatisfied with what she had achieved forced her to work harder. When she stayed with us, she would rehearse to a point of frenzy. We knew many musicians, but I have not seen any of them work as hard and as intensely as Natasha. Her obsession together with her talent, I think, drove her to perfection. I remember asking myself an interesting question: is there a more easy way to perfection?

My reverence for Natasha led me to the reverence for her cello, for Natasha's cello was part of Natasha herself. Always in love with it, when traveling all around the world with performances, she would NEVER let the cello out of her arms. When we got into the car with her, she would always tenderly lay the cello like a little child. Whenever she got out of the car, even

Our wonderful friend, cellist Gutman N.G.

for a short time, she would gently take the cello out of the car and gently wear it behind her back like a backpack. Watching Natasha, I thought that she needed a devoted cello bearer, her own Sancho Panso, like in Cervantes's Don Quixote, who would take care of these physical worries, saving her for the *"high passion for the sounds."* Unlike Pushkin's Onegin, Natasha did have this high passion without any doubt, and she did have it beyond any measure.

I quoted Pushkin in the previous paragraph and the following thought occurred to me. When Pushkin used the word "sounds" in the lines cited, he was of course, as a poet, referring to the sonic structure of the verses. This becomes obvious if we continue the quote: Onegin had no such passion and as a result, *"he could not distinguish iambic from trochee, no matter how hard we fought with him."* When I used the quotation, I remembered our conversations. We talked with her about many things, not only music, but also poetry. One day I was talking with her about verse meters, iambic, trochee... Natasha complained that she had not seen any good explanations of the difference between meters. With my love of rhyming, I immediately wrote five humorous observations about her in the various popular measures: the two-syllable iambic and trochee and the three-syllable dactyl, amphibrach, and anapest. I accompanied each example of the meter with a diagram of the syllabic stress distribution. She was very pleased and I was very happy.

Thoughts of the cello bearer would torture me after each seeing her in the dress room after the performance, say, at the Great Hall of the Moscow Conservatory. In the beginning, the room was full of people; everyone was in high spirits and happy, sometimes even the hero of the day was happy. All expressed their delight, and then departed. The party would end, and everyday life would return. No one would offer her help as a cello bearer.

Each time, poor Natasha would have to pack up her unique, but still rather big and weighty musical instrument behind her back and to drag herself home alone. It was those moments, when I began to have a thought: what if I could get the cello queen's permission to master, under her guidance, the honorable profession of cello bearer. Then, after each concerts, when I was in the hall, I could help her carry her Guarneri cello at least to the car. I can proudly say that my plan succeeded, I managed to gain Natascha's trust. Under her guidance, I successfully completed my internship and, as they used to say in Russia, I got a temporary job as Natasha's cello bearer!!!

Both Tanya and I love music very much. Our long-term friendship with Natasha brought great joy into our lives and contributed to our musical education. It related especially to me because I knew then and I continue to know today much less than Tanya about music. As a result, this friendship killed few birds with one stone.

First, we were fortunate to have a chance to be at her concerts in Moscow quite frequently and we even heard her when Natasha would come to Boston on tour. We also listened to her many recordings of her performances and performances of her brilliant friends. One of those recordings was also a great success with our granddaughters. When I would pick up one of them at school to take her home, I often get an order from my little passenger: *"Hey, Grandpa, play Mozart, please."* This was the CD of a brilliant recital by S. Richter and O. Kagan of Mozart's sonata K376.

Secondly, through Natasha, we befriended few great musicians, her late husband Kagan, in the first place. We were incredibly fortunate to know this extraordinarily sunny man and extremely talented violinist. It is about such a person one our friend joked: *"They do not produce such people anymore, unfortunately!"* Harsh disease does not spare even such good souls like Oleg. Incurable illness struck him. With unimaginable courage, Oleg never parted with his violin and continued to perform even in intolerable pain until he passed away in 1990.

Another gift we got from Natasha was her friend, the great pianist with whom she frequently played, the wonderful, brilliant Eliso Virsaladze. While we were in Moscow, we managed to see and to hear her regularly, as well. Unfortunately, living on different continents does not help friends to see each other as often as one would like.

Thirdly, Natasha built for Oleg the best memorial imaginable. When Oleg was still traveling and playing around the world, they ended up together on tour in Bavaria in the small town of Kreuth. Oleg fell in love with the place and told Natasha that if he could organize his own music festival, he would like to do in this fantastically picturesque place. It has been 30 years since Oleg left, but thanks to Natasha's efforts, international festivals named after Oleg Kagan have taken place in Kreuth. The first took place three

Family duo: Gutman N. (cello) and Kagan O. (violin)

days before Olegs death. Oleg himself was in the hospital and had obtained permission from his doctor to go to Kreuth and play his last concert. He could no longer stand, so his friends brought him and put on a special chair. As a result, he played beautiful music with his beloved friends in the place of his dreams. With incredible willpower, he made his dream possible. Oleg's family believes that this performance prolonged his life for at least a few days.

After Oleg's death, Tanya and I came to one of the festivals in Kreuth at Natasha's invitation from Boston. The trip was unforgettable in many ways. First, Oleg was right; this place just at the border with Austria in the foothills of the Alps is stunningly beautiful. When we admired the incredible natural sights, a question spun in my head, how could a monster like Hitler grow and form in this unearthly beautiful place? I also wondered how one of the most cultured countries in the world could voluntarily submit to the devilish evil. On the other hand, the USSR natives should not be surprised, having lived more than 30 years under a tyrant of Hitler's caliber. Here, according to Tyutchev Fyodor:

> *There is unperturbed order in everything,*
> *A complete consonance in nature, —*
> *Only in our ghostly freedom*
> *We create a discord with it.*

Tanya and I will not forget our musical and emotional impressions of the festival until the end of our lives. Many of the world's best musicians came to the festival. Many of them knew Oleg and remembered him fondly. Natasha surrounded us there with unforgettably touching care. Finally, it was there that we had our last meeting with our very dear and beloved, Verochka Prokhorov. Oh, Natasha, no words can thank you enough for Kreuth.

I have described before how I became a friend with Natasha's cello. When we were in Moscow, I never asked Natasha what kind of instrument was it, and how highly it was valued: I was happy, anyway, that she entrusted me with HER CELLO! Later I learned that in my career as Natasha's cello bearer I raised quite high. She explained that this collectable instrument had been made by Giuseppe Guarneri, the most famous master of the Guarneri dynasty, the Italian masters of stringed instruments. Some connoisseurs put Giuseppe Guarneri on a par with Antonio Stradivari. Guarneri has often been called Guarneri del Gesù (Guarneri from Jesus in Latin), thus emphasizing the divinity of the instruments that he made. Guarneri Del Gesù made many famous violins, and many famous violinists have played them, including N. Paganini, J. Heifetz and I. Stern. However, according to Natasha, her instrument was the ONLY CELLO that came out of the hands of the great master. It seems to me that this is no coincidence. I see the ultimate justice of the world in the fact that musical instruments made by great masters find their way eventually to great musicians. I was honored and happy that Natasha allowed me to carry this priceless instrument for her.

ANTI-WOLF

Vera Prokhorov occupied an exceptional place in Tanya's life before we married, and after that, she began to occupy an equally exceptional place in mine. Tanya met her in the late fifties at the English Department of the Foreign Languages University, where Tanya first studied and then taught. They soon became friends, and Vera became her favorite teacher, then her favorite co-worker, and then her favorite mentor and friend. This outstanding woman until the last days of her life (Verochka died on January 20, 2013) was a very close, very dear, and very necessary person to both of us. The fact that our lives crossed paths seems incredible luck to me. I still cannot forgive myself that I did not talk to her enough, did not ask enough questions about her and about her very special family and friends.

Verochka was born in 1918. Among her family members, one can find phenomenally many of the country's best sons and daughters, people who make up the pride and glory of Russia. Her father was Ivan Prokhorov, the last owner of the famous

Prokhorov Triokhgornaya Manufactory. Even before the revolution, this factory repeatedly won gold medals at international fairs. Her mother, Nadezhda Guchkov, was an English teacher, whose efforts infused the family with music, literature, and art. It was thanks to her mother that Verochka knew English, French and German. Verochka's grandmother's sister was married to the artist Ilya Ostroukhov, art collector and first curator of the Tretyakov Gallery and friend to Valentin Serov. When I visited Verochka, I could not take my eyes away from the portrait of her mother, Nadezhda, painted by Valentin Serov. The charming woman in the portrait reminded me of my favorite women in the writings by Pushkin, Tolstoy, Turgenev and Goncharov.

Verochka's great-grandmother Varvara Prokhorov was a cousin of Konstantin Stanislavsky. A great-uncle on her father's side, Alexander Alyokhin, was the fourth world chess champion. Great-grandmother Maria Botkin, was the wife of the poet Afanasiy Fet. Great-grandfather, Sergey Botkin, was a physician, doctor, and life-medic of Emperors Alexander II and Alexander III. Her granddad on her mother's side was Nikolai Guchkov, the mayor of Moscow and the member of the State Duma. Her great-uncle on her mother's side was Alexander Guchkov, Chairman of the Third State Duma, and Minister of War in Alexander Kerensky's Provisional Government. We can go on and on with this.

After the revolution of 1917, the family lost everything: money, property, factory, houses (grandfather owned several). Verochka told us that some houses they left literally without taking a single thing. However, Verochka's father did not want to leave his beloved factory and stayed to work there, first as a manager and then as a guard. He had a special relationship with the workers. They helped him to buy a house not far from Trekhgorka in Tsaritsyn. Twice the soviet regime arrested him for his "capitalist" past and both times the factory went on strike, the workers would resume the work only after the release of their owner. In general, contrary to what we learned in our childhood about the bestial nature of capitalists, the Prokhorov family was famous for putting the dignity of their workers and the reputation of their business above any personal benefits. list.

The facts, now published, support what was said in the previous paragraph. At the World Exhibition in Paris in 1900, Trekhgorka received a special Grand Prix for care of its workers' welfare. For the progressive organization of factory production in 1912, Verochka's grandfather Nikolai Prokhorov was elevated with all his posterity to the hereditary nobility. That is how our Verochka became a "hereditary noblewoman." Because of this, there may be a facetious logical conclusion. Since Verochka, shortly before her death, declared Tanya and me her named children, Tanya and I, too, can claim hereditary nobility!

However, if we move from jokes to reality, the nobility in the past did not protect her poor father, but only worsened his troubles in soviet time. From such a "merry" life, he started drinking and died quite soon, in 1927. Verochka was only 9 years old. The workers in the factory refused a funeral coach and wanted to carry the coffin from the Botkin hospital where he died to the Vagankovo cemetery close to Triohgorka, walking across Moscow. Having lost her father, Verochka left with her mother and brother. At the beginning of the civil war, her brother, after mobilization went to the military service and soon was killed, as if the losses, the family had already gone through, was not enough. Her mother, however, lived until World War II and died shortly after it ended. Vera's mother was a wonderful woman, and she left to her daughter the fondest memories of herself. Verochka would tell us, how heroic, I would say, her mother was, always trying to provide her girl with a happy childhood. Verochka used to tell us how, the happy years before her father's death helped her through all her later hardships. In their home, packed with literature, music, and fine art, always sounded humor and laughter. In one of the arrests, they asked Ivan Prokhorov to read and sign the protocol of interrogation mentioning the sentence of death. He signed and said: "*I read it with pleasure and signed it.*" After such stories, I had no doubt, where Verochka got her phenomenal sense of humor.

After her father's funeral, the workers volunteered to supply their exploiter's family with groceries, which they brought directly from the village. Verochka would tell us how in the silence of the night, old women would appear at their door like ghosts with a piece of meat, a bundle of butter or a bag of potatoes. Those "ghosts" kept appearing throughout the thirties and early forties and helped the family survive these difficult times. Since then, Verochka told us, "*I believed in the kindness of Russian people.*" Ten years after her father's death, Verochka recalled how during the mass repressions of 1937, Stalin's thugs remembered her father and came to arrest him. "*He is not home any more*", Verochka's mother told them.

The kindness of Verochka herself knew no bounds. We were friends with her in relatively prosperous times, when she had a steady job and a steady paycheck. Nevertheless, Verochka NEVER had any money, she gave it away to everyone who, in her opinion, needed it more than she did. She herself, in her own words, did not need anything at all. Maya Ulanovsky wrote memoirs about life with her in the high-security camp where fate brought them together. She took over her guardianship and called Maya her camp daughter. "*This is the first time I have encountered such a special phenomenon,*" we read in Maya's memoirs, "*the kindness from a principle which was above human abilities.*" It really was kindness not because something, but kindness in genes and blood. "*After all, I am a wolf, Tanechka,*" she used to say, when Tanya tried to persuade her to buy herself a new dress. "*No dress is going to make me look any different.*" Strangely enough, her own image of herself as a wolf somehow sat deep enough inside Verochka. Whenever I heard about it, I tried to argue vehemently against it, though with her passion I would not call her a sheep either. It seems to me that if one were to use the context of a wolf, she should rather have said after Osip Mandelstam:

> *The wolfhound of the century is upon my shoulders.*
> *However, I am not a wolf by my blood...*

Or after Marina Tsvetaev:

> *I refuse to live.*
> *With the wolves of the squares,*

Nature has made the wolf a predator, and our beloved Verochka is an anti-predator, so she is an anti-wolf.

I do not know where the family lived after the forcible dispossession of the rich people in Russia during the revolution. When I met Verochka in the seventies we used to visit her in a very small room of the communal apartment. This room was in the mezzanine of the several floor building, which used to belong entirely to her father. She managed to change that room for another one later. That is how our Verochka found herself in the "den", so well known to all her friends, in which I was fortunate enough to visit. Verochka never called her room anything but a "den". She was consistent: a wolf lives in a den. We used to drop into her den for tea. Her flat mates loved her very much but often were concerned that all she ate was just tea. So they would always try to feed her. The room was so small that it barely had space for a bed, little bookshelf, and a little table with three chairs where she ate and gave tea to her guests. At the same table, Verochka prepared her lessons on English stylistics. She was one of the best teachers in the department, according to Tanya.

Verochka's charming personality, like a magnet, attracted people to the den, and Tanya and I were not the only ones. Natasha Gutman regularly used the den to rehearse. Surprisingly, she did not mind that its size made sitting down with a big cello difficult. When she played, the small space barely allowed her bow arm not to crash into the wall. Nevertheless, we knew that many of Natasha's best performances were prepared in Verochka's den.In 1937, the most important event in Verochka's life happened: meeting the great Russian pianist Sviatoslav Richter. The meeting took place at the house of Richter's teacher G. G. Neuhaus, where Verochka came with her mother for a birthday party for Verochka's aunt, Neuhaus's wife. Richter was staying at the time with Neuhaus, his favorite teacher. Since that meeting until her last breath, Verochka worshipped the pianist. She called him "Svetik" (in Russian "little ray of light") because she thought he radiated light. He came up with his own name for her, Vipa, based on the first three initials of her full name, including the first name, the patronymic and the last name, Vera Ivanovna Prokhorov. She would never allow any criticism of this man in her presence, and he became the life-giving light, the meaning of her whole life.

In 1941, authorities arrested H. G. Neuhaus. Nadezhda, Verochka's mother, convinced everyone that it was not safe for Richter to continue living with the Neuhauses. She insisted that Svetik should stay with them for a while. Richter moved in with the Prokhorovs and "some time" became several years, until the end of the war. He did become the member of the family, however, he continued to live his own life. If we believe N. L. Dorliak, he proposed to her in 1945 and they married. In the extensive litera-

Verochka Prokhorov and Sviatoslav Rikhter

ture on Richter, authors refer to this marriage as a civil one. Even Verochka herself called it that. It seems to me, however, that such a thing as a civil marriage simply does not exist. If it is not a real marriage, then it is a fake one. I strongly believed then and still believe today, that real marriages are made in heaven, not in the registry offices. It pains me to think how our Verochka, so deeply in love with Richter, survived that event. However, we never know enough about the intimate relationships of others to draw any conclusions.

When I first heard Novella Matveyeva's song "The Girl from the Tavern" I thought that the poet must have described her own feelings, and that she was the only woman on earth capable of feeling this way:

> *It was enough for me just to see you,*
> *Just to meet your smile.*
> *And if you went off with another woman,*
> *If you were, just nobody knew where,*
> *I've had enough of the fact that your*
> *Cloak was hanging on my nail.*

But I did meet another such woman in the person of our Verochka Prokhorov. Her love was as selfless and as wholehearted as the love of the girl in Novella Matveyeva's poem.

Verochka never complained, never blamed anyone, and never discussed her feelings, at least with us. When a conversation would touch upon Richter, she always spoke of him in an exaggerated positive way, as of a fact known to everyone in the world. Everyone could always read her feelings between the lines. She kept every letter and every card from him, putting them all into a suitcase, which she kept under her bed. Verochka is no longer with us, and unfortunately, we know nothing more about this suitcase or its contents.

For more than seventy years, she carried her love deep inside her, and this, I believe, must have been excruciatingly difficult for her. However, shortly before Verochka's death, the writer and journalist Igor Obolensky helped her tell about that love. Based on conversations with Verochka, he published a book in 2012, "Vera Prokhorov. Four friends against the backdrop of a century." Although the title mentions four friends: Richter, Pasternak, Bulgakov, Nagibin, it seems to me that this book is mainly about Richter. It reminded me of Bulat Okudzhava's lines.

> *While the red rose*
> *Is still alive in the bottle,*
> *Let me cry out the words,*
> *That I kept for a long time in my coinbox.*

In Verochka's shout published in the book, I can clearly hear the superhuman courage and dedication so characteristic of her: "We were very close until his last day. I had great feelings for him, which began with friendship. When the question of his arrest came up, I realized that Svetik was much more than just a friend for me... However, I never regretted not becoming Richter's wife... I felt pity for Sviatoslav. What kind of wife would I make? I am a completely anti-family-household person. I am the reverse to ideal in this sense. What kind of life could I offer him? The way it happened, we remained friends, very close people. We could talk about everything. There were no secrets between us. We shared absolute trust in each other." I do not think many of us are capable of such dedication. I personally, like most people in the world, take my hat off to Richter as a musician and as a human being. He had a very difficult life, and his courage and resilience in the face of unbearable circumstances can only inspire admiration.

However, the forty years of my friendship with Verochka, I think, allow me to say something not very much in his favor that may cause resentment in many people. During the last 15 years of our life in Moscow, we were regularly in her den, and each visit would make me sad. During these years, not only the USSR but also the whole word acclaimed Richter as a great pianist. He found himself counted amongst the best musicians in the world. He deservedly received the rain of honorable prizes, awards, and titles. How could it be that he, who had become such a celebrity, could not petition for Verochka, so that she could move from her den in a terrible communal apartment, of which there were not many in Moscow, to a modest but decent place? I still do not know how to answer this question. Maybe I expected more from him than what he could have done.

Our Verochka's friendship with Richter gave Tanya and me many happy hours. Wherever the great pianist played, he would never forget to leave a couple of tickets for Verochka. The poor woman tried to go to his concerts at first, but it turned out to be too much for her to handle emotionally. At each such concert, she choked with tears that deprived her of the opportunity to listen to the music. She became helpless. Finally, she made the decision to stop putting herself through this torture and began to offer these tickets to her loved ones. This way we would often become the lucky owners of tickets that were impossible to get in Moscow, neither for love nor for money. At the same time, our Verochka was adamant that people to whom she gave the tickets would use these tickets for themselves and not for someone else. One day a mutual friend got these tickets and at the last moment realized that she could not go to the concert herself. This woman decided to make her close friend happy and gave her the tickets. But our Verochka did not like this person. I remember that after, our friend got a big scolding from Verochka. She felt that such a replacement was an offence to her beloved Svetic.

Let us go back, however, to the fifties. Neither Verochka's many friends and relatives, nor her communal flat mates, who loved her dearly, could keep her out of Stalin's custody. In 1951, she was arrested as a class enemy, and the Special Meeting, forget about the trial, sentenced her to ten years of hard labor camps. The charges used the sadly notorious 58th article of the Code about counterrevolutionary activity. The camp was located in Krasnoyarsk region. Fortunately, Stalin died in 1953, after which the political prisoners who had survived began to return to freedom. At the initiative of Verochka's friends, the writer Yuri Nagibin, in 1956, wrote a petition for the release of Vera Prokhorov. Sviatoslav Richter had also signed this document among others. Our Verochka returned to freedom, with complete exoneration and soon after, she was reinstated at the University of Foreign Languages named after Maurice Thorez. As a ludicrous compensation for her years of imprisonment, she received two months' salary (?!) and a small room in a communal flat in the Arbat lanes. This room she managed to exchange for the one from which they took her to the camp. This way our Verochka returned to her den.

I was always very interested in the years of our Verochka's imprisonment. I did not ask her much about that time, not wanting to evoke painful and difficult memories. However, sometimes Verochka would tell me, catching hold of a context, a story herself. The little that I heard will always stay with me for the rest of my life.

One story is about a bathing day in the camp. The men, who were strong and rough, drove the poor women like cattle into the cramped pre-bathroom and told them to undress. Then they led them, naked in formation, to the shower room. Later the same thing happened in reverse order. *"How could you bear this disgusting humiliation?"* I could not resist asking her. *"Yurochka,"* she answered me, *"they were neither men, nor people with whom one could be embarrassed or outraged. Either they were robots, or, even worse, the devil's spawn. They had no souls, and I didn't care about them at all!"* This answer taught me a lot and I will never forget it.

The second story I remember was about Charles Dickens, who was favorite writer of our beloved Verochka Prokhorov. Surprisingly, in the camp was another woman who had also read Dickens. Verochka told us how one day at the tree felling works, the wardens let the prisoners rest for a while. Verochka was sitting near this woman on the stumps and a conversation ensued. Verochka said, *"What a great writer Dickens was!"* Her companion asked, *"Why do you think so?"* Verochka replied, *"Look around you and take a good look at both those who suffer and their tormentors. After all, Dickens described them all long ago!"* Before I heard this story, the thought had never occurred to me that a great writer could actually help people even in the extreme situation of a concentration camp.

Verochka recounted in her book a curious episode that happened shortly after her arrest, while still in prison. On September 30, 1951, the name day of three Christian saint women-martyrs Vera, Nadezhda and Lubov (meaning in Russian: Faith, Hope, and Love), the KGB received an odd telegram. It had a strange address: Moscow, Lubyanka, to Vera Prokhorov. For those who do not know, Lubyanka was the name of the square in Moscow where the headquarters of the KGB were located. The text of the telegram said: "*Congratulations, kisses, Richter.*" The investigator later said to Verochka "*Well, the enemy has gotten out of hand!*" What depresses me about this episode is that a man with a law degree may easily assume the right to identify himself with the country, while all the prisoners, and all their relatives and friends to label enemies of the country. The investigation was not over yet. Nobody has a right on this stage to condemn the woman under investigation, nor her acquaintance, unknown to him. This man was angry: who dared to congratulate her on her name day. Who needs these silly sentiments? Everyone I do not like is, of course, an enemy of my people!

There was one topic related to the arrest that Verochka returned to in our conversations more than once. It was the story of the denunciation report by her family friend, the Soviet composer Alexander Lokshin. From what Verochka told us, and from what she wrote in her book, there is no doubt that he was the denouncer. The investigation needed three witnesses, and they were Lokshin's wife, Lokshin's sister and Lokshin's close friend. All three met Verochka during the confrontation in the investigator's office, and all three seemed to her extremely uncomfortable. The investigation decided to keep Lokshin himself, for some reason, in a low profile. I wanted to know what the Russian Internet had to say about this today.

Russian Wikipedia article about A. Lokshin included several paragraphs entitled "*Whistle-blowing charges and posthumous exoneration.*" There we read that the accusation in reporting by Lokshin came from three prisoners of Gulag arrested by A. Lokshin's denunciation. All three returned to freedom with complete exoneration after Stalin's death. Apart from Verochka, I personally knew one: the mathematician Alik Esenin-Volpin, of whom Verochka always talked as about her "same-case prisoner" Esenin-Volpin himself had repeatedly declared, including publicly, that it was Lokshin, who put him in jail. Incidentally, the same Russian Wikipedia confirmed that Esenin-Volpin was sent to jail on a denunciation but did not name the informer. However, it did say, that the authorities forced poor imprisoned man for many years into compulsory "treatment" in a mental hospital. The only illness he suffered, according to Vladimir Bukovsky, was "pathological truthfulness." Frankly speaking, I feel saddened by the Russian Wikipedia article's not very convincing cover-up of A. Lokshin's responsibility. I personally continue to believe in what I learned from our great friend Vera Prokhorov and from Alik Esenin-Volpin.

A portrait of Verochka Prokhorov would be incomplete if I did not tell about her long night telephone conversations with Tanya, which took place before my entrance into Tanya's life. The subject of these nightly vigils was often Tanya's dream of becoming a mother. In this connection, I would like to mention here the following remarkable story from Tanya's childhood. Tanya's aunt had given her as a present the book by Chekhov. During an illness, she swallowed it whole. Paradoxically, Tanya liked being sick, it allowed her to read a lot. Impressed by the book, she recommended the Chekhov to her older sister Natasha. "*I only beg you to treat the book with care, I want to save it for my children,*" said Tanya. "*How many children do you want to have?*" asked Natasha, surprised by her eight-year-old sister's concrete plans. "*Twelve!*" replied Tanya without thinking. More than 30 years had passed since that episode with Natasha, a lot of water flowed away, but that dream remained. She had no shortage of suitors, but somehow, she did not manage to meet a suitable candidate for the father of such a brood. Tanya's dream aroused in Verochka incredible enthusiasm, it was impossible to think of a better interlocutor on this subject.

In these midnight conversations, Tanya's dream became even more concrete. "*Tanechka,*" said Vera to her, "*The man you want is on his way, and you will have with him a lovely daughter who looks like you. I am not sure about the twelve children, but this girl I foresee quite clearly.*" Tanya immediately made up her mind, having, of course, obtained Verochka's consent to name her Verochka. And so, until dawn she discussed with Vera what books should be read to little Verochka. Ever after, in all their conversations, the little girl who had not yet been born was referred to as "little Verochka." To this day, I regret that I did not take part in those discussions about what should be done for little Verochka. Maybe then, I could have given her more than I did and still do now. When our Vera was born there was no question of what to call her, of course "little Vera."

I have already written that our last meeting with the elder Verochka took place at Oleg's Festival in Kreuth in Bavaria, I think, in 2005. But Verochka's last letter was delivered by our niece Masha, Tanya's sister Natasha's daughter, whom we had asked to visit older Verochka in Moscow. We received it a couple of years before her death. Masha told us that Verochka dictated the letter, as she could not see properly anymore and could no longer write by herself. I have already written that our last meeting with the elder Verochka took place at Olegs Festival in Kreuth in Bavaria, I think, in 2005. But Verochka's last letter was delivered by our niece Masha, Tanya's sister Natasha's daughter, whom we had asked to visit older Verochka in Moscow. We received it a couple of years before her death. Masha told us that Verochka dictated the letter, as she could not see properly anymore and could no longer write by herself. Tanya and I both shed many tears over this letter. Here it is.

> *My dear and beloved darlings, my Tanechka and Yurochka! Exactly like* **My first friend, my priceless friend!** *(the bolded quote is the first line from the poem, letter by A.Pushkin addressing his close friend I.Pushchin). I always think of you as my closest people, people I am proud of. I think of your courage that helped you to overcome all adversity. There is no space or time around me. For me, you are always with me, in my thoughts. With joy and gratitude, I look at photos of Vera's wedding. I recall Verochka's birth made me happy, we were talking about her so much. I think with love about Galya, who helped you so much. You are a good example of a family, a real family; you create a wonderful atmosphere of friendship, love and help. You are an example for all the others; I see in this the joy and the meaning of life. Families like yours are the guarantee that the humanity has a future. I am happy to live thinking about such future. I want to thank you for your attitude towards Natasha Gutman. She finds in your home the quietude, the peace, the joy that she lacks in her own home. She always speaks of you with love. Your whole family, all of you, are my dearest. A big-big kiss.*
>
> *Your Vera."*

When Verochka passed away, our little Vera. was already 37 years old, but she still remained in our conversations and thoughts as "little Verochka", and the older Verochka until her last day regarded me and Tanya as her children and the little Verochka. as her granddaughter. Thank you, dear Verochka, thank you for being a wonderful mother and grandmother to us! Your presence was invaluable to us. If there is any good in us, we owe a lot of that good to you. May you rest in peace!

TIGER OF KINDNESS

Tzilia Reitburd was another gift I received from Tanya. When someone around her had an unsolved problem in life, this wonderful woman would immediately rush to solve it, sparing neither effort, nor time, nor money. Unsolvable problems never existed for her. Surprisingly enough, she did manage to find a solution for most of the problems she attacked. Tzilia would rush in like a tiger to help people, never waiting that somebody asked. For that, her acquaintances and friends called her the tiger of kindness. This woman was in this respect truly unique.

Striking were Tzilia's unlimited intransigence and fearlessness. Even in the face of the most serious trouble, up to and including arrest, never would she stop. Remember, we lived in a politically ugly country, where most had so much fear locked inside them that horses could not drag it from them. People feared that even closest friends and relatives could denounce them. Such feelings were unfamiliar to Tzilia. She possessed amazing courage. It was not easy for her friends and relatives, who could not stop worrying about her, and indirectly, of course, about themselves. However, those who really loved her had to understand that this was her essence and there is no way to change her. Unfortunately, many in her entourage, because of her fearless actions, were afraid to communicate with her. Some of them tried to find an excuse to end communication with her and thus to protect themselves. This was

Our very close friend Tzilia Reitburd

how the rumor spread around Moscow that Tzilia was only "fearless" because she worked for the KGB. It amazes me how those who started this rumor do not have stabs of conscience. Tanya and I had a very close relationship with Tzilia, and neither of us for a second believed that such a terrible accusation contained even a shred of truth.

It seems to me that Tzilia inherited her rare qualities from her father, Moses Reitburd. We did not know him at all because he died quite early. However, the stories Tzilia told me about him have stuck in my memory all my life that were enough for me to make him my example of wisdom in life. I like telling these stories to most people close to me

The first story about this man seems to me very instructive. Moses would start his day after ablutions, by addressing his wife: "*We had a very happy day today!*" Each time his wife, was initially perplexed, "*What was so particularly good about today?*" To which he would reply, "*We haven't had much grief today yet.*" The amazing thing is that, in fact, fate had not pampered Tzilia's father or his family. His son and one of his daughters suffered from serious mental illness and Moses worked his entire life tirelessly, to provide for the financial future of his sick children. Thanks to his exceptional qualities and abilities, he was able to do this with fortitude and optimism. This, I think, is the highest wisdom that humankind has accumulated. Moreover, his daughter Tzilia, thank God, imbibed this attitude to life, and she, in turn, strengthened it in me. Another lesson I learned from this story was, that the main criterion for happiness is not one's own well-being and success, but THE WELL-BEING OF THE WHOLE FAMILY.

I think it is very important that the family gets together regularly, to talk not about trivial and silly things, but about something more important for everyone and all together. These thoughts brought me nice memories of the Sunday dinners my dad used to try to have with us. I dreamed then that in my own future family I would try to organize something similar. Alas, I never succeeded. In general, however sad it is, but the hustle and bustle of modern life, its intensity on the one hand and superficiality on the other has led to the fact that such things usually never happen in families any more. For example, the wonderful tradition of gathering in the family in the evening to read together a good book aloud is dead. Those geeks who today still want to read books do so alone, or ruin their eyes by staring at a computer screen or, even worse, a mobile phone.

The second story has to do with the ugly political situation in Soviet Union at that time. "The Iron Curtain" included a rule strictly forbidding all citizens to possess foreign currency; violators of this rule could find themselves in jail. The lucky ones who got permission to go beyond the borders and earn money abroad, musicians for example, were obliged to surrender every penny to the state upon returning to the USSR. I personally once found a $20 bill in the street. I was so frightened that I tried as soon as possible to get rid of it by secretly passing it through someone to a foreigner. However, Tzilia's father secretly kept what appeared to be a hundred-dollar bill in his pocket. When his loved ones would talk to him about playing with fire, he would say, "*I know, but I would like to touch something reliable once in a while.*" Tzilia also inherited this fearlessness from her father.

Tzilia's father worked in the textile industry and came up with an idea of how to recycle waste from factories that would otherwise become trash, thereby saving enormous amounts of money. While pushing his ideas, he fought the Soviet authorities. They would arrest him and put in prison, but he managed to surface again, get free, and resume his feverish activity. In this, too, Tzilia reminded me of her father. She was the only child in the family who had tried to be father's helper during his lifetime, and after his death, she tried, not without success, to be his substitute for the family.

Extreemly sociable, Tzilia attracted a huge number of people. This was especially evident when the mass emigration of Jews and the struggle for permission to leave the country began in Moscow. Tzilia's house became the headquarters of emigration at that time. There was a joke in Moscow: "*The emigration from the USSR was Tzilia-petal and Tzilia-directed.*" Our coming-out-of-the-country epic I describe in more detail in a later chapter, where, of course, the reader will see Tzilia's name more than once. Here I just want to say that it was Tzilia, who personally helped Tanya and me to make this very difficult decision.

Tanya and I were incredibly lucky: we became such close friends that Tzilia told us that we were all one family. When Tanya and I decided to get married, Tzilia was another person from whom I needed approval. I can proudly say that I got it and thus joined this family. By the way, when I met Tanya, one of Tzilia's active projects was to marry Tanya off. Through Tzilia's efforts more than one candidate came forward. The last of them was Tzilia's friend, one of the leading architects of Kiev. Just before our first meeting with Tanya, Tzilia arranged for Tanya to meet this man. The architect took a liking to Tanya, and he gave Tanya first-class courting. I could never have offered Tanya anything even close to this. I still cannot understand, and therefore I cannot explain how I managed to beat all such worthy and sometimes high-ranking rivals and win this difficult election campaign.

Tzilia's ingenuity and uniqueness were displayed on a variety of occasions. She was a fearless, speedy driver and regularly exceeded the speed limit. Once she borrowed her sister, Serafima's car and failed to get a power of attorney. Moscow police officer stopped her once for speeding and, of course, asked for her documents. Then the officer asked her *"How can you explain that the car is registered to Reitburd Serafima and the license says Reitburd Tzilia?"* Tzilia, without blinking an eye, answered: *"You know, such things happen among Jewish people!"* The bewildered police officer, evidently not very familiar with the history and traditions of Jewish customs, scratched his head, and then, believing Tzilia, let her go.

Here is another example of Tzilia's unconventionality and broad-mindedness. She had two daughters. From their early childhood a nanny, whose name was Shura, lived in the house. Decades passed, and this simple sweet woman continued to live in the house, when the girls in practical terms no longer needed a nanny. She simply became a member of the family, tried to help in any way she could and became very attached to the girls, adoring them as her own children. Shura did not have a family of her own. Both girls called Shura Mama, sometimes Mama Shura. Among Tzilia's loved ones, many were perplexed as to why the family, with Tzilia's approval, allowed their daughters to refer to Shura as their mother. I remember that I myself, being silly, was also among those who shared this bewilderment. *"Yurochka,"* the wise Tzilia used to say to me, *"it's so wonderful to have a good mother! But when children feel the similar way about another person as they do about their mother, they are doubly happy."* With the years, I came to understand that Tzilia was, of course, right. It was a good lesson for me that when something happens out of the ordinary, but with a good result, it is not a reason to think it is wrong, but rather it is a reason to think, analyze and understand that there is something to it.

When I became friends with Tzilia, it was more than ten years after my parents passed away. Although, according to the age, she could be to me more like an older sister than a mother can, I well remember how she often showered me with maternal care, and how it warmed and touched me. It was always a great pity that my dear parents had not known her. We never had to ask Tzilia for any help, she always saw our needs and rushed to help. This was particularly intense after we started our emigration odyssey with her and Soviet authorities did not allow either family to leave the country. If I happened to run into her for a minute in the middle of the day, she would always try to feed me something tasty. Nora, her daughter inherited this quality and Nora was an even better cook than her mother was.

If mother or daughter could "get" some nice clothes, they always tried to buy them also for our family. If Tzilia found out about an earning opportunity, she would always remember my interest as a refusenik, and tried to arrange that job for me too. Tzilia, never forgetting that our budget was much more modest than hers was, during all the years took care of us financially with extraordinary generosity, she never took money from us for anything. When I tried to pay her expenses for something for us, she would say: "*Yurochka, we are one family!*"

As the summer approached, Tzilia always volunteered to take us to get Verochka out of the sweltering and dusty city. One summer she invited us a to her dacha in Pushkino and did not charge us a penny. One summer when we could not use her dacha for some reason, she made an agreement with her cousin about a dacha for us. From the very beginning of our acquaintance, Tzilia became friends with my Galya and unconditionally accepted her as a member of our family. Not all the people close to us did this.

Whenever one of us fell ill and getting ill in Russia was more dangerous than most anywhere else, Tzilia with her characteristic energy managed, using an incredibly wide circle of friends and acquaintances, to achieve the impossible. She would find a doctor who was impossible to find and then got an appointment with him, even if he was no longer accepting new patients. She would get drugs that were impossible to get, she would arrange admission to a clinic that did not take new patients at the time.

In my recollections, I often return to this unique woman for the simple reason that in my Russian life there was very much of Tzilia. Over the years, I have been lucky enough to meet many wonderful people. However, Tzilia had a special place among them. There were very few people, whom I loved as much as I loved her. From very few people I learned so mach, as from her. There were very few people, for whom I feel such gratitude as I did to her. What was wonderful, she herself never expected gratitude for her good deeds.

Unfortunately, I have to end this chapter about Tzilia on a very sad note. The last time Tzilia and I met was after both our family and hers had left Russia. I think it was in Paris in the nineties, where she and her husband Milan had come from Israel, and Tanya and I from America. During this meeting, just out of the blue, a monstrous and unexpected thing has happened. Milan announced to us that he hated Tanya and cut off all communication with us because of her undignified behavior. He alleged that she had made friends with foreigners only in order to leave sooner herself, and she never cared about the rest of the refuseniks. I do not see any need to give any objections or explanations for this nonsense here. Tzilia, on the other hand, told us that this kind of conflict between close people is idiotic.

Nevertheless, she said to me before parting, that Milan is her husband, and there was nothing, she could do about the situation. It was the first time I heard "cannot" from Tzilia during all years of our friendship. Before this nightmare encounter, the last time we spoke with Tzilia was in Israel for her 70th birthday. I still cannot come to terms with what happened, and the bitterness and pain lingers to this day. On the day that this terrible meeting took place, Tzilia managed to talk to us. That meeting was a farewell forever. I cannot remember this last conversation between us without tears. In Israel, Tzilia had a long and painful illness and passed away in 2020. I could not even say goodbye to her...

A terrible evil has happened: Milan took away from us a very dear person us for no real reason. In the years that followed, we went to Jerusalem twice, and both times, we asked our mutual friends if they thought there was any possibility of seeing Tzilia. Both times, they advised us against even trying. Today, sadly, that question has lost its relevance. We are still in contact with Tzilia's daughters Nora in Boston and Galya in Jerusalem. When contacting them, I felt always closer to Nora, who seems to me much more like Tzilia than her sister does. We know from both that Tzilia was in a nursing home until she died, and towards the end, she did not recognize even Milan anymore... Why did everything happen so unkindly?! I cannot believe, it was what Milan wanted?!

This sad ending to our exceptionally close relationship with Tzilia than her sister does. We know from both that T reminded me of a story from Milan's own life that Tzilia than her sister does. We know from both that T shared with us many years ago. Milan was still young, and he had a disagreement of a political nature with his father. They went so far that Milan stopped talking to his own father and, if I remember correctly, the relationship never came to reconciliation during his father's lifetime. I knew Milan's mother, I can only imagine how much grief their conflict brought to this sweet woman, and I am not talking about the father himself. It seemed that this experience could have taught Milan some more tolerance and kindness. Nevertheless, it did not...

EMOTIONAL MENTOR

People, who are emotionally gifted, always attracted me. In our family, my mother's side, in the Shlifshtein family one could more often see this type of people. Among them, was my mother's younger brother, Semyon Shlifshtein, whom we all called Senya. His emotional depth was always an example to me, and I wanted to be like him. I loved him very much.

First, I loved him because he was a musician, and, in my opinion, these people are often very special. What is more, he had romantic feelings about music. Such musicians constitute the highest category of people. He had graduated with excellence from the Moscow Conservatory in piano, and his teachers predicted that he would be a great pianist. However, by the end of his studies Senya developed debilitating stage fright, which, to the great dismay of all who knew and loved him, shut him out of the performing profession. Instead, Senya became a musicologist. Like a great pianist, he tried to bring to the public his own interpretations of the highest achievements of his favorite composers.

Some of those interpretations were not simple at all. However, Senya had a gift for talking simply about the complex, especially when the conversation was not with music professionals. Unfortunately, our time with Senya was regrettably much too limited. Nevertheless, I learned many music-related things from him. For example, I remember him once asking me about the performer of a concert that I had been to. I told him that the pianist was not famous at all, but that was irrelevant, because at my low musical level it did not matter how good he was. "Yuri," Senya said to me. "*It's just the opposite. The less you know about music, the higher class of performers you should listen to.*" I remembered his lesson well, and I loved my uncle even more since that time.

Secondly, I loved Senya because of his remarkable youthful enthusiasm and capacity for fascination. He retained this wonderful quality to the last days of his life. He applied this not only to music, but also to life in general. In our family, he and I were the only regular visitors to the salon at Balechka's place on Pushkin Street. I remember well his exuberant enthusiasm about the new poems by Y. Visbor and I. Gabai, Yu. Kim and, of course, by A. Galich and B. Okudzhava. As for music, it is impossible to forget his indomitable interest in the works of Dmitri Shostakovich, which emerged in his student years and lasted literally until the last day of his life. Senya wrote enthusiastic articles about every new piece emerging from the great composer's pen. They knew each other personally, and both lived in Moscow in the House of Composers on Ogarev Street. So Shostakovich knew well about his ardent admirer not only from Senya's publications, but also from their conversations. This passion made Senya a target of the Soviet authorities and caused him much suffering and grief.

It all started when, on 28 January 1937, Pravda newspaper published a scandalous editorial "*Chaos instead of music*" about D. Shostakovich's new opera "Katerina Ismailova." Stalin was at the first performance. He did not like it and left long before its conclusion. Throughout Moscow, there were rumors that Stalin himself had a hand in the publication of the editorial. After that, there was a prohibition against performing ANY of Shostakovich's music in the Soviet Union, and ALL music publishers got instructions not to accept for publication any materials about the composer, and certainly any with the signature "Semyon Shlifstein." Our poor Senya found himself in a very difficult situation, both morally and financially.

My uncle could not continue to do his favorite work and could not publish a single line of his musicology research anywhere. Remember, this was his life's major work. For him, this distressing situation lasted until the death of Stalin nearly seventeen years later. Senya had two daughters, one an invalid and the other a little girl, and he was their primary provider. Senya's wife, Liolya, was a humble piano teacher at a music college with meager pay. Senya's brothers and sisters, my parents included, tried to help the beleaguered family by collecting money for them every month. The year 1953 came and "the great helmsman," thank God, passed away. Soon the music of Shostakovich returned to the concert halls and our Senya, in his fifties, was again able to write about music and, of course, about Shostakovich. How could one not admire such fidelity to his beloved affections as his?

My dear uncle Semion Shlifsteyn

Thirdly, I loved Senya for his choice of wife. I admired my aunt Liolya, I found her the charming and the sweetest creature. Liolya and Senya met when they were both studying at the conservatory. According to Senya, she was the most beautiful in the class. I realize that Senya may not be entirely objective here, but I like to believe in it and, in fact, want to believe in it. She had an incredibly enchanting timbre to her voice, so listening to her was always music to my ears concerning both what she was talking about and how it sounded. Unfortunately, life never indulges such wonderful people. As a result, there were few festive gatherings in their house and when there were, they were very modest. Most of the Shlifsteins, on the other hand, loved to eat, cooked well, and loved to treat others. I think they had the genes of their grandparents, whose family business was a cook-shop. In Senya's home they saw no such thing, and they reproached Liolya, from my point of view, quite unfairly for being stingy. I never thought Liolya was stingy. I liked to be at her table even when almost no food was on the table, only tea. Unfortunately, I did not go there very often. We are all strong in the back of our minds, I blame myself for that now. I always felt good in this house. Senya's house was the only one in my surroundings that preserved the Russian cultural tradition of gathering together as a family around the table and reading a good book aloud. I so wanted to be invited to these readings, but I was too shy to ask.

Time was running out. It was August 9, 1975. Senya went to the library in the middle of the day. He was working on another article about Shostakovich. He did not come home at the scheduled time. *"Well, that is all right,"* thought Liolya. *"He is a keen man, he is been working hard and has not noticed how the time has flown by."* When a few more hours passed and Senya did not show up, Liolya got worried and started calling everyone close to him, including us, in the hope that someone had been in contact with Senya. No one had heard anything from him. Night was falling and Liolya got nervous and called the police. They registered a missing person and promised to report as soon as they knew anything. The whole night there was no news. Liolya and her close ones did not sleep a wink. In the morning, Senya's youngest daughter Natasha had to go out. She tried to open the apartment door but could not: something was in the way on the outside. After they managed to open it, they were horrified to discover that behind the door lay the dead body of Senya.

The subsequent details came later from Senyas friend with whom he met in the library in the afternoon. When they met, the friend asked Senya: *"Have you heard the sad news?"* "No," said Senya. *" I do not know anything." "Shostakovich died today!"* Although Senya knew that the composer was already seriously ill, the news shocked him. Any work was out of the question. When he came to his senses, he frantically gathered his papers and rushed home. No one knows how he got home or how he got up to the second floor. He was already at the door of his apartment when his poor heart failed... The next day Liolechka received a telegram of condolence from Shostakovich's widow Irina with kind words.

I often think how fate has wonderfully linked these two people. Senya was only three years older than the great composer and they died on the same day. So, their lives coincided quite precisely in time. Both dedicated their lives to Russian music. They had a lot in common in their musical tastes. Unfortunately, they both suffered in full from the Soviet regime. It is horrible, that Soviet government successfully chose the best representatives of the nation to harass... Concluding the chapter about my uncle Semyon I cannot help mentioning increadible, I would say mystic, coincidence. In the name index WHO IS WHO (Appendix 2 in the English version of this book) alphabetic sorting of the names has brought these two people next to each other!!!

I AM DAD, ONCE AGAIN

Little Verochka, about whom so much was said in the night telephone conversations between Tanya and Verochka Prokhorov, was born, but only in 1976, because the process was more difficult and worrisome than we thought. In 1974, Tanya had a miscarriage. We had a consultation at the Institute of Obstetrics and Gynecology and doctors recommended we try again in a year. With this consultation, we were very lucky. At the Institute, we met Joseph Rozovsky who was knowledgeable, educated and kind and he became a friend of our family. When Verochka started talking she called him "Uncle Osya Solomonych," and Tanya and me just "Solomonych." All three of us used an abbreviated form for the patronymic of the doctor "Solomonovich". At the Obstetrics Institute, Solomonych was the head of the genetics department.

In 1975, Tanya became pregnant again, and now we took care of her like of a crystal vase. Scared of a miscarriage, we tried to follow strictly all the recommendations of specialists and not to take a single step, even a small one, without consulting Solomonych. In 1975, in Russia and in the beginning only in Moscow, pregnant women begin to undergo a diagnostic procedure called amniocentesis. It revealed the health of the fetus and any gene defects at a very early stage without interrupting the pregnancy. The procedure consists of taking a sample of amniotic liquid from the pregnant uterus and then analyzing the gene structure of the cells of the sample. In 1975, our Solomonych was the ONLY specialist in

Soviet obstetrics who introduced amniocentesis to diagnose fetal development. Tanya had this procedure done and we got a green street to go on with the pregnancy.

A funny episode from that time comes to my mind. We were in Tzilia's car and pregnant Tanya was with us. Tzilia was driving, and Tzilia's favorite grandson, Mitya, was in the car. Everyone who knew Tzilia was aware that she was a very daring driver and often allowed herself to exceed the speed limit. Mitya asks his grandmother what has happened, why she is driving so slowly. Tsilya answers: *"Because, Mitya, we are now carrying in our car a VERY VALUABLE LOAD."* Mitya thought for a second and said: *"Yeah, I understand, like new furniture."*

No matter how careful we were, no matter how Solomonych kept his hand on the pulse, all through Tanya's pregnancy we could not help but worry and could not relax. However, what was even sadder was that Tanya had to spend a considerable part of that time in hospitals to preserve her pregnancy. Poor thing, she was hospitalized FOUR times during that time!!! Although all the times, it would happen through influential connections which it seemed to be better than usual, I would not wish anyone under any circumstances to spend so long in any hospital, and God forbid, in the kind of hospitals we had in Soviet Russia.

The last hospital before the birth of little Verochka was one of the best maternity hospital at number 25 in Moscow, on Lenin Avenue. The hospital was affiliated with the clinic of the Research Institute of Obstetrics and Gynecology. Far in advance, we decided to admit her to their Pregnancy Pathology Department in order to decrease the miscarriage risk and to stay under clinical supervision until the delivery. We managed to put Tanya there only because the head doctor was an old friend of our Tzilia. By the way, her name was also Tzilia. She was Tzilia Tsurenko.

Fate tied me to this maternity hospital quite strongly, and there will be many stories about it further on. Here I only want to sketch an idea of the place of Tanya's hospitalization. NONE of the maternity hospitals in Moscow at that time allowed visitors. This supposed ostensibly to fight infections. In Tanya's department, women could spend weeks without seeing their families. Tanya's ward was on the fourth floor. She got to the hospital in early spring when it was still quite cold and sometimes there were even frosts.

Hospital administration did not allow patients to wear their own clothes on the ward; all of the women wore only hospital nightgowns over their naked bodies. However, we all know, there is no limit to what love can do! Wishing to see their close ones, women in any weather wrapped themselves in blankets, opened the windows wide, lay down on broad windowsills and actively communicated. Mothers nursing their babies were exposing their breasts to the cold, but it was impossible to stop them. Bringing things to the women in the hospital was possible only a couple of hours every day according to a strict schedule. During this time, there was an unusual sight: a buzz of shouting, sometimes about even intimate topics like the condition of the vagina after delivery. All kinds of things one could hear there. Once I heard, an overexcited dad shout, *"Tell me please about his nose, his eyes, and his ears? What kind of teeth does he have?"*

Food in the maternity hospital was so scarce that most of the relatives and close ones tried regularly to bring bags of food to pass on to patients. The assortment of food items allowed was strongly restricted to prevent bringing infection to the hospital from the outside world. Much of the contents of such bags could consist of elementary foods, such as UNOPENED paper packages of milk or yogurt bought in the grocery stores. The delivery of these items in overcrowded public transport never concerned anyone in terms of infection transmission.

Another restriction was no less ridiculous. The administration allowed only brand-new books, and the proof of novelty was the presentation of the receipt from the store for the purchase of a particular book. Good books at that time in Russia were an absolute scarcity, and the most part of the new books sold in stores were politically correct junk. Decent published books somehow mysteriously would be quickly gone, not reaching the bookstores. Despite this, the amateurs contrived to collect decent home libraries by hook or by crook, apparently, through the black market. Thus, in the face of fighting infection, the hospital administration successfully deprived the poor patients of an opportunity to read the books they wanted. In other words, they could not get their favorite books from home, from the library, or recommended books from loved ones. The idea that an infection could have entered soviet shops or public transport would never occur to the hospital officials.

I happened to hear a funny story about the paper packages of milk from some cunning people who had passed on food to their loved ones, as I did to Tanya. Many people in Russia believed in the magical benefits of milk and, in particular, in its ability to increase lactation in women after childbirth. For this reason, milk became one of the most given products in maternity hospitals. It was always included in the list of allowed products, while a huge number of items were not on the list.

Of course, any alcohol was subject to a complete ban, which was unbearable for the Russian soul. Firstly, the joy of the event of a child's birth required to "wash this event off" as soon as possible. Secondly, in Russia they believed that the champagne causes the pregnant women's labor birth pangs. The number of bans in the country was innumerable. However, over more than fifty years of Soviet rule, the country's citizens had developed a special ability to circumvent ingenuously almost any prohibition. In the case of alcohol, paper packages of milk played an unusually instrumental role. Skilful artisans used a medical syringe to extract all the milk from the bag. Then, using the same syringe they gently inserted a needle into the same hole and carefully washed the bag from inside with water. Then it remained only to "inject" the bag with alcohol and carefully seal the hole with a tiny piece of tape. After that, the bag of "pasteurized milk" was ready for usage. This was the way women induced childbirth on the eve of the duty of their doctor they wanted to assist the delivery.

Solomonych recommended to Tanya a medicine to preserve her pregnancy. Of course, this drug was not available either in the hospital or in the pharmacy. We called everyone we could and managed to get it. Very happy, we brought it to the chief doctor in the hospital. She told us: "*I don't want to give this medicine to our staff. Tanya will never get it because they will steel it from you. Keep it with yourself and hand it to Tanya when the doctor tells you to.*" In order for Tanya to get this hard-won medicine, we followed her advice exactly.

One day I got a tearful note from Tanya. A nurse came into her room and gave her an injection. Tanya asked her "*What are you giving me?*" The nurse answered, "*Don't worry, I'm giving you what you need!*" and left the room. In the same note, poor Tanechka begged me to get her out of there. In the reply note, I tried to console her and convince her that such attitude to the patient WAS terrible, but, thinking about our child, we could not afford the risk of discharge. Unfortunately, this case was a characteristic feature of Soviet health care organization.

As we are talking about Soviet hospitals, I will take the liberty of a "lyrical" digression that has nothing to do with the birth of little Verochka, but which further describes our sad experience with medical institutions. In the spring of 1976, when our Vera. was born, our Hungarian friend, the Russian translator, Sharah Karig, arrived in Moscow from Budapest. This special woman belonged to the circle of Tanya's friends whom I got as a gift from Tanya. She had come to the USSR to attend the conference of literary translators. Her biography is remarkable.

Let me tell about some details of Sharah,'s background. She belonged to a social-democratic party in Hungary, which had to go underground during the Nazi occupation. The Soviet army liberated Budapest, and naïve Hungarians cheered, celebrating "freedom." As an activist in her party, Sharah, was one of the organizers of the first democratic elections. When she was sorting out the ballots the night after the vote was over, a Soviet soldier showed up at the polling station and demanded that she hand over to him all the election results. In response, Sharah, sharply stated that the demand of the Soviet administration was a gross violation of the rules of free elections, and she refused to do so. Events developed very rapidly. The next day, Sharah, was under arrest and soon she found herself in one of the concentration camps in Siberia. She returned to freedom only after Stalin's death in 1953.

When we asked Sharah, about the camp years, she told us: *"Well, that's all right. Every cloud has a silver lining. I learned Russian in Siberia, so I could translate Russian literature. Thanks to my arrest, I have a profession that I love very much."*

Now I will go back to her arrival in Moscow in 1976. It was a cold and snowy spring, and the authorities did not do proper road cleaning. One day Sharah, slipped on the ice, fell down and ended up with such pain that she found herself in the special ward for foreigners of the Moscow Botkin Hospital. Sharah was very sad that this happened to her out of her country, but Tanya and I, the native Muscovites, convinced her that she would get the best possible clinical care in our capital. We ourselves, not being foreigners, could never dream of such care under such luxurious conditions.

At the hospital, she immediately got X-rays that showed a hip fracture. The diagnosis required immobility and they put her into a cast from her chest up to her knees. After this, the poor woman began the terrible suffering associated with the care required with such immobility. After a week, Sharah begged Tanya to contact the Hungarian Embassy in Moscow to tell them that she could not stand being here any longer and she begged to transport her to Budapest. Tanya spoke with the embassy's employees who did everything necessary to return Sharah to Budapest. I participated in carrying her stretcher to the plane at Vnukovo airport in Moscow.

Frankly speaking, when I saw Sharah off, I grumbled about how spoiled all foreigners were, even the best ones. They are not at all ready to overcome difficulties. Just the next day Tanya was talking to Sharah on the phone. Right off the plane, they took her to the hospital. For hygienic reasons, and to give her a rest, they removed the cast and immediately repeated the x-ray. The doctors could only look in a perplexity at what they had seen. It had NOT shown any fracture!!! The poor quality of the image or the poor skills of the Russian interpreters led the doctors down a false path. In a phone conversation, Shara gave us a wonderful phrase. *"I learned another useful lesson in Russia, Tanechka. If you are very, very healthy, you can spend some time in a Russian hospital. But if not, you'd better try to avoid that institution."* I thought, there was really a reason, that since pre-revolutionary times those in Russia who could, went to the West for medical treatment.

Tanya turned out to be, by Sharah's definition, a very, very strong woman. She bravely went through an incredibly difficult path of preserving her pregnancy and came to the finish line, it was time to give birth. No one, including Solomonych, believed she would give birth safely on her own. We were preparing her for a C-section. On March 14th Tanya started having contractions. We feverishly began to pack. It was still quite cold outside, and we pulled out our warm boots. In my haste, I tried to close the zippers, but one, as zippers like to do, got stuck in the very beginning and did not want to go either up or down. I made a drastic decision: I grabbed a screwdriver and pliers, and we rushed out with her shoe unzipped. When we emerged at the door of the admittance room with tools in hand, midwifes met us with Homeric laughter. "*Wow*," said one midwife, gasping with laughter, "*women now come to give birth with their own tools!*"

Tsilia Tsurenko's subordinate was a very experienced obstetrician named Irina Levantovsky. She had golden hands. In every complicated case of childbirth or surgery, her colleagues always referred to her. Irina would come, and as if by magic, the procedure would be successful. At the same time, the chief doctor Tzilia Tsurenko in recent years had been engaged only in administrative work. Between Tzilia and Irina there was a disagreement about Tanya. The first insisted on Caesarean section, the second said, that the entire clinical picture made her confident, that Tanya would be quite able to cope with natural childbirth. Irina suggested to her boss to bet on a bottle of vodka—the most common type of bet in Russia. After a long and exciting discussion, they decided to try to let her deliver herself but were ready for surgery at any time. I prayed to God that either one or the other happened not at night, but during the day, when Irina would be working in the maternity hospital.

This is how our little Verochka looked

In the meantime, the contractions were getting stronger and stronger. God heard my prayers: Tanya herself gave birth to little Verochka on March 15 at 11 o'clock AM! She came into this world tiny, but pretty and everything was fine. However, for Tanya, all complications possible occurred during the birth. She had to do a manual separation of the placenta, which turned out to be very painful. Exhausted and worn out she was taken on a journey to the corridor. Usually in maternity hospitals, all women who were done with the delivery would stay on a gurney for a couple of hours just outside the delivery room in the immediate vicinity of midwives in case there were complications. With Tanya's "Jewish luck," there was no room available in the maternity ward during the whole day, and she had to stay in the cold corridor for the rest of the day. After all the preceding misfortunes, Tanya could not believe her happiness that our little girl was doing so well. She fell into a psychological state that I would call positive shock, and it took her some time to come out of that state, calm down and start to be peacefully happy.

As for the name, for a long time, until we knew if we were having a boy or a girl, two names were prepared. For a girl, Verochka after Vera Prokhorov and for the boy, Borechka, after Tanya's father Boris Gershman. Tanya somehow thought that we were waiting for Borechka, and until we found out whom our child was, we addressed him as Borechka. I would like to think that little Verochka never felt offended by that.

While Tanya and Verochka were still in the maternity hospital, I started running around like a man on fire, trying to solve all the usual household problems connected to the birth of a baby: crib, pram, bathtub, scales, etc. It is sad and funny that 14 years had passed since the birth of my Galya, but none of these problems lost their urgency. Therefore, in a new cycle I was taking old things out, restoring them, putting them in order and renewing them. Surprisingly, most of the items of the same name in 1962 and in 1976 differed very little, as well as the process of returning these items to new life. Tanyusha reproached me that I do not remember which of these objects I did for Galyusha and which I did for Verochka. However, the huge difference this time was the very active participation of the baby's mother in dealing with ALL the issues, first remotely from the maternity hospital, and then physically at our home.

THEY DID NOT LET ME INTO MEDICINE

I liked my work with computers. I often admired their incredible capabilities and some smart applications. However, I did not really like them, and they repaid me in kind. I was always concerned about how easy it was to use computers for malicious purposes. Examples of such 'harmful' use are an endless number of military applications, helping to kill people efficiently. In addition, I always hated evil use of computers as tools for crooks and thugs. Apparently, until our world improves significantly, this situation will unfortunately not change. If I had to choose a profession again, I would probably choose something that does people good not evil.

Religion aside, I think, good teachers and doctors fall primarily into this category of professions. Improving human health, whether physical, mental, moral or spiritual, is a noble task. The thoughts outlined here began to come to me in the seventies. It was then that I realized that I had made the mistake of following my brother's advice and becoming a computer scientist rather than a doctor. It is difficult for me to explain why I prefer a doctor to a teacher, but I felt clearly that teaching was not for me. As for medicine, it has always attracted me. The very sight of a man in a white doctor's coat always excited me. One of the possible explanations may be the fact that since ancient time people understood that healing was an exceptionally good deed. To my great regret, today such understanding has changed all over the world. I see today more and more attempts to turn health care into big business. The Hippocratus Oath dates from 400 BC and remains an unrivaled ethical document to this day! Not for nothing, most medical schools around the world still use it as the basis for the oath for graduates starting their careers as doctors. Personally, I wish other professions had followed the medical profession's example and instituted a similar ritual.

Ethical standards have changed since the time of Hippocrates, and today not everyone shares the rules prescribed by this document. There are three very serious prohibitions in the Hippocratic text, what a doctor MUST NEVER DO: a doctor may not help a patient to bring death, a doctor may not participate in performing an abortion and a doctor may not perform an operation to remove stones that have formed in the patient's body. These prohibitions mostly relate to the question of who owns a person's life and who has the right to make serious decisions about that life.

Religious believers think that life is a gift from God and that only God can end a person's life or take actions that risk ending life. This is a very serious position, but for some reason a large part of this group of people in special circumstances forget about it and easily give themselves the right of God without asking. This has happened since ancient times to the participants of wars in which people killed their own kind in great numbers to "improve" the life of others. These same people may have been militant opponents to permitting abortions in times of peace. It seems to me that the most horrible type of warfare was the Crusades (II – XV centuries) where mass murder has happened in the name of God. Other examples: in the name of God, the Catholic Inquisition tortured and murdered a huge number of people for "incorrect" beliefs, or zealous anti-Semites killed Jewish people just for being different.

However even much worse, in my opinion, are the people who are convinced that a citizen's life belongs to the country in the person of the ruling political group, and the government has the right to destroy the "bad" citizens" of the country. We saw examples of such "improvement" of the country in Hitler's Nazi ghettos and concentration camps and in Stalin's communist prison camps, where millions of people were exterminated.

A much smaller group believes that human life belongs to a man himself, and he has the right to dispose of it. I myself belong to this third group. While I respect the idea of those who believe that life is a gift from God, I can agree with them and am grateful to God for such an invaluable gift. However, you never take back the gift, and the one to whom the gift was given has, it seems to me, the full right to dispose of his gift.

That is why I would venture to repeal all three prohibitions in the Hippocratic Oath, and the rest, in my opinion, applies in a slightly modified form to all other professions. At any rate, I well remember that reflection on this very remarkable document of antiquity led me to a strong desire to start working in the health care system. When I realized this desire, I was already in my thirties, and to begin a new profession, I thought, it was already too late. That is why I started thinking of a plan to try to apply my knowledge and experience with computers to the world of medicine.

It was the seventies and computers were evolving rapidly. They had become less cumbersome, more affordable, and much easier to use. On the other hand, computer geeks were discovering, virtually every day, new extraordinary possibilities, far beyond mere computation. This progress resulted in the emergence of specialized computing centers in various fields. The first MEDICAL COMPUTER departments and centers appeared in Moscow. At that time, only the largest medical institutions involved in scientific research could afford such a luxury.

I was very active in knocking on their doors, but most of them did not like the shape of my nose. Disliking the shape of one's nose was in the Soviet Union a euphemism for anti-Semitism. In one institution, however, things went quite far. It was the Institute of Experimental and Clinical Oncology (IEKO) of the USSR Academy of Medical Sciences on Kashirskoye Shosse. I managed to pass successfully an interview with the director of the computing center and the head of one of its departments. They liked me and said that everything was all right with my hiring. I was naïve enough to think that this time I am in. The next and last formal step was to get a signature of the Institute's director.

The director at that time was a big man, a full member of the Academy of Medical Sciences (AMS) named N.Blokhin. He had many honors and awards of the USSR: President of the AMS, Hero of Socialist Labor, laureate of State Prizes, deputy of the Supreme Soviet of all convocations, deputy of all Congresses of the Communist Party, etc. When I came in two days later to the Institute to find out whether these people had received the desired signature, they met me in extreme embarrassment. The director received a long list of names of people selected to join the staff of the Institute, to approve with his signature. When they got the list back, they saw that he crossed out my name from the list. He had done this without ever seeing me or knowing anything about me.

Today the Institute is named "Russian Cancer Research Center after N. Blokhin." This man himself reached the rank of academician of the Russian Academy of Sciences. To all his titles, I would like to add the title of the Honored Guardian of Racial Purity of the specialists in oncology science. He died in 1993 in glory and honor and his grave is, of course, at Novodevichy cemetery. When I wrote these lines, I involuntarily asked once again myself, why my own brother was so eager to bury our father in the company of this type people? Recently my brother's daughter, my niece Olya, was struck at the end of her life by blood cancer. She went for treatment not to Blokhin's Center in Moscow, which would be easier and cheaper, but to Israel, where they treat cancer much better. However, even there they could not cope with this ruthless disease, and today our Olechka is no longer with us.

After the failure at the Cancer Center, I stopped my attempts to get a job in Moscow in a medical institution. By this time, Tanya and I had already firmly decided to leave Russia and to wait to realize my dream in my new, fourth life. Looking ahead, my dream came true in the United States, and I worked for almost thirty years in medical institutions in Boston, Massachusetts.

However, this did not mean that I then stopped my attempts in Russia to make my way in medicine. I decided to prepare myself for my new profession and to read the corresponding literature. For this purpose, I went to the best medical library in Moscow, the Central Scientific Medical Library affiliated with the First State Medical Graduate School. Today this school has become a University. Unfortunately, I managed to get no further than the entrance foyer. It turned out that there was no free entrance to their library. In order to get a pass, I had to show a certificate to prove that I worked in a medical institution. The pass that confirmed that I worked in a computer research institute of the Academy of Sciences and my diploma of PhD did not satisfy them. I tried to tell them that I needed to work on the application of computers in medicine, but this did not help either. After much bickering, I had to leave the library, empty-handed and angry. I decided to go for stealth and began to look for a doctor acquaintance, who could arrange a fictitious certificate, saying that I worked in health care. This took some time.

In the meantime, my second life was ending and a new one was going to begin. We submitted our applications for emigration and because of this, I had to stop working at the Academy of Sciences. The traitors of the Motherland might not keep in Soviet Union any intelligent job. Then the Soviet authorities refused to issue me an exit visa, which made us for many years "refusniks". Nevertheless, I did not abandon the idea of making my way to the medical library. Only in 1988, I managed to get this damned fictitious certificate. With that certificate, I went to the library again, and this time everything went like clockwork. I received a new pass to the temple of medical science and boyishly celebrated having defeated the Soviet bureaucrats. Alas, it was not in my stars, I never got to work there. Quite soon after this happy event, we received permission to emigrate and left Russia forever.

I had one more unsuccessful attempt to break into Soviet medicine, connected with acquiring my new specialty of a "janitor-obstetrician." As fate pushed me in this direction, I decided to do something useful in this domain, obstetrics and gynecology. I had already had some experience with education by correspondence, when I could not study normally during daytime. Therefore, I got some books and textbooks and started to study them. Thank God, the Soviet regime could not interfere with that. My enthusiasm for lexicology and work on dictionaries pushed me to the idea of compiling a dictionary of English-Russian terminology for specialists in the field. Such a dictionary did not exist either in the USSR or in the West at that time. Although I did not have much free time, I plunged into this work with enthusiasm. In about a year, I already had a sufficiently completed an index card catalog of the dictionary. I showed it to our friend Solomonych, a well-known professor of obstetrics and asked his opinion. I was very happy when he found it commendable.

Publication of the dictionary under my name in the Soviet Union was out of the question. Not only was it impossible to publish even one line by a Refusenik author, but even references to the names of emigrants and refuseniks were thrown out of all lists of background literature in scientific publications. Therefore, I asked Solomonych to publish the dictionary under his name. Solomonych went with this suggestion to the "Russky Jazyk" publishing house in Moscow, where all the dictionaries were printed. The response was that nobody needed such a dictionary. That was the ignominious end of yet another attempt of mine to do something good in Russia and for Russia.

EPILOGUE TO THE SECOND LIFE

My second life was extremely important in the sense of forming me as a person. First, at the beginning of this life, I became an orphan, lost both of my parents, I had very close relationships with my parents, they played a significant role in my life, and, in many ways, they shaped me as a person. It was an irreparable loss for me. After our father died, my brother tried to play his role. However, he and I were very different in our understanding of how we wanted to live our lives. He was a pragmatist, and I was an idealist. He was overwhelmed with his work and tried to pay no attention to the political turmoil in the country. I, on the contrary, was concerned about all gross violations of law and human rights around me and tried to help those aggrieved by the Soviet power. Therefore, my second life considerably estranged us from each other. My sister Lena emotionally aligned herself with our brother. In 1963, my mother died, after which I felt that I, not knowing yet how to swim, found myself in the cold and troubled waters of life. I had no choice but to swim myself.

At the end of my second life, I managed to build my own wonderful family. This process was not easy and not simple. It included two steps: first marriage, then divorce, and second marriage. However, the result surpassed all expectations. My eldest daughter from my first marriage has always brought me so much joy that it more than makes up for all the pain her mother caused me.

I began my second life frustrated that I did not have a spiritual and cultural mentor in my family. Towards the end of this life, I was fortunate enough to meet several, special people, from whom I learned and whom I could take as examples in life. They were my mother's sister Bella Shlifstein (Balechka) and her brother Semyon Shlifstein, and my great-uncle Veniamin Kagan-. I also learned from great friends including the poet Ilya Gabai, the mathematician Tanya Velikanov, the linguist Vera Prokhorov, Kostya Babitsky, Igor Melchuk and Yuri Apresyan. There were also musicians Natasha Gutman and Alexander Brussilovsky, and simply a person of great soul, Tzilia Reitburd. Each of these wonderful people became my spiritual influences. Some of them are no longer alive, but I want to thank them all very much.

LIFE THIRD
MY EFFORTS TO EMIGRATE FROM THE SOVIET UNION

FEARS

Soviet Russia was one of the few countries in the world where, when citizens traveled abroad, in addition to permission to enter another country, they had to get permission to leave their own country. Obtaining the latter proved even more difficult than obtaining the former. There were two types of exit visas: for those who travel as tourists or "for work" for a limited time, and for those who had decided to emigrate. For the second type, there was a special Soviet bureaucratic stamp known as "exit for permanent residence." The use of the word "permanent" emphasized one-way character of the move: the authorities were deciding for you, that crossing the border was practically without right to return. For those who SUBMITTED a request for permission to emigrate a special name was born: "submitters." The traditional trips abroad for medical treatment or education known in pre-revolutionary Russia practically ceased to exist in the Soviet Union. This remained only available to very high-ranking Soviet superiors.

The authorities also tried to keep the first category to a minimum and permits were a bonus almost exclusively for party and state officials. Such travel required the consent from the local district communist party committee, where the traveler had to go for an interview. To be able to come to such an interview, a person had to receive a recommendation in writing from her or his employer's Communist party committee. Such approval by the Communist party officials was required for everyone, irrespective of whether he or she was a party member or was not (?!). The recommendation had to contain the magic formula: *"politically literate, modest in everyday life"* (?!). It was very difficult for non-members of the Communist Party to get actually such a recommendation, nothing to say, for Jewish people.

The second category received permits through quite different channels, and the decision would come from the KGB. The Soviet code of ethics instructed citizens to have deep contempt of all those who wished to leave "the best country in the world". Everyone had to consider such a desire as an outrage to Soviet patriotism. This practice resulted in those who decided to emigrate feeling a deep sense of shame in front of their remaining friends and relatives. It was for this reason that such a decision was not as easy one to make.

Tim Sobakin's poem "Motherland" was a great help to me in making this difficult decision. Nowadays they publish the text slightly modified, but I present the old text as I remembered it in Moscow in the 1980s, which I like better.

> *It was polar freezing outside.*
> *Solid ice has covered the pond long ago.*
> *And on the ice there walked shivering ducks,*
> *Very angry and, in addition, very hungry.*
> *I asked the ducks, Excuse me,*
> *I do not get it at all,*
> *Why do not you, ducks, fly from here*
> *To warm places far away.*
> *My ducks answered me,*
> *Let the pineapple blossoms there,*
> *In those lands we shall die of sorrow,*
> *For here is our Homeland.*
> *Defeating the rumbling in my stomach,*
> *I thought softly, "Oh, my…*
> *There they are — our simple ducks!*
> *There it is my Fatherland!"*
> *I walked, unsteadily pulling my foot,*
> *I even forgot to put on the shoe on it.*
> *The moon was shining in my path,*
> *And the star was pointing my way.*

Those who publicly announced their decision to emigrate immediately became "persona non grata." The Soviet authorities let them know that "he who is not with us is against us." Few people remember that the Communists borrowed this militant philosophy, of

LIFE THIRD: MY EFFORTS TO EMIGRATE FROM THE SOVIET UNION

course without reference, neither more nor less than from Christ who in Matthew's Gospel, said carelessly, "He that is not with Me is against Me" (Matt. 12:30). Jesus could not have imagined the wicked people who would take advantage of his words. It was this principle that justified the official prohibition to employ or to admit for studies "submitters" in almost all institutions of the so-called "ideological front." Practically, it meant more than that. It meant discrimination for political views everywhere, since any administrator who accepted an unreliable person was himself regarded as unreliable. As a result, the authorities had their way, and the Submitters in Russia could continue neither to study, nor to work, nor to move. For this reason, many people who wanted to emigrate from Russia were simply afraid to make their plans public.

As for myself, I was no exception. I was afraid of many things. I was afraid that both Tanya and I would lose our jobs. Without any doubt, this should have happened with the application and that we would not be able to provide financially for our girls. Although my Galechka was one of the best students in the school, I was afraid that after submitting papers for emigration that she would find all the doors leading to continuing her education upon graduation closed to her. I feared that all of our family and friends would get into serious trouble because of our departure. In addition to all of these fears, was the fear of whether or not we would be able to adapt to the new economy and culture in our new life.

At that time, I did not yet fully understand that fear was the main tool of the country's rulers to keep their power. That fear was a primary attribute of the country they had built, and it became fundamentally inherent in it. Nadezhda Mandelstam, in her letter to her close friend Anna Akhmatova, helped me to understand this. *"Of all the things, that happened to us, the most basic and powerful was fear and its derivative—a vile sense of shame and utter helplessness. The fear was deadening in us everything that would make life bearable, and for every minute of lucidity, we paid with the night delirium—in reality and in dreams"*. When I read these lines, I was in total amazement: this is exactly what I felt! For the last few years in Moscow, I had a persistent dream that caused me fears. I dreamed that, all of a sudden, the administration of the All-Union Power Engineering University found out that I had not received credits for one of my courses during my studies. Therefore, it decided to annul my diploma and to inform the Research Institute where I worked and the High Attestation Commission that had awarded me the PhD Diploma. Fortunately, since that day in 1988 when I crossed the border of the USSR this dream NEVER came to me again!

N.Mandelstam wrote about fears by 1963. And a year before, in 1962, Yevgeny Yevtushenko (the poem "Fears") saw in his dreams that

> *Fears are dying in Russia*
> *As if the ghosts of the years gone by.*

Many people considered this poem to be courageous freethinking, while others considered it to be naïve wishful thinking. Nevertheless, I think, that the poet showed a good face at a bad game. With these lines, he was insulting thousands of people who continued to live in these years under the oppression of fears. In the 1960s and later, fears not only did not die, but also were in their prime. These lines reminded me of when Gorbachev arrived in Washington in the early eighties and said without blinking an eye that all Jews who wanted to emigrate from the Soviet Union had left the country. He said this at a time when around me thousands of Jewish Refuseniks with PhDs and other doctorate degrees were struggling just as I was, earning miserable wages as janitors, elevator operators, and watchmen. Was this how the fears in Russia died? I have already told you how in 1968 the authorities had crippled the life of my friend Kostya Babitsky just because he did not like how the Soviet tanks brought "freedom" to Prague. Was this how the fears in Russia died? In the seventies my friend Ilya Gabay, one of the noblest people I have known, threw himself out a window after the Golgotha of his many arrests in 1973. Was this how fears died in Russia? In 1979, my friend Tanya Velikanov found herself in a concentration camp for her impeccable honesty and her refusal to submit to fear. Is this how fears died in Russia? I could go on and on with the examples like above.

It was because of fear that all emigrants were trying to leave the country. I personally remember how these fears tormented me. Fears for my family, for my relatives and friends were almost overwhelming. In fact, I had many more fears than I have mentioned. I think, it was enough to put all of my fears together to under-

LIFE THIRD: MY EFFORTS TO EMIGRATE FROM THE SOVIET UNION

stand why I was afraid to decide to start the emigration process. However, Tanya came to help me: she was wiser than I was. She had a clear understanding that no matter how grounded my fears about leaving the country were, what awaited us, if we had stayed, would have been much worse for the whole family. She was able to help me to understand this and thereby to move beyond or at least despite my fears.

Slowly but surely I was baked. We recently celebrated 35 years of our life in the United States. The road to a new life was far from quick and far from easy. This chapter is about the difficulties, at times seemingly insurmountable, that we experienced along the way. However, man has a strong backbone. Today I can say in the words of Juli Daniel from his "Romance to my Motherland," written in jail: "*I do not hide neither my evil thought, nor any regrets about my fate.*" Every single day I send my blessings to Heaven that it happened and to the end of my days, I will be grateful to my Tanyusha for her foresight. I must also pay tribute to our dear Tzilechka, for the unconditional support and help that we invariably felt until the day we set foot on American soil.

In those years, Jewish emigration took place exclusively under the banner of family reunification. That is why ALL Jewish emigrants formally went to Israel to reunite with their relatives. The prerequisite for obtaining an exit visa was an invitation from a relative living in Israel. Such an arrangement was an absolute fake and total hypocrisy of the Soviet authorities, who tried to hide the fact that the Soviet citizens had simply fled the country like rats from a sinking ship. 95 percent of the submitters did not have any relatives in Israel, they were seeking fictitious documents. A significant number of these people were not planning to go to Israel, but were planning to settle in one of the countries the doors of which were open to Jewish emigrants. These countries included, first of all, the US, Canada and Australia. This fraud was well known to the Soviet bureaucrats and the KGB, who would turn a blind eye to it for "ideological" reasons. The rest of the world also knew well about it.

The first real step to start our emigration activities happened unexpectedly and quite accidentally. In 1976, Tzilia's eldest daughter Galya and her family immigrated to Israel. She knew about our factual decision to leave and without waiting for our request, she was Tzilia's daughter after all, immediately started to get us a "relative's" invitation. At the beginning of 1977, we received a small envelope in the mail from someone by name Michael Ziman from Israel. Before I opened the envelope, I thought it was some kind of mistake and generally mistook the sender for a man. When I read the letter carefully, it became clear that a woman was writing to us. The letter contained an official invitation to our family. The poor woman was frightened to death that we were all about to move in with her and so attached a little letter to the summons. In it, she assured us that she is NOT a relative to us in any way and, if we came, we could not count on any help from her side. When we read the contents of the envelope, I was horrified. Now there was no way out, for the KGB had become aware of our plans. If that was the case, I wanted to do everything as quickly as possible and spend not one more day in this country. In our naivety, both Tanya and I believed that after we submitted our documents, we would leave at once. Nobody among us ever considered that we would be stuck for an extended length of time.

Our first concern was to arrange things in such a way that no one in our circle would have any trouble or have negative feelings about our departure. We decided not to say anything to those who might not notice our absence for a while. For those who do not really understand how and why emigration happens, we decided to present a simplified version.

In the communal apartment next to ours, lived an elderly illiterate woman from the village, whose name was Ksenia, but I do not remember her last name. Let her last name be Neighbour. We arranged with her to go for walks with little Verochka. They became friends on that basis. Vera called her "Grandma Ksenia" and both of them became attached to each other. What this simple woman was real master in baking pancakes and Verusha loved pancakes very much. Whenever Baba Ksenia was baking pancakes, she would always bring a dozen for Verushka. Our child was happy and sometimes even her parents managed to enjoy the delicacy. Later, in refusal, we made many overseas friends who really enjoyed the pancakes. Then, to everyone's delight, we began to buy pancakes for our guests from Grandma Ksenia. Along with Vera's walks, pancakes added a little to the miserable budget of this nice woman. Grandma Ksenia had once worked as an unskilled laborer, laying sleepers for the railway, and thus earned herself a miserable pension. In the same apartment in the next room lived a drunkard. This man regularly, got drunk and used to beat poor Grandma Ksenia. Whenever this happened, the poor woman would knock on our door and come in to flee from the bully. She begged us not to call the police because, she said, the hooligan in this case would kill her. We decided not to say anything to Grandma Ksenia about our emigrating plans at that point.

In the summer of 1976, Tanya quit her job at the University, supposedly to be with little Verochka. All her friends at the Institute were sure that it was temporary, that the girl would grow up and Tanya would come back to work. However, we did not want her colleagues to know the real reason. I, of course, also had to quit my job. I was working with my colleagues in my research institute, shoulder to shoulder for more than twenty years. That is why I felt that I have to tell my colleagues the truth about my plans. To my great regret, I was no longer able to say goodbye in person to the director of our Institute, Sergey A. Lebedev and to express my deepest gratitude to him. He had passed away by this time, so I said goodbye at his grave in the Novodevichy Cemetery. Most of my colleagues parted with me forever, which was extremely painful for me.

Viktor Zeidenberg, for example, when we were parting, told me with tears in his eyes, that he had never been closer to any one and that he never would. Nevertheless, he was afraid to see me again. In contrast was my parting with the head of my laboratory, Vladimir Melnikov. Until the last day of my work at my Institute, I unsuccessfully tried to talk to him but he was so terribly "busy" that he could not find the time. One day I was walking along Lenin Prospect and noticed Volodya from afar. He had parked his car near the sidewalk and worked on something in it. I was glad to have finally the opportunity to talk to him before parting. When I came close enough, he noticed me, but immediately ducked under the car, pretending to fix there something. I was always a naive man. How did I not realize until this moment, that he DID NOT WANT to see me?! After almost 20 years of us working together, we were on familiar terms. He is no longer alive, and one should not speak ill of the dead. After I left Russia, he managed to become a professor, an academician, twice laureate of the State Prize.

An even sadder story happened to my work of compiling dictionaries. In 1964, the publishing house "Soviet Encyclopedia" published on the initiative of Victor Zeidenberg first Soviet English-Russian computer dictionary in the USSR. The title editor was the director of our Institute Sergei Lebedev. Victor and I were the main authors of the dictionary. In 1974 in Moscow, the dictionary department of the "Soviet Encyclopedia" became the independent publishing house "Russian Language." One of the first books published by the new publishing house was the revised and supplemented second edition of our dictionary, which contained approximately 24 thousand terms. The title page listed the authors: V. Zeidenberg, Yu. Zieman, and A. Zimarev. Victor Zeidenberg came with a clever initiative: the Department of Scientific and Technical Information of our Institute purchased a part of the circulation of this edition for sale to specialists, who were coming to visit.

Before I left the Institute, I had a conversation with the co-authors of the dictionary about my personal plans for leaving. In addition, we discussed plans for final working on the third edition, which by that time was already largely prepared. It was an essential expansion of the second edition. After this conversation, I do not know who and how decided, but the sale of the second edition within the walls of the Institute was stopped. Nor do I know the fate of unsold copies of the dictionary; probably all the books were destroyed. It reminded me sadly known burning of books under the Nazi regime on May 10, 1933.

In the aforementioned conversation, I promised my co-authors, as well as the editors of the "Russian Language" publishing house, that I would do anything they asked of me in order to minimize any unpleasantness associated with my emigration. They asked me to write a letter to the publisher with specific content, which I did. Never in my life have I signed a document more ridiculous than this one. In this letter, I stated that BECAUSE OF MY POOR HEALTH, I a) refuse to continue working on the third edition of the dictionary, and b) refuse all royalties for past participation in this work.

The epilogue to the story of my dictionary is equally disheartening. The third edition of the dictionary NEVER saw the light of day?! In 1987, Publishing House "Russian Language" published an English-Russian Dictionary of Computer Science. The title page of this publication lists the authors: V.Zeidenberg, A.Zimarev, A.Stepanov, and the volume of the dictionary: was 37,000 terms. A mysterious line on the title page reads "Edition fourth, stereotyped, with supplements." How the fourth edition is possible without the third one? In addition, even schoolchildren know that the "stereotype edition" means the edition the same, letter to letter, as the previous one. To the present time, I am amazed how political correctness can be used to go to ANY TRICKS and is often lacking common sense, and often even contradicts it.

MY DESPAIR

After Tanya and my daughters, the person I was most worried about because of our departure was my brother Jan. It was not because I loved him more than I loved anyone else, but because he worked at the Space Research Institute (SRI) of the USSR Academy of Sciences, and his work was more important for him than anything else in the world. In my mind, he was working with kind of people like the main personage in the poem-song "The story of the technologist Petukhov" by the well-known Soviet bard and poet Yuri Vizbor. This man was proudly telling his friend:

> Nevertheless, we are developing rockets,
> We are building the dam across the Yenisei River,
> And also in the field of ballet,
> We are ahead of all the counties at the planet.

Such people repeated patriotic myths so often that they themselves believed in them. These people, it seemed to me, could not allow the brother of a man who had escaped from the Soviet Union "paradise" to join their ranks on the front lines in the holy of holies of the country. I was in despair and the situation tortured me.

The director of the Institute at that time was an interesting man, a physicist who specialized in plasma theory, the academician Roald Sagdeev. Strangely enough, from what I knew, I had an impression of him as a decent person. I immediately had the audacious idea to find a way to see him and to ask him to do everything possible so that our departure would not harm Jan. It so happened that Tanya's very close friend Ladochka Serebryakov

Director of the Space Research Institute Sagdeev R.Z.

had known Sagdeev's wife Frank-Kamenetsky. When I told Ladochka about my worries, she willingly agreed to talk about them with Thema. The chain worked, and I got an invitation to an audience with the director of SRI. During that meeting, I tried to explain to Sagdeev that our decision to leave the country was strictly private, and not only that my brother had nothing to do with it, but, moreover, that he knew nothing about it yet. My interlocutor made the most favorable impression on me. I felt that he was very understanding. He assured me that he would do his best to make sure that my brother would not get into any trouble. I returned home from that meeting very happy.

Unfortunately, our immigration did not turn out the way we wanted or expected. After submitting the documents, we waited about a year to find out that the authorities refused to give us the exit visas. As a result, we were able to leave only after 11 very difficult years of waiting, nervousness, material and psychological trials. However, Sagdeev kept his word. I had met with him in 1977. Fortunately, my brother continued to work successfully at the Space Research Institute of the Russian Academy of Sciences until his last day of life in 2009. More than thirty years after my conversation with Sagdeev, my brother continued to receive most of the honors possible in the Soviet Union. He became Professor, Doctor of Science, Honored Worker of Science and Technology. Even before we got out of the country, he became a Laureate of the State Prize (1984). In 2002, the Institute celebrated his 80th anniversary with pomp. I feel very sad that my brother deprived Tanya and me of the joy of celebrating all his successes together with him. He passed away, and we were not able even to say goodbye to each other!

APPLICATION TO EMIGRATE

Honestly, I felt disgusted to have to be involved in the stupid activity described in the previous chapters. However, it was quite a consolation to feel that ALL of THIS was exactly what we wanted to leave behind. That said, it was unacceptable for us to offend or hurt in the slightest friends and relatives. Besides, I generally held the opinion that, as much as I disliked Soviet Rome, as long as I lived in that city, I should do as Soviet Romans do. Of course, this rule did not apply to my personal life or my personal views and sympathies.

Once we made the final decision to emigrate, leaving our jobs, breaking up with many loved ones and worrying about the difficulties ahead proved emotionally difficult for us. However, in compensation, we both, Tanya and I, immediately felt a great relief in crossing this line and becoming free internally from the oppression of the totalitarian state. We rushed in excellent spirits to the Visas and Permits Office (VAPO) to announce our plans formally. Anticipating criticism about the layout of the typed texts, I brought my portable typewriter with me. When the unfriendly clerk of the VAPO told us we had to type this or correct that, we thanked him enthusiastically and retreated into the corridor. When we appeared at the door of his office just five minutes later with the corrected and supplemented documents, our official was saddened. As a result, soon all our documents were accepted, and we happily left the office. Unfortunately, we had to return to this place many more times.

Having performed this solemn act, both of us felt great relief. After all, what we had done was a Herculean feat. It was not a simple bureaucratic procedure. It was the final cutting of the umbilical cord connecting us to this country. We made an important, difficult and irreversible decision. We were aware that there would never be a way back.

In our joy, we decided to mark the day with something unusual, but pleasant for both of us. We were big classical music lovers, so we decided to go to the Melodia record store on Kalinin Prospect and use all our pocket money to buy good records. We both liked "dusty music," as one of our Moscow acquaintances defined, referring to music covered with the dust of centuries. We succeeded and, tired but satisfied, we returned home and listened to some of our newly acquired records. It seemed to us, that both Bach and Pergolesi, sounded very approving of the action that we had taken that day.

The deed was over, but now there was the very difficult part: telling everything at home. My parents were already dead. First, we had to tell my brother and sister because until today we had deliberately kept in the dark about our actions and plans. The readers probably would ask why. Because my social-cultural and political views were far from theirs and I knew, that I could not expect their understanding. I did not want to upset them prematurely and give them the opportunity to try to talk me out of my plans, which I simply could not give up.

The conversation with my brother was much more difficult and sad than I had anticipated. Jan was really mad. *"How could you do such a thing without consulting me?"* he said. *"With this decision you have not only spat on us all, but you have spat on the memory of our parents."* This was an accusation, in my opinion, extremely unfair and even, to some extent, blackmailing. Well, God be his judge! Moreover, when I told him about my conversation with Sagdeev he was furious. *"How dare you stick your nose into my private affairs, into my private life, which you know nothing about?"* he shouted. My pathetic attempts to explain that my love for him and my worry that my departure might harm his beloved business were my sole motivation, led nowhere. The consequences of that conversation were most regrettable. My brother ceased all contact with my family and me. Our relationship with him remained severed for over thirty years until his death in 2009. Unfortunately, in 1977, I lost my brother forever.

The conversation with my sister Lena, although it did not have such tragic consequences, was also very difficult. She burst into tears and said, *"I had hoped to live my life without meeting a single person who had decided to leave the Soviet Union. And it had to be that such a man turned out to be my own brother!"* Lena's husband Arkady was smarter than my sister was. Being a difficult man to live with, he had given my sister many bitter moments. Nevertheless, he had a broader general outlook. He took the news of our decision to emigrate enthusiastically. For the first time in the history of our relationship, he expressed his desire to come to visit us and talk about our impending departure. When they left, my Tanya said, *"I feel with my heart that Arkady will start the ball rolling. So, for the second time in her life, Lena will be confronted by someone who has decided to leave the Soviet Union, only this time it will be she herself."* Tanya's prediction came true. Lena with her husband and the family of her son Misha came to the United States and settled in New York, not without our help. Our relationship did not end like our relationship with Jan. However, the intimacy between us was gone. I have visited her many times in New York; she has never visited me in Boston. I call her several times a year, but she never calls me. However, I have tried never to resent her, especially now that she is in her 90s and dementia has taken most of her away.

Once during all these years, we did meet Jan. It was in 1998, when we went to Moscow to see for the last time Tanya's sister Natasha, who was very ill and dying. She was very dear to us. We do not know if my brother's children Olya and Lyova might have coaxed Jan. Anyway, Tanya and I received an invitation from my brother to come to his dacha together with his children and to meet everyone there. I was over the moon. However, it did not work out the way we expected it to. The food was excellent, and over a glass of wine I asked my brother hundreds of questions about his life, which he answered with obvious pleasure. But he never asked us even ONE question about our life in the United States!? He had not seen our daughters in over twenty years, and when he broke it off with us, Verusha. was only a year old. He didn't ask ANYTHING about them either!? Tanya and I came back to Boston from Moscow completely perplexed and extremely upset.

At this difficult time, my brother wanted his children, Olya and Lyova, to follow his example and end all contact with us. Fortunately, both of them firmly replied, "No!" As long as I am destined to live, I will never forget their courageous act of keeping the door open to us. Thank you, my dear ones, for not acting like your father and instead, letting us continue to love you.

I have to say that from the very beginning, Tanyusha and I decided to go not to Israel, but to the United States. For all our love of Israel, both of us had the feeling that there was not enough space there for us in the broadest sense. By saying this, we meant space not only geographically, but also politically, linguistically, religiously, socially. Why did we choose the United States? Simply, this country had the widest quotas for accepting refugees from other countris.

SUITCASES

After submitting our applications, both Tanya and I naively hoped to leave the USSR rather quickly. Therefore, we got train fever and started feverishly preparation for our departure. I remember our worries about little Vera, who was one year old at the time. We tried to plan how and where we would wash and dry her nappies on the way. No one knew anything about disposable diapers in Moscow at that time. We learned from the families of other Refuseniks that you could sometimes buy a unique portable heating fan, which other emigrants were using successfully for this very purpose. However, it was very difficult to find and buy one. I ran my legs off and got one miraculously, with a nice named "Tender breeze." However then, we spent the next 11 years stuck in the USSR. As a result, "Tender breeze" lay idle for all those years, and when we left in 1988, Vera. was 12 years old, and at least, this problem already did not concern us any more.

The next problem was suitcases. The Soviet authorities imposed brutal restrictions on the amount of luggage the emigrants could take with them. Each person was limited to take only one suitcase, and the weight of it could not exceed 44 pounds. Therefore, it was almost impossible to use most of the suitcases you had at home. They were too small, too big, or too heavy. In addition, they were certainly too good to be sent on such a journey. The fact is that on the first leg from Moscow to Vienna the emigrants flew on Soviet planes and the suitcases usually arrived in very poor condition. I suspect that the airline cargo handlers had instructions to throw and disfigure the luggage of emigrants as much as possible to teach people never to try to emigrate. I personally never understood this and I think that the fact that we heading to a different hemisphere should please both sides.

Quick-witted emigrants found the solution to the problem. The Moscow military supermarket occasionally "threw" on sale cheap soldier suitcases made of something between cardboard and fiber. They were ideally suited for "leaving for permanent residence" a political euphemism introduced by Soviet bureaucrats into the Russian language to describe emigration. After the collapse of the Soviet Union, many things have changed, including all the structures for obtaining passports and visas. Now Russians do not shy

LIFE THIRD: MY EFFORTS TO EMIGRATE FROM THE SOVIET UNION

away from the word "emigration," and the attitude towards emigration and suitcases, I hope, has changed too. At that time, these wonderful objects got the special name "Jewish suitcases" and we managed to buy a few. They did accommodate about 44 pounds of possessions, added little weight and when we arrived in our new home, it was not a shame to throw them away.

The conversation about the suitcases reminded me of a nice woman from Moscow, a little older than me, whom I had befriended in Boston much later. Her name Irina Zhivov. We met when I was working as a interpreter at the Hebrew Rehabilitation Center for the Elderly in Boston, and Irochka was admitted to us as a patient. We got to talking and it turned out that she had taught German at the Moscow Library Institute and knew my aunt Lidochka Kagan well. The world is a surprisingly small place. I heard very nice things about my aunt from her and I was overwhelmed with pride. I was not surprised to hear that she was a worthy daughter of my idol Veniamin Kagan.

I had many pleasant conversations with Ira and her visiting daughter Masha. In the course of our conversations I found out that before leaving Moscow, Irochka had composed a whole cycle of songs about emigration. She sang these songs herself, accompanying on guitar. I became very interested in these songs and copied them on my computer from the disk Masha brought me for this purpose. I heard many things in these songs, which we all felt, when we were leaving our Motherland. Since then I organized several listening sessions in the wards of patients of our centre that aroused a lot of emotions of old and sick people.

One of Irina's songs had the title "Suitcases." There are a couple of words in the

Under the suitcases: Tanya with our beloved Victoria Leconte

song, that require comment. The third line mentions Kolpachny Lane. The Visa and Registration Office (VARO) was located there then. Now gone, the new Department has a different name. One of lines in the middle of the poem mentions "Clear Ponds Park" which is one of the nicest parks in Moscow.

> Suitcases, suitcases
> Towering up to the sky,
> And the veterans in Kolpachny,
> Walk, — with visas already, or–yet without.
> Where they were standing, where they were sitting,
> Where they registered in special forms —
> Suitcase joy,
> Suitcase melancholy.
> Here are Abrams and there are Ivans,
> Everyone hurries to get across the ocean.
> There are suitcases in every house,
> One heavy suitcase is on my heart.
> The whole clans are on their way, making plans,
> Wipe the sweat off their faces.
> Suitcases, suitcases,
> Suitcases wherever you look.
> Emigrants are amateurs,
> A restaurant is never a choice.
> Pack your suitcases.
> Go away, as long as you are still in one piece.
> There are people who wait for us there; who knows the value of us,
> There will be recompense for our labors.
> Somewhere is Boston, Somewhere is Vienna,
> However, somewhere is Clear Ponds Park.
> Somewhere is sunshine — thunderstorms,
> Somewhere it is raining and fogging.
> All our tears, all our dreams —
> We will hide everything in the suitcase.
> We will hide and we will cry,
> We will laugh at ourselves.
> We must mean something
> Hauling behind our suitcase, like a back sack,
> All that is intact, all that is torn,

All permitted and all that is not.
Suitcases, suitcases —
You are our best friends.
We chafed the wounds on our shoulder,
We rubbed out our boots carrying you.
Suitcases, suitcases —
You are our worst enemies.
Whom you will drink with, what you will say,
Who is going to empty your pocket?
Where you will stand, where you will lie
To rest in the last suitcase in life?
We are neither sober nor drunk,
We just believe in miracles.
Our suitcases just take us up
They take us to the Heavens!

More than 30 years have passed since Irina wrote this song. A lot has changed in life, including suitcases. Now there are no more suitcases carried behind the back like backpacks. The suitcases on wheels replaced them. However, I still remember Irina's "suitcase joy" and "suitcase melancholy," and for me both were very important experiences. Unfortunately, Irochka is no longer with us. I was still working at the Exoneration Center when she, in her words, went to rest "into her last suitcase." However, the memory of this sweet person lives on in me, and I am happy that our paths crossed. From time to time, I turn on my computer, open files with Irina's songs, and we talk with her, remembering our meetings in the hospital.

LYOVA IN ECSTASY

It was no one else, but my niece Olya, who introduced her brother Liovochka in 1977 to her university friend Igor Chapkovsky. I suppose she regretted what she did more than once afterwards. The boy was only 16 years old at the time, and Igor was an enthusiastic proselyte and considered his mission from above to recruit youth into the "Russian Christian Orthodoxy," as he understood it. Our Lyova was and is still today a very emotional, trusting, and passionate person. He dove headlong into the cult that surrounded

Igor, was soon completely under Igor's influence and followed Igor's advice to go for baptizing in the Russian Orthodox Church.

I remember well our conversation with him at that time. I reproached him that he, knowing very little about Christianity and about Russian Orthodoxy in particular, had made a very serious decision in childishly trusting Igor. I had several highly educated believing friends, for whom I had the utmost respect. I suggested that he meet with these people and discuss with them how best to get prepared for such an important step, so that he could do it CONSCIOUSLY. I tried to tell him that he was, after all, a young man who was thinking about getting a higher education and not a semi-literate grandmother from a remote Russian village. In response, I heard that he did not need this kind of help at all, that he had not made the decision with his head, and that he took this step on the dictates of the heart. I remember how much this conversation upset me.

Now, let me say a few words about the use of the word "ecstasy" in the chapter title. I would not want the reader to see it as my rebuke to Lyovochka. The Longman Dictionary of English Language, which I have been using since my Moscow days, gives three meanings for the word "ecstasy." I reproduce the first meaning here: *a state of overwhelming emotion or feeling, often to the point of loss of self-control.* It seems to me that our emotional Lyova felt unrestrainedly attracted to Igor and completely gave himself to him. He was right: the decision came from his heart, and, as they say, the heart wants what it wants.

Later everything got worse. Learning from Igor, our naive Lyovochka unsuccessfully and ineptly tried to convert his parents to orthodoxy. Both emphatically said "NO!" During one of my conversations with Lyovochka at that time, I asked him to try to be more attentive to his mother, not to distance himself from her, to help her, because she, as an abandoned wife at the time, was already feeling forlorn. "You are a Christian now", I told him. I could not believe what I heard from Lyovochka in response. He told me that neither he nor anyone else could help my mother, but that it was her own fault. He said that there was a dark power in her because she did not want to live in Christ!

Then my straightforward brother went on a rampage. He did not say anything to Lyova but said me: *"I am itching to get behind*

LIFE THIRD: MY EFFORTS TO EMIGRATE FROM THE SOVIET UNION

the wheel of my car and drive after that bastard Igor and run him over." I calmed him down as much as I could, even though I was just as angry with Igor as I was with our beloved Lyova. However, when I heard him speak about a dark power in Innulia, it was my turn to get mad. What a mean person Igor was, what a moral monster! At such a difficult time for the boy, and especially for his mother, he had managed to alienate the boy from both his parents and, consequently, from God. I just wanted to rub this fierce Christian's nose in the fifth commandment of Exodus, verse 20:12, which says, *"Honor your father and your mother, that your days may be prolonged in the land which the Lord your God is giving you."* By the way, this commandment does not say to check the darkness or lightness within the parent before commencing honoring. It articulates an unconditional requirement to honor. Even assuming that a dark force had in fact taken up residence in a person, this one in particular needed kindness and understanding. I had the feeling that this "great educator" not only distanced Lyova from his parents, but also literally ripped him out of the world in which he was warm and comfortable. As to our young fool, he on the wave of emotions, rushed passionately to love his mentor, and thoughtlessly believed EVERY WORD he said. The trouble was that our Lyova felt comfortable with Igor.

At that time, Lyova was studying at the geology department of Moscow State University. If I remember correctly, he studied well and was one of the best students in his class. The year 1982 approached, when the great Soviet helmsman Leonid Brezhnev died. At Lyova's University, there was a memorial meeting, and all students had to stand and honor the deceased with a moment of silence. Our dissident refused to do so. The payback this time was severe. A few months before graduation, the administration of the University expelled Lyovochka from the university and deprived him of a diploma. I remember having very bitter, but mixed feelings. I wondered why Lyovochka did it. Lyova honestly told me then that he could not explain it. I personally can imagine that I myself might have acted just as foolishly in his place.

For two years, our Lyova and all of us around him mourned and worried that he would never see his diploma. We all knew that without this piece of paper, especially in a country as politicized as Russia at the time, one was nothing. He tried to manage with various temporary jobs. Then in 1984, they drafted him into the military. Every day we worried something bad would happen to him in the army. And, of course, it did. One day, as part of the routine drill, the soldiers had to do a marching tour, and before that, a colonel inspected and admonished the boys. This inspector was meticulous and, looking under Lyova's military shirt, he found two terrible breaches of military regulation. First, he was wearing a lined Wulen sleeveless jacket, which Innulia had knitted for him in case of cold weather. Secondly, he had, oh horror, a cross on his chest. The Colonel demanded sternly, *"Give me that!"* Without waiting for an answer, he jerked the necklace, which tore, and the cross fell to the ground. Our hero quickly picked it up and resolutely replied, *"I cannot give it to you!"* I draw the reader's attention to the fact that he did not say, "I will not!" but said more politely, "I cannot."

Surprisingly, this time, the case somehow ended with only solitary confinement. Two more years *"passed like an empty dream"*. (quote from Pushkin's "The Tale of the Dead Princess and the Seven Noblemen"). One can only imagine what it was like to serve in the Soviet army with Lyova's character. In 1986, he was about to come back home, but we heard nothing from him. Innulia and Olga looked for him everywhere but could not find him. When they phoned the military unit where he had served, the officer on the other side of the line told them that he had left. The anxiety-filled search went on for quite a long time until the information leaked that our hero went to his spiritual adviser without saying a word to his family. However, and damned spiritual master, of course, did not bother to inform the relatives because everyone in the family had "given their soul to the devil." Thank God, Olechka somehow managed to find him, and we all were reassured that at least he was alive and well. Well, what a prank-player was (in confidence, he still is) our Lyova, God forgive him!

We do not know where he would have ended up if not for a miracle. A very nice, dignified young woman named Sarah came from England to Moscow to study Russian. She found herself under Igor Chapkovsky's wing. If we skip details, our Lyovochka found her lovely and they married. Sarah was both stronger and wiser in practical terms than our Lyovochka, and soon realized what kind of common mentor they had. She succeeded in the impossible. Not only did she cure Lyova from his stupor, but also she got them both out of this cult. I wish readers would understand me correctly here. Sarah saved Leovochka not from Christianity, but from what I would call a totalitarian pseudo-Christian cult. I cannot help saying to Sarah a line from Pushkin's tale *"You did not rescue the swan, you kept the maiden alive; you did not kill the hawk, you shot the sorcerer."* For such deliverance, I think we should all carry Sarah in our highest esteem. It seems to me that Lyova has not yet realized this. What somewhat exonerates our naughty boy is the fact that there were many nice young people swimming around him in the maelstrom, and they all found themselves caught by this powerful cult leader. Thank God, many of them like Sarah and Lyova. managed to get out.

The best example is the girl Katya Koshkin. She left, in spite of Igor's disapproval; she entered medical school and became a wonderful physician, a Doctor with a capital letter. Katya has no family of her own; her families are the patients she treats, just like Janusz Korczak. Once we talked with Lyova about Katya and he told me that he especially appreciated her for having the courage to say to her patients like Janusz Korczak, "*I don't know*". Neither Lyova nor Katya, probably, knew that Korczak called this ability the indispensable quality of a good doctor. Today Katya is the head of a large department in one of Moscow's city hospitals. At one time, she helped Olga and rescued her from a serious stroke. Until the last day of our Olga's life, Katya cared for her almost maternally. Olga was painfully dying of blood cancer, and I was too far away to help her. However, I knew that Katya was beside her, and that made me feel better. The whole of Moscow knows her as a great doctor. Everyone who knows her personally loves her very much. Her patients know they are lucky to have found such a doctor. Having said all this, it is ridiculous and sad to remember today that when she broke out of Igor's clutches and left to study medicine, this "prophet" told her: "*I feel very sorry for your future patients*".

I would like to conclude the story of Lyova's trials by mentioning a much unexpected, very important and very pleasant development for me. I gave Lyovochka the unfinished manuscript of this memoir. Not only that, he came up with a number of extremely useful comments and clarifications, but also my views on *"the affairs of bygone days"* (A.Pushkin, "Ruslan and Ludmila") aroused a strong emotional response in him. In the first place, it related to my chapter about his mother Innulia. This response culminated in a poem he wrote in November 2019, "To Mama." I love the poem and I want to publish the whole thing here.

> *Someone remembers you as a different person,*
> *Someone remembers you alive,*
> *I do not remember.*
> *Probably, it would be nice to wipe my eyes, like glass,*
> *Before I can look into your eyes and see.*
> *Where are the roots?*
> *Just like before, they are lying in the ground,*
> *As if, they do not need a trunk,*
> *As if a leaf is not important to a bud.*
> *We can see the bud well, but we cannot see the flower?*
> *A boot stepped on the sprout,*
> *And that sprout was not brave enough...*

Every time I reread this verse, tears come to my eyes. In the years that I have been writing my book, this Lyova's response I take as the GREATEST COMPLIMENT I have ever received from anyone. Thank you, dear Lyovochka you made me realize that my efforts were not in vain. Together we manage, using Pushkin's words, *"to arouse kind feelings"* ("Monument"). I am very sorry that our Olga did not live to read this poem.

REFUSAL TO LET US GO

A Russian proverb says that there is nothing worse than waiting and catching up, but for me it is even worse to wait when the waiting period is indefinite. After submitting the documents for departure, the agonizing wait for permission began. Every single day after filing, I waited for permission. This went on for about a year, and one day, around the middle of 1978, I found not a permit, but a refusal to let us go. Thus, we entered a special social category of people, called in the USSR Jewish Refuseniks. We were not emotionally ready for this turn of events. As was then customary, in cases of refusal, no one ever provided a specific reason why one could not get an exit visa, nor was a specific period defined after which it might be possible. The postcard I took out of my mailbox from the Department of Visas and Permissions had the same wording as most other disclaimers: *"For security reasons."* There was complete arbitrariness in the decisions on security waivers, but the excuse for of all of them used the same assumption that sometime, somewhere a person had had access to classified information. State secrets should never go across the country border. There existed cases of regime blockers in the country for a monstrously long time. We were Refuseniks for 11 years, and our close friend Vladimir Prestin waited for his exit visa for 17 years!

The prolonged refusal opened a new chapter in our lives. Tanya and I had lost our regular salaries, our meager savings were quickly running out, and we were in constant need of extra work. This problem was even more difficult because of the fact that we had a one-year-old child. We could limit our own needs, but we could not make little Verochka suffer. As a result, I remember going in winter to the Cheryomushki market and buying ONE fresh cucumber there, for which we had to pay the cost of the DAILY RATION for both Tanya and me. Until I started working and could sit with Vera, Tanya ran to her lessons like a young poor student. Chronic lack of sleep reached the point where a couple of times she fell asleep in class in front of an astonished student. I, at this very time, tried not to reject any handy work. I am sad to say that in those difficult years it did not occur to my brother or sister to offer us any financial assistance

With our refusal came many other problems. Since 1961, the Criminal Code of Russia contained Article 209 to combat parasitism. Under this article, the evasion of able-bodied citizens from work was punishable by imprisonment for up to five years. However, while punishing "parasites," no one ever enquired as to why a person was unemployed. The best example of how Soviet authorities used this horrible article was in 1964 when the great poet Joseph Brodsky got under arrest, went to the court, and spent five years in exile with prior compulsory "treatment" in the psychiatric hospital. Nobody really wanted to go down such a path. This is why it was urgent to find work. Dozens of Refuseniks we knew, upper class professionals, had to work as guards, elevator assistants, janitors, couriers, etc., not to find themselves in jail.

We decided right away that, in the first place, it was I who I had to get a job. Little Verochka was only a year old, and Tanya could not think of leaving her with anyone. However, to get even unskilled employment was not easy. Most administrators were afraid and did not want to deal with a *persona non grata*. I continued to think about working in medicine, so we considered the maternity hospital # 25, where our Verochka was born. The chief physician of this institution was Tzilia Tsurenko, an old friend of our Tzilia's. I was hopeful about getting a job there "through connections." Not only did I not mind manual labor, but also I even aspired to it.

What did it mean in reality to be a Refusenik? The authorities saw all those, who wished to leave the Soviet Union, at the time, as internal ideological enemies, and numerous secret official circulars demanded that Soviet administrators not allow such people to work or study at any institution associated with ideology. However ALL skilled professions in the Soviet Union were ideological. The struggle for ideological purity reached the point of absurdity. When the Vietnam War broke out, my Galya started going to kindergarten. I remember well that one day she came home and told us how on that day they (children of 4–5 years old!?) under the direction of the kindergarten teachers had written an angry letter of protest against the war in Vietnam to the American president. I share this to illustrate that the Refuseniks would never get jobs even as cleaners in a kindergarten, lest they harm Soviet children with their ideological poison. In addition, since the Refuseniks were internal enemies, they were under constant surveillance by the KGB. As a result, it was always easy for the authorities to find a reason to put a Refusenik behind bars. In addition, for Tanya and me, this risk, first, doubled because of our proximity to dissidents and, second, tripled because of our friendships with foreigners. Thinking back on all this, I still do not understand what miracle saved us from the Gulag.

This was the situation, when Tanya and I appeared before Tzilia Tsurenko as beggars for my job. The nice woman looked puzzled for a while. Then she told us: "*I want to help you, and I will do it. But I cannot take a Jew to my hospital, lest I be accused of creating a Zionist nest (!?). I will introduce you to the Russian head doctor.*" A few days passed, and poor Tzilia was convinced that no Russian colleague of hers dared to touch a leper like me. Then my Tanyusha took matters into her own hands and made a very smart move. She took pictures of our adorable two-year-old Verochka and went to see Tsilia. Remember that Vera. was born in Tzilia's maternity hospital. After they had cried together over the baby's photo, Tsilia waved her hand and said through her tears, *"All right, whatever happens!"* She called her supply manager and together they found out that they had a vacancy for a janitor. The question was resolved within 15 minutes. That is how my working life in the maternity hospital began.

We prepared ourselves, as best we could, for the Refusenik life, that we knew would be difficult and might last indefinitely. A few months passed and I adjusted to this new world and even learned to find some joy. I worked in shifts: 24 hours at work and two days and nights at home. I even began to like such a schedule. During my free time, I could do something for my soul, and will talk about this later. In addition, during my free days I tried to earn some money in addition to my meager janitorial salary.

Years of experience as a Soviet administrator did not fool my boss, Tzilia Tsurenko, and she knew there would be ramifications for hiring a Jewish Refusenik. Quite soon, after my janitor career began, uninvited guests from the KGB showed up at the maternity hospital and recommended that the head doctor find a way to fire me. The wise and brave woman replied to them that of course she would do, as they wanted. However, she asked them to teach her how to do it tactically. *"Yuri is just a real Russian handyman, after all!"* she told them. These people left and never came back. This example shows how much depended on the courage of people and their attitude towards outrages, and how much their courage helped those around them, even in such a lawless country as we lived.

After organizing a job for me and thus insuring ourselves against criminal prosecution and starvation, we began to try to extract from the authorities any particular deadlines after which we would be able to leave. Tanya managed to get an appointment with the director of our Research Institute. We decided that it was better for her to go than for me, hoping that he would be less rude and more accommodating with the woman. This man had known me for almost twenty years, and we were on a first-name basis. He was well aware that I had always shunned secret work and therefore working at the Institute could not be grounds for refusal. Nevertheless, she heard nonsense from him. *"Your husband is so capable,"* he said, *"that he could hear some secret information just by being within the walls of the Institute. However, it was not our opinion that re-*

fused him, but that of the Ministry of Radio Electronics. I recommend you go there." I knew that being an academic institution we were affiliated secretly with the Ministry.

After that visit, I sent a written request to the Ministry by mail, asking about the reason and the actual deadline for the refusal. In response, I received a formal note on the official letterhead, which contained no information, with a recommendation to go to the Department of Visas and Permits. There was no printed name of the person, who answered in the document and I could not decipher a single letter in his signature. I went to the ministry with this "document" in my pocket. They would not let me pass the checkpoint. Then I politely asked for the name of employee who signed the "answer" I received. I had to wait for quite a long time, and then a man came out to me and said that the Ministry could not give me the name of the employee, as this information was confidential (!?).

After that, Tanya went with the same questions to the KGB lair on Dzerzhinsky Square. There they told that she had come to the wrong place: the KGB had nothing to do with the refusal. They told her that she had to go to the Department of Visas and Permits (DVAP), though everyone knew that this organization never decided anything. It did paperwork for people crossing the border. When Tanya asked them why they were tormenting her and her children, those monsters replied, *"We do not keep you here; take your children and go."* It was a brazen Pharisaic lie. Even if we assume the impossible, that Tanya had really expressed a desire to leave without me, they would never have allowed it. In addition, they knew perfectly well that this was unacceptable to us. It became clear to me that we were fighting windmills.

THE OLD DOCTOR

In 1976, I read a little book by a great man of the world, a saint of the twentieth century, Janusz Korczak (real name: Ersh Henrik Goldschmidt). The book changed me as a person and changed my life. Its title is 'How to Love a Child' and its author is an outstanding Polish humanist, educator, pediatrician, writer and social activist who dedicated his entire life to children. This book fascinated me from the first pages, and since then I have worshipped this man. I would like to quote here a few lines from this little book written by a man after more than a decade of very hard study, work and thinking about children. I think about these words of my idol very often:

> How, when, how much, why? I anticipate many questions waiting to be answered, a lot of doubts needing resolution. To many of them I answer, "I do not know." 'Do not know', in sciences, is the vagueness from which new thoughts arise, being born, each time closer and closer to the truth. Do not know, for a mind unaccustomed to analytical thinking, is a frightening emptiness. I want all to understand and to love the wonderful, full of life and overwhelming surprises, creative 'Do not know' of modern child science."

I think, in fact, that last phrase applies not only to the science of the child, but to any important aspect of human life. Janusz Korczak was an extraordinary man, his life was extraordinary, and his death was extraordinary too. Therefore, I would like to list briefly the steps of his extraordinary life. After all, J.Korczak himself did in his own life what he was advising others to do. In the Gospel of Matthew (23:3), Jesus instructed His disciples concerning the Scribes and Pharisees, "*All therefore whatsoever they bid you observe, that observe and do; but do not ye after their works: for they say and do not...*". This is where the English proverb came from, "*Do as you preach.*" So J.Korczak, in his own life, did what he preached.

Beginning in 1903, he worked in a Jewish children's hospital and as an educator in summer children's camps and was a member of the Jewish Charitable Society for Orphans. In 1905 he successfully graduated from the Medical Faculty of the University of Warsaw and received a doctor's diploma. In 1907, he went to Berlin, where he attended lectures and interned in children's clinics at his own expense and got acquainted with different educational institutions. He also took an internship in France and visited an orphanage in England. In 1911, Korczak founded the "Home for Orphans" for Jewish children, which he directed for the rest of his life. During the First World War, 1914–18 Korczak served as a military doctor in a division field hospital of the Russian Imperial Army. Then he worked as a doctor in the orphanages for Ukrainian children in Kiev. After the war, Korczak also ran children's shelters, taught, published, and gave lectures at the Free Polish University and taught the Higher Jewish Pedagogical Courses. During the Polish-Soviet war in 1918–21, Korczak worked as a medical major in a military hospital. From 1919–1936, he was involved in the work of an orphanage for Polish children. From 1926–1932, Korczak edited the weekly magazine Small Review, a supplement for children in a Jewish newspaper, in which his pupils were actively involved. In pre-war Warsaw, he appeared regularly on the radio in the program "Old Doctor's Talks."

After the German occupation of Warsaw in 1939, Korczak was walking around Warsaw in his Polish army officer's uniform and said: *"As for me, there is no German occupation. I am proud to be a Polish officer and I will walk as I wish."* In 1940, the Nazi invaders moved the Jewish Orphanage with its children to the Warsaw Ghetto. They arrested Korczak and he spent several months in prison. He turned down all offers by his non-Jewish admirers, of whom there were many, to take him out of the ghetto and hide him on the "Aryan" side. Korczak's Polish associate and secretary Igor Neverly, tells of his own attempt of this kind:

> *We rented a room for him in Bilyany, prepared his documents. Korczak could leave the ghetto any minute. At least he could do it with me, when I came to him, having a pass for two persons, a technician and a plumber of the water and sewage network. Korchak looked at me in a way that made me cringe. I could see, he was not expecting such a proposition from me. The doctor's answer was, you would not abandon your child in misfortune, illness, and danger. Remember, I have two hundred children here. How can you leave them alone in a gas chamber? How you can possibly to get over this?*

Looking ahead, when the Nazis liquidated the ghetto, it was Neverly who managed to get the Old Doctor's diary, which he had kept in the all the years of the occupation, out of the House of orphans. He hid it by walling it up in the foundations of one of the buildings in Warsaw. This saved the unique document for posterity. Neverly then wrote and published in 1958 the most complete 4-volume collection of Janusz Korczak's works in Poland. I managed to become the lucky owner in Moscow of this Polish edition. I was so naive then to believe, that one day I will find energy and time to translate all these four volumes from Polish into Russian. This was never destined to happen.

Korchak's attitude to words "I do not know" resonates for me with wise advice of A.Galich concerning the absolute opposite, the sensation of one's own omniscience:

Do not be afraid of jail. Do not be afraid of beggary.
Do not be afraid of the scorching heat and Hell.
And the only thing to be afraid of is a person,
Who says: "I know WHAT IS RIGHT!"
Who says: "Follow me,
I will teach you what is right!"

Janusz Korczak proved with his own life that for the sake of children, one can step into the furnace and into hell. In 1942, the Nazis took the children of the Orphanage to the death camp near Warsaw, Treblinka, where a huge number of Polish Jews were murdered. The great friend and teacher of these orphans stepped with the children into the gas chambers, and thus entered into eternity. It was this unparalleled heroism of the Old Doctor that inspired A. Galitch to write his remarkable poem 'Kaddish' in memory of Janusz Korczak. The word Kaddish means the Jewish memorial prayer. As one of the epigraphs in this poem, A.Galich used the words of the Old Doctor from "Diary" "*I do not wish harm to anyone, I am not able, I just do not know how to do it*".

When I read "How to Love a Child," I felt ashamed that I knew almost nothing about such (!) a person. I also felt ashamed that I knew almost nothing about how to love a child really, when I had such a wonderful Little Drop. I immediately felt a desire to read EVERYTHING written by such an extraordinary person and to read it not in Russian, disfigured by the Soviet censors. It immediately became clear to me that the Old Doctor had a NON-SOVIET mentality, judging only on the fact that he made no secret of his Zionism. It was only much later, that I read, for example, in the book by Betty Jean Lifton "The King of Children. Life and Death of Janusz Korczak," quoting the Old Doctor said: "In *revolutions, as always, gain those who are sly and cunning, while the naive and gullible are left with nothing, and revolutionary programs are a combination of madness, violence and insolence based on disrespect of human dig-*

nity." The more I learned about Korczak the more I wanted to learn Polish quickly!

At that time, a Polish linguist, Elzbieta Janus had come to Moscow from Warsaw to work together with Igor Melchuk. She was a very special person and Tanya and I befriended her. Her visit was a gift of fate for me. She gave me a lot. Of course, she knew a lot about Korczak, she was pleased with my enthusiasm for him, and she helped me to learn how to read Polish. Just a few lessons with Elia worked a miracle. It appeared to be very important to pronounce a word in a right way. This would often give me a phonetic clue as to what the word meant, as in Polish there are many roots in common with Russian and Ukrainian. Thanks to Elia I came to believe that I WOULD BE able to read Korczak's books after some studying!

Thank God, there was a store in Moscow selling books published in socialist countries. There I bought a big Polish explanatory dictionary and tried to "read" it every free minute. It was more about deciphering than reading. I liked this process and began to notice a progress. At that time, I often took Verochka, a newborn baby, for walks in a stroller. I began to take the dictionary with me and when the baby fell asleep, I intensively communed with the dictionary. The first book by J. Korczak, which I dreamed to get through, was "Diary" written in the ghetto. Slowly but surely, I progressed. At some point, I received a precious gift from one of my American friends: a translation of "The Diary" from Polish into English, published in the United States. The work went on considerably more cheerfully. The further I progressed through the book, the easier the process went, and the more important this book seemed to me. Around 1979, I brazenly decided to try to translate it into Russian. In 1981, I completed the translation.

My translation into Russian of the "Ghetto Diary" by Janusz Korczak

LIFE THIRD: MY EFFORTS TO EMIGRATE FROM THE SOVIET UNION

What was the next step? I sought the advice of our close friend, problem-solver Tzilia Reitburd. She found people among her friends in Israel who were interested in the idea of publishing my Russian translation. My American friends helped them to send the manuscript to Israel. In 1982, the Publishing House "Stav" in Jerusalem published Janusz Korczak's Diary translated by me into Russian. I was over the moon, hugging and kissing our Tzilia! Once again, we got the Russian saying confirmed: *"Don't have a hundred rubles but have a hundred friends."* The success put me in a euphoric state. No one knew how many more years we would stay in refusal. I had already begun to dream of working on a complete collection of Janusz Korczak's works in Russian.

So far, I have read with great interest his play "The Senate of the mental patients" (1931), staged by the Warsaw Theatre. The performance had received many positive reviews. In the manuscript under the title, Korczak himself indicated in brackets: (Gloomy Humoresque). The action takes place in an insane asylum, and the patients have organized a sort of parliament and are discussing how to make life better. I think the idea of the play is very interesting, because in a way mentally ill people are freer than the rest of us. They are not familiar with factors such as diplomacy, calculating, and political correctness. Fear of making a bad impression, self-interest, desire for power, rivalry, etc. do not exist for them. My interest in Gloomy Humoresque led me to translate it into Russian, too. Interesting detail: recently, while doing research in my archives, I came across a piece of manuscript of my translation of "The Senate of the mental patients" which I was working on almost 40 years ago. It turned out to be a manuscript, literally. Portable computers and word processors did not exist yet. I wrote it with my own hand on thin school notebooks with printed lines. The notebook, I found, had "No. 7" written on the cover. I no longer remember how many notebooks the whole translation required. After the translation was finished, I typed the text from the notebooks on my portable typewriter "Erica." In this typewritten form, I sent my translation to Israel, along the well-trodden path.

The publication of "Diary" made my name known in Israel, and when Library "Aliya" in the late 80s was preparing a volume of selected works by Janusz Korczak in Russian, they not only reprinted my translation of "Diary" but also published "The Senate of the

Insane". The publication of "Selected Works" happened in Israel in 1988. However, that same year we got permission and left Russia. I had to pass away in my third life and to be born again in the fourth. I had to start all over again in this my new life. Unfortunately, the new challenges of life did not allow my Napoleon plans to prepare a complete collection of Janusz Korczak's works in Russian to come to fruition.

MY LITTLE FROGGY

To teach citizens of the USSR never think about emigration, the authorities created a multitude of difficulties for them on their way out of the country. The primary hardship was financial. In 1977, when we decided to leave, exit visas for Tanya and me cost about 10,000 rubles. I must pay tribute to the humanity of the Soviet government, a child, who did not come yet of age, did not need a visa when leaving the country. To understand better the cost, before I left my job, my annual salary as a Senior Researcher was about 2000 rubles. Thus, just to buy visas for departure, we would have had to set aside the whole of my salary in the Academy of Sciences for five years. We did not have that kind of spare money, of course. Being aware of this, long before submitting our documents, we began saving the required sum of money by cutting down our daily expenses. By 1977, we had saved the required money.

I have to say that these are modest flowers compared to the berries of the Brezhnev years. Since 1972, according to the decree of the Presidium of the Supreme Soviet of the USSR, emigrants leaving the country, in addition to paying for exit visas, had to reimburse the costs of their education they got in the USSR. This decree was in force in 1973 and was officially cancelled only at the collapse of the Soviet Union in 1991. It is noteworthy that the citizens of the USSR, who immigrated to socialist countries, were not required to reimburse the costs of their education, which indicates the purely political, rather than economic nature of this measure to combat emigration from the USSR.

Under this decree, emigrants had to pay the following:
- Graduates from economic, legal, pedagogical, historical and archival Universities and institutes of culture—4,500 rubles;

- Graduates from a university—6,000 rubles;
- Graduates from institutes and faculties of foreign languages—6,800 rubles;
- Graduates of engineering, economic and higher military educational Institutes—7,700 rubles;
- Graduates of medical, pharmaceutical, dental and physical education Institutes—8,300 rubles;
- Graduates from art Institutes (conservatories, theatrical, art and literary
- Institutes)—9,600 rubles.
- Graduates from the Moscow State University—special charges, 12,200 rubles.

In addition to these amounts, postgraduate, residency, and adjunct students and those with academic degrees were charged as follows:

a). Graduates from postgraduate, residency and adjunct schools who yet did not defended their dissertations—1,700 rubles for each year of study;

b). Persons awarded a candidate of science degree—5,400 rubles;

c). Persons awarded a doctoral degree—7,200 rubles.

The arbitrariness with which the Soviet authorities established the given figures causes only bewilderment. For example, Moscow University cost twice as much as all the other universities, perhaps because of the number of floors in the building. The shamelessness with which they robbed even the most educated and least paid world-renowned professionals forced to flee the country, of course, was outrageous. Let us turn just to ordinary working people. I myself, a senior researcher of the Academy of Sciences with a PhD degree earned about 2000 rubles a year. This means that if such a financial scam had continued, when we were leaving, we would have had to pay for both of us more than six years of my salary! A good example is Igor Golomshtok, an acquaintance and an excellent art critic who left the Soviet Union in 1972. He had TWO college degrees. Over the more than twenty years he spent in Russia, he published dozens of articles and books. On leaving Russia, he had to pay almost 30,000 rubles. Even an outstanding art historian of such a scale did not have this type of money. A collection was taken throughout Moscow, and friends and fellow intellectuals collected money for his departure.

Around 1979, it became clear that we were going to be in refusal for a long time. Therefore, it occurred to my wise wife that it made no sense to keep the money set aside for the visas in the savings bank for in this country there was always a possibility that we would lose it after the next reform. The Soviet government had pulled such thievery on the depositors of the savings banks more than once. Besides, if the money was in our account at the savings bank, there would always be a temptation to spend some of it with the goal to replace it later. However, we could get permission to leave unexpectedly, and then we would need the money very urgently. Tanyusha rightly said that it would be better if we invested the money in something that we could redeem easily at any time.

This is how the idea of investing the money on a car came about. There was an acute shortage of cars in Russia in those years. The cheapest car, as I said earlier, cost about five times my annual salary. The ratio of my annual salary to the cost of a car, I think, describes well the standard of living in the USSR. When I got my first job in America in 1988, it was an entry level job with a salary common for new college graduates. Even at that, I could buy two of the cheapest NEW cars on my annual salary. It turns out that when I first started in the US, the pay gap with Russia was more than 10 times. If we consider my salary when I retired in the USA, the gap was more than 20 times. The catchphrase by Ilya Ilf and Eugene Petrov from their novel "The Golden Calf," misled the reader into thinking that the car in Soviet Russia in 1931 was *"not a luxury, but a means of transportation".* Everybody could see it as a mockery or as an element of political fiction and propaganda.

In fact, personal cars were a rarity in the USSR these days, and buying, operating, repairing, and selling them turned into extraordinary adventures. Nevertheless, Tanya's plan did come to fruition, we did manage to buy the car and to get rid of it before we left, and all the adventures described in this chapter are our personal experiences.

To start with, the process of buying a new car in the USSR was ludicrous. Even those lucky enough to have sufficient money to buy a car could not readily purchase one. There was no free sale of cars. It was possible to buy a car only after standing in a queue for sometimes 10 (!?) years. Those who went through the ordeal had to confirm their queue number once a week every Sunday morning. Every week, the line progressed and each week the number of persons in the line decreased until it became two-digits. The confirmation of the queue took place on the outskirts of Moscow in the wasteland near Koptevo market. Here is some simple arithmetic. We have 52 weeks in a year. It turns out that over 10 years, everyone who dreamt of becoming a car owner had to appear 520 times in the Koptevo wasteland!!! The queue rules were brutal: if you missed one confirmation, you were out of the queue. The rite of marking was performed quite early, at 8 a.m. I remember that in wintertime it happened even in the dark. The sight was very impressive. Early Sunday mornings, under the cover of night, thousands of cars from all over Moscow rushed with their headlights through unlit streets of Moscow to a dirty wasteland in Koptevo. We personally took part in this madness when my brother Jan was buying a car. I once told my American journalist friend, Nicholas Daniloff, about this process. He did not believe me, so I invited him to go with me, so he could see everything with his own eyes. To this day, he can't forget what he saw.

For the lucky ones who reached the end of the queue, the last mark was done, after which the person received a postcard telling him when in the next couple of weeks he should come to the shop on Bakunin Street and pay for the car. This shop was THE ONLY ONE selling cars in all of Moscow. There was never any question of choosing the color of the car. You had to take what was available that day.

The ugly situation for buying and selling cars in the country gave rise to a huge black market for postcards, inviting us to come and buy a car. These postcards were quite expensive, and we did not have the money to add to the price of the car, nor could we wait years to get a car. We did not know when we might get permission to leave, but we knew that once we got it, we would need to pay for the visas without delay. Therefore, the only thing that made sense to us was temporarily investing the visa money. So we could buy a car NOW less than one condition: we have to know with certainty that we could quickly get our money back to pay for the visas. For listed reasons, there was no way we could be able to buy a new car

It was also practically impossible for us to buy a used car legally. The legislation of those times was created to prevent a profit in the automobile market. A private person was only allowed to sell a car through the state commission shop without the right to establish the price or to choose the buyer. As a result, very few people traded their cars in the used car shop (look for a fool!) except when people got rid of a total junk. With these rules, of course, people went to all lengths to get around the law. Of course, our Tzilechka, remember, she was a tiger of kindness, found a solution to help us. A good friend of hers, a man who worked at Izvestia newspaper, had to sell fast a nearly new, inexpensive Zhiguli. I do not remember now why he needed to do it urgently. Tzilia told him about our situation, describing us as remarkable and 100 per cent reliable people. She vouched for us, staking her life and her savings. After this, we handed this man the money he wanted for the car. He handed us the car along with a power of attorney for its unlimited use. We agreed that we would arrange for a similar transfer of the car on his behalf to the next "owner" when we urgently needed money for visas. This is how we got our hands on an almost new, cute little light green car, which we immediately fell in love with and named it Little Froggy.

Of course, we were disappointed that we could not formalize our relationship with the Little Froggy legally correct. We were very concerned that the KGB, having gotten wind of the nature of this relationship, might take legal action against us, or even worse, against the official owner of the car. Therefore, we tried to be as discreet as possible. For example, when we saw our foreign friends and did not want to advertise the gathering, we all tried to park a few blocks away from the meeting point. If we drove somewhere with our friends in two cars, we never parked our cars next to each other. Such tricks were certainly annoying, but tolerable. Fortunately, no conflict with the KGB related to our Little Froggy ever occurred.

By acquiring our car, we received as a bonus the unique experience of car ownership in the USSR, which by its nature was quite consistent with the difficult rules of buying, selling and taking care of the car. Almost every step in the daily operation of the car turned into a serious challenge. First, many spare parts were impossible to get. The best example was car tires, which could only be purchased through a queue similar to the one for buying a car. However, this queue was shorter and took only 6–12 months to get through. This outrageous queue led to an epidemic of wheel thefts from cars parked on the street. After all, to unscrew five nuts or bolts and remove the wheels from a car was a 15-minute affair. Russians immediately responded to this problem by the underground manufacture of "secret" nuts (bolts), the installation and removal of which required special tools. Such improvements began to be mass-produced and went to the black market. Of course, we purchased such bolts for our Little Froggy.

A separate problem, I remember, was the windscreen wipers, which you can buy all over the civilized world literally on every corner. In Moscow, these parts wore out quite quickly, especially during winter snowfalls and icing, and it was simply impossible to buy them. These small and cheap parts, unfortunately, required factory fabrication, and it was simply impossible to make them either at home working on a chair or illegally using the state machinery, even if you had golden hands. Anyone dealing with a car knows that it takes one minute to remove and place a wiper. This situation quickly spawned a massive theft of wipers. For this reason, if you left your car unattended anywhere on the street for even 15 minutes, chances are you would never see your wipers again. A similar situation was with the rear-view mirrors mounted on the fenders of your car Therefore, no one was surprised to see in the streets of Moscow or, say, in grocery stores people with wipers or (and) mirrors in hand and a small wrench in his pocket.

As funny as it was, these problems never upset us. Little Froggy left us with the brightest memories. It served us faithfully all the years of refusal up to obtaining permission to leave in 1988. We loved him. More than once during those difficult years we would travel to some wonderful places, our difficult lives would be brightened, and we would rejoice over him and the tremendous difference he made. That joy was exactly what the authorities were trying so hard to take from us. In this sense, Little Froggy helped us hold on to our sanity during those arduous years and in our own little way to resist the authorities.

TANYA VELIKANOV IS ARRESTED

In the seventies, the Soviet authorities went on a new offensive against dissenters who often represented the best of the country. In 1970, Solzhenitsyn won the Nobel Prize. In 1974, his "Gulag Archipelago" was published in France, and in the same year by decision of the Politburo he was arrested and expelled from the country. This act occurred with the full approval of His Holiness Patriarch Pimen of Moscow, as well as of Metropolitan Seraphim of Krutitsy and Kolomna. The latter published an article in "Pravda" with the headline "To a renegade — the contempt of the people." This position by the leaders of the mainstream Russian Orthodox Church seemed incredible, as it repeated not only the views, but also the vocabulary of the godless Bolsheviks. These were the words of the people who had plundered the Orthodox churches for decades, and attempted to destroy them. The protests of the Western Orthodox clergy have not changed anything.

In 1973, Viktor Krasin, one of the organizers of the Initiative Group for Human Rights Protection in the USSR, was arrested and sentenced to 3 years of labor camp and 3 years of exile. In 1974, Gabriel Superfin, one of the editors of the Samizdat periodical "The Current Events Chronicle," was arrested and sentenced to 5 years in a camp and 2 years in exile. In 1975, Sergei Kovalev, a close friend of Tanya Velikanov and one of the authors of The Current Events Chronicle, was arrested and sentenced to 7 years in a camp and to 3 years in exile.

In 1975, the eminent academic physicist, A. Sakharov, received the Nobel Prize. And in 1976, the then Chairman of the KGB, Yuri Andropov, speaking to his colleagues, called Sakharov *"internal enemy number one,"* because of his political views. Also in 1976, Yuri Orlov, a talented physicist and associate member of the Academy of Sciences was arrested for his political views. This scholar was detained in prisoners camps until 1984, and then until 1986 exiled in Yakutia in the Russian Far East along the Arctic Ocean. After Orlov's release from exile, he was expelled from the Soviet Union. And in 1980, Andropov got his hands on Andrei Sakharov. On his way to work he was arrested and without trial was exiled to Gorky.

All these sad events, as well as many others, which I am not mentioning here, were like bombs exploding around me. But in

1979, you could say a bomb exploded right in my yard: they arrested a very close and dear person to me, Tanya Velikanov, one of the most wonderful people I had ever met in my life.

I met Tanya and her husband Kostya Babitsky and we became friends in 1961. Her connection with the dissident movement, which shaped the rest of her life, began in 1968, when Kostya went to a demonstration on Red Square to protest the invasion to Czechoslovakia by Soviet tanks. Tanya's experience with Kostya's subsequent arrest was a turning point in her political views. As the demonstration was being prepared, Tanya decided in advance to go to Red Square to see everything with her own eyes and hear everything with her own ears, hoping then to act as a witness at the trial and thereby, she thought, help the cause and help Kostya. But she was deeply disappointed. Velikanov's testimony in the court records was perverted so much that it only helped the punishers to impose their monstrously unjust judgment on Kostya and his friends in violation of all legal norms and human rights. Since then, Tanya decided for herself to NEVER become involved legally with the Soviet authorities, and to NEVER enter into any negotiations with them. She was very consistent and strictly followed this rule in all further persecutions by the authorities and the KGB. In the following years, both my Tanya and I repeatedly discussed these questions with her in case we ever faced investigation and arrest. Thank God, it did not come to this, but we remembered her advice always, and it helped us through the arduous tribulations of our refusenik life.

It was this very trial, which started Tanya's ACTIVE human rights endeavors. In 1969, Tanya became the one of founding members of the USSR's first human rights organization "Initiative Group of Defense of Human Rights in the USSR." In 1970, she took the lead in organizing the main periodical of Soviet human rights defenders, the "Chronicle of Current Events." For nine years, under her supervision, some thirty issues of the Chronicle reached its readers. In the 1970s, Tanya's apartment in Moscow became one of focal points where information about Soviet political persecutions was gathered. In 1974, Tanya together with her friends and co-defenders of human rights, S.Kovalev and T.Khodorovich openly took responsibility for the dissemination of this publication. In 1976, the administration took Tanya's job from her and there were repeated searches of her apartment. It became clear that it was no longer safe to continue working on the Chronicles in that apartment. At this time, we, along with all her friends, could already see that the situation was inevitably heading towards Tanya's arrest. She saw it as well.

I cannot tell you how difficult it was for me to see this coming. My many years of friendship with Tanya gave me plenty of time to reflect on my own position. I did not want to get actually involved in the human rights movement in this country for many reasons. Chief among them were, perhaps, my sense of hopelessness in achieving tangible results, my unwillingness to make my family's life miserable and, of course, my fear of not being strong enough to stand up to such a brutal regime. At the same time, I admired and knelt before the moral purity and courage of members of the movement, such as Tanya Velikanov. And I always wanted to support them morally and physically and help them in practical terms.

Shortly before Velikanov's arrest, when her apartment was already under constant surveillance, my Tanya and I offered her our apartment to prepare the next issue of The Chronicle. For about a week we shared our home with a wonderful group of friends, one better than the other, who stayed with us, eating and drinking at our place and working from morning till night, trying to bring the truth to people. During short breaks, we had the joy of fellowship. If you ask whether my Tanyusha and I were afraid, of course we were. However, to this day we are happy that we did it.

On 1 November 1979, Tanya Velikanov was arrested. The charges against her included the texts of the Initiative Group's appeals to the UN, issues of the "Chronicle," as well as connections with foreign publishers of the bulletin. The trial lasted for three days from August 27 to 29, 1980. Tanya's relatives only learned about the start of her trial that morning after a phone call from a foreign correspondent. People in the form of the traffic police cordoned off the block in Moscow where the court building was located. No regular traffic was allowed through the block and all the cars were detoured for three days. We all came to the Moscow City Court building all three days, in the hope of getting into the hall. We knew we had to arrive well in advance, because the most frequent reason for not getting to the "open" hearing was "lack of free seats". This lack of seats was specially created using a squad of soldiers from a nearby military unit who had been brought through the back door and seated in the hall before the front door had been opened. Of course, no one except the immediate members of Tanya's family managed to get into the hall.

The trial lasted for three days, and every day the same masquerade was played out. I remember the day after the court closed, August 31, was my Tanya's 41st birthday, and we invited all of our friends and friends of Tanya Velikanov to come and visit us. In 2020, as I write these lines, my Tanya just celebrated her 84-th birthday. Probably that birthday in 1980 was the saddest of all the birthdays we celebrated together with her.

The court sentenced Tanya Velikanov for "anti-Soviet agitation" to 4 years in camps and 5 years in exile. After her arrest, the Committee to Protect Tatyana Velikanov was formed in Moscow, which included Larisa Bogoraz, Elena Bonner, Sofia Kalistratova, Lev Kopelev and others. The Committee collected and disseminated all available information about the Velikanov case, publishing it in special bulletins. In two issues, there were 27 letters in defense of Velikanov, signed by nearly 500 people. A. Sakharov, E. Bonner, and G. Pomerants spoke separately in defense of Velikanov, as well as writers V. Voinovich, G. Vladimov. In collections of documents, such as the one published by the Velikanov Defence Committee, documentary evidence of her innocence was presented. In the second edition, the poem by Vladimir Kornilov appeared and described this outstanding woman. I would like to quote here the whole poem:

TANYA VELIKANOV HAS BEEN ARRESTED

She was so feminine,
So beautiful with her gray hair,
So natural, not like most people around,
It was as if she was a living saint!
Not retrograde, not left,
Condemning no one's sin,
Doing her simple thing,
Defending not somebody, but everyone!
She was the glory of Russia — Velikanov!
Showing us once again, that
Self-sacrifice and honor still exist,
And not only damned fear.

Having known Tanya Velikanov for so many years, I agreed with every line. The only thing that concerned me then and keeps concerning me today is the past tense used by the author, which gave the impression of an obituary, as if Tanya was no longer with us. Not only was she with us in body and soul at the time, but she was also an amazing example of fortitude for all of us, something that the pygmies-fabricators in the KGB could never understand and appreciate.

I cannot help but say here, that I was incredibly lucky to have had much of Tanya Velikanov in my life, and I am proud that she was my close friend. Not only did she teach me a great deal in both word and deed, but also helped me to become a better person just by being who she was. It was in her house that I met Andrei Sakharov, in my mind, one of the saints of our time. It was through Tanya that I made the acquaintance of such wonderful people as Larissa Bogaras, Tolia Yakobson, Pavel Litvinov, Yuri Shikhanovich, Sasha Lavut, Sergei Kovalev, and many others. And I am happy that Sakharov held Tanya in such high esteem. I want to quote him here: *"T. Velikanov is one of those people who in my eyes embody the human rights movement in the USSR, its moral pathos, its purity and strength, its historical significance."* I am so lucky, dear Tanechka, that you were my friend!

CULTURAL ATTACHÉ

In 1979, a very important event happened. The doorbell rang in our apartment while I was at work and Tanya was at home, and she opened the door to a stranger, who spoke English with an American accent. Standing on the threshold, he introduced himself:

> "I am an employee of the American Embassy in Moscow, Philip Brown. Your address was given to me by Tanya Velikanov and she asked me to come and see you. I recently came to Moscow with my family and brought a letter to Tanya Velikanov from Germany from her friend Tanya Khodorovich."

We knew Khodorovich well as Tanya Velikanov's friend and comrade-in-arms in her struggle for human rights. Tanya Velikanov had warned us in advance of Philip's arrival. Tanya invited the guest to our kitchen: we didn't have a dining room or a living room, so we usually hosted our guests there.

It turned out that Phil received a new assignment and came from Washington to Moscow as press attaché at the US Embassy. Later in his stay in Moscow, he got a promotion to cultural attaché. He was with his wife Roberta and two daughters, Sarah and Christine, and they knew no one in town, including diplomats and journalists from their own country. The girls immediately went to an Anglo-American school for English-speaking foreigners accredited in Moscow. His wife Roberta (Bobbi) an active woman in every way, felt very lonely without the Russian language, without a job, without friends and without acquaintances. Phil asked my Tanya for permission to bring her to visit us. Tanya, of course, said yes, and it did not take long for that to happen. At that time, we could not fully imagine what role the Browns would play in our lives.

The ice had broken really. Beginning with the two meetings I described, a beautiful friendship began between our families, and through the Browns, with many wonderful members of the Western world in Moscow. We enjoyed these friendships through our last days in the Soviet Union, and kept enjoying it in our new life in the United States. We became friends with Bobby's and Phil's parents while they were alive as well as with the rest of their family. Our children and our grandchildren are still friends with them today, even though some live in different cities and on different continents. Their girls have married, and Sarah has three children and Christine has two. Both Bobby's and Phil's parents have left this world. When I edit the English translation of these lines, we celebrate 44 years of our beautiful friendship.

The Brown family had one more wonderful member, an amazing dog, named Tar. She was a small water spaniel, as black as tar. It was impossible not to love this kindest and sweetest creature. We began to call her in Russian affectionately Tarushka. Very soon, we developed a tender friendship with her. It seemed to us that Taruska understood everything almost like a human being and that God had given her a human soul. While we were still in Russia, whenever the Browns went home on holiday, they left Tarushka with us. One summer when we lived at the dacha, the doggy enjoyed the country life with us. Her breed was a hunting dog, and running in the woods brought her into a euphoric state.

All of the children in the neighborhood wished to spend time with her. Responding to this, my Tanya used to tell them, "*This dog came to us from America and she only understands English. If you want to be friends with her, you must learn English.*" The effect was astonishing. Amazed parents would come to us and ask, "*How did you manage to change our child so much? He or she never wanted to learn English, and now they have asked us to find an English teacher!*"

Their diplomatic status allowed the Browns to cross the Soviet border without customs inspection, so thanks to them we had a channel of communication with the free world. Nevertheless, we rarely used it, for we were embarrassed to ask our friends to use their official position to help us. Still sometime it was very useful. Browns taught us much about the world in which we were going to live. But most important, their friendship brightened our lives as "outcasts" in Moscow.

BREACH IN THE IRON CURTAIN

Now I want to go back to Moscow in 1979. The Cold War was raging and the Iron Curtain was impenetrable. Not only were Soviet people not allowed to be friends with foreigners, they were not even allowed to meet foreigners. We violated this rule right under the nose of the KGB not only by meeting Phil Brown, the American diplomat, but with the friendship between our two families. We were only able to afford this luxury because we acquired the status of Refuseniks and in doing so, lost much of what we had been so afraid to lose all our lives. Over the years, I have learned many unpleasant things about K.Marx but I am grateful to him for the winged belief in the Manifesto: "*The proletarians have nothing to lose but their chains. But they will gain the whole world.*" If we replace the word "Proletarians" with "Refuseniks," this phrase describes how we felt those years.

What was the best way to survive in Soviet Union as Refuseniks? It was not an easy question, and I still do not know how to answer it. Some would say it was better to sit quietly, not to irritate the authorities, and then you might be allowed to leave sooner. Others would say that it was better to irritate the authorities as much as possible, and to make the authorities want to get rid of you. My Tanyusha and I, probably being active by nature, were more inclined towards the second way.

Tanya befriended few Americans before we met, but for me, the Browns were the FIRST I had ever met, and our friendship with them started a chain reaction. The Browns, after settling in Moscow, introduced us to many wonderful people, some of whom introduced us to many more wonderful people, and so on and on. Unexpectedly, after having lost many relatives and friends, we were soon compensated by an entourage of friends and acquaintances whom I would describe as the best people of the Western world. These people helped us to survive in extremely difficult conditions and made our truncated life in Moscow so much brighter. I would have to name them all here, but luckily, there were quite a many of them, and my memory unfortunately does not retain all their names. Therefore, I apologize in advance for those whom I have missed. I will remember all of them gratefully until the last breath of my life. I am proud that I had the privilege to meet them and know them. In the title of this chapter, I used the word "breach" to refer to a single failure or hole in the Iron Curtain. What happened to us, in fact, led to the formation of MULTIPLE holes, so that the "iron" of this damned curtain weakened considerably. It became a mighty colander for us, its holes giving life through communication with the other planet, to which we were about to move. And this communication went both ways.

Below I have listed those of our liaisons whom I remember with indication of the country they came from. I have deliberately arranged the names in alphabetical order by last name. I wanted to make sure that no one would even think to associate the order with the importance of these people in any of the countries or in our lives.

Bentick William, the assistant to the Ambassador of the Netherlands to Moscow

Blackman Ann, the U.S.A. journalist, representing in Moscow Time magazine, wife of **Michael Putzel**

Brown Philip, in the beginning the Press Attaché, later the Cultural Attaché of the U.S.A Embassy in Moscow

Brown Roberta, wife of **Philip Brown**

Buwalda Peter, the Netherlands Ambassador to Moscow

Buwalda Wilma, wife of **Peter Buwalda**

Daniloff Nicholas, the U.S.A. journalist, representing in Moscow "U. S. News & World Report"

Daniloff Ruth, the U.S.A. free lance journalist and author, wife of **Nicholas Daniloff**

Driscoll Jack, the Editor in chief of the newspaper "Boston Globe"

Gillette Elizabeth, wife of **Robert Gillette**

Gillette Robert, the U.S.A. journalist representing newspaper "Los Angeles Times"

Guroff Gregory, the Cultural Attaché of the American Embassy in Moscow

Handelman Steve, the freelance Canadian and American journalist

Hartman Arthur, the U.S.A. Ambassador to Moscow

Hartman Donna, wife of the U.S.A. Ambassador to Moscow

Klose Eliza, Kevin Klose's wife at the time

Klose Kevin, American journalist befriended in Moscow, contributor to the "Washington Post", and director of National Public Radio

Leibler Isi, the leader of the Jewish movement in Australia, since 1999 in Israel

McCagg Louise, the USA Artist and sculptor

McCagg William, the U.S.A. Professor of History

Nordal Vera, the Principal of the English speaking foreignes in Moscow

Nordal Odvar, the director of a secondary school for children of English-speaking foreigners working in Moscow, and **Vera Nordal's** husband

Pocock Mag, Pocock Ted, the Australia Ambassador to Moscow and his wife

Putzel Michael, the U.S.A. journalist representing in Moscow "Associate Press" agency

Reagan Nancy, the First Lady of the U.S.A.

Reagan Ronald, the 40th President of the U.S.A.

Shultz George, the U.S.A. Secretary of State

Shifter Richard, the assistant of the U.S.A Secretary of State for Human Rights

Veil Simone, the France Minister of Health and President of the European Parliament

LIFE THIRD: MY EFFORTS TO EMIGRATE FROM THE SOVIET UNION

Wagner Steve, employee of the US Embassy in Moscow, husband of **Susan Wagner**, the U.S.A. Human Rights Attaché of the U.S.A Embassy in Moscow.

I would like to end this list by mentioning a book written about the emigration of about half a million Jews from Soviet Russia by a wonderful man, Peter Buwalda. Peter's name is very important in my list and I will discuss this man in the next chapter. Peter talked about his own experience in Moscow with the Jewish emigration from the USSR. I want to recall this book because of the title, "They Were Not Left Alone." Peter is right that we never felt alone, and it was thanks to people like him. It amazes me to this day, how many foreign people, doing extremely important work in Moscow, had the time, energy and will to help us and similar ordinary Jewish Soviet families in difficult circumstances when Soviet authorities only mocked all of us.

It seems to me that this did not happen because there was a cease-fire in the Cold War. It was because the BEST members of the free world were, unlike many of their compatriots, truly INTRINSICALLY FREE. I am proud to say that in the non-free world of Russia, there were people like our Tanya Velikanov or Tzilia Reitburd, even though it was a hundred times more difficult and dangerous for them than for the representatives of the West. Very often, they paid a high price for this. However, these people existed on both sides of the Iron Curtain, which helped keep hope alive. They did not live by official rules, but by the dictates of their hearts.

Philip and Roberta Brown told us that the instructions given to Phil when he got his job in Moscow included a strict rule to report every private meeting with a Soviet citizen to the embassy security services. Phil and Bobby decided for themselves that, risking trouble, they would not comply with this instruction. The free world, thank God, was different from the communist paradise precisely because such a blatant violation threatened only trouble, not arrest. Fortunately, our Brown friends did not even get in trouble because of us. I cannot but admire such people, and so I shall be sure to tell further on in detail of several other extraordinary families besides the Browns, who also became very close friends of ours.

THE CHALLENGES AND JOYS OF A JANITOR-OBSTETRICIAN

The time has come to describe in more detail the specifics of my work in a maternity hospital. The sad irony of my employment is that it allowed me to fulfill my dream of working in health care. Certainly, I entered medicine not through the front porch, but from a back passage, but all the same, I did enter! I used to work with toilet bowls instead of computers, but who knows which is more important in life: a computer or a toilet bowl? The maternity hospital is not exactly a hospital, but still close to one! Anyway, for more than a decade I, along with my colleagues, wore a white coat and breathed the air imbued with the effort to support and preserve human life. It brought me deep satisfaction.

More than that, there is something special in a maternity hospital that I have felt extraordinarily keenly. This something is not available in a regular hospital, or in any other place. It is a unique opportunity to touch directly the greatest miracle of life: the arrival of a new human being into our world. The whole time I worked there, I never stopped being moved by the spectacle of the beginning of life. I could not get away from sad reflections on how hard it was for those babies to leave the warm and comfortable womb of their mothers and to adjust to the new, cold, and not always kind or fair world. My friends laughed at my emotions and called me a gynecologist as a joke. In fact, by doing so they made a gross linguistic mistake. If strictly following the meaning of the word, they would have had to call me a janitor-obstetrician, because our maternity hospital did not treat gynecological diseases, only obstetrics was practiced there. It was my fault for not stopping this semantic miscommunication. However, the term became a part of the lexicon in my circle of friends in the ten years of my maternity practice. Besides, the words "obstetrics" and "gynecology" are often stuck together like Siamese twins, and only meticulous people like me worry about the difference in meaning. At the same time, I must admit that "janitor-obstetrician" sounds more appealing.

Plus, if we think about the specialties of a sanitary engineering versus those of midwifery, I believe we will conclude that there is an undoubted affinity. Therefore, the combination of the two professions into what my friends dubbed me did not bother me. Both professions seem to me important and useful. As to the first, during the years of my work in the maternity hospital, I achieved the highest level of this specialty, janitor of the fifth grade level.

We had a funny episode about this new profession of mine. Our friends, Armenian musicians took Tanya and Vera to the composers' creative house in Dilijan one summer. Busy with my janitor and obstetrical work, I could join them only for a few days. There they met young composer Yuri Harutyunyan, who very much liked our Vera and often took her for walks. One day, after such a walk, he came up to Tanya and said to her, *"You have a wonderful child, she has an extraordinary sense of humor. I asked her what her daddy is doing. She told me her dad works as a janitor!"*

My shifts lasted 24 hours, but after each shift, I had two days off from work. I adapted to this schedule, and found I liked it. I had my own "office" in the basement, a janitor's shop with a workbench and a personal telephone. I did not work non-stop as on an assembly line. I would be called when something broke. During the night, life in the maternity hospital would quiet down and there would be fewer requests for my services. But as woman tend to give birth at night, sometimes the calls increased. The nights were all different, but almost every night I always would manage to get some rest. I would receive a blanket, a pillow, a mattress, and relatively clean bedding from the hospital storeroom. Around midnight, I would make up my trestle bed, lock up the workshop, and lay down to rest between the calls.

A janitor's work never bothered me itself. I even enjoyed it, especially when it would come to fixing plumbing or any hospital equipment because I was interested in learning how it all worked. My grandmother used to say that you had to have hands, not a pair of iron shovels. Luckily, I had both proper hands and interest. My lack of squeamishness made it easier for me to get the job done. Much less pleasant were the frequent calls to remove blockages in the sewers. The blockages were most often caused by the negligence of the staff. Nurses, midwives, and cleaners used the toilets as waste bins, throwing bandages, cotton sanitary pads, inserts and tampons into them. I found however, that the most successful way to clog a sewer fundamentally was to throw a woman's placenta after delivery into the toilet. Our midwives routinely performed this trick. Then they would shout for help! One had to work for a long time up to his ankles in excrement to eliminate the flood. In the most difficult situations, I even had to climb into the sewer wells in the street. Of course, my job did not exclude the risk of accidents. In my first year at the maternity hospital, a valve on a pressurized oxygen cylinder broke. As a result, there was an explosion and I suffered a micro concussion.

However, what I was not prepared for was a completely unfamiliar social environment. I plunged into the company of people who I could not even have imagined existed in any kind of bad dream. It was as if my colleagues grew up reared on a completely different planet, in a completely different culture, with completely different ethics. It is possible that I had managed to live forty years in a microcosm created for me by my relatives and friends, completely unaware of the greater world around me. What horrified me above all, was the unbelievable amount of alcoholism.

I like to drink in good company, especially when the drink is to my liking. I remember well our regular discussions with my dear mother on this subject. I used to repeat to her that when I grew up, I would always have a couple of decent bottles of wine in my fridge. Every time I would say this, my poor mother would get terribly upset and say, *"Well, why wine, why not juice?"* Being naughty and knowing how frustrating it was for her, I would return to the subject with boyish ferocity and tell her: *"Mommy, I'll have juice too, but it cannot replace wine."* However, what I encountered in the maternity ward was shocking, at least first months.

First, my colleagues drank in unthinkable quantities. I knew that Russian alcoholism had begun in antiquity. As early as the 11th century, chronicler Nestor in "The Tale of Bygone Years" told how the Kiev prince Vladimir Sviatoslavovich, or Vladimir the Saint, choosing a faith for Russia, refused to adopt Islam in favor of Orthodoxy, because the former prohibited the use of wine. Nestor cites Vladimir's words: *"In Russia, there is a cheerfulness of drinking. We cannot live without it!"* I don't think poor Vladimir could have imagined the scale of merry drinking in the future Russia. My maternity hospital was a fair example.

I had an electrician working with me who drank sometimes two liters of vodka per 24 hour shift. At the same time, he ate very little. The first time I saw it, I was mortally scared that he was going to die on that shift. But no, he was just unable to stand properly. Of course, no one fired him, because on those shifts when he was drinking less, he did his job well. What was happenning, when a light bulb went out in the delivery room and he was drunk, the midwives would ask me to replace it. This became his pattern and I soon stopped worrying and just faithfully did his job. I must give him credit: he always sincerely thanked me for my willingness to replace him. Who did his job on the other shifts, I cannot say.

The janitor, my colleague, coming on the next shift to mine, also worked at the cemetery digging graves and his tales often deprived me of sleep. His colleagues there would get so drunk that they would catch stray dogs in the area, roast them on a fire next to the open grave and eat them. It is interesting that in conversations with this man I learned that he sometimes even read books and went to the cinema, like all normal people. I am sure, he did not read much and mostly literature trash, but he did read. Anyway, his stories would give me nightmares.

I remember going up from my basement to the main floor one night, attracted by noise. On the floor, I saw two young midwives in a physical fight. One of the two was drunk beyond any bounds. Her bare breasts were falling out from under her tattered robe. At the same time, she was screaming vicious foul language. Her actual vocabulary cannot be reproduced here. But she was loudly expressing the essence of the lethal insult: her girlfriend had accused her of performing oral sexual both of them, for some reason, considered shameful. The assailant tried unsuccessfully to calm her down. Their other friends told me that we should have taken her away from the hospital to avoid a scandal and possible firing. Upon learning that I had arrived at the hospital in my Little Froggy that day, they begged me to evacuate the girl, who lived quite close by. I agreed and the evacuation took place.

However, one of the most terrible memories associated with alcoholism was when we had young women in labor who were completely drunk. Often, they had to be carried on a stretcher from the car to the delivery room. Most of them were 16–25 years old. As a rule, these, so to speak, "mothers" tried to get rid of the baby they did not want and did not need. After the delivery, they would immediately leave without the newborn, never caring what is going to happen to their baby. Our hospital would organize for these poor babies their admittance to a nearby orphan-children's home. This house was an extension of our maternity hospital and our janitors provided services there. For that reason, I would go there sometimes when they had plumbing problems.

Visiting this orphanage was one of my darkest memories about the country I left. Every time I would go there, I would witness the staggering cruelty of the women working with the children. For some reason I never saw any men in the orphanage. The women were of the same age as the mothers of the poor kids. They were angry, irritable, and had little compassion for the children in their care. Some of the children there were 2 to 3 years old. When I would come to their rooms, they would surround me and watch my work with interest. However, they, like mutes, did not say a word. In a while, I understood why: not only did these children not hear a single affectionate word addressed to them, but no one ever addressed them at all. When one of these unhappy women wanted to take a child away from me, she, without a word, would sharply grab him by the hand and drag him so that I was afraid she would dislocate his shoulder. During one of my visits, I could not help myself and asked why they were being so cruel to the children. The answer I got was, *"They are not kids, they are retarded dregs. Do you know who their parents are?"*

From my first days in the hospital, I made it a rule to try to be friendly with everyone, the staff, even the worst drunks. I saw that they felt and appreciated it, without which my life there would have been simply unbearable. It was for that reason that when they had a drink together and offered me one, I never said no, but I always insisted on a smaller dosage. I was very grateful that they immediately accepted my rule, did not object and did not ask why. An interesting general observation: the very simple people around me showed a kind of inner tact. They certainly saw and felt that I was DIFFERENT. However, they never would try to get into my soul, never would bother me with questions about my personal life, and never would expect me to explain, what made me work with them. I was eternally grateful to them for this. This, I think, advantageously made them stand out from many intellectuals in my circle. Post factum reflections confirmed, I think, that I chose some very correct course of action with them and, as a result, both sides valued and appreciated, what each could offer.

After the rampant drinking, the next thing, which was difficult for me to tolerate until my last day in the hospital, was the attitude

LIFE THIRD: MY EFFORTS TO EMIGRATE FROM THE SOVIET UNION

of many of my colleagues towards sex. I cannot help it, but the only comparison that begs me to make is the innate instinct of copulation in the animal world. What I encountered there had nothing to do with human reproduction, human love, not even with human sympathy. Intimacy for many with many was disgustingly habitual and mundane. In fact, it ceased to be intimate, since everybody talked about it to each other without any embarrassment at all. I was involuntarily involved in this business because I was the only happy owner of a bed in the cellar, and my janitor room had a lock from the inside. Every so often, a man would come into my room and ask me to go for a walk for an hour or so, so that he could bring a woman to have fun on my bed. I tried never to refuse them if I could, for I did not wish to play the part of their tutor. As a result, I felt a little guilty about contributing to this outrage.

We had an electrician who was a bit more intelligent than the others, but he was also a master of drinking. He regularly used my couch for the already described purpose. I met his wife, who usually came in on payday to collect his money before he drank it away. She was quite an interesting blonde-haired woman, in her forties, and I rather liked her. One day I asked him about why he cheated on such a nice wife with girls who, in my opinion, were not even worth her little finger. His answer stunned me. *"Precisely because I love my wife,"* he said, *"I don't want to risk her health if she has to have an abortion."* "What about the girls you put on my coach?" I asked him, "Is *it okay to risk their health?"* "It is their own business, they don't mind,"* he replied. One way or another, for more than a decade, I witnessed limitless free sex in the maternity hospital, unrestricted by any moral or hygienic considerations. After such observations it becomes incomprehensible how the country's population has not degenerated from venereal diseases.

The head doctor of the maternity hospital, Tzilia Tsurenko, was obsessed with cleanliness. She regularly toured all the rooms and personally made sure that the cleaners did everything properly. Once I witnessed how she scolded a cleaner for using the same cloth for the floor as for the walls. As a result, it seemed to me that our maternity hospital was one of the cleanest medical institutions in Moscow, and I was proud of it. Nevertheless, once I felt bitter disappointment. Our kitchen was on the top floor, and at night, I got a request about a leak from the kitchen to ward below. After finding the keys, I went upstairs and opened the kitchen door. It was pitch black until I fumbled for a switch and turned on the light. I am not very squeamish, but I got physically sick. The entire floor of the large kitchen was in motion. I did not immediately realize what was going on. I could not see the floor because it was covered with thousands of cockroaches. I had never seen such a horde! I shut the door without turning off the light and stood for about 15 minutes in shock, unable to move either hand or leg. When I pulled myself together and opened the door, the bugs had disappeared like a bad dream. I found the cause of the leak and at least temporarily stopped it. The next day, we got the necessary parts and did the full repair. At my suggestion, the kitchen was completely disinfected.

My immediate superior in the maternity hospital was a man named Sasha Baranov, who acted as a sort of group manager. He somehow got this job position, not knowing how to do anything. However, he trusted me, and never interfered with my work. Technically, I always acted at my own discretion or consulted with a colleague, who also worked for us as a ganitor. He was a very handy man named Sasha Malykhin from whom I learned a lot over the years. However, our boss made all administrative decisions. I was quite happy with this. As a result, my supervisor and I had a good relationship. Nevertheless, one day I could not avoid a conflict with him. A pipe going to the heating radiator was leaking, and it was impossible to fix it. It required replacement, which I knew how to do, but we did not have such pipes. I described the problem to the boss. He said to me, *"You know, we got lucky. The building next to us is in disrepair, and the pipes we need have been lying and rusting in the yard for a long time. Go out and quietly bring one pipe to us. No one there will even pay attention to it."* I answered him: *"It is not my job to get the pipes, Sasha, it is yours, and I do not want to steal them anyway. If you agree to get a pipe from anywhere, I will gladly work with it".* Sasha, got mad at me. The funny thing is that after that Sasha, asked another janitor to do the same thing, and this man was not embarrassed at all, he just went and stole the pipe. On my next shift, we replaced the pipe and the radiator started working again.

Sasha, never knew that I was not being difficult by refusing to steal the pipe, but rather very practical. I was well aware that the KGB was watching me closely and was only looking for an excuse to catch me doing something wrong. The authorities would have been happy to trumpet to the world, "*This is the true face of the Soviet Jew who doesn't care about his country, its just laws, its material and moral values!*" Such scandal would have undoubtedly resulted in a show trial and punishment. In order that I should not doubt the intentions or the attention of the authorities, they regularly gave me reminders. Around the end of my first year of work, the KGB came to my chief physician, Tsurenko, and tried to persuade her to fire me. The courageous woman answered them: "*All right, I will fulfill your request. Just tell me the reason I can use to fire him. He's the best janitor I have got, plus he doesn't drink!*" Funny as it may seem, those rogues never came back, and I continued to work there for many years. No, I had to limit my behavior lest I give them the opportunity to arrest me.

The hardest part for me was that I had to accept once and forever as the sad norms of my working environment and stop fussing about them. A strong consolation was the conviction that all of this was a dear price to pay for the chance to get away for good from all of the outrages described.

THE MOMENTS OF TRIUMPH OF A JANITOR–OBSTETRICIAN

A decade of my work in a maternity hospital has taught me two important lessons. The first is, that even in the most seemingly unpleasant work, by looking and thinking, you can find little joys. Second is, that there is no job in the world where you cannot be creative and get satisfaction from it. By creativity here, I do not at all mean the ability to invent. I am talking here about keeping your eyes and ears open so as not to miss the chance to do something interesting, good and kind. About that, I will try to tell you in this chapter.

First, all the years I worked in the maternity hospital I was eager to do something nice for the women in labor and the new mothers in addition to my immediate janitor duties. I have always had a special sympathy and respect for mothers delivering babies simply because they were involved in the great miracle of the birth of a new human being. I have already explained how, allegedly for sanitary reasons, the poor patients' communication with their loved ones was banned, almost as if they were prisoners. Unfortunately, my position of "janitor-obstetrician" in this respect did not allow me to help much. Nevertheless, to fight the stupid restrictions on transfers, I started working as a smuggler. In the courtyard of the maternity hospital, I would meet the relatives, and they would hand me the forbidden items which I would carry under the hem of my coat to the intended patient. Honestly, since I thought all these prohibitions were silly, I never had any remorse about my "criminal" activities.

However, my greatest help to the maternity patients was the organization of unauthorized visits with their loved ones. I would escort the visitor through the back door of the building to my basement and ask him to wait by the elevator. Then I would take the elevator up to the floor myself, get the patient into the elevator, and we would go down to the basement together. I would then exit the elevator and the visitor would enter the elevator. The two would then take the elevator up and stop it between floors. In this way, it was possible to achieve the privacy of a date. I do not know how my couples spent their time in the "dating elevator," but they did have a good time. I could see that they were happy, and they thanked me without end. As a result I also was happy.

It has always been a special joy of my life to revive objects destined for scrap. The blatant mismanagement of the maternity hospital, as a typical Soviet institution, regularly and generously provided me with opportunities for such joy. The laws in this regard were ridiculous. Anything that belonged to the institution was state property. At a certain point, state property would be considered obsolete and no longer needed. This phenomenon found its reflection in the Russian language. The formal act of recognition of the thing as useless resulted in removal of it from the state property list. There was special verb for the act, "to write-off," and the special adjective for the thing itself after such an act, "written off." In today's Russian dictionaries, you can find the following definition of writing-off: *"removal from the balance sheet, removal of goods or money valuables of an enterprise from the balance sheet and charging them to losses"*. I would like to draw your attention to the fact that the definition does not mention the unsuitability of things for use or repair and, consequently, the decision to write them off involves complete arbitrariness. Suspecting every employee to be a thief, the law prescribed DESTROYING the written off things, so that, God forbid, they would not fall into private hands. It was exactly like the pithy saying "The dog in the Manger"

LIFE THIRD: MY EFFORTS TO EMIGRATE FROM THE SOVIET UNION

about those, who selfishly keeps something that they do not really need or want so that others may not use or enjoy it.

This situation spawned massive criminal activity because the only option to continue using the decommissioned item was to steal it. Even worse, many administrators deliberately wrote off decent working things they liked and then stole them afterwards instead of destroying them. Both the former and the latter were happening frequently in the Soviet economy.

While working as a janitor, several times I experienced the joy of correcting this ugliness. Once my boss, Sasha Baranov, approached me with a request to smash and discard a dozen written off chairs. I told my boss that I could easily find people who would be happy to take these chairs if he did not mind. He told me that he had no right to allow me to do that, but that if I took the chairs away quietly, he would pretend he did not know anything about it. This tacit "permission" threw me into a very nervous state. On the one hand, I had not forgotten that the KGB was watching me. On the other hand, I did not want to ruin decent chairs which were in great need by others. It annoyed me that the authorities were forcing my maternity hospital to destroy ueful things. Even someone as dim-witted as my boss understood this.

That same day I contacted my friends and, of course, found someone who was very interested in the chairs. It turned out to be a close friend of my eldest daughter and son-in-law named Boris Pitel. I was very fond of this person. He lived very modestly and could not afford to buy new chairs. On the nearest midnight (to make less noise), I arranged a date with Boris at the entrance to the basement, where I had brought the chairs, as if to break them to pieces. Under cover of night, Boris and I, in high anxiety, took the chairs, loaded them into the Little Frog and, unnoticed by anyone, drove away. That night both Boris and I felt very happy.

Encouraged by this grand success, after a while I carried out a similar operation. There were little white benches in the hospital, that our mothers used to put under their feet, when breastfeeding their newborn babies. Do not ask me why, once all of them were being written off. My little Verochka was studying at that time at the Moscow City Children's Music School after Prokofiev. Our friend, Slava Smirnov, taught piano there and was giving our little Verochka private music lessons. Slava complained many times that when his little pianists played piano at school, sitting on a regular chair, their feet did not reach the floor. He could not find anywhere in Moscow an easy-to-use low bench for them to rest their feet upon while practicing. When I saw a pile of our white nursing benches in our basement destined for destruction, I thought, "*This is it!*" I showed one to Slava and he confirmed that it was exactly what the doctor had prescribed. And then the rescue operation was repeated a second time, like a fairy-tale dream. Again, about midnight, I drove my Little Froggy to the entrance to the basement, loaded it to the roof with benches and brought them all home. Next day I took them to the music school to the delight of children and teachers alike.

After I used the expression "the dog in the manger", while talking about saving items from the hospital, I realized that I did not know where the idiom came from. Wikipedia told me that more than 2500 years ago, Aesop used this expression in his fable, and its full text was as follows: "*The dog lies down in the hay, he does not eat himself, and he would not let others.*" After reading this, I realized that I plucked my joys in the hospital literally from the dog's mouth.

After twenty years of work at the Academy of Sciences, I plunged into the completely unfamiliar world of the working-class social echelon of the medical establishment. In contacts with members of this echelon, I was in for a big surprise. They started to share with me their personal and family affairs, including the most intimate details, often asking for advice. The stories they told me were often very sad, and each time I would try to offer moral support. To be honest, at first, I was not prepared for this and the first year I felt terribly uncomfortable. I was embarrassed even more, because for the most part the women would come to me, and I had to "profess" them like a priest. Interestingly, I discovered the amazing openness of some of my coworkers. I regularly wondered what it was in me that made them so trusting. However, gradually I got used to the role of comforter and, apparently, did it better and better, as I formed regular clients. As the years passed, I began to enjoy being needed by this group of people.

VODKA LIBRARY

Every dark cloud has a silver lining: it was in the maternity hospital that the Russian "*cheerfulness of drinking*" gave Tanyusha and me a hobby, which during more than forty years was bringing both our loved ones and us, ourselves much joy. The fact is that alcohol in Russia used to play a very special role not found in other countries. It was like a second currency, sometimes even more valuable than money. In many research and medical institutions, alcohol should have been widely used for work. Instead, most of it would become a reward for employees for good performance instead of a cash bonus, which was always exceptionally difficult to process. Plus, the alcohol received would usually be immediately drunk in honor of the supervisor who gave it.

In our maternity hospital, as in any medical institution, this practice flourished. If there was a request for me to fix a leaking sink in the ward and I fixed it, my reward from a nurse or midwife would be 250 ml of alcohol (more than half a liter of vodka!). All our medical staff knew that if they did not perform this ritual, the next time the sink would remain broken for a week after calling a repairperson. The said ritual even applied to the shape of the award bottle. An alcohol reward would ALWAYS be in used red-brown ether bottles, which everybody would affectionately call "little brown-red thing." An amusing psychological point: if a nurse handed a worker, for example, reward money instead of a "little brown-red thing" that person would feel insulted.

Upon receiving a "little brown-red thing" my colleagues would immediately send it into their mouths, almost never diluting it with water. I used to bring it home. Tanyusha and I began to think about how to make the most interesting use of my "little red thing". Then the idea was born of using alcohol for alcohol tinctures, which have traditionally formed an important part of not only Russian folk medicine, but also the Russian holiday table. Historians believe that tinctures and balsams were born in one of the eastern countries around three millennia BC. In Russia, the first mention of alcoholic tinctures dates back to the 10th century. It seems that tinctures appeared in Russia before Christianity. The variety of types of tinctures is endless: tinctures of herbs, buds, flowers, bark, roots, leaves, berries, vegetables, and fruits. The scope for creativity attracted both Tanya and me.

Our first experiment was lucky and everyone, who tried it, was delighted. In the beginning, we called our creation "maternity drink" after the origin of the bottles. However, the success of the

That id how our "books" looks in Boston, MA USA

enterprise exceeded all our expectations, and soon the amount of alcohol that came in red bottles became insufficient. In order to expand production, we had to include into the production process purchased vodka. Pretty soon, first, the name of the tincture was considered too narrow and historically outdated, and secondly the producers realized the necessity of including the material infused in the name of the drink. This gave rise to a new company name: "VODKA LIBRARY OF THE ZIEMANS." We have to say that our library had plenty of readers in Moscow, and many of them were very active. However, the real success came to the library only on the other side of the ocean, where we began to actively continue this endeavor after crossing the ocean. All has happened in accordance with the Latin proverb *"Omnia mea mecum porto"* (I carry with me everything mine).

There is an interesting legend connected with the origin of this proverb, which I learned only recently. In the 6th century B.C., the Persians approached the ancient Greek city of Priene. Crowds of refugees with their belongings in hands were leaving the city. Thieves tried to get lost in this panic and confusion. One of the individuals standing out in the commotion was a man walking lightly and quietly. He was the famous Greek sage and philosopher Bias of Priene. A man approached him and asked, *"Are you so poor that in all your life you have no possessions?"* The philosopher replied, *"I carry everything important to me with me,"* while pointing to his head. The answer impressed the interlocutor, who said, *"For me, everything is my fingers. I carry everything important to me with me, too"*, *"Are you a musician?"* asked the wise man. *"No, I'm a pickpocket thief"* was the reply. Bias became very angry and indignant and struck the thief with his staff: *"You are a thief and you stole my aphorism from me!"* However, we got the aphorism from a speech by Cicero who told the story of Biant. This explains why some people mistakenly attribute it to Cicero.

At the end of this chapter, I would like to mention the American page of the history of our library. Here we were publishing our "books" in a much nicer way. First, we can buy tall elegant Italian bottles called "belissimo" for them. This word means "most beautiful" in Italian. Secondly, I make and print on the computer a branded bottle sticker for each type of tincture. Thirdly, we have significantly improved the aesthetic design of the bottles, and many of them now look like Japanese ikebana. Finally, fourthly, we have significantly expanded the assortment.

At first, almost all of our American friends refused to read "books" from our library, saying: "We *don't drink hard liquor, only wine*." Today, those same people, when they enter the house, ask us from the doorstep about NEW additions to the library. Interest in our library is growing. Now very often, when we ask our friends what they would like to receive on their upcoming birthday as a gift, we hear in response, "*A new book*". That is why Tanya and I just need to keep ourselves healthy and keep publishing new "books" to please our loved ones. Unfortunately, it is becoming more and more difficult with our aging.

MY UNIVERSITIES

Having written the title of this chapter, I suddenly realized that I was unconsciously echoing M. Gorky's biography trilogy "Childhood", "My Apprenticeship", and "My Universities". The description of my first life could have been called "Childhood." For much that happened to me when I was a janitor-obstetrician, Gorky's title "My Apprenticeship" would do. Finally, like Gorky, I was deprived of the opportunity to study at a university. All of my professional education was obtained either by correspondence or completely independently by me. Therefore, the story about what I have learned allows me to call it "My Universities". Not having any talent for writing, I certainly do not dare compare my autobiography with Gorky's in artistic merit. However, readers of my text are likely to have noticed another similarity. Gorky's trilogy taught me that it is possible to express my thoughts and emotions about the world around us, rather than to limit myself to purely biographical material. In this chapter, I will try to share what I learned in medicine, working for more than ten years as a janitor-obstetrician.

Unfortunately, most of my fellow refuseniks, having lost their jobs in their profession, viewed their occupations as watchmen, janitors, and elevator operators, etc., simply as a waste of time, and had no interest or feeling for them. I saw the years of working in the maternity hospital as an opportunity to immerse myself in the world of medicine. I had long dreamed of studying medicine, and I thought I should try to take every opportunity to learn as much as possible about this world. The sight of people in white coats has always thrilled me. And in our institution, everyone, including janitors and electricians, wore white coats! Moreover, our laundry was running smoothly, and I could get a clean coat almost every shift. This allowed me to feel that I belonged, even as a low-level untrained person, to the great army saving human lives. After all, I continued to believe that with a little more time, I would be able to apply my experience and knowledge of computers to participate directly in improving human health. Fortunately, with my move to America, this endeavor and dream was realized.

Among the sad lessons of my university years were the cases in which medical personnel in white starched coats allowed themselves unacceptable indifference, rudeness, and cruelty to our female patients. For example, our routine dictated that as soon as a woman in labor began to have hard contractions the staff would wheel her out of the ward on a gurney and leave her to lie in the corridor just outside the delivery room. This allowed, when the time was right, to quickly wheel her into the delivery room and begin the delivery. One day I was walking down the corridor and one woman in labor began to cry hysterically: *"Oh! It hurts! I am in labor!"* No one approached her. I ran as fast as I could to the doctor on duty and brought him to the screaming woman. Walking up to the poor laboring woman, the doctor, instead of trying to calm her down, sharply asked her using an impolite form of addresing in Russian, *"And what did you come here to do? Did you come to dance?"* I would have liked to see that boor endure such pain.

However, of all our wards, the worst was the abortion ward. It was supplied with the worst dressings, the worst nutrition and with the weakest doctors. It was hard to believe, but in our maternity ward, most abortions were done WITHOUT THE USE ANES-

THESIA AT ALL! As a result, the poor women went through this torture with only a breathing mask that had nitrous oxide in it. To this day, I cannot forget the horrible attitude of the staff towards the abortion patients. Moreover, the staff was composed almost exclusively of women, from whom I always vainly expected compassion and sympathy, but often saw only cruelty and even gloating. It was my duty to replace the empty nitrous oxide tanks in the abortion ward. More than once performing this job, I was a witness of this type of moralizing from, God forgive, the staff women, *"When you were making love, you were having fun. So now pay the price!"* Actually, they used much harsher language, which I hesitate to cite. A couple of times I could not help myself in such a situation and commented: *"Why are you so unkind? You could be in her shoes tomorrow."* I usually got a rude response, like, *"Mind your own business!"*

In order for the "university" lessons to go most efficiently for me, I tried, first, to keep both my eyes and my ears open. Thank God, soon enough I managed to establish a good relationship with most of the hospital staff, beginning with the technical services and cleaners and ending to the chief physician and her deputy. Moreover, I was not shy about asking questions, and most of them were usually eager to answer me.

Secondly, our maternity hospital was a clinical base of the Institute of Obstetrics and Gynecology. On that basis, groups of researchers and medical students regularly came to visit. If a conversation with visitors took place in the same room where I was, say, fixing a faucet, I was all ears and learned many interesting things.

Thirdly, we had the operating room for caesarean sections. It had high ceilings, and there was a large window in the wall to the corridor on the next floor. Through this window medical students who came to us could watch the operations in progress while they were in the corridor. When there were no visitors at the window, and I had free time, it was impossible to tear me away from the window. I watched the great miracle of the appearance of a new person as if I were spellbound. A few years later, I was already well aware of all the steps of this amazing process, so much so that it seemed to me, I could if necessary, do the operation myself. My fellow janitors expressed to me their utmost amazement at how I was not sickened by the spectacle I was witnessing. Not only was I not nauseous, but I was so fascinated, so excited by what I was seeing, that at times it would just take my breath away. However, what bothered me was how my colleagues, closer to me in education and on the social ladder, would treat my interest. I mean doctors, nurses, and midwives, who for the most part had absolutely no idea to what I was so attracted. I sometimes even thought that some of them saw me as some kind of a sexual maniac, who liked to look at the naked inside and outside of a woman's body. Fortunately, I never heard anything negative from any of them, but sometimes they would look at me strangely.

As I grew to know the staff better and they to know me better, the level of my university classes increased. This process culminated when the midwives asked me sometimes to help them in childbirth. It would happen only at night when women often, for some unknown reason to me, tend to give birth. It never made sense that the night shifts were noticeably smaller than day shifts in terms of the number of people working. Our delivery room was a big and bright room on the second floor, with EIGHT chair-beds, even WITHOUT SEPARATING SCREENS. So, up to eight women could give birth simultaneously. There was no built-in supply of either oxygen or nitrous oxide in the delivery room, so I had to be there quite regularly during the day to change the tanks. All gas tanks both empty and full, were stored in the cold house outside. There were 3–4 midwives working in the delivery room during the day and 1–2 doctors on the floor. At night, these numbers were limited to 2–3 midwives and one doctor on duty, who, after running around during the day, would lie down for a nap. More than once, I could see eight women in labor in the delivery room during night "rush hours." Then ONE midwife could serve SIMULTANEOUSLY SEVERAL women in childbirth.

Sometimes during nights like this I was called upon to be a midwife's assistant. In the beginning, my tasks were quite simple, like carrying this or that to a different place, handing something or holding something. However, a couple of times I can proudly say that I was taught how to assist in sewing up a postpartum perineum tear, and I helped doing this! Unfortunately, almost every woman in labor ended up with lacerations. I remember well how my illiteracy in obstetrics lead me to be angry at our midwives: they were professionals who could not deliver a baby without tearing up the mother! Only when I came to America,

I learned that ruptures in childbirth were a natural phenomenon, but not evidence of a lack of professionalism. There are simply two different schools of thought on this subject in obstetrics. In the U.S.A., most births involve making preliminary incisions in the perineum to widen the birth canal as a precaution against brain injury to the baby. After delivery, these incisions are closed. In Russia, on the other hand, they let the tissues tear naturally and then stitch up the incisions. In this connection, I got another lesson that a little knowledge is a dangerous thing. I wanted to go back to our maternity hospital and apologize to the midwives, who were always nice to me, for unfair thinking so poorly of them. Anyway, I was proud of my "promotion" and glad that my relationship with medicine was getting closer and closer.

INTERPLANETARY TRIPS

Over the years, I got used to the world that was new to me, in the sense that I was no longer shocked to enter it every third day. However, this world always remained alien to me. I saw it as payment, albeit expensive, for our brave decision to leave the USSR and become free. Since my school years, my life principle was, "*All good things must be paid for!*" The monologue of the drunken Satin in "The Lower Depths," by Maxim Gorky always fascinated me with phrases like the following: *"A man is free... he pays for everything himself: for existing faith, for lack of faith, for love, for intelligence, a man pays for everything himself, and therefore he is free!"* I felt as if he said this about our family! We did pay in full for our freedom, and we did get it. However, it did not happen until August 10, 1988, when the reckoning was completed, and the plane with Verochka and her parents on board crossed the border of the Soviet Union and landed in Vienna. In the meantime, I continued my life as a janitor--obstetrician, after losing my favorite job, significant part of my beloved family and friends, my financial welfare, and acquired a hostile environment that reminded me of itself regularly. All those years, I realized that, mentally and politically, I could become the prisoner of the Gulag, where many of my friends and like-minded people had ended up. Of course, I remembered that their life there was much worse and harder than my. I still do not know what fortunate circumstances spared me from arrest. In any case, whether it was an oversight by the KGB or their generosity, I thank them very much!

Not all KGB functionaries were unpleasant people. There was a handsome young man who lived in our building, a chauffeur by profession. He was very handy and always fixed his car himself. Several times, he helped me with my Little Froggy. Once we got to talking to him and it turned out that he had worked in the KGB. Moreover, it turned out that he was well aware of my life, of my refusal, of my friendship with foreigners, though I had never discussed anything of the kind with him. He spoke to me very kindly. "Yuri," he used to say to me, *"do you really want to go to cut lumber in the taiga camp? If not, stop shacking up with foreigners and sit quietly. You are a naïve man and do not realize that you are being watched from every street corner around our building. Don't anger God!"* I had no choice but to thank him for his friendly advice.

Our well-wisher could hardly understand that my friends in Moscow from the free world were like oxygen to us when we felt asphyxiated. But not all representatives of the West working in Moscow at that time behaved like free people. The behavior of Western diplomats was a peculiar test in this respect. The Soviet authorities did not allow their citizens to communicate with any foreigners, even from the socialist camp. Certainly, they did not permit Soviet people to enter Moscow's embassies and consulates. This latter prohibition was very easy to enforce, as there was always a Soviet police officer at the entrance to these buildings, who physically prevented Soviet citizens from entering. As a result, the foreigners working in Moscow split into two groups. MOST of them, not wanting to spoil relations with the Soviet authorities, tried to simplify their own lives and accepted the rules, even when those rules grossly violated human rights. They seemed to reason: it is alien to me, but if the citizens accept it, it is their business. The other group, wishing to preserve the dignity of a free person remembered that their embassy was a small island of their country, lived on this island according to laws of THEIR OWN COUNTRY. They reasoned: wherever I am, I want to follow the rules that my parents (and grandparents) taught me. In our experience, the examples of the first group were England and Canada; and the best examples of the second group were the USA, Australia, and the Netherlands.

Here are the facts that confirmed this opinion. During all the years of refusal we had NEVER been inside either the English or the Canadian embassy, and when the need arose, we called by phone, and the embassy employee would come out to talk to us on the street (!?). But we visited each of three "good" embassies dozens of times. All three ambassadors organized an interesting cultural program with film screenings, musical and literary concerts, meetings with interesting people and receptions. Often, we received a personal invitation. Sometimes this invitation had a magical effect on the police officer, and he let us in after a thorough check of our passport data. When there was no invitation, or the police officer was in a bad mood, he telephoned and spoke either to the ambassador himself or to his wife. Then either the ambassador or his wife would come outside, take us by the arm and tell the guard: "*Remember, these are our friends and next time, please let them in.*"

It is worth mentioning how passports were checked in these cases. The police officers would read out thoroughly all the data slowly and quite loudly, as if waiting for our confirmation. There was no doubt that they were talking to a tape recorder hidden inside their clothes. One way or another, they would let us pass and we, crossing the threshold, found ourselves in... a completely different planet. This "flight" caused a strong biophysical reaction each time, as if we had crossed many time zones and found ourselves on a completely different world. This reaction was especially strong when Tanya and Verochka came to pick me up in a taxi from the maternity hospital. I, having previously arranged with one of my colleagues to cover me for a few hours, washed up, went outside to them and in the car hastily changed dirty overalls for a white shirt and suit with a tie, to step on the other planet as a different person.

And, in fact, we felt like quite different people on this planet. There we breathed more easily, felt warmer, and everything was beautiful and interesting. The hosts welcomed us and were glad to see us. However, unfortunately, the authorities could get to this planet and try to poison the joy of its inhabitants and guests. I remember well one such time and will share it below. But first, some background.

We had many musician friends in Moscow, and some of them turned out, like us, to be refuseniks. Like us, they too lost the opportunity to work. They had to forgo all foreign tours, even though some of them had been winners of the most prestigious international music competitions before they applied to leave. In addition, they were no longer allowed to play in most of the major halls of the Soviet Union, where they had previously performed many times and where audiences knew and loved them. If they managed to have concerts at all, it was exclusively in desolate places in the country.

One such musician was the pianist Vladimir Feltsman, the son of the famous Soviet composer-songwriter Oscar Felsman, who was a favorite of the government and the Party, and the recipient of every prize and award possible for a composer in the Soviet Union. When Vladimir was doing the paperwork to emigrate from Russia, he needed a letter from his parents confirming that they had no objections to his departure and no material claims. O. Feltsman wrote to his son Volodya a ridiculous letter, which evoked a sad smile among Moscow refuseniks: "*I, O. Feltsman, would always in my life give all my abilities, all my talents to the party and to the people. I promise to continue doing so in the future. I have no objection to my son Vladimirr's decision to emigrate from the USSR.*"

Oscar Feltsman had a dacha near Moscow in Krasnaya Pakhra, where Tanyusha and I used to visit Volodya and his lovely wife Anna. There were several Jewish celebrities in the village, which brought to life, an anti-Semitic joking parody of a popular Soviet song musiv by A. Petrov words by G. Shpalikov "And I am walking, striding along the Moscow streets...". The parody was making fun of the fact that many Jewish people have a problem with pronouncing hard sound "R". Everyone sang it in a mock version:

> *And I'm walking, striding along the Pakhra streets,*
> *Where nobody around can pronounce rightly the sound "R".*

As for Oscar Feltsman, he was afraid to show his face at the dacha after Volodya submitted documents for emigration, so as not to risk a meeting with Volodya's friends, unreliable people like us. The Feltsman's dacha was one of the pleasant places where the young Feltsmans and we had a good time with our common conductor friend Lyova Markiz. I remember one evening when we were there, drinking late into the night. When we went to leave, we came to the gate in a rather high fence, and found it locked from the inside. Volodya, laughing, said that this happened quite often before. Their housekeeper would go to bed early and, jealously guarding the master's property, would lock the gate and hide the key. Therefore, to return home for a night's sleep, Tanya, Lyova and I had to climb over the fence. Both Lyova and I were under the influence of alcohol, nevertheless we managed with no problems and with no injuries to climb over the fence. However, my Tanyusha had never been capable of such feats. That is why Anya and Volodya Feltsman, Lyova Markiz and your humble servant managed safely to partly heave Tanya across and partly leg her over the fence. I tell this story because the country should know its heroes. Luckily, what we picked up on the other side of the fence contained everything that made up my dear wife. I wish the unique operation could have been seen in the newsreels. But alas, it never happened.

However, in 1981, Lyova left Russia and settled in Holland, and the connection between us, unfortunately, completely weakened. I wanted to talk about Lyova here because when we were walking along the paths in Pakhra after their departure, we often remembered the many good things that we had shared together, not only at this place. During one of such walks, I took a good photo of our Verusha. striding impetuously along the village with her usual vigor. Remembering that Vera was Lyova's friend, I sent it to the Markizes with the following lines:

> I am walking, still without a visa.
> I am calling, "Hello, Markizes!"
> But, alas, the days go by,
> We see only the Feltsmans on our way...

One of the remarkable places in the centre of Moscow, representing another planet, was a building in Spasopeskovsky Lane in the N.Vtorov Mansion. From1933 to the present, the United States of America rented the mansion to house the US Ambassador's residence in Moscow. For this reason, the unofficial English name of the building was "Spaso House," after the nearby Church of the Savior Transfiguration on Sands (Russian verb "spasti" translates in English as "to save"). The name of the house in Russian could not have been more appropriate, as the place repeatedly served as a place of refuge for people hunted by the Soviet authorities, such as dissidents and Jewish refuseniks.

This became possible because during our refusal years the mansion housed, in my view, an outstanding, in many respects, couple: the U.S.A. Ambassador to Moscow, Arthur Hartman and his wife Donna Hartman. They were extraordinary people not only because of their high level of education and culture; they had a very active and interesting life in which they engaged people around them. I think it is also because they did care about not humiliating human dignity. We were fortunate to have known them, to benefit from their kindness and to be "SAVED" in their home.

The Hartmans both knew and loved music and we invariably were meeting them at all the interesting concerts in the Great Hall of the Moscow Conservatory. On top of that, they would invite prominent musicians to their Spaso House and arranged wonderful concerts there. One such concert was a performance at their residence by Vladimir Feltsman, which we shall never forget for the reason I am about to describe.

So on that day when we went to another planet, it was Spaso House, and the program included a piano concert of Volodya Feltsman. The event was particularly enjoyable to us, because we knew well both the pianist personally and his difficult situation. When all guests gathered together Arthur Hartman shared kind words about Volodya, and then he suggested that everyone should retire to the hall for 10–15 minutes so that preparations could be made before the concert. Everyone was glad to do it because the other guests were interesting interlocutors.

15 minutes passed, then 30 minutes passed, but still there was no announcement about the beginning of the concert. The situation began to cause some concern among the guests. Then Arthur Hartman came out, pale as a sheet of white paper, and explained that when Volodya checked the piano, he had found that some of the keys were dead. Looking under the lid, he saw that someone had cut several of the strings of the grand piano. Arthur said this had never happened within these walls before. However, he had already sent for a piano master, who would be able to replace the strings and tune the instrument. He apologized for the delay and urged his guests to be patient. *"We will not allow these barbarians,"*

LIFE THIRD: MY EFFORTS TO EMIGRATE FROM THE SOVIET UNION

he said, *"to take away our music."* And he really DID NOT let them. The concert took place, and Volodya played wonderfully. The Hartmans, as free people, could afford such behavior because inside their residence there was another planet, beyond the control of the Soviet authorities.

That day I learned two important life lessons. The first was that the KGB extended its tentacles to other planets, so once you fly to such planet, you cannot fully relax. The second one was that these monsters were powerless against real free people, no matter how many millions of them they destroyed and how many grand pianos they mutilated.

At this point, in connection with the concert described, I want to quote a limerick about my era of interplanetary travel, wonderfully composed by our son-in-law Vitya Khatutsky and given to me for one of my birthdays: This poem describes accurately what was happening:

> *There was once a janitor in the maternity ward,*
> *Poor fellow has taken to his hills to the United States.*
> *Meanwhile he was visiting the Spaso House,*
> *When not there, he was fixing toilets,*
> *He worked for the good of his Fatherland.*

My birthday present from Victor included nine limericks, each one better than the other. Rhyming is a contagious thing, and I wanted to conclude this chapter with my humorous parody of Mayakovsky's lines from his poem "At the Top of My voice." The English translation of the original lines may look like:

> *I, a toilet cleaner*
> *and water carrier,*
> *by the revolution*
> *mobilized and drafted,*
> *went off to the front*
> *from the idler's gardens*
> *of poetry—the cranky broad.*

My parody, I think, describes well **my status of the janitor--obstetrician:**

> *I, a toilet cleaner*
> *and water carrier,*
> *by the emigration*
> *mobilized and drafted,*
> *went off to the maternity front*
> *from the idler's gardens*
> *of science—*
> *the cranky broad.*

HOPE AGAINST HOPE

In 1973 there was an event in Russia of exceptional importance. The Great Poet's Library published a volume of O. Mandelstam's poems. Until that moment, the citizens of the USSR could only get acquainted with their great poet in two illegal ways.

The first method to read banned material was full self-service. Poetry lovers would retype for themselves and sometimes for their friends the passages of poetry and prose they loved on private typewriters. These were passages that Soviet citizens could not read in the books published in the USSR because they had been censored. This kind of publication we called "SAMizdat" (the roots "sam" would be translated in English as "self" and "izdat", "publish"). Russia never knew what a free press was, and samizdat had existed there probably since the very beginning of the 18th century. In Pushkin's times, poems went around Russia as hand-written copies because typewriters did not exist. The tsarist government persecuted those who had banned material, but never as severely as the Soviet government persecuted those with "samizdat."

The second way to read banned material was to smuggle Western publications into Russia. Thank God, Western publishers appreciated Mandelstam's poetry and, in defiance of the political barbarism of the Soviet authorities, published most of Mandelstam's poetry and prose. Because of it, some books published in the West found their way to Russia, and into Russian hands. This type of publication we jokingly called "TAMizdat" (the roots "tam" would be translated in English as "there" and the word was a euphemism for "in the West," and "izdat", "publish"). These publications came to Russia illegally, like publications from A.Herzen's free printing house in London, which printed forbidden in Rus-

LIFE THIRD: MY EFFORTS TO EMIGRATE FROM THE SOVIET UNION

sia works of writers and poets. However, how much more impermissible was Herzen's behavior than that of the most ardent "anti-Soviet" Russian authors. For example, on the cover of "Polar Star" were the portraits of five Decembrists hung in St. Petersburg thirty years before by decision of the specially formed Supreme Criminal Court. And how much less brutal and vindictive were the Tsarist guards, making no attempt to "get" Herzen, the troublemaker in London. The Soviet leaders and the KGB have always had very different habits.

The persecution of Trotsky, first in Europe and then in Mexico, illustrated the reach of the KGB. Numerous attempts on his life organized by the KGB culminated in the brutal murder in 1940 of one of the main leaders of the 1917 Revolution. The Spanish Soviet agent, Spaniard Ramon Mercader who committed the crime, was tried in Mexico, and sentenced to 20 years in prison. Having served his time, this executioner came to Moscow in 1960, and the Soviet leaders pompously awarded him the gold star of Hero of the Soviet Union... Notably, before the collapse of the Soviet Union, Russia NEVER exonerated or reestablished Lev Trotsky's honor.

The Soviet Union is long gone, but Putin's Russia still cannot abandon the tradition of executing its ideological opponents. Relatively recently, the whole world was shocked by the poisoning of A. Litvinenko. As I am editing these lines, the world is again shoked over yet another villainous first attempts to get rid of one of Putin's policy critics, the human rights activist Alexei Navalny. These attempts ended up in 2024 with brutal mordring of the courageous fighter for human rights in Russia.

A curious semantic fact: because of the unnatural situation with the Iron Curtain, many words of the Russian language have acquired new, invented meanings. A good example is the Russian adverb "there," which in Soviet times became "behind the borders of the Soviet Union." One of the favorite quotations of Soviet propaganda was the phrase by Nikolai Ostrovsky. He was the soviet writer, ardent believer in the communism myth, who was tragically killed by the incurable illness when he was only 32 years old. All schoolchildren in Soviet Union were required to memorize by heart the following quote from his novel: "*The most precious thing a person has is life and you get it only once. Therefore, one has to live it IN A WAY, not to feel excruciating pain for the aimlessly wasted years, not to suffer the shame of an ignoble and petty past, so that, dying, one could say: all my life and all my energy were given to the most important thing in the world: the struggle for the liberation of mankind."*

One of the ways to translate "in a way" into Russian, would be "TAK." There is also a Russian word "TAM" meaning "there." So replacing "K" with the "M" turns in Russian "TAK" into "TAM". In my school years, I liked an anti-Soviet, a parody to this phrase, which you get with mentioned above replacement of only ONE LETTER in one word: *"The most precious thing a person has is life and you get it only once. Therefore, one has to live it "THERE", not to feel excruciating pain for the aimlessly wasted years, not to suffer the shame of an ignoble and petty past, so that, dying, one could say: all my life and all my energy were given to the most important thing in the world, the struggle for the liberation of mankind."* The replacement turned the Soviet propaganda into advice that was criminal in the Soviet Union: If you wanted to live a decent life, you should move beyond the borders of the USSR. For more than thirty years, I lived "THERE" and I want to tell that it is much easier at this planet to follow the good advice of the courageous writer who, in spite of the ruthless illness, tried to do good things.

Fortunately, thanks to samizdat and tamizdat, by the time the volume of O. Mandelstam was published, I was already well acquainted with his poetry and prose and with the memoirs of his widow, Nadezhda Mandelstam. It seems to me that she was a very praise worthy woman in many ways. I know some people are unhappy with the sharp and not always fair judgments she made in her books of some of her contemporaries. In my opinion, we must understand how much this woman suffered in the totalitarian system, how much she helped the poet, and how much she did for the reanimation of his works. We owe her maximum tolerance to everything that grieved us in her work and instead should focus all our intolerance on those who brought to this couple and our country so much bitterness

Mandelshtam N.Ja.
as we remember her.

LIFE THIRD: MY EFFORTS TO EMIGRATE FROM THE SOVIET UNION

and sorrow. I read somewhere that this woman was not only the widow of a great poet, but also the widow of his great poems.

For years, my Tanya and I were During many years I had very close friends, Lenochka Smorgunov and her husband Yuri Freidin. After my marriage with Tanya I gave her this wonderful couple as good friends. Yuri, a very interesting man, had essentially two specialties. Officially, he worked as a psychiatrist, but his soul belonged to literary criticism, and he was professionally engaged in the works of O. Mandelstam. Because of this, he became friends with the poet's wife, Nadezhda. I treasure a photo from Lena and Yuri's wedding, where Nadezhda Mandelstam, as a witness, celebrated with us.

For the first time, Nadezhda Mandelstam published her memoirs in English in New York in 1970 under the title "Hope against Hope." Only recently have I learned that this is a very ancient expression. In the Epistle of Paul, the Apostle to the Romans in the New Testament (4:18), it is used to describe the faith of Abraham, who *"against hope believed in hope, that he might become the father of many nations..."* And in Latin there is a corresponding winged expression: "Contra spem spero" which may be translated into English as "Against all Hope I Hope". The title of the memoir takes on additional significance because of the fact that the author's name in Russian, "Nadezhda", means Hope.

In the late seventies, Nadezhda's health began to deteriorate rapidly. Yuri Freidin, became the chief steward of everything in her life and organized friends and admirers of Mandelstam's poetry and prose to provide round-the-clock care for her.

In 1979, my Galecka graduated from school with honors, but as the daughter of refuseniks she was denied admittance to all higher education institutions, so higher education was closed to her. Instead, she enrolled in a paramedical school. By that time, she was interested in poetry, knew and loved O. Mandelstam, and was an active friend of the Smorgunov, the Freidin. Thus, she was added to the volunteers who cared for the dying Nadezhda. I was very proud that she did this. On December 29th, 1980, Nadezhda Mandelstam's long suffering-filled life ended.

Very soon, after she passed away, I got a call from Yuri Freidin, who asked me to come urgently IN THE CAR to see him. In those years very few people in our circle had cars. I immediately rushed to their home. I learned from Yuri that he was very anxious about the fate of the archive of Osip Mandelstam that was in Nadezhda's apartment. There were, for example, priceless editions of the poet's poems with his written notes in the margins. We feared that the KGB would seal the apartment. Yuri wanted to prevent this by moving the entire archive to his home. We drove to Nadezhda's apartment on Cheryomushkinskaya Street in a terrible rush. We quickly loaded everything we could into my Little Froggy and nervously drove away from the house. In the rearview mirror, we noticed a KGB black "Volga" car pulling up to the entrance.

Though happy that we managed to get such valuable cargo out, we still had to outsmart the KGB. We had to be extremely careful, and we decided that we could not take it to Yuri's house. Yuri ordered us to divide it into parts and distribute these parts among his friends. At that time, it seemed that we had saved the archives. For a few months, everything was quiet. However, the separation of poor Yuri from the documents tormented him so much because he wanted to continue to work on them. Having calmed down, he began to gradually move everything to his home. Yuri had a tall bookcase, which you could not see most of the time because an open door between two rooms obstructed it. That is where he put all the collection. I felt very uneasy about leaving the archive in Juri's apartment. On the other hand, Yuri needed access to the archive for his work on poet's books.

However, as the saying goes, *"The music did not play for long"*. About a week after the priceless materials were returned, the KGB raided Yuri's place. They did not look anywhere else but went straight to the bookcase and confiscated EVERYTHING there. Tanya and I prepared to receive the same KGB guests in our house. Thank God, they did not come. A few days later, the KGB invited Juri for a "friendly conversation." We never learned what was said in this interrogation. However, to my enormous grief, we never saw our friends again. Apparently, the KGB demanded that they stop seeing us, and both Yuri and Lena were afraid to violate this KGB demand. For Yuri, of course, it was risky to see us or talk to us and he could have lost both of his jobs. He fell into a depressive state, which as a psychiatrist, he probably understood.

LIFE THIRD: MY EFFORTS TO EMIGRATE FROM THE SOVIET UNION

In the beginning of our refusal, when we would lose loved ones and people dear to us, one by one, like the Freidins, we too would become depressed. I am sure the Freidins never stopped being the wonderful people we knew them to be. It's just that the ugly system broke people down, instilling a fear in them that only giants like Tanya Velikanov could resist. I was never a superhuman like her and there were few who could live under this regime without feeling terrorized. The authorities simply did their best to keep people in fear and thus control them, often breaking them. For a long time, they denied Yuri Freidin access to his favorite job, and my Tanya and I lost our beloved friends for good. When we left Russia, we were not able to neither say goodbye to them or to thank them for their friendship.

IN SEARCH OF A BETTER UNTRUTH

Probably, what tormented me most about our refusnik's life, was that our children had to share all the hardships that had befallen us as punishment for our audacious desire to leave the country. Galya was 16 and Vera was 2 years old when we received our refusal. Tanya and I understood what might happen to us after making the decision to leave the country, but our girl did not. We had no choice but to make this extremely serious decision for them. WE condemned them to a wait, always questioning "Well. When?" and the answer was so very long in coming. Vera's age made it possible to protect her from much of the pain, but it was practically impossible to protect Galya. Therefore, we tried to prioritize sending Galya out of the country first.

The foundations of many of the components of life in the Soviet Union were built on untruths. What was taught about our country was a lie. What we were taught about foreign countries was an even bigger sea of lies. The information that was available to us on our side of the Iron Curtain about the economy, science, culture, art, and even religions of the world was soaked in Soviet ideology and was therefore false. The process of emigration out of the country was no exception. Most people had to submit false information, including false reasons for departure and false destinations. Jewish applicant had to present invitations from Israel most of which were false. However, the poor Jews had no other way out.

The Soviet authorities knew this, but for some reason they still demanded this false information. Therefore, we began to look for falsehoods that would help us get away from this nightmare. Crazy situations give birth to crazy plans.

One of the craziest plans was our attempt to bribe KGB officers. The amount of such bribes usually exceeded average people's financial capabilities. We are talking here not about hundreds, but thousands or even tens of thousands of rubles. For better reference and comparison, my monthly salary at the Academy of Sciences before submitting the documents for departure was 160 rubles, and my monthly salary in the maternity hospital was about 100 rubles. Our only savings were invested in the Little Froggy, which we hoped would cover all the expenses when the time came to leave. I would like to notice that our car was one of the cheapest. To illustrate the enormous price of freedom, our savings, hidden in the future sale price of our Little Froggy was about 6000–7000 rubles and the cost of the new car of this type was about 10,000 rubles.

During all the years of refusal, the authorities kept us in complete ignorance of the specific reasons why we could not leave. The officials, we repeatedly approached said the same meaningless words: "for security reasons." At some point, my friends found a person in Moscow, who for a rather large amount of money promised to look through my file and to find out what the refusal was based upon. What in my record prevented us from getting an exit visa? We paid the agreed amount, but it turned out to be a waste of money. We did not learn anything new, and this man turned out to be just another crook, profiting from the misfortune of people.

Our next attempt was to get permission to leave for a huge sum. This had worked before for our family. In 1935, I think, Galka's grandfather, David Ravich, Renata's father, was under arrest for his underground communist activities in the Romanian prison in Chisinau. Renata's mother bribed the jailers, and he was set free. However, such tricks appeared not to work with the Soviet authorities. Later he was arrested by the Soviets, and David Ravich served in jale his 17 years and was not released until after Stalin's death. Later, it was surprising to me that my first mother-in-law, talking about her ordeal with her husband's arrests, was indignant that the Romanians were all corrupt and the Soviet Communists were not (!?).

LIFE THIRD: MY EFFORTS TO EMIGRATE FROM THE SOVIET UNION

The offer to leave for a huge amount of money (about 10,000 rubles for one visa) made us terribly nervous for many reasons. First, we simply did not have that kind of money and there was nowhere to get it. The only real option for us was to borrow the money with no clear hope of being able to repay it. Secondly, we were very afraid of the possibility that the KGB having taken our money with the left hand, would not hesitate to arrest us with the right hand as punishment for attempted bribery of a state official. We tried to make inquiries about our "benefactor," and we were reassured that we may trust him. The experience of the previous ten years left us no other hope. Moreover, just waiting and doing nothing was no longer tolerable. At some point, we decided to take a risk and go to our friends with an outstretched hand. I do not want to mention here the names of the people we reached out to, for the simple reason that not all of them found the courage and strength to act with dignity in the ugly political situation of the time. In their defense, I must say that these people's fears of further persecution for helping the enemies of the people were real.

Our rounds to friends to raise the necessary money divided our close people into three groups. People in the first group, regardless of their financial situation, were ready to give their last penny to help us. Some of these people would turn to their friends, whom we sometimes did not even know, and would bring money from them. People from the second group, many quite wealthy, told us that they would be very happy to help us, but, unfortunately, only a few days ago they bought a car, a summer house, a fur coat, a trip abroad, etc., and so at the moment, they did not have a penny to spare. I would be much happier if these people honestly told me that they are scared to help us instead of inventing excuses why they cannot do this. However, the third group was the most unpleasant. Representatives of this group tried to lecture us on the subject of morals and said that, knowing us, they could not believe that we did not disdain to leave by SUCH means. Well, what can I say, perhaps indeed, the one well fed could never understand the hungry one. I am sending my prayers to God, that none of these people will ever experience what we went through during the refusal years.

Incredibly, we collected the required sum and passed it into what we hoped were the right hands through intermediaries.

After this, there was a rather long and nervous wait. When once again we asked about the status of our case, the answer plunged us into utter despondency: *"Nothing is working!"* We naturally asked for our money back, and this time the response left us in a state of shock: the person we were dealing with no longer had our money. He sincerely apologized and promised to try to compensate us for the money at least to some extent. In another communication session with this person, we were given a gold ring with a diamond (!?) to repay our debt. The sale of this ring returned to us only a small portion of the borrowed money. That was the ignominious end of this trickery.

However, we did not come to such a degree of despair as one young man, Galya's friend, most likely, we simply did not have enough courage for such a daring deed. He and his friend went for a hike on the Karelian Isthmus, and they managed to cross the Finnish border by the forest road with their backpacks. However, in those years there was an agreement between the USSR and Finland on the mutual return of illegal border crossers. Galya's friend was lucky not to be caught by the Finnish border guards but the other boy was stopped by the guards and they handed him over to the Soviet authorities. The poor creature was beaten and sent to a camp for three years and we know nothing more about his fate. Galya's friend, however, managed to wend across Finland by forest roads and crossed the Swedish border. Somehow, he spent a year in Sweden, and then moved to Canada and from there to the United States and lived in Boston. However sadly, we learned that he had paid toll for his way to come to the USA. In 2020, the boy committed suicide. We knew this hero well. His name was Pavel Simanovitch.

However, with our family, we tried to take a less risky route. There were always a lot of young men around our Galya, nice and different. One of them came to the decision to make all his future life plans together with her, and she was ready for that. They began to look for a way to leave together. The young man first found a foreign woman and entered a fictitious marriage with her in order get to the other side of the Iron Curtain. After he implemented this stage of the plan successfully, he intended to arrange a similar departure for Galya. The first part of the plan succeeded. The parting was very hard for our girl. She began to live from letter to letter, and it was not easy to get letters. Events developed sadly. Gradually the letters from Galya's chosen one began to arrive less and less often, and then stopped altogether. Our girl was inconsolable. We tried our best to support her, but we could so little! However, we had no choice but to go on, we had no way back: we had burned all the bridges behind us.

The second attempt was to take Galya over the border with the help of a ficticious marriage. This time the young man had no romantic leanings but a purely businesslike approach in mind. His father was a military man and agreed to give the required consent to the departure of his son only on condition that he would not leave from his home. The boy suggested the following departure plan: a fictitious marriage with our Galya, his registration in our flat and joint submission of "spouses" for departure. It seemed that another untruth should have helped both sides, just like in Arkady Severny's song "Good":

> *The lilacs came to bloom in my garden,*
> *You came in a lilac shawl.*
> *You came and I came.*
> *Now it is good for you and good for me.*

In general, the relationship between our "son-in-law" and his father was strained, so Tanya and I tried to take care of our boy as an orphan. For example, the military enlistment office tried to conscript him into the army. We called our psychiatrist friends, put him in a mental hospital and got him a diagnosis that exempted him from the army. Tanya was active in this story as a mother-in-law. She talked to both the psychiatrists and the hospital administrators and got her way. After this, the boy not only checked in with us officially, but also settled down in our apartment with us. He was an orthodox Jew and Tanya fed him kosher food. However, nothing was coming easy for us. By the time the listed steps were all done, the authorities began to intercept the necessary paperwork and calls from Israel. We were literally standing on our heads to get that fateful summons for our couple, and we did finally get it. When a happy Tanya called our "fiancé" to tell him the wonderful news, she heard from him that his circumstances had changed. He had met a woman, fallen in love with her, and wanted to go away with her. So, our whole plan was canceled. What might happen in this situation to our Galya did not seem to bother him. As a result, after much effort, a lot of worry, expenses, and disappointments, we were back to the starting point.

The end of this sad story was very unpleasant. Jewish refuseniks who had lost their jobs at the time were receiving financial assistance in the form of parcels with valuable items from the Western countries and Israel. Refusniks could easily sell those items in the secondhand stores and to get this way some financial income. Our "ex-son-in-law" managed to inform these nice people that our family was NOT going to Israel, and for that reason he asked them to stop sending packages in our name. At the same time, we also received a lecture from him that we had no moral right to use this aid and should pass all the parcels that already came to us into his hands. This man later became one of the leading rabbis in Israel. From time to time, he comes to Boston and lectures on the subject of morality, and crowds listen to him with reverence. It took some time for us to realize that breaking the relationship with this person was our good luck. The similarity with the song "Good" cited above continued:

> *The lilacs finished blooming in my garden,*
> *You left in a lilac shawl.*
> *You left and I left.*
> *Now it is good for you and good for me!*

THE DICTIONARY OF FORBIDDEN LANGUAGE

Tanya and I both grew up in assimilated Jewish families, completely unfamiliar with Jewish traditions, much less with the Jewish religion. Soviet state anti-Semitism led to the situation when every Jew who wanted to make a career in the Soviet Union tried to get rid of everything in his life that just reminded his Jewish origins. There was a sad joke about this in Moscow. A Jew came to the passport office and asked to have his last name changed from "Rabinovich" to "Ivanov." The officer did what he wanted. Some time passes, and this same man again comes to the same passport office and again asks to change his surname from "Ivanov" to "Petrov." The official recognizes the applicant by sight and says to him, "I remember, quite recently you changed your surname to "Ivanov," why do you want to change it again?" The man replies: "If they tell me that they know that I have changed my surname, and ask me what it was before, it's better to tell them that it was 'Ivanov'!"

In the 1980s, we were no longer living the Soviet life, we were not worried about our careers, and we could take a chance on learning Jewish history and religion. Among other things, we wanted to do this out of solidarity with many of our fellow Jews and Jewish refuseniks, who were very concerned about these issues. However, this was not safe for us either, since the Soviet authorities subjected everything connected with Jewish life to various persecutions, including even criminal.

The Biblical language, Hebrew, was especially "lucky" in this sense. The Hebrew letters annoyed the rulers of the country for some reason. When entering the USSR, the customs officers would confiscate any publication in which they found these letters. By the way, I do not know how they managed to distinguish Hebrew from Yiddish, which used the same alphabet. In the Soviet Union, I read somewhere, there was published only a single book in Hebrew: "The Hebrew-Russian Dictionary" (1963) by Felix Shapiro, whose grandson, Volodya Prestin, was our close friend. In 2006, the daughter of Felix, Volodya's mother, Leah Prestin-Shapiro published her book "Dictionary of Forbidden Language" with the Minsk MET Publishing House. I am very proud that when we were in Israel, Volodya and his mother gave us this book as a gift. There she tells many interesting things about the incredibly difficult birth of the historical publication of a unique dictionary, which she rightly calls the creation of a miracle.

In 1956, Felix Shapiro sent the first application for the dictionary and obtained positive responses from the Institute of Oriental Studies, the Institute of International Relations, and the Institute of Oriental Languages. An interesting characteristic of that time was that none of the applications included the words 'Jew,' 'Jewish science', or 'Jewish culture.' All of the applications spoke of the usefulness of the proposed edition to specialists in Semitic languages, particularly in their comparative analysis of languages such as Arabic and Ethiopian. The manuscript of the dictionary was already ready, and the publisher found excuse after excuse to postpone the print run.

When it seemed that all difficulties had been resolved, it turned out that the publishing house did not have a Jewish typeface for typesetting. The author and his close ones inquired everywhere and found the right typeface in the dilapidated printing shop at the old synagogue in Vilnius. However, it did not contain the letter "Hei" Feliks Shapiro had to agree to begin all the words, beginning with this letter, to start with "Het." Necessity is tricky in inventing! At certain moments, it seemed that the fulfillment of this dream was so close, so possible.

The publishing plans for 1957 and 1958 already included the publication of the dictionary, but as the year passed, nothing happened. At some point, the publishing house, on orders from above, refused to print the book from right to left (!?), and poor author even went along with it. What a state these ignoramuses must have brought the country's foremost specialist in Semitic languages to, for him to agree even to such an outrage! In her book, Leah describes the struggle of her father, *a lonely old Jew against a grandiose, united, hostile, bureaucratic, anti-Semitic Soviet power,"* comparing it to the struggle of David against Goliath.

As a result, the David of our time could not endure such a torture. In 1961, illness debilitated him, and he died. However, he managed before his death to proofread the dictionary. On his grave at Vostryakovsky Jewish Cemetery, there is a Hebrew phrase from his dictionary. If you translate it into Russian, it says, "*I pity those who left us irrevocably.*" Indeed, it is a pity and a double pity that people like Felix Shapiro were shackled by the regime. The Soviet authorities seemed to take always care that people like this hero left us too early. Incredibly, Felix Shapiro's core work was not lost. His friends and colleagues were able to bring it to a victorious conclusion.

Around this time, in Moscow, among the refuseniks there appeared several educated daredevils who had learned enough Hebrew to organize underground classes to teach the language. These teachers were heroic educators indeed, and I knew several of them in Moscow. They were remarkable people and some of them ended up in prison for their enlightenment. In the appendix of her book, Leah Prestin-Shapiro provided information about these courageous people who, knowing that it might send them to prison, still conducted Hebrew classes. In the same book she told readers about the trial of one such hero, Leonid Volvovsky.

Immediately after he appeared in the courtroom, Leonid made the following official statement: *"According to the Constitution of the USSR, every defendant may testify in his native language. My native language is Hebrew, and I will exercise my right"*. After these words, angry shouts of indignation erupted from a hall full of "patriots" of the country. However, they did not hear one more word in Russian from Leonid. Any question from the judge he answered in Hebrew. The judge shouted in impotent anger, not in his own voice: *"Let the record show that the defendant speaks a foreign language!"*

I had the pleasure of studying Hebrew in one of these classes during our last year in Russia. I am very fond of dictionaries, and I did a lot of lexicography. My problem in learning Hebrew was the complete lack of dictionaries. Some time after I started my Hebrew lessons, Volodya Prestin, Felix Shapiro's grandson, made me very happy by lending me his grandfather's dictionary. But a few months before that I was able to borrow an absolutely unique edition of another dictionary. A relative of our son-in-law Vitya had rewritten with his own hand page after page of a Hebrew dictionary published in Russia before the revolution. To my great regret, I had to return this handwritten treasure to its owners. My departure interrupted my lessons, and I am very sorry that I did not bring my studies up to the level where I could have used Hebrew even a little. Moreover, in America, I had a new life to begin, and there was really no time to learn a new language. The more so, that my first years in the new country I had to spend a lot of time to improve my rather poor English.

Nevertheless, after coming to America, I continued to reduce gradually my illiteracy in Jewish history and culture. This helped me better understand many things about my own life, such as the anti-Semitism in which I had lived the first half of my life, and why the Soviets not only hated Jews so much themselves, but also pushed the whole world to join them in such hatred. I also learned more about Zionism and the idea of the unification and rebirth of the Jewish people in their historic homeland, the land of ancient Israel. Stalin did not like the Jews, but at first, he supported the creation of the state of Israel in Palestine, I think for two reasons. First, he hoped to have a country in the Middle East that would faithfully serve as his backbone. Second, he planned to move there all the Jews who annoyed him. He was one of the first to recognize the state of Israel in its proclamation in 1948, and he supported Israel for admission to the United Nations. However, it did not work out the way he wanted: the Israelis, having escaped the Communist oppression, did not pursue a pro-Soviet policy, and were oriented to the West and the United States. As a result, Israel immediately turned from a friend of the Soviet Union into its sworn enemy. The odyssey of diplomatic relations between the Soviet Union and Israel is, in my opinion, an interesting topic.

In Israel, there was an underground anticommunist organization, which, shortly before Stalin's death, twice detonated a bomb in the Soviet Embassy in Tel Aviv. The first time it was in response to the execution of the entire party leadership in Prague as enemies of the people (December 1952). This action was obviously anti-Semitic because 8 of the 11 executed leaders were Jewish. The second time, it was in response to the arrests in the "Doctors case" in Moscow, an alleged conspiracy by Jewish doctors in Moscow to assassinate Soviet leaders. Israeli intelligence managed to find and capture the terrorists, and they all ended up behind the bars (February 1953). However, the Soviet leadership blamed everything on the Israeli government, and diplomatic relations were broken off. After the exoneration of the defendants in the "Doctors case" in Moscow, the Soviet authorities agreed to restore relations. However, in 1967, the defeat of the Arab invaders during the Six Day War in Israel irritated the Soviet government so much that relations were broken off again. The collapse of relations lasted for 20 years. The consular relations restarted only in 1987 and the relations on the ambassador's level, in 1991, after the collapse of the Soviet Union.

However, even after relations were broken, Israel continued to be a thorn in the flesh of the Soviet authorities, as well as in the flesh of Israel's Arab neighbors. In 1975, the Soviet Union, followed by the entire socialist camp, sneaked into the United Nations to the applause of the Arab world and put forth a disgraceful and politically illiterate Resolution 3379 that stigmatized Zionism as a form of racism and racial discrimination. This resolution was voted for by 72 and against by 32 of 139 UN members, with the rest abstaining. Among those who voted against the resolution were the majority of civilized countries: Australia, Austria, Belgium, Canada, Denmark, England, Finland, France, Iceland, Ireland, Israel, Italy, Netherlands, New Zealand, Norway, Sweden, Switzerland, and USA. It is important to note which countries the Soviet Union chose as allies, and which it chose as adversaries. The vote at the United Nations was condemned by Bernhard Vogel, a prominent West German Catholic figure *"For us the self-destruction of the moral authority of the United Nations is excruciating!"*

Immediately after the adoption of what was essentially an anti-Semitic, racist resolution, a movement to repeal it began around the world. The U. S. Senate, the Australian Parliament, the European Parliament, as well as the legislatures of Peru and Uruguay condemned the resolution. The Australian government, initiated by a local Zionist organization, declared the resolution inconsistent with the proclaimed principles of the UN, and pledged to work for its repeal and to engage the countries of Asia in this struggle. All of these wonderful people managed to move the world to the victory for justice. On December 16, 1991, the UN General Assembly, by a convincing majority of 111 to 25, with 13 abstentions, adopted a new resolution, No.4686, which repealed the controversial 1975 resolution 3379. There is one detail in this victory for justice that pleases me most. The 30 UN members, who voted FOR the demeaning resolution against Israel in 1975, voted AGAINST it in 1991. I think that this dynamic in the political theatre shows that the situation in the world is changing for the better. I am especially proud to note that US President George W. Bush made a brief introductory presentation to the General Assembly's discussion on the repeal of the anti-Semitic resolution.

Although good prevailed, this story strikes me as rather sad. First, I find it depressing how easy it was for Soviet leaders to do their evil deeds in those years at the UN. Secondly, it seems to me that even though the USSR collapsed, in the mentality of today's Russia there is much of the former evil empire, as my beloved Ronald Reagan believed. Although Wikipedia in Russian Language described all the details of the adoption and cancellation of the shameful document, nevertheless, the world continues to use today the thinking and vocabulary of 1975.

When I read the statements of Russian "scientists" with PhDs there, I could not believe my eyes. One, a "lawyer", called Zionism a *"wrongful phenomenon, a type of racism, whose theory, organizational structure, and activities were incompatible with international law and that it constituted a constant threat to peace and good, neighborly re-*

lations among nations". The second one, a "historian", said that the resolution of 1975 was *"an indictment not only against Zionism, but also against the policy of the Israeli leadership, a policy of expansion and war."* The third one, also a "historian", went so far as to explain the 1975 UN resolution by the *"numerous Israeli attacks and aggression, the genocide of the Palestinians and attempts by Israel to destroy the Arab civilization"*. I do not want to repeat here the names of these racists with diplomas of scholars. Those who are interested may go TODAY to Russian Wikipedia and get them. Shame on the country, that publishes such political garbage on the Internet. A.Galich's Klim at the "Matins in defense of peace" read a speech a widow that he received by mistake:

> *The Israeli aggressors, — I say,*
> *Are well known all over the world!*
> *As a mother, — I say, — and as a woman.*
> *I hold them accountable!*

This, so to speak, pundit attributed the adoption of resolution 4686 to *"...fierce pressure from the United States, which is the center of world Zionism and imperialism."* This publication makes me simply fearful, as if the familiar Stalinist times of unbridled lies and falsification have returned and caught up with me here in America. If it was really the fierce pressure from my new Motherland, I am very happy!

OUR ADOPTED SON

On April 19, 1980, the week of Passover was beginning and Tzilia invited us to celebrate the first Seder of the week, a lovely event she organized at her home for friends. For Tanya and me, this was a new experience. When I had read the Old Testament before, biblical events were very distant from me. At that time, I had not yet understood that the proper way to read the Bible was to compare my own experience with that of humankind over the millennia. The historical significance of this evening for us was neither limited to the novelty of the knowledge and impressions gained, nor to the study of historical or religious material. Most important for me was the discovery that my experience of leaving home and going into the unknown for freedom was akin to that of our people who left Egypt and went into the unknown to become free in the Promised Land. That is when I started thinking that three and a half thousand years later, people are still concerned about the same issues.

The evening was important to me because it drew my attention to the role of Jews in world history and the importance of freedom in people's lives. Today it seems to me that this holiday extends beyond Judaism to an international celebration of the triumph of freedom. In addition, this evening was a step in learning about the culture of the country to which we were about to travel. Most of the friends invited to the Seder were also good friends of ours, whom we loved dearly and with whom we were trying to break free.

But when we went to Tzilia's that night, we could not have imagined that we would meet a man who was destined to become not only our close friend, not merely our relative, but also in the full sense of the word, our adopted son, for God had not given Tanyusha and me a son. This person, Stuart Saffer, was a young and handsome English student, who came to Moscow to celebrate the week of Passover or Pesach with Jews in Russia. Stuart was interested in Zionism and came to meet Soviet refuseniks in Moscow. He had received names from the local Jewish community before his departure, including Pasha Abramovich, a veteran refusenik, who had been seeking permission to leave for over 15 years. We knew Pasha and his family well and often saw them at Tzilia's house. Stewart, on his arrival in Moscow, called Pasha and told him that he would like to celebrate Pesach in the company of Moscow refuseniks. Pasha immediately invited him to a Seder with Tzilia and they arranged to meet on the first day of Passover at the Airport metro station, right next to Tzilia's house. Pasha brought him to Tzilia's, and so we ended up together at the Passover table. After the formal part of the Seder was over, we of course got to talking.

We both liked the boy at first sight. As for my Tanyusha, she had had a soft spot for British accents from a young age, and Stuart was born and brought up in London. Besides, both Tanyusha and I saw this acquaintance as preparation for our future lives. He taught us about life and culture in the West. We also thought that Stuart might be lonely in a foreign country, and we soon started inviting him to come and visit us. More recently, Stuart reminded me of a conversation that had taken place between us that evening. In response to my invitation, Stuart asked me not to worry about him, because he did have acquaintances in Moscow. I replied that acquaintances are acquaintances, and I was inviting him into my family. At the time, of course, I did not realize that my words would be prophetic. Today, Stuart is a very dear member of our family. That is why I would like to describe briefly here the main facts of his biography and, first, how we twinned.

Stuart was born into a Jewish family in London in 1959. As a point of comparison, he is three years older than my Galya. From the age of 9 he was involved in the youth Zionist organization Habonim (Hebrew for Builders). In his last year of high school, this organization paid for his first trip to Israel. In 1980, Stuart enrolled at the University of Leeds, from which he graduated in 1984. His interest in Russia and the Russian language awakened in him at that time. Together with a group of 30 first-year students, he traveled to Moscow for a month. The next year, 1981, being a second-year student, he came to study Russian for three months in the Voronezh Agrarian Pedagogical Institute, now Voronezh State Pedagogical University. We worried that he would get bored in such a "wilderness." Therefore, my dear Galechka went to Voronezh to visit. At the end of 1981, Stuart came to Moscow again, this time for a year, to study Russian at the Pushkin Institute of Russian Language which had opened in Moscow especially for foreigners.

Stuart Saffer in Moscow, 1980

During that year, our friendship deepened. The Pushkin Institute and student dormitory were in the south-west of Moscow. We also lived in the southwest, not far from the Institute. Therefore, from a practical point of view, communication was quite easy. I could walk from my house to the Institute in less than half an hour. As a result, Stuart began to visit us regularly, much to our delight. He was very fond of children and became fast friends with our five-year-old Verochka. They read children's English books together, and he became her second English teacher after Tanya.

Always attentive and thoughtful, Stuart tried to help us, without expecting us to ask him for help. When he realized that we could not buy our favorite books even by Russian writers, to say nothing of the Western ones, he found out about the special bookstore only for foreigners in Moscow called "Beryozka." To buy the books in this store one had to have foreign currency. There one could buy many books that we did not even dream of. Remember, it was strictly forbidden for Soviet citizens to hold currency of ANY OTHER COUNTRY. In addition, there were always police officers standing guard at the entrance to all currency shops, so that Soviet citizens, God forbid, could not show their noses there.

One day, Stuart invited me into one of these shops to buy me a couple of books using British pounds. I happily set off with him. Stuart was walked up first and the police officer asked him for his ID. Seeing his English passport, he dutifully let him in. In doing so, he saw perfectly well that we approached together and were having a friendly conversation. However, when I tried to follow Stuart, the guard blocked my way and barked rudely: *"Where did you come from?"* At this point, I could not contain my irritation, and I sharply replied in his style, *"My mother gave birth to me!"* I do not know how it would have ended, maybe even an arrest for hooliganism, if Stuart had not immediately come up and in a strong English accent explained to him politely that I was his friend and he needed me for advice on buying books. The guardian of the Iron Curtain was apparently in a good mood and let me in.

In the store my eyes danced everywhere, but I behaved decently and forced myself to name just a couple of books, the ones most-most-important to me. Stuart paid his English pounds, and I walked happily out of the shop with him, my precious gift in my hands. I remember, looking at the British banknotes in his hands as he was at the till, repeating to myself a joke of the time, about comparing English and Soviet money. *"What is the equivalent of a British pound in Soviet rubles?"* The answer was: *"One pound of dry rubles!"* The real equivalent of the English pound in those days was a little less than a hundred rubles.

With his commitment and conscientiousness, Stuart grieved that they did not have a quiet enough place at the Institute to study productively. Of course, we immediately suggested that he come to us to work on Russian language and at the same time, he would get a bonus: conversational practice in Russian. He gladly and gratefully accepted our offer. After that, we started to see him at our place quite a lot, and he got an opportunity to observe our crazy refusal life, which made a strong impression on him. Moved by this impression, one evening he had a memorable conversation with us about it. The gist of the conversation was that we had to come up with something together to get out of this country, and he was willing to go to great lengths to help it happen.

A LAST EFFORT WITH UNTRUTH

By the time that Stuart had come up with a viable plan, he had a good grasp of the Soviet system. He proposed that our Galechka should marry him fictitiously so that he could take her to England. However, to go down such a path, he would have to get official written approval from at least two rabbis. He wanted to take it on himself, and if we agreed, he would begin. Trusting him 200%, we of course gave him our full approval. Soon he brought to our house two British (!?) rabbis, who signed the wonderful document in our presence. The signatories testified that Stuart, in entering into this marriage, performed a mitzvah or good, commendable deed, according to Jewish tradition. In signing the document, Stuart promised that he would never use this marriage for his own personal gain. The act, which took place before our eyes, made a lasting impression on me: I had not previously known that the ethics of Judaism were so wonderfully humane. There are 613 kinds of mitzvahs mentioned in the Torah, and the rabbis in London must have decided that what Stuart ventured to do was one of them.

It was the beginning of 1982, five years into our ordeal as refuseniks. We did not want to procrastinate, and as soon as we received the desired document from the rabbis, we applied for the marriage registration. In the centre of old Moscow in the beautiful pre-Revolutionary building on Griboyedov Street, this is now called by its old name: Maly Kharitonievsky Lane. There was WEDDING PALACE № 1. It was there that we decided to make an official Soviet ceremony. We had never forgotten that our ceremony was fictitious. We had several considerations in choosing the primary wedding site in the country for them. First, we thought Stuart's act was so significant that we wanted the setting to be as solemn and beautiful as possible. Secondly, we thought it would cause the least suspicion of impropriety.

The registration of the wedding was not without a funny development. Stuart decided not to say anything to his parents about our trickery, because he did not want to worry them unnecessarily. Incredibly, his parents came to Moscow unexpectedly that very week on a tourist trip. Moreover, Muscovites considered the Wedding Palace to be a significant sight and they were proud to show it to all foreigners. Unbelievably, his parents' excursion to the Palace was on their agenda on the same day as Stuart's registration with Galya! We were just at a loss as to what to do. We were relying on the fact that, according to the Palace schedule, the parents' tour would happen on Griboyedov Street a few hours earlier than our event. Nevertheless, we were terribly nervous until we managed to find out that their excursion to the Palace had happened earlier and we, thank God, had not yet met there. Only then could we breathe a sigh of relief, though temporarily.

The awkwardness continued into the evening of that day, when everyone gathered at our house to celebrate, and we of course we had to invite Stuart's parents. We asked everyone, who came, ahead of time in no circumstances even mention that we were actually celebrating, and for the poor parents there was a version of the birthday of one of us, I do not remember whom. I can imagine what bewilderment such nice people must have had at so little attention to the "newborn" and so many toasts to our London guests. However, all ended well, Stuart's parents were happy with their trip to the Soviet Union, went home, and we bid them a friendly farewell.

After their return home, there was another misfire, this time with the British authorities. There was a phone call at his parents' flat in London from some local administrative office asking for Stuart. I believe his mother picked up and said that he was not currently in the country. The receptionist on the phone requested that they ask him to call about his wife's papers when he got back. The mother, quite surprised, said that this was some kind of mistake, for her son was never married.

Soon after all this, poor Stuart had to go home to England himself. How he got himself out of the mess with our Galecka's papers we do not know, but we felt very guilty. I thought then, how diffi-

Stuart Saffer in 2009

cult it is for a normal honest man to tell untruths, even for noble purposes, and how easily crooks do it! However, Stuart, a piece of gold, soon prepared and sent Galya all the necessary documents so that she could come to visit her "husband" in London. But this never happened either! The Soviet authorities denied her an exit visa. In this sense, our girl became a double refusenik in the Soviet Union.

But our Stuart would not let up. Through the Soviet embassy in London, he requested an entry visa to the Soviet Union in order to come to Moscow to see his "wife" and bring her with him to England. That did not work either; the Russian authorities refused that as well, thus we became triple refuseniks in the Soviet Union

After this, our Stuart took one last decisive step: he tried to get permission for all of us to change our citizenship for British, Galya, Tanya, Vera and me! However, this also failed, we heard a categorical "NO!" from the Soviet officials. At this point, I was especially sad to see the attitude of the staff at the British Embassy in Moscow. Not wanting to spoil relations with the Soviet authorities, they forgot that they were representatives of a great free country within a state of dictatorship and violence. When our Galechka wanted to meet their consul, they were afraid even to invite her inside the embassy building, and the consul, so as not to upset the Soviet leadership, went outside to talk to her. It was disgraceful. I would hope that they later learned some dignity from the Moscow embassies of Australia, of the Netherlands and of the USA.

This was the sad end to all of Stuart's incredible attempts to help us in our tireless efforts to escape the evil empire. I think we should not call these efforts fruitless because during the hardest days of our lives they helped us to keep our faith in human goodness. They also gave Tanyusha and me a wonderful son and our daughters a wonderful brother. In the mid 80's Stuart moved to live in Jerusalem. In 1984, he called us and told us that he met a woman whom he wanted to marry. We quickly arranged for a divorce from Galya and sent him the papers. The woman's name was Miriam and they got married in 1985. She bore him two beautiful boys. Unfortunately, this marriage ended in 1994. From 1989–2008, Stuart worked for JDC (Jewish Distribution Committee), the largest Jewish charity in the world headquartered in New York, but his region was mainly Russia. In 2006, Stuart married again, this time again unsuccessfully. From this marriage, he had his third boy in 2008. Stuart is an amazing, very caring father to all three of his sons. We have visited him several times in Israel, and he has visited us several times in America. His dad died in 1990 and his mom died in 1998, before his second wedding. Both parents' graves are in London. Stuart says he is a very lucky man to have two pairs of parents and refers to Tanya and me as his other parents.

I will never forget the second time Stuart got married. He invited Tanya and me to Jerusalem as his parents. Tanya spoke at the gala and said all the wonderful things she could about our Stuart. When the solemn part was over, a woman who didn't know that Tanya and I were not the groom's actual parents came up to Tanya and said to her enthusiastically: *"You spoke so beautifully, and Stuart looks so much like you!"* This funny detail touched us to the bottom of our hearts.

OUR OWN PARAMEDIC

In the cares and difficulties of refusenik life, we did not have time to notice how our Galya, like the daughter of the czar in Pushkin's tale, *"...grew, grew, rose and blossomed."* The year 1979 came and she finished high school as one of the top students. I must give her credit, in our multi-problem life she always studied surprisingly easily and cheerfully. However, getting her high school diploma added another problem for us. No institutions of higher learning accepted children from refusenik families. What could we do? She, to my great joy, decided to enroll in the Paramedic School at the Institute of Emergency Care after N. V. Sklifassovsky. I had not managed in Soviet Union to work in health care, but in spite of all our troubles, the fact that she was able to do so made me happy. Moreover, I was proud that she volunteered at the frontline of health care in the ambulance.

Count Nikolai Sheremetev, celebtating his birthday, laid the foundation of the "Shelter for Pilgrim", a "stone hospital" and almshouse for the care of his old peasants and courtiers, as well as all the poor and sick residents of Moscow. A man of the Enlightenment, Nikolai Sheremetev was known for his philanthropy. The origin of Russian name "Shelter for Pilgrim" comes from the Evangelical definition of "pilgrim" and the Christian attitude towards a major type of a neighbor to be cared for. The revolution shut down the "Shelter for Pilgrim," but in 1923, the buildings of the hospital and almshouse housed the Institute of Emergency Care. In 1929, the institute was named after the honored pre-revolutionary professor and renowned surgeon, Nikolai Sklifassovsky, who was the director of the first Russian Institute of Physicians' Advanced Training.

Thank God, this dignified citizen of Russia died in 1904 and did not live to see the Bolshevik atrocities. Sklifassovsky's widow and children received a paper from Lenin that the family of the famous doctor could not be "touched." However, in the mess of the revolution the left hand did not know what the right hand was doing. Seeing a portrait of a tsarist army officer in uniform, the bandits thought that the paralyzed widow, Sophia Sklifasovsky, and their daughter, Tamara, were relatives of the Russian general. They hacked Sophia to death with shovels, and took Tamara out into the yard, raped and hung her. No one bothered to find out that Sklifosovsky got the rank of general for his participation in the wars as a doctor who treated all the wounded, regardless of social status. The tomb of the great scientist was desolated during the Soviet years. The authorities looted the house and used it for the Institute of Pig Breeding. The new hosts set up a pig insemination station in the guesthouse, dismantled the cemetery church, and ravaged the fountains, cemetery, and park. The revolution was commiting its bloody work.

Our Galya became a student in the paramedic school. However, before classes started, the administrator wanted to see her. This person was kind and said, *"We looked at your documents. You did well in a good school and made a good impression on our admissions committee. Why did you not apply to an university? People like you do not usually come to us. Can you tell us what the problem is?"* Galyusha told this woman everything as it really was, where, how, and why. She had the impression the woman listened to her with understanding.

LIFE THIRD: MY EFFORTS TO EMIGRATE FROM THE SOVIET UNION

After studying for two years, Galya received her diploma as an ambulance paramedic. During her training, she practiced driving all over Moscow on calls with the ambulance team. In this practice, as far as I remember, there was minimal treatment, but she developed the essential skills necessary to take urgent action to relieve acute conditions and to stabilize patients to keep them alive on route to the hospital.

Quite soon after graduation, she got a job in one of the city hospitals' intensive care departments. Here she really felt like she was on the battlefield because her patients were often on the brink of death. I was incredibly proud of the responsibility she was given and admired how my little girl was involved in saving people's lives every day. Many patients in her department were there after serious operations, as well as those with severe trauma-related injuries. Among the injuries were those inflicted in nightmarish drunken brawls. She assisted in surgeries with major blood loss. To be honest, I did not really understand how my Galyusha could do such a difficult job. I knew well from my own experience that she absolutely could not see MY blood. Even when I would cut my finger, she could not bandage it for me. However, in this job, she could see rivers of blood and managed to do a great job. I was very concerned that my little girl might be overwhelmed both physically and mentally. She proved more than once that though she was small, she was daring, competent, and strong.

The next step in her paramedic career was when she moved to work on a Blood Circulation Machine (BCM). It seemed to me that physically the work was not much easier, but more interesting for her inquisitive mind. Still, she was very tired and after each shift she literally collapsed in bed. However, Galya always remained Galya. Sometimes her friends would call and invite her to a concert. She would find the energy, jump up, put on makeup, and before Tanechka and I knew it, she would be out of sight. She would return late and if something in the evening was interesting, it would take her a long time to settle down. However, the next day she would hurry to her BCM quite early in the morning, as if to a conveyor belt system. Such intense lifestyle of hers continued and of course, Tanya and I were both worried that she would not go off the rails.

VERA IN THE SOVIET SCHOOL

From the very beginning of our refusal, we were very worried that until we left, the ugliness of life would ruin our Vera's happy childhood. After all, she was only a year old when we were refused. We both remember well the story of our dear Verochka Prokhorov and how the Soviet authorities, when she was still a little girl, robbed her family of everything: their material well-being, their house, and her father's business, which he loved dearly. Nevertheless, her parents managed to prevent the authorities from depriving her of a happy childhood. The warmth with which her parents surrounded her protected her from all adversities then, and the same warmth many years later helped her to endure the inhuman ordeal of the Gulag.

That is why Tanya made it her life's task to protect our girl in a similar way. This was not easy, especially in our crazy Moscow life with calls to the KGB, demonstrations and protest rallies, searches, and the arrests of friends. Several times the police detained Verusha along with us, which felt like hours of arrest. Of course, every time she was terrified and wondered how this could be. We had never done anything bad to anybody. As a result, our Verusha. grew up before her time. She was worried about things to which her peers just did not pay any attention. I remember how one day our girl came home and as soon as the door closed behind her, she said, *"There's a black car outside our doorway with three policemen sitting in it, I noticed."*

The abnormalities of our refusal life poured into many of her "whys." Why do we all have to lead a double life, saying one thing among ourselves, and another with our acquaintances? Why do we have to hide our friendships with foreigners? Why did Mom stop teaching students and Dad become a janitor? Why could her sister not continue to study and get a higher education? And the cardinal question, of course: why were the Soviet people not allowed to cross the border and leave the country? With this last question, I remember a sad conversation with little Verusha. One day she asked Tanya and me if birds could cross the border between countries in the sky. Most questions of this sort by a child would have gone unanswered, but to this question we gave her the exact answer, *"Yes, of course, birds are free to fly wherever they want."* Vera's response to our answer blew away a tear in both of us, *"Happy birds!"*

Tanya tried to use every opportunity to reduce, at least partially, Vera's feelings of trauma on any level. She would switch to something more natural and joyful and avoid the political nonsense. When it was time for her to go to school, we decided to teach Vera at home in order to protect her from a potentially unfriendly environment. After all, the Soviet school drummed into children that the USSR was the best country in the world and the only one that provided children with a happy childhood. Our Verusha. did NOT go to the 1st grade class in 1983, when she reached 7 years old. Tanya continued to be responsible for all of Vera's education. We continued to hope naively that we would finally get permission and the problem would solve itself. However, this did not happen, and we lived the refusenik life for five years more.

But we did not live those years in peace. Our "friends" from the KGB, were well aware of Vera's home education, came and frightened us with a terrible threat. *"You are literate people,"* they said, *"and you know that in our country, the interests of the child come first, and therefore the country has a MUST primary education. If you do not send your little girl to school, like all Soviet parents, we will have to take away your parental rights"*. At first, I thought it was an empty threat. However, later I found out that in 1969, Article 59 in the Soviet Code of Marriage and Family stated in the *"Deprivation of Parental Rights"* the following: *"...both parents or one of them, may be deprived of parental rights if...parents evade their duties to bring up their children or abuse their parental rights if it was found one of the following: parents evade their duties to bring up their children or abuse their parental rights, treat their children cruelly, exert a harmful influence on the children by their immoral, antisocial behavior, or if the parents are chronic alcoholics or drug addicts."*. The Soviet lawyers could establish whatever they wanted. They would have no trouble, of course, establishing that we were alcoholics if you recall the Vodka Library of the Ziemans. However, it would cost nothing at all to bring us under the ill influence of our immoral, anti-social behavior, which deprived children of a school education.

We were very frightened and in 1984 rushed to bring our girl to school. Tanya's pedagogical abilities were apparent as Vera was already reading and starting to write in two languages: Russian and

English. Our girl went straight into the second grade of the Soviet school. Tanechka decided that Verochka's school should not be close to our house to prevent the school from learning of our refusal status. Our friends, the Margolises, recommended a school in Moscow with an intense course of French and even told us of a nice second grade teacher. An additional bonus of that school was its proximity to the maternity hospital #25 where I worked. Tanya went to the school and got our Vera enrolled. It required some effort on our side, as the school was not in our neighborhood. However, it was easy to solve such problems in Russia with the help of gifts to the principal. And it worked this time, too. Vera was accepted. She studied at this school until our last days in Russia and was one of its best students.

I want to tell a funny story here about how the school made Vera a pioneer. Few people know that this organization was created in the Soviet Union in 1922 year and was named after Spartacus, the leader of the revolt of slaves and gladiators in ancient Rome in the 73–71st years BC. What has Spartacus to do with the Soviet Union? Karl Marx started this ball rolling. Somehow, thanks to him the name became the symbol of the international communist movement. After Lenin's death in 1924, the Soviet pioneers' organization changed its name from Spartacus to Lenin and everybody started calling the pioneers Young Leninists. According to the Soviet Pioneer Charter, any child aged 9 to 14 years old could become a pioneer. Children would become pioneers at a grand general meeting of the pioneer organization. In front of all the assembled poor children had to promise things that they had no idea about, namely: *"to love my homeland ardently* (is it possible to love on a promise?), *to live, learn and fight* (against whon they had to fight?), *as bequeathed the great Lenin, as taught by the Communist Party."* We never chose listed teachers for our girl! The last thing Tanyusha and I wanted before leaving the country was for Verusha to go through such a theatrical performance.

As soon as Verusha turned nine, the school started "preparing" her to become a pioneer. At the same time, Tanyusha and I began to prepare ourselves to prevent this political game. As soon as each meeting was scheduled, our child would get sick and not show up to school. For some time, our plan of action succeeded. One day Tanya could not take Vera from school and asked me to do it. As I was on duty at the maternity hospital, I got permission to be absent from work for an hour and arranged with Vera that I would wait for her on the street in the car near the school gate. She had to come out of the school by herself. I drove to work in my Little Froggy. At the agreed time, I jumped out of the Maternity Hospital, in janitor's overalls, drove up and stopped at the gate. 10 minutes passed, 20 minutes passed, 30 minutes passed, but no Vera. After getting increasingly nervous, I decided to go after Vera and to apologize for my work clothing. An unfamiliar woman, holding Vera's hand came out to meet me in the doorway of the school. She literally threw herself at me and started shaking my hand; "Well, congratulations! Finally, your girl is a pioneer!" At a loss, I was numb and could not find the words, I completely forgot to apologize for my being dressed inappropriate. Later we found out that the day's meeting took place especially for Vera, who, though the last in her class, had finally become a young Leninist.

In parallel with her middle school, Vera successfully studied piano at the Children's Music School after Prokofiev. She also sang in this school choir. Once their chorus was performing in the Great Hall of the Moscow Conservatory, and I well remember how Tanya and I sat in the stalls and burst with pride, seeing our daughter on such a famous stage. However, along with good music, they sang absolute rubbish like a song by S.Tulikov "Lenin is always with you," to lyrics by L.Oshanin. Since that day, I have remembered the lyrics:

> *Lenin is always alive,*
> *Lenin is always with you —*
> *Be you in grief, in hope, or in joy.*
> *Lenin is your spring,*
> *On every happy day,*
> *Lenin is in you and in me!*

I personally, can honestly say that this man never was WITH ME AND IN ME, and certainly, he never was with Vera, not because she was such a smart kid, but simply because we never taught her that.

MY TOUR TO THE GULAG COUNTRY

Tanya Velikanov served her sentence in a concentration camp in Mordovia; and the camp allowed prisoners, I think, once a year to see their closest relatives. On one of those occasions, Lenochka Smorgunov and I went there as escorts for Tanya's children. Actually, both Lena and I hoped to try to see Tanya. But this did not work: the camp administration did not even want to discuss this possibility. Through Tanya's family, we received instructions on how to get to the camp, including the train schedule. From Moscow, we took aregular train to Mordovia and there we changed to a small, special narrow-gauge train carriage that took us to a dead end where the rails just ran out. When we unloaded with our backpacks, all I saw around us was a small canopy that resembled a bus stop, surrounded by nothing but forests and fields. There was a bench under the shelter, for waiting "for the bus".

The five of us crawled out of the carriage: Tanya's two youngest children, Lenochka, I, and an elderly oriental woman dressed in black. The length of the bench under the awning only just allowed everyone to sit down, and we had to leave our backpacks and bags on the ground. A person working for the camp told us to wait on that bench until a representative of the camp administration came to talk to us. We did this. With my usual sociability, I struck up a conversation with the elderly woman who came with us to the camp. She turned out to be from a small place in Soviet Georgia. Her only son got imprisoned in the camp for 5 years. The woman did not know the details. For the FIRST time in her life, the poor old woman had left her village and traveled thousands of miles away on a long journey. She was carrying a huge black bag filled with Georgian delicacies, all products of her culinary art, including cheesecake, patties with meat, and ravioli, etc. We were all five of us squirming on the not-so-stable bench in impatience.

Meanwhile, it was getting close to lunchtime. Lenochka and I decided to wait with the food until we talked to the administration. Our Georgian grandmother took something like a cheese sandwich out of her bag and started snacking. I observed with interest what was going on around us. From time to time, a prisoner would pass our bench, escorted by a soldier. Sometimes the soldier was leading a German shepherd. It was a warm summer day. The prisoners were all dressed in prison uniforms, the men in dirty grey pajamas, and the women in blue dresses with flowery ornament.

At one point, as a soldier walked past us with a young man, the old woman quickly broke off half of her sandwich and handed it to the prisoner. What happened next is something I will not forget for the rest of my life, and I want all my loved ones to know. The poor fellow just had time to take a bite of the sandwich and the guard jumped up to him, snatched the sandwich from his hands, and threw it into the grass far from the track. He then shoved the boy in the back and hurried him away. About 20 minutes later, another man in a soldier's uniform came up to the old woman and informed her officially that for violating the camp rules, she was DEPRIVED of the right to see her son! Grandma was incapable of comprehending what she had heard. I was afraid she was going to have a stroke. I did not recover from the shock for the rest of the trip.

After a while, we had an unpleasant conversation with the camp administration, in which they explained to us that friends do not have a right to visit prisoners at all. Calling Lenochka Tanya's cousin did not help either. After this conversation, the children were taken away to see their mother, and we waited for them to be brought back. We thanked the communist party for at least allowing that visit. I was so glad that we helped our Tanechka see her children. After all, their visit could have been cancelled. In similar situations, our son-in-law Vitya used to say, *"Thanks, they could have had cut eyes with a razor and they did not"*.

Though we did not get to see a very dear friend, we managed to be very close to her. I left with bitter feelings, like those I experienced in the Kuril Islands, when seeing Japan. The elbow is close, but you cannot bite it. Besides, it was a pity that we did not have permission to go even a few paces away from the shelter and the dead end of the narrow gauge to see more of the horrible place. However, nobody could forbid me to bow my head in memory of those who had not returned from the gulag. Thank God, Tanechka came back alive, and I managed to see her more than once after her return.

OUR GEORGIAN "RELATIVES"

When I talk about Georgia, I mean a country in the Caucasus region of Eurasia that during my life in Russia was one of the republics of the Soviet Union. We tried as much as possible, especially when Vera was not in school, to take her away from Moscow. Our favorite places, where we managed to hide from the unpleasant feeling of being "declassed people" and from the hollowness of refusenik life, were Georgia, Armenia and the Baltic States. Not only little Vera, but also Tanya and I found relief and relaxation there. The friendliness of the local people in these places moved me. Interestingly, in all three places we never encountered anti-Semitism. Moreover, we always felt comfortable discussing our plans to leave the Soviet Union with our friends there. No one ever asked us personal questions about our lives there, and we simply would forget about all of our problems for a while.

Georgia held a special place among our three havens. All the good things said about the cordiality and hospitality of the locals was true for Georgia. That is why Tanya and I used to call our friends in Georgia "our extended family." We spent most of our vacation time there. Our first "love affair" with Georgia happened when we rented a room for the summer in Abkhazia near Sukhumi on the recommendation of our friends the Margolis. We liked the small village of Kashtak so much that we went there for several years in a row and became friends with many Georgian families.

However, even more intense though shorter in time "love affair" with Geogia began thanks to our friendship with Lyova Markiz. It was he who brought Tanya and me there for a magical week in 1979. I do not know another person who, not having lived in Georgia permanently, loved it so much. He loved coming there as a friend, he loved coming there as a musician, he loved giving it to his friends as a gift. Tanya and I were very lucky to get this wonderful gift from him. Having written about Lyova's gift, I recall the lines from Ada Yakushev's song "My Friend Draws the Mountains," which I had once heard her perform in a salon on Pushkinskaya at Balechka's:

He loves to give these mountains as a present to his friends.

Georgia is a mountainous country and the lines sound to me as if they describe exactly like about Lev Markiz and us.

I had impression that half of Georgia was Lyova's friends and good acquaintances, including the mountains. He was the one who introduced us to many nice Georgian musicians. In Georgia, everybody goes with the rule: "*My friend's friend is my friend*". As a result, we became friends with many of his friends. I am very sorry that our move across the ocean left these friendships behind. To my great regret, it also became too difficult to keep in touch with Lyova himself after we left the country.

To support what I said in the previous paragraph, I would like to tell about one episode of my life with Lyova in Tbilisi. One warm evening, Tanya and I were walking down the street about midnight, returning home with Lyova after another concert of his friends. A window on the second floor burst open right above us and someone began waving at us and shouting: "*Lyovochka!*" Lyova looked up and recognized another friend, who invited us with a broad hand gesture: "*Come on, pull over!*" In response, Lyovochka trying not to disturb the silence, pointed his finger first at his watch and then at us. The man in the window with an even bigger hand gesture insisted that we come up. We went up the stairs and the door on the second floor was already wide open. After we entered the hallway, Lyova embraced his friend, and introduced him to us. The host welcomed us into the room. We passed the doorway and could not believe our eyes: there was a table in the middle of the room, already full of delicious viands! The speed with which Georgian hospitality spread knew no bounds.

Lev Markiz in Georgia

Now I would like to return to our small village of Kashtak near Sukhumi. There we rented a room in a house on a hillside 10 minutes' walk from the sea's beach. The owners were elderly Byelorussians, who suggested us to address them as Grandpa Stepan and Grandma Dusya. My memory did not keep their last names, so let it be Belorus. They had lived in this house for decades. The big window in our room looked out to the sea, and it had a wonderful view of the steamships on the horizon. An even more picturesque view opened up from the latrine, which was a hundred feet higher up the slope. Whoever reached it forgot the reason for coming there, getting lost in the view. In the daytime, such climbing was quite pleasant, but in night darkness, one could do it only with a lantern.

In the beginning, the stern and strict Grandma Dusya demanded that Vera. follow many house rules. But soon Grandma became so attached to our girl that she let her do anything she wanted. However, our Vera. became even better friends with GrandpaStepan. They often went to feed the hens and the rabbits together. One day one of the rabbits named Borka fell ill and died. Our Verusha. demanded a full burial. There was a cemetery up by the latrine and I found a piece of marble slab there. I used it to make a gravestone on which I carved Borka's name with a chisel. Vera took care of the grave of her rabbit all the years that we stayed there.

The Georgian feast deserves special description. The pleasant warm climate and fertile land contributed to the abundance of fruits and vegetables and also to the good heartedness of the people who lived in such a fertile land. It seemed to me that one could just poke a bare stick in any place, and it soon would rout, sprout and bear fruit. Vast vineyards everywhere lead to huge bottles of homemade wine in every house. The same is true for meat and dairy products. Most homes had some sort of livestock, and if wealthy, people would also have cattle. This, in turn, resulted in good food and drink. So, the Georgian feast had no equal. Over several seasons in Kashtak, we managed to make quite a few friends, who treated us like close ones. That meant that a lot of very tasty food and excellent freshly made wine accompanied every visit to "new relatives." Almost every garden had wonderful grapes and, accordingly, almost every gardener had large 20-liter bottles of homemade wine in the cellar. Besides, very many people made grape vodka resembling Italian grappa. Georgians call this delicacy "chacha." Every host took offence if we did not pay enough attention to the family's refreshment: he regarded the amount of food and drink as a measure of respect for himself and his family.

As far as wine was concerned, this applied primarily to men; women drank much less. I had special difficulties with drinking in Georgia because of the tradition of long series of toasts in honor of the many generations of both living and deceased relatives, both of our hosts and our own. It was in Georgia that I received my higher education in the art of toasting. My Tanyusha behaved selflessly during such visits, trying to drink from my glass when the hosts would not notice. This way she tried to share the "burden" of the visit with me so that I could go home on my own feet. However, even with her help, it was sometimes impossible to avoid drinking too much, especially when meeting our good friend Boris L Pirveli, the chairperson of the local collective farm. On one of those embarrassing days, little Vera told our friends about what had happened, *"We went to visit uncle Boria, and then at night daddy slept badly and coughed out of the window..."*

However, even when the urge to cough out of the window did not go away in the morning after a fiesta with next boris pirveli there were places in the Caucasus where one could get help. This wonderful remedy for those who drank a lot of alcohol, has existed since ancient times and was popular not only throughout the Caucasus but throughout the world. I personally experienced it with success in the capital of Georgia, Tbilisi. In the 12th century the dish was invented in Armenia. I am not sure whether there is a word in English but in Georgian, they call it "khash." Ancient historians said that Hayk the Patriarch, the legendary founder of the Armenian nation, and Kartlos, the legendary ancestor of Georgians, were brothers. Maybe it is why both cultures share the common tradition of the khash ceremony. Khash is a fatty meat soup with garlic, which must boil for 6–8 hours. Therefore, those places that cook khash begin cooking it in the evening in order to have the first customers early in the morning. Proper khash in Georgia should always go with a shot of chacha. That is why the English translation of "taking khash" sounds like the funny phrase: "taking a hair of the dog that bit you." How strong the hypocrisy in us is: most Russian pages on the Internet shyly hold back this magical power and purpose of khash. Sometime even worse, they call khash the favorite dish of men in the morning (?!). This seems to me an euphemism for the phrase: "All men are drunkards."

Whenever we returned from Kashtak to Moscow, our Georgian "relatives" showered us with gifts of the sunny land in such quantities that we could hardly bring them home. Even little Verusha. carried on her shoulders a backpack full of wonderful food, which was almost impossible to see in Moscow. In relation to these gifts, it is impossible not to recall some Soviet absurdities we had to face.

Georgians always have been famous for supplying Russian and international markets with mandarins, grapes, wine, and grapes vodka. In our time, Soviet collective farms, even in a place as blessed as Georgia, were a dismal sight. The paltry wages of the collective farmers completely deprived the gardeners of any interest in working on the collective farm. Most of people preferred to work in their private gardens and sell the products in the markets. As a result, collective farms could not compete with the private market at all.

The authorities tried to remedy this situation with Soviet methods. At the height of the season for these products, authorities did not allow private individuals to sell their products at collective farm markets. As a result, individual sales became criminal fraud. At first, we were completely puzzled why no one offered mandarins, grapes or alcoholic drinks made of grapes at Sukhumi market. Then our Georgian friends told us that all this was on sale, but under the counter. When you walked in the market and saw a little branch of grapes or a mandarin on the counter next to the scales, as if for the vendor's personal consumption, we were taught to ask in a whisper whether this was for sale. If he nodded yes, we were to tell him quietly how much we wanted and it would be measured under the counter, put it in an opaque bag, and we would be told the price. Also there was a way to buy wine and chacha in the same way. To Tanya and me it was sad to use such tricks, so we limited ourselves to the gifts of our friends.

However, the authorities did not stop there. Checkpoints were rampant at all border crossings into Georgia, as well as at the airport, checking what people took out of the republic. Our Georgian "relatives" told us a story in the spirit of Babel's "Odessa Stories." Enterprising Georgians came up with an interesting way to get their harvest out of the republic at the height of the mandarin season. They stuffed a large coffin with tangerines, dressed up in mourning clothes and staged a funeral procession that left Georgia safely.

This internal customs inspection had touched us before when we were flying from Sukhumi to Moscow. We had also to do some tricks. We would pour wine and chacha from bottles into jars and throw a couple of pieces of apple into them. Then, at the checkpoint, this would successfully pass as "compote for the baby." As for mandarins, our Verusha. was their carrier. We stuffed them in a non-transparent plastic bag into her backpack, and it was passed as "food for the child." The addition of "for the baby" worked like magic. Georgians, as a rule, are extraordinarily child loving and would do anything for children. Our curly-haired child with the little backpack, who always traveled in jeans, endearingly touched them all. That is why more than once at the airport there was this conversation: "*Boy or girl?*" When Tanya answered: "*Girl,*" the reaction was usually, "*Why?*" But it never occurred to anyone to check the belongings of a child.

There was another place in Georgia apart from Kashtak that we loved and where Tanya and Vera went for a couple of years. It was the composers' Creative House in Borjomi. There, too, they acquired "relatives" who brightened up the lives of both of them. I wanted to mention this spa town to tell about a remarkable episode that happened there.

In Georgia there is the cave monastery settlement, the fortress of the 12th century Vardzia, built by the father of the legendary queen of Georgia, Tamara. An excursion to this interesting place was organized for the residents of the Creative House. As a little girl, the queen played in the caves of the then unfinished monastery. The underground complex included 600 rooms, which housed churches, chapels, cells, storerooms, treasury, refectories, and baths. The complex was 160 feet deep in the rock and had 8 floors. Interestingly, in the 12th century, a strong earthquake destroyed much of the complex, and it was later conquered by Turkey in the 16th century. By order of the conquerors, the dead and wounded monks were burnt in the monastery. A thick layer of soot covered the walls and protected the frescos and drawings from age and damage. In the 19th century, after the annexation of Georgia by the Russian Empire, Vardzia was liberated from Turkey, and the Orthodox Greeks restored monastic life there. The Soviet regime established in Georgia in 1921 abolished monasticism and the place became desolate. In 1938, the Vardzia Complex was declared a reserve-museum. In the 1980s, the Patriarch-Catholicos of Georgia Ilia II began a struggle for the revival of monastic life in Vardzia. In the late 1980s, he celebrated the first Divine Liturgy in the monastery. Today Vardzia is a functioning monastery, although the number of brethren is much smaller than in previous centuries.

Tanyusha signed herself and Vera up for this interesting trip. As the settlement is located in the USSR border zone, passport data was required for the registration in order to get the passes. A week after signing up, the passes came for everyone who signed up except for my girls and they were denied the right to go. This was a reminder to us that the KGB does not doze off even in such a warm and welcoming place as Georgia. However, Georgia is not Russia. One of our newly acquired Georgian "relatives," upon learning of this development, literally went berserk and said, "*No, there will be no such thing in our Georgia!*" We do not know what he did, but a couple of weeks later Tanya and Vera received passes and joined the tour. It is wonderful that despite the suppression by the Soviet Government of the national freedoms in Georgia, there were people, like our friend who got the passes for my girls, who never lost the belief that the country still belonged to them, and who were able to prove it in practice and achieve the realization of their principles. I only was very disappointed that because of my work I could not go with them to such an interesting place.

WEDDING IN UPPER SVANETIA

Svanetia, one of the highest historical regions of Georgia, is located on the southern slopes of the central part of the Main Caucasus Range. The northern border of Upper Svanetia runs along the ridge itself with peaks Shkhara (17,060 feet) and Ushba (15,387 feet). We call people living in Svanetia Svans. Censuses before the 30s they considered this ethnic group as a separate nation, but later they were included in the Georgian population, although they have their own language, different from the Georgian language. The ancient geographer and historian Strabo wrote of them: "*The Svans are a mighty people and, I think, they are the bravest and most courageous people in the world. They were always at peace with the neighboring peoples.*" The Svans have never had serfdom. Ptolemy and Appius described Svans as hospitable, enlightened and strong. Many Georgians consider Svanetia the most picturesque part of their country. In Svanetia they say, *"Whoever comes to Georgia without having been to Svanetia has not seen the real Georgia!"* My Tanyusha and I have been to Svanetia, so we can proudly consider that we have seen the real Georgia.

There has never been love between the Soviets and the Svans since the early days when these mountain people got under the Russian rule. The Svans were always a very peaceful people, and yet in 1921, after their succession into the Soviet Union, the outrage of the Svans grew into an armed uprising against the Bolshevik government of Georgia. As Wikipedia now reports, the people were discontent with the arbitrariness and injustice of the new authorities, the undignified treatment of people, and the national and social oppression. In response, the Soviet government organized well-armed, punitive detachments to crush the *"political bandits raised by the Mensheviks to fight the Soviet power"*. By the end of the year, these detachments had received artillery and aviation. The forces has become unequal at all. The army of the big country confronted the partisans, and the Soviet military brutally suppressed the uprising by mercilessly shooting most of the organizers and activists. After this came the repression of the civilian population.

Opposite the house of our Belarusian elderly lived our local friend, a simple Svanetian woman named Zina who was very fond of us. I do not remember her surname; let us call her Zina Svan. Her family lived in upper Svanetia, in one of the villages located on the highest ridge, not far from the highest mountain in Georgia, Shkhara. One of her relatives was celebrating a wedding and Zina asked us to accompany her there in the ceremony. Her native village was about 62 miles up a winding mountain road from Kashtak. As a result, the journey took four hours.

Going and returning the same day back made no sense, not to mention it was probably unsafe. The feast up the mountain went on, unabated, day and night for several days, but Zina arranged everything for us so that we could go home the next day. She touchingly took care of both the roundtrip private bus ride, and the overnight stay up there. We were young and healthy at the time and decided not to pass up chance to visit such a special place. Both Tanya and I were happy we did it and we will not forget this trip for the rest of our lives.

The journey both there and back on the small bus was a special adventure in itself! Please do not condemn me for my bad memory, about some details I may mix up, whether they happened while climbing up or returning down back to Kashtak. We started right from our gate. The bus had to pick up a few more people along the way and then started climbing up along the foothills of the ridge. When we reached these people, we were in for a surprise in the best Georgian traditions. At each stop, as others joined us, they immediately set up the table next to the bus and invited everyone in the bus for refreshments. As usual, the table, covered with a white tablecloth, was hardly visible under all the viands and bottles. So we would have few stops with drinks and snacks before proceeding up the serpentine road.

More than 35 years have passed since I visited Svanetia, and I really hope that the roads there have improved. Then the roads were not for the faint-hearted. They were very narrow, very winding, with walls on both sides: one rising steeply upwards and the other plunging precipitously into an abyss. Even now, when I think back to this journey, I feel a little queasy. I take my hat off in reverence to the Svan drivers. They are virtuosos of their trade and extraordinarily courageous people. These drivers astounded both of us, Tany and me. Svans make jokes about their roads. "*A good road in Svanetia is a road from which you have a chance not to fall into an abyss.*" In the winter snow season all the roads like that are closed, and villages such as the one where the wedding took place, are simply cut off from the rest of the world. .

During the few hours of the serpentine ascent in Svanetia, we were scared out of our wits. Even the unimaginably beautiful scenery around us did not always help us cope with our fear. What was particularly helpful was the amazingly friendly and joyful attitude of the people in the bus. They were all in good spirits and infected us with them. Nevertheless, when the driver finally announced that we were stopping partway up the mountain to get rest and stretch, we all got very excited. Our excitement turned to joy as we realized that we had been met by another car sent down to us from the village far above with a meal of HOT meat pies before we reached the wedding. It was just like a magical fairy tale. Life became beautiful again. Having had a drink and a snack, we passed the final, not so terrible part of our route and drove triumphantly into the village. The word "triumphant" I used here not figuratively, but literally we were delivered right into the arms of the merry people who were already well into their wedding feast.

To call the village picturesque was an understatement. The village was nestled in a picturesque narrow green valley fringed with snowy mountains that looked like they were covered with lace. When the snow glistened in the sun, the lace seemed golden. We got off the bus and, like Pushkin's Onegin, we found ourselves dropped straight from the ship into the ball. Dozens of tables were on the grass, and our bus stopped ten feet away from one of them. Before we knew it, total strangers seated us at a table, filled our glasses, and endless viands were poured onto our plates. All around the feast was going on in full swing. Some were sitting at the table, some were walking around, some singing, and some dancing. Neither before, nor after, have I ever seen such a mass hurricane of merriment and joy, in which hundreds of people were involved.

The picture of the feast we attended would not be complete without mentioning the incredible abundance and variety of food and drink on the tables, which were literally bursting at the seams. Especially for this wedding, an ox, most likely several rams, goats, pigs, as well as countless chickens, geese, and rabbits, lost their heads. All types of meat were served in two forms: one: on their own, in large, enameled basins, used for washing in Russia, and second: as a filling for all kinds of pies and pirozhki, as well as ravioli. Wine and chacha poured down like rivers. If you put together such an excited trip and then gastronomic attack, inexperienced guests like us, become so excited that they are unable to concentrate even on the major things. Neither Tanya nor I could describe how the bride and the groom, and their families looked. Wow, we forgot completely that we had come to A WEDDING!

Obviously, we were absolutely stunned and overwhelmed by the experience. By evening, we felt mortally tired, but we had somewhere to stay for the night. We decided that we, probably, overdid our day's quota of fun, and it was time to find those, with whom we were arranged to stay the night. Some nice people escorted us to the house of a very beautiful middle-aged woman who turned out to be very pleasant to talk to. She had an intelligent and educated speech, which we did not expect to hear on the crest of such a high ridge, remote from all civilization. She turned out to be a teacher in the local school. All members of her family found themselves exiled to this place after the Upper Svanetia massacre of the Mensheviks during the uprising of 1921. Though we were really exhausted, we enjoyed talking to her late into the night.

When we left the house the next morning, the feast was still going on full speed, as if the night had never happened. Once again, we got chance to aware of what strong people the Swans are. We touched again the unceasing gastronomic binge as our breakfast. After that, we got ready to take a multi-hour ride through places of indescribable beauty. We went to pack our bags to join a group of people who had to leave this wonderful place and take a bus down to the foot of the ridge to get back to everyday life.

We naively thought that the way back along the familiar mountain road would be easier, without taking into account the local color and traditions. Our bus companions were in a great mood and continued to celebrate on the way. No difficulties and dangers of the road ever prevented them from singing, cheering and even dancing (!?) in the bus aisle, from which our hearts sank with fear. Thank God, we got safely to Kashtak, happy and eternally grateful to our Georgian "relatives" for this fabulous trip.

HOUSE OF THE MERRY BEGGARS

Another way of hiding our child from the outrages of the refusenik life was the dachas near Moscow, which we rented for the summer. One of them belonged to our friend Tzilia Reitburd's and was in the suburban settlement Pushkino near the Yaroslavl railway. A second was the dacha that we rented in the writer's village of Krasnaya Pakhra, near the town of Troitsk on Kaluga Road. The third was the dacha that we rented in the academic village of Perkhushkovo, near the station of the same name near the Belorussian railroad.

All these dachas were a refuge for us, but to a much lesser extent than trips to places far away from Moscow. There were few reasons for it. First, they were usually uncomfortable and miserable to live in, since we could not afford to rent comfortable accommodation. In most cases, in an attempt to save money, we did not rent a room in the main dacha, but in a small annexe. Most of our dachas did not have gas supply, and we had to cook using gas cylinders, electric stoves or even kerosene stoves. Secondly, the dacha residents around us were not much different from Muscovites, so there was no change in the socio-political climate that all the refuseniks were striving for. Moreover, after the Gorky "Summerfolk", the country developed a disdainful attitude towards the meaningless intellectuals who aspired to a quiet and peaceful bourgeois life at the dachas. Thirdly, in the suburbs of Moscow at that time the supply was disgusting, and we had to bring all the food products from Moscow. All this made our already difficult life even more difficult. Nevertheless, Tanya would manage to organize our life in each of the three places in a way that wil magically turn it into something wonderful. As a result Verusha. would have always a good time

The dacha in Pushkino was wonderful because we lived there FREE: Tzilechka did not want to charge us. In terms of nature, it was the poorest place of the three, and there was not much room to walk. However, the bonus attached to our Pushkino dacha was that Tsilia's daughter Nora Samarov and her family lived in the same village. She had two children at the time: Mitya and Borya. Max was not even in the picture yet. This fact created a reason for endless jokes that near Vera lived two nice suitors who could make her future choice between them a difficult one. When Norochka came to our house, there were shouts: *"Vera, come quickly to meet your mother-in-law!"* Such a neighborhood, indeed, was wonderful. It was not often possible to live so close to the closest people. Besides, Nora's husband Sasha was a booklover, and Tanya with pleasure taught him to read English with the original of V. Nabokov's memoirs "Speak Memory." It was then that she told me and repeats it to this day, that she never had such a capable pupil as Sasha Samarov. To deserve such a praise from a very strict teacher, which Tanya was and still is, was a significant complement time.

Dacha in Krasnaya Pakhra was nice because right outside our fence, there was a small but pleasant forest, and we liked to walk there. In the same settlement, here was also the dacha of Oscar Feltsman. His son Volodya Feltsman and his wife Anya lived there a lot, and communication with them made our life very brightened. I told a little about it in the chapter "Interplanetary trips".

One of interesting things for me about our life in Pakhra was that Vera had an admirer there. He was a middle-aged man who we rarely saw sober. He was a local amateur angler and would often parade down our street passing our fence to go fishing and back home. I had built a sandbox not far from this part of our fence for our girl and she would play there often. One day, walking along our street, he saw our curly-haired Verochka through a fence in the sand-box, stopped and could not take his eyes off her, repeating one and the same word in amazement: "*Pushkin!... Pushkin!... Pushkin!...*" The result was hilarious: we called this drunkard Pushkin amongst ourselves, and he, in his turn, called Vera "Pushkin." After that day, he could never pass by our house, if Verusha was in the sandbox, without stopping and expressing his admiration. His catches were not rich, one or two small fish, and from then on, he would always bring them to Vera.

At that time, our girl was already well acquainted with Pushkin's fairy tales. She remembered many of them by heart and recited many with great enthusiasm. It was then that she gave us her own, more comprehensible than Pushkin's interpretation of the line from "The Tale of Tsar Saltan": "*...I see, my swan is amusing herself.*" When she was reciting the tale, she gave us her own version of the line: "*...I see, my swan is scratching herself.*" This funny perusal of our daughter can be explained with phonetic similarity of two Russian verb third person singular forms: *amuses—teshitsia* and *scratches—cheshitsia*. We had no television set in our house, but when we were visiting our friends, Vera. watched with our hosts a program about Pushkin's life. When our impressionable child came home, she passionately said to Tanya, "*Mom, bad news, it turns out that Pushkin has passed away!*" We had the impression that in our Verochka's mind, the great Pushkin and the dacha Pushkin had become one person in time and space.

The owners of the dacha on Pakhra never lived with us, they usually rented out all the rooms of the big house. We saw the owners' representative a few times to talk to him about the financial side of our relationship. The name of this representative was Varlen. Later we found out, it was abbreviation for the name "VlAdimiR LENin." He was a lethargic type, and Tanya immediately came up with the different interpretation for the abbreviation: "VARiony LENin" (first Russian adjective is for English "cooked"). As a result, in English Tanya's interpretation is "Cooked Lenin". After just a few short meetings with this man, we were unable to form any certain opinion about him. Probably, he was overcooked.

The owners rented out all the rooms in the house except one small dark room that looked like a filthy storeroom. The junk in that room was everywhere on the floor, like a pile of garbage, and covered with years of dust. It was clear that no one had looked in here in a very long time. In this junk, Tanya's eagle eye immediately noticed several books in very poor condition. She was not squieamish to look, and among the Soviet political trash, she suddenly found in a dirty pile one of her favorite books, "A History of England for Children" by Charles Dickens, published in the late 19th century in London in the "World of Charles Dickens" series. It reminded me Krylov's fable, "The Cock and the Pearl Seed."

Tearing up the dung heap,
The rooster found the Pearl Seed.

The funniest thing is that the owners of the house, judging by the abuse of the pearl, which they possessed, probably, like Krylov's rooster, were perplexed:

What you can do with it?
What an empty thing!
I think it is silly
To prais this grain high.
I, really, would be a lot happier
To find a barley grain instead.
Though it does not look so great,
But at least it is nourishing

Tanya lovingly cleaned her favorite book of dirt as much as she could, and the embossed gold of the century before at last gleamed on the emerald-colored hard cover. The fable of the pearl goes back to the times B.C., and the expression "pearls found in dung" was also popular then. The book moved into our room and lived with us until the end of summer. When we moved away from the cottage in autumn, Tanya could not part with the book and sinned by taking it with her and, this way, rescued a treasure. Today this gem of Dickens graces our bookshelf in Boston.

Of the three dachas, the one in Perkhushkovo had the most uncomfortable accommodations, but my Tanyusha managed to keep Vera in particularly good company there. Our dacha was in an academic settlement and belonged to one of the "Chief Jews of the Soviet Union", the historian Isaac Mints, who spared no effort to curry favor with the Bolsheviks. Here I am trying to construct a parody of the name of the highest award of the Soviet Union: the "Hero of the Soviet Union." This man not only composed and edited the fundamental works on the history of the Revolution, the history of the Civil War, and the history of the Communist Party, but also exposed horrors of the world's imperialism wherever he could. A special merit of this "great scholar" was his active participation in the Cosmopolitan Campaign of 1947–1948 and in the Doctors' Case of 1953. It was just he, who collected the signatures of high-ranking and famous Jews in a letter that denounced "murderers in white coats" to assure the Party of the loyalty of the Jewish people. The Soviet authorities, while pinching him from time to time for his Jewish roots, appreciated his diligence: he was a Hero of Socialist Labor, a Knight of three Orders of Lenin, the Order of the Patriotic War, two Orders of the Red Banner of Labor, twice a winner of the Stalin Prize and a winner of the Lenin Prize. He died in 1991, still without deserving the right to have his grave at the Novodevichy Cemetery. His grave was in the Jewish cemetery in Vostryakovo.

On the Mints's property, there was a large house where his daughter's family lived, and a separate small house, most likely for the housekeeper, which we rented. We lived in a small world; in 1970, when Juli Daniel was freed from prison, he was at first not allowed to live in Moscow and its surroundings, and

Our Vera is playing recorder at the performance of merry beggars

LIFE THIRD: MY EFFORTS TO EMIGRATE FROM THE SOVIET UNION

he settled in Kaluga. After this ban was lifted, he rented a large house on the Mints property in Perkhushkovo. As to our "house", it included a room and a small, glazed walkway and unheated terrace. To get to the room where Tanya's mother and Vera slept, we had to cross the terrace. Tanya and I slept on the walkway on a small single mattress that was barely big enough for one person. To fit both of us, we had to lie on our sides, pressed against each other. I creatively extended the bed using old crates from the owners' junk shed that I covered with several layers of our old cotton blanket. Thus, I resolved this difficult problem. Tanyusha and I were still young then and much less choosy.

Very soon, through Tanya's efforts, our cottage became an attraction for children of Vera's age. They used to rush to our barn, which they liked more than their huge, luxurious houses, so we had a busy life. The cottage owner's grandchildren lived those years in the big house with a caregiver. The funny thing was that they would spend their daytime and evenings with us as well. The children read together with Tanya, made music, put on plays, and played games. Tea parties would take place regularly even though we did not have a room with a roof big enough for such gatherings. Therefore, the tea was drunk on the grass when the weather was fine. It would always bother our Galyusha that we did not offer anything sweet with the cups of tea. It was beyond our means to serve sweets, but Tanya found a way by simply boiling water with sugar. ridiculous it is, the children liked our "dessert" better than any fancy jam. We did not have enough cups either, so Tanya made it a ritual that the children would come to us with their own cups. When we would arrive from Moscow on our Little Froggy, a joyful cry would go through the whole settlement: "*Tanya has arrived!!!*" Very soon after that, you could see children with cups in their hands running towards us through the streets.

Someone, looking at our children's gatherings, called our Perkhushkovo barn "the house of merry beggars." In our illiteracy, both Tanya and I thought that the phrase was that person's concoction, and we borrowed that name for our dacha in Perkhushkovo. Only recently, I learned that the phrase "House of Merry Beggars" was the title of a tragic story by the Soviet writer Grigory Belykh. It was his first story, published in 1930, when the author was just 24. The novel describes a real house, located at 7 Ismailovsky

Avenue in St. Petersburg, where he lived all his short life with the boys who lived in this house during the pre-revolutionary years. In 1935, Belykh was arrested on the false accusation of counterrevolutionary activity. The real reason for his arrest, most likely, was his "wrong" poem about Stalin. In 1938, he died of tuberculosis in a prison hospital. After Stalin's death, in 1957, Grigory Belykh got his postmortem exoneration because of *"lack of a committed crime"*...

BIBLE STORIES

For more than a century of militant atheism and militant, brutal and intransigent communist ideology, morality in the country had tragically declined, and the literature on ethics had been reduced to mere political blather. In 1981, I found a book "Bible Stories" by an English children's writer and actor, David Kosoff. The author hosted regular programs for children on London TV using the Bible to help them understand what was good and what was bad. Apparently, the book was a great success with English children. The first edition was printed in London in 1968, and my copy was printed in London in 1975, already the tenth (!?) edition. Such success was understandable. The book retold the Old Testament stories in an entertaining form for children with an emphasis on the problems of morality. In addition, these stories are the basis of many of the greatest works of music and art in the European cultural and historical heritage. I liked the book for its kindness. I love translation work, and I wanted to translate the book into Russian so, that it will become available to Russian children.

The first person I shared this idea with after Tanya was our close friend Tzilia Reitburd, who also loved the idea. She approved strongly of my plan and advised me to start working on the translation as soon as possible, and when the text is on the table, we will find where and how to publish it. My Tanya liked the Kosoff's book, too, supported the idea of the translation and even promised to help me. I think there is no better stylist in language than my Tanyusha, so I was happy to receive her promis. Encouraged by the support of two such talented women, I threw myself into my work.

At the same time, I reached out to David Kosoff. I told him who I was, how much I liked his book and explained that Soviet chil-

LIFE THIRD: MY EFFORTS TO EMIGRATE FROM THE SOVIET UNION

dren did not have books like his. I also told him about my dream to translate his book into Russian and told him how difficult it would be to publish and distribute it in the USSR. In addition, I explained that even if all this succeeded, any royalties would be out of the question. After that, I asked him if he might to let me attempt such a charitable publication.

I knew that the KGB did not like my contact with foreigners, as they repeatedly told me in our "friendly" conversations. So, I asked my American friends, Bobby and Phil Brown, who had diplomatic immunity, to send my letter to David in London. I will never forget how much these wonderful people did for us during their time in Moscow for which I am eternally grateful to them. In this case, it seemed to me that Phil, as the son of a pastor, was especially pleased to help.

The Browns' mail worked perfectly. David received my letter and, again through my friends, sent the sweetest reply. My letter caught him at a very difficult time: his son had recently died, and I thought it was bad time to worry about me. Nevertheless, Mr. Kosoff fully understood and responded to everything I wrote. He asked me not to think about any royalties. He said he would be happy if my undertaking was a success and that the book appeared in Russian. I was inspired. I went to work like crazy and Tanya helped me a great deal. A few months later, the draft of the translation was ready, and I rushed to look for someone to print it.

In Moscow, there was a Russian Orthodox priest, Alexander Men. He was the Father Superior of the Purification Church in Novaya Derevnya, a neighborhood of Pushkino near Moscow. In my circle of friends and acquaintances, he was considered one of the most educated members of the Russian Orthodox Church. He wrote books and articles on theology, on the history of Christianity and other religions, on the foundations of Christian doctrine, and on Orthodox worship. I had read several of his books, and I liked his interpretations. I knew that Father Alexander had been attacked, even within the Church, for his ecumenical views and I liked ecumenical ideas and happy to see him in Kosoff's book. It always seemed to me that the purpose of religion was not to divide, but to unite people. I felt that there was no better person to show Kosoff's book and ask for help with its publication. Now, how could I see him?

Many members of Moscow's intellectual elite regularly visited the Purification Church in Pushkino and knew Father Alexander personally. I was acquainted with some of them. I was very close to the Polish linguist Elia Janus, who helped me in my study of Polish when I studied J. Korczak. A Catholic herself, she nevertheless had great respect for Father Alexander and, being in Moscow, visited his parish regularly. Elia, was a special person whom one never had to ask for help. She knew about my passion for Kosoff's book, she encouraged it and volunteered to arrange our meeting. And she really did it.

One day soon afterwards, I happily went with the manuscript of the Bible Stories in hand for an audience with Father Alexander. He made a most favorable impression on me. The meeting was short. He asked me to leave the manuscript with him and promised Elia to let her know when he was ready to see me again. I was triumphant, I was also very naïve. I believed the job was done and everything goes my way. However, it occurred to be not as simple as that.

At my next meeting with Father Alexander, I was deeply disappointed. He said that he liked the book, but, unfortunately, he could not help me because it was not a Christian book, but a Jewish book. I was speechless and unable to continue the conversation. I left him, frankly, very angry. In my irritation, I foolishly said: "*If even such people also...*"

Somehow, I did not understand it all at once. I did not know much about Father Alexander at the time. He lived in the same country as me, where there was only one approved religion, Communism. He walked on the edge of a knife, and he behaved very bravely. I did not know then that he was Galich's godfather, and that the poet received the blessing of Father Alexander before leaving Russia. I am ashamed of my reaction now. I know now that he embodied the best of Christianity in Russia, an openness to ANYONE regardless of his/her views. I now know that his church in Pushkino would warmly welcome Catholics and Jews alike. Today I understand that he tried to carry his understanding of Christianity to people as much as he could. However, you cannot leap above yourself. His understanding was deeper than that of most of his colleagues, who went so far in their orthodoxy as to call him a heretic and not recommend reading his books. There were priests who argued that his calls for a better understanding of Judaism were a sale of the soul to the devil. Certainly, he could not support the publication of a book on the Old Testament. Any dissent in Russia always resulted in punishment, and the religious have never been an exception. Alas, you cannot go against the wall! Later I learned that the KGB had a case against him. In 1964, KGB agents searched his house. In 1974, KGB chief Yuri Andropov initiated an investigation against him. In 1985, a plan was ready to prosecute him criminally, but it did not happen, only thanks to the patronage of Metropolitan Juvenaly.

This man's life ended tragically. It happened two years after we left the country, in 1990, in a very Russian way. When Father Alexander was in a hurry to get to the church for liturgy, they sent assassins. These beasts hacked him to death with an axe. As usual, despite personal orders from the President of the USSR and the Chairman of the Presidium of the Supreme Soviet of Russia to investigate the crime, the murder remained unsolved.

After I recovered from my failure with Russian Orthodoxy, I decided to talk to a Russian "expert" on Judaism, since it was about the Old Testament stories. The other Christian denominations, it seemed to me, were not worth approaching: their views were noticeably narrower, and they were much less tolerant. At the beginning of the 1980s, one could notice a religious revival among Jews in Moscow. It was mainly among those who had either already started the emigration process or who were seriously thinking about it. Many people in this group had never practiced Judaism before. From my observations, these individuals seemed like zealots, which scared me away. On the other hand, approaching the synagogue with my problem made no sense at all. The rabbis of the synagogue of those days were members of the Anti-Zionist Committee of the Soviet Public, established in 1983 and managed and financed by the communists and the KGB.

I decided to show the manuscript of my translation of the book to Ilya Essas, then the leader of the Religious Jews of Refusal in Moscow. My fears proved correct: the second attempt turned out to be much more unpleasant than the first. This time I had to listen to the humiliating admonitions of the high dignitary. *"How could you even touch a material about which you have no idea? All these questions are ten times more complicated than you think! You are so arrogant to comment on them! Even more, you went to the wrong place. The book you tried to translate has nothing to do with Judaism. It is a Christian book!"* This time I was not angry, I was just disgusted. I took the manuscript and hurried away, saying, *"Not, in this country anymore"*. I felt that I have to forget these attempts as a waste of time. In addition, somewhere inside me I even felt a deep satisfaction. When I considered both conversations together, I realized that I had chosen the right book to translate because it stood ABOVE the differences between Judaism and Christianity. That was what I liked about Kosoff's book.

However, the problem remained unsolved, so I went back to our problem-solver, Tzilechka. She knew Ilya, well and took it with humor. *"Don't worry, we will think of something"*, and she did. Again, her friends in Israel helped her find a publisher for the book. That was the publishing house "Tarbut," which means "Culture" in Hebrew. In 1984, the book was published, and I happily told the author, David Kosoff about it. My American friends helped me to bring some of the books from Israel to Moscow, so I had the pleasure of giving copies to my friends.

I was very happy, despite an act of political correctness, which existed in Israel too. The Israeli publishers did NOT print my very small preface, which included the name of Christ, the words Bible, Old Testament, New Testament, and Christianity. I suppose it couldn't be helped. In this world, you have to pay something for everything. There is no such thing as a free lunch!

I want to close the chapter on "Bible Stories" with a funny and simultaneously sad episode. Vera was eight years old. We had a sleepover with her friend Nadya, the daughter of our close friends Lenochka Smorgunov and Yuri Freidin. The girl was named after Nadezhda Mandelstam. At that time, our Vera had problems with pronunciation of hard "R." There are two words in Russian that sound very similar: "podrushka" (in English "female friend") and "podushka" (in English "pillow"). When she introduced Nadya to our acquaintances, she would loose sound "R" and it sounded: *"Here is my pillow Nadya."*

Tanya was putting the girls to bed in the evening and was about to read my translation of the Kosoff's book to them. When the "pillow" Nadya knew that Tanya was going to read them stories from the Bible, she flatly refused to listen and crawled under the covers. Tanya, of course, was quite surprised. After all, our friends were not the kind of people who considered religion to be *"the opium for the people"*: a definition of religion that became widely known in the atheist world thanks to Karl Marx, who used it in his work "Toward a Critique of Hegel's Philosophy of Right" (1843). How could it be that the girl grew up like that? Nevertheless, Tanya did not let on and said, *"Okay, let's do this: I'm going to start reading. Whoever wants to, listens, and whoever does not want to, does not."* Tanya began to read but kept watching the mound under the blanket. Soon the mound started moving, and at its foot, there was a crevice between the blanket and the bed. After a little while, Tanya could see Nadya s attentive face through the gap.

STARVING CAMELS

In 1983, Tanya Velikanov finally finished her camp term after which she was sent into exile in Western Kazakhstan on the Mangyshlak Peninsula which juts into the Caspian Sea. A year later, I visited her and spent some wonderful, quiet, healing days together. They were wonderful because two of us were together all the time, it was quiet, and nobody prevented us from enjoying each other. They were also great because they allowed me to see once again that Tanya is an extraordinary person. The four years that she had spent in Stalin's gulag had not broken her. I found her just as I had always known her. She was still beautiful, benevolent, and wise, and she had no bitterness towards her tormentors. Amazingly, it felt like she and I just never separated. To me this is the highest achievement of the human spirit, unattainable and incomprehensible to the monsters who tried to punish and change her.

Tanya and I talked a lot about life in Moscow, about our mutual friends and acquaintances. Before our apartment exchange and moving to the new one, we lived with her sister Asya in the same building. We were able to communicate a lot and became very close then. Tanya knew about this, of course. By the time, I went to visit Tanya in Kazakhstan, Asya was stricken with breast cancer, which she was heroically trying to fight. Our conversations pretty much revolved around Asya and her state of health. This was back in 1984.

When I found myself in Kazakhstan, we were already in our seventh year of refusal, and our patience was slowly but surely ending. More than once over the years we consulted with the wise Tanya Velikanov about how we should behave in order to leave Russia as soon as possible. She would always advise us to take the loudest, strongest, most irreconcilable position and to burn all the bridges behind us. I think she deliberately sent us the Browns in the hope that they might help our family leave. The Browns were a wonderful gift from her for which we will be forever grateful. It was very typical of our friend, despite the fact that she knew that she herself would never voluntarily leave Russia, she tried to give us all possible help and support. It was amazing, with what understanding and respect she took our decision to emigrate! She taught us a lesson that we will never forget. In our immediate circle, we knew only two people who were like that: she and Verochka Prokhorov. Both of them were convinced that they would never leave, yet both of them were sensitive and kind enough to be sympathetic to our decision.

Of course, when *"Finally, it was just the two of us,"* (quote from Kostia Babitsky's poem and song dedicated to his Tanya) we talked about our leaving, which was central to our lives at the time. Discussing it with Tanya Velikanov was very important to me. I had always had the utmost respect for Tanya Velikanov's opinion. At that time my "incurable optimism," as Tanya Zieman used to put it, was very low and it urgently needed a recharge. Thank God, Tanya Velikanov, during the years in the camp had not changed her former opinion about our departure. We could not even dream about a better recharger. As I write these lines, it is over thirty years since we came to the United States. Tanya Velikanov is no longer with us. How many times over the years have I caught myself missing Velikanov's recharge! Since then, I have not had, and probably never will have a friend and advisor like Tanya Velikanov.

I was carried away in describing my strong emotions connected with our meeting, and I didn't say anything about the place I had come to. It seems to me that it is the feature of our memory, certainly it is of my. I remember in the first place what was dear to me, not the objective historical picture, not the real facts. So back to the place she had been exiled. It was dull, bare, and gray. Not far from the house where she lived was a shop with no more than a scanty assortment of unpalatable goods. The dirty, half-empty shelves held bread, butter, sugar, stale biscuits, macaroni, cigarettes, and vodka. Cardboard boxes were strewn outside the store, like at a junkyard. But I recall unforgettably depressing impression of the wandering around ragged, as if after the fight, camels with sad eyes. The old cardboard attracted them to the shop and they were standing sadly slowly chewing and eating this garbage. I do not know who they belonged to, but they looked homeless. Believe me, homeless camels look ten times more miserable than homeless dogs. Because of their large size, such unfortunate animals gave the place a sense of incredible squalor and poverty. The Soviet authorities chose successfully the place for exile for one of their most dignified women!

During my numerous trips around Russia, I knew that small country shops in the godforsaken corners of the country were often destitute. So, with the help of our mutual friends, I packed a rather large backpack of snacks that might please Tanechka. I had fun putting this backpack together. It was just another proof of how much we all loved this woman and tried to send her the nicest things. Indeed, she was very happy about all of it. As to me, I felt like a happy messenger.

Even my brief sketch of the village, where Velikanov lived, I hope made it possible to understand why, even though I love walking, I did not want to leave the house for a walk. Those few days that I spent with Tanya, we sat in the house and talked, talked and talked. It was wonderful and I loved it. I could have gotten an exit visa any day, which would have meant that I would leave and most likely NEVER will see her again. However, fate had different plans.

Three years later, at the beginning of 1987 in Moscow we buried Tanya's sister Asya Velikanov. At that time, Tanya's exile was nearing its end and a miracle happened: Tanya got permission to come to Moscow from exile for her sister's funeral! No one expected such humanity from the inhuman power. Poor Asya, alas, could not already rejoice this. However, we were very lucky with my Tanyusha: after a long break, both of us managed to see our beloved Tanechka Velikanov in Moscow in Asya's house.

WITH LITTLE FROGY TO THE BALTICS

The biggest trip with our Little Frog was in 1884 to the Baltic region. First, we visited our good friends the Margolis family in Latvia. Tanya taught two of their children, Katja and Misha, English.

We really liked the whole family: the parents, Natasha and Lionya, and the grandmother Marina Shpet. Our Verochka often communicated with these children. I personally had a fondness for Misha's little sister, round-faced Anechka. When we went to visit them, she would follow me and try to call me, pronounced *"Yuy!"* apparently unable to pronounce the sound "R."

Special mention should be made of Vera's friendship with Misha. Little Misha, also had difficulty pronouncing the letter "R." Instead of "Verochka" yt would say "Veitchka." One day Misha, asked Vera for something, but for some reason Vera did not want to do it. At some point, he lost his patience and resolutely said: *"I am addressing you Veitchka! But I could have said Vejka!"* Humor here requires some explanations about Russian suffixes that carry a lot of meaning. The name "Vera" may take two forms: Ver-ochka and Ver-ka. First means "nice Vera" and second, "bad Vera." Misha, tried to underline the difference between the two.

In fact, Misha, was always very gallant with our Vera, and she liked him. Once, during a conversation with Vera, we mentioned that she would grow up, find a husband and would have beautiful children. To this, our girl immediately said, *"I have already found the man. I am going to marry Misha Margolis, ."* You can imagine how surprised Tanya and I were.

We spent glorious days with the Margolis in Latvia. Our friendship with them lasted until we left for America. We really missed them in Boston. One day Lionya came on a business trip to the US and stayed with us. Everything was very nice. However, something happened I still do not understand what. After he left, we got an angry letter from very annoyed Lionya accusing us of having been carried away by our new life and forgetting about our friends in Moscow, which he felt we no longer needed. For this reason, he did not want now to have anything more to do with us. The unkind style of the letter made us feels unable to reach out and mend the relationship. Both Tanya and I were shocked how it was possible to destroy the good things we went through together all at once. However, you cannot force someone to like you. Plus, as far as I know, all the Margolis children left Russia and live today in different foreign countries...

From Latvia, we drove to Estonia to our very dear friends, Sophia Kagan and her daughter Judith. I was lucky to meet many

LIFE THIRD: MY EFFORTS TO EMIGRATE FROM THE SOVIET UNION

wonderful people with the surname Kagan in my circle. This is one of the most important and historically significant Jewish surnames. It belongs to the high priests, the sons of Aaron. When I described my childhood, I talked about my great-uncle Kagan whom I consider to be a man of special distinction. I also loved and revered the Kagans who we visited in Estonia. Finally, Innulia, my brother's first wife's maiden name was Kogan, undoubtedly of the same surname. Wikipedia lists 44 (!?) famous people who have this surname. This list is curious because I found many people I know well in the list, such as the sisters Lilya Brik and Elsa Triole whose maiden name was Kagan. Moreover, this list did not include such names as Kaganov, Kaganovich, Kaganowskiy, Kogans and many other Kagans!

Our dear friends: mother and daughter Kagan

Sophia Kagan was born and raised in Germany, where she met her future husband, who came there from Russia to study. Matvey Kagan was one of the most educated people of his time, a Jewish philosopher and culturologist. In 1918, the Kagans returned to Russia. Sophia for many years was a friend of Marina Tsvetaev's sister Anastasia. Until our departure from Russia, she remembered much about her interesting life, and we were happy listeners of her own stories. Also, she would always take an active part in every discussion of the life and work of her very special daughter. When I learned that Matvey Kagan died in 1937, I feared that the Soviets had finished him off. Fortunately, I was wrong and was happy to learn that this remarkable man died of angina pectoris. this recalled me the words of A. Galich about Boris Pasternak:

> *How proud we bastards are,*
> *That he died in his own bed...*

Matvei Kagan's friendship and scholarly interests connected him with the famous philosopher, literary critic, and intellectual leader Mikhail Bakhtin. Both women often would tell us about this remarkable man, sent into exile by the Bolsheviks. When Matvey Kagan died in Moscow, Mikhail Bakhtin had been released from exile but did not have right to appear in the primary cities. Nevertheless, at the risk of the additional term in prison, he came to Moscow to attend the funeral of his friend and peer.

Sophia's daughter, Judith, worked with Tanya as a latinist at the Foreign Language University. She was a member of the author's brigade that compiled a Latin textbook for humanities universities. She was a translator of the fundamental philosophical and religious works of such famous authors of the late middle Ages as Martin Luther, Thomas More, Erasmus of Rotterdam, and Heinrich Bebel. In addition, Judith inherited from her father a wide interest in the history of Russian culture. She authored the book about Marina Tsvetaev's father, one of Russia's finest men, Ivan Tsvetaev. This scientist-historian, archaeologist, philologist and art historian was the corresponding member of the Petersburg Academy of Sciences, a professor of the Moscow University, a privy councilor, and the founder and the first director of the Alexander III Museum of fine arts of the Emperor at Moscow Imperial University, now the Pushkin State Museum of Fine Arts. Judith also wrote a book about the end of the life of Marina Tsvetaev. In addition to all the above, she did a lot of research on the poetry of Marina Tsvetaev, wrote about her life, and gave lectures on all of this. I never could understand how one person could manage to do so much.

Both of these wonderful women were given to me by my Tanyusha. Both of them, during all the years of our refusal supported us morally in the difficult decision to emigrate and stayed by our sides, unlike many of our good friends. I remember very well when Sophia told us: *"You made the right decision. I can personally imagine that I will live to the end of my life here, but I wouldn't want to die in Russia."* Sadly, it was not destined to happen: in 1994, Sophia died in Moscow and her daughter did not manage to organize her funeral, as her mother wanted. Her grave is in Moscow.

Talking with them was always pleasant and interesting. Sophia would always serve tea. We received from her a wonderful present, a phrase: *"Do not look at tea as a dish of food. Tea is a form of conversation."* During our political conversations, we would agree most often, which was very pleasant. However, Judith often spoke more forcefully, emphatically and uncompromisingly. At the same time, Sophia, agreeing with us, was always softer and more accommodating. It was not by chance that our Verochka Prokhorov called Judith "the fierce Judith."

I recall the story about Judith by her student, Zhenya Sokolov, who was expelled from the University for being politically unreliable. *"Judith was not a dissident in the conventional sense of the word. She was just herself. In my last days in the University, she told me one episode. One day she learned about her appointment as a group propagandist. Judith refuses to do this explaining, that she does not understand what this means. She got an advice to ask the party committee for an explanation. 'Can you imagine, Zhenya,' Judith said to me indignantly. 'They have sent me to the Communist Party Office. But there are some doors, I never try to open: to the men's room and to the Communist Party Office'."*

Putting aside the purely geographical interest in our trip to Estonia, meeting our friends there was, as always, a joy, and the indispensable element of this joy was, as always, tea, which served as a wonderful means for pleasant and interesting conversation. We spent about a week there, which flew by like the blink of an eye.

Our friends lived in the tiny village of Käsmu, which was pleasant and beautiful and populated, according to the Wikipedia, by only 131 people! We took many walks around the village, reveling in the soul and artistic taste that the Estonians showed in the design and decoration of their houses, and in their gardens. It moved me when the master of a house was trying to create a two-colored fence, trying to choose those two colors on different slats (!) for an hour. Compared to the houses in the Russian countryside, each of these houses looked like a work of art. I was just as impressed by the gardens around the houses. When you crossed the border between Estonia and Russia somewhere in the Narva area it seemed as if one was entering another country.

However, I recall very depressing, even shocking impression, left from the walk to the "beach" in Käsmu. On a lovely clear, sunny, windless summer day we headed for the seashore. On the way, we were picking of the incredibly abundant blueberries. After passing a beautiful green stand of pine trees, we came to a narrow strand of very fine, pure yellow-pink sand, behind which shone a very calm turquoise blue sea. Suddenly, something that was hard to believe appeared before our eyes. What a normal person would take for a luxurious beach, looked like a huge concentration camp. Along the whole shoreline, as far as the eye could see, was a barbed wire fence! There was not a single living soul to either side of the barbed wire fence. As for the sea, it too looked quite solitary, I would say, just dead. We could not see a single floating thing in the water, not a man, not a boat, not a steamer. In this labor camp, the sea itself looked to me as a prisoner!

When, in utter shock, we told our friends about our walk to the beach, they explained it. What we had seen was another manifestation of Soviet paranoia. The monstrous fence was to stop people from defecting across the bay to the West by making it impossible to enter the sea from the shore. There was also a prohibition against any kind of boat in the coastal waters.

ALIENS FROM THE LAND OF DOLPHINIA

I have always thought that Novella Matveeva is a very interesting poet, and some of her lines simply fascinated me. It is very difficult to believe, I once read about it, that the poor woman suffered from fear of open space and NEVER could travel. Poet's incredible imagination created such extraordinary places and images. Here I want to quote a line from her poem "Land of Dolphinia", which imprinted in my memory and heart many, many years ago:

> *Wisteria is blooming gently-*
> *It is more delicate than rime...*
> *Somewhere out there is the land of Dolphinia,*
> *Somewhere there is the Kangaroo City.*

These places, invented by Matveyeva, seem to echo Australia probably because of the kangaroos. I have never seen Australia and, most probably, never would. But in my imagination, I saw cheerfully hopping kangaroos surrounded by flowering wisteria, and dolphins merrily swimming through water brightly shining on their backs. Matveyeva reminded us that there was so much more beyond our borders and even beyond our imaginations. Why do we see so little of our lands, know so little of its diverse cultures, speak so few of its many languages?

I recall a sad and funny British anecdote on this subject. Two enlightened women are standing in front of the kangaroo cage in the London Zoo and hear the guide explaining: *"Here is a representative of the aborigines of Australia"*. Upon hearing this, one of the women turns to her mate: *"To think, my beloved niece married one of these!"*

It was 1984, and the Hartmans invited us to their Spasohaus for another music concert. Arthur was a big music lover and knew a lot about music, so the concert was, as usual, very interesting. Actually, in their house in general we were always very happy. However, this evening something special and important for us happened. Hartmans have acquainted us with recently arrived to Moscow new ambassador Ted Pocock and his charming wife Mag (pet form of Magaret). I learned later that Ted's official assignment in Moscow was as Ambassador of the Commonwealth of Australia to the USSR and Mongolia. I was even a little offended, firstly, that there are not only joint sanitary rooms (bathroom + toilet), but also joint ambassadors, and secondly, that Mongolia did not even deserve a full-time ambassador. Nevertheless, both newcomers made the most favorable impression on us. It is funny, but I recall my thinking this very evening: this couple just came from the extraordinary land of Dolphinia, the extraordinary city of Kangaroo, invented by the extraordinary poet Novella Matveyeva. For this reason, they must be extraordinary people. Very soon, indeed, we were convinced that they really were extraordinary. Ted Pocock was a professional diplomat, Australian politician and public figure. He was representing his country in many parts of the world: Cambodia and Vietnam, South Korea and Mongolia, the Soviet Union and Pakistan, France and Belgium. Wherever Ted found himself, he always would show a particularly keen sense of justice, understanding and sympathy for those whose rights were infringed. He always would advocate legal and ethical rather than political correctness irreconcilably. Those who knew him referred to him as a "compassionate diplomat." No political motives either in his life or in his work would justify lying.

During the Vietnam War, in the 1960's when Ted was working in Cambodia, he became suspicious that contrary to official statements received by their embassy, both weapons and Viet Cong military personnel were being moved across the "neutral" Canbodia and Laos into South Vietnam. Ted was not lazy to get behind the wheel of his beloved green Mustang and to drive with his Vietnamese counterpart to the Vietnamese border near the Ho Chi Minh Trail. They both saw evidence that the public statements were false, and Ted's suspicions were valid. After coming back to Canberra, he bravely contradicted the established opinion of his administrators and reported his observations to his government. In doing so, he was able to accurately predict the outcome of the war. His reward was sending by the Australian government special mail to Saigon. Alas, it made little difference. People wanted to believe what they wanted to believe, even when it contradicted the facts. It appeared that that US military experts repeatedly recommended to President Johnson that the Ho Chi Minh Trail be closed as a military communication playing an important role in the war. Each time he strongly objected. It turned out that Ted Pocock was wiser than our President. We do not know how the war might have ended if he had been listened to, but we may have missed the chance to save many American soldiers on both sides of the front lines who laid down their lives in this war.

As soon as we talk about the Vietnam War and how some of the Communist leaders behaved in that war, I recall a story that happened to me at this time back in Moscow. Not far from our Research Institute, where I was working, there was a kebab house where I occasionally would go with my colleagues during my lunch break. They had a wonderful dish there called "roasted pork brisket", in Russian "koreyka". The word sounds very close to "Korean woman", however the etymology has nothing to do with Korea. Russian borrowed the word from French "carré", which means exactly "roasted pork brisket". However, every time we would go there, we jokingly called this day the Democratic People's Republic of Korea Day.

One such day, a colleague and I sat down at a table, ordered and waited for our order. At our table sat a well-dressed, heavyset man who gave the impression that he had already had a good drink. After a while, he spoke to us and offered to buy us a glass of cognac. Out of politeness, we agreed, but at once, we said that it is our working time and we could only have one drink. When the waiter approached, the man ordered a cognac for us, which was not slow to appear along with our brisket. We happily began to devour both, and an interesting conversation ensued.

This man, a Muscovite, first asked us about our work and, after finding out what we were doing, we thought he was clearly interested. Then he spoke briefly about himself. It turned out that he had been doing some kind of work for over a year in the North Vietnamese army somewhere near Hanoi. He told us that they were in great need of computer specialists there. He is currently on leave for three weeks in Moscow. He complained that his close friends are vacationing in the south now, and he does not have anyone else in town, and he feels lonely and sad.

After telling us about himself, he asked us if we would like to go to work with him in Vietnam for a very decent salary. My colleague diplomatically said that it was a serious offer and he would have to think it over. I answered right away that I do not want to work in the army, and, the more so, during the war. He did not understand my pacifistic motives and told me that their computer centre was in a quiet and very safe place and I should not worry about it. Besides, I told him at once that I am Jewish and I am not a communist party member, so no one would employ me for such a job. In response, he advised me not to speculate about things I did not know about. As for the paper work, he said, it is his but not my concern. If I tell him yes, he is going back to Vietnam in about two weeks and we will leave together!

I will never know how serious everything he said was. All I know is that when we finished our "Korean" business the waiter, a nice woman, took me aside and begged me to get him out of here, put him in a cab and send him home. She told me he had been here already for few hours, and his pockets are literally full of money. She said, it seems to her, he would not stop until he would be drunk out of his mind. My coworker and I decided to take her good advice. Anyway, she said, it would not end well. With difficulty, we persuaded him to do as she advised. As a parting, he gave her a very decent tip and his telephone number for us, and urged us to think over his offer and to call him. For some reason he addressed all his last words mainly to me... I never saw or heard that man again. That is how I almost got the job to fight in defense of communist Vietnam. Now I wish I had told that story to Ted Pocock!

Sweet school-age children of Mag and Ted, Emily and Tieg, also fostered our bond with their parents. Very soon, my Tanya became friends with both children and then their parents asked her to tutor

Pocock family at the Red Square in Moscow

kids in Russian. Remembering well that we were always on the KGB's periscope, and that we needed to avoid accusations of currency dealing, Tanya asked Mag NOT to pay her for lessons at all. Exceptionally considerate and tactful, Mag always would of course find a way to thank Tanya for her work. The English-speaking school where the children studied was very close to our house. So, the children would walk to our house after the school and then would rest, have a snack, then study Russian. Snacks would regularly include thin Russian pancakes, which they both adored. The supplier of pancakes was usually our next-door neighbor, Granny Ksenia who I mentioned earlier. The children told their parents that Tanya was the best teacher in the world. My Tanya thought that Grandma Ksenia's pancakes might have played a significant role in this radical conclusion.

When I think of Ted, I am filled with the deepest respect and admiration. It was a great pleasure to hear and read the comments about him from people who knew him much earlier than I did, people from a very different world, who came from a very different culture, but who thought of him in the same way that I did. It was also a special joy to see charming Mag by his side. This was a woman, on whom I, personally, just had a crush. The full form of her name was Margaret, but no one called her that way. The sympathy of everyone in our family for her prompted us to use the affectionate suffix "ushka" with her name: we called her gently "Magushka" like "Verushka."

Magushka and Ted managed to arrange things at their embassy in such a way that we always felt surprisingly comfortable there. Unlike many of our diplomat friends, it did not feel as if we were in an official ambassador's residence; it always felt like we were just stopping by to visit close friends. They would invite us not only to official receptions and music concerts, but also simply to dinners. Like the Hartmans and the Buwaldas, they often had fine music. Magushka was friends with the Finnish ambassador's wife, the professional pianist Lisa Karhilo. Through Pococks, Lisa. would invite us to her concerts and to the concerts of other musicians at the Finnish embassy.

The Pococks often had other interesting people in their house as well, especially people who were known to be unappreciated by the official authorities. In doing so, the Pococks tried, to the best of their ability, to correct the injustices around them. It was in their house that we were fortunate to meet first the composer, Alfred Schnittke. My musical knowledge may be limited but all the musicians we knew spoke of his music only in superlatives. The very special composer's genius and incredible capacity for work resulted in, on the one hand, the complete rejection of the many Soviet musical bureaucrats, but, on the other hand, led him to fame and recognition throughout the world.

I would like to mention an interesting detail in his difficult life. In 1990, unexpectedly, the Soviets awarded him the Lenin Prize, which he rejected in his own very special way. Being a religious man, he did not want the award, which had the name, according to his words, of an *"ardent atheist."* When I met with him, I always had the uneasy feeling that he was from a completely different world, a world that was not political at all, more educated and interesting, more noble and kind, more emotionally developed and sensitive and, at the same time, more modest and even humble. You can imagine how delighted I was to read the words about Schnittke by Mstislav Rastropovich."*He walked his straight, without a deflection, path to God."* That was exactly how I felt when I thought about him. I am glad that Rastropovich could articulate this so well. Thank you, dear Pococks, for giving us the opportunity to touch such an extraordinary man.

I have already mentioned our visits to our new friends from the free world for cultural events as "interplanetary flights". One such "flight" from Moscow Maternity Hospital No. 25 to the Australian Embassy in Moscow ended in my shame and embarrassment, if not crash. After exhausting working hours as a janitor-obstetrician I "flew" in the evening to the Dolfinia Land Embassy to listen to music there, and then returned to the maternity hospital for the nightly continuation of my shift. Everything was pleasing to the eye in the bright, beautiful hall. There was not much time left before the concert and there were no vacant chairs for Tanya and me, we had to sit separately. I immediately noticed a place in the front row next to our beloved host Magushka. Ted was already sitting somewhere apart from her. Of course, I offered that seat to my Tanya, but she was too shy and preferred to sit in what seemed to be a not occupied seat in the fourth row. As I hesitated, looking for another seat, Mag made a sign to me, gesturing for me to sit next to her. How could I say no to a WOMAN like that?!

I sat down, thankful, and immediately felt incredibly good, like I was in a magical dream. It was as if I had really flown into a fairy-tale Dolphinia. There was wisteria blooming affectionately all around me, which, indeed, looked more delicate than rime. I let my guard down and succumbed to the magical dream. When I opened my eyes,—shame on my not-so-young head—I was horrified to find out that the music was playing, and I was blissfully asleep on Magushka's shoulder! It was even worse than that. I had to confess that I woke up feeling like I had been in paradise. I wanted to fall through the earth and no longer be. When we met with the Pococks after this incident, I was embarrassed to lift my eyes to them. However, the generosity of our friends knew no bounds: they were as sweet to me as ever.

I will never forget another visit with the Pococks with our Galechka, who was heavily pregnant with Masia this time. We joked that if the Galya delivered the baby here that day, it would be an Australian citizen. I well remember Magushka telling Tanya and me: *"It's going to be great, and you do not have to worry at all. We will certainly help your children settle down in Australia."*

Unlike many Westerners working in Moscow, the Pococks never cared whether the Soviet authorities liked or disliked their activities. They would always come to us as if we all lived in a free country. Once, when we had a very dear person, the violinist Alexander Brussilovsky, staying under special circumstances with us, we arranged a home performance and invited the Pococks. Their appearance was dramatic. It had rained heavily that day and the approach to our building was all in deep puddles. Poor Ted fell into one of those puddles and walked up to us with completely wet feet. Ted was cold and worried that he would catch a cold. Tanya immediately played the part of a good Jewish mother, insisting that he take off his wet shoes and socks. Ted got my dry socks and slippers, and for the wet ones she found a warm place where they would quickly dry. The question arose as to where in the apartment he could change. We had only two private rooms. Tanya's mother and Verusha. lived in the first room and Brusilovsky lived in the second. The second also had my workshop, where I tried to earn extra money with my handicrafts in addition to my feeble salary of a janitor-obstetrician. Tanya and I slept in the pass-through room. Tanya decided that Ted should change in the second room, and Ted obediently went there. When he came out of there happy and with dry feet, he said to Tanya, *"I know what you're missing from this apartment, a big Saint Bernard."*

As it happens, the Jewish community in Australia was small but very active. Many members of that community saw discrimination against Jews, wherever it occurred in the world, as a big human rights issue. As a result, many Australian non-Jews acquired this attitude, which I do not think was the case in other countries at all. This explains why Ted and Mag were incomparably more disturbed by this violation of human rights in the country where they lived and worked now than, say, the diplomats in England. What's more, thanks to this situation, the world got from Australia as a gift major Jewish public figures of international stature. We were lucky to become personally acquainted with one, the world-renowned Zionist, Isi Leibler. However, this acquaintance did not turn into friendship until the help of the Pococks.

Isi Leibler was four years older than I. In Isi's childhood, his parents moved with him from Belgium to Australia, where he lived until 1999, when his family made Aliyah to Israel. The literal translation of the word "Aliyah" is from Hebrew "ascent," "ascension," and "exaltation." The term is one of the foundational concepts of Zionism and refers to the repatriation, or the return of Jews to our historic homeland in the land of Israel. The word originates from the return of the Jews to Judah from the Babylonian captivity in the 6th century B. C. In Australia, Isi owned a large successful travel agency. In time, Isi became a prominent Jewish activist with a particular interest in the discrimination against the Soviet Jews. In 1963, in Melbourne, he published the book "Soviet Jews and Human Rights," in which he highlighted the problem of anti-Semitism in Russia. He looked at it, not just as discrimination against one nation, or one religion, but as one component of the broader gross violation by the Soviet authorities of human rights. Moreover, in 1965, at the initiative of Isi Leibler, the question of the Jewish refuseniks of the Soviet Union became the subject of discussion at the United Nations. Eventually, he was elected the President of the Council of Australian Jews and the Vice-president of the International Jewish Congress. In 1988, he came to Moscow to meet and help the refuseniks. By then he already knew the leaders of the Moscow refuseniks, Volodya Prestin and Pasha Abramovich. We owe it to them to get to know such an interesting person.

The year Ted Pocock came to Moscow, he received a new appointment as the Australian Ambassador to France and he and Mag left for Paris. However, when Mag and Ted found out about I. Leibler's visit to Soviet Union, they came to Moscow with the main goal to meet him and to focus his attention on the fate of our family. It was so wonderful to see them again. And, of course, Magushka brought us lots of presents. She knew well how the janitor-obstetrician and his family lived, and her gifts, as always, were very practical and important to us.

The meeting with I. Leibler was particularly fulfilling because we did not have to explain anything to him. He was so familiar with the situation of Soviet Jews; it was as if he had lived as one of us for a long time. Nevertheless, one day my Tanya felt the need to correct him. Speaking to the refuseniks, he warned them against expecting that their life in the West would be easy. Tanya explained to him that every reasonable person who decided to emigrate understood this and was very cognizant of the difficulties ahead. To help such a person, one should not intimidate him even more, but, on the contrary, should support him. Isi agreed that she was right and apologized for not thinking about that.

He turned out to be a very kind and nice man. After learning about my medical problems, he prepared and sent us an official invitation to come to Australia for treatment. Who knows, it could have turned out that I would have left the Soviet Union on this invitation sooner than I did. I personally received a wonderful gift from Isi. He bought me a German electric Philips razor in a Moscow currency store, which I brought with me to America and continued to use until recently (over thirty years!). Funny thing is, a few years ago I bought the exact same American-made razor as a spare. It was already out of order, but the Icy's gift was still working like clockwork.

In 1989, when we were no longer in the Soviet Union, Isi came to Moscow again, this time for the opening of the International Cultural Center after Solomon Mikhoels. It was one of the most important cultural events in Russia commemorating the life of the great Jewish actor, activist, and fiery fighter against fascism, Mikhoels-. By the Stalin's order, Mikhoels was killed in 1948 in brutal assassination. Many very worthy people in the world came to the opening of the cultural center or sent their greetings by mail.

To conclude the chapter about the Pococks, I would like to say that upon their move from Russia to France, these amazing people touched us on many occasions by continuing to take care of us. From the very beginning of their life in France, they tracked down our friends who lived in Paris and made contact with them. I am talking about the violinist Sascha Brussilovsky and the Frenchman Alain mentioned in the chapter on the Committee of Fifteen. When Alan and his lovely wife Anne was getting married, Mag and Ted were invited and sent us pictures of the big event. Secondly, they told Ted's successor, Robin Ashwin, who took over as the new Australian Ambassador in Moscow in 1987, about our family and asked him to keep an eye on us. The new Ambassador seemed to be a good man and complied with the request of the Pococks. Until our last day in Moscow, we saw signs of attention from the Australian Embassy staff.

BECOMING FATHER-IN-LAW

On March 5, 1981, a wonderful event happened in our family. A group of young friends gathered at the home of Dima Zelevinsky to celebrate the anniversary of the country's liberation from the Chief Tyrant of the Soviet Union, Joseph Stalin. At this party, our Galya met Dima's friend Vitya Khatutsky. Only recently, I found out that Dimochka played an important role in this acquaintance. This meeting turned out to be portentous. In 1985, Galya and Vitya got married. During more than 40 years since that day, we have rejoiced over this event, sure that a better partner for our Galya could not be found. Dimochka dear, on behalf of my party and government (it was one of political stamps in Soviet

Russia), I express my deepest gratitude to you. I express it no matter how much you contributed to that good thing that happened in your flat, and it does not matter how consciously you did it. We can now definitely affirm that it was a good thing.

It was at that time, being in deep refusal, that we lived the most difficult years of our lives. I like very much the advice by Alexander Galich in his poem "Don't be afraid": *Don't be afraid of jail. Don't be afraid of beggary...*

I have already mentioned this poem in the chapter about Janusz Korczak. However, for me personally, it was very difficult to follow A. Galich's advice not to be afraid of jail and beggary. I must confess that I was very afraid. I had a family, a wife and two daughters, so I was thinking and worrying not only about myself. No matter what it took, I had to save them from the "joys" enumerated by the poet. When we came close to 1985, it became clear that Galechka and Vitya had made their choice. On the one hand, we liked Vitya a lot and it made us happy. On the other hand, Vitya lived with his grandmother and mother and none of them had expressed an interest in emigration. I was terribly nervous, as I did not understand how to put everything together so that everyone would be happy and content. At some point, I discussed this with Vitya. The result of this conversation literally stunned me. Vitya taught me a lesson for which I will be forever grateful. He said, *"Yuri, let's FIRST decide the main question: whether we want to build a life together with your Galechka and then, if we decide YES, we can discuss where and how we will build it."*

I am still ashamed that such an elementary thought had not occurred to me. However, I am happy to say that soon Galechka and Vitya decided to be together, which made a rather complicated situation much simpler. The wedding celebration was at our house on Maria Ulyanov Street. There were, as far as we remember, about 60 people. According to already established tradition, I took the door to the big room off its hinges and turned it into a table. Even so, I still cannot remember or explain how we managed to place everyone at still such a small table. We decorated the wall above the piano with wedding greetings in over 15 languages. There was a lot of music. My Tanyusha and I prepared and sang fun ditties in Russian style. Here are the lyrics of some of them:

LIFE THIRD: MY EFFORTS TO EMIGRATE FROM THE SOVIET UNION

A mother-in-law is not a gift. A mother-in-law is a hole in the head.
Poor Vitya happened to get into a trap: he has two of them!
Our Galya trained even a fierce mother-in-law of her.
She just plays the violin and never drinks her daughter-in-law's blood.
Galya and Vitya are not on equal footing, it would not be easy for Vitya:
Vitya's father-in-law is nearby, Galia's father-in-law is far away.
Before he used to come to us, just as Vitya, and now he comes, as son-in-law!
Now, no matter how you twist it, you cannot grab him with your bare hands.
Etc.

When Tanya and I sang, Geda played the violin and her friend accompanied her on the piano. Fedya Antsiferov sang, too. Everything was not only fun, but beautiful and delicious. In Moscow, it was difficult to find fancy dressed up food, which really bothered my Tanyusha. In response to her concern, Ruth Daniloff offered us a turkey as a wedding gift. We got very excited, as in Moscow there was a great shortage at the time. The funny thing was that the turkey turned out to be a GOOSE! However, it only added some spice to the festivities. My Tanya is a great master of decorating a feast, transforming even everyday events, not to mention the festive ones, into a holiday. This time, for example, she brought fresh chestnuts from Abkhazia and dried them. So, our goose was covered with roasted chestnuts (!?), served on a Gardner dish with little candles around the edge. We made candle holders out of oranges, in which Vera, under my guidance, made holes the size of the candles. As a honeymoon, the young couple went straight from the table to the train station, boarded the train, and set off for St. Petersburg.

We were done with Galya's wedding, and fortunately my fears that our émigré plans would ruin my daughter's happiness, were in vain. Soon after the wedding, Vitya, his mother, and grandmother decided to leave the Soviet Union, and they

Galiusha and Vitya on the way to the honeymoon trip

applied separately, along with Galochka for papers to leave. We were all in the same boat again. Moreover, they overtook us on this thorny path and managed to leave a year ahead of us!

I want to end this chapter with some humorous poem, I wrote. I did it as a parody of very popular in Russia song for kids about little gray goat living with babushka. The poem is recounting the story of Vitechka's joining our family:

> *There lived with his grandmother our son-in-law to be.*
> *He was an avid fanatic of Ancient Greece.*
> *There you go, there you go, son-in-law to be,*
> *There you go, there you go, Ancient Greece.*
>
> *His mother- and father-in-law loved him very much,*
> *His mother- and father-in-law treated him with vodka.*
> *There you go, there you go, loved very much,*
> *There you go, there you go, treated with vodka*
>
> *Things were moving fast, not bad and not good,*
> *We palmed off him Galka as his wife.*
> *There you go, there you go, not bad and not good*
> *There you go, there you go, palmed Galka off as a wife.*
>
> *Once our son-in-law got an idea of a long walk,*
> *That was when America turned up at the right moment.*
> *There you go, there you go, off a long walk,*
> *There you go, there you go, at the right moment.*
>
> *Since we, together are roasting potatoes,*
> *Grilling and gobbling lamb ribs and lamb legs.*
> *There you go, there you go, roasting potatoes,*
> *There you go, there you go, lamb ribs and lamb legs*

BECOMING GRANDFATHER

For more than a decade, I practiced as a janitor-obstetrician. As a result, this decade proved to be quite fruitful in the fullest sense of the word. During this time, many wonderful babies were born in my hospital. For both the newborns and their mothers, I tried

Great-grandmother, grandfather and aunt are greeting little Anna

to do something good. If I could create a list of these people, I, undoubtedly, should open it with my Tanyusha who gave birth to Verochka In my hospital. However, the next on the list should be my dear Galecka, who gave birth to our granddaughter Anechka with the party nickname Masya. In fact, if we look to my participation in the process, she should be even ahead of Vera because she was the only child in my decade as a janitor-obstetrician, in whose birth I continuously PARTICIPATED from the first to the last moment. I cannot explain why, but I was terribly afraid that something would go wrong, and I felt it necessary to stand by Galecka and to be at her side during the whole process. Our midwives knew me well and respected my worries. They did not treat me as just a janitor and allowed me to be in the room during the whole labor. I was given permission to stand beside them like a sentry. I am sure, they would never allow any other janitor such thing and may be even wish him to go hell in a rude way. Sometimes they chuckled at my need to observe a routine process that they had been performing daily for years. They were completely unaware of my worries and concerns during Galya's childhood, of the fact that I had to be both her mother and her father. If they had known the historical context, it would have been much easier for them to understand my emotions.

The next thing I remember well is funny. Galya's mother Renata had brownish-red hair. There came a moment in the delivery, when I could see the crowning of the head. I loved the red hair of her mother. To my utter horror, her head was as black as night, and I feared that something was wrong with the tissues. It did not even occur to me that I was seeing dark hair on her head. Our midwives immediately reassured me and once again laughed at me. Soon our brand new Anechka appeared before us in one piece, and everything in this girl from the first moment of her birth was perfect and beautiful! Even her first cry sounded like a beautiful song to me.

After this, the midwives took care of my brand new girl: washed, dressed, swaddled, put her in a small crib on wheels and rolled it to the newborn's room. Then they switched to her mother. . They covered my Galusha, put her on a gurney, which they took out of the delivery room and placed for half an hour in the corridor in front of the door. They usually do it to all women after the childbirth in our hospital in case they needed the urgent help of an obstetrician. On her way to the corridor, I tried to distract my Galyechka from pain and worry with conversation. Then I begged the midwives permission to roll the gurney to the nearest phone in the corridor. No one answered at Vitya's, so I dialed our home number. Tanya answered the phone, but I was so excited I could not get a word out: I just choked with tears. It is easy to imagine how I scared the hell out of Tanya. Of course, she thought something terrible had happened. I put Galya on the phone and while I recovered, she explained that everything had happened, as it should have.

On the first evening after the end of my work shift, there was a serious "party" in the kitchen of our house. It is important to stress that I am not talking about a large gathering of close people, but about a spontaneous outburst of emotions and relaxation in which only Tanya, Vitya, your humble servant and, as fate would have it, ONE guest took part. Dear Denis Gulet who worked at the Canadian Embassy had happened to drop in on us that evening. We liked her very much, and we often called her Deniska softly, following "Deniska's Stories" by Victor Dragunskiy. Deniska very happily and naturally joined our exultation. As for the mentioned seriousness of the event, it refers solely to the amount and to the quality of the consumed drink. In the autumn, we brought home from our friends in Georgia a large bottle of homemade chacha. This drink was wonderful! Tanya put a big bottle on the table, and it is hard to believe it, but the four of us drank it all. It is pertinent to note here that the Canadian subject paid great homage to one of the finest achievements of Georgian culture. As the alcoholics in Russia said about it, the chacha "went down" very well. We did not have anything particularly interesting to eat on this day. However, my Tanyusha, first, belongs to masters of cooking something out of nothing, and, secondly, she always kept a stock for a rainy day. One our friend in Moscow had joked on this occasion that if the blockade of the city would begin, those who with Tanya would never die of hunger. That is why this evening we did not go hungry either, and we even had a proper snack after chacha.

In conclusion, I would like to tell our dear Masechka that in the days of her coming into this world we drank so much great alcohol for her to be happy, that she has simply no other choice but to be so.

COMMITTEE OF FIFTEEN

In 1967 after the Six-Day War Soviet Union broke off diplomatic relations with Israel and did not re-establish them until 1990. During this time, more than half a million Jews left the Soviet Union. The embassy of the Netherlands voluntarily represented Israel in Moscow during these years and did whatever it could to help many people emigrate. Thank God, such remarkable people were not only in Holland. In the seventies, an organization was set up in Paris to help families in the USSR that suffered human and civil rights violations. There were 15 members of this committee and so they called themselves the "Committee of Fifteen." For their work, they chose 15 families in the Soviet Union, deprived of human rights. We were Jewish refuseniks, not allowed to emigrate. It was our incredible luck to be included into the list of those fifteen families. But when I looked at the list, I could not believe my eyes. On the same list I saw the name of very famous Soviet physicist and human rights activist A. D. Sakharov, an outstanding personality. I had previously been fortunate to meet him at home of my very close friend Tanya Velikanov. I have always the deepest respect for this man.

The Committee of Fifteen members, disguised as tourists, regularly visited major Russian cities with one sole purpose to support people deprived of human rights, and to let them know that the world had not forgotten them. The Committee members belonged to the highest category of humanity. Each of these people were ready, following the poet I. Gabai, to say

> *I would like to feel someone else's pain inside me,*
> *Like my own heart-oppressing pain.*

This moral support of us could not be overestimated. The Committee also rendered material assistance by bringing us things that we otherwise could never get in this country.

The Committee played a huge role in my family's life. After all, by the time the Committee's envoys started showing up at our doorstep like kind wizards, we were outcasts in our own country. Suddenly and quite surprisingly, we began to receive attention, care, and even, I say, love. Before we knew it, some of these magical people had become our best friends.

Good example of such friends is Alain Rochette de Lempdes. He was very young and still unmarried, but today he is a family man with three wonderful grown children. We have all become dear friends and after relocating to the free world started visiting each other in both Paris and Boston. They are all wonderful people or in their French language, the "crème de la crème." In those years, Alan came to Moscow with his friend Gerard Frances, and these two young, interesting, and handsome Frenchmen began a touching friendship with our family and specifically with little Verochka, who was not even ten years old at the time. The two young men made a vow not to marry until our Verochka got to freedom. Everything happened to them as Ludmila Gurchenko once sang in the popular Soviet film "Carnival Night":

> *In five minutes, people sometimes*
> *Resolutely decide never to marry.*
> *But there are times when in a minute*
> *All things change in a significant way,*
> *Change once and forever.*

Both of Vera's friends kept their vows. When that very minute came that we got permission and took Verochka away to freedom, both of our friends got married. Unfortunately, we gradually lost the connection with Gerard, but we were able to continue our friendship with the dear Rochets and to meet them from time to time, and to contact them by phone, though less often than we would like.

Alan and Gerard were our ambassadors in France, and through them, many people in the world came to know us. It was thanks to them that we were lucky to meet and know Simone Veil, who was famous not only in France but throughout the whole world. Tanya and I could not believe it when we found out that this prominent

LIFE THIRD: MY EFFORTS TO EMIGRATE FROM THE SOVIET UNION

woman was not only coming to Moscow but coming to our small apartment to meet us and to support us.

Simone Veil was born in 1927 to a Jewish family in Nice. She was a year older than my sister Lena. The Nazis exterminated her parents and brother in concentration camps during the occupation of France. In 1944, both Simone and her older sister were arrested by the Gestapo, and they were sent to Auschwitz. Both went through the horrors of the Nazi camps but survived, returned home, and were honored and respected in post-war France. Simone graduated from university law school in France and worked as a lawyer. She traveled many times to the Nazi death camps in Europe to lecture about the crimes committed by the German occupiers.

I so admire Simone's heroic journey and I cannot refrain from enumerating just the main steps of this journey. At the end of the fifties, she was already Attaché to the Ministry of Justice. In the sixties, she was the Deputy Head of the Department in that Ministry. In the late sixties, she served as the Adviser to the Custodian of the Seals. In 1970, she was the General Secretary of the Superior Council of the Magistracy. In 1972, she was the Director of the French Broadcasting and Television Authority. In the mid-seventies, she was the Minister of Health of France. In 1977, she was the Chairman of the Atomic Energy Information Council. In the late seventies, she was again the Minister of Health. From 1979 to 1982, she was the President of the European Parliament. From 1982 to 1989, she chaired various groups and committees in this Parliament. From 1993 to 1995, she was the Minister of State for Social Affairs and Health. From 1997 to 1999, she was the President of the High Council for Integration. From 1998–2007, she served as a member of the French Constitutional Council. From 2001–2007, she was the Chairwoman of the Holocaust Remembrance Foundation and in 2007, she was the Honorary Chairwoman of the Holocaust Remembrance Foundation.

It was a honor for us that this great French citizen, in fact, a great representative of all humanity, in her unusually busy life dedicated to serving the world, lerned about our personal difficulties, and found the time and energy to help us. Moscow is about 1900 miles away from Paris. However, that huge distance never stopped her. She overcame it in order to come to see us—a small, distant and unfamiliar family—so that we would not lose faith in goodness and justice. When we sat with Simone Veil in our little kitchen and talked, her modesty and simplicity stunned both Tanya and me. We had the feeling that we were having a conversation with an old friend of ours. Our whole family will always be full of gratitude for her kindness.

Simone Veil departed this life on June 30, 2017, two weeks short of her 90th birthday. Peace is upon her ashes! Tanya and I were very pleased to learn that French President Emmanuel Macron attended her funeral. After that, thousands of letters asked the President to rebury her in the Pantheon in Paris. With the President's consent, the reburial took place in 2018, and Simone Veil became only the fifth woman to find a resting place together with those whom the French Republic considers its most deserving representatives. It seems to me that this was a remarkably fair and just decision.

Tanya and I want once again to give our thanks to the fifteen wonderful people who put a part of their soul into the Committee and, through the Committee, into us, who were under the Committee's ward. We will never forget what they did for us. We happen to be especially close to Alan Rochette and his family. For more than thirty years now, we have lived in America, and our friendship with the Rochets has continued to warm us all these years.

REPRESENTATIVE OF ISRAEL

Immediately after Israel's triumphant victory in the 1967 Six-Day War, the Soviet leaders, infuriated by the failed Arab aggression, severed diplomatic relations with Israel and closed the embassies and consulates in both countries. Only after the collapse of the Soviet Union in 1990, did the Consulate of Israel reopen in Moscow, and in 1992 the Soviet embassy in Israel was opened again. In the 25 years between these two historic milestones, the Dutch government voluntarily took on the role of representing Israel in the USSR.

During 1986–1990, Peter Buwalda was the Dutch Ambassador in Moscow. We were lucky enough to meet both Peter and his wife, Wilma, shortly after their arrival in Moscow and we became close friends. During our last two years in Moscow until we left in 1988, their friendship helped us survive and brightened our lives during the difficult days of refusal until our very last hour in Moscow. This friendship kept us warm when we were already living in Boston, and they had returned to The Hague. Our family was incredibly fortunate when processing our departure from Russia: we did not have to deal with unknown bureaucratic officials, but with our dear friends Peter and Wilma Buwalda.

Peter, was a professional diplomat from The Hague, and before Moscow, he was ambassador to Egypt and to Sweden. Behind his seemingly northern restraint was a man of the highest European culture, rare nobility and remarkable kindness. He extended these splendid qualities not only to the people he encountered but also to the countries he dealt with as a diplomat. He was a large man in all dimensions. I suppose he must have always had trouble buying oversized clothes. Peter loved music and played the piano well. He had a piano in his residence and when we visited he would often sit down to play. It was always an added joy for us.

Our very dear friend Peter Buwalda

Peter's wife Wilma was Greek. She was a professional singer who came to the United States as a young woman from Thessaloniki. Many people consider this city to be the cultural capital of Greece. It seems to me that Wilma absorbed all the culture of this wonderful place with her mother's milk. During the Nazi occupation of the city, the family fled leaving everything behind them. Wilma told us that her father left with a single object in his hands, "The Divine Comedy" by Dante. Therefore, she was familiar with the feeling of losing everything. When Wilma married Peter, she was singing with the Metropolitan Opera Company. She faced a difficult choice: continue her vocal career, or travel around the world accompanying her diplomat husband. She chose the second. With a rich emotional intelligence and with a hypertrophied sense of justice, she threw herself into helping the *"Humiliated and Insulted"* (the title of Dostoevsky's novel). She was a petite woman, or so it seemed to me when I saw her next to Peter. She retained a very beautiful soprano, but it was not easy to get her to sing for us. Only a few times did I succeed. However, once she blessed us with a little tape recording of her singing. But a terrible thing happened, since our last move, Tanya and I cannot find the tape.

As I mentioned, we were incredibly lucky: fate brought us together their first year in Moscow in 1986. We met during an intermission in the foyer of a musical concert at Tchaikovsky Hall. I will never know what motivated Wilma to come up to me and introduce herself; I would never have dared to do it myself. She told me that she saw something in my face that made her want to meet me. I told her briefly who and what we were. She immediately started addressing me as "Professor!" I tried to explain to her that I had never taught at an institution of higher education, and I did not have the title of professor. However, I did not have luck with my arguments. She told me it was completely irrelevant to her. "*You are MY professor!*" she told me. After this, she told me a Greek saying that, in her opinion, related to my situation. If you translate it into Russian, it is something like: "*Rings can be taken off your fingers, but your fingers are always with you.*" I asked her to write this proverb for me in the Greek version, which she did. The Greek letters were very beautiful. An idea immediately occurred to me. I loved my hobby of wood calligraphy. I was so enthusiastic about my new acquaintance that I thought I would carve a souvenir with the saying. I made my vision come true in a couple of months. I found a good photo of the three of us, Tanya, Vera and me, and I made a frame for this photo, topped with the Greek text of the saying. My gift was ready and I gave it to Wilma. When we visited them, I saw it in one of the rooms of their mansion. Alas, neither Wilma, nor Peter is alive today, and I do not know about the fate of the photograph. I hope it survived in the home of their son Mark, who knew us well.

Peter was very serious about representing Israel in his embassy and helping Jews who wanted to emigrate. For him it was an opportunity to protect basic human rights from people who did not want to know what these words meant. The Soviet authorities surrounded the process of Jewish emigration from the USSR with mountains of artificial difficulties, humiliation and lies. Both Peter and Wilma personally went to great lengths to help unfortunate people make their way through these multitudinous obstacles. For this purpose, they had to do many things, which went far beyond the functions of an embassy located in a civilized country. This, of course, required extra work and money. Endless thanks to the Dutch government for not objecting to such expenditures. I learned about many of the details of this noble activity relatively recently.

For example, the Dutch embassy took it upon itself to forward over the Soviet Union border documents sent for those wishing to leave. All such mail that went through the Soviet mail would be censored and confiscated. Especially great difficulty was in obtaining summons from Israel, which were required prior to submitting documents for departure. The post offices also did not forward important documents from the Soviet Union abroad, which were necessary for the emigrants to arrange their lives in the new country. There were special problems with people who, according to the laws of Israel, did not have the right to enter their country. It never occurred to many people in the West that in order to get out of the country-prison, an exit visa was necessary. Where an emigrant plans to go next was another matter. As a result, the Dutch embassy tried to rescue Pentecostals for whom there was a threat of imprisonment for their faith. These people were trying to get out of Russia on an Israeli visa, which displeased the Israeli government. Yitzhak Rabin summoned Peter to Jerusalem to give him his thoughts on the matter. Peter, knowing the position of his country and many other European countries, did not agree with Israel's views, did not want to discuss these views, and refused to come to Israel to do so. I personally have nothing but admiration for the views of the Dutch embassy and Peter Buwalda personally. When the government persecutes its people unjustly, I believe that any way to save them is good.

As for Wilma, her behavior in Moscow regularly moved me to tears. Seeing a line of people waiting for visas through the window in the courtyard of her embassy, she would personally go downstairs and bring out chairs so that the elderly could sit down. More than once, she complained to us, that she saw young people shamelessly sitting on these chairs, while the elderly, who were too shy to ask for a seat, stood. On such occasions, she would go down again and put things in order. How much better our world would be if there were more Wilmas and Peters!

In 1988, Israeli Prime Minister Yitzhak Shamir began to initiate the restoration of diplomatic relations with Russia. He sent to Moscow a man named Arieh Levin appointed head of the diplomatic group in the Soviet Union and working under the auspices of the Dutch Embassy and Peter personally. As a first step in this direction, Peter allocated a special room with a separate entrance from the street in his embassy. In this room, A. Levin started issuing Israeli visas, and on the door to the room, there was a small sign "Issuance of Israeli visas". Before that, the Dutch consul handled Israeli visas, as if by way of charity. A. Levin in his memoirs describes the event: "*In the Soviet Union, an area of 8.9 million square miles, there appeared a small but official Israeli place where it was possible to get an entry visa to the country*".

In just mentioned memoirs A. Levin describes also an amusing episode connected with the opening of the Israeli room on the premises of the Dutch embassy. He thought it proper that a mezuzah should be on the front door of the room in accordance with ancient Jewish customs. Since he felt he was a guest at Peter's embassy, he struck up a conversation with him about this in the hope of obtaining his approval and permission. Peter, however, said that he needed time to think for himself and to consult with his colleagues in order to make the right decision.

Some time later, they met again, and a very enlightened conversation took place. Peter said that he realized how important it was for both him, Levin, and for the Jews who come to get their visas, that this sacred object blessed the entrance. On the other hand, in the Netherlands, there was a separation between church and state, making the presence of the object at their embassy not entirely appropriate. After weighing both considerations and given the very special situation of having an island of Israel in their embassy, as an exception, he gave permission to proceed with the installation of the mezuzah. When I learned of this story, my already high respect for Peter Buwalda increased even more.

In 1990, an Israeli consulate opened in Moscow and A. Levin became Consul-in-Chief. In 1992, the Israeli consulate moved to same building where it existed 25 years before. The Israeli Consul became after a long break the first Ambassador of the State of Israel to Russia. It seems to me, A. Levin really deserved this promotion. I believe that the restoration of the recognition of the State of Israel by Russia at the end of the 20th century was a correction of a sad historical mistake, and a major step towards ethical, social, and political progress for the entire civilized world. Anyone, I think, should recall with gratitude the outstanding diplomat of the Kingdom of the Netherlands, Peter Buwalda and his friend, assistant, and wife, Wilma Buwalda, who stood at the origin of that step. The leading American journalist of the "New York Times" expressed it very well in his article of June 1988: *"If the American embassy in Moscow was a bastion of political support for the powerless citizens of the country, in the embassy of Peter and Wilma Buwalda, they could find close relatives."*

I do not want to speak for other families, but for our family I can say that Wilma and Peter were even closer to us than many of our blood relatives, and it has happened during one of the toughest periods of our lives.

MUSIC ON THE WATER

Somehow, it happened that there were always many musicians among our friends, although neither Tanya nor I had ever been involved in music professionally. However, we must single out one man among them, who always has and always will occupy a very special place in our hearts. I am referring to Sasha Brussilovsky, a remarkable person, musician, and violinist. Our lives have overlapped and at certain periods, I would even say, intertwined to such an extent that our relationship grew up and I want to promote him from a friend to a family member. He feels to me somewhere between my younger brother and my son. If we consider age, both of my feelings are possible: I am 15 years older than him, and 16 years younger than my older brother is, Sasha is 9 years older than my Galechka.

We met Sasha in the early 1980's. By then, he had dared to upset the Soviet music bureaucrats on several occasions. First, in 1975, he unintentionally disrupted their plans by becoming the winner of the prestigious Jacques Thibaud violin competition in Paris. Organizers of the competition in the Soviet delegation had planned that Sasha's classmate, Irina Ivanov, would receive this award. In winning, Sasha became an accomplice in the "criminal" disobedience of Western musicians to the authority of the Soviets. Secondly, in 1976, Sasha participated in an artistic tour in France during which he spent time with the pianist Mikhail Rudy who was his classmate in the Conservatory. A year before, Rudy, had come in first at the prestigious Marguerite Long piano competition in Paris. Rudy defected in France when the trip ended and became a "deserter" in the Soviet bureaucrats' language. After that Sasha was repeatedly harassed because the authorities felt he must have known of the pianist's intention to defect. As this went on the authorities' patience wore thin and, on the other hand, so did Sasha's.

It became clear to Sasha that the Communists' political wrangling seriously threatened his romance with music, and further tours abroad of his own were unlikely to become possible. Slowly but surely, he was getting closer to making the difficult decision to leave Russia. In 1979, the Brussilovsky family dared to apply to leave, and soon they joined the ranks of those who had been refused. I know it is a sin to say this, but I am glad that we ended up in the same boat, even in such a gruesome way. Otherwise, we might never have met, and that would have been a great loss to me. The Brussilovsky family left Russia at the end of 1985 and settled in France. To my great regret, the very wide Atlantic Ocean separates us today, but a great consolation is that we live in the ONE FREE WORLD with him.

Now we finally got to our first meeting with Sasha and to getting to know each other. Remember, the first thing, the authorities did to slow down the emigration, was to take away from the refuseniks the jobs they loved. In addition, the musicians were robbed of their foreign tours, and, within Russia, they were no longer allowed to play in the prominent music halls for the audiences that loved and appreciated their music. In other words, the artists lost their opportunities to perform music and without this they ceased to be working musicians.

Volodya Feltsman told us the following story, sad and at the same time funny, about one of his concerts during the refusal years. I would like to think that he did not make it up himself, and if he did, I still like this story. Once he went to play in some forsaken remote place in Siberia. It was winter, and it was bitterly cold. When he arrived, the first thing he did was to look for the piano. Failing to find one, he asked the administrators where the instrument might be. They answered that they did not have one and had never had one (???). *"So, what am I supposed to do?"* asked Volodya. *"Maybe you can tell people something interesting,"* they replied.

In these ghastly circumstances, the most effective help was to organize home concerts. That was exactly what my Tanyusha did for all of our friends who were musicians in refusal. If I remember correctly, it was my Tanya, who persuaded Feltsman to invite Sasha to play at their home. Home concerts are wonderful and are how music was played at the old time. Such concerts create a closer connection between the performers and the audience, consequently, with the music being played. We are talking about the chamber music. Once there was such a concert in Volodya Feltsman's little flat on Sadovoe Ring and Tanya, Verusha and I were there. Both soloists were at their best, and Volodya's beautiful wife Anechka, a pleasant and beautiful woman, added to the delight of the audience, being, as always, ornamentation at his concerts. One of the sonatas of J. Brahms for violin and piano was in the program. Volodya played the piano and his friend, Sasha, played the violin.

I remember two funny details of that event. First, our little Verochka, for lack of chairs was sitting on the floor quite close to Sasha. She was so enraptured with his playing that without realizing it, got closer and closer to him. At one point, she was so close to his feet that Tanyusha had to pull her away to prevent him from stepping on her. The second was that Volodya's friend, the composer Kolya Karetnikov, sat next to us, sniffing so loudly that Tanya got angry and grumbled to herself. After the concert, it became clear that what had angered Tanyusha was not a sniffle, but a sob! He had been so moved that he had begun to cry. Later I learned important things about Kolya from the Internet. First, he had a close relationship with the poet Alexander Galich, his godfather. Secondly, leaving Russia, Galich came to get a blessing from his priest, father Alexander, along with Kolya. Thirdly, I found out with sadness, I lived already in the USA, that Kolya left this world in 1994.

That evening we started talking to Sasha, and something immediately drew us to each other. We quickly became friends with him and his family. Sasha's wife, Lenochka, was a lovely, attractive woman with a very pleasant timbre and way of speaking. She studied voice at the Moscow Conservatory with Nina Dorliak, and when Lenochka sang, her voice touched all of us. I will never forget Christmas in the house of our American friends the Daniloffs. We were with the Brussilovskys that evening. Lena looked unthinkably beautiful in a white dress and sang a Christmas aria by my beloved Bach. I thought I was going to fly to Heaven.

Unfortunately, we rarely heard her sing afterwards. Lenochka's fate took a tragic turn when she was struck by a grave mental disease and then, as if that were not enough, she was diagnosed with liver cancer. Shortly before her departure from Moscow, Lena was further overtaken by a crazy and torrid love affair. She had crush with, in my opinion, not very interesting person, an employee of a musical editorial office of Moscow television named Tolya Weinstein. When Tanya and I would try to look at Sasha and this man, it was impossible not to think of the saying: "You cannot compare the God's gift and fried eggs".

To the horror of Sasha and all of us, Lena refused to leave Tolya. Sasha refused to leave without their daughter Alice. Tanya and I tried our best to help each of them. Sasha's life together with Lena was turning to a hell. We suggested to Sasha that he should stay with us while the discussion what to do went on. He agreed to come to live with us. This way we killed two birds with one stone. Sasha got a chance to get some physical distance from the terrible nerve-racking. Lenochka got their apartment at her disposal and thus an opportunity to be with her lover in peace.

In the meantime, we had been trying to convince Lena in the name of her daughter and Sasha not to make any moves until they received the permission to leave with Sasha the Soviet Union. We recommended trying solving her personal problems only after arriving at the other side of the border. That was the situation in the beginning of 1985. I have to admit that when the disease would recede from the unhappy woman, though it never happened often at all, I continued to like Lenochka a lot.

At the height of the heartbreak, Tanya and I thought it might help Sasha to be away from Moscow for a while so that he could quitely plan his next move. Fortunately, we were very lucky. Tanya's sister Natasha had found four extra vouchers on a small steamer on the rivers in the Vologda Region between Vologda and Veliky Ustyug. Four vouchers meant separate cabins on the steamship. In the history of Russia Vologda had been mentioned as early as the 12th century, and Veliky Ustyug, in the 13th century. Veliky Ustyug is located on the Vologda River which is the right tributary of the River Sukhona. Both rivers dry up in summer and navigation on them is possible only in early spring. The vouchers were very difficult to get and practically impossible to buy. We bought them "by connection" and were very fortunate. The Russian North is one of the most interesting places in the world, both in terms of its natural beauty, amazing folk crafts, and unique carved wooden architecture.

It was not easy to persuade Sasha: he did not dare to leave his family in such a turbulent situation. However, we, mainly Tanya, succeeded. The next difficulty for Sasha was to part, even for a short time, with his favourite violin made by Nicolò Gagliano, one of Antoni Stradivari's best pupils. He categorically refused to do it and as a result, we decided that he would take it with him. Now it is time to explain the title of this chapter, "Music on Water". This is the Russian translation of "Water Music", the title for Georg Friedrich Handel's three orchestral suites (HWV348—HWV350). After our voyage, Wikipedia told me curious details of the first performance of this work.

> *On 17 July 1717, King George of England took part in a Thames cruise during which "Music on the Water" was for performance. There was a barge with fifty musicians playing a variety of instruments: trumpets, French horns, oboes, bassoons, flutes, violins, violas and double basses. The king was so delighted with the music that he ordered the concert to be repeated twice before dinner and once after (such were the kings at the time!). The people on the banks of the Thames and in the boats on the water also enjoyed the royal revelry.*

268 years later there was, I think, an equally unusual performance of another work by another great composer, which I would also call Music on Water. It was not the first performance, but it was also very special. We are talking about Sonatas and partitas for solo violin by Johann Sebastian Bach (BWV1001—BWV1006). Here I am going to joke: I will echo the Wikipedia story about the first performance of Handel's "Music on the Water". I will tell the story about special performance of Bach's "Sonatas and partitas for solo violin".

> *In the spring of 1985, the Soviet Refuseniks Tanya, Vera and Yuri Zieman took part in an outing on a little steamer along the Vologda and Sukhona rivers. On this steamer a recital "Music on the Water" was performed. In the cabin of the small ship together with them*

> was a remarkable musician, also refusenik, Sasha Brussilovsky. He played only a violin, but managed to make it magically sing with the voice of an angel. The cabin was so small that it was not easy for the violinist to play. It was so small that there was no room for the listeners, and they had to climb up with their feet tucked on the berths. Yet the Refuseniks were so enraptured by the music that they were willing to listen to the music once before dinner, then instead of dinner, and again afterwards. However, they were ashamed to push their friend for such overtime work. The people on the banks of the Vologda and Sukhona, as well as in the boats on those rivers, had never heard such music in the 9-century history of the region. The listeners were especially grateful to the musician for choosing works of their favorite composer for their "Music on the water."

The previous paragraph mentioned dinner on the steamboat. All four of us were very pleased with the trip, but the food, I have to admit, unfortunately, was in no way in keeping with the natural beauty or the unique cultural attractions. When we would come down from the steamer to land, there was absolutely no way to buy any food additions to the steamer's ration that would please us gastronomically. However, my Tanya was with us, her ingenuity in this respect knew no bounds. Under her leadership, when we went on dry land, we were gathering young spring nettles. The green nettle salad was a regular addition to our meals and protected us from avitaminosis.

We returned home via Vologda, and we had one free evening there. Vera had a coming performance at her music school where she had to play Shostakovich's march and she was not quite ready. When Sasha learned about this, he was so nice that he contacted the local music school in Vologda and got permission to use their piano for a lesson with Vera. As a result, the sounds of Shostakovich's march marked our triumphal return to Moscow from the wonderful voyage, and our child prepared herself for the performance. However, even Vera's Shostakovich did not muffle my beloved Bach. Music on the Water resounds in my ears to this day. I think that on this steamer a miracle happened. Through the will of circumstances, I found myself in a very confined space very close to the wonderful music. Nothing like this had ever happened to me both before and after this time.

LIFE THIRD: MY EFFORTS TO EMIGRATE FROM THE SOVIET UNION

There was one more extremely positive memory about this trip. With satisfaction and pride, I was able to earn Sasha's trust to carry his violin when the steamer stopped and we would go for a walk. My attitude towards his violin was similar to the attitude I had towards Natasha Gutman's cello. We fondly called Sasha's violin "Nikolka" after the name of its maker, Nicolò Gagliano. Such feelings are like an expression of the pleasure I felt for the instrument when it sang under Sasha's fingers. This was my meager and modest contribution to the miracle that took place on the water.

However, as A. Pushkin accurately explained in his poem "To Chaadaev":

Three of us at the Vologda pier

> *It did not take long for us to be deceived with*
> *Love, hope, quiet glory,*
> *Gone are the youthful amusements,*
> *Like a dream, like a morning fog...*

That was exactly what happened to us when we returned to Moscow. Everything the poet listed floated with us in the Vologda area. Our trip really was a happy one. However, it has ended, and we returned to Moscow to all our problems. We came back to our refusenik life and Sasha to his. Also, he returned to his broken family. These problems, unfortunately, did not follow the morning fog.

A year ran by in the vanity and jitters and at the end of the year, the Brussilovsky family got their exit visas. It was a madhouse for a while. Poor Lenochka was pouring her tears over herself and everybody around her. She was telling that she could not part with her coveted one. She became completely beside herself. Tanyusha walked the streets with her and passionately tried to convince her that the best thing for everybody and, above all, for her and her Tolya would be if she and Sasha left now. Then after a while, she would be able to get Tolya out to Paris. Thank God, Tanya's arguments worked, and after a while, we saw them off at Sheremetyevo airport.

Because of Lena's insanity, the move was terribly difficult for everyone. Sasha's friends in Paris helped him find a decent apartment, where he put Lena and Alice. He himself wandered around from place to place. Lena at this time fell into a terrible depression. In 1989, seeing that it was impossible to keep the family together, Sasha filed for divorce. From that time on there was a new period in his life to which I will come back. Until Lena's last day, Sasha continued to take care of her. After a while, Lena did take Tolya to Paris. However, her illnesses kept killing her. In 2000, I think, Lena's suffering ended up and she left this world. Her grave is in France. Their daughter, Alice, married and lives in England today.

LATIN IS OUT OF FASHION THESE DAYS

Latin has been dead for over fifteen hundred years, because it is no longer a spoken language or a native language for any group of people. This was almost the fate of Hebrew which was used only in small enclaves in the Promised Land before the establishment of the State of Israel when it became that state's official language. Yet Pushkin's phrase from Eugene Onegin, which makes the title of this chapter, is not quite accurate. This language is not completely dead because it continues to exist in science (e.g., medicine) and religion (e.g., Catholicism) and to this day attracts the attention and interest of specialists in ancient history, culture, and literature.

I remember well that my father repeatedly taught me how important it was to know at least a little Latin to be able to extract the most basic content elements from texts in many European languages. However, much to my regret, I never took any practical steps to supplement my education with the bit of Latin. In prerevolutionary years, my father studied not in a gymnasium, but in a school of natural and exact sciences. Students at his school nevertheless received a short course of Latin, which he often recalled afterwards with gratitude.

It is interesting that Pushkin described his Eugene Onegin as a "young scamp" studying, as most of us, very little, only a bit here and a bit there. However, later he listed for us what this man really knew:

LIFE THIRD: MY EFFORTS TO EMIGRATE FROM THE SOVIET UNION

> *He knew quite enough of Latin,*
> *To parse the epigraphs,*
> *To talk about Juvenal,*
> *Even to regard "Vale" at the end of his letter.*
> *He also remembered by heart, not without mistakes,*
> *A pair of "Aeneid" verses.*

On top of that:

> *He kept in his memory*
> *Stories of days gone by,*
> *Beginning with the days of Romulus*
> *and ending with the present day.*

Also:

> *He berated Homer, Theocritus.*
> *As a result, had he read books by Adam Smith,*
> *Moreover, he had deep knowledge of economy...*

Well, what can we say about it? Most of us today, who consider ourselves educated people, have not reached the level of the scamp of the Pushkin's time. Few people today can parse Latin epigraphs, let alone read Latin texts. Certainly, for the majority of educated leople it is not easy, even being surrounded with Latin dictionaries. I still like to try to do it, but it is difficult to me! Most people today cannot read the first-century Roman poet Juvenal and do not know what the Latin "vale" means. I was not too lazy to look in a Latin dictionary and in Russian it means "be well."

Pushkin did not specify in what language Onegin remembered the verses of the "Aeneid" by Virgil, the famous poet of ancient Rome. Most likely, he remembered them in the original, though Russian translations have existed since 1770. Unfortunately, most of us do not know either the poet or his poems in any language.

The phrase *"stories of days gone by"* requires a comment. For the word "stories" Pushkin used the Russian word "anecdote" which may have different meanings. During the 18th-19th centuries, it meant a real incident with real people, or historical fact. Modern Russian meaning of the word mostly is "joke in the form of a very short story". Romulus was the founder of ancient Rome, and its first king in 753–716 BC. Therefore, it turns out that Onegin had a solid knowledge of the history of the Western world. It seems to me that today, interest in history in general is steadily decreasing, and especially in the history of the ancient world. As a result, we have forgotten how to learn the lessons of history, which regularly leads to tragic consequences.

Not many of us know the great Greek poet of the 8th century B.C., Homer, enough to scold or praise him. It is such a pity that neither the Iliad nor the Odyssey were on my school literature curriculum. I was pleased when little Verochka in her American school read the Iliad as homework. But of course, very few people today have read and have an opinion on the ancient Greek poet of the 3rd century, B. C. Theocritus.

And the Scottish economist and philosophical ethicist of the 18th century, Adam Smith, one of the founders of economic theory as a science, is at the end of this comparative list, so unprofitable for our contemporaries. I suppose only a few old-fashioned economists know about him today while others, though have no idea "how" the state is getting rich and what it is living on, judge about such things rather self-confidently.

I remember well how, as a boy, I used to revel in Eugene Onegin, and I remember well how, as a boy, I used to revel in "Eugene Onegin", and somehow it did not bother me one bit that Pushkin was INCOMPARABLY more educated than I. I would come across many words, most often names that I did not know, and I, stupidly, just skip them, not even bothering to read the publishers' explanation in the commentary. As I grew older, I naively told myself: *"When I will get older and have more free time I will reread everything I used to like and figure out everything I did not know and did not understand then"*. Now I am 85 years old, and I am still not free enough for such reeducation, and, unfortunately, I am still not at the level of Pushkin's "young scamp." The only consolation is that nowadays, when I am faced with something I do not know and would like to know, I do NOT hesitate to ask the computer. As a rule, every time I get an answer from it and every time, I feel great satisfaction. Such wonderful opportunities, alas, Pushkin and Onegin after him, of course, did not have. Nevertheless, they somehow succeeded with education in humanities much more than we have today with our computers.

LIFE THIRD: MY EFFORTS TO EMIGRATE FROM THE SOVIET UNION

I anticipate the objections of many readers, especially the younger ones, to my conclusion that education in Pushkin's time was much better than today. *"Your Eugene,"* they will say, *"did not know anything, for example, about the Internet, while we know quite a lot.* This is true. However, I measure education not by the number of facts known, but by their importance and relevance. Here, perhaps, different generations have different criteria for importance. When I think about the history of humankind since the Biblical creation of the world, I am amazed with the incredible scientific and technological progress that has changed the world. The Internet is an essential part of this progress. However, at the same time, I feel sad about the regression of humanitarian education as the study of classical literature, philosophy, ethics and ancient languages dwindle. If technological achievements make our lives easier, more comfortable, and entertaining, then the humanities make our life deeper and kinder. For me the second is more important than the first. My beloved Bulat Okudzhava expressed this much better and more poetic than I:

> *You can never bring back the past, and there is nothing to grieve about it,*
> *Builders of every epoch create their own scaffoldings...*
> *It is a pity, we cannot drop in "Yar" today*
> *to dine with Alexander Pushkin,*
> *Even for a quarter of an hour.*

These lines need explanation for readers unfamiliar with Russian history. "Yar" is the name of the legendary restaurant that opened in Moscow in 1826. Its walls would have seen many of the 19th century celebrities like Pushkin, Shaliapin, Giliarovsky, Rasputin, Chekhov, Kuprin, and Gorky. Today there is a hall in the restaurant named after Pushkin. We are talking, of course, about dinner with Pushkin in the figurative sense. Not only did the great poet pass away long ago, but also the poet's norms and calls for culture, literature and education have irrevocably faded into the past. So today, Okudzhava is right: it is no longer possible to have a conversation with ANY ONE at Pushkin's level on important humanist topics. It is interesting that in that poem Okudzhava contradicts himself. In the first line of the stanza, he says that there is nothing to grieve about. I have something to be sad about, and the further I go in life, the more and more this grieves me. At the same time, in the third line he admits that it is a pity that the situation is so unfortunate. That is where I regret along with him.

Now let us return to Latin, which was even more out of fashion in Soviet Russia than in Pushkin's Russia after the Communists urged their citizens with the words of the Marseillaise:

Let us renounce the old world!
Let us shake its ashes off our feet!

Latin, no doubt, was an attribute of the old world. Tanya, however, to my delight, wanted our Verusha to learn Latin. As soon as the girl was born, Tanya met her colleague and friend Latin scholar Judith Kagan and consulted with her when and how to do it. Judith said that she had never taught small children, but that she thought it was okay to start at about seven. As soon as Vera turned seven (1983), Tanya was at her door: she wanted only Judith Kagan as Vera's Latin teacher. Tanya moved Judith with her persistence and our friend said, *"Tanechka, I have never taught such a little one, but I'm willing to try. I hope that love will help me!"* We both really liked that answer, and we started taking Vera to Judith's class. Luckily, both the teacher and the student liked each other. We all saw later that love, indeed, helped a lot!

However, serious difficulties awaited us from the very beginning. We could not find a single Latin book for children anywhere in Moscow. Tanya went to every second-hand bookshop, and everywhere she was looked at as if she was a lunatic. The reaction was: *"Our children do not need it, and we do not understand why you need it."* There was a similar situation with children's Latin textbooks and dictionaries. Our dear Judith had no books for Vera's age either. Through our Western friends, Tanya got a children's Latin textbook which we tried to photocopy. In all Soviet institutions at the time, copying machines were under special surveillance. God forbid, no one would use them to reproduce anti-Soviet literature. Sadly, we were unable to make a copy of a children's Latin book in the Soviet capital. A friend of ours from Austria, a physicist working in Moscow at the time, helped us. He personally made us a copy in his office. By that time, Vera's successful Latin lessons had inspired several parents among our friends and Judith

LIFE THIRD: MY EFFORTS TO EMIGRATE FROM THE SOVIET UNION

agreed to take their children to join Vera's lessons. The whole group of kids began using the textbook we produced for their studies. I am very curious about the books used by Pushkin's contemporaries to teach children Latin. However, in "Eugene Onegin," unfortunately, there is no indication what his tutors read to little Eugene in Latin, when *"first madam followed him, then monsieur replaced her."*

Vera's Latin teacher Ju. Kagan

Nevertheless, our teacher was not the one of those who stops with difficulties. She looked through all the books she had and, not finding anything more appropriate, she chose to my great amazement "Notes on the Gallic War" by Gaius Julius Caesar describing his military campaigns (58–50 BC). I was sure that our girl could not get her teeth into this text. But later I read on Wikipedia that "Notes" is written in Julius Caesar's characteristic precise, concise, and energetic manner. I also learned that it is traditionally the first work of classical Latin to be read in Latin classes for grown ups. Meanwhile, our American friend, Eliza Close, found a CHILDREN'S Latin textbook, published in England. It was a description of a young boy's life in ancient Rome. Now the lucky children in Moscow got proper textbook with which to study Latin.

When I write "children" I mean the group of children who were studying Latin with Verusha, which by that time my Tanya persuaded Judith to take as her students as well. The next children's book we managed to get was "Winnie the Pooh" by A. A. Milne in Latin. The reading of this book by the Latin group ended with a wonderful performance in which our Verusha played the part of Piglet. I am proud to recall my "great" role in this performance: I made a tail for my beloved piglet.

Children progress would cause stirring emotions in me. First, I kept thinking of my father. It is not hard to imagine how he would have rejoiced if he had lived to see it. Secondly, I was happy that, thanks to the lessons with Judith, our Verushka was communicating with one of the most educated people in the humanities that we knew. Thirdly, I was proud of my Tanya, who had initiated and organized their classes, and of our girl, who happily took the plunge. Fourth, I was happy to use each of Vera's classes as an excuse to go into this amazing apartment, where everything was steeped in the history and culture of the past.

Tanya, in order to help more Vera in Latin studies, got Judith's consent and attended the classes in the beginning. As she was an excellent teacher herself, plus she had taken a course in Latin when she had studied at the University, plus she had a lot of love for our child, all this helped a lot. To be honest, I was jealous of both my child and Tanya, both so much involved. At first, I even thought of getting cocky and asking to be with them too, I would sit quietly like a mouse, listen and take good note of everything. However, I never got the nerve to do this. Then I tried to read Vera's notebooks carefully, so that, like Tanya, I could keep up with what they were doing and keep up with them. Soon I realized that with our "multitask" life of refuseniks I had no mental valence or time left for this. I gave up and tried to forget about such a tempting idea.

In addition to working with the textbook, Judith ingeniously invented a theme-project-game for Vera's classes. She selected for her Latin pithy sayings, which had come into many European languages, becoming proverbs. During the lessons, they took apart in detail both the original in Latin and the translation into Russian of each proverb. Doing this, they discussed in both languages every proverb and the meaning of every word. In this process, Vera wrote them in her special notebook. Together with Vera, her parents memorized proverbs too. The game with proverbs went on merrily at home. One of us, taking turns would say proverbs in Russian or Latin, and the other one had to say them in another language. All three of us enjoyed this game and we learned many interesting facts even about proverbs, with which we were previously familiar.

I have already written about how I used to send jocular messages home from my trips. When Vera began her Latin studies, I sent a series of telegrams to her, each of which somehow played on one of the proverbs in her notebook. Each of my telegrams was rhyme in Russian I did not have time to produce the translation into English keeping the rhythm of these rhymes. One part of each telegram was a rephrased saying, and the other — a joke about our family. I will give ten examples without the Latin text, because even in this country Latin also went out of fashion and, unfortunately, never came back.

In 1983, Tanya Velikanov moved from camp to exile in Western Kazakhstan. I went there to visit her and from different places from there, I was sending telegrams with proverbs to Verusha. Here are three examples:

Proverb 1: *An eagle never hunts for flies.*
My text 1: *On my way, the eagle did not shovel flies. I love my girls!*

Proverb 2: *To live is to think.*
My text 2: *To live is to think. I kiss you again.*

Proverb 3: *A gladiators must make a decision right at the arena.*
My text 3: *Gladiators decides everything just at the arena. I am rushing and flying home, not knowing laziness.*

In the winter of 1984, with great difficulty, we got a voucher and Tanya and I went for two weeks to the sanatorium "Porechye" near Moscow. Vera stayed with Tanya's mother. From there I also was sending Verusha a series of telegrams with proverbs. Here are seven more examples.

Proverb 4: *Everybody who writes something reads it twice.*
My text 4: *Though the blizzard is much quieter, it is still not a good idea to open your mouth. Who is going to write anything at all, He will read it twice.*

Proverb 5: Repetition *is the mother of learning and the refuge of fools.*
My text 5: *Mama is skiing through the wood to everyone's surprise. Repetition is the mother of learning, and a haven for fools.*

I draw the reader's attention to the fact that Soviet censorship extended to translations from ancient Latin as well. A good example is how the proverb 5, widely known in Russian, irreversibly lost its second part. It seems to me that the full text of the original expands and deepens the meaning considerably: To this day, I do not know exactly why the proverb underwent circumlocution in Russia. Most likely, as usual, it was the intrigues of the Jews.

My proverb 6 telegram uses the astrologic signs of the zodiac for the members of our family: Virgo (Virgin) for Tanya and Pisces (Fishes) for Vera and Yuri.

Proverb 6: *Delaying the response is the cure for anger.*
My text 6: *The Fishes and the Virgin misses seeing the Fishes. Delaying the response is the cure for anger.*

Proverb 7: *Do not touch my drawings! (After the fall of Syracuse, Archimedes yelled to a Roman soldier demanding to stop working).*
My text 7: *The frost became less, and your mother is glad. Do not grab my drawings.*

Proverb 8: *He, who wants to learn without a book, carries water in a sieve.*
My text 8: *Our Little Frog is as quiet as a mouse, all under snow. Someone who learns without a book, Carries water in a sieve.*

Proverb 9: *As the king, so is the flock.*
My text 9: *The king is always like a flock. We are walking until we drop.*

Proverb 10: *A well-fed bellies are deaf to learning.*
My text 10: *The whole forest stands still under a blanket of fluff. A well-fed belly is deaf to learning.*

The Latin lessons were a great success. Not only did it increase Verusha's interest in a difficult language, but it also contributed to her and her parents' general humanitarian development. For example, I myself did not know until Verusha's lessons with Judith that A. Pushkin in his "Monument" not only used an epigraph from Horace, but he conceived his whole "Monument" as a retelling of Horace's ode in his own era. Thus, practicing the "old-fashioned" language suddenly turned out to be a surprisingly practical way to improve our lives at the very end of the 20th century, dis-

LIFE THIRD: MY EFFORTS TO EMIGRATE FROM THE SOVIET UNION

tracting the whole family from sad thoughts in our uneasy refusal epic.

WITH OUR LITTLE FROGGY TO KALUGA

Our refusenik status not only made our lives very difficult and poisonous, it changed the whole style of that life. We fell into the circle of unreliable Soviet citizens. Before communicating with our relatives and friends who were not involved in the emigration process, we now had to check with them on a case-by-case basis whether they were willing to risk their social status and deal with "lepers" like us. For us, this increased our already high psychological stress and narrowed down our circle even more. However, if our relatives agreed, communication was a great joy, especially when we could find company for our Verusha of her age.

That is what happened in the winter of 1984, when my niece Olya with her husband Aliosha and daughter Masha who was 12 years old, decided that they WANTED to take a trip together with us in our Little Froggy. Our daughter Verusha was 8 years old. It was especially pleasant for me to go with Olya. Firstly, I was glad to have the chance to be closer with her in the light of our separation from her father. Secondly, I involuntarily transferred my love of Innulia to her daughter, who so resembled her mother. Aliosha, much engaged in the protection of old Russian architecture, suggested we visit Kaluga, from his point of view, a beautiful historically interesting Russian city, and we went to Kaluga.

To be honest, I knew very little about Kaluga before that. For one living in the Soviet Union, of course, it was impossible not to know that Konstantin Tsiolkovsky, the "father" of Russian and, some would say, world cosmonautics, lived there. All textbooks during our school years would tell us this. Today the situation has changed, and the whole world agrees that the cosmonautics had, actually,

Our great-niece Masha in Kaluga

several fathers, but what is particularly pleasant is that the West nevertheless recognizes the merits of K. Tsiolkovsky, keeping him among founders of astronautics. I am a small enthusiast of space research in general. It seems to me that we have more than enough unsolved problems on Earth to spend on a purely political and military race in space such unthinkable resources. Therefore, the history of this race caused in me only anxiety.

The second thing I remembered for some reason about this pretty town on the Oka River was a refrain from V. Lebedev-Kumach's bravado song "Two friends" lyrics of which mentioned two Russian towns:

> *Come on, show all your might, Kaluga!*
> *Stride with more joy, Kostroma!*

I am not sure how cheerful Kostroma was at this time, but Kaluga really showed us all its might, greeting us with unbelievable frost. The temperatures were so low that poor Little Froggy's engine flatly refused to start. We even had beg the mercy of the driver of a heavy truck to tow us around the frozen city, until our car warmed up sufficiently, started and agreed to drive again. However, our company kept our spirits up and, despite the freezing weather, was surprisingly resilient and warm. We did a lot of walking, and, I want to praise Aliosha, firstly, for his choice of the city, and, secondly, for the interesting stories about its history. For both adults and girls it was interesting to listen to him. The city on the bank of Oka River, founded in the 14th century, was pleasant for all of us, and fierce frosts didn't prevent us from making friends with it. The local history museum also left a nice impression.

Tanya of mine has a special talent for making life around her look ornate. Thirty-nine years have passed since our trip to Kaluga, and Masha still remembers how Tanya brought "gizmos" from Moscow and decorated a dull Soviet provincial hotel room with them. In addition, she insisted on an excursion to the local market and bought little joys for the girls at the triple price in the form of bundles with nuts and dried fruits. These goblets were also supposed to help create a sense of "movable feast" in the sense intended in the title of Hemingway's novel.

However, of all Tanya's ideas for children on this trip, poetry readings were probably the most successful. She took with her a volume by N. Gumilev and we all, while walking, were learning two of his famous poems, "The Giraffe" (1907) and "The Captains" (1910). We used to do it when we drove our Little Froggy on the way there and back. We did it also when we walked around Kaluga on foot. Tanya surprisingly managed to captivate the whole company, children and adults alike, by this activity, and we all in concord, I would say avidly, read and memorized them. I can say for myself that, of course, I knew both poems much earlier, but I really felt their exotic originality and learned them by heart only in Kaluga. I remember how immediately after Kaluga I realized how little I knew about the poet's life and creative work. It was after this trip that I belatedly began to research them.

Then I learned that the poet's life really was very intense and tragic. From 1906–1914, he lived in Europe and traveled around the world. In 1910, he married Anna Akhmatova. The marriage was not successful and ended in divorce in 1918. At the very beginning of the First World War, in 1914, he volunteered to the front, and returned to Petrograd at the end of the war in 1918. It is notable that although almost all famous poets of that time wrote either patriotic or military poems, only two volunteers took part in the hostilities: Gumilev and Benedict Livshits. In 1920, Gumilev collected the greatest number of votes at the elections to head the All-Russian Union of Poets.

Nevertheless, already in 1921, soviet authorities suddenly arrested Nikolai Gumilev on the basis of the false charges: for participation in the conspiracy of "Vladimir Tagantsev Petrograd militant organization." Three weeks after the arrest there was a ruling of the Petrograd KGB ordering the execution of 56 of the 61 members of "Tagantsev's Conspiracy" and 2 days later, the report was in the paper that all the executions have happened. The KGB then assiduously covered up all traces of their crimes. Since then a century has passed and still nobody knows either the place of execution or the place of burial. In 1992, the case was considered entirely fabricated, and all those convicted in the case of "Petrogradskaya militant organization," including Nikolai Gumilev, were exonerated.

The main themes of Gumilev's lyrics include love, art, life and death. Besides this, there are adventure subjects. Unlike most poets, Gumilev's work is almost completely devoid of political themes.

Yes, he raved about giraffes and brave sailors. The only thing that could irritate the authorities was the fact that he openly declared that he was an Christian Orthodox believer and that he was sympathetic to the monarchy. However, behind irritation, the executioners somehow, felt that he was their enemy. That was the reason they destroyed him.

I want to tell you what it was in Kaluga that so childishly fascinated me in the mentioned verses of N. Gumilev. By the time he wrote "Giraffe", he had not yet had time to visit Africa, he had not yet had time to see with his own eyes how *"far, far away, on Lake Chad an exquisite wandering giraffe"*. However, his phenomenal artistic imagination painted a fantastic picture. I cannot refrain from reproducing here two lines that struck me long before my trip to Kaluga. These very lines continue to strike me today, lines describing the handsome giraffe:

> *He has graceful harmony and contentment,*
> *A magical pattern adorns his skin,*
> *That only the moon dares to match,*
> *Crushing and swaying above the moisture of wide lakes.*
> *In the distance, it is like the colored sails of a ship.*
> *His run is as smooth as a joyful bird's flight.*
> *I know there are many wonderful things the earth sees,*
> *When at sunset he hides in the marble grotto. .*

In addition to the blatant EXDTRAORDINARINESS of this poem, there is an endless sadness, even, I would say, tragedy. The poet speaks to his beloved woman, who cannot understand at all, let alone share his feelings. He is overwhelmed with rapturous emotions and she is crying. He knows that it is not her fault. She simply cannot cope with her mental and emotional condition. "*She has been inhaling a heavy fog for too long and she doesn't want to believe in anything but rain.*" Unfortunately, there was nothing he could do about it. After rereading and remembering these lines in Kaluga, I reflected on how often many of us, having inhaled a heavy fog for too long, then weep and cannot cope with themselves.

Two verses in "The Captains", describing *"discoverers of new lands"*, struck me about the same way with their EXTRAORDINARITY. I also cite them here:

LIFE THIRD: MY EFFORTS TO EMIGRATE FROM THE SOVIET UNION

When he ascended the flickering captain's bridge,
Recalling just abandoned port,
He shaved off, with strokes of his cane,
The foam shreds from his high boots.
Or, having discovered rioting on board,
He snatched his pistol from his belt,
So abruptly that the lace gold starts
To fall down from his pinkish Brabant cuffs.

When Gumilev wrote in his "Captains", *"the sails of ships are rustling,"* sailing ships were rapidly disappearing into history and becoming museum exhibits. Along with them were gone into history the captains in high boots and jackets with lace cuffs, and the more so with cuffs of pinkish Brabant lace with gold. Such lace was woven in Belgium (then called Flanders) beginning in the 16th century. The lace was famous for its quality, using only the finest threads of linen grown in the Dutch area of Brabant. Of course, the poet, who had traveled a great deal, could not have seen any captains as refined as his giraffe.

These captains enthrall him and, through him, the reader. He contrasts them with politicians and lawyers. It is of such captains, he wrote, that *"not the dust of lost charters, but the salt of the sea soaks into their breasts"*. In their difficult and unsafe voyages, he sees the meaning of life.

During his own short life, because he was destined to live only 35 years, the poet sought the exotic and refined. However, there is very little of that in real life, much more of ordinary and grey. When he did not find what he was looking for, he recreated it with his extraordinary poetic imagination and gave us the fruit of that imagination. Tanya managed to turn our trip into a solid holiday, which we all remember to this day. How wonderful that our girls, Masha and Vera, got this holiday as a gift from the poet! How wonderful that we went to Kaluga, and how wonderful that Tanya took with her a volume of Nikolai Gumilev! By inviting the poet to our company, I think she taught the girls another brilliant lesson about the importance of learning to see and enjoy beauty. It was a lesson not only for girls, I myself learned a lot in this trip.

Speaking of lesson, I was very happy to see how Tanya opposed the thoughtlessness of Masha's father Aliosha, who was trying tiresomely to reproach his daughter for her lack of education in the humanities. Even if this was true, he did not know what he was doing, his remarks were only turning the girl away from such an education. We have to give him a credit being so happy that he was sharing his extensive knowledge of Kaluga's architectural history with us on this trip. However, in Tanya's class he turned out to be a bad student himself. Anyway, I would like to think that this trip as a whole left all the participants with the same happy memories as I have

Our excursion to Kaluga was especially dear to me because we had Olga and her daughter Masha very close to us for several days before our departure from Russia. This was very important for us, because despite the touching attitude of both siblings Olya and Lyova, the break-up with their father Jan had put quite a bit of tar in the honey of our relationship with his children. All these years, separated by the Atlantic Ocean, we tried our best not to lose the closeness to them. I was very happy to see how my Galyusha and Olechka became close friends during those years.

In the winter of 2019, a terrible blow, blood cancer, struck our dear Olga. Her relatives did everything possible and even seemingly impossible to help her. They took her to Israel so that Olya could receive a unique treatment unavailable in any other country. Already hopelessly ill, she continued to work in order to pay at least to partially for the treatment. She tried her best to help her daughter and grandchildren, her brother Lyova and his family, and if not to help, at least to do something nice for them. She showed heroic courage in resisting the ruthless disease.

What also touched me to the core was Olya's active interest in these memoirs of mine, that my dear reader holds now in hands. When she was still undergoing treatment in Israel, she insisted that I send her the incomplete, but already written, part of it. By that time, I finished only about 300 or so pages what was about the half of the book. I did as she asked, and Olechka was the first reader and editor of those pages. Those days she was already feeling lousy: the negative reaction to the chemotherapy was very strong, and she was very weak. Nevertheless, she fished out a considerable amount of language errors in that state. An experienced professional editor, she made many valuable comments. Moreover, having learned that my computer has no Russian spelling editor, she, through Galechka,

PERSONALLY ASKED Vitya to help me install it. I was too shy to ask him for it myself, knowing Vitya's busy schedule. This kind of thing moved me to tears. Vitya did what she asked, and I was happily using this mighty program for preparing the Russian edition of the book. Today I appreciate Vitya's help in preparation of the English translation of my memoirs. Many thanks, my dear Vitya!

That was not the end of her helping me. In my immediate family, Olga was following me in age, and there was no one else besides the two of us who knew the facts of the family history as we did. And as for the period when I was no longer in Russia, Olga knew even more and better than I did. I already have mentioned that my memory was beginning to betray me. As a result, Olechka helped me a lot to mend the holes in my punctured memory, and I hoped that this help would continue.

However, alas, it was too good a plan to be true. The poor woman's health was slowly but surely deteriorating. Wild weakness and excruciating attacks of suffocation increased. An ICU doctor in Moscow, Olya's close friend and her leading doctor, and a wonderful person, Katya Koshkin decided to move the poor woman to Moscow, at least temporarily. She had a hope that among family and friends, maybe it would be easier to achieve stabilization, after which she could return to Israel to continue treatment. However, that plan did not work either. Olya did not better in Moscow. Her closest people: her brother Lyova. and his children, her daughter Masha and home doctor Katya were near her. The girl Masha with whom we were so excited reading Gumilev's poetry in Kaluga, *"grew up and blossomed,"* just like the Pushkin's princess in "The Tale of the Dead Princess and the Seven Knights." She turned into a wonderful young woman, a prosperous businessperson, a mother of two wonderful children and a tender, attentive daughter. I was much less worried about until her last day, knowing that she had Masha. Family and loved ones were ready for anything, but no miracle happened. In April, Olechka, exhausted herself, and left a life that had become unbearable.

SYMPOSIUM OF REFUSENIKS

The year 1987 marked the tenth anniversary of our refusenik life. Thousands of Jewish families suffered like we did, thrown out of their normal lives, deprived, as Tanya and I did, of a job in our professions, of education, as our Galya did, of the right to visit relatives and loved ones abroad, as most citizens of the Soviet Union did. This was in blatant contradiction with the obligations of the Soviet government, which had signed more than one international treaty on human rights. One such treaty was the 1975 Helsinki Act, adopted by 35 European and North American countries at the Conference on Security and Cooperation in Europe. To help publicize the blatant violation of universally recognized human rights by the Soviet Union, Jewish refuseniks prepared and held this year the Symposium in Moscow, "Legal problems and humanitarian aspects of the refusal for security reasons of the permission to leave the Country".

The authorities, clamping their hearts (I doubt they have them!), gave official permission for the Symposium, but refused to provide rooms. As a result, we had to hold the meetings in private apartments. There were over 130 people attending with over 50 papers presented. We received Greetings to the Symposium from the human rights activists from England, USA, Israel, Switzerland, Belgium and other countries. We were pleased to learn that many people not only in Russia cared about our fates.

I prepared a paper for the Symposium: "Departure from the country: the legal situation in the USSR and in the United States." Unfortunately, I was not able to read it myself because during the Symposium I was in the hospital with severe double vision. We do not know exactly, what caused this illness, but it could have been a consequence of a broken valve on an oxygen cylinder in my hands during my shift at the maternity hospital. The oxygen in such cylinders was under high pressure, so I could get a serious trauma. Whatever was the case, I managed to get away with this accident quite happily. I had to go to more than one hospital for my double vision. Some details of these misadventures I will describe in one of the next chapters. Because of my inability to be at the symposium physically, my Tanya read the paper.

In the course of preparing this paper, I learned many interesting and useful things. As a non-member of the communist party and a Jew, I had no chance of going to another country. As a result, I had lived in the country for 50 years without ever having crossed the border of the Soviet Union. My natural curiosity helped me to know how it was possible for Soviet citizens to leave their country.

What I did not know at all was what kind of procedures for leaving the country existed in Western countries. Of course, in the first place, I was interested in the United States, where we were going to move. Our american friends, who were working and living in Moscow at the time, helped me a lot. Besides, other papers presented at the Symposium and communication with my comrades-in-arms increased my general education in the field of human rights. Of course, attending the Symposium gave my friends the satisfaction of knowing that we were not sitting idly by waiting for some unknown man to come along and help us. Such a thing as our Symposium was also useful because it brought information about gross violations of human rights to Uncle Sam, calling him for help.

Tanya, unlike me, took an active part in the Symposium. A particularly important role, from my point of view, fell to Tanya to liaise with representatives of the Western press in Moscow and to organize the arrival of Western correspondents at the Symposium meetings. She was able to do such an important and dangerous job in a totalitarian country because of her courage as well as her perfect knowledge of the English language. In the course of this work, she translated the summaries of all the papers into English so that people in the West could read them.

Tanya, standing on the left, is translating at the symposium

As a result, my Tanya being far from an IRON WOMAN had to break through the IRON CURTAIN. I think her activity was helping to lower the curtain not only along the borders of this large country, but also everywhere inside it. Of course, in a totalitarian country like the Soviet Union, it was a dangerous occupation. So, it grieved me wildly at the time that I myself was in a clinically deplorable state and could not support her. We had already been in refusal for more than ten years and had reached a point where everything was at stake, and it was simply impossible to retreat. Tanya risked doing such "anti-Soviet" work not only at the Symposium. She was by then regularly interpreting for groups of dissenters in dialogue with representatives of the West.

It was sad that there were people in the refusenik brotherhood who accused Tanya of getting to know foreigners in order to distinguish her from the rest of the refuseniks and get permits only for our family. This was monstrously unfair and monstrously untrue. It is impossible to believe that the worst of these accusations came from one of our closest friends, Tzlia's husband Milan Menjeritski. In his inflamed brain this ridiculous, I would say, typically Soviet, explanation took shape. I talked about this in the chapter about Milan's wife Tzilia.

It seems to me that the life of rerefuseniks is a kind of test of strength. I can only compare it to exile or imprisonment in terms of difficulty. Not everyone has the strength to endure such a difficult test and to keep his dignity at the same time. Even more, it is not right to expect, let alone to demand such strength and endurance from poor people who are in such a predicament. It seems to me that Milan did not pass the test. I was mad at him for a long time, but then I realized that it was wrong. God is his judge! I do not like to speak ill of people, but I think such accusations can also be born of irritation: People often would like to do what Tanya did, but could not do, for example because they did not speak English well enough.

PARTING WITH GALYA

When Tanyusha and I made the most incredible effort to get Galya's family across the border as quickly as possible, we had good reason to do so. After all, we were the ones who started the whole thing and encouraged them to take such an arduous journey. Galya and Vitya were young, and we were sure that they would be fine. However, Vitya's grandmother was part of the team. The mother of Vitya's mother Geda, was a lovely woman who was already in her 70's and who had little idea what awaited her in the new life. Of course, she was scared to leave for the unknown, and she made weak but touching attempts to dissuade Vitya from his intention. *"Well, what are you missing here,"* she used to say to him. *"Do you want me to buy you a car?"* But after she could not be dissuaded, she courageously agreed to follow her loved ones to the edge of the world. Of course, we were all worried about how she would handle such a big change in her life and how she would cope with it. In addition, they were carrying a two-year-old child, our granddaughter, Anechka, and naturally, we were worried how they would manage to carry out the routine daily operations required by the little girl on the road. It would have been so much easier if we had all gone together!

However, in all the pre-departure worries, we were completely unaware of the worst possible side of obtaining Galecka's permission to leave the country: our separation from her for an indefinite period of time, and maybe even forever. Those were the rules of the game: the authorities never bothered to tell anyone how long it would take to get permission. At the same time, in our circle, certainly, it never even crossed anyone's mind to return to Russia ever. I was so anxious to see Galyusha reach freedom and, I looked so forward to it. However, at the same time I was terribly afraid of her being away from me. Once I remembered a poem written in 1932 by Russian poet Alexander Kochetkov, whom I did not know really well.

The poem's title was "The Ballad of the Carriage filled with Tobacco Smoke." It was this poem which brought the poet wide popularity. It ends with a stanza that quite accurately describes my emotions at that time:

> *Never part with your loved ones!*
> *Never part with your loved ones!*
> *Never part with your loved ones!*
> *With all your blood sprout in them,*
> *Every time, say goodbye forever!*
> *Every time, say goodbye forever!*
> *Every time, say goodbye forever,*
> *When leaving only for a moment!*

Having thought everything through a thousand times, I really prepared to say goodbye forever to my girl and to the people closest to her! At the same time, I truly believed that we were sending them off for a new, happier life. The moment of such a farewell came, surprisingly enough, when in 1987, Galya's family unexpectedly received exit visas. It was a very difficult time for both sides:

those leaving and those staying behind. On the other hand, Tanyusha and I had a sense of great victory: five members of the family out of eight had broken free. Of course, we tried to help them in everything we could during the difficult days of pre-departure rush and nervousness. I have to give credit to Vitya's grandmother, Lydia Oguz, who was absolutely on top of it and behaved heroically. In all the years, I had known her she had always selflessly given herself to her family and in this time of difficulty, she did as well. I cannot help but boast that Lydia admitted me into the circle of people she considered her close ones, and I was lucky to receive a lot of her warmth, attention and care.

The time came to a real and final separation. I remember one sad and at the same time funny detail while going through customs inspection at Sheremetyevo airport. One of my friends helped them to pack their suitcases very well, neatly folding each item. We were already hardened and, we knew how the inspection works. Therefore, we knew it could be a wasted effort. But it was painful for our newcomers to see the real picture. Things from the suitcase ended up on the table in a heap that we had to put back by ourselves later. Unfortunately, their former semiprofessional packer was not with them at the airport.

Among the escorts was Vitya's faithful friend Misha Bershadsky, always ready to help others. He was, for instance, one of the best baby-sitters for our Vera, when we could not stay at home with her ourselves. When our dear deportees looked melancholy at the pile of clothes on the table, Misha was the first to rush to pack them back in the suitcase. Here it was an embarrassment: when Misha, packed the things, they did not want to fit into the suitcase, heavily packed before. Misha, capable in many respects, had little experience in packing, the more so because the suitcase in question mostly contained women's underwear. At that time, Misha, was still a young bachelor. Honestly, he did not have to pack women's underwear very often. I remember well our puzzled assistant with a woman's bra in his hands. Nevertheless, with a collective effort, we managed to shove everything back into the suitcase. Time flew by, and the moment came when our dear family went behind the barrier, where we could no longer follow them. I saw them off with a look that expressed a mixture of joy and sorrow. My eyes were wet.

Geda and Granny flew away and we agreed that the next day we would come to their flat to offer everything left there to the *"Rabbit's Families and Friends"* (A.Milne, "Winnie the Pooh"). The next morning took place with, as in the feuilleton "All Life" by M. Zoshchenko: *"a free distribution of elephants and various garments."* During my school years, I learned, that it were I.Ilf and E.Petrov who in their "Golden Calf" invented the expression *"giving out elephants."* In Chapter 6 of the novel, one of the tricks of the famous Brahmin yoga in his performance had anounced: *"Materialization of spirits and distribution of elephants."* I assume, this was most likely one of the Soviet literary plagiarism and falsifications. The undesirable Zoshchenko published his feuilleton in 1928, and the popular Ilf and Petrov their novel — only in 1931.

The first week after Galya and Vitya left, the phone rang and a man's voice on the other end of the line asked for Victor Khatutsky. It was the military commissar of Moscow's Oktyabrsky district, where Vitya was on the military register. I politely explained to the man that Victor was not at home and he was not in the Soviet Union either. *"When will he be back?"* my interlocutor asked glumly. *"He is due for an urgent military training camp".* Inwardly exulting, I tried, using the vocabulary familiar to this man, but again politely and understandably, to say what I thought about it: *"I understand your difficulties, but I believe that Victor will never return to the USSR, for he has departed for permanent residence."* After a short pause of confusion, the Military Commissar exclaimed *"But that cannot be!"* To this, I replied that he had every right to think so and hung up.

The conversation reminded me of one of my favorite Moscow jokes, only turned inside out. A regular visitor of a French bistro was coming every day and ordering the same thing: coffee and Pravda newspaper. One day the waiter brought him only coffee with a polite apology: *"I'm sorry, monsieur, the Soviet Union no longer exists and so does* newspaper *Pravda,"* he told the customer. The next day everything was repeated again, and this time the waiter replied with some irritation: *"Excuse me, sir, I told you yesterday that the Soviet Union no longer exists, and there is no Pravda newspaper either".* Responding to this, the visitor happily replied, *"Please, repeat, repeat, this, my dear! I like hearing this."*

In literature, and I classify jokes as literary work, things often happen better, more as we want them to, than in life. Personally, like the visitor to the French bistro in the just told joke, I would have been much happier if Pravda newspaper had ceased to exist after the collapse of the Soviet Union as well. The articles in Pravda come to my mind, which today can arouse no other feelings than shame and disgrace. But the newspaper is still alive and well, and in Russia the Communist Party continues to exist, which according to the data of 2016, published in Wikipedia, consists of 162,173 members (!?). After all the bloody crimes committed under the banner of Soviet Communists, these thousands of people have the conscience to keep ranting about prosperity under socialism. Actually, the fact that the Communist Party is not in power in Russia today does not change much. Thank God, my immediate family and, most importantly, my children and grandchildren are on the different planet. However, the latest events in Ukraine today show that planet we all came from is still existing as well as newspaper Pravda.

Having found herself on the other side of the Iron Curtain, Galechka impressed not only us, but also all our friends and relatives in both hemispheres of the world. Having over-exhausting cares and troubles of making a new life for her family of four, including a two-year old child, she found both time and energy, developing prodigious activity in her attempts to do something for us, which might have helped to get the permission for us to leave the country. There was not a door she did not knock for this purpose, there was not a powerful person in the U.S.A. she did not approach about it. She was going to demonstrations and was giving interviews on television. I am convinced that her personal contribution to getting our permission to leave the USSR was extremely significant. In addition, it is hard to overstate, the moral support it gave us. It certainly added to the pressure of the West on the Soviet leaders, who essentially held us, you could say, hostages in the Soviet Union. So many people said to me, *"Yuri, you are very lucky with your daughter, she was behaving just heroically!"* Such words made everything warm up inside me. I really am incredibly lucky with my daughter. Thank you my dear girl, you really showed yourself to be heroic these days. Today, when I am translating these lines into English, my "girl" is sixty two years old.

A HOSPITAL EPIC

This is the story of how I had to stay a lot of time in Moscow hospitals. One day, I was driving my Little Froggy and suddenly, quite close to home, a phantasmagoria began before my eyes. I did not understand what was happening and so immediately pulled up to the curb and stopped. It took some time for me to figure out what it was double vision. The next thing I discovered was that if I closed one of my eyes the double vision would disappeare. It became clear to me that this was a way for me to return home as soon as possible and there together with Tanya to decide what to do next. I did so and slowly, slowly drove home. I was quite scared and so nervous that when I got out of the car, I was all wet with sweat

Tanya, of course, got terribly nervous and immediately called an ambulance. They came and said, *"Go to the hospital immediately!"* On the way, Tanya tried to discuss with them the hospital we could go to for help. However, nobody in the ambulance team listened to her, they told her, *"We will bring him to the nearest one, and figure it out there what to do next."* The "nearest" turned out to be a city hospital on Kashir highway, about which we had NEVER heard ANYTHING and had NEVER knew ANYTHING. Tanya was completely dejected. We arrived at the admission entry of this hospital.

The building seemed at least fairly new and clean, and to that end, thank you. However, something very unpleasant happened on the way from the admission room to the ward. Tanya's keen eye spotted a rat running down the corridor. That was the last drop to fill the cup. I stayed in the ward for the night, and she came home strongly depressed and began to call all her friends tohelp for God's sake. As always in Russia, you can get everything by acquaintance. The next morning through our good friend, also a refusenik, she already had an agreement with the head of the department of the Neurosurgery at the Botkin Hospital to admit me there. This is one of the best hospitals in Moscow, and I have described it already in the sad story of Sharah Karig. Actually, it was probably hard to find a better place to treat double vision in Moscow.

When I was writing these lines, I remembered well the name of this glorious man, the head of the Neurosurgery, Ravikovich, but, to my shame, I could not remember his first name and patronimic. I decided to turn to the Internet: he was the head of the oldest and one of the largest departments of neurosurgery in Moscow. Imagine my surprise when I could not find ANYTHING about this person in Yandex and in Google. It was not just especially important for me to bring here the name of Ravikovich. Simply, knowing well that undesirable people disappear often from history in Russia, I decided to spare no time and to find out why this person, whom I liked so much, did not please the authorities. I looked through everything available on the history of Botkin's Hospital and the history of neurosurgery in the USSR in general. NOTHING!!! When I had absolutely lost hope, the memories of an unknown doctor, whose father was a wartime front comrade of Ravikovich, suddenly appeared on my computer screen. In 1963, this doctor graduated from school, and Ravikovich, then still a boy, advised him, to go to medical school. Although there were only a couple of phrases associated with Ravikovich in this document, I was happy to find them. Firstly, I was happy to get confirmation that at that time, 24 years before I met him, Ravikovitch was already the director of the Botkin clinic department. Secondly, these memories brought back to my memory the name and patronymic, which I had so shamefully forgotten: his first name was Mikhail, of course. Thirdly, the author of those memoirs had already written that all that time Mikhail Ravikovich was the Chief Neurosurgeon of Moscow, which I had never known. If what I had read in these memoirs was true, we were dealing with yet another example of shameless remaking of history in the Soviet Union. To be honest, I did not have time to investigate further.

The next morning there was a detective story of kidnapping me from the hospital at Kashir highway and transporting me to Botkin Hospital. First, Tanya tried to order an ambulance. It turned out to be practically impossible. When it was not a doctor, but a patient, who was ordering an ambulance, the waiting time was at least a week (!?). Then we decided to use just a taxi. Tanya with this taxi came to the entrance, asked the driver to wait for her and went up to the floor. Somehow, after swindling the floor nurse with giving her some important reasons why she urgently needed to take me to another hospital, we hurried out of the room. In Russia, few people take the stairs, and we were at 11-th floor, and there was an elevator. However, we did not want to meet accidentally any of the medical staff, so we went down the stairs. On the

LIFE THIRD: MY EFFORTS TO EMIGRATE FROM THE SOVIET UNION

way I changed clothes in the staircase into the clothes Tanya had brought for me, we left my pajamas on the banister of the stairs. When we got out of the stairwell, we jumped into the waiting taxi car and rushed to Botkin Hospital.

Since they were admitting me through influence, I was immediately looked at carefully by a wonderful doctor, Mikhail Ravikovich. By that time, I forgot to mention, several doctors I knew had already examined me and suggested two possible diagnoses, either a brain tumor or, or a brain aneurysm. Both were very bad, difficult to say which was better. Dr.Ravicovich studied my case very carefully. He joined the opinion of the previous doctors who had seen me. He told us that only a brain tomography could clarify the diagnosis, preferably a magnetic resonance imaging (MRI), if not, then a CAT scan. He said, he did not have these devices in his department and, unfortunately, he could not organize these procedures for us. Therefore, in his hospital such clarification was only possible by opening the skull (!?). However, he recommended the tomography at other place. If Tanya could manage to do this, he would turn a blind eye to our excursion to this place.

Such a statement affected my Tanyusha like a signal "Attack!" Soon we managed to find out how sad the situation was. There was only ONE MRI device in Moscow at that time. Moscow State University physicists had tried to disassemble it, to figure out how this miracle worked and to reproduce it. Therefore, this option evaporated for us. As for a CAT scan, the situation was not much better. In Moscow, there were 25 devices, 20 of which were in closed institutions of party-government apparatus and KGB. If it were possible to get into those places at all, then you would have to pay a VERY big bribe to get in. The other 5 devices were in medical institutions for the regular people. As a result, there was a long queue of patients in need of this crucial diagnostic test, and if I got in line, I would have to wait about five years to get it (!?)

The second option looked almost impossible, but not for Tanya. She bribed half of Moscow and made her way to the International Center for Eye Microsurgery, run by S. N. Fedorov, one of the five lucky owners of a device, and arranged for me to come there for the coveted procedure. I still do not know how much the cost was. Then Tanya came back in a taxi on already the beaten track, she snatched me from Ravikovich, drove me to the Fyodorov Center, I had a CAT scan there, after which they took me to the Botkin Hospital in the same way and brought me back to Ravikovich. The operation "Y" was a success. For those who do not know, the expression is taken from the title of a popular 1960s Moscow film-comedy "Operation Y and Other Adventures of Shurik" shot by Leonid Gaidai.

However, the main success of the operation was that the CAT scan showed neither a tumor nor an aneurysm. No money was enough for such good news. In all the years that followed, Tanya tried so hard to forget exactly how much she paid, that she succeeded well in doing so. Both of us will never forget the wonderful result of our efforts. The following days in the Ravikovich neurosurgery department were no longer so gloomy: we could forget the terrible diagnoses. I had adapted to live with severe double vision. In the frame of my broken glasses, I screened one glass with paper, and removed the other one out. This way I was able to see only with one eye which stopped my double vision and allowed me to walk and to eat, in other words, to live.

There were three other people in my room in the hospital, two walking and one bedridden. The bedridden one was a boy of school age, paralyzed from the waist down. All the class in his school went to the collective farm, as it was a custom, to help to harvest potatoes. The boy bent over another bush and suddenly the paralytic stroke hit him instantly. When they brought him to the hospital, doctors discovered the spinal nerve cord of the boy tied into a knot. He had to have a surgery to "untie" this knot. The boy could not get out of bed or walk, he could not go to the toilet, and was suffering with a bedpan. When I, armed with my special glasses, walked around the ward, I saw that about half of the patients in our department could not walk because of paralysis. However, I did not see A SINGLE wheelchair on the ward! I went with my bewilderment to the charge nurse on the ward, from whom I learned that they had two such chairs in their storeroom, both broken. After getting this nurse's permission, I went to the storeroom to look at these two invalids. After examining the "sick" wheelchairs, I concluded that I could assemble one working chair using the parts of both.

I immediately called home and asked Tanyusha to use the first visit to bring me the necessary tools. Having received them, I set to work. A day later, I rolled one working chair out of the storeroom. However, a new problem arose. The chairs of those days used inflatable bicycle wheels. I searched the whole storage room, but I did not find a tire inflator, and, of course, nobody remembered where it had gone. I was very upset, but then I had an epiphany. Most of the wards on the floor had oxygen lines with taps. From the same senior nurse, I begged a piece of rubber tubing, which I could pull over the faucet and thus be able to inflate the wheels with oxygen! I was aware that the safety officer was unlikely to approve of my ingenuity. Nevertheless, I was obsessed with getting my boy out of bed.

Unbelievably, we did! All worked out as I had intended! My two walking roommates helped me to carry the poor boy from the bed and to put him in the chair. It was one of the best days in my life! I do not know what happened to the boy later, but this day his joy was boundless. I had never seen such a happy face before or after that. Then it was impossible to get him out of the chair until late in the evening. The highlight of the day was when he drove out into the hallway, pulled up to a pay phone and called his mother's house. The mother was stunned. She almost had a heart attack. She could not believe she could hear her son's voice. After all, mobile phones did not exist at that time. There was only one mishap with that wheelchair that day. The boy also wanted to drive the wheelchair to the toilet, but he could not do this. The door to the toilet was not wide enough for the wheelchair to pass through it (?!) Probably no one at the hospital thought of that because there were no working wheelchairs on the ward anyway.

I spent about three weeks in Ravikovich's neurosurgery department. After receiving the results of the CAT scan, they tried to give me hormonal anti-inflammatory drugs, which began to reduce the double vision. By the time they discharged me from the hospital, the double vision had practically disappeared. I was happy to go back home and took with me the fondest memories of the head of the department, Mikhail Ravikovich.

Tanya rightly thought that since we had not received an exact diagnosis, the restoration of my vision did not mean that such an episode could not happen again. And it did: about a month later the double vision came to me again, now, the other eye was the culprit. Having learned by bitter experience, this time we decided not to hurry to the hospital, but to consult a good specialist, not a neurosurgeon but a neurologist. Tanya's sister, Natasha helped us to find such a doctor. His name was Boris Gekht and he was the head of the neurological department of the hospital of the Ministry of Transportation. Through our friends, we managed to persuade him to admit me to his clinic. Having listened to our story and examined me attentively, he suggested a rare and poorly studied neurological diagnosis: Tolosa-Hunt Syndrome which medical science studied and described only in 1961. Curiously, neurologists sometimes call this condition as a "chameleon". The internet explained that the origin of the name has to do with the fact that the symptoms of the disease often mislead doctors: they take it for a brain or vascular lesion. That was exactly what happened to me! Dr. Gekht agreed to admit me to his hospital and reassured us that this disease was well treatable with hormones.

The hospital admitted me and I started treatment. It was the spring of 1988. My room was for two people, and my roommate turned out to be quite pleasant. It was in this ward that I spent my 50th birthday. Tanyusha brought me a flat bottle of brandy, which we drank to my health with my roommate. The hormones were doing their work and my condition gradually began to improve. Tanya and I were glad that we had found such a good doctor. An interesting observation about him: he seemed to us aloof and taciturn. One day Tanya, feeling emotional for some reason, briefly described our refusal situation to him. The person seemed to be changed: he became especially tender and attentive. We could not help seeing his sympathy and support. This has happened not for the first time in our many years of experience, but usually only with nice people.

I spent almost a month in Gekht's hospital and, grateful, could go home with restored vision. However, before they discharged, Dr. Gekht did not advise me to return to my physically demanding "midwifery" job. He found it necessary and possible to give me a temporary disability. This outcome, of course, worried me and I asked him what the word "temporary" meant in his conclusion. He reassured me by promising me a full recovery.

THE NEW HOSPITAL CIRCLE

However, this was not the end of my hospital epic. Just a few days later, Tanyusha noticed a change in the pigmentation of my skin.

It seemed to her that I turned blue. Our medical acquaintances attributed it to a reaction of my liver to drugs which were used for my treatment. However, the cyanosis did not go away, and Tanya's anxiety was growing. She decided that it was necessary to show me to a doctor urgently and wanted only Dr.Gekht to see me. We drove back to the hospital and Gekht admitted me. He took me to the window where there was more light and looked at me and cried out, "*He has got hepatitis—jaundice. Go to the infectious diseases hospital at once!*"

We left the hospital, discouraged, and decided first to go to our Tzilia, who lived a five-minute walk from where we were. Such a foolish decision could only have occurred to us in the utter unconsciousness in which we were both. Clearly, it was much more convenient to choose a hospital from there and order transportation. However, normal people should never visit their loved ones when you have such an ACUTE MEDICAL INFECTION. It was embarrassing, but we put our dear Tzilechka in a big-ass pigsty, may God forgive us! This time just as relentlessly, as always before, Tzilia proved to be an ambulance. Together with her, we opted for the infectious disease department of the Botkin Hospital, considered one of the oldest and best in Moscow for this disease. Besides, I was electrified that the hospital was named after an outstanding physician S. P. Botkin, a classic of Russian medicine and a major infectious disease doctor, and besides, a relative of our beloved Verochka Prokhorov.

The hospital was founded on the donations of a remarkable Russian philanthropist from a family of Old Believers, Kozma Soldatyonkov, an outstanding man, an entrepreneur, a manufacturer, a patron of the arts, and a selfless publisher of the most important books on Russian history. He gave so much to Russia that he was called Kozma de Medici in memory of the famous dynasty of Renaissance rulers of Florence, who were patrons of the most distinguished artists and architects of their time. This Florentine dynasty included four popes and two queens. The Medici of Russia also donated funds for the maintenance of the House of God at the Rogozhsky cemetery, for scholarships and grants to needy students of Moscow State University, for scholarships to students of Moscow gymnasiums, to the Arnoldo-Tretyakov College of deaf mutes, as benefits to brides and recruits, as well as to pay land duties for the peasant society village Prokunino. When Russians were reading the manifesto on the abolition of serfdom, a rumor spread across Russia that in fact, the Tsar did not sign anything, but simply the generous Soldatyonkov bought out all the peasants and let them go free. The Soldatyonkovs were merchants, but in 1892, Vasily Soldatyonkov, Kozma's nephew, brought up by his uncle after the early death of his brother Ivan, received the hereditary nobility, as an award for the service to the country. The Russian Medici belonged to a galaxy of worthy citizens of the country, constituting the pride and glory of Russia. Nevertheless, thank to efforts of the Soviet authorities, we do not see his name in Russian history.

Kozma Soldatyonkov was lucky: he died in 1901, thus avoiding the sad fate of his comrade and colleague I. N. Prokhorov, the father of our Verochka Ivanovna. Soldatyonkov's grave was in the family section of Rogozhsky cemetery. In Soviet times, authorities destroyed the grave, as well as a large tomb of merchants Soldatyonkovs. According to Soldatyonkov's will, his library (8 thousand volumes of books and 15 thousand copies of magazines), as well as a collection of Russian paintings (258 canvases and 17 sculptures) were transferred to the Museum of Count Rumyantsev and, as a national treasure, were kept in a separate room with the name "Soldatyonkov's Gallery." Bolsheviks closed the Museum in 1924. All its exhibits they added to the holdings of the Tretyakov Gallery and the Russian Museum, of course, without mentioning the Soldatenkov name.

According to his will, a large tract of land and a large sum of money was given to build a hospital *"for all the poor without distinction of ranks, estates or religions."* A separate sum of money was designated for the construction of an Russian Orthodox church on the hospital premises, although, strictly speaking, Kozma Soldatyonkov was not a Russian orthodox believer. At another point of his will, he wanted to give money for the construction of the Artisan School, which opened its doors to students in 1909. The hospital began its work in 1910, and at that time, it had only one department: an INFECTIOUS DISEASE department, which the one I got into. In 1911, the church started serving sick parishioners. The hospital kept the name K. T. Soldatenkov until 1920, when it was renamed after S. P. Botkin. With all my respect to this eminent doctor, I am sorry to see that Soldatenkov's name disappeared from everywhere. In 1921, the authorities closed the temple and morgue. Nowadays, the Orthodox Church returned to its building.

I had hepatitis B, not hepatitis A, therefore I needed more severe and more difficult treat. With hepatitis B, there is always a risk of irreversible liver damage. We urgently called for transport, while I, depressed, sat on a chair, trying not to touch anything. The ambulance arrived and we went back to the hospital from which I had so happily escaped a short time earlier.

This time the appearance in the waiting room was dramatic. We had begun to fill out all the required forms when we heard noise and bustling and, at times, rumbling from the corridor. A nurse opened the door and we saw the battle. A sick man was coming in after us, greatly dissatisfied with life and with the course of events. He was behaving, I would say, violently, and I believe he was a psychiatric patient. If anyone tried to approach him, he would grab the nearest chair and threw it at that person. The nurse shut the door tightly so that the noise from the corridor would not disturb us. This sick man really scared everyone, and Tanya and I were no exception, so filling out the intake form was quite nerve-racking. With the consent of the nurse, we waited until everything calmed down, the staff moved the rioter somewhere and we could go into my room. That was how I began my second cycle at Botkin Hospital.

I knew infectious hepatitis can be transmitted with food virus through feces and blood and also through sexual contact. I was at a loss as to how I got this infection. During his first rounds when the doctor came to our room, I asked him about it. The answer literally stunned me, and I found it hard to believe. The doctor said that based on his experience in their department, we can say that about 70% of all cases of infectious hepatitis turned out to be caused by syringe infection. Difficult to believe, this means that because of insufficiently conscientious sterilization of syringes, medical workers of medical institutions of the country IN THE MAJORITY OF CASES are giving with their own hands their patients one of the most severe infections. Pay attention, this situation happens not in the medical center of a remote village but in the best hospitals of the country's capital. In my case, before

I learned about my hepatitis B, I was in three hospitals: the city hospital on Kashirskoye Shosse, Botkin Hospital and the hospital of the Ministry of Transport. One of these three hospitals I have to thank for the syringe infection I received.

The ward I went to was quite large, if I remember correctly, about a hundred people. There was only ONE toilet (!?) for the whole ward. Thus, the patients in the ward had a good opportunity to transmit their own form of infection to each other. In addition, the best medicine for infectious hepatitis is non-acidic berries and fruit. During all the time that I was in the ward, we were NEVER had fresh berries and fruits, which during the cold months of autumn, winter and spring in Moscow were always a sight unseen. Dr. S. P. Botkin was engaged much in infectious diseases. That is why all types of hepatitis got their name after him. I think that if he had visited our department, he would not have been pleased with what he would have seen.

Fortunately, we had many wonderful friends. One day Tanya came to me and brought me some FRESH STRAWBERRIES (!!!) in the middle of winter. It turned out that the Dutch Embassy had received berries. The ambassador's wife, Vilma Buwalda, knowing that I had hepatitis, sent them to Tanya for me. Another time I got bananas from her in the similar way. This story was even more amazing. There was a reception going on at the embassy and one of our friends happened to be there and witnessed the story. Embassy's person serving the table had already put a vase of bananas on it without asking Vilma. Vilma walked around the table, noticed this vase and said to their guests, *"Please don't eat the bananas, there is a sick person to whom the doctor has recommended bananas, and they must be saved for that sick person."* Lenochka Okhotnikova, Sasha Brussilovsky's ex-wife, then already living in Paris, was not less caring. Having learned about my illness, she managed to get some healing fresh fruit juices, unheard of in Moscow, and somehow managed to send them for me from Paris to Moscow. Sadly, neither of the two wonderful women is alive now, but when I think of them, I choke with tears of gratitude.

In connection with my illness and stay in hospital, it is impossible not to mention our wonderful friend and fellow sufferer Volodia Prestin. Among the Moscow refuseniks, Volodya was a veteran: at that time he had been trying to get his family to leave for

Israel for 17 (!?) years. Being a very special person, Volodya never had to be asked for help: he came to our door as soon as he saw he could help us. It was thanks to him that during my illness Tanya was able to leave Verochka with him and leave home either to visit me in the hospital or to attend some important meeting, of which there were so many during our struggle to emigrate.

The story of how Tanya met and got to know Volodya is noteworthy. It happened at Tzilia Reitburd's apartment. The mission of the tiger of kindness led this intrepid woman to a heart attack, and Tanya in her runs stopped by to visit the sick friend. She could not call Tzilia beforehand because the authorities had cut off her phone to interfere with Tzilia's boisterous social activities in the refusenik movement. The door opened, and Tanya appeared caught like a hen in a pluck: there was a search in Tzila's apartment! The searchers put her in a chair in the first room and asked her not to move. At some point, a man showed up, who caught Tanya's attention because the searchers tried to conduct a body search on him, but the stranger categorically declined. Then there was a phone call to the police department to detain the man for disobeying the authorities. In these conversations, Tanya heard his name Vladimir Prestin. This scene took place very close to Tanya, who, by some sixth sense, felt that he had to get rid of something. I quote here Tanya's words from the book "Remembering Volodya Prestin" published in Israel:

> I pointed to the man with my eyes to my lap and a notebook fell on it that I had discreetly tucked under my clothes. Unfortunately, we both did not see that in the corner there was an elevator woman sitting, who had quietly disappeared from the room. As soon as they took Volodya out of the room I was taken away and interrogated and examined personally, and for several hours they were beating me over my quite truthful replies that I did not know this man, that I did not know what was in the book, and why I had taken it, I did not know either...

The examiners, of course, extracted Volodya's notebook from under Tanya's clothes and took it from her.

Volodya's arrest lasted several days, and he came to see us as soon as they released him. At that time, we learned that the book contained the addresses of many refuseniks that needed help, and Volodya was upset that the information had gotten to our tormentors. Volodya became and until his last day remained a very close person to us.

In principle, I have been quite healthy, and in half a century of living in Russia I have been hospitalized only a handful of times. However, in the last year and a half in Moscow, I have broken all records, having been in hospital 4 times! I guess, you can easily learn from a person who you have been close with: I tried, probably, to keep up with Tanya, who had been hospitalized about 20 times during her years of life in Russia!

THE BEGINNING OF THE "FRIENDSHIP" BETWEEN THE TWO PRESIDENTS

From 1977 to 1988, we spent eleven years in "refusal" and regularly tried to appeal to various Soviet superiors, asking them to reconsider our case and not to prevent our departure from the country. On both the lower and the upper levels, we failed utterly: nobody wanted to talk seriously with the traitors of the motherland. This is how we got to the top level. It was the decade of Mikhail Gorbachev's ascent to the Soviet Olympus. As a President of the Soviet Union, this man had publicly described himself, before anybody could smell the collapse of the Soviet Union, as a communist to his bone marrow. Nevertheless, I had the impression that he was different from most of his hardheaded colleagues. In the following paragraphs, I tried to outline what I saw as different and why I had not given up hope and repeatedly appealed to him for help. However, it turned out that I was sending my letters to nowhere. There was never a line from his office in response, nothing not even an acknowledgement receipt of my letters.

In recent years, many interesting documents have been uncovered, about which I did not know in those years, in particular, about Gorbachev's life and activities. Now I am even more certain that he differed favorably from most of his comrades-in-arms in his views on both domestic and foreign policy. I think these very differences pushed him to reshape Russia's domestic life, as well as its relations with the West. However, this does not mean, that he got rid of the virus of Sovietism and that his brain fully recovered from the long and serious ideological trauma. I do not think he was different significantly, but just not as frenzied as his predecessors. However, he was not willing to make even micro-movements to help families like ours. When he was in the U.S.A., he had the audacity to bullshit Americans by claiming that all the Soviets who wanted to leave the Soviet Union had already left. At this very time, our entire family and THOUSANDS of others were wandering around in Moscow without permission to emigrate.

The evidence of fact that he was not quite like most of his colleagues was confirmed with his biography. Both M. S. Gorbachev's grandfathers, peasants, were victims of repressions in the 1930s: his paternal grandfather for not fulfilling the sowing plan, and his maternal grandfather for Trotskyism mentality. The family was well aware of what Bolshevik terror was, and despite this, Mikhail Gorbachev devoted his whole life to Soviet party-state work. He reached the top, becoming General Secretary of the Communist Party of the Soviet Union Central Committee in 1985 and President of the Soviet Union in 1990. During the state of emergency in 1991, there was an attempt to throw Gorbachev out on the pretext of his illness, and he ended up under house arrest in Crimea. Upon his return from Crimea, Gorbachev himself resigned as party general secretary, and later that year he cancelled his membership in the Communist Party. For a communist to the "bone marrow", this was an act of courage. His disappointed colleagues, by the end of 1991, initiated a criminal case for treason against Gorbachev in connection with his signing resolutions of the USSR State Council of September 6, 1991, recognizing the independence of Baltic republics of Lithuania, Latvia and Estonia. However, the Prosecutor General of the USSR closed this case. On December 25, 1991, Gorbachev, in an address to the nation, declared the end of his presidency of the USSR and signed a decree transferring control of strategic nuclear weapons to Russian President Boris Yeltsin. After this, a historic event happened: the national flag of the USSR over the Kremlin went down.

What else set Gorbachev apart from his Soviet comrades-in-arms was his intense interest in Europe and America. Probably no other Soviet leader had ever made so many friendly visits to the

West. In 1971, he went to Italy, in 1972 to Belgium, in 1975 to Germany, in 1976–1977 to France, in 1983 to Canada, in 1984 to England, in 1986 to East Germany, and in 1987 to Romania.

In addition, a special place in Gorbachev's ties to the West was his personal relationship with U. S. President Ronald Reagan. Interestingly enough, fate decided that these two presidents were destined to decide the fate of our family's emigration: Reagan because of his belief in human rights, and Gorbachev because he sought to improve relations with Reagan, and in order to do so, he had to compromise his country's position on refuseniks. Reagan made Soviet human rights one of the main points of discussion in all of their meetings. Gorbachev only grudgingly made concessions in response to Reagan's strong demands.

In the mid-80s our friend Buwalda, the Dutch Ambassador in Moscow, insisted that Vera write a letter to their Queen Beatrix asking her to help us leave the Soviet Union. We listened to his advicewe and we helped Vera to do this. In 1987, our child wisely asked why we did not write a similar letter to President Reagan of the USA. We agreed, and with Tanya's help, the text of the letter came up. After this, Vera wrote it with her own hand. Below is the original text of the letter.

> *April 4th, 1987. Moscow*
>
> *Dear Mrs. and Mr. Reagan,*
>
> *We hear your names and see your pictures so often now, people are so excited about your coming to this country and are hoping that you will help to solve their problems. That is why I decided to write this letter. My name is Vera Zieman, but everybody calls me "Moscow's Orphan Annie", though, unlike Annie, I have my family and it is about its fate that I want to tell you. When I was just born, my parents decided to emigrate but were refused by the authorities. We became refuseniks, which meant we were thrown out of normal life. My Mother, who was a professor of English, (she taught me English), lost her job, my Father, a Senior Computer Scientist lost his job and has been working as a janitor. As a result of all our misfortunes my father got gravely ill. My elder sister, who lives in*

> Boston now, tries desperately to help us get permission to leave the USSR. I wish and wish I could do something too. So, I made up my mind to venture to ask you for help.
>
> Respectfully,
>
> Vera Zieman.

Our friends at the American embassy in Moscow helped to send this text to President Reagan. As a result, our name got in front of his eyes, and we do not know what really helped this to happen. As a result, when it came to the emigration of our family, we had not waited for anything from our own president. But about five thousand miles away from Moscow, over a huge ocean, on an unfamiliar continent, the country chose a President who did care that the authorities were depriving an unknown Yuri Zieman of his elementary rights. This President, running ahead, forced the Soviet authorities so, that Yuri Zieman received these rights after all. In this connection, I recall a poem by Dmitry Prigov:

> Here has been elected the new President of the United States.
> Here has been scolded the old President of the United States.
> Why do we care? — Well, the President of the,
> Well, United States,
> But still it is interesting — the President of the United States.

We were not just curious we were vitally interested in what the overseas President thought of us. Until my last breath, I will remember President Ronald Reagan of the United States with gratitude for giving my family and me three completely new lives in freedom. At the end of the book, I will try to tell you how he did it. There is a special word "summit" for a meeting of heads of government or leaders of two countries. Gorbachev's annual summits with Reagan in the four years 1985–1988 led to a noticeable warming of relations between the US and the USSR. This warming, of course, played into our hands (I mean our family here).

The first meeting and personal acquaintance of the two leaders, including a one-on-one walk, took place in November 1985 in Geneva, when relations between the USSR and the United States were at a standstill. The two heads of state had not met for six years because of the war in Afghanistan. At that time, President Reagan did not really believe in the reality of peace between his free country and Russia's totalitarian "evil empire".

The first time the American President used this expression in reference to Russia was in 1983 in Florida, about two years before Geneva, in his speech to the National Association of Evangelicals of the United States. I know that many Soviet and former Soviet citizens condemn President Reagan for such a sharply negative label. But such people simply could not take a sober look at the crimes that took place in the country in which they grew up, especially if those crimes did not affect them personally. These people were easily turnning a blind eye to the fact that those who were victims of crimes were not hundreds, not thousands or tens of thousands of their fellow citizens, but hundreds of thousands and millions. At the same time, the well-known Soviet dissident and refusenik Natan Sharansky languished in prison cells since1977 accused of treason and anti-Soviet propaganda only for his convictions. In one of these cells in 1983, he read an article in "Pravda"denigrating U.S.A. President Reagan for calling Russia an evil empire. I am quoting here Nathan Sharansky's reaction to the article he read:

> I remember what an explosion of enthusiasm this article provoked in us political prisoners. Finally, there was a leader in the West, who wanted to call things by their proper names and show the true essence of the Soviet Union. We dissidents always knew and felt that the most important thing is not to give in to illusions and not to let the Soviet Union deceive us. We had to believe that the day would come when the West would finally see what the Soviet Union really was.

John Gaddis wrote in his book "The Cold War. A New History," published in English in the U.S.A. in 2007, Reagan's impression about Gorbachev in Geneva: *"I saw in his face for the first time a warmth and sense of style rather than the coldness based on hatred that*

I had seen in most leading Soviet leaders before." Although the Geneva meeting did not lead to any formal agreement, I think the progress made was tremendous. Jack Matlock, the U. S. Ambassador to Moscow, 1987–1991, assessed the significance of the Geneva summit: *"Reagan and Gorbachev came to the conclusion that they could work together as equals. It was at this summit, that they developed a personal relationship of mutual respect that later developed into a true friendship. To this day, if someone criticizes Reagan in the presence of Gorbachev, the Russian President corrects such critics."* It seems to me, however, that Mr. Matlock went too far replacing the reality with his wishful thinking. It was from this quote that I borrowed the word "friendship" in the title of this chapter on summit meetings. My opinion explains why I put the quotation marks with the word "friendship." I wish Mr. Matlock was right, but I think he was not.

AN AMERICAN WITH RUSSIAN ROOTS

Among the foreign friends, that I had made while being a Refusenik, Nick and Ruth Daniloff deserve special mention. They were both interesting people, both journalists, and they lived very close to us, three blocks down Lenin Avenue toward the center. We had many common interests, we shared a lot of worries, excitements and joys, had many wonderful walks together, discussed books together, listened to music together and had fun together on holidays. As for Tanya, to all this it is necessary to add, that from the young years she had a soft spot for everything connected with England. And Ruth was a real British woman, as British, as it is possible to be. She had met Nick in Oxford when he was studying there.

If we talk about holidays, one of the funniest was Nick's 50th birthday in 1984, which we celebrated together. Tanyusha and I sang ditties that we had composed together with our friends. These lyrics we dedicated to Nick. Unfortunately, only one verse has survived in my memory:

> *If you were married to a Russian woman,*
> *Even to an ugly one,*
> *We would never consider you*
> *As convict of your Motherland.*

Nick came to Moscow with his family to represent "US News and World Report" magazine. He has an interesting family tree with Russian roots of which he was very proud. His great-great-grandfather, Alexander Frolov, was a member of the Southern Decembrist Society and participated in pre-revolt activities. Although he did not go to the Senate Square, his punishment was severe: 20 years of hard labor and indefinite settlement in Siberia. While he was in exile, his sentence was reduced to 15 years, and then to 10 years. However, he happened to be was lucky. When Alexander II ascended the throne in 1855, he immediately released all the Decembrists who had survived, including Nick's great-great-grandfather, who returned to Moscow, where he lived and died in 1885. While in Moscow, Nick was very interested in everything that connected his family members with Russia. He was proud of the fact that he inherited from his great-great-grandfather the ring, handcrafted in exile in Siberia by Alexander Bestuzhev.

Alexander II did a lot for Russia in general, but he became famous in history as a "liberator," mainly because he put an end to serfdom in Russia. I like the way V. Klyuchevsky wrote about him most of all: *"He did not want to seem better than he was, and often he was better than he seemed."* I feel sad that the "liberated" terrorists of the "People's Will" at their congress passed a death sentence on such an emperor. They hunted him for a long time and after seven (!?) attempts finished with "the liberator" in the end. After that, a considerable number of members of the organization went to jail and many of them to execution. The bloody way of building *"socialism with a human face"* leads me to despondency. The slogan in Italic is referring to the reformist and democratic socialist program of Alexander Dubček and his colleagues, agreed at the Presidium of the Communist Party of Czechoslovakia in April 1968. The revolutionaries of the type of "People's Will" brutally murdered an inconceivable number of people in different parts of the world along the way. Among the victims, there were many decent people. It would be appropriate to call such socialism *"socialism with a hangman's face"*.

Nick's grandfather, Yuri, was a military general, and he participated in the First World War. In March 1918, General Daniloff headed a group of military experts in the negotiations of the Bolsheviks with Germany on the Brest Peace Treaty. Later he retired, left for Kiev and joined the White Army. After the Civil War with the forces of Wrangel, he evacuated from Russia and moved to America in 1919. I got the impression that Nick respected his grandfather, but he really loved his grandmother. There was a serious political disagreement in the family as to the attitude towards Bolshevik Russia. On the one hand his grandfather and father, who believed righteously that the Bolsheviks had ruined the country, and that to cooperate with them meant to aid the enemies of Russia. On the other hand his patriotically minded grandmother, Anna, with the maiden name Frolov, was the granddaughter of Decembrist A. F. Frolov. She, also righteously, could not renounce Russian culture and everything that was so dear to her in pre-revolutionary Russia. It was she, who taught Nick the Russian language.

Nick's father, Sergei Daniloff, left Russia with Nick's grandfather and settled in France. After all his forced post-revolutionary wanderings, he did not like to remember Soviet Russia. When Nick's family was already living in America, he had the foresight to advice Nick, not to show his nose in Russia. *"You will be arrested, and no American passport will help you,"* he told his son. Sad as it was, he was looking straight into the water. The Soviets did arrest Nick, and I will tell you in this chapter how it happened.

Nick's memory preserved his angry father's remarks that the Bolsheviks had stolen his country from him. This annoyance stayed with him for the rest of his life. Nick's father had begun to develop dementia as he grew old in Paris. Nick tried to interest him in his journalistic connections with Russia. Whenever he uttered the word "Russia" in this conversation, his father would exclaim with irritation, *"Russia is shit!"* It would repeat again when Nick brought his son, little Caleb, to Paris to see his grandfather. It started repeating at every meeting, until Nick, who did not share his father's resolute point of view at all, decided that it was better for him not to talk to his father about Russia.

Although Nick was aware of many horrifying facts of Soviet Russia's history, he himself had a touching, fondness and excitement for his Russian genes, and it seemed to me that he, like his grandmother, believed in the high purpose of the country. I remember meeting him on the platform of the Kazan railway station, when he was returning from a trip to the places of exile of his Decembrist ancestor. He drew my attention to the sign on the wagons of the train like "Vorkuta-Moscow" and asked me if I felt excited when I read those words. He was slightly saddened when he heard my reply that if I felt anything, it was sadness, since Vorkuta was famously one of the main cities of the Gulag. I was born and lived for 50 years in the country. Even with all my love to the Russian culture, I would rather join Nick's father and grandfather in their opinion about Russia, than himself and his grandmother.

In my Refusenik life, I was always trying to earn some money in addition to my meager salary as a janitor-obstetrician. For some reason, this kind of additional work Russians call "hack-work." I can honestly say that even this type of work I tried to do with the utmost conscientiousness, without any shirking, whether it was manual work, which was the majority, or intellectual work. All my relatives and friends knew about it and tried to help me in it. The word "refusenik" never appeared in the Soviet media, as if the concept did not exist. Also, nothing, done by the refusenik, should ever appear in Soviet media, as if this never happened. Therefore, when I published, I usually had to do it either under another's name or under a pseudonym. For this purpose, I even invented a pseudonym, Yuri Tanin (the surname ment "Tanya's"). My sister worked in the Academy of Sciences of USSR and she helped me publish several popular articles and translations in academic editions. I must say that during my refusal, I made mountains of translations in different specialties, and Tanya helped me substantially. To all those who helped me in this difficult time to earn, even a penny, I am unspeakably grateful.

I brought this up here because the Daniloffs, understanding my situation, were also so nice as to offer me regular part-time work. The first job I did for them was carpentry. One of their rooms had a bay window and there I constructed a built-in cabinet table. This order was certainly an expression of their kindness. They had not commissioned a professional cabinetmaker, who would certainly have done a better job than I did. But I felt OK because it would have cost them considerably more. They decided to help me in this way, and I remember it with gratitude.

The second job was more interesting for me and took advantage of the fact that Russian was my native language. Nick had several Russian newspapers and magazines subscriptions. He made a list for me of the issues that interested him in his reporter's work and asked me to look through the available Russian publications and to mark articles and notes related to these issues. That was how I started working at Nick's office on a regular basis. A side effect of this work was that I became more aware of the most important events in both domestic and international life.

The Daniloffs had a funny dog with the name Zeus. The name pushes one to imagine a huge strong dog with a thundering bark. However, Zeus was a small, cat-sized, smooth-haired foxhound, a small hunting dog for hunting foxes. This type of hunter must be quite small "in cross-section" to be able to fit through rather narrow foxholes. In addition, Zeus' bark was high pitched. Because of such smallness, few people in Moscow called him Zeus, many would use Russian diminutive suffix "ik" which comes to "Zeusik". In addition, poor Zeusik for some reason hated ringing telephones, and whenever the telephone rang, Zeusik ran to the phone so that I was afraid that he would shatter it into small pieces. I would say, although the dog was rather nervous, he was quite friendly. All our family made friends with Zeusik, which was very good, for at that time we did not yet know that he would become a part of our lives.

SPECIAL GIFT FROM THE KGB

Nick, as a reporter, had a special interest in small Soviet district newspapers, and he always asked his friends and acquaintances traveling in Russia to bring him one if they came across it. Because of his ability to communicate with people in Russian and his sociable nature, he got to know a number of people who would bring him provincial newspapers from their travels around the Soviet Union. One of these acquaintances by the name of Misha was often in Kyrgyzstan and he brought local Russian newspapers to Nick several times.

It was August 1986, Nick's term in Moscow was coming to an end, and a new correspondent, Jeff Trimble, and his family had already arrived to replace him. Misha called and said that he had brought Nick the latest papers. They arranged the meeting place, and Nick went there. As had happened before, Misha handed him a bag of newspapers. The meeting was close to their house and Nick walked home. However, no sooner had Nick left the meeting place than six men attacked him, arrested him, and took him in handcuffs to Lefortovo prison charged with espionage. Inside the envelope Misha gave him were photos of Soviet soldiers in Afghanistan and a map marked as confidential. During the first interrogation in the prison, Nick learned that the charge was so serious that it could result in capital punishment (!). I do not remember Nick ever mentioning Misha's last name. For the sake of an index of names, let him be Mikhail Decoy.

I think, the blatant impudence of the KGB has crossed all bounds. It was hard to find a man among Western journalists who was more loyal to the Soviet Union, and I would even say, more emotionally committed to it. It was unbelievable, that such a man was thrown to prison and, and even threatened with the death penalty WITHOUT ANY REASON at all! No one doubted that the espionage version was a gross fabrication. Nick himself described it in Russian shortly after his arrest: "*It was all whitened with whitewash.*" The whole world, journalistic in the first place, went wild.

Nick knew that according to the consular agreement between the USSR and the United States, the accused in such a situation had the right to make a telephone call to his loved ones, and he insisted on that right. He was allowed to call Ruth and tell her what had happened to him. To Ruth's credit, she simply rang the alarm bells and got the Western journalists in Moscow on their feet. Not only did she notify the American Embassy of the details that she had heard from Nick, but she also tried to speak personally with most of the journalists she knew.

As soon as Nick found himself in prison, we tried to help Ruth in any way we could, understanding how important it was to free her from household chores, so she could focus on the struggle to free Nick. Their apartment became the headquarters of this struggle, and dozens of people would come there to Ruth, wanting to get involved in the campaign to free Nick Daniloff. An unexpected problem occurred: little Zeusik did not like these frequent visitors and the endless phone calls. Each time he raised such a racket that Ruth could barely calm him down. Tanya and I suggested that we take the doggy with us to our place. We did but had to reduce the number of visitors and phone calls so as not to turn poor Zeusik into a nervous wreck.

About a week before Nick's arrest, a Soviet physicist, Gennady Zakharov, a UN representative in New York, went to jail with evidence of espionage. I learned from Nick later that Zakharov confessed to spying during the first interrogation and gave the names of the KGB officers who had worked with him at the UN. The KGB never wanted to leave its failed residents abroad, so they tried in every way to get Zakharov from the Americans. Thus, a compromise exchange resolution, though far from fair, was on the table. I personally was with the hardliners in the exchange discussion, who demanded the unconditional release of Daniloff and the trial of Zakharov. However, since the release of an innocent prisoner was involved, any price was appropriate. Curiously enough, Nick noticed an interesting change in his life around the tenth day of his imprisonment. The warden manager made a visit and ordered additional blankets and better rations for him.

Zakharov soon went to trial in New York, and pleaded no contest to the charge, using the legal trick "nolo contendere" which was invented specifically as a bargain for a guilty person not requiring a guilty plea. The deportation of the spy sent him out of the United States with a five-year ban on reentry. Thus, strictly speaking, the verdict sacrificed justice to politics. That same day, September 29, Moscow released Nick and closed the case without any conditions. The Daniloffs immediately flew to Frankfurt and from there to the US. Immediately after this exchange, the media informed the world that a Reagan-Gorbachev meeting would be held in Reykjavik on October 11–12. Nick described these events in his book "Spies and Spokesmen." The presentation of the book to the public was in Washington in 2008.

Due to the urgent departure of the Daniloffs from Russia, they could not take Zeusik with them. The dog needed a vaccination certificate to cross the border, and there was absolutely no time to get it. The doggie owners did not want to stay in THIS COUNTRY even for a day. We agreed that we would keep Zeusik at our house for a while, and Daniloff's friends in Boston would vacci-

Daniloffs in the White House

nate him, and we would send the dog back home at the first possible opportunity. That was exactly, how it happened.

There is one more episode with Zeusik. One day we got a phone call from Nick's successor Jeff Trimble's wife. She wanted us to bring Zeusik over to the apartment where Nick used to live. Tanya and I decided that they must have found a way to send the doggie to its owners and rushed to do it. It turned out to be not the case. There was a big buzz around Nick's story in the press and a magazine photographer came to the Trimble's to take a picture of the "hostage dog." Jeff and his wife wanted to be in the picture themselves and that was the reason for their calling us. We handed Zeusik over to the Trimbles for a half an hour and thereby helped them, as they both very much wanted, to go down into history.

There is no doubt in anyone's mind, starting with Nick himself, that President Reagan played a crucial role in Nick's release. I am sure, President Reagan, who had always been attuned to human rights, heard the alarm bell that Ruth rang. I am almost certain he made it clear to the Soviets that the impending meeting with Gorbachev in Reykjavik could not take place under these circumstances. I was personally very pleased that shortly after the Daniloffs returned to the United States, the entire family, including both of their children, got invited to the Reagan White House. Their story ended there, and it did not reflect well upon the Soviet Union, as usual.

Concluding this chapter I would like to explain its title. Nick returned to the United States as a national hero. His family was invited to meet the President of the United States in the White House. He got invitations vying with each other to tell his detective story, and each time he received a very handsome fee. In addition, he soon took the job as director of the School of Journalism at Northeastern University in Boston. This seemed to me to be quite a fair compensation for what he and his family had gone through. All of this greatly improved the family's financial situation and as a result, they bought a piece of land in beautiful Vermont and built a beautiful home there. Both Nicks family and our family loved that house very much, and we spent many happy days there together. We all thanked the KGB for such a wonderful gift.

I have to end this chapter on a sad note. Old age befalls everyone, and the Daniloffs were no exception. Nick retired, and as they got older, it became difficult for them to live in their flat in Cambridge which both they and Ziemans loved. Daniloffs moved to an assisted living home for seniors. As for our beloved home in Vermont, it was sadly abandoned. However, the joyful memory of this wonderful place stays with them and with us.

CONTINUATION OF THE "FRIENDSHIP" BETWEEN THE TWO PRESIDENTS

The second meeting of the two presidents was entirely Gorbachev's initiative and took place in October 1986 in Reykjavik, Iceland. At this summit, Gorbachev and Reagan could not reach agreement and sign the treaty, which was due to fundamental differences over major U.S.A. research in the Strategic Defense Initiative (SDI). This research caused much of the consternation of the Soviet leadership. They were very concerned about the U.S. development of ballistic missile interception in space. Nevertheless, the meeting progressed significantly in the work to reduce the missile race and came close to an agreement on complete nuclear disarmament. However, at the time, Reagan did not yet believe in the sincerity of the Soviet side's intentions. After the summit, he wrote to British Prime Minister Margaret Thatcher *"The Russians are not interested in WAR. They are interested in VICTORY threatening with nuclear weapons."* How well he read the Soviet diplomatic wiles! In addition, Reagan managed to put on the agenda of the discussions at this summit the topic of human rights and Jewish emigration from the Soviet Union.

Reagan's third meeting with Gorbachev took place in late1987 in Washington and lasted three days. Remarkably, in the first two hours, Reagan managed to get Gorbachev to talk about how human rights, in particular, the right to emigrate, largely determined relations between the two countries. I view this part of the meeting as a personal gift to me from President Reagan. No one knows for sure, but it is quite possible that this conversation was one of the last drops that broke the cup of patience of the Soviet leaders and they said with irritation, *"To hell with you, take your lousy Jews and get out!"*

Internationally, this summit was significant because the two Presidents signed the historic Intermediate-Range Nuclear Forces

Treaty (INF Treaty). The US and USSR pledged under this treaty to eliminate all systems of ground-based ballistic and cruise missiles of medium (620–3,400 miles) and shorter (310–620 miles) range, and to not produce, test, or deploy such missiles in the future. For the first time in history, both sides agreed to eliminate a large class of weapons. Pursuant to this treaty, both countries have destroyed 2,692 missiles and respective launchers. The significance of this scale of disarmament cannot be overestimated.

The meetings and negotiations of the Presidents of the two great powers led to a warming of relations between the USSR and the USA. The biggest achievement in this direction was the exchange of New Year's addresses by Gorbachev to the American people and by Reagan to the Soviet people, for three years (1986–1988). All people could watch these addresses on TV. It was sad for me to make sure that the English text of the transcripts of both Presidents' addresses was EASY to find on the Internet, but the Russian one I COULD NOT.

On January 1, 1988, a TV crew from an American company, I do not remember which one, came to see us. They wanted to show in their program how our whole family was watching and listening to the New Year's greetings of the USA President to the Soviet people on the big screen. I recall the funny circumstances surrounding this visit. The journalists were in for a big disappointment and the collapse of all their plans for we had no TV at home at all! These people refused to believe that this could happen. Seeing how dejected they were, Tanya suddenly remembered that when our close friends, the Brussilovskys left the Soviet Union they had a portable television for the car with a screen the size of a small paperback book. They had no time to find someone willing to get this thing and knew that we were not friends with TVs. Therefore, they asked us to give the TV to anyone who wanted it. The Brussilovskys left in 1985 and it was 1988. In the three years that elapsed, we NEVER turned this machine on and, frankly, we could not even remember where it was. However, out of respect for the American correspondents, Tanyusha found it and dragged it into the room. You should have seen the faces of these people, it was as if they had had a great grief. This thing was much smaller than their cameras and they did not want to film us sitting around this toy. It was the sad end of their attempt to show to the whole world our interest in address of the American President to Soviet people. We also left the Brussilovsky's tiny TV set behind leaving our apartment for good, for anybody who wanted it.

President Gorbachev, also, unknowingly, gave me a personal gift during the third meeting. In his spare time, he took a walk through the streets of Washington, D.C., during which he began fraternizing with passing Americans. No Soviet figure before him had dared to take such a step. For the first time, Americans faced not a political robot stuffed to the gills with an ideology they could not accept, but a normal, friendly human being. It is true that the President talked to people he met through an interpreter, probably, because he did not know English well enough. Nevertheless, he made a positive impression about himself on ordinary Americans and on their President, to say nothing, on myself. The reader may ask why I view Gorbachev's flirtation with Americans as a gift to me personally. The answer is that President Reagan responded to this and the effect of his response on our lives exceeded all expectations. The next meeting between the leaders of the two powers, scheduled in Moscow in 1988, was fast approaching. And President Reagan during this visit also decided to do something unheard of: he announced that on his way from Vnukovo airport he wanted to stop by for a cup of tea with the Zieman refuseniks!!! For those who do not know, our street overlooked Lenin Avenue, which foreign important guests, arriving to Moscow Vnukovo Airport, always used to drive to the center of the city. Therefore, the intended visit of the President was easier by the fact that we were in his way.

SOVIET-STYLE HOSPITALITY

On both sides of the Iron Curtain, the news of President Reagan's visit was like a bombshell. The Soviets began to take immediate emergency action. President Reagan planned to enter the Soviet Union from Finland. Gorbachev, taken by surprise, sent Soviet Deputy Foreign Minister Alexander Bessmertnykh to Helsinki to intercept the American President. He met Reagan in Finland and threatened the US President: *"If, Mr. President, you meet the Ziemans, this family will NEVER leave the Soviet Union. We are not going to control your activity. If you are so concerned about human rights, draw the appropriate conclusions yourself."* With this demarche, the Soviet leadership put the cold north wind over the warming Soviet-American relations.

Meanwhile, the deadline for the fourth Moscow summit approached. President Reagan planned to arrive in Moscow on May 29, 1988. Shortly before that date, aware of Reagan's relentless nature, the Soviets began feverishly to prepare for his visit to our family. It never occurred to those pygmies that there might be political leaders for whom the well-being of just one family might be more important than a political objective they had set. Then on our Maria Ulyanov Street began a phantasmagoria. New asphalt arrived to cover the whole street, the lawns were redone and flowering plants in full bloom were planted along the street. We lived in the mezzanine of a nine-story building. A special team of workers rewashed and repainted all nine floors. Our street was not very wide and, *"thanks to the communist party"* (Soviet political stamp), the trolleybus still continued to work. However, they set up temporary road signs on the street, prohibiting traffic stops.

These very days a funny story had to do with the American correspondents attempted to interview our Verusha about the meeting of the two Presidents. These people came to us with their cameras and found nothing smarter than to ask a 12-year-old child, *"What do you think about the upcoming summit in Moscow?"* Vera, I think, answered to this stupid question brilliantly: *"I don't think about it at all!"* I personally could barely keep from bursting into laughter at such a conversation. As a result, it was the second time that American media also failed.

Meanwhile, the U. S. Embassy in Moscow worried because their staff was responsible for the security during the President's visit. Special people visited us to take a thorough look at our apartment. They were interested in everything: the plan of the staircase and of apartment, the location and position of doors and windows, and even the telephone and electrical outlets. Tanya asked these people if she could offer President Reagan a meal. It was recommended that she limits the offering only to tea. But even that option bothered them after all. What a disgusting world we live in, where there are so many cold-blooded murderers, where one has to suspect the murderer in everyone!

The evening before the Reagans arrived, our lovely friend from the American Embassy, Susan Wagner, came to visit us. Susan was in charge of human rights. She officially informed us that President Reagan after much thought and to avoid any complications with our departure, had decided to cancel his visit to us. He asked Susan to convey his apologies for the change of plans. It turned out that he knew about our girl's musical classes, and he asked us to hand her his gift on his behalf: musical records which he had prepared for the visit and had brought with him to Moscow. I remember that among them was a tape of Andrew Lloyd Webber s musical "The Phantom of the Opera," based on the novel of the same name by the French writer Gaston Leroux. It was first performed in 1986 in the London's West End and then in 1988 on Broadway in New York.

After the official announcement, we spent a pleasant evening together. She told us that the President was very upset that the scheduled visit would not take place. However, everyone in the embassy, including the President himself, was in a good mood. He had made the necessary concessions, and it looked like he had brokered a deal and that we would get permission to leave Russia very soon. Susan also informed us that the Reagans were holding a reception for dissidents at the ambassador's residence the following day and they were personally inviting me, Tanya, and Vera. We received a document with an official invitation to this reception so that we would have no trouble getting past the police cordon at the entrance to the Spaso House.

On one of Susan's earlier visits to Maria Ulyanov Street, she had had an accident with a Soviet-sized water-filled deep pothole in our yard. She came after heavy rain that filled the pothole to the top with water. It looked no different from the many other puddles around it. The front tire of Susan's Volvo station wagon hit the hole and fell into it to the axle. It was impossible to get the wheel out of the hole. She had to call the embassy for help. Susan's husband, Steve, was an embassy administrator and he managed to get a tow truck with a crane. Steve himself drove this marvel of technology to our place to get his wife's car out of the hole. No one had ever seen such a machine in the Soviet Union. Crowds of curious and sympathetic onlookers from all the surrounding houses instantly gathered around. Tanya noticed that the windows overlooking the yard opened and admiring neighbors peeped out. I remembered one jolly drunkard from the nearby house, quickly ran home and came back with a classic snack for vodka, a pickle. As I understand it, the incident had interrupted his meal. This man, like most people around him, had figured out that Steve was a foreigner, and he wanted to express his sympathy for him. He handed Steve a salted cucumber and joyfully said, apparently, the only "foreign" word he had learned since the Spanish Civil War: "*No pasaran!*" During the time of the War, Soviet propaganda often used this exhortation in the Russian context to mean, "*We will not let it go!*" I remember how proud our Steve was to receive such a gift.

The next day, the day the Reagans arrived in Moscow. There was a total frenzy around our house. In the morning I looked out of the window, under which I always left our Little Frog, and it wasn't there!!!! I was worried behind belief and was about to report the theft of the car to the police right away. My wise wife, suspecting that I had forgotten where I had left it, went and carefully looked around everywhere. I became very upset: she apparently assumed early Alzheimer's in me. But I obediently went and, to my horror, found my beloved green car about little more than 400 yards from our house, in a place where I had never parked it. I ran up to it, expecting to find it all mangled. No, it looked fine on the outside. I immediately opened it and started it up, once again, everything was working, as it should.

We will never know HOW they did it without the key, but as they say, *science can do many tricks*, and the KGB can do even more. After I wrote this winged phrase, I wanted to know its exact meaning and origin. It turned out that the saying occurred for the first time in the 19th century. It came to us from card games and tricks, and the word means, most likely, "a trick to win." The phrase's structure itself was in Russian original, like a trick, quite cunningly: it repeated deliberately each letter in it exactly two times.

The second question, we will never know the answer to, is WHY they "stole" our car. We can assume that it was simply out of a desire to let us know that they could. Another assumption, perhaps a silly one, is that they did not want me to show the American President that I owned a car. However, all such speculations are of little importance. Anyway, I was happy that my Little Froggy had been found! Also I was glad that our acquaintance, who was the formal owner of the car, did not have to go into any conversations with the police.

From the morning of that day, a rapidly growing crowd began to gather under our windows. Somehow, all these people got wind that there might be a chance to look at the living President of the United States. We can not rule out the attempts of the authorities to use the situation for anti-emigration propaganda. They could tell the crowds that we were traitors of the Motherland and wanted to meet the head of a major imperialist power. Frankly, this gathering seriously frightened us. The windows of our apartment were so low that it would have been easy for angry patriots from the street to break in and physically express their displeasure. We feared such a riot. It was unlikely that in such a case the police would have stopped the intrusion of uninvited guests. Numerous representatives of the "Soviet police" who had also appeared under our windows somehow already knew that the President was not coming. They tried to persuade the gathered crowd that there would be neither bread nor circuses and asked them to go home. But nobody listened to them: the people knew very well the price of the promises of the authorities. If they said nothing would happen, something would surely happen. No one left.

I cannot remember without tears the support of our true friends in these difficult hours. In the morning, Wilma Buwalda, the wife of Peter Buwalda, the Dutch Ambassador in Moscow, called to find out what was going on. Tanya told her how we were living under siege by crowds and militia, were very worried and unable to leave the house. Within half an hour, a limousine of the Ambassador of the Netherlands rolled up to our house with flags fluttering. Wilma deliberately broke protocol with those flags because she was not accompanied by the ambassador and the flags were to be flown only when he himself was in the car. This extraordinary woman got out of the limousine with a plastic bag in her hands, proudly marched to our entrance and rang our doorbell. The police officers saluted to Mrs. Buwalda and saw that she safely reached the door to our apartment. We rushed to hug her and tried to tell her that such a demonstration might make the authorities angry, and that she and Peter might get into trouble because of us. "*What are you talking about?*" exclaimed Wilma in her operatic voice. "*We are free people!*" The plastic bag held pizza that she had grabbed when she found out we could not leave the house to shop for food. Wilma was worried that we were starving. In any case, her pizza turned out to be extremely tasty and very welcome.

Equally touching was the assistance of Bob Gillette, a correspondent for the American newspaper "The Los Angeles Times". Over the years that he worked in Moscow, we became convinced more than once that he was an extraordinary man. It was never necessary to ask him for help: Bob always saw what he could do and did it. This time was no exception. Bob knew the ways of the Soviet secret police, as if he had lived his whole life in Russia. He knew what was happening to us, and he came to us without calling, just to be there for moral support. The Soviet "guardians of order" always behaved more reservedly in the presence of foreigners. Bob spoke a little Russian, and he even tried to come out to the crowd and explain that Reagan had canceled the visit. However, they did not believe him either. Only in the afternoon, tired of waiting, people began to disperse. It was only after everyone had left that Bob, after saying goodbye to us, went home. He left only when he knew we were safe.

FOURTH SUMMIT

Ronald Reagan and his wife Nancy arrived in Moscow on May 29, 1988. Like all U. S. Presidents had always been, Reagan was № I person among the leaders of the country. Noteworthy detail, it was not Gorbachev and his wife who met the President and First Lady at Vnukovo Airport, but the Gromyko spouses. In Soviet Russia at that time there was no position of the president. Formally, the Chairman of the Presidium of the Supreme Soviet of the USSR played the role of the president, and it was this position that A. Gromyko fulfilled. However, Gromyko, like all previous rulers in this position, was never leader № 1 of the Soviet Union. The most important position in the USSR was traditionally held by General Secretary of the Communist Party Central Committee, at that time M. Gorbachev was in this position. He could not help to use this bureaucratic trick in such silly way to elevate himself above the U.S.A. President.

In his first two working days in Moscow, Reagan had a series of intense formal and informal conversations with Gorbachev. At a reception in the Kremlin, they toasted to improved U.S.-Soviet relations. However, behind that, President Reagan managed to carry out a few items of his own agenda, which had been planned before leaving the United States. On May 30, he invited the dissidents to the Spaso House and addressed them with a very significant, very touching speech. The same occurred the next day, May 31. As part of this program, Reagan met with students at Moscow State University, and on the same day spoke to cultural representatives at the USSR Union of Writers. Only for the last two days, he gave himself entirely to Gorbachev.

I want to draw the reader's attention to Reagan's initiatives because they were not so much about relations between our countries, as about the spiritual, social, cultural, and economic life of the citizens of Russia and their rights to freedom. As far as I understand, the Soviet authorities did not welcome such independence of the American president and were not very happy about his initiatives. Therefore, the final permission for some of these meetings was postponed, sometimes literally until a few hours before the events themselves. At most of these meetings, no major Soviet leadership ever appeared, despite the fact that the Reagan family was accompanied by the upper echelon of U.S. leaders, who had traveled with him to Moscow. Among these were Secretary of State George Shultz, Presidential Military Adviser Colin Powell and Chief of Staff to the President of the United States, Howard Baker.

Immediately upon President Reagan's arrival in the Kremlin, high-level talks began. The U. S. Senate had ratified by this summit the bilateral disarmament treaty agreed at the previous meeting, and the leaders of the two countries refined the details of the treaty. The withdrawal of Soviet troops from Afghanistan was also discussed. To me personally, it was very important that the two Presidents discussed human rights in that meeting. In addition, they agreed on cultural and educational exchanges. However, for the Soviet press, unfortunately, these were much less important agreements, and I have not found any details about them.

It was my special pleasure that in honor of the meeting of the two leaders a concert in the Spaso House by the a quintet of American jazz star pianist Dave Brubeck was given. I have not yet forgotten how Soviet Communist Party officials referred to jazz as "ideological poison." Thank God, we have lived long enough to see that the General Secretary of the Communist party Central Committee listened to a great ensemble, happily stomping to the beat. And I was doubly pleased with how the 67-year-old jazz player responded to the enthusiasm of the audience. "*I wanted to fly to the moon,*" Brubeck said after the concert.

It is so remarkable that the four meetings between the two leaders resulted in the Cold War between the countries beginning very slowly to fade and to go into the past. The most telling episode to support this statement came during Gorbachev and Reagan's joint walk on Red Square. Someone asked Reagan *"Mr. President, do you still consider the Soviet Union an evil empire?"* The President replied, *"No, I meant a different time, a different era."* I want to pay tribute to both superpower leaders for making this change happen.

Ronald Reagan was 77 years old when he arrived in Moscow for the summit. One has to wonder at his energy and activity level at such an age. He was in Moscow for five days, and he and Gorbachev had an intense political and social program each day. In addition, he held several meetings devoted to problems worrying him, and he was not afraid to provoke discontent in the Soviet authorities. He knew for sure that the Soviet authorities would not approve of these meetings. The problems discussed at the meetings included Soviet Union's observance of human rights, and the granting of social, religious, and economic freedoms to its citizens.

As I wrote these lines, Soviet power no longer exists in Russia. Much water has flowed since then. However, the problems that worried Reagan and the entire Western civilization, have, unfortunately not disappeared. Although the legal position of Russians has improved tremendously since the communists left power, it still lags far behind the West in that respect. Today's authorities in Russia still neither observe even basic human rights and freedoms, nor even allow talking about them. Many Russian dissidents are in jail today. Russians are still not willing to change much, first, in their thinking and then in the country's legislation. I was not able to find on the Russian computer search engine Yandex any text of Reagan's speeches that Bolsheviks did not like at the Gorbachev time and which Putin, probably, likes them today even less. By contrast, I found much information about these speeches in American sources on Google. The entire world had extremely depressing views about the human rights in Russia, caused by the brutal crackdown on demonstrators in the streets of Moscow in July-August 2019, on people peacefully protesting the constitutional violations in the last election. The entire civilized world was indignant at the unsuccessful attempts of Russian authorities to kill Russian politician Aleksei Navalny just for criticism of Putin. Later this courageous man was arrested and put to jail and killed there.

Concluding this chapter I could not help to add to the English version of my book the most recent, most horrible violation of human rights and international laws by Russia that happened after the Russian version has been already published. In February 2022 Putin started the bloody war in independent country of Ukraine that has taken already lives of many thousands of people, both Ukrainians and Russians.

DISSIDENTS AT THE HIGH RECEPTION

On May 30, 1988, the Reagans met with the Soviet dissidents and Tanya, Vera, and I had been invited. Of course, we regarded the invitation as a great honor and were very excited, anticipating attending alongside distinguished representatives of the country. Among the hundred invited guests we were especially pleased to see many friends and acquaintances, people whom we knew personally. Tanya and I thought that President Reagan's speech was amazing and it made a lasting impression upon us as well as many others. Lev Timofeyev, a scientist, economist, writer, and journalist, who was at the meeting, articulated it very well. He had just returned from prison for being "anti-Soviet" in his economic and literary writings one year before the event. Timofeyev was released early, not because of exoneration, but because he was pardoned. He said in an interview right after Ronald Reagan's speech. *"Today was a precedent of great importance. To be able to hear SUCH THINGS from the President of the United States in the heart of Moscow is a symbol that means a lot to us."* I think that most of the guests at that reception thought the same thing. Many would agree that this meeting in Moscow was a remarkable event in the history of the struggle for human rights.

That is why, I have chosen to quote here the full text of a very special address by the President of the United States to the "Humiliated and Insulted" (The title of the famous novel by

F.Dostoyevsky, 1861). I found this text from the archives of the President Reagan Library most of which are stored on the Internet. They published it there under the title "Remarks to Soviet Dissidents at Spaso House in Moscow".

> *Well, thank you all, and welcome to Spaso House.*
>
> *After the discussions we have just had I thought it might be appropriate for me to begin by letting you know why I so wanted this meeting to take place. You see, I wanted to convey to you that you have the prayers and support of the American people, indeed of people throughout the world. I wanted to convey this support to you that you might in turn convey it to others so that all those working for human rights throughout this vast land, from the Urals to Kamchatka, from the Laptev Sea to the Caspian, might be encouraged and take heart.*
>
> *In one capacity, of course, I speak as a head of government. The United States views human rights as fundamental, absolutely fundamental to our relationship with the Soviet Union and all nations. From the outset of our administration, we've stressed that an essential element in improving relations between the United States and the Soviet Union is human rights and Soviet compliance with international covenants on human rights. There have been hopeful signs; indeed, I believe this a hopeful time for your nation.*
>
> *Over the past 3 years more than 300 political and religious prisoners have been released from labor camps. Fewer dissidents and believers have been put in prisons and mental hospitals. And in recent months, more people have been permitted to emigrate or reunite with their families. The United States applauds these changes, yet the basic standards that the Soviet Union agreed to almost 13 years ago in the Helsinki accords, or a generation ago in the Universal Declaration of Human Rights, still need to be met. If I may, I'd like to share with you the main aims of our human rights agenda during this summit meeting here in Moscow.*
>
> ***Freedom of religion*** *— in the words of the "Universal Declaration of Human Rights", Everyone has the right to freedom of thought, conscience, and religion. I am hopeful the Soviet Government will permit all the peoples of the Soviet Union to worship their creator as they themselves see fit, in liberty.*

Freedom of speech — again in the words of the Universal Declaration of Human Rights, Everyone has the right to freedom of opinion and expression. It is my fervent hope for you and your country that there will soon come a day when no one need fear prison for offenses that involve nothing more than the spoken or written word.

Freedom of travel — I have told the General Secretary how heartened we are that during the past year the number of those permitted to emigrate has risen. We are encouraged as well that the number of those permitted to leave for short trips, often family visits, has gone up. And yet the words of the Universal Declaration go beyond these steps. Everyone has the right to leave any country, including his own, and to return to his own country. It is our hope that soon there will be complete freedom of travel.

In particular, I've noted in my talks here the many who have been denied the right to emigrate on the grounds that they held secret knowledge, even though their secret work had ended years before and their so-called secrets had long since become either public knowledge or obsolete. Such cases must be rationally reviewed.

And finally, institutional changes to make progress permanent. I've come to Moscow with this human rights agenda because, as I suggested, it is our belief that this is a moment of hope. The new Soviet leaders appear to grasp the connection between certain freedoms and economic growth. The freedom to keep the fruits of one's own labor, for example, is a freedom that the present reforms seem to be enlarging. We hope that one freedom will lead to another and another; that the Soviet Government will understand that it is the individual who is always the source of economic creativity, the inquiring mind that produces a technical breakthrough, the imagination that conceives of new products and markets; and that in order for the individual to create, he must have a sense of just that, his own individuality, his own self-worth. He must sense that others respect him and, yes, that his nation respects him, respects him enough to grant him all his human rights. This, as I said, is our hope; yet whatever the future may bring, the commitment of the United States will nevertheless remain unshakable on human rights. On the fundamental dignity of the human person, there can be no relenting, for now we must work for more, always more.

> *And here I would like to speak to you not as a head of government but as a man, a fellow human being. I came here hoping to do what I could to give you strength. Yet I already know it is you who have strengthened me, you who have given me a message to carry back. While we press for human rights through diplomatic channels, you press with your very lives, day in, day out, year after year, risking your jobs, your homes, your all.*
>
> *If I may, I want to give you one thought from my heart. Coming here, being with you, looking into your faces, I have to believe that the history of this troubled century will indeed be redeemed in the eyes of God and man, and that freedom will truly come to all. For what injustice can withstand your strength, and what can conquer your prayers? And so, I say with Pushkin:*
>
>> *It's time, my friend: it's time! The heart wants rest—*
>> *the days slip by, the hours take away*
>> *fragments of our life: and you and I*
>> *plan how to live and, —just like that—we die.*
>> *No happiness on earth, yet there's freedom, peace.*
>> *I've long dreamt of an enviable fate—*
>> *I've long thought, a weary slave, to fly*
>> *to some far place of labor and true joy*
>
> *Could I play a little trick on you and say something that is not written here? Sometimes when I am faced with an unbeliever, an atheist, I am tempted to invite him to the greatest gourmet dinner that one could ever serve and, when we finished eating that magnificent dinner, to ask him if he believes there is a cook.*
>
> *Thank you all, and God bless you.*

On that memorable day, President Reagan quoted in his speech only a couple of lines by the great Russian poet. However, it seems to me that the verse he chose was very appropriate, and since the whole thing is short, I have the audacity to replace the lines, quoted by the President with the full text, which, it seems to me, describes our situation with surprising accuracy. I found on the Internet the translation of the Pushkin's poem into English done by A.S. Kline, and that is what I quote.

The party in the Spaso House took place on May 30, 1988, and, getting ahead, on August 10 1988 an Aeroflot plane took off from Moscow Sheremetevo airport and whisked us away from Russia for good, to *"Some place where I will work to my delight"*. Thus "the tired slave", contrary to the will of Gorbachev, REALIZED his plan.

I cannot help remembering in this connection another wonderful limerick, composed by our son-in-law Vitya and describing this time events:

> *Gorbachev told the KGB:*
> *No way, the slave may move to the States!*
> *However, the slave said goodbye,*
> *And Gorby with forehead huge birthmark*
> *Remained home.*

It just so happens that Reagan's address to the dissidents at the meeting was preceded by short introductions from three Russians, all three of whom Tanya and I knew quite well personally

The first was Sergey Kovalev, a PhD of biology, a friend and associate of Tanya Velikanov in the fight for human rights. I often was meeting him in her company, and I have the fondest memories of him. On charges of "anti-Soviet agitation and propaganda", Kovalev served seven years in camps and three years in exile. After he was released from prison, he became a professional human rights activist, first in the USSR Supreme Soviet and then in the State Duma.

The second was a veteran refusenik and one of the organizers of Hebrew studies in Moscow, Yulius Kosharovsky. A funny detail: Tanya was helping Yuli, on the way of preparation his speech, to formulate in English his greeting to the President of the United States. Our Verusha played the role of the audience at the rehearsal. Before his struggle to emigrate from the Soviet Union, Yulius was a designer of electronic systems for airplanes and missiles. For more than 17 years, he fought with the Soviets for the right to repatriate to Israel. Finally, in 1989, he got the permission to go and left Russia. An active person by nature, Yulius became a prominent politician and political leader in Israel.

The third person to speak before Reagan at Spaso House was the Orthodox priest Gleb Yakunin. We owed our acquaintance with him, as well as many other wonderful things in our lives, to Tzilia Reitburd.

The official Soviet reaction to the American President's "impertinent" speech emerged that same evening. This response reminded to all of us that we should not have any delusions about what country we were in, who we were dealing with and from whom we were trying to run away. Poor Ronald Reagan honestly thought the evil empire was over. However, it was still alive and rather powerful. Reagan's kind words woke up the well-preserved old dame, who immediately began to spew her usual evil. The president did not understand Russian, but someone on his team must have told him how the Soviet leaders perceived his kind moves. I would very much like to think that despondency did not replace his enthusiasm.

That same evening, immediately after the reception at the Spaso House, Soviet officials met in the press center, led by Gorbachev's advisor Fyodor Burlatsky. Foreign Ministry spokesperson Gennady Gerasimov was quick to warn Soviet citizens that it was a delusion of the President of the United States, that the dissidents and refuseniks were the cream of the cream of our society. Rather they were the dregs of it. Already in the evening, on the news of the television program Vremya, Henry Borovik even cited evidence to support Gerasimov's statement. He, for one thing, unearthed among the guests of American President one dissident who had allegedly collaborated with the Nazis. Not surprisingly, I could not find even a mention of this person's name anywhere. Secondly, without any reason, he flung mud at Sergei Grigoryants, claiming that his arrest was for illegal economic manipulations. I used to know many dissidents, and we all knew well Grigoryants, as a noble and honest man. Nevertheless, they imprisoned him in camps twice, and, as a result, this innocent man spent nearly ten years incarcerated. Working as an interpreter for dissident groups, Tanya also knew Grigoryants well. Both times, they arrested him for "anti-Soviet" truth seeking. However, the years of the Gulag did not break him. Upon his return to freedom, he fought steadfastly for truth and justice, founding the magazine "Openness" and becoming its editor. In Stalin's years, we saw mountains of such lies, such slander and such filth. G. Borovik, this servant of Soviet high-ranking criminals, continued to do so even in the 1990s!

LIFE THIRD: MY EFFORTS TO EMIGRATE FROM THE SOVIET UNION

OPIUM OF THE PEOPLE

In 1918, the Bolsheviks, having gained absolute power, promulgated under Lenin's leadership the first Soviet constitution. I was not lazy to read this interesting document, which promised freedom of conscience, i.e. the right to choose a religion and many other things that should be in the laws of any civilized country. However, the Soviet government had its own understanding of what the law is and what freedom is. The Russian popular proverb describes well their understanding: *"The law is like a turn shaft, as you turned it, so it came out"*. Today, few people know that the word "turn shaft" people used for a simple turning mechanism of harness for two horses. Most of the promises of the Bolsheviks were originally beautiful words, that later turned out lies.

In fact, as far as religion was concerned, a bloody war with the church immediately began, accompanied by the most brutal robbery of it. If in 1914 there were about 75 thousand active churches, chapels and houses of worship in the country, by 1939 there were about a hundred. In March 1922 "peace-maker" Lenin wrote in a secret letter to Politburo members: *"Seizure of treasures, especially from the richest laurels, monasteries and churches, should be unconditionally carried out with ruthless determination. Nothing should stop it, and we have to do it in the shortest possible time. The greater number of reactionary bourgeoisie and reactionary clergy we manage to execute on this occasion, the better."* In the frame of this program, authorities were deciding themselves most often without a trial who was reactionary and who was not. As a result, there was no end to shootings. When the flaming Leninists were drowning Russia in blood, on their banners, among other things, they were writing, *"Religion is the opium for the people!"*

From my school days, I remembered this Marxist slogan from his 1843 work "Towards a Critique of Hegel's Philosophy of Law." Of course, Lenin was not slow to adopt this phrase. As a boy, together with most Soviet people, I knew nothing about religion, opium, or Marx. Nevertheless, of course, I admired the wise words of the founder of Marxism. In those years, I, of course, did not find time to learn about each of these subjects, as I had no idea, how easy it is to fool an illiterate person. Today I learned a little bit. I cannot resist quoting at least one phrase from Marx

"Religion is the sigh of the oppressed dumb animal, the heart of a heartless world, just as it is the spirit of a soulless order. Religion is the Opium for the people." I wonder if the author of this phrase could have imagined that it would lead to such long-term cruelty!

I find it hard to imagine that the educated Marx was not aware of how many millions of people found and still find in religion solace and comfort in their grief or adversity. It is just as difficult to imagine that he did not know that for many thousands of years, millions of people of the ancient world used poppy seeds (opium) for pain relief and anesthesia, and that the father of world medicine, the great Hippocrates, approved its use. Therefore, opium from ancient times not only intoxicated people, but also cured their ailments and relieved their suffering. However, none of this mattered to the great intriguer. He wanted one thing; to lead millions of uneducated people, and he succeeded.

Finally, the militant atheists, armed with Marx, did not know or did not want to know that the "great scholar" had borrowed this statement from the great Enlightenment thinker Jean-Jacques Rousseau. The original can be found in Rousseau's novel "Julia, or the New Eloise," published a century earlier, in 1761: *"The piety... is opium for the soul; it revives, enlivens and sustains when taken sparingly; in too strong a dose it lulls, or leads to madness, or kills."* Rousseau's words, unlike Marx's, seem to me more precise, pleasant, and kind.

Fighting against the opium for the people, the Soviet authorities taught that opium could be also different. They would always consider Russian Orthodoxy as the least harmful opium. After all, most of the Orthodox believers were, as they say, at hand. It was easy to keep them in check, to punish "bad" behavior, to destroy the disobedience and to award "good" behavior. However, two varieties of opium were the most terrible.

They considered Judaism as the most pernicious opium at the time. If I remember correctly, in Moscow, when we were still living there, there was only ONE functioning synagogue on Arkhipov Street (today the street has regained its former name: Bolshoy Spasoglinischevsky Lane). At this synagogue, ONLY since 1957, the ONLY legal Jewish religious yeshiva school in the Soviet Union functioned. I remembered well this synagogue because it was the ONLY place in Moscow, where one could buy matzah for Passover. The chief Jew in the Soviet Union at the time was the rabbi of this synagogue, Levin Yehuda Leib. He was also the head of the yeshiva. He worked well with the Soviet authorities and was an active and honorary member of all the anti-Zionist committees in various countries. The Soviets were happy to launch him to represent soviet Jews at all anti-Zionist gatherings around the world.

I wanted to find on the Internet and quote here the number of Jews living in Moscow in order to relate it to the only synagogue in the city. But Soviet Russia was an interesting country: the figures quoted by various "experts" are between 225,000 and 5,000,000 differ from each other by more than a factor of ten. No one knows what to believe!?

Only elderly pensioners dared come to the synagogue, since the appearance of a working person at the synagogue service was enough to get him kicked out of work. Similarly, a student's appearance in the synagogue was enough to expel him from his university.

The next most harmful opium, as I understand it, was Catholicism. This religion became very popular in Russia after the Patriotic War of 1812 and the cultural rapprochement with France. In the 1930s, the Soviet authorities closed most of the Catholic churches and schools, and simply shot most of the people connected to catolicism. Only few foreigners left, primarily French, and they were deported. Here I must express my deepest gratitude to the party that it spared at least some of these people. In all of Soviet Russia in our time, there were only TWO Catholic churches, one in Moscow and one in Leningrad. In Moscow, it was the Church of St. Louis on Malaya Lubyanka Street. The Church had a Catholic school, which the authorities closed in the 1930's and had never allowed to reopen. Therefore, Catholic education could only take place underground.

Historically, Jews were always hated. It is not just about Russians and Soviets. I would like to point out here that the aforementioned faithful French King Louis, being a patron of the arts, earned his sainthood by his intransigence towards other religions and to the adherents of different faiths. It was he, who led the 7th and the 8th Crusades supported by Pope Gregory IX, the Bishop of Rome. This Pope condemned the holy book of Judaism, and in 1242, 22 cart loads of Talmuds confiscated from Jews were burnt in Paris. Similar but smaller actions were repeated several times thereafter. So, today's Popes have much to apologize for, and today's French people have much to be ashamed of.

Tanya and I had our own experience with the Catholic world. In 1983, we met a very nice man named Vladimir Nikiforov. He came to visit us on the recommendation of one of our mutual acquaintances, whom exactly, I cannot remember. He was very polite and very modest, both Tanya and I liked him from the first moment. Vladimir turned out to be a Catholic, and he described the deplorable situation with Catholic believers. He was involved in underground Catholic classes for children. When Tanya heard that Vladimir was teaching goodness to children, she loved him even more. Vladimir vividly described to us the acute lack of any teaching aids and books: all Catholic publications were banned, especially books for children. Our mutual acquaintances told him that we new some employees of the American Embassy in Moscow. He dared to ask us to put him in touch, through our diplomatic friends, with the Chaplain of the U. S. Embassy, so that he could ask him to help him procure teaching aids.

After using the word "chaplain", I became interested in its origin and its exact meaning, which I find interesting. We call a chaplain a clergyman who combines a ministry with some additional (usually secular) position. The origin of the word comes to us from the legend of one of the most revered saints in France, Martin the Graceful, who lived in Tours (year 316). One day this saint met a beggar who implored the saint to give him some of his own clothes to cover his tatters. Martin cut his cloak in two and gave one to the beggar. The second part of cloak became a relic and people called it a "capa." Today, the capa is a part of Catholic priests' vestments. In addition, the word denotes the red cloaks of bullfighters. The Kings of the Franks used to take the capa with them going to military campaigns, where it was supposed to protect them from danger. The priest who went with the army eventually became known as a chaplain, that is, "guardian of the capa".

In the beginning of the 21st century, in some countries the institution of "humanity chaplains" emerged, called to provide moral support to people who do not adhere to any religious beliefs at all. Today, in most countries, military chaplains have the status of career officers and provide religious and counseling services. As a rule, these chaplains do not carry weapons.

So, let us go back to Nikiforov. When we met Vladimir Nikiforov he told us very little about himself, and we learned his interesting story only later. I think, we can explain this, on one hand, just by his modesty and, on the other hand, by his concern about the conflict of his religious views with the Soviet authorities. Not being a Jew, he was able to enter the Faculty of Mechanics and Mathematics of the Moscow State University, from which he graduated in 1970. For some time, he worked on the research of information systems. His first religious experience was with Orthodoxy, and his spiritual mentor was Alexander Men. Father Alexander's historical-religious and ecumenical interests attracted inquisitive seekers like Vladimir who soon became a faithful assistant to the rector of the church. There, Vladimir was called chancellor, a word that in Latin means "secretary at the barrier that separates the court from the public."

Unexpectedly for his friends, in the mid-1970s, Vladimir converted to Catholicism and in 1981, was secretly ordained as a priest, possibly in the Baltics. When Father Alexander found out about it, he asked Vladimir not to appear in Pushkino any more. That was sadly the end of their friendship. When Vladimir came to us on Maria Ulianov Street he was already a priest, but he did not tell us, so we did not know it.

Immediately after our first meeting with Vladimir, we contacted one of our American friends at the embassy. This man arranged with the chaplain to meet Vladimir at our home. We sat in our kitchen, and Vladimir explained to the chaplain his problems, and the chaplain showed complete understanding and promised to help. To everyone's delight, Vladimir's pupils began to receive teaching materials. Everything seemed to be going well.

However, our joy was short-lived. A few days passed and we got a phone call from a friend of Volodya's who told us the terrible news: Volodya is in jail! This news put both Tanya and me in a state of shock. Only a couple of days later another call rang, and this time the news was bad again. The caller was a man, just released from jail, where he had met Volodya. Volodya asked him to call us and to tell us that he had to give our names during the interrogation and to admit that we had helped him to get in touch with the chaplain. At this point, Tanya and I got terribly nervous. We realized that the risk of our arrest becomes very high now, which may kill all our plans of emigration. Also our hearts sank at the thought that the KGB might grab our American friends by the hand and use the fact for their own dirty purposes, claiming that they *"were not doing what they had been sent to Moscow for"*. We seriously lost our peace of mind.

I must confess that at the time, not only was I tortured with fear caused by this development, but I also condemned Vladimir for giving out our names. Subsequent life experience has taught me that I HAD NO RIGHT to make such a judgment. For many years, I was in close relationships with many dissidents, some of whom were under arrest many times. There were always moralists who regarded such behavior by the arrested as betrayal. In the last years of my life in Russia, I often had terrifying, intrusive dreams in which I was imprisoned. It was not the imprisonment itself that terrified me, but the fact that I might not be strong enough to endure the torture in a dignified manner and protect my friends. Over the years, I came to a clearer understanding: people who live in freedom can never imagine what a person living behind the bars must endure, even more when he is in jail for his beliefs. In this case, my personal fears could in no way justify accusing a courageous man, and I have to offer Vladimir my belated apologies. I am happy to say that we are very fortunate: the Soviet authorities never got to Tanya and me on this matter.

Unfortunately, we never met again with Volodya after his return from imprisonment. When I was writing these lines, I decided to look on the Internet, in case there was something about him. And it turned out that there was much, and what I learned, pleased me a lot. In 1988, he got political asylum in Sweden and left Russia around the same time that we did. He subsequently moved to England, got a PhD from the University of London, and worked part-time as a chaplain there. His interests and area of research was the sociology of religion, including such issues as religion and science, religion and conflicts, religion and sexuality, and religion and psychotherapy. I was especially pleased to learn that he had published a book in New York on Mikhail Bakhtin's philosophy.

TO SEPARATE OR NOT TO SEPARATE

Already in 1918, the first Soviet Constitution clearly ordered the complete separation of church and state. However, Soviet rulers never followed the letter of the law, especially in regards to the religions in Russia. I was personally acquainted with three Russian Orthodox priests: Gleb Yakunin, Alexander Men and Vladimir Nikiforov, and they were the most worthy citizens and patriots of Russia. However, life in the Soviet Union was anything but happy for the three as they constantly reminded the Soviet as well as the church authorities of the regular and blatant non-observance of the country's constitution regarding religion and religious freedom.

A young graduate of the Agricultural Institute, Gleb Yakunin, under the influence of the priest Alexander Men, decided to become a priest as well. In1962 he was ordained a priest of the Russian Orthodox Church. First, he got appointment to serve in Zaraisk, and later in Dmitrov. In 1965, together with priest Nicolas Eshliman, he sent to Patriarch Alexis I an open letter, which described in detail the illegal suppression of the Soviet state authorities of the rights and freedoms of believing citizens. Copies of the letter were sent to Nikolai Podgorny, Chairman of the Presidium of the USSR Supreme Soviet, Alexei Kosygin, Chairman of the USSR Council of Ministers and Prosecutor General of the USSR Roman Rudenko. In addition, he sent 100 copies of the letter to all the ruling bishops of the Moscow Patriarchate.

The pain for the freedom of faith taken away from the citizens of Russia cost Gleb and his colleague and friend dearly. In 1966 on the instruction of His Holiness, the Patriarch they were both relieved of their offices and prohibited from serving. In 1979, they arrested Gleb and kept him in prison until 1985, after which they exiled him to Yakutia. In 1986, he got under amnesty and released. At the railway station friends, former parishioners, and Western journalists greeted him. Tanya was present at this joyful event as an interpreter. In 1987, Gleb, reinstated by theMoscow Patriarchy as a priest, served in St. Nicholas church in the village of Zhegalov in the Moscow region. In the 1990s, Gleb first became a member of the RSFSR Supreme Soviet and then a member of the Russian State Duma, where he tried to defend the interests of both believers and ordinary clergy.

But the music did not play for long. In 1993, the Holy Synod demanded that he, as a representative of the clergy, not participate in the parliamentary elections. Gleb refused to obey this demand, and the Synod deprived him of his priestly ministry. Gleb appealed to the Moscow Patriarchate for reinstatement to the rank of priest, but they rejected his request. For unruly behavior, Russian Orthodox Church excommunicated Gleb Yakunin in 1997.

Another priest I knew personally was Alexander Men. He was only 6 years old when his father was arrested on false charges and sentenced to more than a year behind the bars. After prison he was forced to work in the Urals until the end of the war. Already a student of the Fur Institute, Alexander decided to become a clergyman, but continued studying at the Institute in order to acquire a worldly profession. However, he was not able to do this: shortly before the final state examinations in 1958, the Institute administration expelled him for his religious beliefs. He was ordained to the diaconate in the same year and ordained to the priesthood after graduating from the Leningrad theological seminary in 1960. In 1965, he graduated from the Moscow Ecclesiastic Academy after studying by correspondence.

The beginning of the 1960s' space race led, for some reason, to an intensification of the persecution of the church. At that time, Alexander held underground classes on the history of Christianity. In 1964, the KGB came to Alexander's home to search. Yuri Andropov, the KGB boss, took a personal interest in him. If not for the patronage of Archbishop Juvenaly, Men would have been arrested.

At that time, Alexander Men became one of the founders of Christian "samizdat." He also published many of his articles and books in the West. The seven volumes of his "History of Religion" are world famous. In the 80s and 90s, his little church outside of Moscow was the center for Moscow's intellectual elite. Alexander became one of the most popular Christian preachers. It was sad that both the Soviet leadership and the top brass of the Russian Orthodox Church were equally irritated with him. The popularity of Father Alexander in the West, his intellectualism, and his ecumenism: the desire for rapprochement and better understanding between the different branches of Christianity, annoyed authorities from both camps. Both wanted to keep the Iron Curtain strong, so that the world would be less aware of their shady dealings.

Everyone who knew Alexander Men and his writings worried for his safety. He repeatedly received threatening notes during his speeches and the worries were not in vain. Bolsheviks hated special people, and he was so special. In 1990, as he was hurrying to

LIFE THIRD: MY EFFORTS TO EMIGRATE FROM THE SOVIET UNION

church for the liturgy, a man ran up to him and handed him a note. Father Alexander stopped and took out his glasses. While he read the note, another man jumped out of the bushes and violently hit him from behind on the head with an axe. Bleeding, he barely made it to the gate of his house before fell down dead. It was very much a Russian style hired murder. President Putin to have an alibi personally ordered an investigation to find the killer. However, as everybody would expect, this animal *"could not be found"*.

When I think of this brutal murder, it is hard for me not to remember how in southwest Moscow in September 2005, in broad daylight, the Russian business mafia shot and killed Zhenya, the husband of Tanya's sister Natasha. He did not want to "share" with them enough the profits of his successful business. In Zhenya's case, no one even expected Putin to express his concern about the villainous murder of the talented Jewish designer. When I asked Zhenya's daughter, Masha if she knew any results of the investigation, I heard a very sad answer: "*Yurochka, I do not even want to mention this story, as long as they do not touch me and my children!*" In other words, the mafia had achieved its goal to keep people in fear and by doing so, to continue safely their horrible criminal activity.

I often think about the fate of the Russian Orthodox Church and its believers in Russia. If you look at the history of the country, since ancient times, the Church never tried to separate itself from the state and had often acted as a servant to the rulers. The Bolsheviks, after coming to power immediately after the Revolution, unceasingly carried out, as part of the general Red Terror, pogroms killing, torturing, and robbing the Church and believers. In spite of these facts, the leadership of the Church not only continued in its role as servant of the rulers of the empire of evil, but even increased its vile activity. And they were well rewarded. Patriarch of Moscow and All Russia, Alexis I threw out Gleb Yakunin for intransigence after receiving his letter from the Orthodox Church and threatened him with a harsher punishment if he did not repent. Gleb did not repent and continued to fight for the truth of the Church and ended up in the Gulag. I read on Wikipedia that this "devoted to God" patriarch was FOUR times awarded one of the highest decorations in the country, the Order of the Labour Red Banner. He received these decorations while he worked for the KGB, tragically, from the very people who were killing, torturing, and robbing the Church and its believers.

An amusing coincidence: when Alexis I, in 1962, was presented another high award by Brezhnev in the Kremlin, the director of my employer, the computer research Institute, S. A. Lebedev was also in the group to be awarded. All present were invited to sit down before the photographer, and everyone was afraid to sit near the Patriarch, lest something bad happen. Our Sergey Lebedev saw the last free chair and, without thinking, sat down next to him. After reading about it, I was once again happily convinced of how much he differed from the majority of those whom the Soviet authorities liked to reward. Alexis I sat on the Moscow Patriarchal throne for more than 25 years, the longest in the history of the Russian Church. He traveled halfway around the world and died in glory. I wonder who signed the required permission from the administration, the party committee and the local trade union committee, which was necessary for every Soviet citizen for every trip abroad.

One of the later Patriarchs of Moscow and All Russia, Alexis II, went much further. When Gleb Yakunin accessed the secret archives of the KGB as a member of the Supreme Soviet, he discovered and made public a list of more than ten highest leaders of the Russian Orthodox Church, who served as secret informants and as KGB agents. Alexis II who worked part-time for the KGB since the 1960s under the name of "Drozdov" had begun this list. It is hard for me to imagine a greater moral failure than the church fathers selling their souls to the devil. They have long managed to hide their nefarious activities from their parishioners. It would seem that they should have known better than I that God can see everything. But nothing stopped them from such extreme godlessness, which is far worse than honest atheism. And as for Alexis II, the Soviets were stingy in paying for his extra efforts: only THREE Soviet decorations were hung on his chest. He must have underperformed and sent too few of his wards and believers to prison.

THE DEJECTION OF AN ALIEN

US President Reagan's visit ended on June 3, 1988, after spending a week in Moscow he flew back to Washington. That week was emotionally very intense and very special for me. Returning to my metaphor of interplanetary travel, I would say that all these previous journeys were always short, lasting only a few hours each time. Here, on the other hand, thanks to intensive communication during these days with our American friends, I began to feel myself belonging to this group of people, and these people were very different from Soviet citizens. In other words, during this week I myself began to feel like an alien. For these days, my daily expectation of the authorities playing dirty tricks on me stopped. Attention and care from our new friends in the West allowed us THIS WEEK to stop feeling like ever punished refuseniks. The only sad circumstance these days was our inability to share this joy with our loved ones. The fear of meeting foreigners in my surroundings made them distance themselves from us and to pretend that nothing bad was going on with me. Of course, you cannot blame them for their reticence and distance because they really had every reason to be afraid. As I suspected, while the Reagans were in Moscow, the Soviets tried to put a good face on a bad game. What would happen next was never certain. Subsequent events showed that this was in fact the case.

Our Western friends in Moscow expected, as well as Reagans, only good things for our family. They believed that the American President had compromised with the Soviet rulers by deciding not to visit the Ziemans. They were sure that quid pro quo and we would be given permission to emigrate in the near future. However, they forgot that Soviet people had their own logic and ethics, different from commonly accepted.

It was several months before the Reagans arrived, that I mailed a letter to the Supreme Soviet of the USSR, the country's highest office of state power, similar to the parliament in many countries. The letter was a polite complaint letter, asking it to stop torturing us and let us go. I had sent many such letters during the years of refusal, and I HAD NEVER RECEIVED AN ANSWER TO ANY OF THEM. There is a phenomenon of the black hole in physics. It is a region of space-time, whose gravitational attraction is so great, that it absorbs without a trace all nearby objects. Many Soviet institutions, with which I had to deal during our refusal years, seemed to be black holes. Immediately after the Reagans' departure, I made phone calls to many such black holes trying to find out where my unanswered letter to the Supreme Soviet of the USSR had gone.

The response on one call was not typical for the soviet bureaucracy. The person at the other end of the line let slip that my answer was in Moscow City Hall. I was not a fool, I was sure that it was just another excuse and another lie to get rid of me.

Nevertheless, we had no choice but to continue our "Road to Calvary" (the title of the novel by A. N. Tolstoy). We went hand in hand with my Tanyusha to the reception room of the Moscow City Hall on Gorky Street, which now has its old name Tverskaya Street. We stated our problem to the receptionist. So many times before bureaucrats were sweeping us from one official to the other, that what we heard this time did not surprise me at all. They said that the City Hall does not deal with emigration cases, and we should address to VPD, Visa and Permits Department. However, by that time, we were already old birds, that you cannot catch with chaff. We knew exactly, that the function of VPD was only to accept the emigration documents, and there our response COULD NOT BE THERE. Our patience was running out, and we said in unison that we would NOT leave the City Hall's office until we knew exactly where the answer to our letter was.

After maybe another hour or so, a man came out and asked us to follow him. I was sure that he would lead us to another robot programmed to tell us boolshit again. Literal translation of the Russian equivalent of "to tell boolshit" would be "to hang pasta on your ears". I am always interested in the exact meanings and origins of phraseology. Of the several variations of the etymology of Russian noodle expression I just used, the most convincing and interesting one says that "noodle" comes from the French "la poche", which translates to "pocket". The French word sounds similar to "lapsha" in the Russian transcription. Pickpocket thieves liked to use the word and, probably, they brought to Russian the verb "oblaposhit", equivalent of English "to pickpocket."

Following the man, we came to a rather large room, in which there was one desk alone, at which a man with glasses was sitting. This man, after inquiring about our names, reached into a drawer of his desk and pulled out a piece of paper. "I have in my hands," he said, "an answer to your inquiry to the Supreme Soviet of the USSR. I shall read it to you now." When we heard this, I got an urge to ask him, why must he keep a letter addressed NOT TO HIM in his desk instead of sending it to the addressee? I hardly held myself back. The official held the paper in his hands in such a way that there was no way we could see what was written there. The thought even ran through my mind that it was all a theatrical performance and that we would never know what was really going on. The person read in a monotone and unconcerned manner, that, once again, we cannot get an exit visa now, that we were entitled to have the decision reviewed, but not before 1992. It was June 1988.

My Tanyusha went white, as a sheet of paper, with impotent anger. Noticing her reaction, the bespectacled man said, "I don't understand why you're getting so upset. You have been waiting for so many years, in just four years you can make another request." On the official's large desk was an old-fashioned grey marble paperweight. Tanyusha hissed softly through her teeth to me: "Now I am going to throw this paperweight at his head". I was frightened out of my wits, took her under my arm and immediately led her out of the office, just in case. We were both in shock and rushed home. I tried to console her, poor thing.

When we got there, we immediately called Galeczka in Boston and told her about our visit today. She, too, could not believe what she had heard. *"Are you sure you understood this man correctly?"* she asked us. We replied that there was no doubt about it. As a next step, our Galecka did her best to let know about our sad news as many people in the West, as possible. After all, all of our family and friends on the other side of the iron curtain were already cheering and getting ready to meet us. Exactly the same reaction was in Moscow with our friends, only they were getting ready to say goodbye. Both there and there, everyone was perplexed, and we dejectedly returned to the reality of the world of refusal.

TWO WORLDS — TWO SHAPIROS

In my life schedule, every day for ten years, I religiously performed the same ritual: I went to our mailbox every time, hoping to find in it a little postcard from the Department of Visas and Permissions allowing us to leave the country. Many people who knew me laughed at my sentimentality and naivety. Somehow, it was happening that every day when I did NOT FIND the desired card in my mailbox, I would say to myself, well, maybe TOMORROW...

It was June 1988. Unexpectedly, our very close friends, Tzilia and Milan received permission to emigrate. It was one of our most difficult partings. We had gone through all the troubles of refusal years together with them; Tzilia was our first adviser and helper. With their departure, we felt a kind of orphans. Additionally, our sadness was compounded by the fact that they were going to Israel and not to America. This meant that it was very uncertain if and when we would be able to see them again. We spent their last twenty-four hours in Moscow with them day and night. We had mixed feelings: we were extremely happy for them, but we did not want to be apart.

Before they left their Moscow apartment for the last time, we sat down at the table and had our last meal with them in Russia. Time was running out and Tanya was already very nervous that we might be late. She started rushing everyone. At one point, she got up from the table and said. *"Whatever you want, but we are going!"*. Then little Borya Samarov, Tzilia's grandson, who was not yet very good with hissing sounds in Russian, jumped up from his chair and, raising his index finger, said very expressively to Tanya: *"Well, that is what I say, we are the ones going and you are the ones staying!"*

Against Borya's order we went, of course, to the airport to see them off. There the minutes flew particularly fast, and before we knew it, the moment of physical separation had arrived. Our dear friends were gone behind the barrier, and we did not know if we would ever see them again. We returned home feeling such mixed emotions.

No sooner had we crossed the threshold of our apartment, than the phone rang. It was the secretary of the French Embassy calling. He wanted to inform us that they had just returned from a press conference at which they had heard that the Ziemans had received permission to emigrate. The news threw us into kind of positive shock, although previous experience had taught us that it could have been false information. However, 15 minutes later somebody from the Australian Embassy called and confirmed the news!

A little later Bobbi Brown called, excited and happy. Her husband Phil had just spoken to the American ambassador, Jack Matlock who had also informed him of the permit. He told Phil: *"I hastened to tell you, not the Ziemans, so as not to rob you of this joy of being the first messenger of wonderful news."* Next, we received a call from the BBC Moscow team, who for some reason showed interest. And very late that night, I got a phone call from Boston, from a happy Galya, who had already been informed about the wonderful news from the office of the US Secretary of State George Shultz. It seemed that it was not false data, so it was time to rejoice. It was a huge victory and people from all over the world rejoiced and reached out to share their joy with us. The only people we did not hear from were the Soviets who had tormented us for eleven years.

This difference reminded me of a real story that happened in the 1940s in Moscow, which gave birth to the aphorism "Two worlds—two Shapiros." I would like to say that in this story, the comparison of the behavior of the two worlds does not sing the glory to Soviet ideology at all. Many legends surround this interesting story, and now it is difficult to determine, what in this story is true and what is fiction. More than 70 years have passed since, and the generations growing up both in the West and in the East know little of it. My favorite version is set out in the book, "The Anti-Soviet Soviet Union" by Vladimir Voynovich, and I quote from this publication.

> *One day in the 1940s, United Press International (UPI) correspondent Henry Shapiro walked past the Telegraph Agency of the Soviet Union (TASS) building and saw smoke billowing from it. He rang the doorbell. No one answered. He made a phone call. The man on duty, Solomon Shapiro, answered the phone. "You have a fire!" Henry told him. "And who is speaking?" Solomon asked. "Shapiro!" The Soviet Shapiro thought somebody was playing a trick on him and hung up. The American Shapiro reported by telephone to New York that the TASS building in Moscow was on fire. The Soviet Shapiro received by teletype the UPI message. He opened the door to the corridor and looked. This immediately convinced him that the usually lying American press was not lying this time: the corridor was all in smoke. The fire people arrived and, somehow, put out the fire, but the event gave birth to a joke: "Two worlds—two Shapiros."*

Henry Shapiro served as UPI's representative in Moscow from 1937 to 1973 and was one of the most experienced, educated, and knowledgeable American correspondents in Moscow. As for Solomon Shapiro, he was an ordinary Soviet official whose brain, most likely, successfully absorbed the poison of the Bolsheviks propaganda. On one of the Russian Internet pages we can still read the following vulgar interpretation of the popular aphorism about two worlds: *"This is how they talk about the difference in mentality, habits of inhabitants of different countries, representatives of different nationalities."*

This purely false propaganda phrase really describes the difference between mentalities. However, the author, of course, does not mean two different worlds, two different planets. He is talking about the residents of different countries and representatives of different nationalities that have nothing to do with the story at all. The act of publishing such a phrase tells us that little has changed ideologically in Russia since the collapse of the Soviet Union. What strikes me, in fact, is the similarity of the two situations. In the capital of pre-war Russia, a major Soviet institution learned of a fire in its own building from the report of their Moscow correspondent in a Western agency (?!). Almost half a century later in the capital of post-war Russia, a family of refuseniks learned of their own authorities' decision to allow them to emigrate from a report by Western diplomats (?!) working in Moscow and informed of this by their offices in the West. Unfortunately, there are today, I think, like in the described story, the same different worlds and the same different Shapiros!

THE COVETED POST CARD

The days went by, but the DVP was silent. After 11 years of trials, we needed a rest and our friends helped us to get a voucher for a few days to the Composers' Art House in Ruza. Now we had to wait to receive official permission that could come at any minute and so we felt that we could not leave Moscow. After some hesitation, we still decided to go, but asked our close friend Volodya Rabinovich to stay in our flat while were away and to check our post box. We agreed that we would call every day, and if we got a postcard, we would come back immediately. The authorities were in no hurry, and the postcard did not arrive while we were away. It was nice that we had taken some time to rest before we returned to the Moscow commotion.

LIFE THIRD: MY EFFORTS TO EMIGRATE FROM THE SOVIET UNION

Now my trips to the mailbox were not so bleak, and we really hoped to get the desired postcard any day. And we did! One unremarkable day in early July, I opened my mailbox, and I took out an unremarkable rectangular piece of paper, which informed us that our visas were ready, and that we could come to the office to get them. It was incredibly mundane, as if we had waited not eleven agonizing years, but only a few days. What was remarkable, it was Monday, the Fourth of July 1988. There is a saying in Russia: Monday is a hard and unlucky day, so let us live it. For me since that time Monday is one of the most wonderful days of my life. After the United States of America became my adopted homeland in 1988, the Fourth of July became a very special day for me also because it was the day the United States declared its independence from the Kingdom of Great Britain. I am happy about this coincidence: my family gained their independence on the day our country was born. I see this as a blessing from above upon our emigration.

Without wasting precious time, we picked up our exit visas at the DVP, received all the necessary instructions on what we needed to do to leave Russia as soon as possible, and started really getting ready to leave. I personally had the feeling that we needed to hurry before the authorities changed their minds and took away our permits. I did not want to spend an extra hour in Russia.

For the summer, as always, we rented a dacha, this year in Perkhushkovo. My mother-in-law, Maria, always tried to get away from the heat of Moscow in the summer. This year was no exception. She went to Perkhushkovo in the spring and did not show herself in Moscow all summer. We agreed that during closing of our life in Russia before departure, we would bring Vera to her, and Tanya's sister Natasha helped. This allowed us to focus on the pre-departure fuss. There really was a lot of fuss and Tanya and I began to do it at full speed.

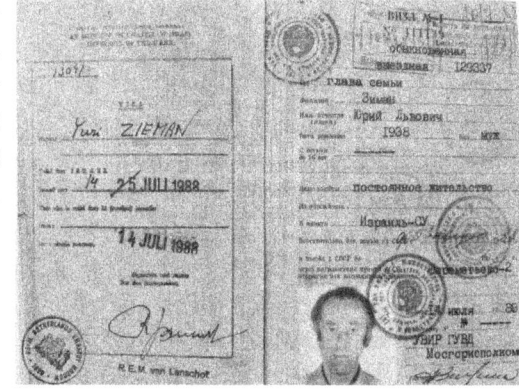

My exit visa
I longed for 11 years

The day before we took Vera to the dacha, Tanya and I were running around and Vera was at home alone. The phone rang and Vera picked it up. A gentle female voice asked, *"Is this Verochka?"* Vera answered in the affirmative. *"Could you please give a reciever to one of your parents?"* the woman asked. Vera explained that we were both out. *"Would you please tell them, my friend, I called from DVP and we are waiting for them. All their documents are ready."* When Tanyusha and I got home and heard Vera's story about the call, we started laughing. After all, when you are called from such an institution, you expect to hear the voice of a shrew, and the woman who spoke to our Verusha, sounded like a close relative. It was very unexpected and funny.

One of the first things we had to do, as soon as possible, was to buy plane tickets to Vienna. There we were to meet the representatives of the Jewish Agency for the repatriation of Jews to Israel. These same people also could help emigrants, like us, who wished to travel not to Israel, but some other country. Airline tickets were an eternal problem in the Soviet Union at the time. We made enquiries and found out that the soonest that we could get tickets to Vienna was September. For us, waiting that long was completely unacceptable.

At that time in the Soviet Union, one could resolve any complicated problem only through acquaintance. One of Tanya's sister Natasha's patients turned out to be an Aeroflot pilot. He managed to get us tickets to Vienna for August 10. It was mid-July, so we had less than a month. If one takes into account that in any Soviet institution even nice people, who sympathized with us, were afraid to express their kind feelings to "traitors of the fatherland", it becomes clear how difficult was it to obtain every necessary document. For us it was even more difficult, since we did not have much time for this.

For example, Tanya was very worried that the headmistress of Verusha's French school would put all possible obstacles in our way to get a certificate about what classes the girl had taken at her school. It was the middle of July, and Tanya really wanted Verusha to start classes in an American school on September 1. Sometime prior, our friends had given us a beautiful old French lithograph of a map of Paris. Tanya decided that the map would be a nice gift to the headmistress of the FRENCH LANGUAGE school. With this litho under her armpit Tanya went to the school for the certificate herself. As soon as Tanya put the litho of Paris on the headmistress's desk and said that the school was a good memory of ours, the woman noticeably softened. She had previously stated that the task was difficult and demanded a lot of work. After being gifted with the beautiful map, the task became simple. Tanya returned home with the certificate she needed.

THE DINNER THAT NEVER TOOK PLACE

No sooner had we rejoiced over the purchase of the plane tickets, than our dear friend Peter Buwalda, the Dutch ambassador in Moscow, informed us that he had spoken to Armand Hammer and that Mr. Hammer was going to take two families of long-standing refuseniks straight from Moscow to New York on his private plane. Two families had been chosen: the Ziemans and the Charnys. Benjamin Charny, a mathematician who formerly worked for the Soviet space program, was a long-term refusnik. Hammer was a well-known American millionaire. This businessman had fallen in love with the Soviet Union back in the 1920s and had been in Moscow often since then to meet with Soviet leaders. In the late 1970s, he built a huge International Trade Center (ITC) on the Krasnaya Presnya Embankment of the Moscow River, which everyone called the "Hammer Centre."

Armand Hammer did not enjoy a good reputation among our American acquaintances in Moscow. Greg Guroff, cultural attaché at the American embassy told us that in the mid-1980s, Hammer had come to Moscow and met with Eduard Shevardnadze, then Soviet Foreign Minister. He, Greg, personally asked him to intercede for us, and Hammer promised to do so. Later, Greg found out later that he NEVER DID it.

Of course, it would have been nice for us to leave as soon as possible but even more importantly, to go straight to the US, bypassing the transfer in Vienna, and thereby getting rid of all the bureaucratic procedures with documents related to entering the US. A couple of days later we got a phone call and Tanya answered it. The person on the other end of the line introduced himself as Hammer's secretary. He told Tanya that his boss asked him to call and tell us that Hammer was leaving for New York in three days and had invited us to fly with him in his private Boeing! Actually, at this time we were in many ways far from ready. Remember, it was not just a departure. It was the departure FOREVER! We could not leave in such agony the country of our roots, a country with so many connections, and not being able even to say goodbye to our loved ones.

Tanya asked this gentleman to tell Mr. Hammer that we were deeply touched by his offer and that we thanked him sincerely for his kindness. However, unfortunately, that we could not leave Russia in so fast, and she explained our reasons. Then a brilliant idea came to my Tanyusha's mind. Soviet authorities allowed emigrants leaving the Soviet Union to take only two pieces of luggage with them. Tanya said that Mr. Hammer would do us a great service if he would take a couple of our suitcases on his plane, and we would find a way to retrieve them in New York. She asked that the request be passed to his boss. He promised to do so and to let us know the decision. The answer came soon enough and confirmed our worst assumptions. Armand Hammer responded that he could not take our suitcases, as his Boeing was already overloaded (?!). In order to expiate his unwillingness to help us, he sent through his secretary an invitation to dinner. We could not help but think that he was ready to take on board two adults and a child, whose weight even without luggage significantly exceeded the weight of two suitcases. The great entrepreneur could have tried to find some more decent and more plausible reason for his refusal. But who needs this?

Tanyusha and I accepted the invitation and met him at his office in the Hammer Centre. He asked about our reluctance to fly with him. In this conversation he did not forget to mention that he had spoken to President Reagan about us. Tanya repeated the explanation she had given him through the secretary, but this sentiment seemed alien to this man. She added that we already had both the permit and even the plane tickets, so we do not need his help so desperately. But it would be so wonderful, if he tried to take out those, who did not yet have a permit. As an example, she named Yuli Kosharovsky and Vladimir Kislik. He responded that he had talked to Gorbachev and she, Tanya, should not worry: the Soviet leader promised him that SOON everyone who wanted to go would be able to leave. For our friend Volodya Prestin, this "soon" happened one long year later, but Mr. Hammer did not seem to care about such trifles. I had the impression that he was not very happy that we did not fly with him. Maybe that was why he forgot that he had invited us to have dinner with him and never said a word about it. We thanked him again and parted. We never got the dinner.

After sober reflection, it seemed that our supposed benefactor's motives may have been for his own benefit. The situation of refusal as an example of gross violation of human rights had finally attracted the attention of the influential people of this world. Both our family and Czarnys were good examples of these violations. Hammer, of course, considered himself among the influential people, most probably wanted to be in the center of this attention. He intended to play the No. 1 role in the triumphant appearance on American soil of two long term refusenik families, around whom the world has made so much human rights abuse noise Our suitcases were in no way up to the task he had set for himself. Arriving of our luggage only, apparently, would steal a moment of glory from him.

As a result, our opinion of this man was far from the best. I was curious and decided to find out more about him on Google. Much of what I read there did not please me at all. Armand was born to a family of Jewish immigrants from Odessa. His father, Julius Hammer was a physician by trade, was a founder of the Communist Party USA (!) and had Party card number one. Armand was born in 1898, same year that my mother was born. In 1920, his father performed an illegal abortion and his patient died. As a result, he was sentenced to three and a half years in prison. Armand, then a medical student, assisted him in the operation. The son tried later to explain his father's prosecution by his ties with the Communist Party. Obviously, this was a lie. During his residency in medical school, Armand went in 1921 on a short trip to the Soviet Union on his father's business. This business trip lasted until 1930, so the young doctor apparently forgot all about his chosen noble profession.

In his very first year in Moscow, Hammer had a four-hour conversation with Lenin. The leader of the world proletariats charmed the young businessperson so much that he wrote after the meeting: *"If Lenin had ordered me to jump out of the window, I probably would have done so."* Hammer's connections with Soviet leaders, as defined by Radio Liberty, created his reputation as a "Kremlin liaison." That radio wrote that his activities in the Soviet Union were of interest to the FBI. At the urging of the director of that organization, J. Edgar Hoover, they opened the file number 61–280 on Hammer, which piled up not by the each day but by the each hour during the years of his "work" in Russia. The materials of this case showed that his activities in the Soviet Union went far beyond Soviet-American business. I wonder how on the basis of such documents our entrepreneur did not go to jail in the United States. Most likely, his billions and Soviet diplomacy helped.

Meetig the prominent leaders of the world would always tickle Hammer's vanity throughout his life, and he liked to talk about these meetings. He reminded me of a wonderful epigram by R. Burns, which was nicely translated by S. Marshak into Russian, and was very popular in my childhood. I give below the original text. In attempts to make the Burns' text more decent the "Improved" Russian translation, as well as many later English publications replaced in the last line "cunt" to "curls". In my opinion, copyright does not allow us to make such meaning changes.

> *Of lordly acquaintance you boast*
> *And the dukes that you dined wi' yestreen,*
> *Yet an insect is an insect at most*
> *Tho' it crawl on the cunt of a queen.*

I just wanted to move the action of the epigram to a world that is much closer to me and Hummer, and also to Burns' original. I am aware of the fact that our acquaintance, a millionaire, is described well enough with the original text. Nevertheless I could not help to offer my lame modern plagiarism of the epigram that sounds s like this:

> *You boast of your acquaintance-celebrity*
> *And of the dignitary that you dined with yesterday.*
> *But an insect is still an insect*
> *Though it crawled on the cunt of a queen.*

Hammer had never been squeamish about the way he made his money. We learned many of the darker aspects of his business only after the collapse of the USSR, when the secret archives of the KGB were uncovered. Radio Liberty described his activities in the

Soviet Union as follows: *"For every one of his legal actions, there were ten illegal ones".* He became a great expert in laundering dirty money. Our businessperson made his first million during the Prohibition years in the United States on the successful sale of a drug that contained a high percentage of alcohol (remember, he had an MD diploma in his pocket!). After I discovered this, it became clear to me, that it was this kind of unscrupulousness that made the American entrepreneur similar to the Soviet executives. I thought how wonderful it was that God saved me from having dinner with this man and flying with him across the Atlantic Ocean.

Armand Hammer died in 1990. It is not customary to speak ill of the deceased, and I apologize that I had to tell such unpleasant things about him here. However, I advise those readers who are interested in details of our billionaire's biography to turn to American publications and the Internet. Even in the Russian Internet, you will find many interesting things on this subject. I would like to end our Hammer epic with my paraphrase of a verse of a popular Soviet song by I. Dunayevsky to the words of M. Isakovsky from the movie "The Kuban Cossacks." This cinematographic fake was released in Moscow in 1949. It showed the happy life of Soviet collective farmers. I was in fourth grade and rather silly at the time, and I have to admit, I loved everything in this movie, and I happily sang the songs, including "The Way You Were." Now I want to use a paraphrase of the verse from that song, addressing one last time Armand Hammer

> *The way you were, the way you still are,*
> *Manipulative, whether you lie down or stand up...*
> *Why, why did you meet us,*
> *Why did you grow up like this in the States?*

For the first two years that we lived in the US, Hammer was still alive, but we knew nothing about him and, truth be told, we were not very anxious to find out.

LAST DAYS IN RUSSIA

The final two weeks in Russia were crazy. The difficulty was not in preparation and packing to leave. After all, the authorities allowed us to take so little that we did not have to worry about it. In fact, when we departed, we left almost everything we owned and flew away with what we were wearing. However, some of what we wore did not meet Tanya's standards. For example, I did not own a single decent suit, and it was impossible to go and buy a suit, Tanya wanted, in Moscow at that time. As always, friends came to the rescue. Our friend Valya Chilikin sent us to his friend, a seller in clothing shop and he gave me a grey suit of Finnish nationality. It was the suit that made my debut in my new, fourth life. I wore it all our days in Europe and the first days in America at all official places where I had to be decently dressed.

The main difficulty, in fact, was in saying goodbye to everything that had become close and dear to us during half a century of living in Russia, and there was quite a lot. The political situation in those days made emigration from the USSR a one-way street. Those who left the country and those who stayed in the country had almost no chance to see each other ever again after the separation. Neither death, nor the birth of a new family member, nor a desire to visit the burial place of a relative or loved one on the other side of the Iron Curtain was a sufficient reason to obtain an entry visa to the USSR or exit visa from the USSR. That is why it was a lasting separation FOREVER

So, the process of separation was incredibly difficult. The correspondence between the separated was also very difficult, just next to impossible. Tanya was leaving her mother and her sister's family in Moscow, and I was leaving my brother's family and my sister's family. Losing these people was a bitter payback for the start of our new life. Today, as I write these lines, many of them are no longer alive. And only some of these people later emigrated also.

Tanya and I were very lucky in life: we had many GREAT friends, some of whom were family to us. We shed many tears when we were saying goodbye to them. To the elderly and not so healthy, we went to bid farewell because of their limited mobility. The rest passed through our flat in an endless stream during the last weeks of our life in Moscow. We simply did not close our front door. Some of the people who came were among those who had begun to think about emigration, and they came as a family, so each family member could ask us, now experienced refuseniks, their questions. Many of them could not free themselves from work or household chores during the day and came in the evenings. Some of them stayed past midnight. As a result, in the last weeks we were sleep-deprived. At the end, we had seen over 200 people and had drunk bottles of liquor beyond count.

Our farewell to my colleague at the maternity hospital, Sasha Malykhin, a janitor, was very touching. His life was not easy. He had had poliomyelitis as a child, which left him with a leg that he dragged and a very awkward gait. His wife, who also worked in our maternity hospital as a dispatcher, had been struck by an eye disease that left this lovely woman half-blind. They had two small children. And despite these challenges, Sasha was surprisingly handy, the best locksmith in the maternity hospital. From him I learned a lot. He was the only person in the maternity hospital to whom I told the real story of my refusal and our departure. Tanyusha collected quite a few of the things we had to leave for this family. On one of the frantic days of pre-departure farewells, the bell rang and Tanechka opened the door. She saw at the threshold all four Malykhins. They had come to see us for the last time, and Sasha's crooked fingers were holding a bottle of olive oil, an incredible rarity in Moscow in those days. Sasha knew that Tanya was very fond of this oil. It was a lovely gift and a lovely farewell.

Our wonderful helpers, mother and daughter Nadya and Vica

We were leaving an apartment full of stuff, and we did not have the energy or time to try to sell anything and make some money. Still, we were able to get help from our wonderful friends. Nadya Dudnichenko and her daughter Vica, whom Tanya taught English, voluntarily took it upon themselves to dispose of all that we had not given away, cleaned the apartment and gave the keys to the house management. Vica took some time off from work to be able to help in the pre-departure hustle and bustle.

I have already mentioned that I was preparing an English-Russian dictionary on human reproduction. By the time we left, the materials of this dictionary were thousands of standard index cards that filled several file cabinet drawers. Taking the contents of those boxes with us on the plane was out of the question, despite the fact that they were the result of a year's intense work. At the time, I naïvely thought that I would be able to find a publisher to print my dictionary. So, our lovely Vicochka volunteered to make sure my efforts would not go to waste. She copied by hand the text from all the cards on multiple sheets of paper, which I was able to put in a folder and take away with me. To this day, what she did touches me to tears. I have to confess, I feel terribly guilty, for my new life in America, turned out to be so intense, that it left me no time, energy, or mental valence to tackle my vocabulary. Viculia, my dearest, forgive me that I have not been able to follow through on my dream yet. Believe me, whenever I see on my desk the dictionary rewritten by you, I feel grateful and happy. From an emotional point of view, your intentions and help were for me invaluable. Thank you, Vicochka, thank you very much!

LAST HOURS IN RUSSIA

The day was coming. August 10, 1988, was the day of our physical parting with Russia. We had to report before dawn the day before for the customs inspection of our luggage at Sheremetyevo airport. It was before dawn, because everything connected with emigration from the Soviet Union was ugly and mindlessly difficult. The authorities deliberately created endless difficulties for those who tried to leave the country: if you wanted to betray your homeland and people, you would have to suffer.

The inspection of departing Jews lasted many hours, and there were cases where poor people missed their flight because of these long inspections. Therefore, most of the emigrants preferred to go through the inspection and to get rid of their suitcases the day before departure. Early morning, every day there was a line at the airport of families of departing emigrants. The thoroughness of the search was humiliating and surpassed every conceivable limit. The customs officials checked each item of clothing to see if it had jewelry in its seams. The customs officials stuck their noses into the anus and, in the case of the women, also into their vaginas to make sure there were no diamonds in the way. One would have thought they were inspecting criminals who had robbed a bank.

LIFE THIRD: MY EFFORTS TO EMIGRATE FROM THE SOVIET UNION

Nevertheless, some people still tried to take with them family heirlooms that they had managed by incredible effort to save in difficult times of their lives: disease and ruin, war, and misfortune.

We had permission to check in only one suitcase per person and the weight of each suitcase could not exceed 44 pounds. Such a restriction posed a huge problem for me. Since the 1950s, I had kept the programs of all the concerts, performances, exhibitions and other memorable events that I had attended and I had accumulated several hundred of them, and I regarded this collection as a treasured socio-cultural diary. I sorted them out by years, so that we could make excursions into the past with our friends and remember when and what we were interested in, and what we enjoyed in our lives. In all seriousness, if I had the talent for writing, my collection could have been the basis for an interesting book about Moscow's theatrical, concert, and exhibition life. I treasured this collection and could not imagine leaving Russia without it. Due to severe limitations on allowed luggage, this undertaking did not make my Tanyusha happy at all. However, I must give her credit: when it came to packing, she was incredibly generous and agreed to allow one of the three suitcases for my programs. I was over the moon about it.

Some of our good friends accompanied me early on the morning of August 9 with our suitcases to be at the beginning of the line. Tanyusha stayed home with Vera and stowed her carry-on luggage for the next morning. We arrived at customs to learn that we already had to wait for hours. When they called us in for the inspection, the customs officers refused to inspect our luggage because they demanded that BOTH of the departing adults be present. We had nothing to do, but to give up our position in line to the next family and urgently call Tanyusha, who rushed to join us by taxi. This adventure was very anxiety-producing and took several more hours of waiting.

It was in the late afternoon that the "happy" moment arrived, when the customs officer invited us again to start. An extremely unfriendly woman, already well-acquainted with us from the send-offs of several of our friends who had left before, evoked an association with cobra from "The Shaggy Alphabet" by my beloved kids poet B. Zakhoder:

> *There is a cobra curled up behind the glass.*
> *She looks dumb and unkind.*
> *You can tell at a glance:*
> *There is little brain and lot of poison!*

The funny thing is that the room at Sheremetevo airport, where the customs inspection was located really behind a glass barrier separating that place from the public. All our friends who came with us to customs that day could watch, though not hear, what was going on with our luggage through the glass. Emigrants tired and tortured by the ordeals and difficulties of departure and the general hostility of the staff, often did not behave in a very delicate or polite manner. However, that did not give anyone among the customs personnel reason to resemble a venomous snake.

An amusing scene played out when the customs officer glanced at my opened suitcase with the theater programs. I was worried that the suitcase contained programs of well-known performers who became "enemies of the people" who had scandalously left the Soviet Union such as brilliant musicians Mstislav Rastropovich and Galina Vishnevsky. I really was horrified when I imagined that the Cobra might make now a political cause. I pictured a nightmare picture of a customs official throwing out of my suitcase very dear to me documents showering the floor of the inspection room like freshly fallen snowflakes. However, I was lucky; the unexpected nature of the situation helped me: the poor official had probably never seen anything like it before. After looking through a few programs lying on the top, in complete amazement demanded an explanation from me, "What is all this???" I mumbled something probably not very intelligible about my emotions. He turned around abruptly, hid behind the partition for a moment and brought Cobra over. "*Look,*" he told her, "*a suitcase full of theater programs, I'm not kidding!*" Cobra was not impressed by the turn of events. She waved her hand at Tanya and me, and her face said: "*What the hell do you expect from crazy people!?*"

Our next step with customs turned out to be not without incident. Our niece Olya volunteered to pack our suitcases before the inspection, about which we were extremely happy. Tanya specifically asked her to check thoroughly that all the clothing pockets were empty, to avoid trouble with the customs officials. We were all tired and exhausted. During the inspection of the suitcase there was a knitted blouse in Tanya's suitcase, and from the pocket of which, oh my God, the customs person took out a Jewish amulet and a woman's watch on a silver bracelet, which our Olechka out of fatigue had failed to notice! This led to a scandalous summoning of Cobra, and a report was made accusing us of smuggling and then the confiscation of both items. And then we were required to pay a rather large fine.

I have a very sad memory of this because it caused me to have a ridiculous panicked reaction. I was afraid that, taking advantage of this "violation," the authorities would revoke our visas and we would have to go back to our refusenik life, only in much more unbearable conditions. My fear was that knowing that we had been so close to leaving for good, that we had ruined many important things in our lives and had irreversibly burned all bridges behind us to have to turn back now would be unbearable. Under the oppression of this dreadful fear, I jumped on my poor Tanya with the ridiculous suspicion that she had deliberately put these two silly objects in the pockets of her blouse, hoping to take them away with her. But no, three weeks before, Tzilia and Milan had left Russia, and of course, we had seen them off. Customs had not allowed Tzilia to take the two items with her, so she had shoved them into Tanya's hands, saying: *"Do what you like with them!"* It was a very hard separation, and Tanya had unconsciously slipped them into her pocket and had forgotten all about them. She had never worn the sweater again, and Olechka, putting it into the suitcase, had not noticed that the pockets were not empty. After I realized all these details, I still could not shake off the shame of my behavior. Forgive me, my dear Tanyusha! Thank God, this storm passed us by. The next day we left Russia, leaving all our troubles, worries and fears on the other side of the Iron Curtain.

The suitcases we sent that day did not arrive in America until a month later. One would have thought that they had not flown across the Atlantic Ocean in a jetliner, but had swum across it on the back of a giant turtle. However, that was not the most upsetting thing. When Tanyusha saw our suitcases, she started crying. The fiber "Jewish" suitcases had straight through cuts and looked like somebody had ripped them open with a knife. Some missing small items must have fallen out through the cuts. In Sheremetyevo, the inspection of each suitcase ended with a pile of our stuff on the table, and Olechka dutifully stacked each item again, trying to restore order. When we opened the suitcases in Boston, the contents again looked like they were on the customs table. Do not ask me why, but the suitcase with the music programs reached us in the best condition. My feeling was that we paid for the opportunity to get on the plane, to fly over the Iron Curtain, to leave and to NEVER have to deal with such ugliness again. This kind of payback was a very effective cure for the ailment of nostalgia. I like this principle: to pay for everything yourself. I'm glad we learned Satin's monologue from Gorky's "The Lower Depths" by heart in Soviet school: *"A person is free... he pays for everything himself: for faith, for unbelief, for love, for intelligence, man pays for everything himself, and therefore he is free!"*

On the day of our departure, our dear friends Wilma and Peter Buwalda were not in Moscow, but they made sure that everything went smoothly before we left the city. On the day of our departure, his right-hand man at the Embassy, William Bentick, came to the airport at Peter's request as moral support. Thanks to his special diplomatic privileges, he was able to be with us from the first to the last minute in a place where mere mortals did not have permission to be. Even as we approached the aircraft, we could see him waving to us through the glass doors. The presence of our friend, such a high-ranking diplomat, radically changed the attitude of all the Soviet officials at the airport towards us, beginning with the small fry and ending with the Cobra itself. Maybe that is why we got off so easily with our "smuggling" incident.

Then the first real "interplanetary" flight in my life happened. It started out very mundanely. We did things that I had done many times in my first three lives. We stepped onto the airfield with our hand luggage in our hands and boarded the Aeroflot plane, which looked nothing like the spacecraft whose destination was the Austrian capital, Vienna. Having fastened our seatbelts we relaxed, tired but satisfied, thinking of the forthcoming miracle: landing on the other planet. And the miracle, as in a fairy tale, did happen!

FRANKLY ABOUT VIENNA

Fleeing pogroms and discrimination, Jews fled Russia and Eastern Europe long before the formation of the Soviet Union. In 1881, the Jewish community of the United States formed the Hebrew Immigrant Aid Society (HIAS) in New York City. This non-profit organization survives to this day, and there is almost no Jewish family in the United States of America that has not benefited from HIAS at some point. In 1975, after the communist victory in Vietnam, there was a mass exodus from Vietnam, Laos and Cambodia. At the personal request of US President Ford, HIAS then helped resettle 3,600 people from these countries in 38 different states. I would like to draw the reader's attention to how active the Jewish community in the USA was in its efforts to help the refugees and how understanding the American government was in this problem. I am very proud that I now live in a country that in most cases tries to support all those in every corner of the world whose rights are violated.

By arrangement with HIAS, all Jewish immigrants would fly to Vienna, where they would meet the staff of this wonderful organization and get help to move forward to the country of their choice. That is why we flew to Vienna, where we were supposed to meet with representatives of HIAS. When we got off the plane at the airport in Vienna, HIAS officials were, indeed, waiting for us, to help us get in touch with the US administration and arrange the necessary papers to get permission to enter the US. Additionally, some very pleasant for us surprises expected us in Viena.

First, we immediately saw a lovely English couple, Brenda and Lawrence Elton. These people, had received our names and learned about our refusenik ordeal through their Jewish community, were coming to visit us in Moscow as support. Somehow, they had heard about our leaving Russia and came from London to Vienna to rejoice with us in our having escaped from the Communist captivity. My eyes filled with tears of tenderness and gratitude. On the second day in Vienna, we were able to enjoy some time with them.

Secondly, to our surprise, we also saw at the Vienna airport our familiar BBC correspondents who had come to visit us in Moscow and who had interviewed us on those crazy days when the Reagans were going to come to visit us. We spent most of our time together with these people on our first day in Vienna. They came with a film camera to capture our first impressions of the free world. They were with us most of the time and proved to be wonderful guides in the extraordinary Austrian capital city. Our impressions of this fabulous city exceeded all expectations.

How silly I was in the early school years, when I happily sang the post-war song by A. Ostrovsky on words by S. Mikhalkov "Home Land", which talked about such a wonderful city:

> I beat the Germans in the streets of Vienna,
> It has good gardens and palaces.
> But Vienna, I will be honest with you,
> Is good not for the Russian soul.

What a rabid Russophile and politician intriguer the author of this abominable song had to be! He disparagingly agreed that the palaces and gardens of Vienna were worth something, but the main memory of one of the most beautiful capitals in the world is how he himself, the hero, beat Germans in it. Incidentally, I am not sure that the story about beating Germans in the streets of Vienna is a true story. After all, the poet never fought on the front lines. He was a war correspondent and went into the reserves in the rank of lieutenant colonel. Usually those who beat Germans on the streets, if they survived, served at most up to the rank of senior lieutenant. If you believe this expert on the Russian soul, I will be honest with you, that I think my soul is certainly not Russian, both genetically and consciously. After my first acquaintance with Vienna, I was completely delighted with the city. Mikhalkov is also infamous as the irreplaceable servant to Bolsheviks, in particular, as the author of the words to numerous versions of the hymns of the Soviet Union. With every change of the authorities, the ideology was also changed, and he was never late with composing new words of the hymn, which the new authorities liked. For this exceptional ability, his colleagues in the writer's shop sarcastically called him "hymnyuk" which in Russian means "hymn man". The word sounds in Russian very negative because phonetically it is very close to "hovnyuk" — "shithead" in English.

Thirdly, there was one more surprise in Vienna, that both of us would call wonderful: a close friend of our children, Galya and Vitya, an Austrian physicist and the nicest person, Manfred Jeitler, tried to meet us. I use the word "tried" because being a very modest man, Manfred was hesitant to push his way through the crowd of such determined men, hardened by their profession, as today's press correspondents are. Nevertheless, despite our very short stay in Vienna, we were able, to our mutual pleasure, to walk and talk with him while strolling through Manfred's native city.

Fourthly, at last, by importance it should, probably go first, we had to arrange as soon as possible with the American representatives in Vienna all our papers to entry the United States. We really had to hurry, because I came to this country, frankly speaking, with a still not cancelled and not confirmed, but horrible diagnosis of brain tumor or brain aneurysm. Now, in hindsight, I think it was really crazy for such an ill person to try to come to a new country to start life all over again with only literally $100 in the pocket. But to my great good fortune, doctors at Boston Hospital sent me urgently to brain MRI. On the basis of this test results they DID NOT confirm my scary diagnoses. I turned out to have just an acute inflammation of my eye nerve, which was successfully treated with hormonal therapy. I received the therapy that gave me over thirty five happy and productive years in blessed America. I was terribly pleased that the American doctors did confirm the diagnosis given to me by only one Moscow doctor, Boris Gekht and we were afraid to believe him then. How wonderful it was, that Tanya managed to organize CAT scan to me in Moscow after which we decided not to cut open my skull in order to understand what the next step should be! However then, during the days in Vienna, my prospects were not so bright at all.

Now, let us go back to our tour in Vienna, led by BBC journalists. Since we had only a few hours for this tour, it was literally a "gallop through Europe." At the same time, our guides kept hurrying us, enigmatically repeating that we should leave the evening free for the big surprise that they had prepared for us. And if we add to it that the excursion was preceded by flight over the ocean, and before it there was a week of sleepless packing and saying goodbye, we could not imagine how we were following our guides, physically exhausted, but with our mouths open with excitement and admiration. Of course, we did not have a chance to enter any museum even for a minute. Nevertheless, our guides led us through some inconceivably beautiful streets, and it seemed to me that the palaces and towers we passed were all smiling at us. To my senses the whole air was saturated with the greeting "Welcome!"

After this we walked through what one would call a small market in the city center and gastronomic Vienna did not lose face either. In my head, a man of dictionaries, all kinds of lexical combinations with the adjective "Viennese", familiar to me in Moscow, like schnitzels and sausages, coffee and buns, waffles and strudels immediately came to mind. I remember when we stopped outside a large outdoor ice cream stand. At that moment, another myth that, I had learned as a child, was shattered to the ground: myth that Russia has the most interesting and delicious ice cream in the world. The kiosk we stopped in front of offered to the customer, I counted, more than 20 different kinds of ice cream! Each one looked to me more delicious then the other.

At some point, our guides said it was time for a surprise. They led us to the Vienna State Opera building and happily announced that we were all going to listen to Mozart's The Magic Flute. Where else but in Vienna to listen to this jewel of a great musician, which was first played in Vienna in 1791, a little less than two hundred years before we came to Vienna. The building, which we approached, did not exist then. It was built only in 1869, and the premiere took place in the Teatro Widen. This theatre does not exist today, in 1801 in its place was built a residential building. The seriously ill Mozart attended the premiere, and the success of the opera slightly lifted his depressed mood. Nevertheless, two months later the composer passed away.

The invitation was very touching and completely unexpected for us. Mixed feelings were tearing us apart. On the one hand, we were dead tired and were falling asleep. On the other hand, in this situation it was impossible for many reasons to say "no". Anyway, we entered the hall of the Vienna State Opera, flooded with light. Of course, the entire interior could arouse nothing but admiration, but to be honest, we did not have enough energy even for adequate admiration. I wanted to sit down as soon as possible. Tanyusha, Vera and I found ourselves on the left side on the first balcony close enough to the stage, and the BBC team settled symmetrically on the other side. That way they probably got more opportunities to film us from the other side of the hall. Time ran out and we all positioned ourselves in our seats. The show started.

The lights went out in the hall, and soon after that came one of the most embarrassing moments of our lives. Tanya and I both, as if we had prearranged, slipped into the realm of Morpheus and only our child, burning with shame for us, continued to look with all eyes and listen with all ears. We ignominiously slept through most of Mozart's magical music, waking up only to the highest notes of the Queen of the Night's trills and then falling back into the abyss. It was our shame, and I do not know how much our BBC friends recorded for history from the other side of the hall. I hope that the darkness in the room saved us from that. At any rate, we did not see any of this on the videotape we were given afterwards. I do not remember at all how we got back to our hotel room, but we did, and we had no trouble sleeping that night at all.

The next day we finally got a chance to spend time with our dear friends Manfred and the Eltons. What a mutual pleasure it was to walk around an unfamiliar city with people we knew very well! And the next morning we left Vienna very early. Our plane flew to Boston, Massachusetts, with two stopovers in Frankfurt am Main in Europe and New York in America. The break between flights in both cities was very short, so we spent it at the airport without even going into the city.

REUNITING WITH GALECHKA

Our first-ever flight across the Atlantic Ocean was surprisingly uneventful, so it was hard to believe that we had landed in New York. We got off the plane and made our way to the John F. Kennedy Airport lounge. Unbelievably, in the crowd of people gathered to greet us were familiar faces.

First, we saw Bill and Louise MacCagg, wonderful New Yorkers who came to Moscow in 1973, and befriended Tanyusha. As a historian, Bill was writing a book about Stalin and was interested in the Soviet Union. His wife Louise was a sculptor. This couple became very dear and close to us, and they were very helpful throughout our years in America. The friendship between our families included many wonderful days together. Bill came back to Moscow in 1977 for the International Book Fair. They were the first Americans who Tanya and I became friends with, even before the Browns. Unfortunately, Bill had severe stomach cancer and he is no longer with us.

Another familiar person we knew from our Moscow life, waiting for us, was Yuri Chekanovsky. He left the Soviet Union for New

York, and in recent years, contacts with him have somehow come to an end, but I remember him fondly. Yuri had held quite a high position in Moscow, working as the director of food supply of a large district of Moscow called Leningradsky. All of the food shops of the district were under his command. It is not difficult to imagine how privileged his life in Moscow was. One day Yuri was a guest of ours, and we treated him to a tea of American origin called Earl Grey, given to us by foreigners in Moscow. It was a good quality black tea with bergamot leaf that Yuri had a great passion for. With all his unbelievable ability to find in Moscow almost any foodstuffs, he could not get such tea in the whole Soviet Union. He literally drank cup after cup with us in our kitchen and could not stop.

Later that night, Chekanovsky went home and immediately called us. Talking, he could not restrain his laughter. It turned out that he was speeding on the road and a police officer had stopped him. The first thing police did in such a situation was to check whether the driver was drunk. In those years, the police had a simple device for such testing: they demanded that the person breathe into a test tube with a special solution. If the exhaled air contained alcohol vapors, the solution would change its color. This test was given to Yuri, and the solution changed its color in an unexpected way. No one in the Moscow police had ever seen such a color. *"What crap have you been drinking?"* asked the officer in amazement. That was how we found out how unusually bergamot leaf stains the solution in the test tube.

As much as we enjoyed talking to our friends who lived on opposite side of the Atlantic Ocean, I was really thinking about being able to get out into the city and see at least with one eye the skyscrapers of Manhattan. Although I had never managed to see New York City, I had read so much about it and had seen so many photographs, that I could not wait to see all this with my own eyes. A silly line from the poem "Broadway" by my beloved Mayakovsky, who was looking around from the Brooklyn Bridge, immediately came to my head:

> *I am excited about New York City.*
> *However, I do not want to pull my hat off my temple.*
> *The Soviets have their own pride:*
> *We look down on the bourgeois.*

LIFE THIRD: MY EFFORTS TO EMIGRATE FROM THE SOVIET UNION

How much trash was in the mind of this extraordinarily talented poet! Without fear of accusations of plagiarism, I wanted to walk to the top point of the Brooklyn Bridge about which the poet said: *"It is (just) a thing, really."* It did happen many times but later, not this day and I did shout in reverence from there:

> *I am excited about New York City.*
> *I do want to pull my hat off my temple.*
> *In clemency, a tear flows down to my beard.*
> *From this height, I can see all of Manhattan.*

The announcement of the flight to Boston ended these reflections and we hurried to board. After a seemingly short flight, our plane came in for landing in Boston. Interesting, the airport is located at the very shoreline of the bay and the landing strip starts very close to the water line. So, planes landing fly about a dozen feet above the water and look as if they are about to dive into the bay. That day of my first landing, I was scared out of my wits. Since then, it has been 35 years, and I have flown into Boston many times, but every time I have landed, I have been nervous. Anyway, on August 12, 1988, everything turned out OK, and we safely pulled up to the terminal building and got off the plane, without swimming in the Boston bay.

To say that we were emotional as we entered the waiting room is an understatement. When we saw the crowd of family and friends smiling at us with *"Welcome to the USA!"* placards and flowers, we were overwhelmed, relieved, and transported. We hugged, kissed, and we laughed and cried at the same time. It was an experience that I cannot find words to describe. I had the feeling that we had risen from the underworld, and, suddenly, there was a reunion with loved ones who we had given up hope of ever seeing again. I could not move a step away from my Galechka, in fear that something would separate us again. Twelve year old Verusha was holding the 3-year old Masya in her arms, and never wanted to hand her to anyone. Tanya and I, happily watched it all through a veil of uncontrollable tears of tenderness.

Having listened to tons of wonderful kind words and showered ourselves with love from our acquaintances, friends, and relatives, we headed to the exit with heaps of gifts in our hands. The crowd that greeted us followed us to the car. Then another shock overtook us. At the exit from the airport was a miracle of imagination and creative impulse of the engineers of the American automobile industry: a limousine, or limo for short. The Jewish community activists who volunteered to help our family get settled in Boston, led by the lovely man, Jerry Shulman, decided that we should drive into Boston from the airport in luxury. Thanks to everyone who tried to make the beginning of our life in America as pleasant as possible.

To understand, what represents limo, it is necessary to imagine the longest passenger car made of elastic material and then stretched in length twice more. Aesthetically this construction seemed to me quite ugly that day, until today, my attitude to it has not changed. Having graduated from the technical college, having studied courses of strength of materials and theoretical mechanics in my time I should say that this automobile is an incredible engineering achievement. When I look at it, I am amazed that such a huge span of the floor between the supports — front wheels and rear wheels — does not break in the middle at the first bump in the road. Difficult to believe, but it DOES NOT!

In this miracle of technological progress, we safely drove from the airport to the house, where our Galechka had prepared for our first night a cozy apartment, which she and Vitya were renting from friends. No sooner had we crossed the threshold of the apartment, than another miracle happened. The phone rang in the apartment. I do not remember, but I think our Vitya picked up the phone. On the other end of the line, they said that it was the White House and that President Reagan and the First Lady wanted to verify personally that the Zieman family had made it safely to the United States!!! They asked that Tanya and I please come to the phone. It just astounded everyone. Tanya and I, unable to believe our ears ran to the phone. I gave Tanya the phone because she was the better English speaker. Tanya took the receiver and an unbelievable thing happened: Ronald Reagan, the President of the United States of America, really talked to Tanya! She heard his simple, but warm kind words and congratulations on the successful completion of our emigration story. He then handed the phone to Nancy Reagan, and she did the same. Afterwards, Nancy told Tanya that both the President and she wanted to hear my voice and congratulate me personally, as well. I took the receiver, and they wished me the same. Everyone who was in the apartment was in shock. How wonderful that all of our family members could share such joy with us!

EPILOGUE TO THE THIRD LIFE

As I write these lines, we started our fourth decades since we have left Russia. All this time I have had the feeling that I, like Lewis Carroll's Alice, have found myself in Wonderland. Like her, I fell asleep, and in the miraculous dream, I crawled through a narrow hole in the iron curtain, like Alice slipping down the rabbit hole. Russian poet writing for children, Boris Zakhoder, retold brilliantly, in my opinion, into Russian the book "Alice in Wonderland". It seems to me, that in this retelling B.Zakhoder very successfully and in the spirit of this magic fairy tale precedes the "Chapter One" with his own "Chapter without a Number", in which, as well as in all book, he has many nice contrivances. I think all of these contrivances must have been to the author's liking. In particular, in this chapter he has, for example, a reflection about the title of the book he retold:

> *... If it were up to me, I would call the book "Alice in the Land of Imagination", or "Alice in the Land of Astonishment", or "Alice in the Land of Nonsense", or, at the very least, "Alice in the Land of Miracles". However, as soon as I said a word about this desire, everyone began to shout at me, that I do not dare. That is why I did not dare!*

I like all the variations he offered for the title of the book. I, indeed, consider the United States a wonderland. If it ever comes to describing my life in America, maybe, I will borrow one of his titles. Then I will give the title to my sequel book, without fear that some one will shout at me in a frightful way not to dare do this. It would be something like "Yuri in the Imagination Land," or, "Yuri in the Wonderland," or "Yuri in the Land of Miracles." It seems to me that there is no perfect place to live on this planet, but I feel that this country is one of the best places to live. It saddens me that many former Russian citizens do not notice the wonders of the United States at all and take them for granted. It is my faint hope that this description of my first three lives in Russia will help such people to remember their own lives in the Soviet Union and to see the wonders of the American Wonderland. If that happens, I will be content.

If my hands and head come to describe my next life in America, I will tell about the many miracles that happened to me in my new homeland. One miracle happened at the very beginning of my fourth life. Though it has happened already in the USA and not in Russia, I think, I have to describe it in this epilogue because the story about this miracle seems to me very appropriate completion of the main theme of my third life, the last one in Russia.

The miracle happened on October 5, 1988. Our whole family got the invitation from Ronald and Nancy Reagan to visit them at the White House! Before we could even set our own lives going in Boston, all our family headed to Washington, DC. In the popular Russian romantic song "Brigantine," music by Georgy Lepsky and lyrics by Pavel Kogan, written in 1937, there are the following lines:

> *In trouble, in joy or in grief,*
> *Just close your eyes partly.*
> *In the filibustering, distant blue sea,*
> *You will see the brigantine hoisting her sails.*

The poet died at the front line of the Second World War at the age of 24, not having had time to sail away on a two-mast sailing ship from the Bolshevik terror. Tanyusha and I are very lucky people. We did make it in time. When we *"in trouble and in joy or in grief close our eyes partly,"* in each of our lives we see our dear friends who come to our aid. Such was the case on this visit to the very unfamiliar Washington, DC. We fell into the arms of our wonderful friends Liza and Bob Gillette. We lived in their house; they fed us, gave us drink, caressed, and took care of us in this new world. At the appointed time, they drove us to the White House gate, and after the appointed time, they picked us up at the same gate and brought us to their home. I cannot help to ask myself: *"How came that we happened to be such lucky people?"*

Some nice people led us in friendly rows, from the gate into the holy of holies of our new country. We found ourselves in a big room and someone came to us and politely asked to wait a little while for

At the steps of the White House with Reagans

the President and his wife to join us and very soon they did. From the first few seconds our impression of both of them was most pleasant. Both of them said many kind words, the gist of which was how happy they were for us, that we had finally reached our goal. *"Welcome!"* The President immediately invited us to move to his Oval Office, where he said we would be much more comfortable to talk. I remembered the name of the office well from press, radio, and television reports, as well as from photographs in the press.

The construction of the White House building was completed at the end of the 18th century. James Hoban, the Irish architect was the author of the project. The third US president, Thomas Jefferson, moved to the building in 1801, and since then it has been the official Presidential residence. I liked the neoclassical style of the 19th century building. In 2007, the American Institute of Architects ranked it as second after the Empire State Building in "America's Favorite Architecture" list. From that day until today, I loved the White House architecturally and I quite agree with that decision.

Shortly after the conversation began in the Oval Office, the President apologized, it unexpectedly turned out that he had a very brief meeting with reporters. Taking advantage of this, he wanted, if we did not mind, to introduce them to our family. We, of course, agreed, and we all walked together through the wide glass doors to the steps down to the White House Rose garden. We saw a crowd of journalists with notebooks and cameras around the steps. A funny detail: On the steps, there were small pieces of paper with our names on them: who should stand where. A fuss lasted for half a minute as everyone found their name and stood up as the organizer had intended, after which the President addressed a short introduction to the crowd. I would like to quote here in full what the President said then on the steps to the rose garden:

> Ladies and gentlemen of the press,
>
> We just wanted to come out here for a few seconds and introduce our friends to you — newcomers to our country — the Zieman family and their daughter and son-in-law, who have been living in America. And now the family is reunited. They came out of the Soviet Union and are reunited here in the United States, and we are very happy to have them with us...

At that moment, the unbelievable has happened: one of the journalists interrupted the President halfway through with a question that had nothing to do with the words he was saying. As if this impudent man was thus saying to the leader of his country, "I don't care about your friends. You would better tell me why your administration made this or that decision?". For better understanding, we should explain that just at that time a political scandal with violation of arms embargo against Iran by U.S.A. administration was unfolding. First of all, I was shocked, how a civilized person, and I naively thought that all journalists were educated people of culture, could afford such behavior, and all the more so against the background of such beautiful scarlet roses. Well, secondly, I was shocked again, this time in a positive way, by tolerance and politeness of the President. Rather than put the heathen savage in his place, Ronald Reagan calmly answered the question, he was asked, and then tried to go back to human rights and our arrival in the United States. Unbelievable, but story, like in a bad dream, repeated itself with the next insolent.

Giving up his intended plan to talk to the press, the President calmly accepted a few more questions about the scandal, just as politely answered them, and then let the crowd of these moral freaks know that the meeting was over. He threw the door wide open back to the Oval Office and held it as a host would until we all made our way inside. After that, he closed the door tightly, took a deep breath and, turning to me, said sadly, *"Now I hope you understand, Yuri, what a hard job I have!"* With his entire demeanor in this brief episode, he bought me lock, stock, and barrel. It seems to me that the leaders of many countries have something to learn from this President. For myself, I realized once again that I could NEVER do the job at the level of the leader of the country.

Throughout the brief meeting on the steps of the White House rose garden, I was in a state of extreme tension, as if it was not Reagan, but I who was leading the meeting with reporters. When the President shut the door tightly behind us and ushered us back into the Oval Office, I was personally very relieved. Our conversation with the President of the US was surprisingly friendly and straightforward. The way that President Reagan spoke to us set me at ease. Oddly enough, I felt like I was talking to old friends, and I was excited about the continuation of our conversation.

After meeting with the press people, Colin Powell, joined the Reagan family for our conversation. At first, I was upset that the conversation took the form of an official visit with the presence of a man unfamiliar with our emigrant odyssey. However, I turned out to be wrong: the "stranger" behaved himself quite delicately, limiting himself to rare and quite delicate, but friendly remarks. Nancy Reagan behaved in a similar manner.

As for President Reagan, he was very active in asking us about our life in Russia. He was interested in all the details: how we worked there, how our children studied there, how we spent our free time. He asked me questions about the job I had in Russia and what kind of work I would like to do here. He asked me if I had any difficulties in getting the job, I was interested in, to let him know and he would try to help me. I politely thanked him and remarked that we had different professions, and I would not like to get my first job in my new home country through acquaintance and not by recommendation in my domain. It seemed to me that we had a complete understanding on this subject.

He told us that it saddened him greatly that the political differences between our two countries had led to alienation and even animosity between ordinary citizens of those countries. He told us a story that happened to him recently. He had attended a soccer match between college soccer teams from the United States and the Soviet Union at an American university. First, he praised the high level of sportsmanship of the Soviet team. Secondly, he shared with us his memories of that match. *"I was impressed,"* he said, *"that if it was not for the different color of the uniforms, I would have never been able to tell the difference between the students from Russia and the students from the United States. Both were nice people. Why cannot they both be friends and travel freely to see each other?"* Many sympathetic people in the United States ask this rhetorical question. It would be wrong to blame everything on the Communists then in power. However, even though the Russian Communists are no longer in power today, things have not budged an inch.

As long as I am destined to live on earth, I will remember with gratitude this meeting and this conversation. When we lived in Moscow, we had very short visits to other planets, which I described in my third life. More than 35 years have passed since the fourth life began. I still have the feeling that we have moved to another planet inhabited by another type of sentient man (Homo sapiens). I must honestly confess that I like this planet much more than the previous one and I pray daily that the rest of my close ones move to this planet.

APPENDIX 1
WHEN AND WHAT

1938 — I was born
1941 — German attack on Russia
— My father and my brother were mobilized in the army
— Evacuation from Moscow
1945 — Return from evacuation at the end of the war
— Starting school
1947 — My niss Olga was born
1953 — Stalin passed away
1955 — Graduation from school
1956 — My Father passed away
— Starting work and studying by correspondence
1961 — My first marriage
— Lev was born
1962 — Galya was born
1963 — My Mother passed away
1964 — The first edition of my computer dictionary was published
1965 — Galya starts kindergarten
1966 — Translation of J. S. Bach's Matthew Passion test
1967 — Galya in Koktebel
— Alexander Ginzburg's third arrest, hunger strike, wedding
— I am helping Arina Zholkovsky
— Construction of the loo in Tarusa
— My Dictionary of English Terms on the Use of Digital ComputingSystems was published
1968 — Building the house in the Arkhangelsk region
— Soviet troops in Czechoslovakia, Kostya's arrest and exile
— My conscript epic,
— My post-graduate studies

1969 — A. Gladky comes into our life
1970 — My PhD thesis
1971 — Kostya returns from exile
1972 — First Kuril Expedition
— Masha Klimenko was born
1973 — Second Kuril Expedition
— Meeting Tanya Markish
1974 — My second marriage
— My brother Jan leaving his family
— Tanya's Father passed away
— Second edition of my computer dictionary was published
— Apartment exchange and move to Maria Ulyanov Street
— The denunciating report on me
— Tanya brings her friends into my life
1975 — My uncle Semyon passed away
1976 — Vera was born
— My attempts to enter the medical world
1977 — Submission of documents for emigration
— Ending working in my Research Institute
— My first meetings with the KGB
1978 — My friends refusniks
— The Committee of 15 in France
— The Jewish community in Florida
— My foreign friends Browns, Hartmans, Pococks, Kloses, Gilletts, and Buwaldas.
— Starting working in the maternity hospital
— Brain concussion after the oxygen tank explosion
1979 — Tanya Velikanov was arrested
— Galya graduated from high school
1980 — Nadezhda Mandelstam passed away
— Trips to friendly Georgia and Armenia
— My translation of Janusz Korczak's Diary was published
1981 — My trip to the GULAG labor camp
— Galya graduated from the Sklifasovsky paramedic school
1982 — My nephew Lev was kicked out of the University

APPENDIX 1: WHEN AND WHAT

1983 —Tanya Velikanov's transfered from camp to exile
1984 —My translation of D. Kossoff's book "Bible Stories" was published
1985 —Vera was interviewed by American journalists
—Galya and Vitya get married
—My granddaughter Masya was born.
1987 —Khatutsky family's departure
—Tanya Velikanov was released from exile
—3rd edition of my computer dictionary was published without my name
—The beginning of the epic with my double vision
—Asya Velikanov passed away
1988 —President Reagan attempts to visit us
—Permit from the Visa Office
—Pre-departure bustling
—We cross the iron curtain in the plane
—"Magic Flute" by Mozart
—Our arriving in Boston
—Phone call from White House
—First steps on the new planet
—Meeting President Reagan

APPENDIX 2
WHO IS WHO

This appendix is a list of the names of all the people mentioned in the book. The list is sorted alphabetically and gives very brief information about the person. If it is a relative, friend or acquaintance, I indicate the role they played in my life. If it is a well-known person, I usually give a brief reference about them from Wikipedia.

Aaron—biblical high priest, elder brother of Moses.
Abraham—the most revered biblical patriarch.
Abramovich Pavel—veteran-refusenik, our good friend currently living in Israel.
Aesop—legendary Greek poet and fabulist.
Akhmadulin Bella—Soviet and Russian poet, short story writer, and translator, known for her apolitical writing stance.
Akhmatov Anna—Russian poetess of the Silver Age, translator and literary critic, one of the most important figures of Russian literature of the 20th century.
Aksakov Sergey—Russian writer, official and public figure, literary and theater critic, memoirist.
Alexander II—Emperor of Russia of the Romanov dynasty.
Alexander III—Emperor of All Russia, father of the last Russian monarch Nicholas II.
Alexander the Great of Macedonia—the outstanding commander of the ancient world, the creator of the world power, which collapsed after his death.
Alexandrov Alexander—Soviet and Russian mathematician, physicist philosopher; climber, organizer of education and science in the system of higher education.
Alexei Mikhailovich—the second Russian tsar of the Romanov dynasty.

APPENDIX 2: WHO IS WHO

Alexis I—bishop of the Russian Orthodox Church; Patriarch of Moscow and All Russia, theologian, teacher, occupied the Moscow Patriarchal Throne more than 25 years—the longest in the history of the Russian Church.

Alexis II—Bishop of the Russian Orthodox Church, Patriarch of Moscow and All Russia.

Alyokhin Alexander—Russian chess player who played for the Russian Empire, Soviet Russia and France, the fourth world chess champion.

Alzheimer Alois—German psychiatrist and neurologist after whom senile dementia is named.

Andreev Nikolai—Russian sculptor.

Andropov Yuri—Soviet statesman and politician, head of the USSR, Chairman of the State Security Committee.

Antsiferov Fyodor— ur friend from Moscow times.

Apelles—ancient Greek painter, friend of Alexander the Great.

Appius Claudius Cecus—Roman statesman and military leader, lawyer and writer who built Rome's famous aqueduct, the first Roman aqueduct.

Apresyan Yuri—Soviet and Russian linguist, our good friend from Moscow times.

Archimedes—ancient Greek mathematician, physicist, and engineer of the 3rd century B.C.

Arkhipov Abram—Russian painter, painter, wanderer, his name was on a street in Moscow, where there was a synagogue, in 1994, renamed the Bolshoi Spasoglinischevsky Lane.

Arnold Vladimir—Soviet and Russian mathematician, one of the greatest mathematicians of the XX century.

Ashwin Robin—Ambassador of the Commonwealth of Australia in Moscow, Ted Pocock's successor.

Azef Evno—Russian revolutionary provocateur, one of the leaders of the Social Revolutionary Party and simultaneously a secret police officer.

Babel Isaac—Russian Soviet writer, translator, screenwriter and playwright, journalist, war correspondent.

Babitsky Konstantin—Russian linguist and human rights activist, my friend.

Babitsky Natalia—daughter of Konstantin Babitsky.

Bach Johann Sebastian—great German composer, organist, conductor, and music educator.

Baev Tanya—human rights defender and the only participant of the 1968 Red Square demonstration who managed to avoid imprisonment.

Baker Howard—American statesman, chief of staff of President Ronald Reagan.

Bakhtin Mikhail—Russian philosopher, culturologist, literary critic, theorist of European culture and art.

Balmont Konstantin—Russian symbolist poet, translator and essayist, one of the most prominent representatives of Russian Silver Century poetry.

Baranov Alexander—my supervisor at the Maternity Hospital No. 25 in Moscow.

Baratov Vera—my brother Jan's second wife.

Barenblatt Grigory—Soviet and Russian scientist in the field of mechanics, son of Nadezhda Kagan and Isaac Barenblatt.

Barenblatt Isaac—Nadezhda Kagan's first husband.

Barto Agniya—Russian Soviet children's poetess, writer.

Beatrix Wilhelmina Armgard—queen of the Netherlands.

Bebel Heinrich—German humanist poet, translator, satirist, teacher.

Beethoven Ludwig—great German composer.

Beletsky Arkady—cellist and teacher, our friend from Moscow times.

Belorus Evdokiya—landlady of the house where we lived in Sukhumi.

Belorus Stepan—owner of the house where we lived in Sukhumi.

Belyaeva Elena—my cousin, my mother's sister Elizabeth's daughter.

Belykh Grigory—Soviet writer.

Bentick William—Assistant to the Ambassador of the Netherlands in Moscow.

Bershadsky Michael—Friend of our elder son-in-law Victor Khatutsky from Moscow times.

Bessmertnykh Alexander—Soviet Minister of Foreign Affairs.

Bestuzhev Alexander—Russian writer-byronist, critic, publicist of Romanticism era and Decembrist.

Bias of Priene—one of the most revered Greek sages.

Blackman Ann—American journalist and author, contributor to Time magazine, wife of Michael Putsel.
Blank Galina—Juli Blank's wife.
Blank Juli—my late close friend, companion in my Kuril expeditions.
Blank Yuri—software engineer, son of our friend Yuri Blank.
Blokhin Nikolay—Russian oncologist-surgeon and public figure.
Blokhintsev Leonid—specialist in nuclear physics, professor of the Moscow University.
Blokhintsev Varvara—wife of Leonid Blokhintsev.
Bogart Humphrey—one of the greatest actors in American cinema.
Bogoraz Larisa—Soviet and Russian linguist, human rights activist, publicist.
Boltaev Maria—mother of my wife, Tanya Ziman.
Bonaparte Napoleon—Emperor of the France, general and statesman, who laid the foundations of the modern French state, one of the most prominent in the history of the West.
Bonner Elena—wife of Andrei Sakharov.
Borkin-Yolkin—surname of the participant of our apartment swap in Moscow, when Tanya, Galya and I ended up living together.
Borodin Leonid—Russian poet and prose writer, publicist and dissident.
Borodulina Maria—the rector of the University, where Tanya first studied and then worked.
Borovik Henrik—Soviet diplomat and international journalist.
Botkin Maria—wife of the Russian poet Afanasiy Fet.
Botkin Sergei—famous Russian physician, pathologist, physiologist and public figure, who created the doctrine of the body as a whole.
Botticelli Sandro—Italian painter, Renaissance master, representative of Florentine school of painting.
Boyarsky Eric—geodesist, a friend of mine since I studied at the University.
Braginsky Stali—Soviet theoretical physicist, geophysicist, and author of the theory of geomagnetism.
Brahms Johannes—German composer and pianist, one of the central representatives of the Romantic era.

Brezhnev Leonid—Soviet statesman and party figure who led the USSR for 18 years.
Brik Lilya—"muse of Russian avant-garde", mistress of one of the most famous in the XX century literary and art salons in Moscow.
Brodsky Joseph—Russian and American poet, essayist, playwright, translator and teacher.
Bronstein Ilya—Soviet mathematician and historian of mathematics.
Brown Philip—press attaché and later cultural attaché of the US Embassy in Moscow, our close friend.
Brown Roberta, wife of Philip Brown.
Brubeck Dave—prominent American jazz composer, arranger, pianist, and leader of the Dave Brubeck Quartet.
Bruevich Nikolay—First director of my IPM&CT, specialist in theory of precision mechanisms.
Brushtein Alexandra—Soviet writer, playwright and memoirist.
Brussilovsky Alexander—Soviet and French violinist and music teacher.
Brussilovsky Alice—daughter of Alexander Brussilovsky.
Buanarotti Michelangelo—Italian poet, painter, architect, sculptor, thinker, one of the greatest masters of the Renaissance and early Baroque periods.
Bukharin Nikolai—Russian revolutionary, Soviet political, state and party figure.
Bulgakov Elena—Mikhail Bulgakov's wife.
Bulgakov Mikhail—Russian writer, playwright, stage director and actor.
Burlatsky Fyodor—Soviet political scientist, journalist, publicist.
Burns Robert—Scottish poet, folklorist, and author of numerous poems written in Plain Scottish (south-east) and in English.
Bush George Herbert Walker—the 41st president of the United States.
Buwalda Mark—son of Wilma and Peter Buwald.
Buwalda Peter—Ambassador of the Netherlands in Moscow.
Buwalda Wilma—wife of the Ambassador of the Netherlands in Moscow.
Caesar Julius Gaius—the ancient Roman statesman and politician, general and writer. 1st century BC.

Caravaggio Michelangelo—Italian artist, one of the greatest Baroque masters.
Carroll Lewis—English writer, mathematician, logician, philosopher, deacon and photographer.
Catherine the Great—the reigning empress of Russia from 1762 to 1796.
Cervantes Miguel de—Early Modern Spanish writer widely regarded as the greatest writer in the Spanish language.
Chapkovsky Igor—Buddy of my niece Olga Klimenko.
Charny Veniamin—Jewish refusenik-veteran who received a permit at the same time as us.
Chekanovsky Yuri—Our friend from Moscow times, living today in New York.
Chekhov Anton—great Russian writer and playwright.
Chernyshevsky Nikolay—Russian literary and social critic, journalist, novelist, democrat, and socialist philosopher.
Chilikin Valentin—dentist in Moscow, a good friend of ours.
Chombe Moise—Congolese and Katangese politician and statesman, a leader of pro-Western anti-communist forces during the Congolese crisis.
Christ Jesus is the central figure in Christianity and the Messiah predicted in the Old Testament to be the atoning sacrifice for the sins of men.
Chukovsky Korney—Soviet poet, one of the most popular children's poets in the Russian language.
Cicero Marcus Tullius—Roman politician, orator and philosopher.
Cimarosa Domenico—Italian composer who was a central figure in opera, especially comic opera, at the end of the eighteenth century.
Copernicus Nicolaus—Polish and German astronomer, mathematician, mechanic, economist, Renaissance canonist, author of the heliocentric system of the world, which marked the beginning of the first scientific revolution.
Curie Marie—Polish and French experimental scientist (physicist, chemist), educator, public figure.
Curie Pierre—French physicist, one of the first researchers of radioactivity.
Daniel Yuli—Russian prose writer and poet, translator, arrested in the Soviet Union for publishing his works in the West.

Daniloff Caleb—American journalist, son of Ruth and Nicholas Daniloff.
Daniloff Nicholas—American journalist and writer, professor, contributor to "U.S.A. News & World Report", and our good friend.
Daniloff Ruth—American journalist and writer, wife of Nikolas Daniloff.
Daniloff Sergei—father of Nicholas Daniloff.
Daniloff Yuri—Russian military leader General, grandfather of Nicholas Daniloff.
Dante Alighieri—Italian poet, thinker, theologian, one of the founders of literary Italian language, politician.
David—Old Testament character, the third king of ancient Israel.
Davidson Cibelly Cherilyn—our close friend, the editor of the English translation of the present book.
Decoy Duck Michael—the soviet the soviet acquaintance of N. Daniloff working for the KGB.
Delaune Vadim—Russian poet, writer, dissident.
Dickens Charles—great English writer.
Dobroklonsky Alexander—church historian, rector of the Imperial Novorossiysk University.
Dolukhanov Zara—Soviet, Armenian and Russian chamber singer, coloratura mezzo-soprano.
Dorliak Nina—Russian Soviet chamber and opera singer (soprano), teacher, wife of Svyatoslav Richter.
Dorodnitsyn Anatoly—Soviet mathematician, geophysicist and mechanic.
Dostoyevsky Fyodor—one of the greatest Russian writers, thinkers, philosophers and publicists.
Dragunsky Viktor—Russian Soviet writer, author of novels and stories, a classic of Soviet children's literature.
Dremlyuga Vladimir—Soviet dissident, participant in the demonstration on Red Square on August 25, 1968 against the entry of Soviet troops into Czechoslovakia.
Driscoll Jack X—American journalist and author, editor-in-chief of the "Boston Globe", our good friend.
Driz Ovsey—Jewish Soviet poet who wrote in Yiddish.
Dubcek Alexander—communist politician in Czechoslovakia.
Dubnov Yakov—Russian mathematician, professor.
Dudintsev Vladimir—Russian Soviet writer.

Dudnichenko Nadezhda—Mother of Victoria Leconte, our very close friend.
Dunayevsky Isaak—Soviet composer and conductor, music teacher, author of music to films and many popular Soviet songs.
Edelman Galina—Soviet artist.
Einstein Albert—German-born theoretical physicist, widely acknowledged to be one of the greatest physicists of all time.
Eisenhower Dwight—34th president of the United States from 1953 to 1961, during World War II Supreme Commander of the Allied Expeditionary Force in Europe.
Elijah the Prophet—one of the most revered biblical prophets in the kingdom of Israel in the ninth century BC.
Elksnin Valentina—secretary of director S. A. Lebedev of the institute where I worked.
Elnitsky Lev—Soviet and Canadian linguist and translator, our friend from Moscow times.
Elnitsky Svetlana—linguist, literary critic and educator, ex-wife of Lev Yelnitsky, our friend from Moscow times.
Elton Brenda—Lawrence Elton's wife.
Elton Lawrence—our friend in London.
Engels Friedrich—German politician, philosopher, historian and entrepreneur, one of the founders of Marxism, friend and associate of Karl Marx and co-author of his works.
Erasmus of Rotterdam—the greatest scholar of the Northern Renaissance, nicknamed "the prince of the humanists".
Erastov Konstantin—Soviet linguist and translator, famous Moscow polyglot.
Erebus—the personification of eternal darkness in Greek mythology.
Esenin-Volpin Alexander—Russian-American poet and mathematician.
Eshliman Nikolai—Russian Orthodox priest, fighter for the rights of clergymen and believers.
Essas Ilya—long-time renunciate Jewish religious activist in Moscow.
Evstigneev Anna—our neighbor in a communal apartment in Moscow.
Evstigneev Vadim—the son of our neighbor in a communal apartment in Moscow.

Fadeyev Alexander—Soviet writer, one of the co-founders of the Union of Soviet Writers.
Fedorov Svyatoslav—Soviet and Russian ophthalmologist, eye microsurgeon.
Fedynsky Maria—my grandniece, Olya Klimenko's daughter.
Feinberg Viktor—philologist, prominent figure in the dissident movement.
Feltsman Anna—wife of Vladimir Feltsman, our friend.
Feltsman Oscar—Soviet composer-songwriter, father of Vladimir Feltsman.
Feltsman Vladimir—Russian and American pianist, our friend from Moscow times.
Fet Afanasiy—Russian lyric poet and translator, memoirist.
Ford Gerald Rudolph—38th President of the United States.
Frances Gérard—French engineer, member of the Committee of 15.
Frank-Kamenetsky Thema—The then-wife of Roald Sagdeev.
Freidin Nadya—daughter of Elena Smorgunov and Yuri Freidin.
Freidin Yuri—psychiatrist and literary critic, co-chairman of the "Mandelstam Society", our close friend from Moscow times.
Freiman Grigoriy—Soviet and Israeli mathematician, number theory specialist.
Frolov Alexander—great-grandfather of Nikolos Daniloff, Decembrist.
Frolov Anna—Nikolas Daniloff's grandmother.
Frumkin Alexander—Soviet physicochemist, organizer of science, author of pioneering works in modern electrochemistry.
Gabay Galya—Soviet and American educator, wife of Ilya Gabay.
Gabay Ilya—prominent member of the human rights movement in the USSR, a teacher, poet, writer, screenwriter, my friend from Moscow times.
Gagliano Nicolo—Italian violin-maker; one of **Antonio Stradivari's** best pupils and followers.
Gaidai Leonid—Soviet and Russian film director, actor, scriptwriter.
Galanskov Yuri—Russian Soviet poet and dissident.
Galich Alexander—Russian poet, screenwriter, playwright, prose writer, author and performer of his own songs.
Garibaldi Nadya—My granddaughter, the Vera's daughter.

Garibaldi Natalie — My granddaughter, the oldest Vera's daughter.
Garibaldi Nicola — My granddaughter, the youngest Vera's daughter.
Garibaldi Vera — My youngest daughter's married name.
Gekht Boris — Soviet doctor.
Gerasimov Gennady — Soviet diplomat and international journalist.
Gershman Boris — father-in-law in second mariage, Tanya Ziman's father.
Giliarovsky Vladimir — Russian writer and newspaper journalist.
Gillette Elizabeth — Wife of Robert Gillette.
Gillette Robert — American journalist.
Ginzburg Alexander — journalist and publisher, active participant in the human rights movement in the USSR, member of the Moscow Helsinki Group, compiler of one of the first collections of samizdat ("Syntax"), member of the editorial board of the journal.
Giorgione (Giorgio Barbarelli da Castelfranco) — Italian painter of the Venetian school during the High Renaissance.
Gippius Zinaida — Russian poet and writer, playwright and literary critic, one of the prominent representatives of the Silver Age.
Gladkov Galina — classmate of Leonid Ziman and Ilya Gabai.
Gladky Alexey — Soviet mathematician, specialist in formal languages and grammars.
Gladky Jakob — son of Aleksey Gladky and Renata Ravich.
Glovinskaya Marina — linguist, our friend from Moscow times, wife of Yuri Apresyan.
Goethe Johann Wolfgang — German writer, thinker, philosopher and naturalist, statesman.
Gogol Nikolai — great Russian writer.
Goliath — Old Testament character, an enormous Philistine warrior, a descendant of the giants, who was fought by the future King David.
Golomshtok Igor — Soviet and British art historian.
Gonchar Andrey — Soviet and Russian mathematician, specialist in theory of functions and approximation theory.
Goncharov Ivan — famous Russian writer and literary critic.
Goncharov Natalia — poet A. Pushkin's wife.

Gorbachev Mikhail—Soviet and Russian statesman, party and public figure.
Gorbanevskaya Natalia—active member of the human rights movement in the USSR, Russian poetess and translator.
Gorky Maxim—one of the world's most famous Russian-Soviet writers and literary figures.
Goulet Denis—employee of the Canadian Embassy in Moscow.
Goya Francisco—Spanish painter and engraver, one of the first and brightest masters of fine arts of the Romantic era.
Gregory IX—Pope of the 13th century, founder of the Inquisition and advocate of the Crusades in Russia.
Grieg Edvard—Norwegian composer, pianist, conductor, public figure.
Grigoryants Sergey—Soviet dissident, former political prisoner, journalist and literary critic, founder and head of the "Glasnost" Human Rights Foundation.
Gromyko Andrei—Soviet diplomat and statesman.
Guarneri Giuseppe—great Italian master of stringed instruments.
Guchkov Alexander—Russian politician and statesman, Military and Provisional Minister of the Provisional Government, great-uncle of Vera Prokhorov.
Guchkov Nadezhda—mother of Vera Prokhorov.
Guchkov Nikolai—Moscow mayor, grandfather of Vera Prokhorov.
Gumilev Nikolai—Russian poet of the Silver Age, the founder of the Acmeism school, prose writer, translator and literary critic.
Gurchenko Lyudmila—Soviet and Russian film actress, pop singer, director, screenwriter and writer.
Gurevich Ella—daughter of our friend Lubov Loewiecky.
Gurevich Grigory—Professor of Geometry, Moscow Pedagogical State University.
Gurevich Semyon—professor of journalism at Moscow State University, son-in-law of Lubov Loevetskaya.
Gurevich Vladimir—Russian journalist, grandson of Lyubov Loevetskaya.
Guroff Gregory—cultural attaché at the US Embassy in Moscow.
Gutman Natalia—outstanding Soviet and Russian cellist and teacher.

APPENDIX 2: WHO IS WHO

Haass Friedrich Josep—"Holy doctor of Moscow" who spent 25 years until the end of his life to humanize the penal system in Russia.
Hammer Armand—American entrepreneur and art collector.
Hammer Julius—American physician, father of entrepreneur Armand Hammer.
Handelman Steve—Canadian journalist and writer.
Hartman Arthur—US Ambassador to Moscow.
Hartman Donna—Arthur Hartman's wife.
Harutyunyan Yuri—Armenian composer.
Hayk—legendary ancestor of the Armenian people, as well as the founder of the legendary Haykazuni dynasty.
Hegel Georg Wilhelm Friedrich—German philosopher and one of the most influential figures of German idealism.
Heifetz Jasha—American musician, one of the world's greatest violinists.
Henry IV of Bourbon—King of France founder of the French royal dynasty of Bourbons.
Herzen Alexander—Russian publicist-revolutionary, writer, pedagogue, philosopher.
Heyerdahl Thor—Norwegian archaeologist, traveller and writer.
Hilbert David—the great German mathematician, one of the most influential mathematicians of the 19th and early 20th centuries.
Hippocrates—ancient Greek healer, physician and philosopher who went down in history as the "father of medicine."
Hirsch Evan—pianist and piano teacher who has become a close friend of ours in the USA.
Hitler Adolf—German politician and orator, founder and central figure of Nazism, Reich Chancellor of Germany, Supreme Commander of the German Armed Forces in World War II.
Ho Chi Minh—Vietnamese communist revolutionary, state, political, military and party figure, first President of the Democratic Republic of Vietnam.
Holofernes—according to the biblical Book of Judith, an Assyrian general who led an invading army in Judah.
Homer—ancient Greek poet and storyteller, creator of the epic poems *The Iliad* and *The Odyssey*.
Honegger Artur—Swiss-French composer and music critic.

Horace—the name commonly known in English for Quintus Horatius Flaccus—the leading Roman lyric poet during the time of Augustus.
Ilf Ilya—Russian and Soviet writer, playwright and screenwriter, photographer, journalist.
Ilia II—Catholicos-Patriarch of All Georgia.
Iordanskaya Lydia—Soviet, Canadian linguist, our friend from Moscow times.
Iron Abram—the teacher of blacksmithing class in my school.
Isakovsky Mikhail—Russian Soviet poet, songwriter, prose writer, translator.
Ivan the Terrible—the first tsar of all Russia.
Ivanov Irina—classmate of Alexander Brussilovsky at the Conservatory.
Janus Elzbieta—Polish linguist, a very close friend of ours.
Jefferson Thomas—the third president of the USA.
Jeitler Manfred—Swiss nuclear physicist, our friend from Moscow times.
Jeremiah the prophet—the second of the four great prophets of the Old Testament, author of both the book of the prophet Jeremiah and the book of Lamentations of Jeremiah.
Jodl Alfred—military leader of Hitler's Germany, Chief of Staff of the Operational Headquarters of the Supreme Command of the Wehrmacht, Colonel General.
Joliot-Curie Frederic—French physicist and husband of Irène Joliot-Curie,.
Joliot-Curie Irene—French physicist, daughter of Marie and Pierre Curie.
Judith—Jewish widow, a character in the Old Testament book of Judith.
Juvenal Decimus Junius—Roman satirist poet.
Juvenaly Metropolitan (Poyarkov)—hierarch of the Russian Orthodox Church.
Kadzasov Sandro—Soviet and German linguist working at Moscow State University, our friend from Moscow times.
Kagan Elena—sister of my grandmother, Berta, the first wife of Veniamin Kagan.
Kagan Judith—Latinist at Moscow Foreign Language University, our close friend.

Kagan Lydia—my aunt, the youngest daughter of Veniamin Fedorovich Kagan.
Kagan Maria—the second wife of Veniamin Kagan.
Kagan Matvey—Russian Jewish philosopher, father of Judith Kagan.
Kagan Nadezhda—my great aunt, V. F. Kagan's eldest daughter.
Kagan Oleg—Soviet violinist, husband of Natalia Gutman, our friend from Moscow times.
Kagan Sophia—mother of Judith Kagan.
Kagan Veniamin—husband of his father's aunt Elena Yefimovna Kagan.
Kalistratov Sofya—Soviet lawyer, member of the Moscow Helsinki Group, known for her human rights documents and speeches at political trials of Soviet dissidents, friend of Tatyana Velikanov.
Kapitsa Pyotr—Soviet physicist, scientist, engineer and innovator.
Karatsuba Anatoly—Soviet and Russian mathematician, creator of the first in the history of mathematics fast method of multiplication of large numbers.
Karetnikov Nikolai—Soviet composer, representative of the domestic postwar avant-garde.
Karhilo Lisa—pianist, wife of the Finnish Ambassador in Moscow.
Karig Sharah—Hungarian literary translator, friend of Tanya Ziman.
Kartlos—legendary ancestor of the Georgian people, the founder of Kartli, from the family of Fogarma.
Kasatkin Leonid—Soviet and Russian linguist, our good friend.
Kazavchinskaya Tamara—philologist, wife of Sandro Kadzasov, our friend from Moscow times.
Keitel Wilhelm—German military leader, Chief of Staff of the Supreme Command of the Wehrmacht, Field Marshal General.
Kennedy John—35th President of the United States.
Kerensky Alexander—Russian politician and statesman; minister, then minister-chairman of the Provisional Government.
Kharitonov Mark—Russian writer, essayist, poet and translator, friend of Leonid Ziman.
Kharms Daniel—early Soviet-era Russian avant-gardist and absurdist poet, writer and dramatist.
Khatutsky Anna—my eldest granddaughter, the daughter of Galina and Victor Khatutsky.

Khatutsky Galya—My elder dauhter.
Khatutsky Geda—mother of our elder son-in-law Victor Khatutsky.
Khatutsky Victor—our eldest son-in-law, Galina Khatutsky's husband.
Khlebnikov Velimir—Russian poet and prose writer, one of the greatest figures of the Russian avant-garde.
Khodorovich Tanya—linguist and dialectologist, participant of the human rights movement in the USSR, member of the Initiative Group.
Khomanko Vitaly—our acquaintance whom we met only in the USA.
Khrushchev Nikita—the first secretary of the Communist Party of the Soviet Union, and Chairman of the Council of Ministers.
Kibrik Alexander—Soviet and Russian linguist, our good friend.
Kikot Miroslava—friend of my wife Tanya Ziman.
Kim Yuliy—Soviet, Russian and Israeli poet, playwright, bard, participant of dissident movement in the USSR, friend of Leonid Ziman.
Kingdon Clifford William—English mathematician and philosopher.
Kislik Vladimir—famous acquaintance, refused veteran (1973–1989), who served three years in GULAG on trumped up charges.
Kissinger Henry—American statesman, diplomat, National Security Advisor and Secretary of State.
Klimenko Alexey—Soviet Architectural Monument Preservationist, husband of Olga Klimenko.
Klimenko Olga—my niece, my brother Jan's daughter.
Klose Eliza—Kevin Close' wife at the time.
Klose Kevin—American journalist, contributor to the Washington Post, and director of National Public Radio.
Klyuchevsky Vasily—Russian historian, professor at Moscow University; Chairman of the Imperial Society of Russian History and Antiquities at Moscow University.
Kochetkov Alexander—Russian poet and translator.
Kochin Ira—wife of Grigory Barenblatt, daughter of Nikolay and Pelageya Kochina.
Kochin Nikolai—Soviet mathematician and physicist. One of the founders of modern dynamic meteorology.

Kochin Pelageya—Soviet hydrodynamic scientist, wife of Nikolai Kochin.
Kogan Bluma—my brother Jan's mother-in-law, Inna Ziman's mother.
Kogan Gennady—brother of Jan's brother Inna Ziman's first wife.
Kogan Inna—maiden name of Inna Ziman.
Kogan Pavel—Russian Soviet poet of Romanticism.
Kolmogorov Andrey—Russian and Soviet mathematician, one of the greatest mathematicians of the XX century and one of the founders of modern probability theory,.
Kopelev Lev—Soviet and Russian literary critic (Germanist), dissident and human rights activist.
Korczak Janusz—Polish paediatrician and educator, head of a home for orphans in the Warsaw ghetto, who died together with his children in the Nazi gas chambers.
Kornilov Vladimir—Russian Soviet writer, poet, essayist and public figure.
Korolev Lev—mathematical engineer, my boss and friend at my Research Institute.
Korolev Galina—wife of Lev Korolev.
Kosharovsky Yuli—Soviet Jewish refusenik.
Koshkin Ekaterina—Soviet and Russian doctor, a friend of my niece Olga Klimenko and her family.
Kossoff David—English actor, writer and social activist.
Kosygin Alexey—Prime minister of the USSR.
Kovalev Sergey—Soviet dissident, participant of the human rights movement in the USSR and post-Soviet Russia, Russian politician and public figure.
Kozlovsky Ivan—Soviet and Russian opera and chamber singer (tenor), director of opera.
Krasin Viktor—Soviet economist and human rights activist, dissident.
Krylov Ivan—Russian publicist, fable writer, poet, publisher of satirical-educational magazines.
Kulikov Galina—Soviet journalist, a friend of my brother Jan since his school years.
Kuprin Aleksandr—Russian writer.
Kuznetsov Sergey—General of the Gulag of the KGB of the USSR.

Labkovsky Naum—Soviet poet, author of lyrics to the song "Field Post".

Lander Alexander—son of Elena and Victor Lander, my friends from my work at IPM&CT.

Lander Elena—engineer and veteran veteran of my Research Institute, my colleague and close friend.

Lander Victor—husband of Elena Lander.

Landsberg Grigory—Soviet physicist, professor at Moscow State University.

Lavut Alexander—Soviet mathematician, human rights activist and dissident.

Lebedev Alice—Sergei Lebedev's wife.

Lebedev Sergey—one of the pioneers of computer science and technology in the USSR, the director of ITM&CT, where I worked for about 20 years.

Lebedev-Kumach Vasily—Russian Soviet poet and lyricist of many popular Soviet songs.

Leconte Victoria—student of Tanya's now living in Paris, a very close friend of ours.

Leibler Isi—leader of the Jewish movement in the Commonwealth of Australia.

Lelewel Joachim—Polish historian of the 18th and 19th centuries.

Lemeshev Sergei—Soviet opera singer, lyric tenor, opera director and teacher.

Lenin Vladimir—Russian Marxist revolutionary, creator of the first socialist state in world history—the USSR.

Lensky Georgy—Soviet and Russian artist, poet, bard and teacher.

Leontiev Nina—Soviet and Russian linguist and my friend from my Moscow days, in her house I met Tanya Markish.

Leontiev Anatoly—brother of Nina Leontieva.

Lepsky Georgy—Soviet and Russian artist, poet, bard and teacher.

Lermontov Michael—Great Russian Romantic writer, poet and painter.

Leroux Gaston—French writer, journalist, recognized master of detective.

Levantovsky Irina—Deputy Chief Physician of Maternity Hospital No. 25, Oktyabrsky district, Moscow.

Levin Aryeh—Israeli diplomat, first Israeli Ambassador to the USSR after the restoration of diplomatic relations in 1991.

Levin Mikhail—Soviet theorist in radio physics.
Levin Yehuda Leib—Rabbi of Moscow Choral Synagogue and head of yeshiva.
Levintov Ernestina—my aunt, a Spanish philologist, adopted daughter of Veniamin Kagan.
Levintov Ida—piano teacher, wife of Joseph Levintov Jr.
Levintov Joseph Jr.—Soviet physicist, adopted son of Kagan Veniamin.
Levintov Joseph Sr.—employee of the publishing house "Mathesis" in Odessa, first husband of Maria Kagan.
Levitan Isaac—famous Russian artist.
Levitin Yuri—Soviet composer, author of the song "Field Post".
Levkovich Elizabeth—Soviet microbiologist, collaborator of Nadezhda Kagan and second wife of Grigory Sinai.
Lifton Whitie Jean—author of the biographical book about J. Korczak, The King of Children.
Lisitsa Valentina—American pianist of Ukrainian origin.
Litvinenko Alexander—operative, lieutenant colonel of Soviet and Russian state security, who fled to England and was killed by KGB there.
Litvinov Pavel—Soviet and American physicist, educator; member of the USSR human rights movement.
Livshits Benedict—Russian poet, translator and researcher of Futurism.
Lloyd-Webber Andrew—English composer, author of many musicals.
Lobachevsky Nikolai—Russian mathematician, one of the founders of non-Euclidean geometry, the leader of university education and public education,.
Lokshin Alexander—Soviet composer.
Long Marguerite—French pianist and teacher.
Lopshits Abram—Soviet mathematician, student of S. O. Shatunovsky and V. F. Kagan.
Loren Sophia—Italian film star, actress and singer.
Louis the Holy—king of France in the 13th century, led the 7th and 8th Crusades, canonized shortly after his death.
Loyevetsky Lubov—old friend of my parents and older generation Kagans.

Lukin Vladimir—Russian politician and historian, political scientist, friend of Leonid Ziman.
Lumumba Patrice—Congolese left-wing nationalist politician and the first Prime Minister of the Democratic Republic of the Congo.
Luther Martin—a Christian theologian, initiator of the Reformation, a leading translator of the Bible into German, one of the founders of the German literary language.
Lysenko Trofim—Soviet biologist, founder and largest representative of the pseudoscientific trend in biology.
Mach Ernst—Austrian physicist, mechanic and positivist philosopher.
Magomayev Muslim—Soviet, Azerbaijani and Russian pop and opera singer (baritone), actor and composer.
Malykhin Alexander—locksmith at Maternity Hospital No. 25 in Moscow, my colleague.
Mandelstam Leonid—Russian and Soviet physicist, one of the founders of the national scientific school of radio physics.
Mandelstam Lydia—wife of Leonid Mandelstam.
Mandelstam Nadezhda—wife of poet Osip Mandelstam.
Mandelstam Osip—Russian poet, prose writer and translator, essayist, critic, literary critic, one of the greatest Russian poets of the XX century.
Mandelstam Tanya—granddaughter of Lydia and Leonid Mandelstam.
Mann Thomas—prominent German writer, essayist, master of the epic novel.
Margolis Anna, daughter of Natalia and Leonid Margolis.
Margolis Katia—daughter of Natalia and Leonid Margolis.
Margolis Leonid—Soviet biologist, our friend from Moscow times.
Margolis Mikhail—son of Natalia and Leonid Margolis.
Margolis Natalia—wife of Leonid Margolis.
Marjasin Alexander—our friend, one of the heads of the State Electrotechnical Factory VEF, Riga.
Markish Peretz—Soviet Jewish poet and writer who composed in Yiddish.
Markish Tanya—my wife Tanya Ziman's name in her first marriage.
Markish Yuri—nephew of the poet Peretz Markish, adopted by him, first husband of Tanya Ziman.

APPENDIX 2: WHO IS WHO

Markiz Lev—Soviet and Dutch musician: violinist and conductor, our close friend from Moscow times.

Markov Andrei, Sr.—Russian mathematician, academician, who made a great contribution to probability theory, mathematical analysis and number theory.

Marshak Anna—Soviet microbiologist, wife of V.Yu.

Marshak Samuel—Russian and Soviet poet, playwright and translator, literary critic, screenwriter.

Martin the Graceful—bishop of Tours, one of the most revered saints in France.

Marx Karl—German philosopher, sociologist, economist, founder of scientific communism.

Matlock Jack—American diplomat, US Ambassador in Moscow.

Matthew the Apostle—one of the twelve apostles, the closest disciples of Jesus Christ, a character of the New Testament, is considered the author of the first canonical Gospel—the Gospel of Matthew.

Mavrina Tatiana—Soviet artist and children's book illustrator.

Mayakovsky Vladimir—Russian, Soviet poet, futurist, as well as playwright, screenwriter, film director.

Mayantz Lazar—chemistry professor, a good friend of ours.

McCagg Bill—American professor of history, a close friend of ours.

McCagg Louise—American artist and sculptor, a close friend of ours.

Medici—dynasty of rulers of Florence, from the 13th to the 18th century, patrons of outstanding artists and architects of the Renaissance.

Mei Lev—Russian writer: poet, prose writer, playwright, translator.

Melchuk Igor—famous Soviet and Canadian linguist, an old friend of ours from Moscow days.

Melchuk Svetlana—daughter of Igor Melchuk.

Melnikov Vladimir—Soviet computer design engineer, my supervisor at IPM&CT.

Men Alexander—one of the most interesting people among Russian Orthodox priests in Moscow.

Menzheritsky Emil—Soviet electrochemist, husband of Tzilia Reitburg.

Menzheritsky Galina—daughter of Tzilia Reitburd and Emil M.

Mercader Ramon—Spanish communist and Soviet state security agent, famous for assassination of Lev Trotsky.

Michelson Faina—my aunt, my mother's sister.
Michelson Mikhail—my uncle, the husband of my mother's sister, Faina Michelson.
Mikhalkov Sergei—Soviet and Russian poet, playwright and publicist, war correspondent, screenwriter, fable writer, public figure.
Mikhoels Solomon—Soviet actor and the artistic director of the Moscow State Jewish Theater.
Mikoyan Anastas—Russian revolutionary, Soviet state and party figure, one of the most influential Soviet politicians.
Milkis Julian—renowned Soviet and American clarinetist, both in the field of classical music and jazz. A student of the legendary Benny Goodman.
Milne Alan Alexander—English writer, the author of the stories about Winnie-the-Pooh Bear with sawdust in his head and many poems for children.
Mints Isaac—Soviet historian, specialist in the history of the USSR.
Mohammed—Arab religious and political figure, founder of the Muslim religion and preacher of monotheism, the central figure of Islam.
Molotov Vyacheslav—Russian revolutionary and Soviet political, state and party figure. One of the top leaders of the VKP(b) and the CPSU.
More Thomas—English lawer, philosopher, humanist writer.
Morits Yunna—Soviet and Russian poetess and translator, screenwriter.
Morpheus—god of good dreams in Greek mythology.
Moses—the most important Old Testament prophet and lawgiver, the founder of Judaism, who organized the exodus of the Jews from Egyptian slavery.
Mozart Wolfgang Amadeus—great Austrian composer and virtuoso musician, one of the most popular classical composers.
Muge Sergey—biologist, husband of Ksenia Velikanov.
Nabokov Vladimir—Russian and American writer, poet, translator, literary critic and entomologist.
Nagibin Yuri—Russian novelist, journalist, screenwriter, memoirist.
Navalny Alexei—Russian opposition leader, lawyer, politician and public figure who has gained notoriety for his investigations of corruption in Russia.

APPENDIX 2: WHO IS WHO

Neighbor Ksenia—our staircase neighbor in the last apartment in Moscow.

Nekrasov Nikolai—Russian poet, prose writer and publicist, classic of Russian literature.

Nestor the Chronicler—Old Russian chronicler, monk of the Kiev-Pechersk monastery.

Neuhaus Heinrich—Soviet pianist and teacher.

Neverly Igor—J. Korczak's secretary at the Orphanage in the Warsaw Jewish Ghetto.

Newton Isaac—the great English physicist, mathematician, mechanic and astronomer, one of the founders of classical physics.

Nice Liolya—neighbor and friend of Lander family.

Nice Tim—Son of Liolya Nice.

Nikiforov Vladimir—chaplain of the University of London, professor of sociology of religions, our acquaintance from Moscow times.

Nobel Alfred—Swedish inventor, entrepreneur, scientist, businessman, also poet and playwright, who left much of his wealth to the establishment of the prize for achievements that confer the greatest benefit on mankind in physics, chemistry, peace, physiology or medicine, and literatur.

Nordal Odvar Vera Nordal's husband, our friend.

Nordal Vera—American teacher, director of a secondary school for English-speaking foreigners working in Moscow, our friend.

Obolensky Igor—Russian journalist and TV presenter, writer.

Ogarev Nikolai—Russian poet, publicist, revolutionary, closest friend of A. I. Herzen.

Oguz Lydia—the grandmother of our eldest son-in-law Victor.

Okhotnikov Elena—Soviet singer, wife of Alexander Brussilovsky.

Okudzhava Bulat—Soviet and Russian poet, bard, writer and screenwriter, composer, one of the most prominent representatives of the art song genre.

Olesha Yuri—Russian Soviet writer, poet and playwright, journalist, screenwriter.

Orlov Yuri—Soviet physicist and human rights activist, a member of the dissident movement, the founder and first head of the Moscow Helsinki Group, and a professor at Cornell University.

Oshanin Lev—Soviet songwriter.
Ostroukhov Ilya—Russian landscape painter and art collector, associated with the artist group "Peredvizhniki." One of the heads of the Tretyakov Gallery, great-uncle of Vera Prokhorov.
Ostrovsky Alexander—Russian playwright whose work was an important stage in the development of the Russian national theatre.
Ostrovsky Arkady—Soviet composer-songwriter.
Ostrovsky Nikolai—Soviet writer, revered by the Bolsheviks as a national hero.
Otman Nelli—Head of the geological party of my Kuril Expedition.
Paganini Nicolo—great Italian violinist, violist, guitarist and composer.
Pakhmutov Alexandra—Soviet and Russian composer.
Pankov Victor—programmer from IPM&CT, who worked with me.
Pasternak Boris—One of the greatest Russian poets of the 20th century.
Pergolesi Giovanni Batista—Talian composer, violinist and organist, representative of the Neapolitan school of opera, one of the earliest and most important composers of comic opera.
Peter the Great—the Last Tsar of All Russia and the First Emperor of All Russia.
Petrov Andrei—Soviet composer.
Petrov Yevgeny—Russian Soviet writer, scriptwriter and playwright, journalist, war correspondent.
Petrovsky Ivan—Soviet mathematician and educator, rector of the Moscow University.
Picander—the pseudonym of Christian Friedrich Henrizi, German poet and librettist, friend and colleague of Johann Sebastian Bach.
Pimen, Patriarch—14-th Patriarch of Moscow.
Pinkas Sally—pianist and music educator who has become a close friend of ours in the USA.
Pirveli Boris—our friend in Abkhazia.
Pitel Boris—Friend of Galya and Vitya Khatutsky.
Plakida Nikolay—physicist, nuclear researcher, constant organizer of our Khibin hikes.
Platonov Vladimir—Soviet, Belarusian and Russian mathematician.
Platonov Vyacheslav—Specialist in African culture, human rights defender, who "worked" in the Gulag.

Plekhanov Georgy—Russian theorist and propagandist of Marxism, a philosopher, and a prominent figure in the international socialist movement.
Pliny the Elder—Ancient Roman writer, erudite microbiologist.
Plisetsky German—Russian poet, translator.
Pluzhnikov Vladimir—my classmate and friend in high school in Moscow.
Pocock Emily—Meg and Ted Pocock's daughter.
Pocock Meg—wife of the Australian Union Ambassador in Moscow Ted Pocock.
Pocock Ted—Ambassador of the Commonwealth of Australia in Moscow.
Pocock Tig—son of Meg and Ted Pocock.
Podgorny Nikolai—Soviet state and party figure, Chairman of the Presidium of the USSR Supreme Soviet.
Pontryagin Lev—the Soviet mathematician, one of the greatest mathematicians of the XX century, infamous for his militant anti-Semitism.
Pope Alexander—eighteenth-century English poet, one of the greatest authors of British classicism.
Posse Konstantin—Professor of Mathematics, St. Petersburg University.
Powell Colin—politician and U.S.A. Army General, U.S.A. Secretary of State, and U.S.A. National Security Advisor.
Prestin Vladimir—veteran of the Jewish refusal movement and our close friend.
Prestin-Shapiro Leah—daughter of Felix Shapiro and mother of Vladimir Prestin.
Prigov Dmitry—Russian poet, artist, sculptor. One of the founders of Moscow conceptualism in art and literary genre.
Prokhorov Ivan—father of Vera Prokhorov, the last owner of Prokhorov's manufactory.
Prokhorov Nikolai—Prokhorov's grandfather Vera, owner of Prokhorov manufactory.
Prokhorov Varvara—Vera Prokhorov's great-grandmother.
Prokhorov Vera—Tanya's English stylistics teacher in the University of Foreign Languages, later our mentor and very close friend.
Prokofiev Sergey—Russian and Soviet composer, pianist, conductor.

Ptolemy Claudius—astronomer, astrologer, mathematician, mechanic, optician, music theorist, and geographer of ancient Greece early in our era\.

Pushkin Alexander—the great Russian poet.

Putin Vladimir—Russian statesman and politician, the current President of the Russian Federation and Commander-in-Chief of the Armed Forces.

Putzel Michael—American journalist and writer for the Associated Press, our good friend.

Rabin Yitzhak—Israeli politician and military figure, sixth and eleventh Prime Minister of Israel.

Rabinovich Vladimir—friend of our elder son-in-law Victor Hatutsky and the whole family.

Rashevsky Pyotr—Soviet mathematician, geometer.

Rastropovich Mstislav—outstanding Russian cellist and conductor.

Ravich David—my father-in-law in my first marriage, Renata's father.

Ravich Leah—my mother-in-law in my first marriage, Renata's mother.

Ravich Renata—my first wife, my Galecka's mother.

Ravich Yakov—brother of Renata Ravich, killed in WWII.

Ravikovich Mikhail—Head of Neurosurgery at S. P. Botkin Hospital in Moscow.

Reagan Nancy—First Lady of the United States, wife of Ronald Reagan.

Reagan Ronald—is the 40th President of the United States.

Reformatsky Alexander—Soviet linguist, specialist in phonology, transcription, graphics and orthography, morphology, semiotics, terminology, history of linguistics.

Reich Arkady—the husband of my sister Reich Elena.

Reich Elena—my sister.

Reich Michael is my nephew, son of Reich Elena and Reich Arkady.

Reitburd Moses—Tzilia Reitburd's father.

Reitburd Serafima—sister of Tzili Reitburd.

Reitburd Tzilia—Soviet lunar geology researcher, activist of the Jewish refusenik movement, our very close friend.

Renoir Auguste—French painter, graphic artist and sculptor, one of the main representatives of impressionism.

APPENDIX 2: WHO IS WHO

Repin Ilya—Russian painter, teacher, professor, full member of the Imperial Academy of Arts.
Ribentrop von Joachim—Hitler's Foreign Minister during WWII.
Richter Svyatoslav—prominent Soviet and Russian pianist.
Rochette Alain—French electronic engineer, a member of the Committee of 15, a close friend of ours.
Rochette Anne—Alain Rochette's wife.
Romulus—one of two brothers, the legendary founders of Rome.
Ronkin Valery—Soviet engineer technologist, active dissident and human rights activist.
Roosevelt Franklin D.—32nd president of the United States.
Rosenstrom Alexander—husband of my niece Maria Weissman, poet, novelist, screenwriter, director, producer, editor, publisher.
Rosenzweig Victor—Head of the Laboratory of Machine Translation at the Institute of Foreign Languages.
Rousseau Jean-Jacques—French-Swiss philosopher, writer and thinker, musicologist, composer and botanist of the Enlightenment.
Rozovsky Joseph—Soviet obstetrician, our good friend.
Rubinstein Nikolai—Russian composer, pianist, conductor and music educator.
Rudy Mikhail—Soviet pianist who did not return to Russia from a tour in France.
Rudenko Roman—General Prosecutor of the USSR.
Saffer Stuart—very close friend of ours currently living in Israel.
Sagdeev Roald—Soviet and American physicist, former director of Space Research Institute of USSR Academy of Sciences, where my brother Ziman Jan worked.
Sakharov Andrei—Soviet theoretical physicist, one of the creators of the first Soviet hydrogen bomb, public figure, dissident and human rights activist.
Samarov Alexander—American statistician, Tzilia Reitburd's son-in-law.
Samarov Boris—second son of Nora and Alexander Samarov.
Samarov Dmitriy—eldest son of Nora and Alexander Samarov.
Samarov Max—youngest son of Nora and Alexander Samarov.
Samarov Nora—daughter of Tzilia Reitburd and Emil Menzheritsky.
Sapgir Genrich—Russian poet and fiction writer of Jewish descent.

Scarlatti Alessandro—Italian Baroque composer who wrote more than 60 operas, is considered the founder of the Neapolitan opera school.
Shlifshtein Bella—My Aunt, My Mother's Sister.
Schnittke Alfred—Soviet and German composer, teacher and musicologist.
Shultz George—U.S.A. Secretary of State.
Schweitzer Albert—German and French Protestant theologian, cultural philosopher, humanist, musician and physician,.
Sechenov Ivan—Russian scientist-naturalist, physiologist, teacher and educator.
Selvinsky Ilya—Soviet poet, dramatist, memoirist, and essayist.
Semyonov Alexander—my colleague at my Research Institute in Moscow.
Seraphim, Metropolitan—Bishop of the Russian Orthodox Church, Metropolitan of Krutitsy and Kolomna.
Serebryakov Lada close friend of Tanya Ziman's.
Sergei Aleksandrovich, Grand Duke—fifth son of Alexander II; Governor General of Moscow.
Serov Alexander—Russian composer and music critic.
Serov Valentin—Russian painter and graphic artist, master of portrait, member of the Imperial Academy of Arts.
Sevez Francois—French general who signed (as an official witness) the Act of Unconditional Surrender of Germany.
Shakespeare William—the national English poet, writer and playwright, often considered the world's greatest.
Shaliapin ee bass voice.
Shamir Yitzhak—Israeli politician, eighth and tenth Prime Minister of Israel, was Chairman of the Knesset.
Shapiro Genrikh—Russian Empire and Soviet mathematician, algebraist.
Shapiro Henry—American journalist who worked in Moscow for many years.
Shapiro Felix—Russian and Soviet philologist-lexicographer and teacher, author of the first Hebrew-Russian dictionary in the USSR, grandfather of our friend Vladimir Prestin.
Shapiro Pavel—friend of my father-in-law in first marriage, David Ravich.

Shapiro Solomon is an employee of the Telegraph Agency of the Soviet Union (TASS) in Moscow.

Sharansky Natan—Soviet dissident and later Israeli politician, human rights activist.

Shchepkina-Kupernik Tatiana—Russian and Soviet writer, playwright, poetess and translator.

Sheremetev Nikolai—Russian count, founder of a family, who built a hospital in Moscow, which became the basis for the Institute of Emergency Care. Sklifassovsky Institute.

Shatunovsky Samuil—Russian Empire and Soviet mathematician, algebraist.

Shestopal M. G.—Soviet mathematician, teacher and translator.

Shevardnadze Eduard—Soviet and Georgian politician and diplomat.

Sheveleva Raya—my aunt, my father's sister.

Shifter Richard—Assistant Secretary of State for Human Rights.

Shikhanovich Yuri—Soviet and Russian mathematician and pedagogue, human rights activist.

Shirshov Anatoly—Soviet mathematician.

Shlifshtein Elena—music pedagogue, wife of my mother's brother Semyon Shlifshtein.

Shlifshtein Natalia—daughter of Elena and Semyon Shlifshtein.

Shlifshtein Semyon—My uncle, my mother's brother, musicologist.

Shostakovich Dmitri—Russian and Soviet composer, pianist, teacher, musical and social activist, one of the greatest composers of the twentieth century.

Shostakovich Irina—wife of Dmitry Shostakovich.

Shpet Marina—Leonid Margolis' mother-in-law.

Shulman Jerry—American lawyer, a friend of our family.

Shulzhenko Klavdia—Soviet, Russian and Ukrainian pop singer, actress.

Shura-Bura Mikhail—Soviet and Russian scientist who made a significant contribution to the formation and development of programming.

Simanowicz Pavel—friend of my daughter Galina Khatutsky.

Sinai Alexander—son of Elena Vul and Yakov Sinai.

Sinai Grigory—Soviet doctor, microbiologist, second husband of Nadezhda Kagan.

Sinai Yakov—famous Soviet and American mathematician and educator, son of Nadezhda Kagan and Grigory Sinai.
Sinyavsky Andrey—Russian writer, literary critic arrested in the Soviet Union for publishing his works in the West.
Sklifasovsky Nikolai—famous Russian surgeon and pedagogue, director of the Imperial Clinical Institute in St. Petersburg.
Sklifasovsky Sophia—wife of Nikolai Sklifasovsky.
Sklifasovsky Tamara—daughter of Nikolai Sklifasovsky.
Smirnov Slava—piano teacher, teacher of Vera Ziman in Moscow.
Smith Adam—Scottish economist and ethical philosopher of the 18th century, one of the founders of economic theory as a science.
Smith Bedell—American military leader and statesman who signed the Act of Unconditional Surrender of Germany.
Smith Fenwick—an American flutist and educator we became friends with in the USA.
Smorgunov Elena—specialist in the history of the Russian language, our close friend.
Smorgunov Praskovya—mother of Elena Smorgunov.
Smulevich Anatoly—Russian psychiatrist, psychopharmacologist, friend of Tanya Ziman.
Sobakin Tim—Soviet and Russian children's writer, poet, journalist and editor.
Sokolov Evgeniy—student of Judith Kagan in the University.
Soldatenkov Kozma—Moscow businessman, councilor of commerce, textile manufacturer and major book publisher, owner of an art gallery.
Solzhenitsyn Natalia—before her marriage—Svetlov Natalia, the name by which I knew her.
Solzhenitsyn Alexander—Russian writer, playwright, essayist-publicist, poet, public and political figure.
Sonya Golden Hand—famous Odessa Jewish (Russia) adventuress of the 19-th century.
Spartacus—leader of the revolt of slaves and gladiators in ancient Rome in 73–71 BC.
Squire John—20th-century English poet.
Stalin Joseph—the leader of the Soviet state after Lenin.
Stanislavsky Konstantin—Russian theater director, actor and teacher, theorist, theater director, theater reformer, creator of the famous Acting System,.

APPENDIX 2: WHO IS WHO

Stepanov Andrey—Soviet programmer, my colleague from my Research Institute, co-author of the first English-Russian dictionaries on computers.
Stern Isaac—American musician, one of the world's greatest violinists.
Stolte Adele—German soprano singer and vocal teacher, famous performer of Bach and his contemporaries.
Strabo—the famous historian and geographer of ancient Greece and ancient Rome.
Stradivari Antonio—the great Italian stringed instrument maker.
Superfin Gabriel—philologist, member of the human rights movement in the USSR.
Susloparov Ivan—Soviet general who signed the Act of Germany's unconditional surrender for the Soviet Union.
Svan Zina—acquaintance of ours from Sukhumi.
Svetlov Mikhail—Russian/Soviet poet.
Svetlov Natalia—Russian public figure, widow and closest assistant of writer A. I. Solzhenitsyn, my friend from Moscow times, after her marriage to Solzhenitsyn she became Solzhenitsina.
Sychiov Maria—IPM&CT employee I was friends with.
Tagantsev Vladimir—Russian geographer, professor, shot on trumped up charges of conspiracy against Bolsheviks, later exonerated.
Taneyev Sergei—Russian composer, pianist, teacher, scholar, musicologist.
Tarasov Alla—Soviet Russian theater and cinema actress and teacher.
Tarasov Mikhail—Soviet state and party figure. My brother Jan's friend.
Telemann Georg Philipp—German composer, Kapellmeister, music critic and public figure.
Thatcher Margaret—Prime Minister of Great Britain, leader of the Conservative Party.
Theocritus—ancient Greek poet of the 3rd century BC.
Thibault Jacques—French violinist.
Tikhonov Andrey—Soviet mathematician and geophysicist. Founder of the Faculty of Computational Mathematics and Cybernetics of Moscow State University.

Timofeev Lev—Russian writer, journalist, scientist, economist and public figure, dissident.
Titian Vechellio—Italian painter, the greatest representative of the Venetian school of the High and Late Renaissance.
Tolstoy Alexei—Russian and Soviet writer and social activist, author of socio-psychological, historical and science fiction novels, novellas and stories, works of journalism.
Tolstoy Lev—great Russian writer.
Tomsky Nikolai—Soviet muralist sculptor, teacher, professor. President of the USSR Academy of Arts.
Trimble Jeff—American journalist who replaced Nicholas Daniloff in Moscow.
Trotsky Lev—Russian revolutionary, Soviet state and political figure, ideologist of Trotskyism.
Truman Harry—33rd President of the United States.
Tsalenko Maria—wife of Mikhail Tsalenko.
Tsalenko Mikhail—mathematician, active fighter against anti-Semitism.
Tsiolkovsky Konstantin—Russian and Soviet philosopher, inventor and school teacher, one of the founders of theoretical cosmonautics.
Tsurenko Tzilia—Head and Chief Physician of Maternity Hospital No. 25, Oktyabrsky district, Moscow.
Tsvetaev Anastasia—sister of M. I. Tsvetaeva.
Tsvetaev Ivan—Russian scholar-historian, archaeologist, philologist and art historian.
Tsvetaev Marina—famous Russian poetess of the Silver Age, prose writer, translator.
Tulikov Serafim—Soviet Russian composer and pianist.
Turgenev Ivan—great Russian writer.
Tvardovsky Alexander—Russian Soviet writer, poet, prose writer and journalist.
Tyurin Andrey—Soviet mathematician.
Tyurin Dmitry—son of Natalia Svetlov and Andrey Tyurin.
Tyutchev Fyodor—Russian lyricist, thought-poet, diplomat, publicist.
Ulanovsky Maya—participant of the dissident movement in the USSR, translator, writer.

APPENDIX 2: WHO IS WHO

Ulyanov Dmitry—revolutionary and party activist, younger brother of Alexander and Vladimir Ulyanov.

Ulyanov Pyotr—Soviet and Russian mathematician, Professor of Moscow State University.

Ulyanov Maria—Russian revolutionary, Soviet party and state leader, younger sister of Vladimir Lenin.

Ushakov Dmitry—Russian and Soviet linguist, one of the organizers of the Russian orthography reform.

Utyosov Leonid—Russian and Soviet variety artist, singer, reciter, conductor, orchestra leader, entertainer; actor.

Uvarov Irina—Soviet theatre historian, widow of Julius Daniel.

Van Gogh Vincent—French painter, one of the greatest representatives of post-impressionism.

Vasily III—Grand Prince of Vladimir and Moscow, Tsar of All Russia.

Vedernikov Alexander—Soviet Russian opera and chamber singer (bass) and teacher.

Veil Simone—French magistrate, Holocaust survivor, and politician.

Velikanov Ksenia—sister of Tatyana Velikanov.

Velikanov Tatiana—Soviet dissident, an active participant in the human rights movement in the USSR, and one of the founding members of the Soviet Union's first human rights organization, the Initiative Group for Human Rights Protection in the USSR.

Vernadsky Vladimir—Russian, Ukrainian and Soviet naturalist scientist, thinker and social activist. Academician of the Imperial St. Petersburg Academy of Sciences and Creator of scientific schools and the science of biogeochemistry, one of the representatives of Russian cosmism.

Veronese Paolo—prominent Venetian Renaissance painter.

Vinogradov Ivan—a prominent Soviet mathematician and number theory specialist, was notorious as a militant anti-Semite.

Virgil Publius Maronus—famous poet of ancient Rome.

Virsaladze Eliso—Soviet, Georgian and Russian pianist and music educator.

Vishnevsky Galina, Soviet opera singer (soprano), actress, theater director, pedagogue.

Vivaldi Antonio—Italian composer, violin virtuoso, teacher, conductor, Catholic priest.

Vizbor Yuri—Soviet singer-songwriter, poet, film actor, writer and journalist, screenwriter, documentary filmmaker, playwright, artist.
Vladimir Svyatoslavich—prince of Kiev who organized the Baptism of Russia.
Vladimirov Vasily—Soviet and Russian mathematician.
Vladimov Georgy—Russian writer and literary critic.
Vogel Bernhard—President of the Central Committee of German Catholics.
Volkonsky Andrey—Russian composer, harpsichordist and organist.
Volvovsky Leonid—Jewish renunciate, an acquaintance of ours.
Voroshilov Kliment—a Russian revolutionary, Soviet military leader, statesman and party figure, participant in the Civil War, one of the first Marshals of the Soviet Union.
Voynovich Vladimir—Russian prose writer, poet and playwright.
Vtorov Nikolai—Russian industrial, one of the richest men in pre-Revolutionary Russia.
Vul Benzion—Soviet physicist, specialist in the physics of dielectrics, semiconductors and quantum electronics, father-in-law of Yakov Sinai.
Vul Elena—Yaakov Sinai's wife.
Vyshinsky Andrey—Soviet statesman, lawyer, diplomat, Prosecutor of the USSR.
Wagner Steve—employee of the US Embassy in Moscow, husband of Susan Wagner.
Weil Peter—Russian philologist, journalist and writer emigriroted to the West.
Weinstein Anatoly—music editor on Soviet TV.
Weinstein Mikhail—American French horn player.
Wierzbicka Anna—Polish and Australian linguist working on semantics.
Wiesel Elie—American and French Jewish writer, journalist, social activist.
Wilker Sophia—Soviet and Israeli-American violinist, conductor and teacher.
Wood Boris—the teacher of the carpentry class in my school.
Wrangel Peter—Russian military commander, participant in the Russo-Japanese War and World War I, one of the main leaders of the White Movement during the Civil War.

Wul Benzion—Soviet physicist, specialist in semiconductors theory.
Wul Elena—wife of Yakov Sinai.
Yablonsky Sergey—Soviet and Russian mathematician, one of the founders of the Russian school of mathematical cybernetics.
Yakir Iona—Soviet military leader, 1st rank commander, prominent military leader during the Civil War, shot in the false case of Tukhachevsky.
Yakir Pyotr—Soviet historian, participant of the human rights movement, son of Iona Yakir.
Yakir Sara—wife of Jonah Yakir.
Yakobson Anatoly—Soviet poet, translator, literary critic, human rights activist.
Yakunin Gleb—Soviet and Russian religious, public and political figure, dissident, priest of the Russian Orthodox Church.
Yakushev Ada—Soviet poetess, bard, radio journalist and writer.
Yershov Yury—Soviet mathematician.
Yesenin Sergei—Russian lyric poet of the 20th century.
Yevtushenko Yevgeny—Russian poet, prose writer, director, screenwriter, publicist, orator and actor.
Yuvenaly—Bishop of the Russian Orthodox Church—Metropolitan of Krutitsy and Kolomna, Patriarchal Vicar of Moscow Diocese.
Zakharov Gennady—Soviet spy, Rear Admiral in the reserve.
Zakhoder Boris—Russian writer and poet, translator, screenwriter, one of my favorite authors in the world of children's literature.
Zalewski Piotr—janitor in J. Korczak's house of Jewish orphans, shot by the Nazis.
Zaretsky Mikhail—violist of the Boston Symphony Orchestra.
Zeidenberg Victor—my friend and colleague at IPM&CT, my co-author of the first dictionaries in the USSR on computers.
Zelevinsky Dmitriy—friend of our son-in-law Victor Khatutsky from Moscow times.
Zhdanov Andrey—Soviet party and state leader, one of the main ideologists of Bolshevism.
Zhivov Irina—colleague of Lydia Kagan at the Library Institute.
Zholkovsky-Ginzburg Irina—philologist, teacher of Russian for foreigners at Moscow State University, wife of Alexander Ginzburg.

Zholkovsky-Ginzburg Sergei—adopted son of Irina Zholkovsky-Ginzburg.
Zholkovsky Alexander—Soviet and American linguist, literary critic, writer and educator.
Zhukov Georgy—Soviet commander Marshal of the Soviet Union, after World War II—USSR Minister of Defence.
Zieman Tanya—my beloved wife.
Zieman Vera—my youngest daughter (maiden name).
Ziman Berta—my grandmother, my father's mother.
Ziman Galya—my eldest daughter (maiden name).
Ziman Hanah—my mother.
Ziman Inna—my brother Jan's first wife.
Ziman Jan—my brother.
Ziman Lena—my sister (maiden name).
Ziman Leonid—my cousin, son of my aunt Bella Shlifshtein.
Ziman Lev Jr.—my nephew, brother Jan's son.
Ziman Lev Sr.—my father.
Ziman Michael—our namesake in Israel who sent us a challenge.
Ziman Sarah—my nephew Lev Ziman's wife.
Ziman Yakov, Jr.—father of Ziman Leonid.
Ziman Yakov, Sr.—my grandfather, my father's father.
Zimarev Alexey—Soviet engineer, developer of computer elements, my colleague at the research institute I was working, my co-author of the first English-Russian dictionaries on computers in the USSR.

APPENDIX 3
WHO IS MENTIONED WHERE

Aaron 437
Abraham 383
Abramovich Pavel 397
Akhmadulina Bella 191
Akhmatov Anna 112, 311, 481
Aksakov Sergey 90
Alexander II 510
Alexander III 438
Alexei Mikhailovich 87
Alexis I 539, 541, 542
Alexis II 542
Alzheimer Alois 522
Andreev Nikolai 90, 91, 581
Andropov Yuri 346, 431, 540
Appius Claudius Cecus 419
Apresyan Yuri 148, 164, 175, 182, 263, 308
Arkhipov Abram 534
Arnold Vladimir 74, 75
Azef Evno 111, 113, 581

Babel Isaac 69, 416
Babitsky Konstantin 134, 136, 137, 140, 141, 148, 164-166, 182, 192, 194, 195, 206-208, 210-216, 308, 312, 347
Babitsky Natalia 137, 141, 215
Bach Johann Sebastian 169-175, 319, 467, 468

Baev Tanya 210, 211
Baker Howard 525
Bakhtin Mikhail 438, 538
Balmont Konstantin 112
Baranov Alexander 362
Barenblatt Grigory 70-73, 95
Barenblatt Isaac 69, 70
Barto Agniya 41
Beatrix Wilhelmina Armgard 506
Bebel Heinrich 438
Beethoven Ludwig 130
Belorus Evdokiya 413, 414
Belorus Stepan 413, 414
Belyaeva Elena 89
Belykh Grigory 427, 428
Bentick William 353, 562
Bershadsky Michael 490
Bessmertnykh Alexander 519
Bestuzhev Alexander 510
Bias of Priene 368
Blackman Ann 220, 353
Blokhin Nikolay 305
Blokhintsev Leonid 148, 188, 189, 190
Blokhintsev Varvara 188, 190
Bogart Humphrey 121
Bogoraz Larisa 165, 210, 349, 350

Boltaev Maria   447, 583
Bonaparte Napoleon   30, 340
Bonner Elena   349
Borodin Leonid   195
Borodulin Maria   263, 264
Borovik Henrik   532
Botkin Sergei   493-496, 499-502, 583
Botticelli Sandro   112
Boyarsky Eric   182, 184, 185, 187
Braginsky Stali   148
Brezhnev Leonid   70, 327, 340, 542
Brik Lilya   437
Brodsky Joseph   182, 191
Bronstein Ilya   66
Brown Philip   350-353, 355, 429, 584
Brown Roberta   351, 353, 355, 429
Brubeck Dave   525
Bruevich Nikolay   117
Brussilovsky Alexander   308, 446, 447, 463, 464, 468, 469, 470, 502, 518, 519
Buanarroti Michelangelo   112
Bukharin Nikolai   65
Bulgakov Elena   91
Bulgakov Mikhail   91, 92, 279
Burlatsky Fyodor   532
Bush George Herbert Walker   395, 584
Buwalda Mark   460
Buwalda Peter   353, 355, 444, 458, 459, 460-463, 523, 551, 562
Buwalda Wilma   353, 444, 458, 459-463, 523

Caravaggio Michelangelo   112
Chapkovsky Igor   325-328
Charny Veniamin   551
Chekanovsky Yuri   567, 568
Chekhov Anton   90
Chernyshevsky Nikolay   62
Chombe Moise   167, 168
Christ Jesus   311
Chukovsky Korney   48, 130
Cicero Marcus Tullius   369
Cimarosa Domenico   112
Copernicus Nicolaus   66
Curie Marie   73
Curie Pierre   73

Daniel Yuli   109, 192, 194-196, 221, 313, 426
Daniloff Caleb   511
Daniloff Nicholas   354, 509, 510-514, 516
Daniloff Ruth   354, 509, 516
Daniloff Sergei   511
Daniloff Yuri   510
Dante Alighieri   459
David   392
Davidson Cibelly Cherilyn   2
Decoy Michael   514
Delaune Vadim   210
Dobroklonsky Alexander   63
Dolukhanov Zara   172
Dorliak Nina   277
Dorodnitsyn Anatoly   222
Dostoyevsky Fyodor   134, 216
Dragunsky Viktor   454
Dremlyuga Vladimir   210
Driscoll Jack X   354
Driz Ovsey   110
Dubcek Alexander   210
Dubnov Yakov   66

APPENDIX 3: WHO IS MENTIONED WHERE

Dudintsev Vladimir 134
Dudnichenko Nadezhda 557
Dunayevsky Isaak 165, 166

Einstein Albert 64, 65, 66
Eisenhower Dwight 32
Elijah the Prophet 216
Elksnin Valentina 134
Elnitsky Lev 164
Elnitsky Svetlana 235
Elton Brenda 563, 567
Elton Lawrence 563, 567
Erasmus of Rotterdam 438
Erastov Konstantin 237
Erebus 169
Eshliman Nikolai 539

Fadeyev Alexander 130
Fedorov Svyatoslav 495
Fedynsky Maria 479, 480
Feinberg Viktor 210, 211
Feltsman Anna 376, 377
Feltsman Oscar 376
Feltsman Vladimir 376, 377, 378
Ford Gerald Rudolph 563
Frances Gérard 456
Frank-Kamenetsky Thema 318
Freidin Yuri 148, 383, 384, 385
Freiman Grigoriy 222
Frolov Alexander 510, 511
Frolov Anna 511
Frumkin Alexander 66

Gabay Galya 115, 116
Gabay Ilya 108-116, 292, 308, 312
Gagliano Nicolo 469

Gaidai Leonid 496
Galanskov Yuri 109, 195
Galich Alexander 134, 174, 292, 396, 430, 437
Garibaldi Nadia 1
Garibaldi Natalie 1
Garibaldi Nicola 1
Gekht Boris 498, 499, 565
Gerasimov Gennady 532
Gershman Boris 254-256, 302
Gillette Elizabeth 354
Gillette Robert 354
Ginzburg Alexander 109, 191, 192, 194-199
Giorgione 112
Gladky Alexey 148, 217-219, 223, 238
Glovinskaya Marina 148, 175
Goethe Johann Wolfgang 113, 114
Gogol Nikolai 90, 91, 92
Goliath 392
Golomshtok Igor 341, 589
Gonchar Andrey 222
Gorbachev Mikhail 312, 504-509, 516-519, 524-526, 531, 532, 552
Gorbanevskaya Natalia 210
Gorky Maxim 49, 50, 59, 129, 170, 369, 373, 423, 562
Goulet Denis 454
Goya Francisco 112
Gregory IX 535
Grieg Edvard 130
Grigoryants Sergey 532
Gromyko Andrei 524
Guchkov Nadezhda 277
Gumilev Nikolai 112, 481
Gurchenko Lyudmila 456

Gurevich Grigory   66
Guroff Gregory   354, 551
Gutman Natalia   271, 308, 469

Haass Friedrich Josep   256
Hammer Armand   551-553, 554
Hammer Julius   553
Handelman Steve   354
Hartman Arthur   354, 378, 379, 444
Hartman Donna   354, 378, 379, 444
Harutyunyan Yuri   357
Hayk   415
Henry IV of Bourbon   196
Herzen Alexander   380, 381
Heyerdahl Thor   136
Hilbert David   74
Hippocrates   303, 534
Hitler Adolf   26-32, 46, 272, 304
Holofernes   111
Homer   471, 472
Honegger Artur   112
Horace   174

Ilf Ilya   130, 342, 491
Ilia II   418
Iordanskaya Lydia   148, 163, 164, 185, 218
Ivanov Irina   463
Ivan the Terrible   87

Janus Elzbieta   430
Jeitler Manfred   564, 565, 567
Jeremiah the prophet   90
Jodl Alfred   32
Joliot-Curie Frederic   73
Joliot-Curie Irene   73

Judith   111-13, 115
Juvenal Decimus Junius   471
Juvenaly Metropolitan   540
Kadzasov Sandro   148, 170, 236, 237
Kagan Judith   438, 439
Kagan Lydia   323
Kagan Maria   61, 63, 66, 68, 69, 72, 74, 150
Kagan Matvey   437, 438
Kagan Nadezhda   69, 70, 71
Kagan Oleg   271, 272
Kagan Sophia   437, 438
Kagan Veniamin   62-69, 95, 308
Kalistratov Sofya   349
Kapitsa Pyotr   134
Karatsuba Anatoly   222
Karhilo Lisa   445
Karig Sharah   493
Kartlos   415
Kasatkin Leonid   148
Kataev Valentin   130
Kazavchinsky Tamara   170, 236, 237
Keitel Wilhelm   33
Kennedy John   567
Khatutsky Andrew   1
Khatutsky Anna   1
Khatutsky Galya   383, 446, 488, 489, 492
Khatutsky Geda   488, 491
Khatutsky Victor   379, 393, 488, 490, 491
Khlebnikov Velimir   90
Khodorovich Tanya   347, 350
Khrushchev Nikita   27, 85, 159, 168
Kibrik Alexander   148

APPENDIX 3: WHO IS MENTIONED WHERE

Kikot Miroslava   213
Kim Yuliy   114, 115, 183, 292
Kingdon Clifford William   66
Kislik Vladimir   552
Klimenko Alexey   479, 480
Klimenko Olga   83, 84, 146, 305, 328-330, 561, 562
Klose Eliza   354
Klose Kevin   93, 354
Klyuchevsky Vasily   510
Kochetkov Alexander   489
Kochin Ira   72, 73
Kochin Nikolai   73
Kochin Pelageya   73
Kogan Bluma   48
Kogan Gennady   48
Kogan Inna   48
Kolmogorov Andrey   74, 76
Kopelev Lev   349
Korczak Janusz   329, 338-340, 430
Kornilov Vladimir   349
Korolev Lev   123-125, 219-223
Kosharovsky Yuli   552
Koshkin Ekaterina   329
Kossoff David   428, 429
Kosygin Alexey   539
Kovalev Sergey   346, 347, 350, 531
Krasin Viktor   109, 346
Kulikov Galina   88
Kuznetsov Sergey   196

Labkovsky Naum   38
Lander Alexander   118
Lander Elena   117-120, 122, 123, 137, 217
Lander Victor   118, 119
Landsberg Grigory   66

Lavut Alexander   350
Lebedev Alice   129, 130, 131, 132, 134
Lebedev-Kumach Vasily   165, 480
Lebedev Sergey   121, 129-135, 542
Leconte Victoria   557, 558
Leibler Isi   354, 447
Lelewel Joachim   210
Lenin Vladimir   70, 135, 167, 172, 197, 199, 222, 404, 445, 509, 519, 533, 553
Leontiev Anatoly   236
Leontiev Nina   148, 235-237
Lermontov Michael   213
Leroux Gaston   521
Levin Aryeh   461, 462
Levin Mikhail   74, 75
Levintov Ernestina   150
Levintov Joseph Sr.   68
Levin Yehuda Leib   535
Levitan Isaac   90, 93
Levitin Yuri   38
Levkovich Elizabeth   71, 72
Litvinov Pavel   210, 350
Livshits Benedict   481
Lizarevich Alexandr   65
Lloyd-Webber Andrew   521
Lobachevsky Nikolai   66
Long Marguerite   463
Lopshits Abram   66
Loren Sophia   125
Louis the Holy   535
Lumumba Patrice   166, 167, 168, 169
Luther Martin   112, 438
Lysenko Trofim   133, 165

Malykhin Alexander 362, 557
Mandelstam Leonid 66, 74
Mandelstam Lydia 74
Mandelstam Nadezhda 182, 311, 312, 382-384
Mandelstam Osip 64, 65, 86, 109, 112, 380, 382-384
Mandelstam Tanya 74
Mann Thomas 113, 114
Marjasin Alexander 30, 31
Markish Peretz 235
Markish Tanya 214, 235-240, 246, 247, 264
Markish Yuri 235, 264
Markiz Lev 376, 413
Markov Andrei, Sr. 62
Marshak Anna 148
Marshak Samuel 64, 65, 122
Martin the Graceful 536
Marx Karl 94, 352, 533, 534
Matlock Jack 509
Matthew the Apostle 172, 174, 311
Mavrina Tatiana 129, 599
Mayakovsky Vladimir 113, 167, 254, 379, 568
Mayantz Lazar 100
McCagg Bill 354
McCagg Louise 354
Medici 499, 500
Mei Lev 112
Melchuk Igor 145, 147, 148, 162-164, 182, 188, 217, 218, 308
Melchuk Svetlana 164, 218
Men Alexander 429-31, 537, 539-541
Menzheritsky Emil 561
Michelson Faina 39

Michelson Mikhail 39
Mikhalkov Sergei 564
Mikoyan Anastas 70
Milne Alan Alexander 491
Mints Isaac 426, 427
Molotov Vyacheslav 29, 31, 66
More Thomas 438
Morits Yunna 214
Morpheus 567
Moses 148
Mozart Wolfgang Amadeus 112, 566, 567
Muge Sergey 165

Nagibin Yuri 279
Navalny Alexei 527
Neighbor Ksenia 444
Nestor the Chronicler 358
Neuhaus Heinrich 277
Newton Isaac 64, 65
Nice Liolya 120
Nice Tim 120
Nikiforov Vladimir 536-539
Nobel Alfred 75, 171, 346
Nordal Odvar 354
Nordal Vera 354

Obolensky Igor 279
Ogarev Nikolai 90, 292
Oguz Lydia 490, 491
Okhotnikov Elena 502
Okudzhava Bulat 59, 142, 171, 191, 221, 279, 292
Olesha Yuri 130
Orlov Yuri 346
Oshanin Lev 26
Ostrovsky Alexander 213
Ostrovsky Arkady 564

Pakhmutov Alexandra 26
Pasternak Boris 75, 164, 279
Pergolesi Giovanni
   Batista 319
Peter the Great 87
Petrov Andrei 376
Petrovsky Ivan 67
Petrov Yevgeny 130, 342, 491
Picander 173
Pimen, Patriarch 346
Pirveli Boris 415
Plakida Nikolay 148
Platonov Vladimir 222
Platonov Vyacheslav 195
Plisetsky German 164
Pluzhnikov Vladimir 51
Pocock Emily 443
Pocock Mag 354, 443-446
Pocock Ted 354, 443-446
Pocock Tig 443
Podgorny Nikolai 539
Pomerants Grigory 349
Pontryagin Lev 222
Pope Alexander 65
Posse Konstantin 62
Powell Colin 525, 575
Prestin-Shapiro Leah 391
Prestin Vladimir 391, 502,
   503, 504
Prigov Dmitry 507
Prokhorov Vera 89, 277, 278,
   279, 280, 295, 302, 308, 499
Ptolemy Claudius 418
Pushkin Alexander 46, 75,
   129, 163, 328-330, 380, 403,
   421, 438, 469-471, 530
Putin Vladimir 526, 527, 541
Putzel Michael 353, 354

Rabin Yitzhak 461
Rashevsky Pyotr 66
Rastropovich Mstislav 445, 560
Ravich David 138, 386
Ravich Leah 139, 219
Ravich Renata 137-150, 165,
   217-224, 238, 239, 247, 386,
   604
Ravich Yakov 139
Ravikovich Mikhail 493, 494,
   495, 496, 497
Reagan Nancy 354, 524, 570,
   575
Reagan Ronald 1, 220, 354,
   395, 506-509, 516-528, 530-
   532, 542, 543, 552, 563, 570,
   574, 575
Reformatsky Alexander 147
Reich Arkady 320, 321
Reich Elena 25, 43, 45, 49, 86,
   99, 321
Reich Michael 321
Reitburd Moses 286
Reitburd Tzilia 286-288, 308,
   339, 344, 355, 396, 397, 499,
   503, 532, 561
Renoir Auguste 142
Repin Ilya 91, 92
Ribentrop von Joachim 29
Richter Svyatoslav 277, 278,
   279, 280
Rochette Alain 456
Romulus 471, 472
Ronkin Valery 195
Rosenstrom Alexander 115
Rosenzweig Victor 148
Rousseau Jean-Jacques 534
Rozovsky Joseph 295
Rubinstein Nikolai 90

Rudenko Roman   539
Rudy Mikhail   463

Saffer Stuart   397, 402, 403
Sagdeev Roald   317, 318, 320
Sakharov Andrei   134, 346, 349, 350
Sapgir Genrich   191
Scarlatti Alessandro   112
Schnittke Alfred   445
Schweitzer Albert   171-174
Sechenov Ivan   90
Selvinsky Ilya   75
Seraphim, Metropolitan   346
Serebryakov Lada   317, 318
Sergei Aleksandrovich, Grand Duke   113
Serov Alexander   112
Serov Valentin   90
Sevez Francois   32
Shakespeare William   169
Shaliapin Feodor   90
Shamir Yitzhak   461
Shapiro Felix   391, 392, 393
Shapiro Genrikh   66
Shapiro Pavel   165
Shapiro Solomon   547
Sharansky Natan   508
Shchepkina-Kupernik Tatiana   169
Sheremetev Nikolai   403, 404
Shestopal M.G.   66
Shevardnadze Eduard   551
Shevelev Raya   26
Shifter Richard   354
Shikhanovich Yuri   350
Shirshov Anatoly   222
Shlifshtein Bella   26, 39, 114, 116, 292, 308
Shlifshtein Elena   150, 293, 294
Shlifshtein Natalia   294
Shlifshtein Semyon   26, 149, 150, 292-295
Shostakovich Dmitri   292-295, 468
Shostakovich Irina   294
Shulman Jerry   570
Shultz George   354, 525
Shura-Bura Mikhail   223
Simanowicz Pavel   388
Sinai Grigory   71
Sinai Yakov   71-76, 95, 188
Sinyavsky Andrey   109, 192
Sklifasovsky Nikolai   404
Sklifasovsky Sophia   404
Sklifasovsky Tamara   404
Smith Adam   471
Smith Bedell   32
Smorgunov Elena   148, 383
Sobakin Tim   310
Sokolov Evgeniy   439
Soldatenkov Kozma   500, 501
Solzhenitsyn Alexander   134, 189, 190, 216, 346
Solzhenitsyn Natalia   189, 190
Sonya Golden Hand   69
Squire John   65
Stalin Joseph   27-33, 45, 85, 86, 91, 100, 117, 130, 135, 165, 182, 222, 292, 293, 304, 386, 393
Strabo   418
Superfin Gabriel   346
Susloparov Ivan   32, 33
Svan Zina   419
Svetlov Mikhail   130, 609
Svetlov Natalia   148, 188, 189
Sychiov Maria   137

APPENDIX 3: WHO IS MENTIONED WHERE

Taneyev Sergei 90
Tarasov Mikhail 88
Telemann Georg Philipp 170
Thatcher Margaret 517
Theocritus 472
Thibaud Jacques 463
Tikhonov Andrey 222
Timofeev Lev 527
Titian Vechellio 112
Tolstoy Alexei 113, 544
Tomsky Nikolai 92
Trimble Jeff 513
Tsalenko Maria 247
Tsalenko Mikhail 222, 247
Tsiolkovsky Konstantin 479, 480
Tsurenko Tzilia 361, 363
Tsvetaev Anastasia 437
Tsvetaev Ivan 438
Tsvetaev Marina 112, 216, 232, 437, 438
Tvardovsky Alexander 116
Tyurin Andrey 188
Tyurin Dmitry 188, 190
Tyutchev Fyodor 272

Ulyanov Pyotr 222
Ushakov Dmitry 110, 113
Uvarov Irina 221

Van Gogh Vincent 248
Vasily III 87
Veil Simone 354, 611
Velikanov Ksenia 165
Velikanov Tanya 166, 212, 214, 308, 312, 346-350
Vernadsky Vladimir 66, 247
Veronese Paolo 112
Vinogradov Ivan 222

Virgil Publius Maronus 471
Vishnevsky Galina 560
Vivaldi Antonio 112
Vladimirov Vasily 222
Vladimir Svyatoslavich 358
Vladimov Georgy 349
Vogel Bernhard 395
Volvovsky Leonid 392, 393
Voroshilov Kliment 39, 88
Voynovich Vladimir 134, 349
Vtorov Nikolay 377
Vyshinsky Andrey 66

Wagner Steve 355
Wagner Susan 355
Weil Peter 612
Wierzbicka Anna 182, 185
Wrangel Peter 511
Wul Benzion 74
Wul Elena 73, 74

Yablonsky Sergey 222
Yakir Pyotr 109
Yakobson Anatoly 350
Yakunin Gleb 531, 539-542
Yershov Yury 222, 613
Yesenin Sergei 47
Yevtushenko Yevgeny 312
Yuvenaly Metropolitan 431

Zakhoder Boris 559
Zeidenberg Victor 117, 120, 122, 137
Zhdanov Andrey 164, 165
Zhivov Irina 323
Zholkovsky Alexander 148, 164, 182, 191
Zholkovsky-Ginzburg Irina 189, 191-199

Zholkovsky-Ginzburg Sergei 199
Zhukov Georgy 33
Zieman Tanya 347-350
Zieman Vera 321, 357, 377, 414, 416, 417, 423, 447
Ziman Galya 147, 162, 188, 190, 206, 212, 218, 219, 223-239, 246, 247, 302, 385, 388-390, 402-405
Ziman Hanah 23, 25, 26
Ziman Inna 48, 59, 84, 86, 146, 149, 159, 327-30, 437, 479
Ziman Jan 25, 38, 44, 47, 48, 84-89, 95, 146, 320, 343
Ziman Lena 39
Ziman Lev Jr. 48, 84, 146, 147, 321, 325, 326-330
Ziman Lev Sr. 23, 25-27
Ziman Sarah 329

www.ingramcontent.com/pod-product-compliance
Lightning Source LLC
Chambersburg PA
CBHW070817230426
R18182700001B/R181827PG43662CBX00002B/1